All Said and Done

Simone de Beauvoir

Translated by Patrick O'Brian
Introduction by Toril Moi

Paragon House
New York

First Paragon House edition, 1993

Published in the United States by

Paragon House
90 Fifth Avenue
New York, N.Y. 10011

Library of Congress Cataloging-in-Publication Data

Beauvoir, Simone de
    [Toute compte fait. English]
    All said and done / Simone de Beauvoir ; trans-
lated by Patrick O'Brian ; introduction by Toril
Moi. — 1st Paragon House ed.
      p.   cm.
    ISBN 1-55778-525-2
    1. Beauvoir, Simone de, 1908-   — Biography.
2. Authors, French—20th century — Biography.
3. Feminists — France — Biography.   I. Title.
PQ2603.E362Z47513   1993
848'.91409 — dc20
[B]   92-32335
                                   CIP

All Said and Done

Also by Simone de Beauvoir

Earlier volumes in this autobiography
Memoirs of a Dutiful Daughter
The Prime of Life
Force of Circumstance
A Very Easy Death

Other works
The Long March
Brigitte Bardot and the Lolita Syndrome
Djamila Boupacha
Blood of Others
She Came to Stay
America Day by Day
Must We Burn De Sade?
The Second Sex
The Mandarins
All Men are Mortal
Old Age

For Sylvie

Introduction

In *All Said and Done*, the fourth and last volume of her autobiography, Simone de Beauvoir takes another look at the course of her life, and pronounces it good: "What is certain is that I am satisfied with my fate and that I should not want it changed in any way at all." There is a striking contrast between her insistence here on her own satisfaction with every aspect of her life, and the dismally depressing end of the previous volume, where she cried out her despair at feeling old and unloved (see *Force of Circumstance*, vol. 2). It is hard not to suspect that the relaxed confidence of this opening chapter is deliberately intended to efface the impression of unhappiness produced by its predecessor.

Returning to her childhood, Beauvoir declares that it was immensely happy and stable, and that her mother "had a warm and loving relationship" with her. It is as if she has forgotten her long descriptions, in *Memoirs of a Dutiful Daughter*, or *A Very Easy Death*, of her mother's intrusive and domineering personality, her envy of her two daughters' friendship with each other, and her efforts to control every aspect of her daughter's life. In *All Said and Done*, on the other hand, Beauvoir claims flatly that she had no emotional problems at all until the age of thirteen: it was only during her teenage years that her mother and father changed in their behavior toward her, turning her adolescence into a nightmare of rejection, exile and betrayal. As for her relationship with Sartre, she reiterates her conviction that meeting him "was the most important event in [her] life," before declaring that she lost none of her freedom, and none of her happiness in the process. Readers of *The Prime of Life* and *Force of Circumstance* may well feel inclined to question this upbeat account.

On an emotional level, the unshakably positive outlook of

Beauvoir's final volume would appear to have its roots in her own happiness. Dedicating her book to Sylvie Le Bon, later to become her adoptive daughter and literary executor, Beauvoir dwells on the pleasure she takes in her relationship with the young woman. "Once again a piece of great good fortune was offered to me," Beauvoir writes about her meeting with Sylvie, using the exact turn of phrase which in *Force of Circumstance* introduced her relationship with Claude Lanzmann. Protecting her against loneliness, the friendship with Le Bon allows Beauvoir to declare—not quite truthfully—that "since I was twenty-one I have never been lonely." The close relationship between the two women provides a firm base for Beauvoir's public life as an intellectual and writer, and as Sartre's official companion.

All Said and Done is above all an account of Beauvoir's activities as the *grande dame* of French intellectual life in the 1960s. Published in 1972 when Beauvoir was 64, the text—in contrast to the intimate confessions of *Memoirs of a Dutiful Daughter* or *The Prime of Life*—often reads like a chronicle of Beauvoir and Sartre's public engagements. Traveling together to the Soviet Union, Japan, Egypt and Israel, the two writers are treated like royalty. Occasionally the lists of engagements carried out and sights seen are broken up by an unexpected anecdote: Sartre, we learn, never experienced nausea in his life until he tried *sushi* in Tokyo in 1966.

Politically, Beauvoir's major commitment in the late 1960s was her involvement with the Russel tribunal, set up to investigate reports of U.S. war crimes in Viet Nam. By the early 1970s, however, her political interests had started to focus on the emerging women's movement, and *All Said and Done* contains some valuable additions to *The Second Sex*. Insisting on the necessity of struggling for feminism and socialism at one and the same time, Beauvoir throws in her lot with the tradition of socialist feminism represented in Britain by Juliet Mitchell in *Woman's Estate*. But she also has much sympathy for the work of many U.S. feminists, singling out Betty Friedan's *The Feminine Mystique* and Kate Millett's *Sexual Politics* for positive attention. Rejecting all patriarchal myths of femininity, Beauvoir opposes every form of feminist separatism: "I do not believe that there are specifically feminine qualities, values or ways of life," she writes. "To believe this would mean acknowledging the existence of a specifically female nature—that is to say agreeing with a myth invented by men to confine women to their oppressed state."

Feminism for Beauvoir is the product of a cultural tradition profoundly marked by patriarchal ideology. Unlike some feminists, she refuses to believe that traditional thought is "male." Instead of rejecting our cultural traditions outright, Beauvoir favors a thorough revision of the patriarchal culture against which feminists define themselves: "We must very carefully distinguish," she writes, "between those things which have a universal nature and those which are marked by masculinity."

During the writing of *All Said and Done*, Beauvoir is at the pinnacle of her fame, but she is also at the end of her career. "I no longer feel that I have a distinct purpose," she writes. "And I know that none of my future books will transform the body of my work as a whole: it will be the same corpus with a volume added." *All Said and Done* accordingly reads like a text in which Beauvoir is more concerned with producing a monument to her life as a public intellectual, than with freshly exploring her inner tensions and torments. The confidence with which she lists her favorite things—books, films, food, landscapes, monuments, buildings—is breathtaking. It is as if, after a lifetime of cultural anxiety (I am thinking of her account, in *The Prime of Life*, of how she trained herself to like classical music, for instance), Beauvoir finally feels free to tell her readers to take it or leave it: if we don't like her descriptions of churches in the French provinces, she is not going to lift a finger to make them more palatable to us. Challenging us to accept her as she is, Beauvoir makes herself less seductive, less deliberately pleasing than ever before.

"I always remained faithful to my fundamental project," Beauvoir writes in this volume, "that of knowing and writing." To find the truth and tell it to the world was always her greatest passion. Her curiosity and her love of truth pushed her to study philosophy, to explore the world, and to pioneer new sexual arrangements in her own life. But the truth is not always lovable, and for Beauvoir, ultimately, love mattered at least as much as truth. Just as she identified with Maggie Tulliver in *The Mill on the Floss*, or with Jo in *Little Women*, Beauvoir wanted her readers to identify with her. Her ideal reader is a friend, somebody who loves and understands her in spite of her flaws and limitations. For the author of *All Said and Done* to write is to communicate, and to communicate is to be loved.

At the end of her memoirs Beauvoir lays down her pen, secure in the knowledge that she has succeeded in turning her writing into a bulwark against exile and loneliness. "I wanted to make myself exist for others by conveying, as directly as I could, the taste of my own life," she writes. "I have more or less succeeded. I have some thorough-going enemies, but I have also made many friends among my readers. I asked no more." This is no longer the voice of the brilliant but naive young student at the beginning of *The Prime of Life*, nor of the distressed middle-aged woman at the end of *Force of Circumstance*; it is the voice of a woman who has finally come through the major struggles of her life.

Toril Moi

Prologue

When my book *Old Age* came out there were some readers and
critics who blamed me for not having dealt with my own old age at
greater length. It seemed to me that this curiosity often arose more
from a sort of cannibalism than from any genuine interest; but even
so it does encourage me to go on with my autobiography and to
finish it. The nearer I come towards the end of my days, the more I
am enabled to see that strange thing, a life, and to see it whole: that
is what I shall try to do at the beginning of this book. Then again,
ten years have gone by since I broke off my tale, and I have many
things to speak of.

In the earlier books I followed a chronological sequence; and this
has its drawbacks, as I know. The reader has the feeling that he is
never being given anything but the non-essential, the side-issues – a
series of forewords: the heart of the matter always seems to lie
somewhere farther on. Page after page he hopes to reach it; but he
hopes in vain, and at last the book ends without ever having come
to a full close. By imprisoning it in words, my account turns my
history into a finite reality: and it is not a finite reality. Yet at the
same time it scatters it abroad, breaking it up into a string of set,
distinct moments, whereas in fact past, present and future were
inextricably bound together in each one of them. I may write 'I got
ready to leave for America': but the outcome of that once-living
project, its then future, has now sunk and vanished behind me, just
as a plan that no longer has any vitality would disappear. Again,
every stage of my life was haunted by those I had lived through
earlier – my life as an adult by my childhood and adolescence, the
war by the years before the war. By following the sequence of time,

I put it out of my power to convey these interconnections, this dovetailing; so I failed to give my past hours their threefold dimension: they march by, devoid of life, reduced to the flatness of a never-ending present, cut off from what went before and from what came after.

Yet there was no other way I could have done it. For me life was an undertaking that had a clear direction, and in giving an account of mine I had to follow its progress. The circumstances are not the same today. Obviously I am not condemned to self-repetition: the world has moved on since 1962, and I have had fresh experiences. But no public or private event has made any fundamental change in my position: I have not altered. And then there are still plans and projects that mean a great deal to me: but they no longer form a single, clearly-laid-down intention. I no longer feel that I am moving in the direction of a goal, but only that I am slipping inevitably towards my grave. So now I do not have to take the passage of the years as my guide: to some extent I shall follow their sequence, but it is around certain given themes that I mean to group my recollections.

1

Every morning, even before I open my eyes, I know I am in my bedroom and my bed. But if I go to sleep after lunch in the room where I work, sometimes I wake up with a feeling of childish amazement – why am I myself? What astonishes me, just as it astonishes a child when he becomes aware of his own identity, is the fact of finding myself here, and at this moment, deep in this life and not in any other. What stroke of chance has brought this about? If I look at it from outside, my birth in the first place seems unlikely. The penetration of that particular ovum by that particular spermatozoon, with its implications of the meeting of my parents and before that of their birth and the births of all their forebears, had not one chance in hundreds of millions of coming about. And it was chance, a chance quite unpredictable in the present state of science, that caused me to be born a woman. From that point on, it seems to me that a thousand different futures might have stemmed from every single movement of my past: I might have fallen ill and broken off my studies; I might not have met Sartre; anything at all might have happened. Tossed into the world, I have been subjected to its laws and its contingencies, ruled by wills other than my own, by circumstances and by history: it is therefore reasonable for me to feel that I am myself contingent. What staggers me is that at the same time I am *not* contingent. If I had not been born no question would have arisen: I have to take the fact that I do exist as my starting point. To be sure, the future of the woman I have been may turn me into someone other than myself. But in that case it would be this other woman who would be asking herself who she was. For the person who says 'Here am I' there is no other coexisting possibility. Yet this necessary coincidence of the subject and his history is not enough to do away with my perplexity. My life: it is both

1

intimately known and remote; it defines me and yet I stand outside it. Just what, precisely, is this curious object?

Like Einstein's universe, it is both boundless and finite. Boundless: it runs back through time and space to the very beginnings of the world and to its utmost limits. In my being I sum up the earthly inheritance and the state of the world at this moment. Any good biographer is aware that to make his hero known and understood he must first deal with his hero's period, civilization and society; and that he must go back along the line of his hero's ancestors as far as he can. Yet even so, all this information put together amounts to the merest trifle compared to the inexhaustible multiplicity of relationships that every element in an existence maintains with the Whole. What is more, of these elements each has a meaning that differs according to the point of view from which it is seen. The statement 'I was born in Paris' does not mean the same thing to a Parisian, to a person from the provinces, and to a foreigner. The apparent simplicity of the statement is scattered and dispersed among the millions of individuals who have varying relationships with the city.

And yet life is also a finite reality. It possesses an inner heart, a centre of interiorization, a *me* which asserts that it is always the same throughout the whole course. A life is set within a given space of time; it has a beginning and an end; it evolves in given places, always retaining the same roots and spinning itself an unchangeable past whose opening towards the future is limited. It is impossible to grasp and define a life as one can grasp and define a thing, since a life is 'an unsummed whole', as Sartre puts it, a detotalized totality, and therefore it has no *being*. But one can ask certain questions about it. How is a life formed? How much of it is made up by circumstances, how much by necessity, how much by chance, and how much by the subject's own options and his personal initiatives?

One thing that helps me to reflect upon my own is the fact that I have told it. 'Tell, oh tell!' says one of Robbe-Grillet's heroes. Very well: it is true that the tale evolves on a plane other than that of the experience as one has lived it, but the tale exists in reference to that experience and it may allow certain leading characteristics to be distinguished. Although the experience implies infinity, it takes on the form of a given number of words – words that could be counted, if one set oneself to it: but these words have reference to a knowledge that in its turn embraces the infinite. When I write 'I was born in Paris', the reader to whom I am speaking understands the

2

sentence without my having to locate Paris in the history of the world or upon the map. There is also the objection that 'telling' means setting the hard outlines of the written phrase in place of the fluid ambiguity of actual experience. But in fact the images called up by words are floating and imprecise; the knowledge words convey is not sharply defined. In any case I do not intend to lead the reader through a waking dream that might bring my past back to life, but to examine my history from the standpoint of certain given concepts and notions.

There is one of these that will act as my leading thread – the notion of chance. It has a distinct meaning for me. I do not know where I might have been led by the paths that, as I look back, I think I might have taken but that in fact I did not take. What is certain is that I am satisfied with my fate and that I should not want it changed in any way at all. So I look upon these factors that helped me to fulfil it as so many fortunate strokes of chance.

The first was obviously that of my birth. As I have already said, it is useless to speculate upon the series of hazards that tossed me into this world. I set off from the fact that I was born on 9 January 1908, the daughter of Georges and Françoise de Beauvoir. Seen from the outside, this fact (quite overwhelming for me in its unique quality) is perfectly commonplace. By marrying, she at twenty, he at thirty, and by having a baby a year later, two young bourgeois were conforming to the customs of the particular world in which they lived and of their time. It was laid down in advance what this child's state should be – French, bourgeois, and Catholic: only its sex was unforeseen. Seeing that my parents were in easy circumstances, it was very likely that I should not die prematurely and that I should be blessed with good health. A clearly-defined future lay before me – watchful care; a family of immediate and of more distant relations; a nurse, Louise; the flat in Paris; the country house in the Limousin; and almost certainly the coming of a second child.

From the very beginning my birth set me up as a socially-privileged child and guaranteed me a great deal more in the way of opportunity than the daughter of a peasant or a working-class family. Another piece of luck that I cannot define so exactly was the way in which my earliest childhood developed.

Nowadays all pediatricians dwell upon the importance of the first two years in the building-up of a personality. A baby's tears and

3

crying usually becomes a means of communication with those around it towards the age of eight months; it becomes conscious of their effectiveness and it uses them as signs: a reciprocal relationship grows up between it and the adults. This relationship does not come into existence when the baby is unloved, left alone, or thwarted: where this is so, if it does not die it becomes an autistic or schizophrenic child. To a lesser degree, indifference, neglect and want of stimulation give rise to a feeling of insecurity and cause the baby to turn in upon itself. Speaking of Flaubert, Sartre has shown how a child well-cared-for and well-fed but handled without loving kindness and so treated that no dialogue is established with him, acquires a passive make-up. Obviously this was not the case with me. I do not know how I was weaned, nor how I was first taught cleanliness, nor how I reacted to that teaching. But my mother was young and cheerful, and she was proud of having successfully produced a first child: she had a warm and loving relationship with me. Around my cradle there was a large family of attentive relations. I looked out confidently upon the world: the grown-ups smilingly put up with my whims, and this persuaded me of my power over them. My sanguine nature encouraged this exactingness, a quality that was with me from the beginning and that has never left me since – I have always insisted on carrying my desires, refusals, acts and thoughts right through to the end. One does not insist unless one reckons on obtaining what one calls for, both from others and from oneself: and there is no getting it unless one does call for it. I am grateful to my earliest years for having given me this excessive frame of mind. When I was crossed, I would be shaken with fury: where did these rages come from? I have not explained it satisfactorily in my Memoirs and I cannot do any better now. But I still think they were good for me. I set off on the right foot. To be sure, that in itself is not enough. A life is not the mere growth of the original seed. It runs the continual danger of being halted, broken, damaged or turned aside. Yet a happy beginning does encourage the subject to get the best that can be got from his circumstances; if the beginning is unhappy, a vicious circle comes into being – the subject lets his opportunities go by, he shuts himself up in refusal, loneliness, and gloom.

A comparison of my fate with my sister's is very revealing: her road was far harder than mine because she had to overcome the handicap of her early years. In the photographs that were taken of me at two and a half I have a determined and self-confident expression; hers at the same age show a frightened, timid look. Being the younger daughter, she was less surprising and less amusing than the elder; and my parents were sorry she was not a boy. She must have had fewer smiles and less attention than I. She was an easily-disturbed and even an anxious child; they said she was more 'affectionate' than I was – she needed comforting. She was called peevish, and that plunged her deeper into sulks; she often used to cry without any apparent reason. It took her a long time to make a complete break with her childhood.

Mine was calm and happy. In spite of a few squabbles, my parents got along well together, and this strengthened the feeling of security I had gained in my cradle. And then again, generally speaking there was no conflict between the image of myself that I derived from those around me and my own inner knowledge of the subject.

A child is an alienated creature. He receives the world, the time and the space within which he has his being from the grown-ups, and even the language he uses. Since things belong to demi-gods and bear their mark, for the child they are not only tools but also the sign of hidden realities with mysterious depths. That is where the 'wonder' of childhood lies. The poetic transfiguration of childhood carried out by the bourgeois nineteenth century is so much stuff: there is nothing poetic about a child whatsoever. But it is true that for a child the world possesses a fascinating strangeness – always providing that he is lucky enough to be able to gaze upon it and explore it.

The price he has to pay is that he receives his image and even his very being from others: he looks upon this as the essential and himself as the non-essential. Yet at the same time he sets himself up as a subject. He therefore stands at the centre of a world, a world in which he sees himself, with regard to grown-ups, as a relative being. He perceives himself as something that is *seen*. He may experience this state in a great many different ways.

There are some children who may be said to have no childhood at all. At the age of five, a little bootblack has a worker-employer relationship with his customer, not that of a child with an adult. Even if he takes his earnings back to his parents, at the time he actually wields the brush he is an autonomous individual, perceiving himself by means of direct activity without the mediation of any

5

outside person. There are others, especially in large, poor families, who are so uncared-for that they scarcely attain self-awareness at all: extreme cases, in India for example, may turn into wild children who go back to a state of nature. It is impossible for a child who is browbeaten, pitilessly dominated, exploited and terrified, to carry out the reflective process of becoming conscious of himself. In our society, however, the great majority of children, as I have said, experience both alienation and autonomy at the same time: even the most alienated looks upon himself as fundamentally necessary, and he has fleeting glimpses of himself as a self-known being. If his role seems to him flattering, he eagerly falls in with it: he plays a part, becoming an imitator. In *Words* Sartre describes his own histrionics.[1] But there were moments when he discovered that he had an existence apart from these pretences: he discovered the naked truth of his being as it was for himself, and looking in the mirror his face distorted with confusion and distress. He found his salvation in reading and in writing – independent activities. Others, like my sister or the young Flaubert, find themselves saddled with a most disagreeable self-image; they either put up with it or they rebel. Many compromises between resentment and anger are possible. Violette Leduc was often ill when she was a little girl, and she felt that she was a burden and a living reproach to her mother: she believed herself to be guilty. On this level I was privileged too. Sometimes I would fly into a rage at being treated as a child when I thought I was a fully-developed person; but in general I liked my role. When I was about seven my fits of temper stopped and I submissively played the part of a good little girl. But at that time those activities which allowed me to fulfil myself as an independent subject increased in number.

During my earliest years, my feelings for my parents and Louise were supported by my freedom, since I actually experienced them; but these feelings were so natural to me that they seemed wholly necessary, and the behaviour that expressed them was imposed upon me; it was a response to what was called for and to what was expected. There was only one freely-created relationship during this period, and that was with my sister. The family pattern followed by my parents required that they should have another child quite soon;

[1] 'My truth, my character, and my name were entirely governed by the grown-ups; I had learnt to see myself through their eyes.'

6

and as chance[2] would have it, this child was a girl. Would things have turned out differently for me if it had been a boy? I cannot tell. In any event, I do not think I should have benefited; indeed, I should probably have been worse off. I believe I should count the fact of having had a sister, younger than myself but close to me in age, as one of my pieces of good luck. She helped me to assert myself. I invented the mixture of authority and affection that marked my dealings with her. It was I, of my own initiative, who taught her to read, write and count. It was I who worked out our games and our living relationship. Of course, my attitude towards her arose from my being what I was: I was a happy, well-adjusted child, self-confident and open; there was nothing to prevent me from heartily welcoming a younger sister, one of whom I was not in the least jealous. I was an active, bossy little girl, and I longed to get away from the passivity of childhood by means of effectual action: she provided me with the best possible opportunity. Yet still I can properly speak of invention, since although the grown-ups guided me in my behaviour to them, at the beginning my sister required nothing of me, and when I was confronted with her I drew upon no pre-existing pattern of any kind – I followed my own spontaneous impulse.

As for the rest, my freedom consisted of accepting the lot laid down for me, and of accepting it cheerfully, even zealously. My piety had ardour in it; and straight away I became the best pupil at the Cours Désir. When my parents were reduced to near-poverty, they set their faith on the cultural values rather than the 'conspicuous expenditure' that my father might have preferred. As my chief amusement they offered me reading, an inexpensive delight. I was passionately devoted to books. I loved my father and my father loved books: he had filled my mother with a religious respect for them. They satisfied my curiosity – a curiosity that was active in me as far back as I can remember and that has never faded. Just where did I get it from? Freud holds that curiosity is rooted in the sexual instinct. Yet it seems to me that my interest in 'unsuitable things' was rather an offshoot of my eagerness for knowledge: and that I look upon as one of the basic data.

Perhaps there is no point in trying to explain it. All children have

2 A child's sex depends on the paternal spermatozoon, of which there are two kinds: in each particular case it seems entirely a matter of chance which of the two should fertilize the ovum.

a natural tendency to explore the world. The question is rather why in some cases this spontaneous impulse is broken. Several reasons occur to me – physical weakness, torpor, want of attention and therefore of stimuli, routine or overmuch loneliness, being forced to wearying tasks too early, worries and obsessions of every kind, and a disturbed emotional balance. A maladjusted child is too much taken up with himself to turn towards the outside world. My sister had an open nature, but she was less extremely eager for knowledge than I was. Zaza was lively and intelligent, but her involved relationship with her family, then her childhood love-affairs, and then still later her nostalgia for them, left her less free and disengaged than I. Until I was ten or twelve I had virtually no problems: I could devote myself entirely to my inquiries. I was not a forward child, an early developer. When I was about twelve I was still playing shop with my sister and my cousin at Meyrignac. I was quite happy to read childish books; but even they gave me glimpses of what interested me more than anything else – possible fluctuations in the human state, and relationships between people. The mechanical side of things did not attract me; I did not want to know how they were made or how they worked. I liked history for telling me about the customs of nations long ago – it did not bore me until later—and even pre-history and paleontology. I was interested in cosmology and geography, and I devoured books of voyages. When I learnt English I had the delight of discovering another literature and another country. I wanted to recapture the past and to grasp the whole circumambient universe, from the stars to the very centre of the earth.

Insofar as chance is defined as a meaningful junction of two causative series that no finality directed towards one another, it had scarcely any influence on my first ten years; the only time chance stepped in was when my parents gave me a sister rather than a brother. I had a high opinion of my cousin Jacques, and some admiration for him; but he did not play an important part in my childhood. The first important stroke of chance, as far as I was concerned, was the appearance of Zaza at the Cours Désir: this happened when I was rising ten. Both of us necessarily had to go to a Catholic school; but neither for her nor for me was it necessarily this particular one. What is more, we might well have been put in different forms and then, since my parents and the Mabilles had no point of contact, we should never have known one another. And in

8

that case my childhood would not have been lit up by a great friendship, since I never had anything but the mildest feelings for the other girls I knew at school.

What was not a matter of chance was the way I profited by our meeting. I was an open, sociable child, and I got along fairly well with her – fairly well, but no more. I saw Zaza's value straight away and I did my best to set up an alliance with her; I sat next to her in class, and I no longer talked to anyone else. What my childhood had made of me stood me in good stead; although I was not so unselfconscious as Zaza, nor so lively, and although I admired her for everything in which she differed from me, yet still I was not paralysed by shyness, and I succeeded in interesting her. I do not remember whether it was I who persuaded my mother to ask Zaza to the house or whether it was Madame Mabille who took the first step. At all events it was I who brought about this friendship: Zaza readily agreed, without suspecting how much of myself I was committing to it.

Would my life as an adult have been different without her? It is very hard for me to say. Through Zaza I came to know the joy of loving, the delight of intellectual exchange and of daily intimate alliance. She made me give up my role of the good little girl; and she taught me independence and disrespect, but only superficially. She took no part in the conflicts that set their mark on my adolescence; I never involved her in the tumult that was working inside me. Indeed, I carefully hid from her the fact that I was reading forbidden books and that I was calling religion and morality into question; for a long while I did not frankly tell her that I no longer believed in God. Our friendship had hardly any influence on outside events. Certainly it was because of her that I took up mathematics; I found them entertaining, but they led nowhere. Her father did recommend the Collège Sainte-Marie to my parents, and it was there that I met Garric and Mademoiselle Lambert. Garric was no more than an illusive shadow for me: Mademoiselle Lambert encouraged me to read philosophy, and that determined my way of life. But I should certainly have taken that course in any event, for it was my fundamental vocation. Through Zaza I met Stépha and indirectly Fernand; both of them brought me a great deal, but nothing really essential.

So did the happiness I knew with Zaza leave no lasting trace upon my life? I am not sure about that. From the time I was sixteen my own family filled me with a longing for escape, with anger and resentment; but it was through Zaza that I discovered how odious the bourgeoisie really was. I should have turned against the bourgeoisie in any case; but I should not have felt the falseness of their attitude towards things of the spirit, their stifling conformity, their arrogance and their oppressive tyranny – I should not have felt it in my heart nor paid for it with my tears. For me Zaza's murder by her environment, her milieu, was an overwhelming, unforgettable experience. And then how grey and dismal and lonely my youth and adolescence would have been without Zaza! She was my only thoroughly happy connection with life outside the world of books. I was apt to defend myself from hostile forces by means of a tight, withdrawn pride; and from this I was preserved by my admiration for Zaza. Without her, I might have turned out a mistrustful, bitter twenty-year-old instead of being ready to welcome love and friendship – the only attitude likely to arouse them. I cannot imagine myself at twenty other than I was – but nor can I imagine my childhood without Zaza in it.

She would have liked to live, to love, perhaps to write: what were the causes of her shipwreck, her death? What was the nature of her misfortunes? In the first place I believe there was that of her early childhood. Her father thought less of her than he did of her elder sister: Zaza was passionately attached to her mother, who was kind but whose time was very much taken up. Under an offhand, easy appearance, Zaza was in fact, extremely vulnerable, and she also lacked self-confidence: this was borne out by the last words she ever said – 'I am a reject.' She was torn apart by contradictions that she was not strong enough to overcome and that destroyed her: when she was fifteen her love for her mother was in conflict with that which she felt for her young cousin, and then later for Pradelle. Her basic fragility made these conflicts lethal.

When I was about twelve or thirteen I could have changed the course of my life. My father was disgusted by the poor quality of the teaching we were given at the Cours Désir and he thought of sending us to a lycée. Our schooling would have been sounder, and it would have cost less. My mother might have given way if I had sided with him. So there were two paths opening before me. But as it generally happens, it did not seem to me that I could really choose – my choice was dictated. I did not want to be parted from Zaza. What is more, I clung to my past, to my schoolfellows as a whole, and to the classrooms in which I had spent so many of my days. Within a familiar framework, I was sure of myself; the idea of confronting an unknown world terrified me. Our easy programme at school left me a good deal of free time, and I liked that. I knew that in the lycées the time-table was much more demanding. So without any hesitation I joined in my mother's protests.

My father could not override them; he had always left the care of our education to my mother, and this suggestion of a change was in itself an unlooked-for interference on his part. Yet if there had been no Zaza, and if he had managed to persuade me to go to a lycée because of grave financial pressure or other reasons, how would things have turned out? To begin with, uprooted and over-whelmed, I should no doubt have done indifferently and my vanity would have been wounded; but the way I worked later shows that I was capable of adapting myself to change, and in time I should have taken a good place in the school. In the stronger competition I should have stood out less than I did at the Cours Désir, but on the other hand a lycée would have given me many opportunities – intelligent teachers and open-minded companions. I should not have been forced to hide my intellectual development as though it were a deformity. I should have reached my goals sooner and more easily. And perhaps I should now be asking myself, with a retrospective shudder, 'But if I had stayed at the Cours Désir, would not all my chances have been ruined?'

I stayed, not by any deliberate choice, but because the whole of my earlier life required it of me. My real freedom in those days lay elsewhere – in the hard, intensely exciting work that throughout my awkward age helped to make me what I am. Among my pieces of good fortune I count the fact that my parents' different views on morality drove me into contestation. I made up my mind to be answerable to myself alone. I got rid of certain taboos. My intention of working, of reading hard, grew stronger: so did that of writing. I admitted to myself that I no longer believed in God. I shall speak of my atheism later on. But right away I will state that Father Martin's blundering played no great part in my development. It separated me from him, but not from religion; I still clung to that for some time. But I had learnt to think, and my faith had lost its pristine simplicity: it had become that dubious compromise which satisfies many people and which amounts to believing that one believes: I was too direct to put up with it.

11

When I was born, I was on rails. As I have said, my parents became members of the 'new poor' in 1919: the points shifted, and I found myself on a different set of rails – the line that suited me best. That too was one of my pieces of luck. I did suffer from our poverty a little, both directly and even more through my parents' fits of ill-humour. But without it, I should have found it harder to go on with my studies when I left the Cours Désir.

At this juncture I had to make a certain number of decisions; but here again it does not appear to me that I really made any free election – I followed the path that my earlier life pointed out for me so imperatively. I had wanted to teach ever since I was a child. When it was suggested that I should become a librarian, I refused: the austerity of Sanskrit and philology disheartened me. My father wanted me to be a civil servant; I persuaded him to let me go in for teaching – for teaching at the higher level. It took me a year to realize that I did not want to specialize in mathematics, nor in letters, but in philosophy: I convinced Mademoiselle Lambert that my idea was sound, and through her my parents. After this, it was circumstances that decided the choice of the subjects for my degree and of the theme for my diploma; but these were decisions without any great significance. A more important move on my part was deciding to sit for the *agrégation*[3] as early as 1929; but once again this was determined by my situation – I had the right to offer myself as a candidate; I was stifling at home; I wanted to put an end to it as soon as possible.

So throughout the years of my childhood, adolescence and youth my freedom never took the form of a *decree*: it was the carrying through of an initial project, continually resumed and strengthened – the project of knowing and of expressing. It branched out into secondary designs and into manifold attitudes towards people and the world, but all these had the same origin and the same meaning. I put my name down for Garrigue's social teams; I sought and cultivated a friendship with Jacques; I saw a lot of my fellow-students at the Sorbonne; I secretly haunted the Montparnasse bars; I made friends with Stépha; I benefited from Herbaud's kindness to me. I was never inert: I called out for life and welcomed it. My search often led me into blind alleys. But I also made some most rewarding

[3] A competitive and very difficult examination for admission to posts in the lycées and universities.—Tr.

discoveries. And this attitude of mine increased my chances of a decisive encounter.

From my childhood until the time I came of age, I moved on from one discovery to the next; my life was an adventure. Yet at the same time it followed given cycles, as all life does. This was particularly striking during the years I spent at the Cours Désir. I went there almost every day, making the same journey by foot or by métro, and there I found the same teachers and the same companions. My Sundays were repetitions of the foregoing Sundays and the summer holidays those of the year before. This routine fell to pieces after my *bachot*.[4] The Collège Sainte-Marie, the Institut catholique and above all the Sorbonne were great new experiences. I discovered the Bibliothèque nationale. I grew accustomed to unknown faces. But still I was firmly pinned in my parents' home and compelled to follow their rhythm of life. It was only after my *agrégation* that the old framework was entirely broken.

The development of my life during those twenty years was marked by a twofold continuity. My physical being was subjected to its metamorphosis. And at the same time I was going through a continual apprenticeship. Time, in those days, was a positive factor of accumulation: as I had an excellent memory I did not lose a great deal of what I had gathered together. Yet it should not be forgotten that a certain loss of pace is to be observed in every individual, even if he progresses steadily from birth to maturity. In his eighties Tolstoy said that there was little more than a single stride between himself then and himself at the age of five, whereas between the five-year-old and the new-born Tolstoy there lay an immeasurable distance. There is a great deal of truth in this seeming paradox. The metamorphosis of the human grub into a speaking individual has something amazing about it. After that comes the achievement of language, rational thought, reading, writing, and the elements of knowledge, and this too amounts to a most surprising feat: but less so. Subsequently the progress goes on, but it does not advance at the same rate. From the point of view of schooling, one learns more in *seconde*[5] than one does in *huitième*,[6] and more at the Sorbonne than in *seconde*; but these acquisitions play a less important part in

[4] The *baccalauréat* or school-leaving certificate that gives admission to the university.—Tr.
[5] In this class, the pupils are about sixteen.—Tr.
[6] In this, about nine.—Tr.

the general building-up of the person. (Yet for me, although it was in the context of this loss of pace, there was one exceptionally favoured year – the year in which I left the Cours Désir and in which thanks to Jacques I had the overwhelming revelation of contemporary literature.)

As I grew older, so my position in relation to the adults changed, as did their behaviour towards me; and these changes in their turn reacted upon me: I had to readjust to the way in which the grownups adjusted to me. My mother stopped taking me on to her lap; she began to treat me seriously, which I found gratifying: I assumed the character of a good little girl. Under Zaza's influence and also no doubt because of my age, towards twelve I became restless, troublesome and irreverent. The harsh reactions of the good ladies at the Cours Désir brought about a private rebellion within me: I renounced their morality and the God who underwrote it. I was most uncomfortably aware of the gap between my teachers' and my parents' image of me and my own truth. Later, at the beginning of my life as a student, I came to a muddled working knowledge of Necessity, in Sartre's meaning of the word – fate in externality of freedom. I had made myself freely; and, with the approval of one and all, I thought I had made myself into an eager, hard-working student: and there I was, turned into a monster. At this I became sullen at home, closed-in, gloomy and hostile. Fortunately the acquaintances I made, my meetings with other students, and my friendships helped me to recover a more cheerful image of myself.

All through my childhood and my young days, my life had a distinct meaning: its goal and its motive was to reach the adult age. At twenty, living does not mean getting ready to be forty. Yet for my people and for me, my duty as a child and an adolescent consisted of forming the woman I was to be tomorrow. (That is why *Memoirs of a Dutiful Daughter* has a fiction-like unity lacking in the later volumes. As it does in novels dealing with apprenticeship to life, in that book time runs straight on from beginning to end.) My life in those days seemed to me an upward progress. It is true that nothing is gained without something being lost: everyone knows that in fulfilling oneself one necessarily sacrifices some possibilities. The adjustments carried out in a childish mind and body are harmful to those one would like to carry out later. The interests then formed thrust others out; and in me eagerness for knowledge overlaid a great many of them. The possession of an object takes away its newness. Regression in children means that they are sorry to grow up. For my part I lost my mother's caresses, I lost the carefree irresponsibility of my first years and my sense of wonder at the world's mysteries. Sometimes the future frightened me: was I one day to lead my mother's dull, grey kind of existence? Would my sister and I become strangers to one another? Should we eventually stop going to Meyrignac? But generally speaking the balance was decidedly favourable. The only thing in my young days that was repugnant, scandalous in the strict sense, was death: I liked growing older: I was moving forward. Then later on, I wanted to escape from my family. For me, at that time, growing older meant both ripeness and freedom. Even in my gloomiest days my sanguine nature urged me to put my trust in the future. I believed in my star; I believed that what would happen to me could not but be good.

Many children and adolescents long for the grown-up state as they would long for a release. But others dread it. It was far harder for Zaza to grow up than it was for me. The idea of leaving her mother wrung her heart. The magic of her childhood made her look upon her adolescence as grey and dreary and the prospect of a 'prudential' marriage horrified her. For a working man's son, it is cruel to become a working man in his turn – that is to say a man condemned to do nothing any more, other than carrying on with the same life. Many young people fight against this transition to adulthood by means of revolt, delinquence, running away, drugs, violence, or a challenge to death that may go as far as suicide. For my part, the idea of earning my own living by work I liked filled me with delight: all the more so since my being a woman seemed to foredoom me to dependence.

What would have happened if the position of my family had been different? There are many suppositions I could make. Suppose in the first place that my parents, though ruined, had behaved differently: if my mother had been less tactless and oppressive, the narrowness of her understanding would have troubled me less; resentment would not have overlaid my affection for her and I should have borne my father's withdrawal better. If my father, even without intervening in my struggle with my mother, had continued to interest himself in me, that would have helped a great deal. If he had openly taken my side, demanding that I should be allowed various kinds of freedom – and my mother would in that case have yielded – my life would have been so much the easier. I should still have

15

been against their way of living and thinking, even if both had behaved in a friendly manner; I should still have more or less stifled at home and I should have felt myself isolated; but I should certainly not have felt rejected, thrust out and betrayed. It would not have changed my destiny; but it would have spared me a great deal of pointless sadness. This is the only period of my life that has left me with regrets. As for the crisis of my awkward age, it was I who stirred it up; and it was fruitful; I tore myself away from the safe comfort of certainties through my love for the truth; and truth rewarded me. Between seventeen and twenty I was deeply hurt by my parents' attitude towards me; and it was a pain from which I derived no benefit whatsoever.

If they had kept their money, we should have lived more pleasantly; their mood would have been less gloomy. But I was eleven or twelve when their habit of mind changed for the worse, and by then I was already formed. My mother was so timorous and at the same time so despotic she would never have known how to discover diversions for us and she would have disliked letting us amuse ourselves without her. No doubt I would have spent more of my time in games and sports: the reason why I was so passionately devoted to croquet at La Grillère was that there was no other kind of amusement of that sort in my life. But in that case my make-believe games with my sister would have been more or less sacrificed, certainly not my work or my reading. Even if I had been better dressed and therefore more at my ease, I should have loathed social gatherings. No: money would not have changed much in my childhood nor in my adolescence. And if I had not been obliged to take up a profession, I should still have succeeded in carrying on with my studies.

Only in one respect might the course of my life have been turned from its path, but that was an important one: Jacques would have taken more interest in me if I had been better dressed, more ornamental, and if I had had that ease which money generally gives. My poverty would not have been an impediment to the marriage he thought of at one time. I will not speculate on his having married me without a fortune: he would have had to be so thoroughly unlike himself, so thoroughly another person, that the hypothesis has no meaning. But such as he was, he would willingly have married me if I had had a dowry. If he had proposed marriage before I met Sartre, how should I have reacted?

It is difficult to dream retrospectively about one's life: to do so convincingly one would have to control all the variables. Yet had my father been satisfied with his position he would not have seen me as the image of his failure and he would not have withdrawn from me; and even if I had been harassed and badgered by my mother, the house would not have seemed to me a hell nor Jacques a rescuer from it. Perhaps I should only have regarded him as a friend, and one whose faults I should not have overlooked. Even in those days, when I dreamt of sharing his life, the idea sometimes horrified me. I should have hesitated. Yet if he had spoken to me of love, then the emotion and the physical attraction that would have grown up between us would no doubt have persuaded me.

What if it had? Would Jacques have drunk less and would he have managed his affairs more intelligently? I do not believe that I should have filled the emptiness in him: he was not ready to receive what I had to bring. I should soon have discovered his poverty of feeling, and he would not have satisfied me intellectually. I should have been very fond of him, however; and of the children we should have had. I should have experienced the torment that so many young women know, bound hand and foot by love and motherhood without having forgotten their former dreams.

There is one thing that I am quite sure of, and that is that I should have dealt with that situation. My first eighteen years had made me into a person who could not possibly have betrayed them. It is impossible to imagine that I should have renounced my ambitions, my hopes and all that was essential to give my life a meaning. At some given point I should have refused to bog down in the bourgeois way. Separated from Jacques or not, I should have returned to my studies, I should have written, and in the end I should certainly have drifted away from him. I should have had to overcome a great many difficulties; and it may be that confronting them would have been more valuable to me than the easy opportunities that were in fact my lot. More than one future can be imagined for the girl I was, although it is not in the power of the woman she has now become to conceive herself as other than she is.

What real importance did Jacques have in my life? Far less than Zaza. My introduction to modern art and literature would certainly have taken place during my years at the Sorbonne, in any event. Thanks to him I did come to know the 'poetry of the bars', and I went to them often; for me it was a valuable relief from pressure, but it was one that did not bring me a great deal. My relationship with Jacques meant more pain than joy. What he stood for in my youth was in fact its share of dreams. Before then I did not day-dream much: Zaza, books, nature and my plans were enough for me. But at eighteen, unhappy at home and maladjusted, I dreamt: not of being someone else but of sharing a life that seemed to me admirable, like Garric's, or thrilling, like Jacques'. That dream lasted a long while, yet I never really believed in it entirely. My feelings for Jacques were inflated, exaggerated, whereas those I had for Zaza were genuine. Although he was unusual he was in no way outstanding, whereas Zaza was an exceptional being.

Now that I think of Zaza and Jacques and many others, I see what a great deal of ignorance there was in my relations with them: I thought I knew them through and through, but they had hidden sides whose existence I did not even suspect. Going into Zaza's room when she was not there, for example, I would feel quite moved; I would wonder just what life tasted like to her: but it never occurred to me that there might be more in it than ever I knew. I lacked imagination, experience and discernment. I had a childish belief in what people said and I did not wonder at all about what they did not say. I was thunderstruck when I learnt about Zaza's adolescent romance, about Jacques' affair, and when Fernand gave me to understand that he slept with Stépha. Yet Zaza would not have been what she was, she would not have been the Zaza I loved, without her passionate attachment to her young cousin – a love that was to be crossed. It was my own life that was impenetrable to me, and that at a time when I thought I saw the whole of it clear.

I was blinder still to the social and political context in which it was being formed. My story was typical of a French bourgeois girl belonging to a poor family. I had access to the consumer-goods that my country and my period held out to me, in so far as they suited my parents' budget. What I should learn and what I should read was laid down for me by society.

To begin with I knew society only through my parents; then I came to know it more directly, but still without taking any interest in it. This want of concern was conditioned by the state of the world as it then was; it was the security of the years after the war that allowed me to worry so little about what was happening. My companions at the Sorbonne forced me to take at least some notice of current events. I came to understand the disgrace and shame of colonialism. Stépha converted me to internationalism and anti-militarism. I now accepted to the full the disgust I had long felt for the fanaticism of the right wing, for racism, for the bourgeois values and for every form of obscurantism. I was charmed by the idea of Revolution. I slid leftwards: every candid intellectual must necessarily, in the name of the universalism he is taught, wish for the abolition of classes. But my personal adventure meant more to me than the adventure of mankind as a whole. I did not realize how much the first depended on the second; and I continued to be very poorly informed about humanity.

How should I have developed if I had not met Sartre? Individualism, idealism and spiritualism (in the philosophical sense) were still hanging about me; should I have got rid of them earlier or later? I cannot tell. The fact is that I did meet him and that that was the most important event in my life.

I find it hard to decide how far our meeting was owing to chance. It was not entirely fortuitous. By going to the university I had given myself the greatest possible number of opportunities for such a meeting to take place: the ideal companion I dreamt of at fifteen had necessarily to be an intellectual, one who was as intensely eager as I was to understand the world. Then again, from my first days at the Sorbonne, my eyes and my ears had been on the alert to find the fellow-student I could sympathize with most fully. And my generally open attitude won me friendly contacts; I gained Herbaud's liking, and through him, Sartre's.

Yet if he had passed the *agrégation* a year earlier, and if I had sat for it a year later, should we never have known one another? Not necessarily. Herbaud might have acted as the link between us. Indeed, it has often occurred to us that if our meeting had not happened in 1929 it might well have come about later: the group of young left-wing teachers to which we belonged was not very large. In any case, I should have taken to writing; I should have seen a great deal of other writers, and because of his books I should have wanted to know Sartre. And because of the solidarity that bound anti-nazi intellectuals together between 1943 and 1945, my wishes would have been realized. A bond, perhaps different but certainly very strong, would have been created between us.

Although to some extent it was chance that brought us into

contact, the commitment that has bound our lives together was freely elected: a choice of this kind is not a decree but a long-term undertaking. For me it first came into evidence in the form of a practical decision, that of staying in Paris for two years instead of taking a post. I adopted Sartre's friendships and I moved into his world, not as some people said because I am a woman, but because it was the world I had longed for for many years. Besides, he adopted mine just as I adopted him; he liked Zaza. But presently none of my past was left to me except my sister, Stépha and Fernand; he had a greater number of friends, and they were linked to one another by emotional bonds and intellectual affinities.

I took great care that our relationship should not deteriorate, gauging just what I should or should not accept from him or from me myself, so that our understanding should not be endangered. I would have agreed, unwillingly though not despairingly, to his going to Japan. I am sure that two years later we should have come together again exactly as we had promised. One important decision was that of leaving for Marseilles rather than marrying him. In all other cases my resolutions coincided with my spontaneous impulse: but not in this. I very strongly wished not to leave Sartre. I chose what was the hardest course for me at that moment in order to safeguard the future. This was the only time when it seems to me that I gave my life a wholesome change of direction and avoided a danger.

What would have happened if I had accepted his proposal? The supposition is meaningless. I was so made that I respected others. I knew Sartre did not want marriage. I could not want it all by myself. I did sometimes exert pressure on him in little things (and he on me), but I should never have been capable, even in thought, of forcing his hand in any serious matter. Supposing that for reasons I can scarcely imagine we had been obliged to marry, I know we should have managed to live our marriage in freedom.

Freedom: to what extent did I make use of it during the ten years that followed? How much did chance and circumstance step in?

I took some steps that the situation required of me: I asked to be moved nearer to Paris, and I was posted to Rouen, not far from Sartre, who was teaching at Le Havre. After that, asking for an appointment in Paris and accepting it followed naturally. I entirely agreed that Sartre should spend a year in Berlin. Both of us were of the opinion that he should teach a terminal class at Laon rather than preparing students for the *Ecole normale* at Lyons, rightly supposing that that would get him back to Paris sooner.

My lot, during this period, was much the same as most other people's: I too worked simply to carry on my life. Like theirs, my days were repetitive; and sometimes I found this wearisome. But I was favoured. Most people cannot hope to escape from their routine before the long-awaited and dreaded day when they retire. For them the only freshness in life is that which comes with the birth and the growing up of their children; and the novelty of that fades steadily in the monotony of every day. For my part I had a great deal of spare time; I read; I made new friends; I travelled – I went on making discoveries. I continued to pay close attention to the outside world. My relationship with Sartre remained living and immediate; I was not chained to a home and household cares; I did not feel myself indissolubly bound to my past. And I kept my eyes steadily on a future full of promise: I was going to be an author. It was essentially in my apprenticeship as a writer that my freedom was committed and engaged. Here there was no question of a smooth upward progress like the one that had led me to the *agrégation* in philosophy, but rather of a faltering struggle – efforts without advance, retreats, a timid moving forward.

Chance, in one form or another, helped to fill my life with people: Colette Audry might very well not have happened to be in the same lycée as myself; neither Olga nor Bianca nor Lise might have attended my classes. Seeing that I was deeply interested in people, it would have been quite out of the ordinary course of things if none of my fellow-teachers and none of my pupils had attracted my attention; but instead of these contacts I might have made others that would have been more rewarding or less, and that would have given my life a different tinge. It was chance that brought these meetings about rather than others. But now this same chance could not do a great deal either for or against me, for at this time the essential basis of my life was fixed and settled.

My freedom did come into play in the way I cultivated these friendships. I am particularly interested in working out just what share my freedom had in my relationship with Olga, because it was unusually complex.

It was I who took the initiative in going out with her from time to time. I was touched by her affection; and encouraged by Sartre I persuaded her parents to send her back to Rouen, whereas they had wanted to keep her at Caen. I had meant to coach her for her degree in philosophy, but I did not succeed, and I resigned myself to her laziness: I *could* not do otherwise. As Sartre has shown, the practico-inert puts up with arbitrary demands: a friendship is not only a matter of day-by-day experience; it also falls into the past and becomes a set reality that we are compelled to accept; and this particular reality insisted on continuation. There was no question of my breaking with Olga, nor of going on obstinately struggling with her. Later I found myself face to face with other impossibilities. 'Setting myself in total agreement with Sartre was too necessary for it to be possible for me to see Olga through any eyes but his.'[7] It was in me that this necessity had its origin; I elected it continually. But this choice was in contradiction with others, and that is why I found myself torn apart in the trio that we had brought into being. I could not break away, but within the trio I felt ill at ease. It was Olga who dealt with the situation by becoming closely attached to Bost. From that time on I was perfectly happy to satisfy all the requirements of our friendship – a friendship that was no longer a constraint to me but one that I could live freely.

At this point something happened that might have broken my life for good – my illness. This was in no way the effect of chance. I was tiring myself beyond all measure, and I did not take precautions straight away, as I ought to have done. The illness was also an escape: I was running away from our trio – it had just broken up, but tensions remained. Nor was it a question of chance that the illness could not be cut short – in those days antibiotics did not exist. My surviving was, at least on the plane of medical knowledge of the disease. The doctors said it was two to one against my recovery.

It seemed to me during those ten years that I was building up my life with my own hands, and that was not entirely untrue; yet I was being conditioned by society, just as I was in the earlier period. I consumed the goods society offered me; and society allotted me a given salary: the margin of decision it allowed me was very narrow. In my profession I enjoyed the comfortable status of lycée teachers at that time, and I could take certain steps on my own; but the programmes, the time-tables and the number of pupils was decided without reference to me. As far as culture was concerned I was

[7] *The Prime of Life.*

allowed to choose; but only among the books, the films and the exhibitions society put at my disposal. What is more, it often happened that when I thought I had discovered some new form of behaviour for myself, I was only complying with a pattern: going to winter sports or spending my holidays in Greece was merely following the example of a great many French petits bourgeois. Yet when I looked with a remote and distant eye and saw myself as a member of a community, an item in a collectivity, I was put out of countenance. At Rouen, when Stépha said 'How well these French do eat!' and later, when Fernand said 'These swine of Frenchmen', I refused to believe that their words had anything to do with me. When I was a little girl I would not be classed among the children – I was *me* – and now in just the same way I refused to be defined as a Frenchwoman: here again I thought I was *me*.

A country's position depends upon its own history and upon the history of the world, and I was therefore under the domination of events: I refused to concern myself with them. I did keep more or less abreast of what was happening, but I did so with a good deal of detachment. In *The Prime of Life* I ought to have given a better account of the things I did not know, of the extent of my ignorance, in order to draw a more exact picture of my life. A person is shown as clearly by what he does not grasp as by what he does; sometimes even more so. Both Louis XVI and the last Tsar, by writing in effect 'Today, nothing' in their private diaries when revolution was breaking out all round them, tell us more about themselves than by any of their words or deeds. As I have said, between 1929 and 1939 the whole of the French left wing suffered from political blindness. It was easy for me to share this blindness, since I did not feel the pressure of history in such a way that it worried me at all. And I wanted to be blind: I wanted to believe that nothing, ever, could disturb my happiness. The Popular Front meant a good deal to me; and that was because it brought hope and not threats. I was stirred by the war in Spain, but I did not think it had anything to do with me personally. The use I made of my freedom was to fail to appreciate the truth of the time in which I was living.

In 1939 this truth suddenly stared me in the face. Then I knew that I was undergoing my life, suffering it, for I had stopped agreeing to what was prescribed to me: the war tore me apart; it separated me from Sartre; it cut me off from my sister: I moved from dread to despair, then to anger and disgust shot through with

23

flashes of hope. Every hour of every day I saw just how much I depended upon events. They became the very stuff of my daily life. Most of them I knew nothing about, because of the censorship: the dark side of the moon, the unseen part of my existence, has never been so impenetrable as it was during the war. But I passionately tried to know what was happening and to understand it: I no longer distinguished between events and my own personal fate.

The share of freedom that remained to me was slight. During the winter of 1939 I did manage to go to Brumath to see Sartre; but there again I was only copying a great many other women. In June 1940 I left Paris. My lycée was being evacuated to Nantes and Bianca's father offered me a seat in his car – my departure was a matter of course. I very soon came back to La Pouèze, taking advantage of an opportunity that cropped up: this return too was dictated to me. My attitude during the occupation was prescribed to me by my past – by my whole scale of values and my convictions. My political commitments always expressed the ideas I had worked out for myself during the course of my life: at this point the question was to choose the form of conduct that would translate them most faithfully in hitherto unknown circumstances. In later days that was a problem I often found hard to solve. In 1940 there was no possible hesitation on the intellectual plane: I was incapable of doing anything but hate Nazism and collaboration. My line of conduct also required that I should try to react to the situation without letting myself be crushed. Once a fellow-prisoner had reassured me about the fate of Sartre I determined to place all my hopes on a happy future. I turned to Hegel to make the course of history comprehensible to me; and I welcomed and sought out every possible kind of distraction. Above all I set about finishing *She Came to Stay* and I wrote *Blood of Others*. What I did not find was a way of converting my opposition to Nazism into acts. It was Sartre, after he had come back from his camp, who took the necessary steps: the first, the setting up of the resistance group *Socialisme et liberté*, astonished me to begin with, but he persuaded me of its soundness and from that moment on I took part in his political activities. I adapted myself to the war-time shortages by turning my worries into a kind of obsessive game. Circumstances led us to leave Paris in July 1944; in spite of the difficulties we came back of our own initiative to be present at that splendid and joyful event, the Liberation.

There was nothing fortuitous about the friendships we made towards the end of the war. We came to know Giacometti through Lise, or possibly through Leiris, with whom Sartre worked in the CNE[8] and whose books we liked. Leiris brought us Salacrou, Bataille, Limbour, Lacan, Leibovitz and Queneau, all of whom belonged to the intellectual resistance. Sartre had written an article on Camus, and he introduced himself one day when *The Flies* was being acted. Genet, who knew that we liked *Our Lady of the Flowers* came over and spoke to Sartre at the Flore. Supposing I had not known Sartre, should I have made friends with these writers? No doubt I should. By that time I should certainly have had one book published; I should have been a member of the CNE and perhaps there I should have met Sartre.

In 1945 I was back on my rails and there were few decisions for me to take. The most important was making up my mind not to go back into teaching nor to accept any bread-and-butter job, so that I could devote myself entirely to writing. All I had left to do was to create opportunities. My objective reality as a writer, a member of the *Temps modernes* team, the *grande sartreuse*,[9] brought me a great many; my only task was to decide which to accept and which to reject. In this way, without ever having asked to go, I was invited to Portugal, Tunisia, Switzerland and Holland. I did make more effort for our journey to Italy; I insisted on its taking place, in spite of the unfavourable circumstances. As for my visit to America, it was Soupault who laid it on for me; I more or less begged him to do so. After that Sartre and I worked out some of our journeys together: others were urgently pressed on us, particularly those that took us to Cuba and Brazil in 1960 and to the USSR in 1962. Our stays at La Pouèze were the result both of Madame Lemaire's invitations and our own wishes. Those we made in the south of France were organized by me, and I suited them to Sartre's personal tastes. I left my hotel and set myself up in a room in the rue de la Bûcherie, moving on, after I had accepted the Prix Goncourt, to a small flat near the Montparnasse cemetery. In 1951 I bought a car and learnt to drive: there was nothing original about this move – the automobile industry was coming to life again and a great many French people wanted a car.

[8] *Comité national d'écrivains*, the national committee of resistance writers.—Tr.
[9] An obvious pun on Grande Chartreuse, and Simone de Beauvoir's well-known nickname.—Tr.

Since my life was spreading wider and wider in the world, since I knew more people, and since opportunities came my way more and more often, the part played by chance diminished to something very small. The things that happened to me were either extensions of my past or repercussions from it. Yet it was chance that brought me into contact with Algren in 1947: nothing was more unlikely than my meeting with him. It was natural that Sartre should have known Richard Wright in America, and it was also natural that Richard Wright should have introduced me to New York intellectuals. But he never mentioned Algren, who lived in Chicago. It was Nelly Benson who advised me to see him when I was having dinner with her – an invitation I had very nearly refused. In Chicago Algren was within a hairsbreadth of not answering the telephone when I rang him up; and in spite of the liking we felt for one another I should not have seen him again if Sartre had not asked me to stay on in America for a while. Even so, there would have been nothing between us if I had not been free enough to want the affair: I should not have telephoned him suggesting that I should take up his invitation to come back to Chicago. After that I wanted what happened: we suited each other because of what we were and because of what each represented for the other. But I wanted it within certain given limits that almost necessarily condemned it to an early end. I have told what it brought me in *Force of Circumstance*.

Chance had far less to do with my relationship with Lanzmann. He might not have been one of the *Temps modernes* team; yet his age, intellectual make-up and political ideas made it the obvious place for him. At that point too I felt free and unattached and I wanted something to happen to me; my liking for Lanzmann (which I knew he returned) was quite ready to turn into a deeper feeling. Circumstances and our difference in age meant that after a few years it ceased, giving way to a deep friendship. In this case too the outcome was inevitable.

From then on I knew that the course of the world was the very texture of my own life, and I carefully followed its progress. I was still widely ignorant, for want of adequate information: among other things, I had no idea of the extent of the repression at Sétif in 1945, and until 1954 I knew nothing about the true situation in Algeria; nor did I know what was really happening in the USSR and the people's democracies. Even if one does not know a great deal, one must take up a stand; and that does not happen without hesitations and mistakes. As for our relations with the Communist Party and the socialist countries, there I followed Sartre in his fluctuations. From time to time it was shatteringly clear that we were bound to reject certain grossly discreditable things – the Soviet camps, the Rajk and Slansky trials, Budapest. Our attitudes towards capitalism, imperialism and colonialism were sharp and clear: they were to be fought against in our writing and if possible by acts. I was intellectually committed in this struggle, but on the practical plane I was not very active. I find the boredom of congresses and committees hard to bear. Still, I did take part in the Helsinki congress of 1955. That same year I wrote a book on China, where I had spent two months; the book was intended to make the Chinese revolution more widely known. On various occasions I signed manifestoes and attended meetings. I did a few small things during the war in Algeria and against Gaullism. On these last two points my intellectual convictions forced themselves upon me with as much clarity as my rejection of Nazism in 1940: how were they to be translated into action? I asked organizations engaged in the struggle and militants like Francis Jeanson. All I did was to follow their advice: but obviously I had in the first place elected to ask for it, and that was a free choice.

It is essentially in the field of literary creation that I have made use of my freedom: a writer writes from the basis of the being that he has made of himself, but writing is always a fresh act. In *Force of Circumstance* I have given an account of how my creations were born and how they developed up until 1962; there is no point in going over it again in this book.

When I reflect upon the general course of my life, I find it has a striking continuity. I was born in Paris and I have always lived there: even during the years in Marseilles and Rouen, my roots were still in Paris. I have moved several times, but I have always stayed in more or less the same district: today I live only five minutes away from my first home. Paris has changed immensely since I was young, but still I can find my youth in many places – the Luxembourg, the Sorbonne, the Bibliothèque nationale, the boulevard Montparnasse, the place St-Germain-des-Prés. I no longer write in cafés, but I still work with much the same rhythm and according to the same methods. I do not go for long walks any more, but I drive about in my car. My occupations have always been the same – reading, the cinema, listening to records, looking at pictures.

27

Yet there is one field in which this continuity has to a great extent been interrupted – that of the friendships I shared with Sartre. Sometimes it was death that broke them. I have told how some wore thin or fell brusquely apart while others were coming into being. In most cases – in that of Camus, for example – their history seems plain from beginning to end. But there is one that puzzles me: the case of Pagniez. For years he was Sartre's best friend; they liked being together and they saw one another continually. No clash or disagreement ever set them definitely, clearly against one another; how can they have drifted so far apart as never to meet at all? When they were young they had differences, but these were only differences of view and attitude – shades of opinion that never formed part of any praxis. The moment these slight differences express themselves in choices, which immediately form a practico-inert charged with fresh demands, it is understandable that paths that to begin with were almost identical should diverge at great speed. The fact that Pagniez was a lover of the past and Sartre an extremist was merely amusing – two ways of experiencing their state as petit-bourgeois intellectuals. But when Pagniez revealed himself as a conservative and a reactionary while Sartre was discovering the class-struggle and taking it with the utmost seriousness, then it was clear that an understanding was impossible. Yet still one might have thought that for the sake of the past a mutual forbearance could operate: for a great while there was a tolerance of this kind between us and Madame Lemaire. We did try with Pagniez. 'You write,' he said. 'I set up a happy home for myself; and that is not such a bad thing either.' But we soon saw that it was not all he thought it was; otherwise he would never have harboured such bitterness against Sartre. We had not seen him for years when in 1960 he refused to support his colleagues Pouillon and Pingaud, who had been suspended for having signed the manifesto of the 121.

Yet there are some very old bonds in my life that have never been broken. Its essential unity is provided by two factors: the place that Sartre has always had in it, and my faithfulness to my original design – that of knowing and of writing. What did I aim at in this project? Like all living individuals, I sought to overtake my being, to rejoin and merge with it; and in order to do so I based myself upon those experiences in which I had the illusion of having achieved this. Knowing meant directing my awareness towards the world, as did the meditation of my childhood, withdrawing the world from the void of the past and from the darkness of absence: when I lost myself in the object upon which I gazed, or in moments of physical or emotional ecstasy, or in the delight of memory, or in the heart-raising anticipation of what was to come, it seemed to me that I brought about the impossible junction between the in-itself and the for-itself. And I also wanted to realize myself in books that, like those I had loved, would be existing objects for others, but objects haunted by a presence – my presence.

All search for the being is condemned to failure; but this very failure can be accepted. By giving up the vain hope of making oneself a god, one can be content with simply existing. Knowing does not mean possessing; yet I never tire of learning. A writer's works may live on and on, and I wanted to share a perennity in which I should myself be embodied, but above all I wanted my contemporaries to hear and understand me. It is my relationship with them – cooperation, struggle, dialogue – that has meant most to me throughout my life.

All in all, my lot has been very fortunate. I have been frightened at times, and at times I have rebelled. But I have never suffered oppression; I have not known exile; nor have I been afflicted with any infirmity. I have not experienced the death of anyone essential to me and since I was twenty-one I have never been lonely. The opportunities granted to me at the beginning helped me not only to lead a happy life but to be happy in the life I led. I have been aware of my shortcomings and my limits, but I have made the best of them. When I was tormented by what was happening in the world, it was the world I wanted to change, not the place I had in it.

'One is born manifold and one dies single,' says Valéry, in effect. Bergson too emphasizes that in fulfilling ourselves we lose most of our potentialities. That is not at all the way I see myself. Certainly when I was twelve I was tempted by paleontology, astronomy, history, and every fresh branch of learning I chanced upon; but they all formed part of the larger project of discovering the world, a project that I followed steadily. Very early the idea of writing made my future clear and luminous. To begin with I was amorphous, but I was not manifold. On the contrary, what strikes me is the way the little girl of three lived on, grown calmer, in the child of ten, that child in the young woman of twenty, and so forward. Of course, circumstances have caused me to develop in many respects. But through all my changes I still see myself.

Mine is a striking example of how dependent the individual is upon his childhood. My early years allowed me to make a good start. After that it was my luck that no accident occurred to cut short the unfolding of my life; another piece of good fortune was that chance favoured me extraordinarily in placing Sartre upon my path. My freedom was used to maintain my very first projects; and it has continually devised and contrived ways of remaining faithful to them throughout the variation of circumstance. Sometimes these inventions have assumed the appearance of a decision, but of a decision that always seemed to me self-evident: I have never had to *ponder* over important things. My life has been the fulfilment of a primary design; and at the same time it has been the product and the expression of the world in which it developed. That is why in telling it I have been able to speak of a great deal other than myself.

And where exactly am I now? What new things have these last ten years of my life brought me? That is what I shall try to clarify here.

The first thing that strikes me when I look back at the ten years that have passed since I finished *Force of Circumstance* is that I do not feel that I have aged. Between 1958 and 1962 I was aware that I had crossed a frontier. Now that frontier lies behind me, and I have resigned myself to it. It may be that some illness or infirmity will oblige me to cross yet another; I know the threats that the future holds, but I am not obsessed by them. For the time being, the passage of the years has come to a halt for me: as I see it, there is not much difference between being sixty-three and fifty-three; whereas when I was fifty-three I felt at a staggering distance from forty-three. Now I mind little about my personal appearance: I take care of it out of consideration for those around me. In short, I see myself as settled into old age. Like everybody else, I am incapable of an inner experience of it: age is one of the things that cannot be realized. Seeing that my health is good, my body gives me no token of age. I am sixty-three: and this truth remains foreign to me.

My life has scarcely changed since 1962. It is strictly dependent upon the same past, a past that defines both my present and its opening towards the future. My past is a datum, a base from which I project myself and which I must surpass: it has provided me with the mechanisms assembled in my body, the cultural tools that I use, my knowledge, my areas of ignorance, my tastes, my interests, my relations with others, my duties, and my occupations. To what extent does this repossession of my past by the practico-inert amount to a limitation and a restraint? What room does it leave my freedom?

As I have just said, the practico-inert bears arbitrary requirements. 'I *can't* do that to him.' 'You mean you don't *want* to.' This is a very usual exchange between lovers, and generally it is the first speaker who is right. One cannot always want what one would like: it would mean self-betrayal. That is why people whose life is fixed and settled often live it unwillingly, shut up in a house they long to escape from or imprisoned in a calling that no longer interests them. If the break with the past is both very strongly desired and at the same time rigidly forbidden, it may happen that the subject finds that suicide is his only way out. That was Leiris' case, as he describes it in *Fibrils*: he could neither betray the woman he had lived with all his life nor give up the one who had just opened fresh horizons for him. It may seem absurd to spare two beloved beings by carrying out an act that will agonize both; but at this point the absurd is the only answer. One shatters the rational world by blind violence: for want of a solution, it is a radical means of escape. People do not often reach these extremities, but they do often sustain the burden of earlier commitments in submissiveness or a state of revolt. As for me, I may say I never feel either. I have always hated being bored and little by little I have succeeded in getting rid of all wearisome forms of drudgery. *Live with no time out*: a slogan of May 1968 that touched me more than the rest, because it was the one I had adopted in my childhood: I am still faithful to it. My days now are to a great extent the prolongation of those of former times; but that is with my whole-hearted agreement. For example, I have lived in the same place for fifteen years. It is true that moving would raise problems and that there is some inertia in this staying where I am. But it is also true that I cannot imagine any other flat that would suit me better: this place is rich in memories and that gives it a priceless charm in my eyes. I deliberately elect to stay here.

The past dwells in me and hems me about. But I do not look back towards it more often than I used. I have always liked going over shared memories with Sartre, with my sister and my friends. I prize some that belong to me alone very highly in spite of their stereo-

typed poverty. In my living emotion they still have life. It is a great
good fortune to have had feelings that last: the moments when I
experienced them intensely in the past were not illusory; the future
they promised me has come about, and they have kept their value to
the full. It seems to me that in a life that has been cut by violent
breaks, looking back cannot have the same gentle pleasure. If I
retain my former links with someone, links perhaps a little different
but still warm, then all we experienced together colours these
images of earlier times, strengthening their significance, giving them
their weight. Then there is another way in which the past delights
me at times: it is when I revisit places I have loved. When I come to
speak of my travels I shall say how important these confrontations
are to me.

I am neither a slave to my past nor am I haunted by it; I do not
retain a sufficiently sharp image of it to be able to gauge the alterations that take place around me; I cannot therefore grasp the passage of time as it fleets by. When I am in a country that I have not
seen for a long while, the changes are obvious to me; but what I
seem to see is a sudden replacement of one scene by another rather
than a transformation. But if on the other hand I watch the various
stages of a development day by day, I adjust myself to it so
thoroughly that I do not notice it. From my window and from
Sartre's I see huge buildings, great blocks that did not exist ten
years ago. When they began to rise they did not spoil the landscape;
and I had forgotten it by the time they were finished.

From this point of view, History is no less disappointing. As the
present asserts itself, so the earlier moments are swallowed up in the
darkness. Seeing that one is swept on towards the future, one rarely
has the time to look back. Once I was compelled to return to the
past, however. Every year the young barristers solemnly set up a
mock trial at the Palais de Justice to practise their eloquence. In
April 1967 they chose Frantz, the hero of *Loser Wins*, as their
prisoner at the bar. Was this torturer to be acquitted, condemned to
death, or given some lighter sentence? Many of the barristers spoke
very well. The prosecutor delivered an extremely violent indictment
of torture: there was to be no mercy for those who had resorted to
it – they were to be put to death. It was in this same Palais some
years earlier, during the Ben Sadok trial, that the lawyers present at
the hearing were indignant because some witnesses spoke out
against torture. Now the memory of these horrors was so entirely

32

lost that they could be publicly denounced. The independence of Algeria was claimed as a Gaullist triumph, whereas for three years de Gaulle had carried on the war and had covered the torturers. As far as I was concerned, the Algerian war rose up again with extraordinary clarity precisely because of the silence in which it had been buried ever since those days.

What shows me the number of my years most decisively is the complete change that has come about in my scale of ages. This scale does not affect those who are close to me. Perspective has nothing to do with one's actual perception of space (a fact well brought out by the theory of forms), and the friend I see at a distance does not shrink in size; at twenty yards she is still five foot three. In the same way she remains identically herself throughout the years. It is well known that in time as in space some quite unusual circumstance is required for another vision – for Proust to see an old woman instead of his grandmother. Everything is entirely different where acquaintances or strangers are concerned: upon them I do set an age. But this age has not had the same value throughout the course of my life. I shall take just one example – my view of the woman of forty.

When I was a child I made a rough classification of adults according to their generation; there was that of my parents, and they were the grown-ups; then that of my grandparents, and they were the elderly people; and then there were some quite revolting freaks, the ancients, whom I put in much the same class as the sick or crippled. People of forty were already fairly old. By the time I was twenty, the forty-year-olds seemed romantic – they had a life behind them, they had a sharply distinct personality; and I pondered about the somewhat battered but deeply experienced woman that I should be one day. But it seemed to me entirely out of place that people of such an age should presume to have affairs or even to flirt. I was at a party at the Atelier when I was twenty-five, and I looked at all the 'well-preserved' creatures there, thinking of them as so many old hags. Even when I was thirty-five it shocked me when I heard older people referring to the amorous side of their married life: there comes a time, thought I, when one should in decency give up that sort of thing.

I was forty when I went down the Mississippi with Algren and I felt very young; I was forty-four when I met Lanzmann, and I did not feel old. As I have said, it was after fifty that I seemed to have crossed a frontier. By this time forty meant young middle age to me, an age still rich in hope; and I understood Colette's heroine saying nostalgically, 'I am no longer forty, to be moved by a fading rose.'[10] And the other day, when I was talking to a fresh, lively woman of forty-five, she seemed to me as young as when I had met her for the first time, twenty years before. Seen from the top of a mountain the hills and valleys lose their relief; so now differences in age grow less for me, or even disappear altogether. There are the young; then until about fifty, the grown-ups; then the old people; and then the ancients, who no longer seem very far from me.

But there is one sign of ageing that is even more obvious to me, and it is one that I am continually coming up against – my relationship with the future. When old people are interviewed, they may affect a certain optimism, but they do point out some of the unpleasant sides of ages. It astonishes me that they never mention that shrinking of the future which Leiris describes so well in *Fibrils*. It is true that some people do not feel it. My friend Olga said to me, 'I have always lived in the present and in eternity; I have never believed in the future. Being twenty or being fifty is really much the same thing.' For others life is a burden and the shortness of the future makes the burden lighter. My case is different: I used to reach out towards the future; I went happily towards my meeting with the woman I should be tomorrow; I was eager because I foresaw in every acquisition the source of a memory that would never fade. Now I can still fling myself whole-heartedly into short-term plans – voyages, lectures, meetings – but the full impulse that urged me on has been broken. As Chateaubriand put it, I am reaching the end: I cannot allow myself strides of too great a length. I often say 'Thirty years ago, forty years ago.' I should never venture to say 'In thirty years.' And this brief future is a blind alley. I am aware of my own finity. Even if it is increased by two or three books, the body of my literary work will remain what it is.

Yet up until now my world has not stopped growing larger. I mentioned this phenomenon when I was speaking of the years after the war: it has increased in scope. The effect of outside events on my history has grown less: what happens happens within it, and the share of chance is reduced to almost nothing. Most of the new people I have met wrote to me because they liked my books: it was I who initiated the relationship, by a kind of repercussive effect.

10 I quote from memory.

34

Because my life has spread wider and wider in the world, it has become the meeting-point of many converging lines, and this is the explanation of the increasing number of coincidences that I have noticed for some time. What is so boring about novels, says J.-B. Pontalis, is that the same people are perpetually meeting one another. That is true. But it is much the same thing in the real world, I find. A forty-year-old woman with whom I have friendly relations marries a man I knew at Madame Lemaire's when he was sixteen. Violette Leduc goes out from time to time with one of the two homosexuals that Lise was fond of. I could quote many other examples. It all arises from the number of people I have come to know and from the narrowness of the circle of intellectuals I belong to.

In their rhythm, in the way I fill them, and in the people I see, my days resemble one another. Yet my life does not seem at all stagnant to me. Its repetitive side is no more than a background against which new things perpetually appear. I read every day: but not the same book. I write every day: but writing continually sets me unforseen problems. And with an anxious concern I follow the unfolding course of events: they never repeat themselves, and now they make part of my own history.

One of the advantages of age is that it allows one to see the progress of certain lives in their continuity and their unexpected developments. Many have surprised me. I should never have imagined that time would have changed that beautiful, bewildered 'stunner' of the Flore into a capable businesswoman; nor that that casual, rather wild-looking girl would have become the leading French expert on Kafka; nor that the handsome Nico, grown up, would make very fine films. I did not imagine that Paulhan, so little of a conformist and so apparently indifferent to honours, would ever put on the tail-coat of an Academician. Nor that the man who wrote *Days of Hope* would accept a ministry in a technocratic France bound to Franco by links of friendship. The reason why these developments astonished me was obviously that I saw them only from the outside; I did not know the background upon which the aspects visible to me were superimposed; as far as these men and women were concerned, I knew nothing whatsoever about their childhood, the key to every life.

It is quite another thing where my friends are concerned. I am reasonably well informed about their past, their roots, their opening

35

to the world and their potentialities; when striking events occur in their lives I have more or less expected them; and it does not seem to me that these happenings change those they happen to. To make sure of that, I should really have to begin standing back from them, so that I could see them. That is not what I usually do: I live in a clear, unambiguous alliance with those who are close to me; and for me to be able to view them from the outside, as untransparent beings, something has to go wrong with my relationship for a while. Then they can be seen as either above or below what I expected of them, or in any case different. But this distance soon vanishes.

Naturally, insofar as they are wedded to the course of events or are confronted with unexpected situations, my friends evolve. They may call everything into question; there may be crises, breaks, fresh commitments. I have seen instances in Sartre, Leiris, Genet, Giacometti, and many others. But that does not prevent them from remaining true to themselves. I have never seen them undergo a radical change before my eyes.

I have also noted a great stability in what is called people's character – their reactions, taken as a whole, in analogous circumstances. The passing years bring changes in the individual's situation, and this affects his behaviour. I have seen shy or sullen adolescent girls become happy young women in full flower. I saw Giacometti's mood change and darken because of his disease and his immense weariness. I watched the extraordinary decline of Lise and Camille. But generally speaking men and women, once they are settled into adulthood, remain consistent. Sometimes, indeed, they repeat their own conduct when they think they are being quite different. In his *The Traitor*, Gorz denounces his own muttering; and he does so in a mutter.

In fact, even when he claims that it is not so, no man wishes himself other than he is, since for all living persons, being means making oneself be. Looking back, a man may blame some parts of his conduct; but that does not lead him to change them. In his *Journal*, Amiel continually laments his idleness; he says that he is fighting against it and yet he goes on sinking deeper and deeper. In fact he elects to be this idle man moaning over his idleness. That does not mean that every man likes what he is. As I have said, if a man has been ill-loved in childhood, and if he adopts his parents' view of him, then he builds up a disagreeable image of himself that he can never throw aside. But it is the subject who secretes this distaste for himself, and although he suffers from it, yet at the same time he agrees with it. This ontological approval allows some people proudly to claim characteristics that seem to me inadmissible blemishes. 'I respect money; I do not fling it about.' 'It amuses me when people I know are in a mess.' 'I am not one of those hysterical creatures who have to know the truth at all costs.' Straight away I think 'He is a miser. He is an evil man. That is a woman who lies to herself.' But the people in question would cry out against these descriptions of themselves. It is almost impossible to persuade others of faults that seem to us obvious: if they agree with our observations, it is because their values do not coincide with ours and our criticism therefore leaves them untouched. Take the case of Fernande Picasso saying, 'If people do not snigger when I go by in the street, I feel that my hat has no style.' The idlers who thought they were humiliating her only strengthened her notion of her own elegance.

I too feel this acceptance of myself. A friend of mine who is a graphologist analysed my writing and she drew a picture of me that I thought flattering. 'You like it because you choose to be what you are,' she said. 'But it could be taken the other way round.' And indeed, my way of centring myself upon my work and carrying my plans right through to the end could be called strength of will, steadfastness, perseverance: they could also be seen as blind obstinacy and a narrow stubbornness. Is my desire for knowledge openness of mind or a frivolous curiosity? For my part I accept myself without any holding back. When I 'recognize' myself, it makes me smile. During a certain period I explored the world of music as systematically as once I explored the Provençal landscape: I realized what I was doing, but that in no way diminished my extreme eagerness. What I have said about others is equally valid as far as I am concerned: it is hard to wound me. If criticisms or reproaches are unjustified they have no effect. If they are well-based, I take them as compliments. It does not worry me to be called an intellectual or a feminist: I accept what I am.

One of the meanings of paranoia is a refusal to abandon the subjective position: we are all more or less affected by it; we are all more or less blind to our inert presence in the Other's world. Yet from time to time some incident destroys my pellucid familiarity with myself. Friends point out words I have uttered or things I have done without noticing it; I said or did them without the least suspicion of having done so, and this realization disturbs me. Or else they blame me for having done something that I was aware of but without seeing that it was out of place. Or they tell me of some characteristic that I had not observed. For example, a woman I know said, 'You seem to think it quite natural: but it isn't.' How true. My way of thinking, feeling, doing, is quite natural in my eyes. I find it hard to admit that it is in my eyes alone.

However, there are times when I find it fascinating to see myself from the outside. There are tests which confront me with a reality, one that I pursue and that escapes me. I took a Rorschach test: after the psychologist told me the result I let myself slide into the world of the fantastic – I went to see a clairvoyant who was supposed to tell me the truth. She told me nothing new. But I was astonished to find that I had shown myself to her without ever having meant to, and at seeing myself from the outside as both the projector and the projected. Another disturbing experience is reading the account of a dialogue in which I have taken part, written by the other person: even if every detail is correct, the substitution of his point of view for mine takes me aback: he had a face, I did not – now he has lost it and I have put one on. He wrote down the words I uttered, but according to his grasp of them. I know that this reversal takes place every time I talk to anyone. On the whole, I mind little about the images people may form of me; they are so contradictory and often so inconsistent that I do not worry about them. But even so I am rather disturbed when I personally confront an audience. I feel that these external consciousnesses have turned me into an object. What object I do not know, and for a moment I am intimidated.

Building up a picture of myself: I am not interested by this pointless and in any case impossible undertaking. What I should like to do is to provide myself with an idea of my place, my locus, in the world. Being a woman, French, a writer, sixty-four years old in 1972: what does that mean? To give an answer, one would first have to know the historical meaning of the moment in which I am actually living. It is a period before a war? Are we on the eve of vast revolutions that will do away with the system? Will the young people of today see the coming of a true socialism; or the triumph of a technocracy that will perpetuate capitalism; or a form of society unlike anything I can imagine? These questions remain unanswered; for me the meaning of my period is uncertain, and that helps to obscure the meaning of my own personal existence.

When I was young I thought my life was an unusually successful experiment in the human state.[11] For a great while now I have known that it is nothing of the sort. I have not shared in the lot of the vast majority of mankind – exploitation, repression, extreme poverty. I am privileged. When I compare myself with other privileged people there is none I envy; but there are some I know who have no reason to envy me either. For many years I retained a feeling of superiority with regard to the earlier centuries. When I read the life of some writer of former times and I looked at the books he had read I felt a kind of uneasiness: all the science, the history and the psychology he had studied were so very much out-of-date! Partly because of him, quite often. Even so, for me this backwardness took away from his value. And now at this point I look at myself with the same eyes: without yielding to the futurist excess that has seized upon my contemporaries, I have to confess that the coming generations have a great advantage over me. They will understand my period, whereas my period does not understand itself; they will know a great many things that I do not know; my culture and my view of the world will seem out of date to them. Apart from a few great time-resisting works, they will despise all that I have been fed on.

Still and all: Stendhal watching the horse-races on the Corso has no reason to envy the modern tourist who wanders down that same street, now made commonplace and ugly. Every historical period is an absolute entity, one that cannot be compared with others by any universal criterion. The varying destinies of mankind do not challenge one another. The future's wealth does not impoverish me.

No: but it does make my position relative. I have finally and completely lost the childish illusion of standing in the very middle of the world.

Others remain to me. At present I am concerned with recovering my life – reviving forgotten memories, re-reading, re-seeing, rounding off incomplete pieces of knowledge, filling gaps, clarifying obscurities, gathering scattered elements together. Just as though there had to be a moment when my experience was to be summed

[11] 'I had a vague notion that as soon as an object formed an integral part of my history it benefited from a peculiarly favoured light. A country remained virgin, unseen, until I beheld it with my own eyes.' (*The Prime of Life*, p. 369.)

39

up, and as though it mattered that this summing-up should be done. Some primitive peoples suppose that after their death they will remain for ever exactly as they were at the moment it struck them – young or old, strong or decrepit. I am behaving as though my life were to carry on beyond my grave as I have managed to regain it in my last years. Yet I know very well that 'I can't take it with me.' I shall *all* die.

I mind it less than once I did. I no longer feel the haunting anxiety of death that was so very strong in my youth. I have given up rebelling against it. Speaking of physical pain, Freud says, 'It could be called vile and shameful, if there were anyone to blame for it.' This applies to death too: the emptiness of heaven takes anger away. My indignation is now directed only against evils stirred up by men. Yet the idea of my end is with me. Beneath my feet there stretches a road: behind me it emerges from the darkness and in front of me it plunges into the night. I have travelled more than three quarters of its length, and the space left for me to traverse is short. Ordinarily the picture is static: but sometimes a conveyor-belt hurries me towards the abyss. The last time I saw a coffin lowered into a grave – it was Madame Mancy's – the thought came to me with brilliant clarity, 'Soon it will be my turn.' When I sleep I no longer have those comforting nightmares in which after my death a voice still speaks, saying 'I am dead.' But I do sometimes wake up swimming in confused anxiety: the taste of the void is deep within me.

The void: I no longer find the idea overwhelming, but still I do not get used to it. People have said to me, 'Why fear it? Before you were born, that too was the void.' The analogy is unsound. Not only because knowledge to some extent lights up the past whereas darkness hides the future from me, but above all because it is not the void that is repugnant: it is annihilation. The connection between existence – consciousness and transcendence – and life in the biological sense has always puzzled me, although it seems to me nonsensical to claim that the one can be separated from the other. Existence continually races on towards a future created by this very motion itself, and for existence it is a crying scandal when the extinction of life brings it up short. The scandal is to some degree wiped out when it is existence itself that brings about the extinction, as in the case of heroic deaths or suicides. But nothing seems to me more horrible than dying in perfect health, without having wished for death. By lessening our vital strength, old age and disease often help us to tame the idea of the end.

Sometimes I am astonished at myself: there is more difference between this body and my corpse than between my twenty-year-old body and my body of today, still warm and living. Yet forty-four years lie between me and twenty and surely much less between me and my grave.

When I reflect that my corpse will outlive me, the thought brings about a strange relationship between me and my body.

Does the semi-indifference to my death that I observe arise from the fact that the final term still seems to me remote? Or am I less attached to life than I was? I believe the true reason lies elsewhere: if I die in fifteen years or twenty it will be a very old woman who vanishes. I cannot feel moved by the death of that octogenarian; and I do not wish to outlive myself in her. The only thing I find wounding when I think about my end is the pain I shall cause some few people – those very people whose happiness is most necessary to me.

My relations with others – my affections, my friendships – hold the most important place in my life. Many date from long ago. My links with Sartre and with my sister have not changed. I still often see Olga, Bost, Lanzmann, Bianca, Violette Leduc. Less often, but regularly, Pouillon, Gorz, Gisèle Halimi, Gégé, Ellen Wright, and some others. Some of my friends I meet only now and then, because our occupations have led us in different directions, but Michel Leiris or Jean Genet, for example, are just as living for me as ever, and I follow their doings with close attention.

This is another field in which permanence does not mean stagnation: I see the same people in order to share the perpetual newness of the world with them. We exchange our ideas about the subjects that interest us and we pool the information we have amassed. Since our points of reference, our plans, our values and our aims coincide, our divergencies have a meaning: each throws light on a different aspect of what we are discussing – an event, a film or a book. I can also benefit from the conversation of people whose co-ordinates differ from mine, so long as we are in agreement on what I consider essential points. In this way my friendship with Lena in the USSR and with Tomiko in Japan came into being.[12] Although they

12 See pp. 280 and 317.

approached the world with the same requirements as myself, they saw it from a different point of view; and seeing it through their eyes enriched me. On the other hand I see no point in talking to people whose attitudes are radically unlike my own; words do not have the same meaning for them and for me, and they never allow us to come together. In any case, I have no time to waste with people I do not care about; I should rather spend more with those who are close to me. I have put so much of myself into their lives that their projects, their successes and their failures have become mine. I very carefully read the books or articles they write; and I share in what happens to them. To a certain degree my existence embraces theirs, and it is the richer for doing so.

Sartre's life is as closely a part of mine as ever. At present he lives in the boulevard Raspail, five minutes from me; from his study on the tenth floor there is an immense view over Paris, with the Montparnasse cemetery in the foreground; I work at his place every afternoon, and as evening comes on I watch the sun set, sometimes in astonishing splendour. We spend the evenings in my flat. His activities since 1962 are too well known for me to deal with them here. I shall speak of just one episode, that of the Nobel prize.

At the beginning of autumn 1964, Pace, an Italian philosopher with whom Sartre had often had discussions, wrote to him: he wanted Sartre to send him the speech he would make on receiving the Nobel prize. Was there then some question of giving it to Sartre this year? Yes, we learnt, there was. He was inclined to refuse it, and I encouraged him. Our middle-aged friends urged him to accept, but the students I asked reacted violently – what a profound disappointment for the young if he were to let himself be given the prize!

Sartre made up his mind. He had a proud horror of 'honours': he had no notion of going to make an exhibition of himself at Stockholm. Who were these academicians who took it upon themselves to select him? Their choices had a political tinge: never had the prize been awarded to a Communist. If Sartre had been one he might have been able to accept, since by making that decision the Swedish Academy would have shown its impartiality; but he was not a Communist and giving him the prize meant not that his political positions were acknowledged but that they were looked upon as of no importance. He did not mean to allow himself to be brought back to the fold. He wrote a letter in which he very politely begged

the Academy not to inflict a prize on him that he would be obliged
to refuse.

The letter had no effect. We were having lunch in a café near my
flat when a journalist (he had no doubt been keeping watch on us)
came and told us the news. Sartre decided to explain the reasons for
his refusal to a Swedish journalist he had met through Claude
Gallimard at the Mercure de France. In this statement, which was
read in Stockholm by his publisher's representative and which was
printed in many papers, Sartre recalled that he had always refused
official distinctions because he felt that a writer should not let himself be turned into an institution; and then again he regretted that
the Nobel prize was reserved 'for the writers of the West and for the
rebels of the East'.[13]

Sartre did not want to talk to the press before this statement had
been communicated to the Swedish Academy. He came to see me at
five o'clock, and his mother telephoned us – she was living very
close to him – to say that there was a crowd of journalists waiting
for him outside his block. Some of them guessed he had taken
refuge with me and they rang on my bell until two in the morning.
In order to have some peace, Sartre went out and let them photograph him, but he said only a few words.

As soon as I woke up, I saw photographers and a television-van
in the street, Sartre was seized upon the moment he went out. The
journalists and television men followed him as far as his flat.
Finally, when he reached the door, he said to them, 'I have no wish
to be buried.' That afternoon the woman who keeps a pork-
butcher's shop next to his block said to me compassionately, 'Poor
Monsieur Sartre! Two years ago it was the OAS. And now the Nobel
prize. They never will leave him in peace!'

Of course the press accused Sartre of having arranged the whole
thing out of love for publicity. They hinted that he had refused the
prize because Camus had had it before him: or because I should
have been jealous. He must obviously be very rich to despise twenty-
six million francs.[14] What took Sartre aback even more was the
letters from people who wanted him to take the money and to give
them some of it, or all of it, or even rather more: they would use it

---

[13] Sartre said 'It was given to Pasternak and not to Sholokhov.' Our friends in the
USSR completely misunderstood the words. They thought Sartre was deserting the
'liberal' for the 'Stalinist' side.
[14] Old francs: rather more than £20,000.—Tr.

43

for the protection of animals, for the preservation of a certain species of tree, to buy a business, repair a farm, or to treat themselves to a voyage. They all accepted the principles of capitalism; big, well-established fortunes did not shock them, nor did Mauriac's having devoted the whole prize to putting in a bathroom: but the fact that Sartre should scorn such a sum filled them with frustration.

Some time before this, Sartre had brought out *Words*, a book he had outlined much earlier under the title of *Jean sans terre*. I never come upon his books in all their freshness – I have always read the drafts. However, after two or three years they become new again. This one seemed to me both very familiar and quite unknown. I knew about that childhood and the people who were concerned with it. What I did not know – and nor did the writer himself before he had put it into writing – was his present distance from those earlier times. Dealing with himself in the past and in the present, both alternately and simultaneously, his linguistic invention created that relationship between the adult and the child which forms the book's originality and which gives it its value. Here I saw a living example of the transition from a contingent history to the timeless necessity of a written text. I saw the imaginary character – the vampire – who guides the writer's hand actually taking the place of a flesh-and-blood individual. I do not know how many times I went through *L'Idiot de la famille*, reading long sections out of sequence and discussing them with Sartre. I went right through it again from the first page to the last during the summer of 1971 in Rome, reading for hours on end. None of Sartre's other books has ever seemed to me so delightful. It is a suspense-story, a detective's investigation that ends in the solution of the enigma, of the question 'How did Flaubert make himself?' In this book the writer explores the fields that interest him, more freely, more happily, than he had ever done before; and his exploration is concerned with what a man owes to his childhood and his period. With the relationship of what he says to what he has actually experienced in life, and with the nature of language, art and the comic. I should need whole pages just to point out the main headings. This book is as deep, thoroughgoing and solid as *The Critique of Dialectical Reason*, and at the same time it has all the charm of ease and gracefulness. It is obvious that Sartre had fun writing it, and if the reader can make the effort to follow he will have fun with him.

My sister no longer lives in Paris. At present her husband is in the

Council of Europe, which has its headquarters in Strasbourg: they bought an old Alsatian farmhouse in a village, and they have turned it into a charming, comfortable home. From morning until night, even in their very cold winters, she shuts herself up in her studio and she paints. She has always refused both the shackles of representation and the barrenness of abstraction: she has discovered an increasingly delicate equipoise between formal invention and allusion to reality. I did not see her very successful exhibitions at the Hague and in Tokyo, but I did like the pictures – Venice was their inspiration – that she showed in Paris in 1963, and even more the collection based upon the festive atmosphere, the exuberance and the tragedies of May 1968. For a long time now she has produced excellent engravings, and she was particularly successful with the illustrations for *The Woman Destroyed*; she showed them in an exhibition that also included her subtle watercolours. Recently she discovered an interesting technique of painting on altuglass and polyester; but she has not given up oils. She is able to carry on all these activities together because she almost never takes a holiday. During the summer, in her house at Trebiano in Italy, she works in a big sunlit studio. We meet quite often in Paris and sometimes I go to her house to see her latest pictures and her roses.

The oldest of all my friendships, that which bound me to Stépha, did not survive our long separation; it was a great joy to me to see it come to life again.

Stépha and Fernand reached the United States at the beginning of the war and they settled in New York. He went on painting and she took various jobs. I had not seen them for a great while when I rang on their bell in 1947. Fernand opened the door; he had not changed much. When I walked into her room, Stépha was so moved that she fell off the divan she was lying on. I spent many hours with them during that stay. I saw them again for a short while in 1948 and 1950, when I was passing through New York on my way to Chicago. After that they settled in a small town in Vermont, where they taught. Neither Stépha nor I are particularly endowed for a relationship kept up by letters and we let a silence fall between us. In 1965 she went to Austria to see her mother, and on the way she stopped in Paris; I happened to be in the USSR just then and she was rather unfairly vexed at my absence. My sister stood up for me, but Stépha grew obstinate. 'No: if people don't care about you any more, there's no point in going on.'

45

But when *The Woman Destroyed* came out I sent her an inscribed copy. She wrote to thank me and to say she would be staying in Paris during the spring of 1969.

On the telephone we arranged to meet at my place: she was living with her brother-in-law, not a hundred yards away. I waited somewhat apprehensively for her ring on the bell. Was I going to see the Stépha of my twenties, grown older; or someone else? And who would that someone else be?

I opened the door. There stood a very little old woman leaning on a stick; straight away I recognized Stépha's blue eyes, her pinkness, her nose, her cheekbones and her broad laughing mouth. I cried, 'You haven't changed!' There were tears in her eyes and we kissed one another. 'How tall you are!' she said. She had shrunk a great deal and now she was a head shorter than I. Moving her hand from her forehead to her waist she said 'From here to here, I'm twenty-five.' Her hand left her waist and pointed to her feet. 'But from here to there, I'm a hundred.' She was suffering from severe arthritis and she could not walk without a stick. She said she thought my expression was not the same as it used to be.

We talked about Fernand, about her son, of whom she is very proud, and about her work. She loves her job as a teacher, a job she has worked at for twenty years: her pupils have a great deal of respect and affection for her, and she makes use of this to try to arouse their political consciousness. 'I love the young,' she said warmly. She liked living at her brother-in-law's because he had three children between twenty and thirty, all of them extreme left-wing militants. She never tired of hearing them talk about the great adventures of May.

I often saw her after that, sometimes by myself, sometimes with Sartre. We would walk along the boulevard Raspail, taking little steps, and we would lunch in the local cafés. We talked as easily as if we had never been separated: we had the same opinions and the same tastes. And everything interested her. I admired her vitality and her spirit. Her legs caused her a great deal of pain, yet she was always cheerful. She had made up her mind not to retire but to accept a post she had been offered in Philadelphia. She would spend her holidays at Putney, where the quietness suited Fernand. But she wanted to keep in touch with the young and to take advantage of the resources of a great city.

She has carried out this plan and it has pleased her as much as she thought it would. She is one of those rare people who have put so much of themselves into their activities that old age does not bring them low: for them the world remains filled with interests, values and aims, until the very end of their life. I do not think it likely that we shall see much of one another any more. As for me, who so hate seeing my past fray away, recovering this friendship of my youth was of the greatest value.

While I was correcting these proofs, Violette Leduc died at Faucon. Nevertheless I shall speak of her under the heading of my living friendships, because for these last ten years her life was closely mingled with mine.

As I have said, the failure of *Ravages* in 1955 plunged her deep into dejection. Presently she fell a prey to that hallucinatory state she began to describe in *La Folie en tête*. Little bits of string, torn pieces of newspaper, dog's droppings, empty cigarette packets – the street was filled with the signs that a malevolent organization strewed along her path to make game of her. In spite of the bolts she had put on the doors, people got into her room at night: when she woke up she noticed that her fur coat had grown shorter, that there was a stain on the wall, that the corner of a photograph had been turned up. As she worked she heard creaking overhead: there was a spy hiding up there and he was reading her manuscript: in the papers and on the radio she discovered malignant allusions to what she had written. I tried to reason with her, but without being able to shake what for her were obvious facts: she no longer attempted to gather her evidence into a coherent system. They were jeering at her; they wished her ill: but she did not know who was persecuting her nor why: she had little more than vague suspicions. I was seriously worried when she began to react violently to what she thought were attacks directed against her: she insulted people who bumped into her in the métro or who looked at her strangely. I persuaded her to see a psychoanalyst: he gave me to understand that he thought it a hopeless case. One afternoon in November 1957 I was working at Sartre's flat in the rue Bonaparte when the telephone rang. It was Madeleine Castaing, a friend of Violette's who had an antique shop on the corner of the rue Jacob and the rue Bonaparte: Violette was with her, in a terrible state: she asked me to come. I went. Madeleine Castaing, driving past Sartre's house, had noticed Violette leaning against the wall, deathly pale, with her eyes fixed. She got out, touched her shoulder, and Violette fell to the ground, shrieking. Madeleine Castaing made her get into the car and took her to the shop. I found Violette in tears; she gave me a confused explanation of how she had been waiting for Sartre outside his door to complain of what he had written about her in *Les Temps modernes*: speaking of Tintoretto he had mentioned ugliness and she saw quite plainly that his words were directed at her. After that she had two or three more crises so violent that in the end they frightened her. She agreed to undergo treatment. On the advice of a psychiatrist I took her to a nursing-home at Versailles: in spite of my formal opposition the doctor submitted her to a series of electro-shocks. After that she had a sleep-cure in the home that Dr Le Savoureux ran at La Vallée-aux-Loups: [15] she found him and his wife sympathetic and she liked walking in the splendid park. She became capable of leading a normal life once more. At one time she had seemed so deeply affected that I doubted whether she would ever get well. One of her oldest friends had been so afraid that he had stopped seeing her. But there was something so strong in her and she loved life so passionately that in the end she over-came her aberration.

She never quite gave up her way of interpreting things however. The world was still filled with signs and symbols put there by invisible persecutors. But now she did not let herself be beaten: she began working again. Often I admired her spirit. In her books she has described the care with which she did her household work: she spent hours cleaning and polishing; she did her shopping with scrupulous attention to details; she spent a great while preparing her meals. And for hours on end she filled the squared pages of her notebooks with her delicate sloping hand. In the summer she rented an old and beautiful but dilapidated house at Faucon in the Vaucluse. Every morning she went out into the woods, hung the basket with her frugal lunch on a branch and wrote until the evening. When one knows the effort that is required to confront a virgin page, the tension needed to set one sentence after another, and the weariness of spirit that saps one's courage at times, this steadfast, dogged energy leaves one amazed – all the more so since Violette Leduc was persevering against a background of failure.

She undertook the story of her life. When we met in Paris I read her drafts with her and we discussed them together. In 1964 she

15 At one time it belonged to Chateaubriand.

48

finished *La Bâtarde*, which at once had a great success. In my preface I have said what I like in the book – the writer's fearless sincerity, her fastidious sensitivity, and the art with which she mingles real life with the life of dreams. Her success completely changed Violette Leduc's existence. Until then she had been condemned to loneliness and poverty: now she was rich and surrounded by friends, some of them sincere and others more or less self-seeking. She let the novelty of her position go to her head; but often she felt the contrast with anger. She associated mainly with homosexuals and she cheerfully went to transvestite bars with them – to Madame Arthur's and the Carrousel. Some plied her with attentions, and for a while she would let herself be affected; but then she would suspect them of making game of her and react violently. Luxury fascinated her; and the very wealthy men who took her up, usually for snobbish reasons, brought her mythical father-figure to life again: she found their elegant manners and their refinement enchanting. But at the same time she saw their faults, and her good sense, her moral healthiness revolted fiercely against their sophistication. On this subject I shall tell just one particularly significant anecdote. Raoul Lévy, then a well-known producer, asked Violette to dinner in a splendid country house: César, the sculptor, was there, together with writers, artists and Raoul Lévy's personal friends – some thirty people all told. They all had drinks in the huge dining-room. Then suddenly they noticed that there were only fifteen of them at table, sitting round a paella: the master of the house and his particular friends were having their dinner in the kitchen. Violette Leduc got up, tucked her napkin into her belt, turning it into a parlour-maid's apron, seized the dish of paella, and imitating a well-trained servant she took it to Raoul Lévy, who was sitting with his back to her. 'Would Monsieur like a little paella? Is Monsieur pleased with the service?' He started. 'What are you doing?' – 'If you can play at being a servant, I can play too.' He produced an embarrassed explanation: 'It's just a misunderstanding – next time there won't be so many of us – next time you shall eat in the kitchen too.' More than once she did things of this kind, tearing herself away from the social whirlpool of Paris and setting herself up again in her pride. When she was with me she laughed at her own frivolity, but I quite understood that after so much privation it amused her to see fashionable restaurants and night-clubs. She liked clothes. She wrote articles on the important dressmakers

49

in *Vogue*: and once again she took pleasure in dressing – with her blond wig, her miniskirt and her coat in the latest fashion, she had a great deal of style – but the contrast between the age marked on her face and her youthful appearance made people stare after her in the street.

She found dealing with money difficult: in her books she has said how attached she was to it. She loathed the idea of letting her royalties lie there in her publisher's hands, doing nothing; but if she took out important sums there was the danger of a great deal going in tax, and that she found revolting. With her friends' advice, she hit upon a compromise. But although she did treat herself to clothes and a certain amount of travelling, she remained very economical. She had no wish to go back in her old age to the semi-poverty she had known before *La Bâtarde*. She kept on her 'hide-out' in a working-class block. The only important outlay she allowed herself was to make an old dream come true – the dream of having some place in the world that was her own. She bought the house at Faucon she used to rent in the summer and she had it done up. This was not a simple business: she fought with the contractor and with the builders. At times she felt there was something malignant about the house; but in the end she made friends with it. She loved the great view with Mont Ventoux framed in her window. She became passionately attached to her garden; she had rare flowers and bushes planted and she took a delight in looking after them herself. At first the villagers were surprised by her shorts, her necklaces, her immense straw hats and her make-up, but finally they adopted her. She had real friends among them.

Even during her social period, she never stopped working. She wrote *The Lady and the Little Fox Fur,* a long short-story based on the theme of loneliness, like *La Vieille Fille et la mort.* In *La Folie en tête* she carried on with her autobiography: reading it was a curious experience for me. I knew about the happenings that Violette Leduc spoke of; I had often been concerned in them and indeed I had sometimes played an important part: it was disturbing to see myself as an object in an account of events that I had experienced as a subject and as a consciousness.

Tired of parties, entertainments and the turmoil of Paris, Violette Leduc took to staying longer and longer at Faucon. In 1969 she settled there entirely, and there she recovered the particular delights of her childhood. At one time she had loved books, music, pictures,

50

architecture; but these last years art and literature had almost lost their interest for her. The greater part of her mind was turned towards the real world – towards people, things, the slight differences of colour in the sky, the smells of the earth. 'What is it I love with all my heart? The country, the trees, the forests. There, with them – that is my place,' she wrote in *La Bâtarde*.

In Violette Leduc there was a striking contrast between her imaginary life, filled with hallucinations and obsessions, and her attitude towards reality. She dreaded death: at the least shiver, the least feeling of illness, it seemed to her that life was running out of her. Yet she underwent the two operations required by the most terrible of diseases with an astonishing serenity. The first time they told her that the tumour they had removed was benign: she believed it. I knew the truth and I hardly knew what to do; I was afraid she would have a relapse and that that would mean hideous torture. And indeed a little later she had to have a breast removed: she put up with it calmly. 'The surgeon says it was cancer, but a cancer of no sort of importance,' she told me. What worried me, the day I went to visit her in the nursing-home, was that she had seen her greying hair and her scalp in the looking-glass as a brilliant red: this had already happened once at Faucon. She could not understand it. I said it was an illusion: she would not have that. 'But why didn't you call the nurse and make her look?' She thought for a while and then smiled. 'I think that deep down my unconscious didn't really believe it.'

That seems to me a profoundly true observation and one that explains how the frail Violette Leduc came to have such resistance. Her unconscious was determinedly sanguine; it did not believe in old age nor in death nor in the hallucinations she invented for herself. When she went into hospital at Avignon in the spring of 1972 she was convinced that she was merely suffering from an upset liver. When she left she wrote and told me how happy she was to be home again and to know that her illness had not been at all serious. A little later I was told on the telephone that she had just sunk into a coma: the doctors had let her leave the hospital because there was nothing more they could do for her. She died without having recovered consciousness, without suffering and apparently without anxiety. She was buried, as she wished, in the graveyard of her village.

At Faucon she had drafted the end of her autobiography. I think it will soon be possible to publish some passages from it. I hope so, because in her case it is impossible to separate the books and the flesh-and-blood woman who wrote them. She turned her life into the raw material of her works, and that gave her life a meaning.

There is a great deal more that might be said about Violette Leduc: I did my best in the preface to *La Bâtarde,* and I do not wish to repeat myself here.

In *Force of Circumstance* I spoke of some friendships that were taking shape round about 1960. They have grown stronger. The young man from Marseilles who introduced himself to me as a 'classic case of maladjustment' and who took very great risks to help the FLN during the war in Algeria has become a teacher of literature. He has held posts in the provinces, in Guadeloupe and Cambodia; and he has told of his experiences in a book.[16] He is bearded, hairy, intensely eager for change of element, of scene, but very accessible to anything that is suggested to him; and his rebellion has preserved all its freshness. He was appointed to a lycée near Paris and there he tried above all to teach his pupils freedom: this brought him into conflict with the authorities. In the summer he gave his lessons on the lawn. He did not report absent pupils; he did not follow the programme; he encouraged challenge, dispute, questioning – *contestation.* He was suspended in February 1972 without any exact motive being given. On March 2 *Le Monde* devoted an article to him, with the heading *Supported by the pupils, criticized by the parents – an unusual teacher at the Gonesse lycée.* He lived in the lycée buildings, and he was so interested in his pupils that he let them come into his room and listen to records and argue among themselves or with him whenever they chose. Naturally the parents talked about drugs and orgies: it was the *Fédération Armand* that insisted upon his being suspended. A child's parent said to the *Monde* reporter, 'I don't know whether you've seen him, Monsieur, in his shepherd's cloak. He doesn't dress like a teacher.' He does in fact wear a long white coat he brought back from Afghanistan.

My Canadian friend, Madeleine Gobeil, has given up producing. She lectured in a Canadian university and she undertook literary programmes on the television. She also did a series of articles and interviews published in the papers over there. She often comes to France, and she is living here now, working at a thesis on Michel Leiris.

16 Cl. Courchay: *La Vie finira bien par commencer,* Gallimard.

I went on seeing Jacqueline Ormond, too. She was disappointed by what happened in Mali, and she went back to live in Switzerland. She wrote one novel[17] based on her private phantasms, and she began another, with her African experience as its inspiration. Then she went to teach in Niger, where she was not at all happy. One morning I received a copy of her second book, which was published in Switzerland: a note from the publisher told me that she had died a few days before. The news was extremely sudden, but it did not surprise me very much. I think I know how she left her life and why.

Towards the end of the Algerian war I received some letters from a social worker[18] named Denise Brébant who insisted upon seeing me. My refusals did not discourage her: 'I am as obstinate as Lise,' she said, alluding to the former pupil to whom I gave that name in *The Prime of Life*. I gathered that it was not just a question of idle curiosity: she was helping the FLN and she wanted to consult me about it. After that her little flat often acted as a shelter for Algerians: she was risking her job and she had no other resources whatsoever. We became friends. She was about my age and she had had a difficult life. She came of a peasant family, and as her parents had been brought up harshly they in their turn were hard to their six children and to themselves. The eldest girl married when she was eighteen to get away from them. The son went off to fight in Spain, and there he was killed. They sent Denise to school at Senlis. She was a very good pupil and when she was fourteen the mistress offered to pay for her to go to a teacher's training college. Her parents refused: first they made her work on the farm and then they put her out: she worked in a garage, a factory, and then for a chemist with a crippled wife. Moving this heavy invalid, Denise, who was then eighteen, put a kidney out of place. (Some years later she had an operation.) Although she gave her parents everything she earned, they beat her for the least trifle. A patch on one of her lungs forced her to spend a year in a sanatorium. When she came out at the age of twenty-one, she went to Paris to try her luck. She found a job as a governess and private tutor in a family. She stayed there seven years, and during that time she was able to take lessons in French, literature and history, and to read enormously. She joined the Salvation Army. In the evenings she went round the

17 *Transit*, Gallimard.
18 *Assistante sociale*, a highly-qualified government official.—Tr.

53

fashionable restaurants and night-clubs collecting money; as she was young and pretty she collected considerable sums. At Fouquet's they even let her go into the private rooms. 'Ah, here is the little Salvation Army girl!' said the regular customers. Chiappe, the chief of police, Gaby Morlay, Marie Bell and Sacha Guitry were very open-handed; but not Jean Gabin nor Raimu. She found the meetings entertaining but in the end she realized that the down-and-outs did not benefit from them. She dropped the Salvation Army then and there. At the beginning of the war she joined the *Secours national*, a welfare organization. She went on with her studies in the hope of becoming an *assistante sociale*. 'A peasant's daughter? You'll never get there,' said an instructor disdainfully. Nevertheless she sat for the competitive examination in 1948: she passed fourth out of five hundred candidates and she had the pleasure of being given the highest marks for the essay she had written on social service carried out during the war. She told me proudly that it was read aloud in public by the minister of health: this was an elegant revenge for the scorn she had had to bear. She was passionately interested in her profession and she worked far beyond her official hours, helping the needy from her own pocket. In her sector she often saw the slums into which the Algerians were herded and the kind of persecution they were subjected to: she took their side. It was then, as I have said, that we met. It was owing to her that I was able to come close to forms of wretchedness and distress that otherwise I should have known only from a great way off.

I very much liked *Elise or the Real Life*, Claire Etcherelli's book that Lanzmann ordered me to read. It describes the workers' world, which novels touch upon so seldom, and at the same time it deals with a beautiful and tragic love between an Algerian and a French girl in the Paris of 1957, a Paris sick with racism. I wanted to know the author: lovely black hair, lovely green eyes, a voice and an air that I liked at once. She was the daughter of a Bordeaux docker who had been shot by the Germans in 1942: she was brought up by her grandfather, a gypsy who sold old horses to the people who ran bull-fights. She had not learnt to read by the time she was nine. As a ward of the nation she was given a scholarship to a religious school; there she soon caught up and she carried on brilliantly to the level of the *baccalauréat*; but she refused to sit for it because she was disgusted by the snobbery of the bourgeois girls who were her classmates. She was married at twenty-two; she had a child and after three years she divorced. She came to Paris and worked on the assembly-line in the Citroën works, then in a ball-bearing factory, and then as a servant, a job she found much less arduous than a factory-worker's. The couple who employed her guided her towards office work. When I met her she was in a travel agency, and four years in that job had enabled her to write *Elise*. Writing had been her passion ever since she was fourteen. It was her good luck that she had had her secondary schooling before the 'annihilating' years she spent in the factory.

I interviewed her for *Le Nouvel Observateur* and some time later she received the Prix Fémina, which meant that she could buy clothes (she possessed only one solitary pullover) and move from the slum she lived in. At present she has a flat on the twenty-first floor of one of the towers that has just been built in the XIIIth arrondissement: from her window you see Zola's Paris with its old buildings and old factories, and the roofs of the Austerlitz railway station. The Seine and the rocks of the Vincennes zoo show in the distance. She says that at this height one feels a great way from the world; even the song of the birds does not reach up there. She lives with her two children, the son she had by her husband and another whose father was the Algerian she calls Arezki in her novel.

Success breeds ill-will. She has been accused of faking the story of her life. After the disappearance of Arezki she is supposed to have married an important Algerian civil servant who kept her very comfortably. The fact is she married an Algerian by a ceremony that was not valid in France. But she never lived at his expense – far from it; and after a few months she left him.

After the Fémina she had various jobs and she wrote a second novel called *A propos de Clémence*; it is about the kind of life the Spanish exiles lead. In one of the papers I said how good I thought it was. Clémence belongs to the same race as Elise, both gentle and hard, giving and holding back. Frail fleeting happinesses dart across the sadness of her life and hope pierces through the grey uncoloured sky. It is a novel as charming as the first, but unhappily it was not so successful.

It often happens that when I have enjoyed a book I feel that I should like to meet its writer. I found it interesting to talk to Albert Cohen and Arthur London and to listen to Papillon. I liked *La Gloire du vaurien* very much; when it came out I met Ehni and we see one another from time to time. I do not share his love for the small peasantry, nor his attachment to things of the past. I am sorry that in his plays[19] he confines himself to decrying the faults of left-wing people. But I do like his vitality and his utter lack of affectation, and when we talk we are usually in agreement.

Before I found Stépha again, I had for some years been friends with her son Tito. We had known one another a great while. The day he was born in 1931 I was with his father and some friends at the Closerie des Lilas, near the nursing-home where Stépha was having him. I saw him grow into a cheerful, turbulent little boy, and then he went off to America with his parents. He came back to Paris in the fifties with his wife, a Frenchwoman: they had a daughter. I introduced him to friends and I drove him about in my car: I liked him very much. When he went back to the States he worked as a journalist and he travelled in Latin America, writing a book on it. Now and then he sent an article to *Les Temps modernes*. I knew he had had a divorce, that he had married the daughter of a Spanish refugee, and that he was teaching at Berkeley. Politically he was very active. He set up a committee against the war in Vietnam; he often spoke on television to denounce the crimes committed by the American soldiers and to insist upon their withdrawal. He took part in the Russell tribunal's first inquiry in Vietnam, and both on the way out and the way back he stopped in Paris – it was then that we really became friends. When he returned to Berkeley he joined the Black Panthers as an active member: unlike Carmichael's movement, they accepted whites. He was also very closely connected with the Weathermen.[20]

Following an incident of a racial nature he occupied the administrative buildings with his students: he was looked upon as a dangerous agitator and he was expelled from the university – an exceptional step that made a great deal of noise in the papers and aroused many protests. He sold everything he possessed and gave himself up entirely to the revolutionary struggle; his wife left him, not choosing to risk the life of a refugee again. He has not told me about his activities in detail; I only know that he was imprisoned for having taken part in the great Chicago demonstration against the Vietnam war – every day he underwent prolonged beatings with a rubber truncheon. When he was let out he went right back to the struggle.

[19] This does not apply to *Eugénie Kopronime*, in which he cheerfully sets about Western culture.
[20] They take their name from one of Bob Dylan's songs.

56

It was through him that Sartre and I came to know Angela Davis'
and Jackson's lawyers: he saw Angela Davis several times in
prison. When the Black Panthers slowed down their activities tem-
porarily, he decided to devote himself to his own personal work for
a while. Since he had already written several books he was able to
obtain a grant from an organization in London, and that meant he
had enough to live on. He often goes to England, but he lives in
Paris and we often see one another.

People still send me a good many letters, and generally speaking I
answer them. Some are interesting enough for a correspondence to
follow; but usually I cannot spare the time for that kind of relationship. For the same reason I will not open my door to people who
ask to come to see me without any valid motive. To tell the truth, I
find it hard to understand the pertinacity of some readers who want
to meet me 'for five minutes'. A writer works for years and years,
trying to communicate the most important things he has to say as
well as ever he can: how could an hour of talk possibly provide the
equivalent of even one of his books? When it is a question of giving
'personal' advice, I cannot – I am incapable of it, since I have no
exact knowledge of the person who asks for the advice. My attitude
often causes resentment, and this surprises me. 'Oh, you aren't
interested in me,' says the cross voice of someone who is no more to
me than a sound at the other end of the telephone. 'You owe nothing to me in particular,' writes a young woman, 'but each one of us
owes himself to everybody.' Maybe. But *everybody*: that makes a
good many people – too many, and I am forced to choose. I do see
the French or foreign students who are working for a diploma or
writing a thesis on my books and who have clearly-defined questions to ask. And I always receive the militants from various countries who want me to help in social or political action. Sometimes
firm relationships spring from these meetings: ever since 1971 I
have been in contact with members of the *Mouvement de Libération de la Femme* and there are some I see very often.

I am especially happy when I am with the young. I am grateful to
them for escaping from the falling-away and the alienation that the
adults accept. I find their intransigence, their radicalism and their
insistent requirements comforting, and the freshness of their view
delights me – everything is new for them and nothing is to be taken
for granted. In a speech where I hear nothing but the droning of a

57

politician, they detect blunders and incongruities that make them laugh or that fill them with indignation.

Stupidity still surprises them; they are scandalized by scandals. Changing our way of life seems a matter of urgency to them, because it is their own future that is in question. I am happy when I am given a chance to take part in action with them. About ten years ago I happened to be fairly disengaged and I entered into personal relations with some of my young readers. Some I have lost touch with: but there are others whose development I have followed with interest. Girls who were at the lycée have moved on to the university; those who were at the university have become teachers. They were in rebellion against that society; now their positions have grown far clearer – they are Marxists or Maoists, and apart from a few shades of difference we are in agreement on the essentials.

One of these friendships has played an important part in my life. I was wrong in 1962 when I thought nothing significant would happen to me any more, apart from calamities; now once again a piece of great good fortune was offered to me.

A girl in a class preparing for the *Ecole normale* wrote to me in the spring of 1960, saying that she would like to meet me; her letter was short and direct and it convinced me that she had a sincere liking for philosophy and for my books. I replied, telling her that I should get in touch with her at the end of the holidays. And so I did: in those days I had much more spare time than I have now. In November I sent Sylvie Le Bon a note asking her to call. I took her out to dinner at a local restaurant. She was very shy; she wrung her hands with nervousness, she squinted, and she answered my questions in a strangled voice. We talked about her studies and in the end I got her to confess that she had won the first prize in July. She liked her class and she had pleasant companions in it.

I did see her again, but for two years our meetings were brief and widely-spaced. I frightened her less; she no longer squinted; she smiled and even laughed: she had an agreeable face and I liked her being there. She did not seem to me to have any personal problems. When I asked her about her relations with her parents she avoided the subject – they lived at Rennes; they had sent her to Paris to prepare for the examination; there was nothing to tell about them. She talked mostly about her lycée, her teachers, her fellow-pupils, her programme and her work; and when she spoke about them it was clear she was so very much alive that quite apart from her anxiety about her work she had a wholly personal outlook upon the world. She interested me and I felt in tune with her.

One day to my great surprise I found a long letter from her mother in the post. She had chanced upon Sylvie's private diary, and she had found, she said, an entry showing that I thought she beat her daughter. She assured me that she had never raised a hand to her; she listed all the sacrifices she and her husband had accepted to allow Sylvie to carry on with further studies. This story seemed very suspicious: I had never uttered the words attributed to me and they did not belong to my vocabulary. I wrote a civil but distant note saying that Sylvie never spoke to me of her family. I hesitated whether to tell Sylvie about the incident; but we were not sufficiently intimate for me to take the risk of setting her against her mother – I knew nothing whatsoever about their relationship. I said nothing.

The school year ended. Sylvie spent the summer in Morocco with a friend. She did not write. When the schools opened again she let a month go by before telephoning. When we met she reproached me vehemently for what she looked upon as a betrayal. Her mother had showed her my letter, reading her a few lines and preening herself on having an alliance with me – an alliance that as a matter of fact I had directly refused. I explained, but Sylvie was dogged: her mother had already made several attempts at interfering with her friendships during the course of her life and she resented it so much that some of her resentment spilled over on to me. I saw that her relations with her parents had not been so neutral as she had given me to understand.

When I had regained her confidence she told me a certain amount about her childhood. Her earliest years had been happy. When her mother was young she had cherished ambitions that she had not been able to fulfil, and she wanted to get even with the world through her daughter. She had the little Sylvie given piano, singing and dancing lessons at the town theatre. She appeared on the stage. She showed me photographs, taken when she was eight or nine – Sylvie dressed in white tulle, crowned with white roses, made up, her feet in ballet-slippers, and smiling as she stood on her points. I recognized her face, but I could scarcely believe that the grave student sitting next to me was this dressed-up and rather affected little girl. She was the child Madame Butterfly clasps in her arms before dying; and she was one of the choir that greets the waking

Rip Van Winkle. Her school work did not suffer: in the primary classes she won all the prizes.

As she rose in the school she could no longer keep a high place in form and her mother was obliged to agree to her giving up the stage. She was able to work more: she managed to come top in French, but her marks in her other subjects were still poor. Her parents did not conceal their vexation. Her relations with them deteriorated; she became shut-in and taciturn. Her mother resented the fact that by giving up the theatre Sylvie had thwarted her dreams: she grew possessive, jealous and ill-tempered. Sylvie told me about all this rather unwillingly; she disliked the subject and I did not persist.

The reconciliation that followed our almost-quarrel brought us closer together. But it was during the autumn of 1963 that I really began to grow very fond of Sylvie. *Force of Circumstance* had come out, and Sylvie, without diminishing its scope, grasped the true meaning of the epilogue, which was so widely misunderstood. During my mother's last days and after her death, Sylvie was a great comfort to me, in spite of her youth. I saw more of her: our conversations became longer and more free.

She was successful in the competitive examination for Sèvres[21] and now she lives in the boulevard Jourdan. She liked it very much at the college. There was nothing of the examination-passing swot about her and she worked easily, without constraint. She got along well with some fellow-students whom the authorities considered 'unruly elements'; they used to go out together, drink red wine, play practical jokes on the 'lemons' and the 'squares', and defy the establishment. They were often reprimanded for their want of discipline, but since they passed their examinations brilliantly they were girls of high standing.

Sylvie used to tell me about what she called her 'wild doings', about what happened when she went out, about her reading and the people she saw, about everything that happened to her. She had keen eyes for people and things, she was sensitive to their various shades of difference, and she described them in happily chosen words. She interested me, and she amused me. An experience was the richer for being shared with her. In the year of her *agrégation* I often took her to the cinema, the theatre and exhibitions of painting. In the spring and early summer we went for long drives together. Yet I still did not know her very well, for she was somewhat reti-

21 The women's higher training college.—Tr.

cent, and on many occasions she surprised me.

After having spent the day in the Sologne we had dinner and stayed the night in an hotel in the middle of a park. I went to bed early and I was already far away from this world when I gave a start: someone was touching me on the shoulder. It was Sylvie standing by my bed. 'Get dressed and come quickly! It's so beautiful!' she said in an enraptured voice. I rubbed my eyes: what was up? She led me to the window. A vast round moon was shining in a very perfect sky; the smell of grass and flowers – a smell of my childhood – rose from the ground; a group of young men were sitting on the lawn, playing a guitar and singing in an undertone. 'I've never seen a moon like that,' cried Sylvie. Yes: it was a lovely night and I liked the music; but I had not the least desire to put on my clothes and go out. 'Oh, I shouldn't have woken you up,' said Sylvie, much distressed. In fact she was quite right to have done so, because she had shown me a side of herself I had never suspected – capacities for enthusiasm and passionate feeling that her great reserve had hidden from me. A few glasses of red wine at dinner had allowed her to break through this barrier. I went back to bed. She returned to the park, and she liked it so much there that she stayed, sleeping in the car under the stars.

Another evening, in much the same circumstances, she surprised me even more. After a long run in the car we had checked into an hotel not far from Paris and we were having dinner. I cannot remember what prompted the remark, but I said to her, laughing, 'Oh but you're entirely crazy!' As I meant it, this was complete nonsense, an antiphrasis, because no one seemed to me more sensible and better-balanced than Sylvie. The meal ended drearily; I supposed that the car and the open air had tired her. When I knocked on her door the next morning to have breakfast with her, I found her fully dressed; and she was wearing dark glasses. I was amazed that she was ready so early. In fact, as she confessed a little later, she had not slept at all: she had spent the night weeping with fury. The reason why I went about with her was that I was amusing myself, just as one might amuse oneself with a fool, a buffoon: I thought she was a half-wit. It took me some time to convince her that she was mistaken. Why had she so entirely misunderstood a harmless joke? In the end she told me. Mad, cracked, mentally sick, abnormal, twisted: that was the chorus she had heard all through her adolescence and she had been unable to bear hearing it repeated by me. I could not understand how her parents had come to have such an opinion of her, and she told me the whole story.

As I have said, when she was in *troisième* at about the age of sixteen, she was on bad terms with them. That year she made friends with another girl in the same class, the daughter of a teacher and a very brilliant pupil: they exchanged diaries in which they described their daily life and eagerly expressed their feelings. These diaries fell into her parents' hands – disaster. Sylvie was reproached for her 'unhealthy emotionalism'; she was stated to be 'unnatural': her friend Danièle's people were told and they too uttered shrill protests – how could their daughter, such an outstanding girl, have a crush on so intellectually commonplace a friend? They complained to the teachers and to the headmistress, and it was decided that when the school opened again after the holidays steps should be taken.

That summer was hell for Sylvie. Danièle wrote her long letters almost every day: but Sylvie's mother opened them, read out certain passages with angry or sneering emphasis and forbade her to reply. She had to use stratagems to slip a few lines into the letter-box, and she could only do so at long intervals. Sylvie had developed intellectually in her friend's company: and now with eager enthusiasm she read everything she chanced upon. The friendships and the games that she had found amusing the year before now bored her. Her mother insisted upon her spending her days on the beach and it angered her to see Sylvie always buried in a book. Violent quarrels were perpetually breaking out between them. When her father joined them on Saturdays he took his wife's side. Oppressed, lonely, shocked at finding herself turned into a black sheep, Sylvie sank into a despair that she was never to forget in later years.

In order to separate her from her friend when term began, they made Sylvie go through the same class again, although she was perfectly capable of moving up into the next. She was so humiliated and disgusted that she wept bitterly all night. To take her revenge against her people, the lycée and Danièle's family, she determined to beat them on their own ground. She set herself to work with a sullen perseverance and soon she was top of the form in all subjects. However she was not given the first prize – nobody got it – on the pretext that she had been in that class for two years. This fresh injustice increased her fury. She was deeply unhappy, because their families kept a close watch over them and she was unable to spend more than a quarter of an hour at a time with Danièle.

Danièle left for Paris in the following year and they lost touch with one another. Sylvie went on working furiously and from that time on she won the first prize every year. That made me understand why she had talked so much about her work when we first knew one another and why she had done so in such a way as to call a great many things into question: during her years at the lycée, that had been her only refuge. She had devoted herself to work not out of the obedient docility of a good pupil but out of resentment – she had worked with a dark fury, by way of challenge and defiance. The state of affairs at home grew no better. Her parents were proud of her in public; in private her stubborn attitude exasperated them: they wanted to interfere in her life and that she would not bear. They meant to 'break her spirit' but she was untameable. More than once they threatened to send her to a reformatory. Their conflicts became more and more violent. During one scene her mother tore up her favourite books, and Sylvie did not speak to her for a fortnight. Her story woke echoes in me. But I was older and less dependent on my parents when I suffered from their ill-will, and it had not taken such a gross and savage form.

The better I knew Sylvie, the more akin I felt to her. She too was an intellectual and she too was passionately in love with life. And she was like me in many other ways: with thirty-three years of difference I recognized my qualities and my faults in her. She had one very rare gift: she knew how to listen. Her observations, her smiles, her silences, made one feel like talking, and even talking about oneself; I told her about my past in detail, and day by day I keep her in touch with my life. There is no one who could have appreciated more than I what I have received from her. I loved her enthusiasms and her anger, her gravity, her gaiety, her horror of the commonplace, her uncalculating generosity.

Since she had proved to herself that she could attain it, success at school no longer interested Sylvie. But she loved to learn and to understand, and she had a lively, exact intelligence: she took a very good place in the *agrégation*, and that meant she could spend a fourth year at the college before going on to teach in the provinces. First she was posted to Le Mans and then to Rouen, in the same lycée where I had taught: when she spent the night there, she stayed in the hotel near the station where I had lived for two years, and she drank her morning coffee in the Métropole bar: all this gave me a certain feeling of being reincarnated. At present she has a post in the suburbs.

This means that we can see one another every day. She is as thoroughly interwoven in my life as I am in hers. I have introduced her to my friends. We read the same books, we see shows together, and we go for long drives in the car. There is such an interchange between us that I lose the sense of my age: she draws me forwards into her future, and there are times when the present recovers a dimension that it had lost.

Some of the people I spoke of in my earlier volumes – those who played a part in my life, sometimes important, sometimes less so – have died during these last years. Here I should like to speak of their deaths and in some cases to finish the portraits I drew of them.

When I was young, Camille's beauty, her independence, the furious strength of her ambition and her immense eagerness for work filled me with an envious wonder. In reality she was completely different from the character that had fascinated me. But there is no doubt that she did in fact possess immense charm. She dazzled Olga. Marco was astonished by his own friendship for her. Madame Lemaire, so very unlike Camille, was delighted by an evening she spent in the rue Navarin. A talented journalist, younger than Camille, was deeply in love with her; and he remained very fond of her for a long while, even after their affair had come to an end. Dullin worshipped her; he believed in her genius and followed her advice. He had formed her taste and he taught her his sense of the theatre. She succeeded in making very good adaptations of *Julius Caesar*, the *Plutus* and *Le Faiseur*. The lectures she gave at the school were often interesting. The pupils did not like her because with them she was domineering and arrogant: they made fun of the way she dressed and her mincing voice. But when she put on *'Tis Pity She's a Whore* by way of practice everybody acknowledged her talent as a producer. Sartre and I thoroughly liked being with her. She irritated us when she talked with an artificial naïveté about Lucifer and the 'presences' who protected her, and we thought her affected when she played with Friedrich and Albrecht,[22] objects she went so far as to take with her in a suitcase during the flight from Paris. But when she gave up her myths and histrionics, she could

[22] Two dolls she named after Nietzsche and Dürer.

64

observe and describe and tell a story very well indeed; she really amused us with her parodies and her imitations.

She decorated the studio in the rue Navarin marvellously; then she did the same in the beautiful flat in the rue de la Tour-d'Auvergne where she lived with Dullin. She loved ceremony and she turned all our meetings into special occasions. We had delightful moments with her in Paris, at Rouen and Toulouse and in her pretty house at Ferrolles. We thought she was writing busily, and in spite of the failure of *L'Ombre* we believed in her. It touched us to read the quotation from Emily Brontë that she wrote in her notebooks: 'Lord, let my memory never fade.'

Our relationship chilled at the beginning of the occupation. Camille went over to Nazism, accepting the persecution of the Jews without turning a hair. And then again she gave us her *Histoires démoniaques* to read; it was so childish and futile that we could not recommend it to a publisher, and that she resented. Why were we interested in Mouloudji's writing and not in hers? We were less candid about *La Princesse des Ursins;* but she must have felt that we were not very deeply moved by this 'magnificent flop' as one critic called it. On the first night the theatre was icy: in the middle of the show the revolving stage stuck and a scene had to be left out – the audience did not even notice. Behind the curtain Dullin was in tears. The play was massacred. At that point we understood that Camille would never be a writer. She no longer spoke of the novel based on her own experiences that she had told us of in Toulouse. The subjects of the plays that she did talk to us about were heartbreakingly silly. She wanted to write about a shipwreck symbolizing the loss of all the old values: the gods would announce a fresh set. She wanted Sartre to define them. In *L'Amour par intérêt* she meant to show that a liking for money and ambition could lead to genuine love: the hero of the tale was to be Peter the Great and the heroine Camille, slightly disguised. We were amazed. Camille was grown up; she was deeply experienced; she was ironic and even cynical, a woman who discussed people and things with realism. She was an intelligent reader; she talked about the authors she liked in an interesting way, and she was witty at the expense of bad writing. How could she possibly take pleasure in these puerile imaginings? How could she display such a total want of the critical faculty?

No doubt her narcissism helped to blind her. And then, although

65

we had supposed she was intensely eager to write, in fact she was exceedingly idle – she played at working and she did not work. Even so, we were surprised at the gap between her conversation and the pieces she wrote. There was something wrong somewhere. But what?

Was it because of this rift that she took to drink? To begin with her stories of getting drunk made us laugh: on the stage at the Atelier she indulged in some very strange capers. During a boring dinner-party at Ferrolles she escaped again and again to gulp down tumblers of red wine with Zina. 'I was sick,' she told us cheerfully. 'I hid behind a big fan and puked on the lawn, saying "This is very Spanish." ' But after the failure of *La Princesse des Ursins* we no longer found her excesses at all funny. Dullin did his best to stop them; she used to hide bottles in the theatre and he tried to take them away – they quarrelled. When she was drunk she made advances to all the actors and pupils. In the end Dullin persuaded her to go into a home for a cure.

The effects did not last long. She started getting drunk and causing scenes again. Dullin no longer had a theatre. He went on tour in Germany; she went with him and she made herself extremely objectionable to the whole company. She told us herself how one night in an hotel on the banks of the Rhine the actors were sitting on a terrace, singing and laughing among themselves: she called out to them from her balcony, saying they were to be quiet because they disturbed her meditations. She also told us how she had got drunk at an official reception of great importance to Dullin, and how she had said the wildest things. And I was told that another evening, when she was completely intoxicated, she grew so furious that she threw a bundle of banknotes into the fire – the company's pay. She told us she drank because she knew Dullin was ill and the idea of his death terrified her. Yet she made his life a hell with her extremely violent scenes about his artistic work, about money, about anything or about nothing at all. At one time he had left her everything he possessed. He changed his will. He appointed an executor, asking him to watch over Camille, whom he now sadly called 'my poor child'.

She almost never went to see him in hospital and she was not with him when he died. None of his friends went to fetch her on the day of the funeral: she came alone, and nobody spoke to her. In February 1950 his friends and pupils organized a ceremony at the

Atelier, a homage to Dullin. I have told how we went to Camille's flat and found her drunk, sobbing, her face all swollen; Ariane Borg was with her, shocked and horrified. She wept throughout the ceremony: no one looked at her, no one made the least gesture towards her. I am not sure that this ostracism was the best way of showing one's faithfulness to the memory of Dullin.

Camille seemed to get a grip on herself. In her bedroom she set up a little altar to Dullin – photographs, flowers an artificial rose stuck into a skull. She said that when things were difficult he gave her advice. In March she wrote to us: 'These last weeks I have lived through one of the most typical periods of my life and perhaps one of the most beautiful. Typical and beautiful because I see the plan and the meaning of my life as continuous and complete (not at all finished, but seen as it were by a kind of clairvoyance right up until my death). I move with a serene gravity that goes with a fair amount of gaiety and a kind of sprightliness (I don't much care for that word, but for me it has an added occult power and meaning that gives it a rather different sense).'

She would have been penniless if Sartre had not helped her: she looked upon this help as a kind of grant to allow her to carry out her literary work. In order to deserve it, she used to talk to us at length about the tasks she had in mind – *L'Amour par intérêt* and another play about witchcraft at Loudun; a romancero in several volumes that would deal with her life and her people's; and above all a book on Dullin – his life, works and ideas. She tried to get official subsidies to turn the huge flat into a Dullin museum: she had magnificent costumes, models of scenery, and some of Dullin's manuscript production-notes. We did not suppose that she did much work, because she was perpetually going to and fro between Paris and Ferrolles, where she had a well-established reputation as an alcoholic – she used to get drunk with the postman. She also spent a good deal of her time setting things in order. We saw her quite often. She went to the cinema, the theatre, exhibitions and concerts, and she read; her conversation was interesting except when she thought herself obliged to speak about her Work.

She lived entirely alone. Zina had married long before, but she went on living in the rue de La Tour-d'Auvergne with her husband, who worked in a garage. Then he set himself up at Belleville, and Zina divided her time between her home and Camille's. But Camille took to knocking her about more and more often in her alcoholic fits: one day she opened the door to us she had a black eye. In the end she went away.

Camille was friends with a girl she called the Corsican, a girl who was more or less in love with her. But their relationship soon fell to pieces. Camille went back to her isolation; she told us she did not dislike it much. In July 1951 she wrote, 'I am in a state completely different from this time last year. Near to a certain power of managing my balance of mind and thoroughly used to the essential solitude, although it is rather bitter at times. Solitude of living, not fundamental solitude, because thanks to you two I do not feel alone in the world; and then ... there are the "presences". Nothing disturbs them any more and they have never worked so well. And then there are also what I call the "half beings", I mean Friedrich and Albrecht, and Nell.[23] I talk aloud with the first two; and I wrangle with Nell almost all the time ... she is terribly jealous of the little ones ... Nothing is like my life any more – my true life, not the one I led with my parents, but the one I had when I was six and seven and eight, and before too and of course later; yet even when I was more eager for contact with real life (don't forget I had my first lover when I was nine) than with the one I am leading now ... Perhaps you will think I have grown childish again, in the bad meaning of the word. But I don't believe it is so, apart from that little "mentally retarded" side I have always had and which I dare say will be with me until I die, if all goes well.' A little later that summer she wrote us an optimistic letter: she was accepting the idea of living like a hermit. Her health was satisfactory and she thought she had made a great deal of progress from the point of view of mental balance; among other things she said she had grown almost entirely inured to loneliness.

Yet this solitude must have weighed on her, because three years later, when a doctor she trusted persuaded her to go into a nursing-home for another cure, and Sartre went to see her, she told him how she liked being there – there were nurses who looked after her; she was interested in the patients in the near-by rooms, and in the sight of an old man dying; it even amused her to see the ward-maids going by with their bed-pans.

She relapsed straight away. She told us herself that she always had a bottle of red wine at her bedside; as soon as she opened her eyes in the morning she drank off a tumbler full, otherwise she

[23] Her dog.

would be sick and she was unable to get up. She took care to be sober when she saw us, but we often felt that she had only just got over a heavy bout and that she had to make a great effort to keep up the conversation. In a letter in 1956 she said, 'There are times when I *cannot* and therefore should not even try to do certain things. That is something I am absolutely obliged to accept ... The other evening I wanted to see you at all costs, and because of that I only showed you the wrong side of myself and also the *negative* aspect of everything I had been, done or thought since the last time we met. I do so regret this generalized gloom and moaning, which is only the farther dried-up shore of a cheerful stream; stones and obstacles do not turn it aside – on the contrary, they change it into happy little waterfalls. I scarcely mentioned anything of real importance (my book, for example), and that only by chance.'

Camille had never been gifted for give and take: she would ask a few quick questions; we would give brief answers; and then she would launch into a monologue. In the days when she still saw a great many people, and read, and acquired information, her soliloquies were full of meat. But you cannot live shut in upon yourself without paying for it. The mind grows rusty; interests diminish: Camille was no longer much concerned with anything, apart from her health. She was capable of spending hours telling us about the symptoms and the treatment of her diabetes. Being anxious to justify the allowance Sartre made her, she was always careful to keep us abreast of her work: she was filing old papers for her romancero; she had had a brilliant idea for her book on Dullin – she was going to replace most of the text by photographs. No doubt she knew how little conviction these words carried. Our meetings tired her. She desired them less and less.

One day when we were waiting for her in my flat we heard heavy, uncertain footsteps in the street; they came nearer, then moved away. She took a quarter of an hour to find my door. She was staggering and she could not articulate properly. She went upstairs to the bathroom, and although she was usually so modest she left the door open: we heard her urinating loudly. We had begun to walk down the boulevard Raspail to dine in the boulevard Montparnasse when she collapsed on to a bench. Sartre went to find a cab. She behaved fairly well during dinner, but it cost her a good deal. Little by little the things that prevented us from seeing one another increased in number. She did not want to see anyone. After

The Prime of Life came out I received a letter from a doctor in Toulouse who had been in love with her when they were young: he asked me for her address. She saw him once, but after that when they made appointments she slipped out of them. Now and then she went to see Zina. Zina too drank very heavily: she fell seriously ill, and having dragged on for some months in hospital she died there, in 1964. When that happened we spent an evening with Camille at my flat: she was quite overwhelmed by Zina's death. A little later she wrote to us that it had caused her 'more than sorrow'; she had gone through a period of 'obsession', and she had passed an appalling, hideous month.

She no longer asked us to her flat, and we no longer took her out to restaurants. She still wore her long hair down her back – it had become reddish – and she dressed in very conspicuous old clothes: everyone stared at her. We stayed in my place, where she could talk more at her ease. More than once she told us how wearisome she found her chastity: one day, when she had been drinking, she went out into the street to look for a man. She brought one back to her flat, but she was overcome with disgust and she put him out. A little while after, he met her, slapped her and threw her to the ground.

The concierge did most of Camille's shopping and saw to her housework. The greater part of the flat was unused: she lived in her bedroom and the round drawing-room. I had not been there for years when she wrote and telephoned, urgently begging me to come and see her: this was in June 1967. I mistook the door and rang the neighbour's bell, opposite. 'Knock hard. Her bell is out of order and often she doesn't hear,' said the woman, giving me an odd kind of a look.

I knocked, I drummed on the door: in vain. I went to find the concierge, who came and thumped even harder: in vain. From the garden we threw pebbles at the windows with their closed shutters: in vain. I telephoned. 'Oh, I thought we were to meet at your place,' said Camille in a fairly steady voice. This was nonsense, because in that case she ought not to have been *there*. She said she would leave the flat door open. I went in, and looking at the dining-room and drawing-room I was unable to believe my eyes: it was as though I had taken leave of reality and had plunged into some fantastic tale. Between the still-recent past and the present moment there was as great a distance as that between a fresh young girl and a woman of a hundred. Camille's carefully planned setting, her decorations and

70

furniture, had turned into a jumble of filth. Layers of dust covered the yellowing mirrors, the greyish walls and the floor. Scraps of tulle and muslin, weird pieces of theatrical finery, were thrown over the furniture and the ornaments. One expected to see spider's webs in the corners. A voice called out, 'Do sit down.' I lifted the papers and rags off an armchair and sat in it. The door was ajar, and through the gap I could see the foot of a bed in the next room. I heard a strange grunting, heavy footsteps; then more grunts, and the thud of a falling body. A few more moments went by and Camille appeared in the doorway of the dining-room: she had rouge smeared above her upper lip and under the lower: she was wearing black satin pyjamas and the open top showed a pink cotton brassière. Her reddish hair was covered with a scarf. She was sucking her lower lip and disjointed words came from her mouth. I gathered that she was talking to me about the Friends of Dullin society, the Dullin exhibition, and Ferrolles, where she never went any more because the house was so deeply mortgaged. Gradually her speech grew clearer and her remarks more coherent. She talked to me about *Les Belles Images* and Walter Scott. But presently she showed signs of tiredness; the upper part of her body swayed to and fro: she was obviously dropping with sleep. I stood up. At the door she told me she wished she had white hair, because men followed her in the street, attracted by her figure (in fact she was horribly fat), and when they saw her face their disappointment was obvious. Before shaking hands she asked me, with a rather defiant air, 'What do you think of miniskirts?'

When I came back from Copenhagen in the autumn of 1967 I found a note from Camille dated ten days before, telling me that she was threatened with a distraint: to deal with it she needed some money within four days – a moderate sum that I could easily have lent her. But I was in Denmark. The next day she telephoned and asked me to get in touch with her 'little concierge', Madame C. The concierge told me that as Camille had not paid her rent or her rates for a long while the distraint had taken place, and in appalling conditions. Camille had kept the bailiff waiting for twenty minutes; then she had come into the drawing-room on all fours, wrapped in a disgustingly filthy dressing-gown and stinking of wine. She rolled on her back, sobbing and shrieking. When the distraint had been carried out, Madame C helped her back to bed: Madame C never used to go into the bedroom, and she found it full of empty bottles, and

71

heaps of paper that might very well have caught fire, seeing that Camille warmed herself with an electric stove. There was no sheet on the mattress and it was black with filth. Thousands of maggots were crawling in the dustbins, where Camille threw the remains of her food. She would not allow anything to be touched. At nine in the morning she had wine sent up: she telephoned the grocer, who brought her good, expensive stuff. Since the distraint she had eaten nothing. Madame C put food on the dining-room table and called Camille: next day she found the dishes untouched. Sometimes at night Camille could be heard singing. 'I don't want to say anything to the other tenants,' said the concierge. 'People are so ill-natured – they laugh. It's more unhappiness than anything else; what you might call a kind of moral decay.' She was very fond of Camille, who was such a lady and so cultivated in her lucid moments and who talked to her so kindly and politely. I said she would have to be sent to a nursing-home and I asked Madame C to urge her to agree. I telephoned Camille to persuade her: Sartre would see to the expenses. She refused stubbornly. She did not want to see anyone, above all not a doctor. She refused to leave her room

Sartre sent Madame C money to pay Camille's debts and to go on looking after her. She telephoned me every day. During four days Camille did eat a little, but then the position grew worse: she was drinking six bottles of red wine every twenty-four hours. 'You are killing yourself,' Madame C told her. 'Why shouldn't I? I've nothing left to live on.' She no longer left her bed, and she relieved herself in the dishes. I advised the concierge to tell the social health department and have Camille taken to hospital. 'No. I want to go on taking care of her.' Three days later Madame C made up her mind to follow my advice. Camille was incontinent; the room was full of excrement – she even had it in her hair. She lay on the floor, surrounded by oysters that she had ordered and then left to rot. That morning she still had the strength to demand the caviar that Madame C had refused to buy her. The concierge called for an ambulance. The doctor would not go into the bedroom because he did not want to tread in the filth. 'We've never seen anything like it,' said the ambulance-men. 'This isn't a woman, it's a heap of filth.' She was in a semi-coma and she let herself be taken away without protesting. She had bed-sores and they had to cut away the dressing-gown she wore next to her skin. At the Lariboisière hospital they cut her hair and put her into a bath. She was as thin as a woman who had been deported in the war, and her belly was enormously swollen.

I went to the hospital the next day. The house-physician was not there. The sister in charge told me that Camille was 'under observation' for diabetes. I sent to ask whether she would like to see me; she said yes, and the sister pointed vaguely to a kind of ward with eight beds in it. I could not make out which was Camille. I eliminated several patients, such as the young and the white-haired old women, and only one remained – a dark woman with short hair and a big shapeless face. I came nearer: she was talking to a nurse and I recognized Camille's voice. She was wearing the regulation rough canvas nightgown; her wrists were very thin and her face was puffy. She apologized for her hair: 'They have cut it and I haven't the strength to comb it.' I asked her whether she was being properly treated. 'It's like prison. They won't give me any of the things I want.'

'What would you like?'

'Milk. It's the only thing that could put me on my feet again. And the male nurses are very rude: they called me filthy – as filthy as a dung-hill.'

'Oh, surely not. How could they?'

'Oh, they are extremely ill-mannered,' she said with a very dignified air. She also told me that sometimes her hands clenched of their own accord and if she were holding a glass she could not give it back to the nurse. When that happened, the nurse was rough with her. I suggested she should go into a nursing-home. She thought it over. 'No. I'd rather stay here,' she said. I asked her whether she slept. 'I sleep all the time. I'm in a coma.' She wanted the concierge to bring her blankets and socks, 'Not expensive ones – the Saint-Pierre market will do.' She did not complain of having been taken away from her room. She did not seem to think herself in any danger.

For some days I had news of her from the concierge, who went to see her and who did her shopping: her condition was stationary. Then on 12 December, at four o'clock in the morning, the telephone rang. It was the hospital: Camille had just died. At eleven on the morning before she had asked for a bottle of burgundy and they had refused. That night she suffocated. They tried mouth-to-mouth resuscitation, but it was no good. Four days later she was buried. There were only five of us at her grave, Dullin's executor, the secretary of the Friends of Dullin, Madame C, Sartre and I. Madame C was the only one whose eyes were red.

She cleaned the flat. She carried down four hundred and fifty bottles out of the bedroom: the mattress was entirely rotted, and under it she found two splendid theatrical costumes, rotted too. All the other souvenirs of Dullin had been bought by the Bibliothèque de l'Arsenal.

She handed Camille's papers over to me: there were not many. Not the least trace of her literary work, not even a page of rough draft: that did not surprise me. But what had happened to the letters Sartre had sent her in former days? There were only a very few left. And where had Dullin's gone? I found some letters from people I did not know and the drafts of Camille's replies. Occasionally some of the people who wrote suggested meeting, but she refused, pleading her 'mystical seclusion'. She spoke of her 'Work' and of her 'enormous study' on Dullin. There was another letter that had come the day before her death: the mortgages on the house at Ferrolles had reached such a pitch that it had been sold to peasants in the village.

Camille also left a kind of private diary. It was a strange collection of separate, different-sized sheets of mauve, transparent paper covered with thick irregular writing: the ink was green, violet or red. It was almost impossible to read them because of the changes and additions. These notes were written between 1960 and her death. Camille had moved on from the cult of Lucifer to that of a number of curiously chosen saints: she was sorry that the Communion of Saints was thought so unimportant and that All Souls had so much overshadowed All Hallows. At the top of each page she marked the date and the name of the saint to whom she consecrated her day. In capital letters she wrote *Prayer*, and recorded whether it had been ordinary or very good. As well as the saints, she invoked the Father and Jesus, asking for their protection. She mentioned the Presences very often. 'That will really please Mama,' she wrote. She felt that she was 'inspired' and 'drawn on' by an inner force that urged her to go to the grocer's just before he closed or to fetch a chicken at the cook-shop at the very moment it came out of the oven. For she was above all concerned with food and health. She wrote down what she had eaten at each meal, how many glasses of mineral water she had drunk, the medicines she had taken, and the nature of her sleep. Two or three times she did speak of her reading – Walter Scott and

Michelet – and of music – Berlioz heard on the radio. She almost never mentioned her drinking bouts; yet sometimes she did say that she had just been through a period of 'heavy weather' or one of 'darkness'. From time to time she realized the filthiness she was living in. In 1964 she spoke of cleaning her bedding: it was a necessary condition for her 'work'. Another time she decided to get the concierge to empty her dustbins. The contents of the dustbins, she said, showed that she had just passed through a 'period of darkness'. Having them emptied would give her the feeling of receiving an 'absolution'.

I had not expected the papers to be as childish as all that. It still surprises me. The emptiness we detected in her when we read her pieces had invaded the whole of Camille; and drink and loneliness had completed the destruction – she had sunk into formlessness. But how is that primary weakness to be explained? Her childhood alone could give the answer. She had told us about it in a legendary form, but we did not know the truth. Since I do not possess that key, the whole of Camille's story and the shipwreck of her last years remains a mystery to me.

After Bourla's death Lise could no longer bear living in France. She became attached to a charming GI after the war, an assistant producer in Hollywood, and she decided to marry him. He did not want to get married, but she was pregnant and she persuaded him to take the steps necessary for her to join him in the States. She did so in 1946 and a little while later she had her baby, a girl. When I stayed with them in their villa in California in 1947 I realized that the marriage was not going well. They were in financial difficulties: she took this as an excuse to steal from supermarkets, which worried and angered her husband. She found looking after her house and the baby altogether too much. She deliberately took no care of her appearance, draggling about the house like a slut. In Hollywood she still retained the aggressive, provocative attitude she had had in Paris; when Jack took her to a party she purposely dressed in any old clothes, wearing thick walking-shoes or sandals. She set about well-known directors and successful producers, criticizing, contradicting or laughing at them. She filched sausages and sandwiches from the sideboard, filling a big bag; once the bag burst. She laughed heartily: Jack did not laugh at all. Sometimes she would also take a fountain-pen, a watch or a brooch. Jack begged her to give up these tricks; but it was no good. He was very well-mannered, he had great self-control, and he was always polite to her; but there were moments when his irritation showed through. She accused him of truckling to Hollywood customs and of taking himself too seriously. She had bursts of overflowing affection – she would fling her arms round him, lift him off the ground and say she adored him. But without warning her voice would turn to a whine and she would complain and sulk and nag. She would even be physically violent. In a letter that reached me a little after my return to France she told me how Jack had come back from a party later than he ought to have done and how she poured a bucket of water over his head: the gesture, she said, was too commonplace by far, and she was sorry for it.

So I was not too surprised when in September 1949 I heard that their relationship had grown far, far worse. 'I am going to write you a very sad letter. It would take a long while to tell you about the causes of my hopelessness. To put it shortly, I believe my marriage with Jack is on its deathbed . . . I am so wretched that it hurts me to think about it . . . He told me he had been in despair at having to marry me, that he did not like to refuse because he was fond of me but he had hoped with all his heart that the steps he had to take would not succeed . . . from the very beginning our life together has been spoilt by money difficulties . . . I have always felt that fundamentally Jack rejected me.

'A little while after you had gone a bad period began. The world grew small and empty; the baby had reached an unbearable age and my only delight was seeing Jack in the evening and loving him. I often had fits of despair . . . they took the shape of a kind of resentment, of a hatred for Jack that burst out on any trivial excuse . . . Jack resented my being a shrew, but he never helped me to overcome it with love and friendship . . .'

Lise had always felt that people did not help her enough nor give her enough; Bourla alone did not come in for that reproach. But what would have happened if their union had lasted?

At all events, things did not turn out well as far as Jack was concerned. In October she wrote to me, 'It is rather like a story that has come to a dead end, a makeshift, a remedy against utter loneliness in this country. Jack has been through a very bad period. He told me how much he despised me and how unbearable it was living with me. "I may have to live with you, I do not also have to like you." Now I do not care one way or another whether I keep Jack or lose him.'

She decided to study at the university. Intellectually she was unusually gifted and she did very well from the beginning. She far preferred the world of the university to that of the cinema. She was especially fascinated by a couple of homosexuals – Willy, a teacher of English literature, and Bernard, a young student. She wanted to share their life; she followed them about and watched their movements. One day she managed to hide in a cupboard in their bedroom, so as to be present at one of their nights together. That amused them, and Willy in particular became very friendly with her. She left Jack for a few days to go and live with them at their house. In her letters she spoke warmly of Willy, and at length.

She went to lectures for ten hours a week, and after 1950 she taught French in the university, also for ten hours a week. There she made friends, whom Jack liked no more than she liked his. She went back to live with him, but she did not think their marriage could last much longer. Her attitude towards her daughter Mary was ambivalent. All her letters began with ecstatic remarks about her charm: she was sorry for those of my friends who knew nothing of motherhood. But the last page would give a rancorous description of the weariness and the anxiety involved in bringing up a child: she accused Mary of being a tyrant. As for Willy, her enthusiasm often lapsed into bitterness: he was a disappointment to her. She yearned to go to bed with him, not out of physical desire, but in order to have a hold over him. Speaking in the name of existentialism she told him that homosexuality was not an entity and that he would prove his freedom by having relations with a woman. He was not convinced. She lost her temper, raised her voice, and even went so far as to hit him.

When I saw her at Algren's flat in the summer of 1950 we discussed her problems. The gap between her and Jack was widening. In November she left him. 'I have lived through what were really the most horrible weeks of my life, apart from those after Bourla's arrest . . . I broke with Jack of my own accord after a fortnight of living with him when I came back from Los Angeles. I have made up my mind to live alone. I have rented a hideous little flat. Los Angeles is a vile kind of a place, I do assure you. Willy was panic-stricken; he thought I had broken because of him and straight away he broke with me . . . In the evenings I gritted my teeth with despair and I waited for the storm to pass. Jack came to see me now and then, but that was even more horrible than not seeing him at all.'

Jack gave her a little money, but he hardly had any himself. Willy came back, but only to tell her how Bernard was making him suffer. She found life bitter indeed. She did make a new friend, a young physicist named Bertie, whom she liked very much; but he did not want to be drawn into an affair with her. He was attracted to her, but she frightened him. She knew perfectly well why he was frightened. At that point she wrote with great clear-sightedness, 'I have acquired a better technique with people: I do not break their spectacles any more, nor do I threaten them with my fist. The tyranny is subtler; but it is there.'

However, thanks to Bertie she did feel less unhappy. She wrote a charming tale in English (she did not manage to find a publisher) about her relationship with her daughter. But when Jack told her he wanted a divorce she was completely overwhelmed. 'I am entirely turned in upon myself; I cannot manage to communicate with any- one at all. On the one hand it is as though I realized that I was incapable of loving anyone, and on the other as though I did not want to. I am too afraid of putting myself into danger. It must be the backlash from the business with Jack: but no, it goes deeper than that ... When for some unbelievable reason Jack asked me to begin the legal proceedings, I really felt utterly alone in the world: I very nearly collapsed. All I had ever done no longer had any mean- ing. These three years seem to me to have been an absurd waste of time, for since I have not even a husband left to me, it is not teaching French that is going to give me the contentment I need.'

She was working very hard indeed to earn her living: 'A kinder- garten in the morning; my university lectures and private lessons in the afternoon; and I am a waitress in a drugstore in the evenings and on Sunday all day long. I work about fifty-five hours a week, but even so I hardly keep my head above water. When I am free I look after a neighbour's two children because she does the same for Mary when I am working. If this goes on, I think I shall go mad.'

Thanks to Bertie, it did not go on. His love for Lise overcame his apprehensions. 'Generally speaking, I am the one who makes the pace with Bertie,' she wrote, 'but in fact there is no doubt he likes it very much, although he admits he is utterly terrified of being eaten alive. But he has an immense belief in me and he thinks I am going to be a great writer. And for my part I think he is going to be a great physicist. So everything is for the best in the best of worlds.'

A little later she moved in with him. When she returned to America from Paris in the summer of 1954 she told me that Bertie had bought a splendid house right out in the country on a hill-top that had been made into a garden. She seemed completely happy. But a year later I received a letter that shook me deeply. 'My knees began to go to pieces. I could not stand upright any more and I had appalling pains in my joints. They have operated on both my knees, cutting five inches of bone from each thigh and grafting them on to my tibias; and they have refashioned both my kneecaps. The operation lasted five hours and I came out in plaster from my toes to my hips – plaster for two months and a half, and then another month in plaster when I came home at last. At the best I slept for two hours at a time with pills, and I would wake up with shocking headaches and pains in my legs ... Two hours after my divorce from Jack was made final, plastered and in a wheel-chair I married Bertie. I am well now, and today I rode a bicycle for the first time.'

She was well: she decided to study law and become a barrister. Was she happy? Her letters always began with an enthusiastic description of her life – Bertie was an angel and the garden was magnificent. Then she would burst out against Mary, saying that she made her life impossible; and she found fault with her position – turning into an American housewife was not at all what she had hoped for.

In her relations with me, she oscillated between affection and ill-will. Her letters were cordial, but she would slip in unpleasant remarks. When I was given the Prix Goncourt she facetiously reproved me for having robbed the younger candidates. I took no notice. But when I heard that she said things about me that were as disagreeable as they were untrue, I stopped writing. For some years I had almost no news of her, apart from the fact that she had had a little boy. Then I heard about her from friends we had in common. She adored her son, but she behaved so temperamentally and so tyrannically towards Mary that the little girl was psychologically disturbed. The psychiatrist advised that she should be removed from her mother. Lise agreed and the child was given into its father's care. I saw Jack and his daughter in Paris not long after: Mary was a very pleasant, agreeable adolescent and she seemed to have recovered a perfect mental balance.

At the end of 1960 I met Willy in Paris. He told me that Lise had wanted another child, but she was seized with convulsions during the delivery and the baby was born strangled. She was all the more wretched about it because the doctors forbade another pregnancy. She wrote to me a little later to tell me of her baby's death. She added, 'I have a curious kind of blood disease, something is lacking, some protein, and I find life hard all the time; but apart from that we are very happy.' She sent me a photograph of herself and her little boy. She was still quite good-looking, but her face no longer had that mixture of tenderness and violence that had given Lise her charm: it had become Americanized and it had hardened in every way. I replied with a friendly note and then again our correspondence came to a halt.

Some time later I heard that Lise had started to suffer from fits of asthma. It was flower-pollen that upset her most. She had had all the plants in the garden dug up and the hill covered with cement. Indoors she could only stand wood and stone; the rooms were icily bare. And in these rooms she had collected a striking number of objects of every kind – typewriters, fountain-pens, pencils, watches. Meanwhile her asthma grew worse. She decided that she could not tolerate the atmosphere of Los Angeles, where in fact the air is heavy with fog and dust: Bertie agreed to move with her to San Francisco. There she adopted a little girl, so that Michael should not be an only child. Her asthma worried her less. But she had what were said to be troubles of an epileptic nature – troubles that took the form of convulsions or of terrible headaches.

A psychiatrist who knew her told me that her asthma, her convulsions and her migraines were very obviously psychosomatic. She had been marked by her childhood, by her condition as a stateless person, and by the terrible shock of Bourla's death. The break with Jack had been another blow. Bertie's devotion had not been enough to heal all these wounds. She wanted to be happy and to make him happy; but the unhappiness had penetrated deep into her body.

At the beginning of April 1967 I had a message from Lise telling me she was in Paris. She asked me to ring her up at the Hotel Scribe. I telephoned. I did not recognize the big, male voice that answered. Did she have a cold? She was surprised: not at all, she said. She was passing through Paris on her way to Moscow with her husband, who was to attend a scientific congress. We agreed to lunch together the next day.

The next day towards one o'clock I watched the empty street with a certain anxiety. How much would Lise have been changed by age and sickness? Would contact be possible? It was strange, waiting for the past to come to life again in the shape of an unknown face. For a long while I stood at the window: at last, very late, a cab drew up a few yards from my block. A woman got out: she was wearing horn-rimmed spectacles, a long, startlingly blue skirt, tall boots and a terry blouse that showed enormous arms; in her hand she held a brush and as she walked she passed it fussily over her faded blonde hair. A little man with baskets in his hand and a camera slung over his shoulder trotted after her: her husband. Shouting echoed in the hall. 'Castor! Castor!' called Lise in her powerful voice. I opened the door. She kissed me, crying out and laughing. She was like one of those neurotic, drink-sodden American forty-year-old women I had seen in many films. The boots and the skirt more or less hid her legs and her enormously swollen knees. 'I was late on purpose because I wanted to see what you would say,' she cried, with a challenging air. And then, noisily enthusiastic, she brought present after present out of the baskets: a very ugly little brooch, a big round clock whose battery lasted a year and that never needed winding, a packet of labels, some gummed paper whose various uses she explained with noisy eagerness, a set of pictures of watches, each with a male or female Christian name: she burst out laughing when she showed me the watches and I had a most uneasy feeling that her illness had completely dulled her mind.

'The clock was my birthday present to Bertie,' she told me. 'He wanted to keep it and we had an argument: that's why we were late.' I felt exceedingly awkward and tried to give it back to Bertie. No, she said, he could buy another clock in San Francisco: he nodded agreement. He had not yet opened his mouth.

She looked round. 'Well, and what's been happening to you?' she asked. 'What are you doing?'

'Still the same thing: I write.'

'But why?' she asked in a anguished tone.

I produced the only argument that might seem valid to her. 'Because it brings me in money.'

'Ah, now that *is* a reason,' she agreed.

With Bertie carrying Lise's bag and Lise holding her hair-brush, we went to the restaurant. She called for snails and ate them, miming greed and crying, 'It's ter-rific!' It was as though she were caricaturing the young woman she had once been, for fun. Everything she said was excessive; all her gestures were exaggerated. Her movements seemed to be outside her control: she would fling herself forwards or backwards with startling suddenness.

She ate little. 'I'm not allowed to drink, nor to smoke, nor eat much; and as that fellow there is very jealous, there's not much left for me,' she said, laughing, with a coquetry that the uncomeliness of her person made shocking. On the other hand she talked prodigiously: almost entirely about her children. She adored her little boy, and for his own good she had decided that he was not to be an only child. In fact, when she adopted Lily, Michael went out of his mind with jealousy: he began disobeying, breaking everything, throwing things Lise liked into the dustbin, and setting fire to the curtains. She could not tame him so she sent him to a military academy as a boarder. 'To begin with Bertie didn't like it. He said to me, "Oh no, you're not going to start that again, not as it was with Mary." But then he understood,' she ended, smiling at her husband, who made no reply. I had the impression that he had made up his mind to 'understand' a very great number of things. She spoke tenderly of Lily. 'A little girl is so interesting!' But immediately afterwards, she complained that for eighteen months on end she had had to be after the child from morning till night to teach her what she ought to do and what she ought not. When I asked her whether she had read any interesting books she cried 'Read? What are you thinking of? I don't even read a paper! You don't know how absorbing it is, it takes up all your time, training a child!' Lily, like Michael, took her revenge for this solicitude by breaking things, throwing them about, burning them. 'But now she is good,' said Lise. And she showed me a photograph of her: a pretty little girl, but in her eyes there was the 'bewilderment of trained animals'. Then she told me about her dog, a huge bitch that she adored: she said proudly, 'I have taught her to make her messes sitting on the lavatory, like a person. It was hard, but I trained her all right.' This love for 'training' was something new in Lise, and I found it frightening.

Lise had talked so much that Bertie and I had drunk our coffee before she finished her strawberries and cream. 'I'll carry them with me,' she said. I protested – we could stay there at the table for a while. But she wanted to eat them in the street. Once more she was parodying the ways of her youth. The huge quantities of drugs she had to take had emptied her within, and she was concealing this hollowness by a mechanical imitation of her former behaviour. An

hour later, when she took a taxi, she complained of a violent headache. Afterwards I heard that she went to bed as soon as she
reached their hotel.

When she came back from Moscow she was wearing a rather
short and very ugly grey linen dress, decorated with blue pompoms.
'Really, you know, I should not complain,' she said. 'It might have
been worse – I can still walk.' She was delighted with her journey
but in fact she had seen nothing: she had spent almost all her time
in her bedroom. She emptied a big plastic bag on the floor and gave
me envelopes from a Moscow hotel. Then, still with huge gestures
and in a very loud voice, she described her life in San Francisco: it
was utter loneliness; she did not know anyone at all. She had almost
not set off on this journey because there was no one to whom she
could entrust Lily: but at the last moment Bertie's mother had
agreed to look after her. Before saying good-bye Lise said to me,
'Now I come to think of it, just why did we quarrel?'

'Because of the things you said.'

'Oh, maybe. When I have had a drink or two I say anything at
all.' I knew she never drank anything, but I did not dwell on it.

When she was back in America she wrote to me. Her letter was
amusing, and there were coloured drawings and collages on the
envelope – it was one of those pleasant things she had loved to
make in earlier days. She was working for her final examination in
law and at present she was studying testamentary legislation. 'To
judge by people's wills,' she ended, 'ours is a curious species.' If she
was capable of going on with her studies, she must be less affected
mentally than I had thought; no doubt the fatigue and the upset of
travelling had made her worse in Paris.

One morning a year later there was a violent ringing on my bell.
At first I did not recognize the little man in a round hat who was
carrying a square box slung on his shoulder: he looked like a fisher-
man. Behind him stood Lise: she flung herself upon me with loud
cries of friendship. She undid some pretty presents: an electric wrist-
watch, a Parker pen in the latest style, checked shirts for Sartre.
Bertie was going to a congress at Poitiers. Before that they were to
travel in Italy. We made an appointment.

I saw Lise three or four times during the ten days she spent in
Paris. She seemed to me rather less swollen and rather less maladjusted than at her last visit. Yet she had just had an appalling
headache, lasting forty-eight hours. She spread an unpleasant

chemist's shop smell all round her: as soon as she began to get tired she sweated all over, her legs trembled, and she had to take a medicine with an ether base. She still gesticulated a great deal. She dressed with an astonishing lack of taste. She was wearing a green bandeau in her hair, a white frock with green spots and an orange corduroy coat. Her attitude towards Bertie had grown less friendly. In my flat she made him sit on her lap and she petted him, which he bore with a certain air of constraint. But she was also capable of talking about him in his presence in the most unpleasant and humiliating way: he never flinched. Yet once he did murmur, 'What have I done now?' when Lise was upbraiding him in an angry tone. She claimed that sometimes he lost his temper to the extent of hitting her: she had learnt karate to defend herself. So had he. They fought a mimic battle in the street that embarrassed me deeply. Lise had even less respect for others than in her youth. At the end of a meal she took a little waterproof bag from her pocket to fill it with the ragout she had not eaten. 'Everyone does this in America,' she told me. 'They say it's for the dog, but nobody believes it.' I persuaded her to take nothing but a little fruit. They left me after a lunch together to go to the Galeries Lafayette: Lise wanted a bear for Lily and some brooms for herself – she did not like the kind they sold in America. The day before they left she still had not found the broom she longed for: they meant to look for it the next morning, before the plane took off.

Lise had been more agreeable to me than usual. The wife of the tutor who guided her studies liked my books and she had influenced her. She congratulated me heartily on *The Woman Destroyed*, which she had read aloud with Bertie. He filmed us together in the street. She lifted me into the air and twirled me about. She burst out laughing. 'Poor Castor! She's all embarrassed.' Most of our conversation had been about her health: we had also talked about her mother for a short while – Lise had brought her over to the States, where she was very unhappy, because she did not speak a word of English. They quarrelled: according to Lise, her mother had been entirely in the wrong. She died of cancer in a hospital without their having seen one another again.

Lise sent me a gloomy little card from Venice: she was not pleased with Bertie and she was bored. She let him go back to America by himself and she stayed in Paris for a few days. During the summer we did not write. At the end of November I had a letter from Bertie. 'I have something terrible to tell you.' 'They are divorcing,' I thought. And then I read the next line: 'Lise is dead.' On Monday she had gone to bed with 'flu. On Thursday Bertie had suggested fetching a nurse while he took the children for a walk. She refused. When he came back he went into her room and found her dead. I never learnt anything more.

A month later I received a parcel with Lise's name and address on it as the sender. For a moment I sat there staring stupidly at this present from beyond the grave. It was one of those fruit cakes that are made in the States for Christmas and that have to be ordered well in advance. She had had it sent to me two days before she fell ill.

Giacometti had been ailing since 1960. He had violent pains in his stomach and they worried him. Dr P, his physician and friend, assured him that he was only suffering from plain gastritis. But nevertheless it weighed on Giacometti's mind. He worked more furiously than ever and this overwork helped to pull him down: sometimes he would faint in his studio. He was dissatisfied because he had not yet been able 'to wring sculpture's neck', to dominate it entirely; he was worried about his health; and he was much less cheerful than before, less open to the outside world. Our meetings no longer had the same warmth: to us he seemed remote.

At the beginning of 1963 specialists told Giacometti that he had a stomach ulcer and that it would have to be dealt with. We saw him at the nursing-home a few days after the operation, which had gone very well. His face was relaxed; he had a sense of release and he was waiting impatiently for the moment he could get back to work.

A little later his wife Annette asked to see Sartre. She thought that in many ways he was like Giacometti, and that he was in a better position than anyone to answer the question she was asking herself: should Giacometti be told that he had cancer or not? She had spoken to the surgeon, who asked her coldly, 'Is it a matter of finance? Do you want him to make certain provisions?' 'No, no, not at all.' 'Are you a believer?' 'Not in the very least.' 'Then why should you tell him?' She argued the point. He flared up: he asserted that from the psychological point of view there was nothing more dangerous for a man with cancer than knowing it. If Annette told Giacometti, he and Dr P would deny it. She wanted Sartre's advice. 'As far as I am concerned,' he said, 'I have made Castor

85

promise to hide nothing from me.' In his opinion, when a man had undertaken to live, trying never to lie to himself, he had the right to look his death in the face and to make use of the interval allowed him with a clear mind. In any case, it was not a question of telling Giacometti that he was condemned to sudden death. The operation might have cured him. And in any event, at his age cancer developed very slowly.

During this discussion we talked about a very different case, that of Pagniez' wife. The doctor said, 'She will be dead in a year.' Pagniez wished to keep it from her, and we approved. She had no decisions to take; she had to stay in bed; she was much weakened and her mind was somewhat clouded – why inflict a year of mental agony upon her? She went on believing that she would soon be well and she died peacefully. Pagniez knew that in deceiving her he was acting in her interest, but for his part he suffered from an untruth that now divided them, whereas before they had always been completely open to one another.

Annette had much the same kind of feeling. Sartre helped her to make up her mind. When she left us she had almost decided to tell Giacometti.

She didn't do so at once. We dined with him two or three times and he did not seem to have any suspicion. We were embarrassed and almost ashamed at knowing something very important about him that he did not know himself. We felt that it was unworthy of Giacometti that he should cherish an illusion. Annette was in torment. The act that we put on seemed to us a betrayal.

They left for Stampa. One evening we had a telephone-call from Switzerland; it was Giacometti thanking Sartre for the advice he had given Annette. He had just learnt the truth. His surgeon had given him a letter for the Italian doctor who looked after him in Switzerland. The Italian was not very good at French, and with surprising stupidity he asked Giacometti to translate the letter for him. It was a case of cancer, wrote the surgeon, but the operation had been entirely successful and the patient had no suspicion of the nature of the disease. Nobody made any remark at this point. At first when they were alone, Annette and Giacometti spoke guardedly; he did not know whether she had been told before nor whether she had entirely understood the letter; and for her part she wondered whether its meaning had been quite clear to him. In the end they reached a perfectly frank understanding, and on the telephone Giacometti seemed wonderfully happy about it. Had he known nothing whatsoever up until then? Probably not. He had had doubts and he had to face them without an ally. Now he was no longer alone. There is less distance between suspicion and certainty than there is between division and understanding. That was why he now felt so much happier in himself. When he came back to France we talked in the same cheerful, relaxed way as we had done in the past.

On the other hand, he more or less broke with Dr P. Not only had P seen fit to lie to him, but he admitted to Giacometti that some years earlier he had detected shadows in an X-ray. 'I said nothing because I did not want you to start living as though you were an invalid,' he explained.[24]

In January 1964 Giacometti's mother fell ill and died. He was completely overcome. He had always loved her deeply. It had given him great joy when, some years earlier, she had replaced the picture of his father over her bed by a picture of him. He had painted a very fine portrait of her in 1958, a picture filled with tenderness.

We did not see much of him that year. When we came back from the USSR in July I was astonished to hear from Olga that he was angry with Sartre because of a passage about him in *Words*. She had heard him say to his friend Lotar in a Montparnasse bar, 'I'm glad Sartre won't be back before July. By then I shall have gone. I shan't see him until the autumn and by then I shall have had time to forget.' He was very gloomy, she added. When she asked him whether his work was going well he answered, with an ominous look, 'I need ten years.' There was supposed to be an important exhibition of his works in New York the following year and Lotar asked him if he meant to go. 'Next year? Oh, if only it were to-morrow,' he muttered. And then, correcting himself, 'Even if it were tomorrow, I shouldn't go to New York.'

He had it out with Sartre in October. 'I was not angry, but bewildered,' he said. In *Words* Sartre had described a conversation in which Giacometti told him how, when he was knocked down by a car in the Place d'Italie, the thought had flashed through his mind, 'At last something is happening to me.' And Sartre observed, 'I admire this readiness to welcome everything. If one likes surprises, one should like them to that point.' But the meaning of the event

---

[24] Later he bitterly regretted a silence that might perhaps have cost Giacometti his life. He died not long after.

had been entirely different. Giacometti was getting ready to go to Zurich and he was sorry that he would have to leave a woman he loved: he walked out of her house in the Place des Pyramides and a car knocked him down: in the ambulance that was carrying him away he felt delighted about the accident that would keep him in Paris. If Sartre were capable of making such an inaccurate tale out of this story, then Sartre had stopped being Sartre. 'But it was *your* account that I used,' objected Sartre. If Giacometti's reaction had really been as unimportant as he now said it was, we should scarcely have taken any notice of it; and to tell the truth, it is difficult to see, in that case, why he should have told us about it at all. The gap between the two versions obviously originated in him, but we could not explain it to our own satisfaction. In any event, we found it surprising that he should have taken the matter so to heart. It is true that at that time he was very much concerned with recovering his past. He had always taken pleasure in looking back on his childhood and adolescence; but now he was perpetually calling them to mind.

In 1965 there were great exhibitions of his works in London, New York, and in the neighbourhood of Copenhagen. Although he loathed travelling he went to all three with Annette. Yet, as she told us later, he was a compulsive worrier and even the smallest thing would cause a state of extreme anxiety. When they were crossing the Atlantic she went into his cabin one morning and found him sitting on the bunk, his eyes staring. 'Stay if you like,' he said. 'But be quiet.' That was not like him at all. He would also relapse into long brooding meditations. In the photographs taken in New York he had aged a great deal, and his expression had hardened. It was not mere chance that his last busts, portraits of his friend Lotar, had something terrifying about them: into those great frightened eyes he projected his own dread.

That autumn his doctor found that Giacometti's heart was strained and he advised him to go to a Swiss nursing-home, as he had done every year since his operation, but earlier than usual this time. He set off by himself. A telegram summoned Annette: his lungs were affected and he was in a bad way. She found him very much altered. It was as though once he had taken to his bed his body had given up the struggle. Did he know that his end was at hand? He cast up his accounts: 'As for my work, yes, there I have succeeded,' he murmured. These words were a comfort to his friends, who had so often seen him full of self-doubt. He remained in a semi-coma before breathing his last on 1 January 1966.

I was not really sad. His obsessions and his memories had taken him over completely and we had already lost him. He had achieved all the fame he could ever have wished for. And it seemed to me that his work was completed. Indeed, it might be that what he was now attempting – the preservation of the general and abstract meaning of the human face at the same time as the elucidation of its individuality – was in itself a contradiction.

In 1968 there was a great exhibition of his works at the Orangerie. Above the entrance stood his name in large letters, with the dates of his birth and his death. I looked at them for a long while, with a kind of unbelief. He had plunged straight into History, as embalmed and as remote as let us say Donatello: and because of that my own life was flung far back towards the beginning of time. The rooms were not very well arranged: first came the masterpieces of his maturity; then the surrealist period; then his maturity again. In my opinion his paintings and drawings became more and more beautiful as the years went by. But in sculpture his greatest period was that which came after the war, from 1945 to 1952. After that time, there were successful pieces, but generally speaking his research did not come to fruition. Yet his last bust, the bust of his friend Lotar, is of an extraordinary intensity. The public did not know what to think: no doubt Giacometti did not seem to them either sufficiently modern or sufficiently conventional to be captivating. On the other hand, almost all the people who go to the Fondation Maeght at Saint-Paul-de-Vence admire him. In that environment the great statues of walking men take on their full meaning. There are now sculptures or paintings by Giacometti in many museums and every time I come up against one I am deeply moved.

After a charge of explosive went off in the doorway of the building in which she lived, Madame Mancy left her flat; she was no longer living there when a second blast destroyed it entirely. She settled in an hotel in the boulevard Raspail. She did not find this move too disagreeable. She had had six flights of stairs to climb in the rue Bonaparte, and although she had help, the housework tired her. The hotel set her free from these obligations. She had her own furniture, her ornaments and her favourite books. She liked the company of the young chambermaids. Sartre no longer lived with her, but he found a small flat just at hand and he saw her very often. She spent three or four happy years there. She saw visitors, read, watched the television and above all listened to music. She came from a musical family; she was an excellent pianist and had a fine voice: she had hoped to make a career as a singer. Her taste in painting was very poor and she only read easy books but on the other hand she had a passionate and discriminating love for music. She was not frightened by the moderns: it was with her that I first heard Berg's *Wozzeck*, played on the radio. In fine weather she went for walks in the immediate neighbourhood or took a cab to the Tuileries. When she was in bed at night she loved thinking back over her childhood and youth. 'I am never bored,' she used to say. She was careful of her appearance and conscious of it; she nearly always dressed in navy-blue with a touch of white about it; her high heels made the most of her fine legs. When she was eighty her figure was still slim and elegant, and as her white hair was hidden under her hat, men sometimes followed her in the street.

In her childhood she had been crushed by Madame Schweitzer, who later became a delightful old lady but who, as a mother, was domineering and selfish: the photographs of the young Anne-Marie show a lost, bewildered girl. She made a joyless marriage and she was soon left a widow: she came back to live with her parents and she worked for the examination as a labour inspector, because she wanted to be independent. She accepted the proposal of an engineer who had long wished to marry her, because by so doing she thought she was acting in the best interests of her son. There was no joy in this marriage, either. 'I have been married twice and I am a mother, but I am still a virgin,' she said when she was old. 'Uncle Jo' was a masterful man, as hard on others as he was on himself, the austere incarnation of the bourgeois virtues; he behaved perfectly to his stepson; but the boy shared none of his ideas and when he grew up there were often clashes between them. When Uncle Jo read the beginning of *L'Enfance d'un chef* he sent his copy of *Intimacy* back to Sartre. There was never any question of his meeting me. Madame Mancy had a submissive, devoted nature; she was full of gratitude because her husband had assumed the care both of her and her child; she always thought that he was in the right. Yet she regretted the tender intimacy in which she had lived with her son in earlier times and she tried to remain close to him. Without telling her husband she often asked us out to tea together. And during the war

I saw her by myself. But it was only in the last years of her life that we felt a real affection for one another. She did not say so, but she disapproved of my way of life. It was less her preconceived notions that troubled me than her apparent spinelessness. She spoke in short, interrupted sentences, making an excessive use of the word 'little' in order to weaken her meaning. For example, in a tea-room she would ask the waitress 'Where is the little powder-room?' Her tone of voice was usually plaintive. She said she suffered from a great many little aches and pains, and she never admitted to having any pleasure. As she saw it, life was a collection of wearisome duties. She never presumed to give a personal opinion on any subject whatsover: her absent husband still governed her thoughts.

But I did admire her delicacy and judgment when Uncle Jo died of a heart-attack. Sartre was then in America. Madame Mancy did not tell him: she did not want him to cut his journey short. She ardently longed to live with him, and when he came back he agreed. She found a flat in the Place Saint-Germain-des-Prés. She turned the best room into a study for Sartre and kept the drawing-room for herself, together with a little room where she slept. Eugénie, the old woman from Alsace who helped with the housework, slept in the back bedroom. 'This is my third marriage,' said Madame Mancy happily.

But their living together did not give her all the pleasure she had expected. Her husband's views had influenced her deeply, and she often had disagreements with her son; he did not make much of them, but they vexed her. If he happened to contradict her she would fly into a brisk but short-lived temper, for she was one of those people whose irritation mounts suddenly, like milk on the boil. And sometimes it was she who provoked him. She had a more social idea of the literary life than we: she had dreamt of receptions in which she would be the hostess. She would have liked him to run after honours and publicity. It was she who signed a paper in 1945 asking for the Légion d'Honneur for him. One day she was called upon by a young man who said he was an American: according to him his sister, a student in an American college, revered Sartre, and her veneration was shared by her fellow-students; he had promised to bring them back photographs of their idol. Flattered, Madame Mancy gave him pictures of Sartre as a baby, a child and an adolescent. They appeared on the back page of *Samedi-Soir* as illustrations to a venomous article. That evening, ashamed of her blunder, she received us in tears. Sartre comforted her. But he was wasting his breath when he begged her to avoid all contact with the press for the future: she often talked too much. Then, aware that she had been incautious, she resented the reproaches that Sartre never uttered.

She was completely devoted to her son, just as she had been to her husband, and she liked to believe that she was necessary to him. She watched over his physical comfort, but she also wanted him to follow her advice. His behaviour worried her, for she respected rank, the established order, and the acknowledged values. Like many women whose existence is 'relative', she lived in a constant state of worry. It distressed her profoundly if Sartre were attacked in the papers. She quite lost her head when we gave a lecture or had a play put on. The rehearsals were often stormy; she heard rumours, and she was consumed with anxiety. She was afraid that Sartre might offend the theatre management, the producer, the audience. On first nights she was in torment if she overheard a criticism or if she thought the applause lukewarm. In many other contexts she would urgently ask us whether 'everything was going well'. We always answered yes, and usually it was true. She suspected us of 'keeping things back', and she questioned all kinds of people. It was above all Sartre's political attitudes that seemed to her deplorable and dangerous.

In time this friction and these misunderstandings diminished, and then they disappeared. In the end she adopted her son's opinions. This was not merely because she was biddable: by rising up against the prejudices that had oppressed her youth and against the ideas that her husband had forced upon her, she was taking her revenge upon all the people who had dominated her so harshly. Towards 1962 she felt entirely liberated. 'It is only now, when I am eighty-four, that I have really broken free from my mother,' she told us. Although she was so timorous in small things, she showed a determined solidarity with her son during the Algerian war. She bore the two attempts at blowing up the building in which she lived with equanimity, and all their consequences for her.

The publication of *Words* was a source of great joy to her. She was shocked by Sartre's portrait of Monsieur Schweitzer, and she did not recognize her son in the little boy he described. 'He understood nothing about his own childhood,' she said to a friend. But she was moved by the way in which he spoke of her and by the evocation of their earlier relationship. On the other hand, she foresaw that she would not like the next volume, in which he would speak of his stepfather. He did not write it: she thought he would do so after her death. She knew very well that her second marriage had broken something between them and she often explained to me the reasons that had urged her to it; I assured her that Sartre understood them, but it was no good – she remained uneasy.

From now on she had a fresh occupation: to complement *Words* she undertook to recount her own story and Sartre's childhood as she herself had experienced it. Month after month she wrote on: 'It's odd: I used to think we were a very united family,' she told us. 'I see us all again, gathered round the lamp in the evening, my parents, my brothers and me. But now I realize that in fact we did not talk to one another. Each was quite alone.'

She had always been more or less of an invalid. With age her complaints increased in number: she had rheumatism, headaches, high blood-pressure, and her heart was weak. Formerly she had always been a little sorry for herself, but now she did not complain at all. Yet once she did confess to Sartre, 'If I were always to suffer as I suffered yesterday, I'd rather die right away.' The pain had made her weep. All this meant that her life was much impoverished. The doctor forbade her to go out in bad weather; even when it was fine she was afraid of a fit of giddiness in the street; and she refused to let anyone go with her on her walks – out of pride and consideration for others she did not wish to feel a burden. So she stayed in her room. Reading and the television tired her eyes and gave her a headache. When she listened to music she was so moved that it was bad for her heart – many times she was on the verge of an attack. She was cheerful when we visited her: at Christmas and on New Year's Day she drank champagne with us and laughed as heartily as could be. But referring to the happy old age of the hero's mother in *The Age of Discretion* she said to me, 'I'm not in the least like her: as far as I am concerned I don't find old age gay at all.' She thought about death a great deal. She had already given some of her jewels and ornaments to those around her: 'I should rather you had them in my lifetime,' she said. She did not wish for death because for her her son was a sufficient reason for living, but I do not think she feared it.

In 1968 her giddiness became more and more frequent: sometimes she fell down in her room. A well-known radiologist, Dr M, and her local doctor looked after her most attentively; they struggled with her high blood-pressure, and they tried, without very much success, to ease her pains.

On Christmas Day we drank champagne with her. When I went to see her on Thursday, 2 January, she told me that she had been unwell the day before, and the day before that: she had been sick. That Friday evening I was working in Sartre's flat when there was a ring on the bell: it was the manager of the hotel: Madame Mancy had had a heart-attack and she was suffering a great deal. The cardiologist had said that in case of accident she should be taken to the Fernand-Widal hospital, where he would look after her himself. He was away from Paris, but even so they took great care of her and her pain decreased. When Sartre saw her the next day she was pleased that the pains were gone; her mind was perfectly clear and she was a little over-excited – the effect of some drug, no doubt.

When I walked into her room on Sunday I had a shock: she no longer had her false teeth, her hair was uncombed, and she looked ten years older than usual. Now and then she would forget a word and replace it by another: 'If I had to stay two mountains here, I should fall really ill.' This vexed her and she said, 'I'm growing senile.' But in fact she was in full possession of her faculties and her memory was unimpaired. She spoke of something that had happened a year before. It looked as though she were going to recover.

During the days that followed she spoke without any difficulty, but her mind did wander a little. The patient who shared her room went away at about seven o'clock on Tuesday morning and came back in the middle of the afternoon. On Wednesday Madame Mancy told Sartre that the woman 'sold corpses'. The day before she had gone to Corsica to buy the corpse of an American and she had brought it back in the afternoon. 'Perhaps they are watching out for my body,' she said; and she asked whether the police should be told. When I saw her the next day I thought her very tired. She complained of a pain in her arm: her neighbour had opened a window during the night and she had caught cold. This explanation did not satisfy us. 'This is no place for old people,' she said. As early as six in the morning a troop of doctors began busying themselves with her: all day long they gave her injections and medicines – it was exhausting ... 'If I were left here for two months, I'd never get over it.' She also said, and in a strange kind of voice, 'I should never have believed it would be like this.' *It*: the end, death? Or was she merely disappointed at not having a room to herself, as Dr M had promised her? The experience both astonished and interested her: she had never been in a nursing-home or a hospital. Towards the end of our visit she wandered a little. At that time there was a lot of talk about sending men to the moon and she said, 'If you go there, don't tell me beforehand: I should worry too much.' To some degree she was joking, and it was also a way of asking whether we were going to set off on a journey; but her voice was serious. She made it clear to us that she wanted to go to sleep. That day I had the feeling that there was no hope.

On Friday morning Sartre was told on the telephone that his mother was at the Lariboisière hospital: she had had a severe attack of uraemia and they were better equipped to deal with it there. On reaching the Lariboisière she had a stroke, with hemiplegia, a usual consequence of an infarctus. The pain in her arm that she had spoken of the day before was no doubt the sign of a disturbance in her circulation. Sartre found her in a cubicle in the big reanimation ward, unconscious, covered with instruments to make her heart beat, her arm fastened to a perfusion apparatus.

Madame Mancy was taken back to the Fernand-Widal hospital, where she was given a room by herself. A variety of instruments kept an artificial life going in her. She was comatose. Her right side was paralysed and her lower lip slightly distorted: it did not disfigure her, but her face was that of a dying woman – the eyes closed, the nostrils pinched. She remained in that state for two weeks. Twice I saw her open her eyes a little, but I did not have the impression that she saw us. Twice, when I was not there, she brought her good hand from under the sheets, took Sartre's wrist and squeezed it; she tried to smile, but her mouth would not obey her; she signed to him to go away. There is no doubt that she had recognized him: but from what distance, from the heart of what darkness?

When we arrived at the hospital and asked how she was, the nurses always said 'No worse than yesterday.' But on the chart there was written 'Condition comatose.' On the morning of Thursday, 30 January, they told me on the telephone, 'Things are not going well.' And they told Sartre 'Her condition is unchanged'; which was not in fact contradictory. When we reached the hospital entrance a woman with reddened eyes, a distant cousin, hurried towards Sartre. 'I have just seen your mother. She had a very peaceful death.' 'Death?' cried Sartre, catching his breath. 'Yes: half an hour ago, very quietly. Hurry if you want to see her. They are going to take her to the Lariboisière.' It was as well she had warned us: for we met nobody in the corridors. We opened the door of the room and we saw Madame Mancy, completely white, with her mouth slightly open but no longer distorted: she had recovered her living face. The nurse confirmed that she had 'gone' without realizing it. Sartre saw her again the next day at the Lariboisière. He was struck by the fierce hardness on her face. He had the impression that life had crushed and dulled a woman whose nature inclined her to passion, steadfastness and even violence, but that it had done so without breaking her. I saw her face for the last time on the morning of the funeral: they were her features, but they no longer expressed anything at all.

She had often said 'I do not want a church service.' She was vaguely a deist but she belonged to no religion and she did not believe in immortality. We took her straight from the hospital to the graveyard, where her family and friends were gathered. The next day we went to the hotel to clear her room. There was not much there because when she left the flat she had got rid of almost all she possessed. Sartre gave the television and most of the clothes to the chambermaids. We packed the things we meant to keep or to give to others in suitcases. It took only an hour for the last traces of a life to be wiped out for ever.

The day after she had the stroke Dr M said to Sartre, 'As a doctor I must keep your mother alive as long as possible. But if I were her son I should want her to die.' That meant that if she survived she would remain paralysed, with her mind impaired. It was a fate that she had always dreaded more than death. My mother had been put to the risk of appalling suffering for a few days more of life. What is the basis of this savage code of ethics which insists upon reanimation at all costs? On the pretext of respecting human life doctors arrogate to themselves the right of inflicting any kind of torment and every kind of degradation upon human beings: it is what they call doing their duty. But why will they not agree to call the meaning of this word *duty* into question? An old lady wrote to me not long ago, 'The doctors want to keep me alive although I am sick and paralysed. But why, Madame, why? I do not say that all old people should be killed, but surely those who wish to die should be allowed to do so. There should be as much right to free death as to free love.' And indeed, why? Why? I have asked a great many doctors and not one of their answers has satisfied me.

During the last years of her life, Madame Mancy's development had brought us closer together. Madame Lemaire's attitude, on the other hand, moved me farther from her. The political differences that had once seemed unimportant to us took on a great significance during the Algerian war. They implied different outlooks upon the world so directly opposed that it was hard to discover any common ground. After the dismal dinner-party in the summer of 1962 at which Madame Lemaire had behaved in so unfriendly a manner I did not see her for a long while. Feeling remorseful, I telephoned and went to her flat in the rue Vavin one evening: the flat belonged to a part of my life that was over and done with and I thought it somewhat sinister – a dead and buried past in which the present had no place. Madame Lemaire was very welcoming; I tried to talk to her about Sartre and me; I asked her questions about herself. But the conversation flagged. She took small interest in my doings; she spoke little of hers. We said we should see one another again but we both knew very well that this meeting was the last. Two years later Jacqueline telephoned to tell me that her mother had just died: she had broken a leg the year before and since then she just kept going: in spite of her sorrow, Jacqueline seemed to think that she had died without regret. So the news hardly touched me at all.

Nor was I moved in the spring of 1971, when I heard that Pagniez was dead. He had survived his retirement only a few months. Not only had we ceased meeting ever since, for apparently childish reasons, he had broken with Sartre, but he had followed paths diametrically opposed to ours. He had strongly disapproved of the Manifesto of the 121 and we knew that when he spoke of us he did so with more criticism than liking. As for us, his way of life had made him a total stranger.

To tell the truth, of all the deaths that occurred among people I knew during these last years, only one really moved me very deeply, and that was Evelyne's. But I have no wish to speak of it.

Why have I accepted these deaths so calmly? I see one primary reason. Biologically one may speak of a programming of living beings, a programming that depends upon the species, and in each species upon both hereditary and individual factors. In his *Flaubert* Sartre shows that this notion can be applied to a human life as a whole: some people die by accident before the programme is completed; others live on after its completion, having nothing more to do on earth. In the instances that I have just spoken of, those who died seem to me to have been survivors of this kind: Camille and Lise because of their decay; Madame Mancy and Madame Lemaire because of their great age; and Giacometti because he had been much changed by disease. Yet this explanation does not satisfy me. When Dullin died in 1949 he was a man who had come to the end of his course; our relationship had been no more than superficial; and yet I was overwhelmed. 'A whole section of my past collapsed and I had the feeling that my own death was beginning,' I wrote. My death began long ago now, and I have grown used to seeing my past desert me. No doubt it is because I am resigned to my own disappearance that I also accept that of others. Of course the death of some few people who are very dear to me would shatter this indifference: they would leave an emptiness in my life that even in imagination I can hardly bear.

Before speaking of my occupations during these last years, I should like to mention a subject that I have never touched on before – my dreams. They are one of the pleasures I like best. I love their total unexpectedness and above all their gratuity. Their setting is in my story, they flower on my own past, but they have no dimension in the future – I forget them. As they come to me, they are unmarked by experience, that is to say by ageing: they rise up and they vanish in an everlasting youth, never gathering in a series or an accumulation. That is why in the morning I often try to bring them together again, to reform them from the shreds that float behind my eyelids, glittering still but fading fast. I try to go back to sleep; I turn on my other side, for my sleep and the visions that inhabit it change according to whether I feel the coolness of the pillow under my cheek or its gentle warmth. But sometimes I wake up suddenly. At once I am torn from the world of phantasms and of a childhood in which wishes are fulfilled, fears acknowledged and all repressions ignored; I am pitched into an existence filled with practical requirements, one in which the past imperatively thrusts activities upon me: sometimes this transition so wounds and disturbs me that my heart begins to thump.

In 1969 and 1970 I noted down some of my dreams: I shall not tell many of them, nor shall I attempt to give them a Freudian interpretation – it is only when they form part of a whole analysis that dreams can reveal their deeper meaning to the psychologist. I shall confine myself to describing mine and to singling out some of the themes that appear most frequently.

Very often I am walking from one place to another. The landscape is beautiful but there are obstacles that I have to get over and I wonder whether I shall reach my goal. I feel very well and happy, because the walk is so delightful, and at the same time I am slightly anxious. This is how it was in a dream I had and that I wrote down in November 1969. I was in Israel with Sartre, but we were walking in a green and rolling countryside more like Switzerland. We had left our baggage at an hotel in a village and we were going back to it: the village could be seen from the top of a low hill – low, but nevertheless provided with a ski-lift. We walked on, along roads and paths, and all at once there was a house barring our way. This very often happens in my dreams: I go into the house and look vainly for a way out; I have no right to be there and I lose my head; sometimes I am being chased. That night I did find a door that gave on to a courtyard, and from the courtyard we carried on along our road. The dream stopped there.

Political events often influence my dreams. This was so on the night of 7 November 1969. I was at home, in a flat (which was like none I had ever seen) that I shared with Sartre. I received a blue telegram, written by hand in black ink: 'Possess exact and shocking information about dance.' I did not understand. I read it again: instead of *dance* there was *Greece*. A great many people were there. I had to pack my suitcase and get rid of a bundle of washing. While I was busy doing so, the flat filled with people – a German who was obviously a former Nazi, some Greeks, one of them a girl, not pretty but very agreeable, who started talking to Sartre. She went away and he leaned out of the window to say good-bye. I leant out too. In the square there was a crowd and coaches full of police; a riot broke out; the people ran and the police chased them, club in hand. Once more the flat was invaded and I saw the girl again. I told the Greeks to make themselves comfortable and shut myself in my bedroom to work. I stayed there a long time. Then, wearing a dressing-gown, I went into the bathroom, where the girl had hung up a flowered bikini and brassière. I found Sartre in the sitting-room again and I was worried – his tooth-ache[25] had got worse and it prevented him from speaking. The Nazi came out of another room: he wanted to talk to Sartre, who refused. Everyone went away. Half an hour after waking up, I suddenly saw the blue telegram again, very clearly.

Quite often I, who am so little given to social events, have social dreams: I am in the midst of an agreeable gathering of people who like me. On 9 November I found myself in a group of homosexuals with Jean Marais and Cocteau, and our relationship was as friendly as could be. At the beginning of my dream on 11 November, I was also among charming people and I felt very happy. I was going to leave in a car, with Sartre. I packed a suitcase and settled myself in the car – but not without some difficulty, for an embroidered blue skirt that I had bought long ago in Greece hung out over half the seat. In the end I managed to shut the case properly. And then there I was with Sartre, walking and without any luggage: we were at the foot of a very steep reddish-brown mountain with a white flag flying on top of it. It looked impossible to climb, but I found steps cut into the rock and we went up easily. From the top there was a splendid view over a desert. But at the other end of a very short tunnel[26] the landscape was quite different: it looked more like a piece of Switzerland or Germany. Below us, in steps, there were little hotels with terraces. We went down and sat at one of the tables. They refused to give us anything to eat, but they did bring us a drink.

On 17 November I was with a group of friends. With the idea of having a picnic we had bought some very expensive food. We went through lovely green gardens with children playing in them and we thought we would sit down on a lawn. It is forbidden to stop more than five minutes, we were told; and I wondered vaguely 'Are we in the USSR?'[27] Then we thought we would go to a restaurant, but we had already spent too much money. Then came a transition I forget. I was alone in a cab, going to look for something somewhere: it was long and tiring. When I was in front of my own door again, dropping with weariness, I found that I had forgotten or perhaps lost my key. I should have to set off again, and that filled me with despair. But a charming young woman who was wearing Sylvie's fur coat, although she was not Sylvie, suggested going with me. We found a

25 He had had tooth-ache the day before.
26 In the Crimea above the sea there is a kind of natural gate: on the one side you see a white, arid, steep coast, and on the other an immense stretch of rolling landscape altogether more gentle.
27 We often came up against prohibitions of this kind in the USSR.

taxi in the middle of a piece of waste ground and I felt comforted.

On the following nights I had many dreams in which I felt loving presences all round me. Often Sartre was there and we were going for a walk. Once an evil great man attacked our friends and I plunged a knife into his throat. I fainted away, thinking 'I've killed a man! It's unbelievable.' When I came to I wondered anxiously whether they would congratulate me or bring me to trial; I was quite disappointed when nothing happened at all.

In real life I do not pay much attention to clothes, but in my dreams they take on an importance that astonishes me. Among many others, I will speak of one: it is quite unusual because of its reflective and critical aspect. I was getting ready to give my lessons at Rouen and all at once there was a gap in my memory: I could not remember my pupils, nor the lycée, nor the subject I was to teach; and I no longer knew what clothes there were in my cupboards. In the mirror I saw that I was wearing a yellow blouse and a tartan skirt: I did not recognize them. I became frightened. I had a telephone-message sent to Rouen saying I could not come and I asked for a doctor. There were a lot of people round me and I still felt this emptiness in my head – I could not think what clothes I possessed. I said to the doctor, 'I cannot understand it at all. *Unless I am asleep.*' Then I corrected myself. 'But that's not possible: when you dream everything changes all the time, and you have all been here a long while.'

I have had many pleasant, confused dreams of journeys, sometimes with Sartre and sometimes with groups of people; one of the most agreeable took place in London and the English countryside. Here is one, more anxious than the others, which dates from 18 December. I was with friends; my sister and a couple of writers were there, and I felt very happy. Suddenly I had to leave in great haste: it was less tragic than a deportation but still very, very unpleasant. I stuffed clothes into a large blue suitcase: it was too small because 'in those parts' it was very cold and I had to take a great many things. My friend the woman writer[28] gave me a huge bag belonging to her husband; it was transparent and amber-coloured. I emptied my wardrobe into it: I took some woollen dresses (which in fact I do possess) and some sweaters, which I stopped wearing long ago. My sister said to me, 'But you're not going right away?' I replied, 'Yes, I have to,' and burst into tears.

[28] Unidentified. I thought vaguely of Elsa Triolet, who never was one of my friends.

On 10 December I dreamt that I was having breakfast with two people, one of whom was my sister, although she was a very young girl and did not look in the least like her. Her nose and her right arm were the burnt branches of a tree. She did not seem to mind, but I said to myself, 'She will never be able to marry. Those burns are too ugly.'[29]

A dream I often have (and not only since I had an accident – I dreamt it before) is that I am driving a car and I suddenly realize that I do not know where the brake is; I cannot find it, and I wonder anxiously how I shall stop. It usually ends by my crashing the car gently against a wall; I get out unhurt, but having been thoroughly frightened. At the end of December I got into a car that had handlebars instead of a steering-wheel: they were on the right, but I was sitting in the left-hand seat when the car started; I tried to steer it, but it was very awkward and of course I could not find the brake. In the end someone got in through the door on the right and took things over. Another night the car was just an armchair; I steered it by pressing either on one arm or on the other; it glided along at a great pace, taking many turns – a kind of slalom – and here again I could not manage to stop it.

In 1970 I gave up writing down the dreams in which I was travelling with groups of friends – there were too many of them. In these dreams I had difficulty in packing my bags and I was afraid of missing the train; but in the end I did catch it, I was with my friends again and I felt very happy. In May I noted down two nightmares: three days earlier I had heard of the arrest of our Egyptian friend Lufti el-Kholi. I was in Cairo with Sartre and we were walking about with Lufti and his wife: the atmosphere was threatening. There was a dense crowd of people and I had the feeling that it was impossible to breathe; in dusty little stalls there were stuffed animals, falling apart with decay, among them a hippopotamus. I felt an unbearable distress: the air was heavy with menace.

Another night I saw my mother, a young and beautiful figure without a face, standing on the shore of a luminous stretch of water that I had to cross to reach her. I thought of the pond in front of Algren's garden; but there was no boat to cross by. It was also a fjord and one could only get round it with great difficulty; one would have to venture into the water, where there was the risk of

[29] Looking over this dream again, I think of an impression I had of my mother when she was dying—she was like a piece of dried branch.

drowning. Yet I had to warn my mother of a great danger that was threatening her.

In June I had an astonishing vision of the rue de Rennes, with the roadway and the pavements, from the Montparnasse station down to Saint-Germain-des-Prés, covered with a splendid red carpet. Above it the sky was a tragic black. I said to myself, 'How beautiful it is! I must write this down in my diary.' And straight away I thought, 'There's no point: nothing will come of it.' Suddenly I became aware that this was the occupation. Sartre was free, but he was more or less condemned to death.

In September too I had a dream centred about a vision. For some months I had been far away from Paris, far from Sartre, in an unknown town; I did not know what to do with myself and I looked at a map with the idea of setting off on a journey. I was going along a broad avenue when all at once a voice stopped me: 'Wait!' The façades of the houses on each side of the road lit up, or rather scenes were projected on them, brilliant colours that no doubt made a film when they were all seen together. 'It is no good leaving,' I said to myself vaguely. 'There is plenty here to keep me busy.' Someone (and later I learnt that he had the right to speak, because he was the chief of the Resistance) said to me, 'Stay. You will be given some job as a cover – painting safety-pins blue or something of that kind – and you will have all the time you need to watch the show.' It was a continuous show and it would have filled a lifetime. Then there were some vague detective episodes. In the end I found myself in a car with an unknown man: it ran into the raised strip in the middle of the road; I felt a bang on my head and closed my eyes. When I opened them again there was no car any more and I was alone in the middle of an extraordinary landscape: it was the same avenue as at the beginning of the dream, but it was covered with snow. The whole world was blanketed with snow and on this whiteness stood out tall grey forms – human forms, perhaps. In the sky there were grey wafts of smoke and a machine was plunging to the ground. It was a tranquil disaster and I watched it unmoved. (When I woke I remembered the episode in *On Trial* where the police scatter the ashes of Slansky and of the other men who have been hanged over an immense snowy plain.)

In the autumn of 1971 I again wrote down quite a number of dreams. Here is the one of 20 October. I was with Sartre in a somewhat vague Saharan town and we were leaving it in the twilight in order to sleep at an oasis: this oasis had an unknown name, but in my mind it was Ouargla. On a broad sand-coloured road we overtook a man and a woman in gaudy fancy dresses, walking one behind the other. I asked them whether we were on the right road for Ourgla: no, this road came to a dead end. We went back to the town we had left, to sleep there. And suddenly I realized that I did not know where we were. Touggourt? No. I asked Sartre for the *Guide bleu*: in a rather bantering tone he told me he had sent it to Paris. I saw that he was not in the least interested in this journey and I felt wretched. He talked to some people I did not know and then disappeared. I wandered about the town, which was full of tourists: nobody knew its name. I found that it was called Mersepolis: [30] but where was it? I found some maps in a filing-cabinet: they were maps of France. There were arrows on the walls and mysterious names that seemed to me either Turkish or Swedish. I began to cry. Under a very blue sky and an enormous sun I caught glimpses of splendid monuments and red roofs in the African style, and I wept. Why was Sartre not with me? Suddenly there I was with him in a car: friendly tourists were driving us about. But I wanted to leave them and begin the journey Sartre and I had planned. When we were passing in front of an hotel Sartre said he was hungry; he got out of the car and we sat there waiting for him. Suddenly angry, I got out too and went into a huge hotel where I looked for him in countless dining-rooms: it was a kind of Ritz and at the same time a family boarding-house. At last I found him in a corner, sitting there with a plate in front of him. 'I am going to eat something too,' I decided. There were appetizing hors-d'oeuvres and a beautiful chestnut cake. 'I've had enough; I've finished,' said Sartre crossly, and we went back to the car. There the dream ended.

6 November. I was in an agreeable place – later it turned into Rome – with a great many friends. I was sleeping, and Sartre was asleep in the next room. A door giving on to the corridor opened and a small girl kissed me awake: I remembered what we and the Pouillons had decided the day before. I got up and I had just put on my dressing-gown when Lise came in, very young and domineering. She sent the little girl away and settled down in an armchair. I told her to go away: I wanted to wash and dress and go and wake Sartre. She refused, and she seemed to me rather hysterical. I do not know how this scene ended. I was dressed and out of doors, and I

30 Persepolis was much in the news at that time.

104

wondered where Sartre lived (there was no longer any question of his being in the same house as myself.) I knew that I knew, and that it was not far away, but I could not manage to bring it to mind. I decided to go down a flight of steps leading from my hotel and at the bottom I found the two windows and the door of his little house. I wanted to have breakfast with him, but it was after eleven and he had already had his. Somewhere Lise was watching me. All at once I was among friends on a plateau from which I could see a very beautiful landscape: I was in Rome but I had forgotten the address of my hotel; all I knew was that it was called the Madrid. I went into a very grand hotel that was also a travel agency, hoping that someone would tell me; but nobody answered my questions. Outside there were taxis, all of a very old model: none was free – they were reserved for taking tourists about. And the drivers did not answer me either. I determined to set off on foot: there was a valley to cross and I thought I should find Rome on the other side, and my hotel. It was very fine, the air was sparkling and I was in no hurry; I said to myself that it would be pleasant to spend the morning walking. I asked Lise – who no longer resembled herself at all – whether she would like to come with me and she said coldly, 'It's too late.' I took a few steps to the right, opened a door and found myself in a big hospital ward full of sick people and babies: I noticed one nurse carrying a very young baby with a large adult's head and a tiny body. I walked out: there was a path leading towards the valley. I ran down; it was a wonderful day and I skipped and skipped again, my heart filled with joy. I passed through an area with very beautiful ruins of baroque buildings; I took pleasure in seeing them, but I did not linger. I knew the address of my hotel now: it was just next to the Minerva. The dream came to an end before I reached it.

The next night I dreamt again. I was in a lecture-hall, a kind of amphitheatre, together with a fairly large audience. There I met a woman – unidentified – whom I had lost to view for a long while, and I was much moved: I had a red place at the corner of my eye and she was affectionately concerned about it. A man came in and sat in one of the higher seats. He was wearing a hat and spectacles; his face could not be seen clearly. Someone said to me, 'It's Solzhenitsyn.' Next to him sat another man – fairly young, in spite of a grizzled beard – an interpreter. The audience told Solzhenitsyn that we knew his books well and that we liked them. Through the interpreter he asked, 'Whose fault was it that my father is dead?' And each of us raised his hand: 'It was my fault. We are all responsible.' Then he asked, 'What part of Russia was I born in?' and I answered rather at random, 'In the north', which was right. At that point I left: my mother was waiting for dinner in our old fifth-floor flat in the rue de Rennes (it comes back to me quite often in my dreams). I was in a village called Villemomble (though I did not make the connection between that name and the suburb where Sylvie teaches). It was about sixty miles from Paris, and I did not know how I had got there nor what I should do to get back. I caught sight of some coaches and buses: but they were all in a parking-place and they were out of order. I went into a station: all the booking-offices were shut – no trains. I set off along the road, hoping to stop a taxi, and I chanced upon a little coach; I got in, and it took me back to the place I had started from. I wandered about aimlessly. I went into a graveyard. There I had an astonishing vision: it was like those dreams that one sees on films and that appear to me so unreal. On the ground there were a great many coffins covered with black cloth; men in black tail-coats and top-hats stood in lines on either side while others formed a procession in the background: under their top-hats some had skulls. It was a very beautiful and a very striking sight. Almost at once I rationalized it: these skulls were not men's – they were stone sculptures. A nun standing by a grave asked me whether I should like to go to Rennes with her; I could take a train for Paris the next day. I refused: I had to be in Paris that evening. I had no doubt of getting there; I was not worried. She said I was quite right: this village was so beautiful that it was worth staying for a while. I left the cemetery to go for a walk. On the top of a small grassy hill I noticed a high tower, like the keep of Gisors, and I walked towards it . . .

Two days later I dreamt of travelling again. I went to the station with a couple of friends (unknown). The station was empty; there was no train. We waited on the platform without much hope. All at once the train was there; the woman darted into it, the man ran off and came back with the luggage, just in time to get in with her in an odd compartment with two seats. And without having boarded the train there I was in the corridor: the train had started. I thought, rather crossly, 'Never mind. I shall get out at the next stop.' The train was going from Rouen to Paris, but it stopped on the way. Through the window I looked at a very beautiful countryside, as dry and golden as the Sahara; it delighted me. At the first stop I got out without paying any attention to my friends, whom I had completely forgotten during the journey. It was eight in the evening and the station was empty: the town had a Russian name. Was I going to have to spend the night there? I asked a woman the times of trains: she could not tell me. The station square was dark. Was there an hotel, and how should I spend my evening? I had not so much as a book with me and it was too late to buy one. I did have some money – ten thousand old francs, in the form of a pink paper, very like the one that had recently summoned me to an examining magistrate. I wondered why I had not gone on as far as Paris while I was about it; but the idea of being held up there left me unconcerned – there was nothing urgent for me to do in the place from which I had just come.

Two nights later, Sartre and I and some friends went into a big café. At a nearby table a banquet was going on – former Nazis, who started to insult us. Then they stopped and we had lunch. Suddenly we were outside, in the middle of a hostile crowd of fascists. We were waiting for a plane that Sylvie was to bring to the esplanade for us with all possible speed: it did not come. Maheu was there and I was talking to him when I noticed that Sartre had vanished: he was lost in the horde of fascists, and one of them was holding him by the collar of his overcoat and tightening it round his neck to throttle him. I rushed at him shrieking, and the man let go. 'They can't even kill,' observed Sartre. I took him by the arm and began to run so fast that his feet did not touch the ground. We passed in front of some policemen, who looked mocking but not malevolent: they would not have liked Sartre to be murdered. I reached a street lined with very gloomy cafés: I thought of the Coupole and the Guillaume Tell, but they were quite different. I went into one of them – lit by candlelight and almost empty – and left Sartre in a corner. I ran off to find Sylvie and Maheu again. They had vanished. I said to myself, 'Maheu is so well known that I shall easily find him.' I asked some people, who gave me vague answers. I went back to see Sartre. But the landscape had changed and I could no longer tell where I was: there were broad avenues, monuments, new buildings – Le Havre, no doubt. In the end someone told me where the Guillaume Tell was. I woke up before getting there.

Some nights later I was getting ready to go off with Sylvie on a motor-cycle that someone had lent me. It was in a garage near a

107

petrol-station where I was to fill up before setting off. (I was the one who was to drive and I was a little uneasy at the idea of riding all night: Sylvie found it entirely natural and amusing.) But first we had to pack: our baggage had to be light, because we lived on a hill and we would have to carry it down on foot, taking a fairly steep path. I put the things in a cardboard box and the clothes in a suitcase, among them a beige suit with a touch of red: a hem had come unsewn, but I said to myself that in Paris my mother would mend it. I went outside to rest in a deck-chair: there were other people in the square and they too were stretched out in deck-chairs. I ate a sandwich while I read. A woman in a blue summer dress was lolling next to me: 'There is nothing to see in this country,'[31] she said, 'apart from ...' and here she mentioned some unknown names. I thought she was stupid: 'What about Grenada and Seville?' I said to myself. I stood up to go: she asked me crossly, 'Am I bothering you?' 'No. I have to go.' Then I found myself looking at my suitcase.

A few nights later I had a dream in which many of my familiar themes were present – a dream that now and then became a nightmare. It began with an argument with Sartre: I quite often have them in my dreams. There was some medicine that he ought to take, but he had none left and instead he drank some yellowish substance unknown to me. I reminded him that he ought to go back to the doctor as soon as possible. He said he was completely fed up with him and he would never go again. I set about him violently, predicting all kinds of disasters: he would not yield. Then I began to sob (I made an effort to get the sobs to come: the whole scene was somewhat unreal). Still he would not yield. I reproached him with stubbornly clinging to a decision that made me very unhappy; I should not have done the same to him. He remained unmoved.

Suddenly there I was with a person who was both Sylvie and my sister, in the lounge of a big hotel: probably in Spain. There were friends with us; we had reserved three rooms and our bags had already been taken up, but we did not know where the rooms were. There was a long queue in front of the reception-desk, but an old chambermaid with a wrinkled, very kindly face, said something, in their language, to the clerk, who gave her the keys: she opened a door on the ground floor for us. In the first room I caught sight of a

[31] In Italy I had been struck by hearing French people say, 'Oh, Palermo! There's nothing to see there. Broadly speaking, there is nothing to be seen in Sicily.'

suitcase that did not belong to me; in the next, a bearded man was sleeping on the bed and accidentally I touched his naked foot. He was a painter, sent here by his people to make a new life for himself. But where was our room? There was a great deal of confused noise in the hall: nobody attended to us any more. Then I was with my sister Sylvie on a railway-platform; we and a great many other people were waiting for a connection: it was an underground or rather a suburban train. I grew cross: it would have been better to take another line – generally speaking, this was the shorter journey, but the trains never ran well. We were waiting in a hutch where our baggage had been put. A train was signalled and there was a wild rush. We climbed in: we had forgotten the luggage. We ran back to the hutch: my sister found a very valuable briefcase, but the suitcases had vanished. 'It doesn't matter,' she said. 'They will follow.' The train was leaving and we did not manage to catch it. We wandered along the platform. In the tunnel women were sweeping snow away. Engines went by, trucks, vans and even a herd of cows. I asked a railwayman when the next train would be: one o'clock in the morning. I collapsed. We walked out. A provincial town with evening coming on; it was warm. Were we perhaps quite close to Paris; could we take a cab? Not at all. Paris was a great way off. Someone suggested telling us of a good restaurant where we could have dinner. There the dream stopped. In it I felt a distress that came near to anguish.

A few days later I had a dream totally unlike the others. I was in a place belonging to some very wealthy people: we were on a huge tree-planted terrace overlooking a river: the Seine, since Paris could be seen in the distance. I was walking with a stupid girl: we were of the same age. I told her that this park reminded me of the one at La Grillère, but in order not to look as if I were showing off I added that this was far finer because of its being so near Paris. I asked her whether she liked it in Paris; she answered that what mattered for a 'wife' was having a crèche nearby. She irritated me, because whenever she spoke of herself she always said 'wife'. We walked into her house: it was a positive palace. She showed me her room, hung with violet velvet and carpeted with grey – it was lovely; but I thought the big gilded drawing-rooms were boring. Suddenly I realized that she was a married woman with a child. People were walking about in the drawing-rooms. All at once Courchay appeared, bearded, hairy and dressed in the long white coat he had worn two days

109

before during the demonstration in favour of free abortion. I was pleased to see him. On the table there was a dish of raw eggs taken out of their shells. Someone took a fork and stabbed the whites. 'Don't do that!' I cried. They were embryos, and if they were touched they would become handicapped children. This dream was obviously influenced by the conversations we had had on the subject of our demonstration.

Still another dream in which I run after trains with Sylvie. We were to meet Sartre in London to make a journey and I was very much afraid of missing him.

A dream I have very often is that of falling. I suddenly notice that I am on top of a scaffolding – or of a wall or ladder – and that I am going to fall. 'This time it's all over; I shall be killed,' I say before I am saved just in time. I am afraid, but it is a fear that I do not wholly believe in. One night not long ago I was in a very beautiful town abroad; it was surrounded with cliffs and there was a great rock and some ancient buildings in the middle of it. Here festivities were going on, and at the same time they were a demonstration. I walked about with some friends; I got somewhat lost and then I found myself with Sartre and many others on an enormous platform set up in the middle of a square. A kind of meeting or a ceremony of a political nature was being held. Suddenly I realized that I was on the very edge, a hundred feet above the ground; I was stretched out on a sheet, as though I were in a bed, and I felt that I was going to fall: I tried to cling to one of the widely-spaced pillars and to creep back, but the slightest movement was dangerous. At that moment a woman dressed in white – perhaps a wedding-dress – did fall, turning over and over and hitting the ground with terrible force. 'It is my mother,' I said to myself, yet it was not exactly myself who said this, but rather a character whose part I was acting. I moved back, stood up again, and found Sartre and our friends. 'My mother has just been killed,' I announced, but without feeling anything, as though I were playing a part. Someone shouted, 'These American swine are really too much!' and I marched towards the middle of the town, as though I could make use of this accident to raise a riot. Then there I was at the station again. All the demonstrators were to catch a train to go home. But I was without my luggage; a chambermaid was supposed to bring it from the hotel, but I did not know what hotel and I was worried. 'We have plenty of time,' said Sartre. 'The train doesn't leave until half past three.' But what was the time now? I was called; they gave me a ticket with my name written on it. But what about my luggage? Had it already been put aboard without my being told? Should I get in without it? At that point I woke up.

A few nights ago I was in Italy with a great many other people. I was dancing in a square with a young Italian working-man, dressed entirely in green with a roll-neck pullover; he was a very talented poet; a kind of Rimbaud, I said privately; but then I corrected myself – I was not able to take all young poets for Rimbauds. This one was rather psychotic, someone observed. 'Somewhat like Deschanel.' 'But he is much more interesting than Deschanel,' I replied. Everyone dispersed, but they were to meet again in a little while. I was in a bedroom with two or three people I knew quite well, and I decided to change my dress. I took down a woollen frock – one that I do in fact possess – and I wanted to put it on; but I set about doing so with such modesty that I became entangled. 'Never mind,' I said, and I took everything off but my slip – there was nothing indecent about that. But I had only got one arm through the sleeve of my dress – I was now standing on a platform in a square – when a number of cars appeared: it was the mothers of prisoners who had come to ask our committee for help. I felt extremely awkward at having to receive them half-dressed.

There is one dream that often recurs and that is more or less distressing. In a foreign town or in a district I do not know well I desperately search for a lavatory. I cannot find one. I go up and down stairs, I hurry along corridors: I find one, but it is locked. I go on looking. This time I find one and go in. But just as I am going to settle down I notice that the room is full of people or that they keep coming and going. Sometimes I am already sitting there when they appear: I am either deeply embarrassed or I do not mind at all.

Some nights ago I went for a long trip with Sartre and Sylvie in a helicopter. Or rather the helicopter was Sartre himself: he flew quite low and we clung to the skirts of his coat. We passed over a splendid lake and he put us down on the shore. 'Go and look at the island,' he said. We went along the bank as far as a platform from which the whole lake could be seen. In the middle there was an island with a building in the centre of it: a fort, no doubt. We came back and I should very much have liked to take to the air again. But Sartre said he was tired: he started to climb up a mountain, and we

111

followed him. Our feet sank into wet clay. I know that something else happened after that, but I forget what it was.

Among the dreams I had before 1969 and that I did not write down I remember there were many in which I flew through the air or swam in the water. In the swimming dreams I was rather frightened. I was obliged to cross a given stretch of water. I thought I could wade across, then suddenly I found I was out of my depth and I was afraid of drowning; but I made shift to keep afloat and reached the other side. The flying dreams were charming. It would often happen that going down stairs to escape from someone or merely to go faster I would just place my fingers on the rail and glide down through the air with my feet not touching. Or I would fly in the street, skimming the roadway; or, with a splendid feeling of euphoria, in the countryside. I have had a great many dreams like those I have described: I wander in foreign towns, I take lifts, I hurry down streets looking for someone I do not find. I lose myself in subways, I pass through tunnels in which I suffocate, I climb staircases that have no end. I run for trains, sometimes catching them, often missing them. I am possessed by joy at the sight of beautiful landscapes. I also have a great many scenes with Sartre, scenes that go farther than those I have described. I want him to do something – to give up going off on a journey without me, for example. He refuses: I implore him to agree; I even go so far as to faint; unmoved, he takes no notice.

I have observed that in my dreams I have moments of euphoria of a kind that I do not experience in my waking state, because they imply a total letting go: perhaps some drugs may produce dreams of this nature. My dream-anxiety never reaches the pitch of the real distress that I have in fact undergone at various times. In some way or another I keep it at a distance. It often seems to me that I am acting out a psychodrama rather than really living.

Some themes have vanished. One of my earlier nightmares was that all the teeth in my mouth caved in: I never have that now. Nor do I dream of those beings, mineral and yet at the same time alive, whose mute sufferings were unbearable to me; and as I have said, I no longer die in my dreams. When I am asleep Sartre has always been either the companion of my ordinary life or the stony-hearted man unmoved by my reproaches, tears, prayers, or fainting. This fainting is obviously suggested by my lying down; and in these dreams too it is with some remoteness that I suffer from Sartre's attitude – there is something implacable and unreal about it, as though I were carrying a hypothesis through: it being given that he does not care for me, how should I react? How far might things go? As I have said in *A Very Easy Death*, my mother often appeared in my dreams whereas my father did not: sometimes, in earlier days, she was a beloved presence but more often I dreaded falling into her power again. Now it may happen that I have an appointment with her in our old flat in the rue de Rennes: I feel unhappy about it and in any case we do not meet – either I do not get as far as the house or she is not there. When she does appear to me she is usually young and a great way off. As for my sister and my women friends, they have little more than episodic and interchangeable roles to play in my adventures.

The theme of happiness often recurs – friendly meetings in which my heart is full of joy, or walks in marvellous landscapes: another usual theme is that of the obstacle across my path that I manage to surmount: and another is that of failure – the missed train, the empty station, the baggage lost. I cannot really see the meaning of my dreams of clothes, suitcases, and trains. In these travel dreams there is surely a foreboding of my death, but I do not make any direct association. Generally speaking I anticipate my nocturnal adventures with pleasure as I go to sleep; and it is with regret that I say good-bye to them in the morning.

2

Writing has remained the great concern of my life. What have my relations with literature been during these last years?

I finished *Force of Circumstance* in the spring of 1963. The book was published shortly after I came back from my holiday that autumn. It was warmly received and widely read; yet I was very much taken aback by some of the observations that it aroused.

Some critics alleged that in writing the book I had abandoned all aesthetic considerations and that I had chosen to offer the public a raw, untreated document. That is completely untrue. It is not for me to determine the worth of my book on the literary plane; but I did not deliberately intend that it should not be on that plane. I did refuse to have the notion of 'a work of art' attached to my auto-biography, and I have explained my reasons – that is a consumer's term and to me it is shocking that it should be applied to the works of any creative writer. But that does not mean that from now on I have decided to make a botch of mine.

Some theoreticians maintain that a testimony cannot belong to literature because, in words reduced to an instrumental role, it holds a prefabricated content. Its author, according to the distinction put forward by Barthes, can never be a *writer*, but only *one who writes*. It is true, as Valéry has pointed out, that a work of literature can only exist if language is involved, if the meaning seeks self-expression by means of language, thus bringing about discovery of the Word itself. But why should the intention of bearing witness prohibit verbal discovery? In order that a thought may unhesitatingly flow into a sign, a discipline must have set up an imperative and unequivocal relationship between signs and ideas. In chemistry water $= H_2O$, neither more nor less. The expression is wholly perspicuous, the object in view being not a reality but a concept. But when words hark back to things themselves they have complex relations with them and their combinations produce unforeseen effects. In his article on artistic realism,[1] Jakobson reminds us that Gogol thought the inventory of precious objects belonging to the prince of Moscow poetic, and that Krutchennylk, the futurist, thought the same of a laundress's bill. No work that has reference to the world can be a mere transcription, since the world has not the power of speech. Facts do not determine their own expression; they dictate nothing. The person who recounts them finds out what he has to say about them through the act of saying it. If he produces no more than commonplace, conventional observations, then he is outside the scope of literature; but if on the other hand his living voice is heard, then he is within it.

Whether it is a question of a novel, an autobiography, an essay, an historical work or no matter what, the writer attempts to set up communication with others by means of the uniqueness of his personal experience; his work must make the existence of this experience evident and it must bear the mark of that experience – and it is by means of his style, his tone of voice and his rhythm that he communicates his experience to his work. No particular kind of writing is on the face of it privileged; none is condemned. In all cases, if the work is successfully accomplished it is defined as a unique universal in the imaginary mode. By means of this work the author provides himself with a fictitious constitution: Sartre is referring to this operation when he states that every writer is inhabited by a 'vampire'.[2] The *I* that speaks stands at a distance from the *I* that has been experienced, just as each sentence stands at a distance from the experience out of which it arises. If the public had not confused them, *Force of Circumstance* would not so easily have given rise to misunderstanding – misunderstanding that I think far more deplorable than the error I have just explained.

I had hoped the book would give offence. Too often I had been congratulated for my optimism at times when my heart was ablaze with anger. In *Force of Circumstance* I breathed out this anger; I reminded my readers of the horrors of the Algerian war: I wanted to distress them. Nothing of the kind. By October 1963 the tortures and the massacres were already ancient history that worried nobody. I did give offence, but for a completely different reason: I

[1] Published in 1921: translated in the winter 1966 number of *Tel quel*.
[2] *Des rats et des hommes.*

spoke about old age without glossing it over. I did not then know to what a degree the subject was taboo nor how shocking was my sincerity. The violent reproaches that I found in some letters and criticisms surprised me: they overwhelmed me with all the platitudes I subsequently cried out against in my study on *Old Age* – every season has its beauty; reaching fifty means reaching the magnificence of autumn, with its full-flavoured fruit and its golden leaves! A woman who ran a 'lonely hearts' column stated that a thorough face-lift would cope with all my problems. For my edification, a female journalist held up the example of a woman of my age who was always ready to open a new eating-place, night-club, or fashionable dressmaker's shop: this 'Paris steam-engine's' secret was that 'she was very unostentatiously a believer'. I would not have mentioned these pieces of nonsense but for the fact that the same sound could be heard even from readers who usually liked my desire for intellectual clarity: according to them I ought, in order not to betray them, to have pretended that I felt young and that I should go on feeling young until I drew my last breath.

Their reaction is comprehensible. Many turn me into an image and at the same time identify themselves with me. They would like to think that I am immutably dedicated to serenity – that I prove by my example that it is not impossible to preserve it when confronted with every kind of adversity and particularly with old age, which is not an accident but rather our common fate. If I am frightened by age, then that means it is frightening; which is something they do not choose to admit. Yet the fact is that unless it comes to a premature end every life reaches a point where it is evident that a certain frontier has been crossed, and that there is no going back. In the event of serious illness, accident or bereavement, this may happen very early; or, where the subject carries on with his occupations uninterruptedly and in favourable circumstances, very late. As far as I am concerned, my ageing became apparent to me between 1958 and 1962. I was sickened by the crimes that were being committed in the name of France; I turned nostalgically back to my past, and I realized that there were many planes upon which I had to say good-bye to it for ever. If you have really loved life and if you love it still, no renunciation is ever a matter of course. I am not sorry for having said so. Where I was mistaken was in the outline of my future: I had projected the accumulated disgust of the recent years into it. It has been far less sombre than I had foreseen.

116

The last words in my book were misunderstood, and even now they still arouse criticism – ironical, indignant, hostile or distressed. To some extent this was my own fault; the epilogue was badly constructed. In looking back over my life, I first spoke of what had mattered to me most – my relationship with Sartre, writing, the course of history in our time. Then I spoke about my age. But the statement 'I have been swindled' did not refer to these particular sections: it was the last item in the whole of the balance-sheet that I had drawn up. It was not the outcome of seeing my own reflection in the glass but of my very deep distress, my revolt at the horror of the world. When I compared this state of mind with my adolescent dreams, I saw how those dreams had led me astray. 'We were promised nothing,' says Alain. That is untrue. Bourgeois culture is a promise: it is the promise of a world that makes sense; a world whose good things may be enjoyed with a clear conscience; a world that guarantees sure and certain values forming an essential part of our lives and giving them the magnificence of an Idea. It was by no means easy to tear myself away from such splendid expectations.

My disappointment also had an ontological dimension. In *Being and Nothingness*[3] Sartre says, 'The future does not allow itself to be overtaken; it slips into the past in the form of what was once the future ... This is the cause of the ontological disappointment that awaits the for-itself every time it opens on to the future. Even if in its content my present is precisely identical with the future towards which, beyond being, I projected myself, it is nevertheless *not* the present towards which I was projecting myself, since I projected myself towards that future qua future, that is to say as the point at which I should overtake my being.'

The discovery of mankind's unhappiness and the existential failure that cheated me of the absolute I had hoped for when I was young – those were the reasons that caused me to write the words 'I have been swindled'.

In the course of a conversation during an interview,[4] Francis Jeanson asked me whether, in writing them, I had not yielded to a kind of 'literary dramatization'. My reply was Yes, in a certain sense I had. Later this question made me reflect upon the relation-

---

[3] I quoted this passage in *Old Age*, but I cannot help quoting it again here, together with those lines in which Mallarmé speaks of 'that scent of melancholy left in the gatherer's heart by the gathering of a dream, even when there is neither disappointment nor regret'.

[4] Published at the end of the book that he wrote about me.

ship between literary truth and the truth of living experience. Since verbal expression is not the translation of an already-formulated text but rather a discovery based upon an undefined experience, words are never anything but one 'way of putting it'; and there could be others. That is why writers loathe being 'taken literally' – a thoroughly expressive phrase that really means being taken, bound and gagged by written words. These words reduce my thoughts to a set, unmoving form, whereas in fact they have never come to a stop. The 'dramatization' lies in having put a full stop after the word 'swindled'. I do not repudiate the word; but it is not the 'last word' on a life that has in fact gone on after it. I measure the extent of my former illusions and I see reality with clear eyes: but this comparison no longer stupefies me.

As I have already said, the most serious misunderstanding arose from the fact that readers did not fully realize the distance that lies between the flesh-and-blood writer and the character he brings into existence by the act of writing – a character endowed with a fictitious constitution. This character transcends time; as he writes, the present is tantamount to eternity: his statements have a definitive nature – there is no going beyond them. The living person, on the contrary, is in a state of change; his moods fluctuate, and for him the moment fleets away. It is a mistake to suppose that in his immediate contingency he can be defined on the basis of what he elects to say in the mode of necessity. Because I wrote certain disillusioned words, some of my readers look upon me as a woman broken by age and disappointment. There were even some psychiatrists who put the end of my book down to an access of depression and who kindly suggested helping me to overcome it. Yet it is common knowledge that the writers of light-hearted books are often melancholy people and that those who produce sad or bitter works may be overflowing with vitality. The beginning of my book, in which I relived the happiness of the Liberation, was written at roughly the same period as its end. A person who is psychologically torn to pieces, who is shattered and desperate, does not write anything at all: he retreats into silence.

This explanation is intended for those candid readers whom I worried and upset. But I am perfectly well aware that the true reason for all these misinterpretations was my opponents' desire to give them currency, and their interest in doing so: it suited their book to take these passages for an admission of failure and a disavowal of my life, in spite of all the statements that fundamentally denied any such interpretation. I shall come back to this point when I define my present attitudes at the end of this book.

At that particular time, I hardly cared about the fate of my book at all. My mother had just been taken to hospital: her illness and her death filled my mind entirely. A few days after she was buried, I suddenly knew that I must write about her last days; I also knew what my account was to be called, how I was to dedicate it and what poem I should quote at the beginning. I spent that winter writing it. Almost every night I saw my mother in my dreams. She was alive, and sometimes I was filled with a happy astonishment because they had managed to save her; more often I knew she must die, and I was afraid.

A surgeon whom I shall not name stated that it was he who had operated on my mother; this he did in the presence of a friend of mine, unaware that she knew me. He had in fact never come anywhere near my mother. This lie enabled him to assert that my sole reason for spending so many hours with her was to collect material. Two or three reviewers were indignant at my having 'taken notes' at the bedside of a dying woman. This concept of writing is based on an utterly out-of-date naturalism. It has never occurred to me to 'take notes' about events or situations that have impressed me and that I have tried to bring to life on paper at a later time. Before actually setting down to it, I had never thought of writing *A Very Easy Death*. At those times when my life has been hard for me, jotting words down on paper – even if no one is to read what I have written – has given me the same comfort that prayer gives to the believer: by means of language I transcend my particular case and enter into communication with the whole of mankind; but although the pages that I wrote at the time may have helped me to recover certain details, I did not need them to remind me of the days I had just lived through – those days were imprinted upon me for ever. If I had been a mere unmoved observer, I should never have touched so many readers.

Apart from a few people who denigrate me on principle, the reviews were very favourable. And I received a great many warm, cordial letters, telling me that in spite of its sadness my book had helped the writers to bear the loss of someone they loved, either in the present or in their memory of the death. It is because of these testimonies that I value the book. All pain is shattering; but what makes it unbearable is the fact that the person who undergoes it feels cut off from the rest of the world; when the pain is shared, at least it is no longer a banishment. It is not out of morose delectation, nor out of exhibitionism, nor out of provocation that writers often tell of hideous or deeply saddening experiences: through the medium of words they render these experiences universal and allow their readers, deep in their private unhappiness, to know the consolation of brotherhood. In my opinion one of the essential functions of literature, a function which means that nothing else can take its place, is the overcoming of that isolation which is common to us all and which nevertheless makes us strangers to each other.

This book too was of an autobiographical nature. When I had finished it I inwardly promised that I should not speak about myself again for a long while. I began thinking about characters and themes very far removed from my own life: I wanted to set them in a novel in which I should deal – though through central figures unlike myself – with a subject that concerned me directly: the subject of growing old. Before I began this work, I took great pleasure in writing a preface for Violette Leduc's *La Bâtarde*. I liked all her books, and this one more than the rest. I read them again, trying to make out just what it was that gave them their value and trying to pass on that understanding. I have written no other critical essays, apart from the one I devoted to Sartre: I wonder why. Immersing oneself in another writer's work, turning it into your whole world, trying to discover their cohesion and their diversity, to plumb the writer's intentions and to display his methods – all this means travelling outside oneself; and I have always delighted in changing my surroundings.

Neither Sartre nor I care for taking part in what are called 'literary manifestations'. Yet during the autumn of 1964 we did so. We had a liking for *Clarté*, a magazine published by young Communists who were trying to bring about a 'loosening up', a 'thaw', among the party's intellectuals. Buin, the editor, asked me to participate in a public discussion at which 'committed' writers would confront those who supported the *nouveau roman*: the audience would pay to come in, and the profits would put the magazine on its feet again. I agreed. Semprun and I were to defend the notion of commitment against Claude Simon, Yves Berger and Janvier, the critic. Some time later, when we were speaking about this discussion, Buin gave me to understand that Simon and Berger looked upon it as an opportunity for 'knocking Sartre on the head': they had already done their best to do so in an interview published in *L'Express*. I said that in this case Sartre should answer them himself, and that I should come only if he came too. Sartre and Buin agreed. Right away devious, underhand plots began to be hatched! Janvier, alarmed at the idea of Sartre's speaking, withdrew in favour of Axelos. Axelos was a 'Marxian' ideologist; and writing about the Nobel prize awarded to Sartre, he had said that Sartre would as willingly and as easily have lived under Hitler as under Stalin: there was no question of our involving ourselves with him. 'Take it or leave it,' said Buin. 'We'll leave it,' said I. Buin felt strongly about his plan and he said that Axelos should not appear on the platform. In a rage, Claude Simon cried off too, and he covered Sartre with insults in *L'Express*. He brought pressure to bear on the *nouveau roman* writers, urging them to boycott the meeting. Nevertheless, Faye and Ricardou agreed both to come and to speak.

There were six thousand people in the amphitheatre of the Mutualité and in other rooms equipped with loudspeakers. German television was there, and we roasted in the heat of its lights. We were all of us greeted with ovations. Buin was the chairman and he opened the proceedings; then Semprun spoke about the writer's responsibilities. In an affected and aggressive tone, Ricardou read out a few pages in which he made use of Barthes' distinction between 'one who writes' and the 'writer': in his opinion only the *nouveau roman* authors deserved the second title at present. I made an improvised reply and went on to give some of my ideas about literature. After this Faye spoke without much warmth and Berger with extreme vehemence. Sartre came last. His was the most interesting contribution when it came to be read; but he was over-whelmed with heat and tiredness; and his delivery was somewhat flat and his argument rather difficult to follow. Nobody convinced anyone else, of course: at the end of these so-called 'exchanges' of ideas, each person retains his own. But the audience seemed pleased, and *Clarté* survived a little longer.

All that year I worked steadily at my novel – steadily, but without much conviction. When I came back from my holidays in October 1965 I re-read the draft: I thought it horrible and I saw that it was impossible for me to make it any better. It had long dead passages that could not be cut out because of the construction and

121

that no amount of work could bring to life. I stuffed it into a cupboard without even showing it to Sartre.

I turned back to an earlier project dealing with this technocratic society. It is a society that I keep as much as possible at arm's length but nevertheless it is one in which I live – through papers, magazines, advertisements and radio it hems me in on every hand. I did not intend to take certain given members of this society and describe their particular experiences; what I wanted to do was to reproduce the sound of it. I ran through the books and magazines in which this sound is recorded; and there I found not only processes of thought and formulas whose totally hollow want of sense impressed me deeply, but others whose premises or implications seemed to me revolting. Keeping nothing but pieces written by 'authoritative' authors, I compiled a collection of nonsense as dismaying as it was amusing.

In this world that I dislike, no character could speak in my name: in order to display it I had to stand back and view it from a certain distance. I decided to look at it through the eyes of a young married woman sufficiently in agreement with those around her not to sit in judgment but also sufficiently honest to feel uneasy about her complicity. I provided her with a 'with-it' mother and a father who was a lover of the past; and this double allegiance accounted for her uncertainties. Because of her father she is doubtful about success and money, the accepted values of her milieu. Her ten-year-old daughter asks her a question that leads to serious self-interrogation on her part; she cannot find the answer and although she wants to pierce the darkness her struggles are in vain. The difficulty lay in making the ugliness of the world that stifles her show through the night of her ignorance, and to do so without stepping in myself. In my earlier novels each character's point of view was perfectly clear and the book's meaning arose from the opposition of these views. In this, it was a question of making the silence speak – a new problem for me.

Did I solve it? When the book came out in November 1966 a great many people felt that I did. For twelve weeks it was on the list of best-sellers, and about a hundred and twenty thousand copies were sold. Many critics, almost all my friends and most of the people who wrote to me liked it. The young, in particular, either wrote or said, 'Yes, that is exactly our story; that is just the world we live in; and like Laurence we too feel imprisoned, caught in a trap.' And there were some readers who congratulated me on having changed and freshened my style and technique.

Yet there were other correspondents and some reviewers too, who said reproachfully, 'This is Françoise Sagan's world, not yours. This is not real Simone de Beauvoir.' As though I had palmed off goods on them that did not correspond to the label. What disappointed some readers was the fact that they could not identify themselves with any of the characters. There were Communists who objected that the world I described was devoid of interest; and they regretted the absence of a 'positive hero'. No doubt they would have preferred Laurence to move on from error to truth by way of a clear-sighted 'self-discovery'.

In his review of *Les Belles Images*, François Nourissier made one observation whose insight I appreciated only later. What would the kind of people I described and who were to form the greater part of my readers think of the book? Some of them made nothing of it. They were amused or bored, but they did not feel that it concerned them in any way. Others accused me of being too hard on the bourgeois – the bourgeois were neither so stupid nor so ill-natured as that.

As for the stupidity, I had gathered most of the remarks I put into their mouths from the works of those 'thinkers' whom our technocrats most respect – Monsieur Louis Armand, for example. And as for moral baseness, I considerably understated the case, so as not to be accused of prejudice: since privileged people are quite at home in their roles they are not aware of the selfishness, greed, desire to succeed whatever the means, and hardness of which I have seen so many staggering examples among them. I have very seldom been blamed for the opposite attitude – that of being too kind to my unsavoury heroes. I did not attribute my extreme distaste for them to Laurence; but as they show themselves in their own words and actions, they cannot but be repulsive. Except perhaps to those who are like them.

There has been a good deal of misunderstanding about Laurence's father: it has often been supposed that I liked his way of life and that I shared his ideas. Nothing could be more untrue. He is seen through Laurence's eyes and to begin with she has a blind admiration for him; but gradually, during their journey in Greece and then when they are back in Paris, her eyes are opened. This phoney philosopher is still another who does not want to know anything about mankind's unhappiness: he makes use of his culture to ensure his moral comfort, and he prefers this comfort to the truth. He is much less unaffected by money and success than he says he is and he does not shrink from surrendering his principles. His remarriage with his former wife displays the collusion between the traditional and the new bourgeoisie – it is one and the same class. Laurence's disillusionment does not take the form of words but it is expressed by her body, setting off a violent attack of anorexia.

How could people possibly have attributed this old egoist's nonsense about the happiness of the poor and the beauties of frugality to *me*? Jean-Jacques Servan-Schreiber was the first to make this blunder;[5] and others, not presuming to question his acuity, followed him. A magazine based on the teachings of Lanzo del Vasto reprinted the relevant passages with applause. A teacher who knows what I think told me that to his astonishment they had been set for the *baccalauréat* as an expression of my own views, the candidates being required to make admiring comments!

It is dangerous to ask the public to read between the lines. Yet I did so again. I had recently received the confidences of several women in their forties whose husbands had left them for others: in spite of the differences of character and circumstance, there were interesting likenesses in all these stories – the women could not even remotely understand what was happening to them; they thought their husband's behaviour contradictory, abnormal and deviant, and the rival unworthy of his love; their world was falling to pieces and they ended up by no longer knowing who they were. Like Laurence they were struggling in total ignorance, but they were doing so in another manner; and I had the idea of speaking about their darkness and making it evident. For my heroine I chose a likeable but emotionally intrusive woman who, having given up any career of her own, cannot manage to take an interest in her husband's. Intellectually the husband is her superior by far, and he has long since stopped loving her. He becomes deeply attached to a woman barrister, more open and more alive than his wife and very much closer to him. Gradually he breaks free from Monique so as to start a new life.

For me it was not a matter of spelling out this commonplace story but rather of using Monique's private diary to show how the victim

---

[5] In *The American Challenge*. Speaking of these passages, he blames me for a love of the past that I do not possess.

tries to escape from the truth. Here the difficulty was even greater than in *Les Belles Images,* for whereas Laurence makes timid attempts at reaching the light, the whole of Monique's efforts tend to obscure it; from one page to another her diary contradicts itself – but it does so through fresh omissions and new falsehoods. She herself weaves the darkness in which she sinks far down, so far that she loses her own image. I hoped that people would read the book as a detective-story; here and there I scattered clues that would allow the reader to find the key to the mystery – but only if he tracked Monique as one tracks down the guilty character. No words have their real meaning, no details their true validity unless they are reset in the context of the diary as a whole. The truth is never confessed: but if only one looks close enough it gives itself away.

At the same time as *The Woman Destroyed* I published two other tales. *The Monologue* was also concerned with the relationship between the truth and the spoken lies. Certain letters I had received showed me how truth can burst through words intended to conceal it. The women who wrote to me cried out against a child's ingratitude or a husband's indifference; in doing so they were in fact drawing their own portraits – the portraits of an encroaching, possessive mother or of an unbearably shrewish wife. I chose an extreme example: a woman who knows she is responsible for her daughter's suicide and who is condemned by all around her. I tried to build up the whole mass of sophistries, prophecies and forms of escape by which she attempts to put herself in the right. She succeeds in doing so only by twisting reality to the point of paraphrenia. To challenge and deny the judgment of the outside world, she wraps herself in her hatred for the whole of mankind. Through this false and grossly biased speech for the defence I wanted the reader to see her real face.

In *The Age of Discretion* I returned to old age, one of the themes of the novel that I had put aside. I had been much struck by a remark of Bachelard's on the sterility of elderly scientists. How is it possible for an active person to go on living – to outlive himself – when he feels that he is reduced to impotence? I imagined an intellectual couple, hitherto very close to one another, but now divided because they do not both bear the weight of their years in the same way. The crisis breaks out because of a conflict with their son; but what really interested me was the relationship between the parents. Of the three tales, this satisfies me the least. Silences form no part of its construction, and it is spelt out, according to my earlier technique. And then the subject was too big for so short a piece: I scarcely did more than touch upon it.

Two themes are present in all three of these stories: isolation and failure. In the last tale the failure is overcome and the dialogue renewed, because even during the crisis the heroine still retains her love for the truth. But Laurence – and Muriel even more – desperately tries to lie to herself and therefore destroys all possibility of communication with others: perhaps one day Laurence might have the courage to face reality and once more enter into contact with her fellow-beings; but as for Muriel, I hardly see any way out other than madness or suicide.

When the book was published, at the end of January 1968, the public bought it as eagerly as they had bought *Les Belles Images*; I had a great many letters from writers, students and teachers who fully appreciated my meaning and who congratulated me on having broken fresh ground once more. But on the whole the book was even less understood than its predecessor, and this time most of the critics flayed me.

For a long time my sister and I had wanted her to illustrate some new work of mine: hitherto none had been short enough. The title-story of this book, *The Woman Destroyed*, was of the right length, and it gave her ideas for some very fine engravings. I wanted people to know about the existence of this edition, which was a limited printing signed by both of us, so I agreed to let my text, together with my sister's pictures, appear in *Elle* as a serial. Immediately I was overwhelmed with letters from women, destroyed, half-destroyed or in the act of being destroyed. They identified themselves with the heroine; they attributed all possible virtues to her and they were astonished that she should remain attached to a man so unworthy of her. Their partiality made it evident that as far as their husbands, their rivals and they themselves were concerned, they shared Monique's blindness. Their reactions were based upon an immense incomprehension.

Many other readers interpreted this story in the same over-simplified manner, and they said that it was trivial. By their reviews, most of the critics proved that they had read it very imperfectly. Monsieur Bernard Pivot, having seen no more than the first installment in *Elle*, hastened to tell the readers of the *Figaro littéraire* that since *The Woman Destroyed* was appearing in a women's magazine it was therefore a shop-girl's romance with pink bows on it. Many other articles echoed this phrase, although in fact I had never written anything more sombre than *The Woman Destroyed*: the whole of the second part is one long cry of agony, and the final crumbling of the heroine is sadder than death itself.

My critics' stupidity did not surprise me. But what I did not understand was why this little book should have unleashed so much hatred. In a public debate that was broadcast by the French radio, Claire Etcherelli defended the book against Pivot; at one point she almost walked out: 'The way you are behaving has no relation whatever to literary criticism,' she said in a voice that trembled with indignation – he was being coarsely facetious to get laughs from the audience. During a discussion with Pierre-Henri Simon, Kanters launched a venomous attack upon me: in a saccharine tone Simon objected that since *A Very Easy Death* I no longer made any claim to produce serious literature. On the radio one of my disparagers said, 'Ever since I caught a glimpse of Simone de Beauvoir in the rue de Rennes I have been sorry I wrote that article: she was creeping along, looking faded and haggard. One should pity the aged. That is why Gallimard goes on publishing her, by the way.' A moment later, without realizing the contradiction, there he was, exchanging knowing winks with his companion – 'Her novel is a best-seller.' 'Oh, certainly – it's a belle-seller.' So my publisher was not actually out of pocket! Although I knew how Mathieu Galey loathed women, his caddishness still took my breath away: 'Oh yes, Madame, it is sad to grow old,' he wrote in his column. Many of them were very sorry that this latest book was so unworthy of *The Mandarins* and *The Second Sex*. What hypocrisy! When those books were published they savaged *The Mandarins* and they dragged *The Second Sex* in the gutter. Indeed, it is because of the positions I took up then that they hate me so today.

Apart from a very few exceptions, I do not mind what the critics say: I rely on the judgment of certain friends who are particularly hard to please. But I was sorry that because of the reviewers' ill-will part of the reading public did not want to see what I had written and that others began my novel with their minds already set against it. There are some women who find my ideas upsetting: they eagerly accepted what the critics said about me and took advantage of it to adopt superior airs. 'She waits until she's sixty before discovering something obvious to any ordinary housewife,' said one of them: I never could find out what discovery she was talking about. I was more affected by the reaction of others who were fighting for the cause of women and who were disappointed because my stories had nothing militant about them. 'She has betrayed us!' they cried; and they sent me reproachful letters. There is no reason at all why one should not draw a feminist conclusion from *The Woman Destroyed*: Monique's unhappiness arose from her having agreed to be dependent. But I really do not feel obliged to choose exemplary heroines. It does not seem to me that describing failure, error and bad faith means betraying anyone at all.

My sister was interviewed on the television about one of her exhibitions, and the interviewer said to her, 'Why did you choose to illustrate this book, which is the most commonplace your sister has written?' She defended it hotly and added, 'There are two sorts of people who like it – simple people who are moved by Monique's tragedy, and intellectuals who grasp what it is all about. The people who don't like it are the semi-intellectuals who haven't enough discernment to understand it and who are too pretentious to read it with a candid mind.' This was not entirely true, I am sure. But the fact is that I was supported by those I respect most; and the people who attacked me have never given a valid reason for doing so.

As in the case of *Les Belles Images* one of the objections was 'This is not real Simone de Beauvoir: it is not Simone de Beauvoir's world: she is talking about people who do not interest us.' Yet many readers claim that they see me in all my female characters. Laurence in *Les Belles Images*, disgusted with life to the point of anorexia, is supposed to be me. The angry university-woman in *The Age of Discretion* is also supposed to be me. 'But everybody thinks so,' said a woman-friend. 'It's you, and Sartre, and Sartre's mother. As for the son, they hesitate between various names.' And of course *The Woman Destroyed* could not be anyone but myself. 'To have written this story, one must have experienced this situation. So in her memoirs she did not tell the whole truth,' said some people. Others went farther. One woman wrote to ask whether the chairwoman of her literary club was right in saying that Sartre had broken with me. Replying to questioners, my friend Stépha pointed out that I was no longer forty, that I had no daughters, and that my life was unlike Monique's in every way. They allowed themselves to be convinced: 'But,' said one of them crossly, 'why does she fix it so that all her novels seem to be autobiographical?' 'She's only trying to make them ring true,' replied Stépha.

In the spring of 1966 a young man named Steiner asked me through friends to write a preface for a book he had just finished – *Treblinka*. I had never seen it, but *Les Temps modernes* had published an outstanding article on his experiences as a parachutist. I read the proofs of *Treblinka* and I was deeply impressed. I was acquainted with pretty well all the books about the death-camps that had appeared in France, and this was quite unlike the others. In writing it, Steiner had based himself upon a few little-known documents and above all upon the evidence of a handful of survivors: he remained at an objective distance from his own feelings and from the experiences he described; in an ice-cold style and with savage humour, he looked at the subject from the technicians' standpoint in order to understand how they had managed to put eight hundred thousand men to death, one by one. What I found particularly interesting was the fact that the course of events was a perfect illustration of Sartre's theories on serialization: [6] both in the ghettoes and the camps, the Nazis serialized their victims with Machiavellian ingenuity, so that they turned against one another and were reduced to impotence. When at the cost of terrible sacrifices the deportees of Treblinka did at last make a final desperate effort and succeed in forming a group, they became a powerful force and rebellion broke out. I met Steiner, and I surprised him very much by asking whether he had had *The Critique of Dialectical Reason* in mind when he was writing *Treblinka*. He had never read a word of it. He had confined himself to reporting the facts. I foresaw that these facts would not please everybody, and in my preface I tried to protect Steiner from the charges of antisemitism that some people would certainly bring against him. I reminded the reader that not one single class of deportees had been able to stand out against the Germans; among the Russians in particular, the members of the Communist Party and the political commissars were put on one side and exterminated – in spite of their ideological and military preparation all they could do was to suffer their fate. In spite of these precautions, Steiner was in fact criticized for representing the Jews as cowards. A full-scale campaign was launched

---

[6] Serialization takes place when individuals, each separately experiencing a condition common to them all, become hostile to one another; as in the case of a panic or a traffic-jam.

against him. In order to defend himself he gave somewhat vague and imprecise interviews that brought fresh misunderstandings into being. In *Le Nouveau Candide* Rousset tried to shoot him down, saying that his book was not a factual document but a novel. I was personally involved in these attacks. To defend *Treblinka*, I had a discussion with Lanzmann and Marienstrass, and it was published in *Le Nouvel Observateur*. I emphasized the fact that the book's authenticity was guaranteed by former deportees such as Daix, Martin-Chauffier and Michelet as well as by the historian Vidal-Naquet, who had gone deeply into the subject. I explained why the non-resistance of six million Jews might arouse problems for the younger generation that had not experienced the war: many young Jews wrote to tell me that they could breathe more freely now that thanks to Steiner they had come to understand a tragedy hitherto incomprehensible to them. Rousset sent the *Nouvel Observateur* a letter in reply and then I in my turn answered him. Many people wrote to me expressing their support; but some were sorry that I should have written the preface for *Treblinka* – I was even asked to suppress my contribution in the translations that were to appear: I refused. In spite of certain hostile reactions, in France Steiner was awarded the Prix de la Résistance.

In May 1967 I had finished the three stories of the collection called *The Woman Destroyed*. I wondered what I should do next. Almost at once I had an inspiration: when I tried to deal with the question of old age in the form of a novel I had failed; now I should do so in the form of a study – the counterpart of *The Second Sex,* but dealing with old people. Sartre was warmly in favour of my plan.

Why did this theme mean so much to me? In the first place, I had been struck by the furious outcry I had aroused when I spoke of growing old at the end of *Force of Circumstance*. Tired, worn-out clichés had been tossed at me, and I wanted to rip them to pieces. I found them all the more disgusting since I knew about the condition in which most old people live today. Here again it was primarily the idea of demystification, doing away with cant and humbug, that attracted me so strongly. But the reason why I made up my mind to embark upon this book was that I needed to understand a state that is my own, and to understand it in its implication for mankind as a whole. I am a woman, and I wished to throw light upon the

130

woman's lot; I was on the threshold of old age, and I wished to know the bounds and the nature of the aged state.

Before studying the feminine question systematically, I had read a very great many books, I had a tolerably wide experience, and I found an abundant documentation straight away. But when I began to look into the problem of old age, I was empty-handed. I went to the catalogue-room of the Bibliothèque nationale and looked at the most recent entries under the heading Old Age. First I came across Emerson's and Faguet's essays and then I found more solid works that provided me with the beginnings of a bibliography. Step by step it grew richer, and I read almost all the treatises and gerontological periodicals published in France in recent years. I sent to Chicago for three enormous epitomes that the Americans have devoted to this study. As I explored, so the book took shape in my mind; and, with more or less difficulty, I wrote the various chapters.

Some critics have spoken of *Old Age* as a book written at second hand: that is wholly unfair. A book written at second hand is one that confines itself to compiling from works about the subject in question. That is what I did in my first chapter, which deals with the biology of old age: I studied the relevant books and I did little more than summarize them. But in the whole of the rest of the book, my work was original. Of course I made use of books, articles, papers and so on – I was not writing a work of imagination. But in the first place I had to discover them, find out how to turn them to account, and carry out fresh syntheses. There is a book on old age in primitive societies, but I do not think it wholly satisfactory: I hardly used it at all. I did employ the admirable working-tool that Claude Lévi-Strauss kindly made available to me – the laboratory of comparative anthropology in the Collège de France. His colleagues pointed out various monographs with sections on the state of the aged: I read them all, trying to establish the relationship between this state and the relevant civilization taken as a whole. The analysis of this material, the reflections it aroused, and the conclusions I drew – all this was work that no one had done before me.

It was impossible for me to borrow from any book on the lot of the aged in historical societies, for none existed: the old were passed over in silence. The few clues that could be extracted were often hard to interpret, and at least at first they seemed confused and contradictory. And then there was the question of knowing where they were to be found. I launched into a positive treasure-hunt. Generally speaking, my research was fairly well-directed, and it was not too hard for me to discover the answers to my questions. Sometimes I was lucky: I would quite unexpectedly chance upon a goldmine. But it would also happen that books from which I expected information gave me none. In that case I would turn to the specialists: some of them gave me useful guidance.

I found it fairly easy to gather a considerable mass of information on the present state of the aged. And I had many interviews with people whose calling gave them a thorough knowledge of the subject.

As for the second part of the book, it is an entirely personal piece of work.

The very heart of a book of this nature is the kind of question the writer asks himself: my own experience and my own reflections alone led me to fix upon those I dealt with – what is the relationship between the aged person and his image, his body, his past and his undertakings; and what are the reasons for his attitudes towards the world and to those around him? To answer these questions, I based myself upon old people's letters, private diaries and memoirs; I turned to the inquiries that had been carried out and to statistics; I asked others for their evidence, and I interrogated myself. Interpreting this mass of data, putting it all into perspective, and drawing the conclusions was entirely original work. In many cases the ideas I expressed and the positions I took up ran counter to a great deal of accepted opinion.

The book came out at the end of January 1970. A little earlier the report of the *Inspection générale des affaires sociales* on the social problems of the aged had been published. From this it appeared that their condition had grown even worse during the preceding ten years, for the derisory increase in their pensions had not kept pace with the rise in prices. *France-Soir* devoted its front page to a study of the report. All at once the question was very much in the news. My book appeared just when the public was ready to receive it: but I had started writing it more than two years before.

I wanted the book to reach the greatest possible number of people, so breaking with my ordinary habit I agreed to give two interviews on Radio-Luxembourg. These brought me very touching letters from grossly under-privileged old people who had heard them. My correspondents provided most striking confirmation of my darkest conclusions: the official figures were still too sanguine by far. The government's negligence,[7] red tape and the extreme complexity of the regulations were reducing great numbers of old people to despair. Even those who were well enough off to buy my book gave me a very sombre picture of their condition: several of them called for the right to 'free death', that is to say euthanasia. Since we are not allowed the means of living, they said, then at least let us choose our death. Three or four comparatively well-off people in their eighties did assure me that the burden of their years was not overwhelming: that is a small number indeed, when it is set against the quantities of heart-broken letters I received.

On the whole the book was very well received by the critics: both the right wing and the left acknowledged that the treatment of the old at present was a scandal. But whereas the left-wing critics praised me for having emphasized the economic and social aspects of the problem, those of the right preferred to look upon it as a question of biology and metaphysics and to feel that society played only a secondary part. There was also a disagreement between those who were of the opinion that I had written an anti-*De Senectute* and those who thought I was going back to Cicero and Seneca. Obviously it is the first who were right. I do admit that in some exceptionally favoured cases old age may bring certain advantages; but the vast majority of old people are condemned to a degraded existence.

The reactions that encouraged me most came from a certain number of gerontologists. Generally speaking, specialists do not much care to see others treading upon their preserves. These, on the contrary, congratulated me for having broken what they too called the 'conspiracy of silence'; and several of them offered me their collaboration.

Naturally enough, some mistakes crept into the book – a very long book that I wrote without any help at all.[8] Three or four correspondents pointed them out, more or less acrimoniously: but nobody has contradicted me upon any important point whatsoever.

---

[7] At the end of 1970 an old lady named Madame Cocagne killed herself because the postal-order to which her pension entitled her had not been sent for months.

[8] Among other things, I confused Sigogne, a French poet who lived at Dieppe, with an Italian antiquary born at Modena. I said that Marivaux married late in life—he did not. When as a child I saw de Max in the role of Nero he looked so ancient I thought he was eighty: in point of fact he was fifty.

An account of my mother's death, two works of fiction, two pre-
faces, one long study: even without mentioning the draft of the
novel that I put aside, I wrote a good deal between 1963 and 1970.
Yet sometimes during this period I went through phases when the
idea of holding a pen sickened me. After I had finished *A Very
Easy Death* I felt utterly incapable of writing; I had felt an irresist-
ible urge to write this account, but when I had finished it literature
seemed to me pointless – I had swung over towards death and the
silence of death. Then again I was paralysed by the want of com-
prehension with which *Force of Circumstance* had been received:
words had betrayed me and I no longer trusted in them. I wrenched
myself out of this disgust because fresh subjects forced themselves
upon me; but my relationship to writing is now more ambivalent
than it was in former times. It is still necessary to me, but sometimes I like giving myself a break from it: I do so when I am staying
in Rome, for example, where I could have all the spare time I want
to work. I have never been able to write when I am caught up by
what is actually happening, whether it is very happy or whether it is
distressing. Nowadays, even at times when I am quite free, I sometimes give myself holidays.

Yet in the long run, idleness bores me: my days seem colourless. I
no longer feel that I have a distinct purpose. And I know that none
of my future books will transform the body of my work as a whole:
it will be the same corpus with a volume added. I am aware that
what I said in *Old Age* now applies to me: in the last stage even
progress has something disappointing about it – one does move
forward; maybe, but one makes little headway, and that with no
hope of going far beyond what one has already accomplished. I
should not like to give up the exalting feeling that writing still gives
me at times – the impression that by creating a book I am creating
myself in the imaginary dimension.

I have continued to help in the running of our magazine, *Les Temps
modernes*. I have not written any articles for it however: I have only
published two of my shorter works in it, *A Very Easy Death* and
The Age of Discretion. I have read and sifted a great many of the
manuscripts sent in. I regularly attend the meetings at which the
editors discuss the line to be followed and the contents of the various issues. These meetings usually take place once a fortnight. We

are all friends, so the work merges with the pleasure of conversation.

In 1962 Francis Jeanson took Marcel Péju's place on the editorial committee; this did not mean any alteration in the policy of the magazine. *Les Temps modernes* changed publishers. After the death of René Julliard his firm was taken over by Nielsen, who ran Les Presses de la Cité, a house that was primarily concerned with making money: he was not interested in our magazine. Claude Gallimard suggested that we should go back to him. He put part of a house in the rue de Condé at our disposal; Beaumarchais had once lived there, and it was now occupied by the Mercure de France publishing house. Our office moved in.

There was a gap in the magazine, and one that we wished to fill: the members of the committee were so much taken up by their own work that they no longer had the time to carry out the arduous and somewhat thankless task of writing pieces on literature, art, and reviewing books on history or economics. We had thought that young people would have more free time and that they might be happy to seize this opportunity of expressing themselves. At the beginning of the autumn of 1964 we had a meeting in my flat – a crowded and somewhat incongruous gathering. There were the budding novelists, Annie Leclerc and Georges Perec;[9] the poets Velter and Sautereau, who wrote in collaboration; a professor of law, Nicos Poulantzas, who was writing important works on political economy;[10] a number of students, particularly some who were studying philosophy – Jeannine Rovet, Sylvie Le Bon, Dollé, Peretz, Benabou and Régis Debray. Many of these were disciples of Althusser, and they, instead of providing us with the reviews we were looking for, wanted to turn *Les Temps modernes* into a forum for the expression of their own ideas. This first discussion was all rather confused. Those who looked upon themselves as the group's theoreticians said, 'We should find out what common views have brought us together.'

The question remained unanswered. But those who attended the second meeting – there were fewer of them, and Régis Debray among others never came back – seemed ready to undertake the

---

[9] A little later she published *Le Pont du Nord* and he *Les Choses*, followed by other works.
[10] He subsequently published *Fascisme et dictature* and *Pouvoir politique et classe sociales*.

work we suggested. From that time onwards the group met every week: with Sartre and me on alternate weeks, otherwise by themselves. They scattered during the vacations and then at the beginning of term they started working again. The 'theoreticians' published leading articles and they thought of bringing out a regular 'Marxist column'. After one issue, this plan came to nothing. There were quite important ideological disagreements between them and the members of the editorial committee. Although they knew nothing whatsoever about the Chinese cultural revolution, they supported it unconditionally: before we took sides, we insisted upon having some information: they maintained that this was overscrupulous. Then again, at the end of the university year almost all of them had to prepare for examinations and they had no time to do anything else. On 26 June 1966 we parted, and with one consent we agreed not to prolong the experiment.

Jeanson's time was entirely taken up by running a Maison de la Culture, and he left the editorial committee of *Les Temps modernes* in 1967. He was not replaced. So now the committee numbered no more than eight; and we were not all in complete harmony. When Kravetz, and others after him, called for 'the Sorbonne for the students' in numbers 64 and 65, and made a violent attack upon official university lectures, Pontalis and Pingaud were strongly opposed to his propositions. They did not make this publicly evident, but in private they did not conceal the fact that they were shocked and distressed by some of the positions adopted by the magazine. They openly stated their disapproval when Sartre published the 'psychoanalytical dialogue' and explained why he thought the document fascinating – an opinion shared by all the other members of the committee. This dialogue had been recorded by one of Dr X's patients: three years after the end of a long analysis he had burst into the doctor's house, armed with a tape-recorder. Reversing the situation, he insisted upon the doctor's answering his questions: faced with the machine, the doctor showed every sign of extreme alarm. Sartre approved of the 'sick man's' claim for reciprocity.

In a note, Pontalis objected that the Censier watchword 'Victims of analysis, rise up!' implied a radical rejection of psychoanalysis. Pingaud felt that the tape-recorder man's 'move into direct action' did not provide a suitable opportunity for calling psychoanalysis into question. Both in the one and the other there was to be seen the

136

same tendency that had caused them to defend the tradition of official lectures.

The matter went no farther. But as the magazine – spurred on primarily by Sartre and Gorz – more and more deliberately adopted a left-wing line, Pontalis and Pingaud left in 1970. It was Gorz's 'Destroy the University', the leading article in the April number, that made up their minds. 'The position, signature and form of this article make it appear to define the collective opinion of the *Temps modernes* team. 'As we cannot accept these propositions, we have regretfully decided to leave the editorial committee,' they wrote. We too regretted their departure; but our intellectual and political disagreements had become too grave for friendship to overcome them. Now we make up a reduced but homogeneous team, although on some points our views may not exactly coincide. We carry on with our work of information and analysis.

3

When I was a child and an adolescent, reading was not only my favourite pastime, but also the key that opened the world to me. It foretold my future: I identified myself with the heroines of novels, and through them I caught glimpses of what my life would be. In the unhappy phases of my youth it preserved me from loneliness; later it broadened my knowledge, increased my experience and helped me to a better understanding of my state as a human being and of the meaning of my work as a writer. Today both my life and my work are accomplished: my work is complete, even though it may go on; and no book can possibly bring me any shattering revelation. Yet I continue to read, and to read a great deal. In the morning and in the afternoon before I settle down to work or when I am tired of writing I read; I read if I happen to spend the evening alone; and I read for hours when I am in Rome during the summer. There is no occupation that seems more natural to me. Still, I do ask myself this question: if books can no longer bring me anything decisive, then why am I still so very fond of reading?

The delight of reading: that has not grown dull. I am still wonderstruck by that metamorphosis of little black marks into a word – a word that projects me into a particular world or that brings this world within the four walls of my room. The most lumpish text is enough to bring the miracle about. *Yng lady, 30, exp. sht-typ. seeks work three days a week.* My eyes scan this advertisement and all at once France is peopled with typewriters and young ladies out of work. The miracle is within me, I know: the wonder-worker is myself. If I do not react to the printed lines they remain mute: for them to come to life I have to provide them with a meaning, and my freedom must lend them its own temporality, retaining the past and going beyond it towards the future. But since

I spirit myself away during this operation, it seems magical to me. There are times when I am aware that I collaborate with the author in bringing the page I read into existence; and helping to create the object I enjoy gives me pleasure. This is a pleasure that is denied to the writer himself: even when he re-reads them, the words born from his pen escape from him. The reader is more fortunate; he is an active partner and yet the book showers unexpected wealth upon him. For the same reason painting and music give me joy of a similar nature; but in this case the immediate data of the senses play a more important part. Here I do not have to carry out that extraordinary transition from sign to meaning that so astonishes children when they start spelling words out – a passage that has never stopped delighting me. I draw my bedroom curtains; I lie on a sofa: my surroundings disappear and I am no longer aware of myself: all that exists is the black and white of the pages before my eyes. And now comes that astonishing adventure that Taoist philosophers tell us about: leaving a lifeless shell on their bed, they take flight, travelling for centuries from mountain-top to mountain-top, travelling across the whole world and even into the heavens. When they come back to their body, they find it has lived for no greater time than the length of a sigh. Motionless, I too travel under distant skies, through days long past; and it may be that centuries go by before I come back to myself some two or three hours later, there in the place from which I have not stirred. There is no experience that can be compared with this. Day-dreaming is poor and thin, because of the poverty of its images; and as one runs through them memories soon come to an end. Rebuilding the past by means of a conscious effort is not a task that enables one to enjoy the object attained, any more than creation is. Whether memories spring up of themselves or whether they are consciously evoked, they never tell me more than I already know. Dreams surprise me more; but as they run on, so they fade; and the memory they leave is disappointing. Reading alone creates new and lasting relationships between things and myself; and it does so with a striking economy of means – just this one volume in my hand.

I like losing all awareness of myself when I read. But in summer I often read in the open air. The narrative carries me away, a great way off; and yet at the same time I feel the breeze and the sun on my skin, I breathe the smell of the trees and now and then I glance at the blue overhead: although I am far away I am still locally present. And at times like these I do not know which means more to me, the countryside all round or the story I am being told. I like reading in the train, too. My eyes take in the landscape that runs by on the other side of the window; they do so almost passively and then they turn back to the page they are bringing to life. These alternating pleasures, both of which delight me, form an enchanting combination. Very often I read for the mere pleasure of reading rather than for having read: I am something of a book-swallower. Then it may happen that my first reading has been too hurried, and as soon as the book is finished I have to go right through it again from beginning to end.

Yet I do not read just anything at all. Unless I am looking at them from a sociological or linguistic point of view, I do not linger over small advertisements. What conditions have to be fulfilled for a piece of writing to absorb my attention at present?

These are of many kinds, and the nature of the profit I draw from them varies widely. In some cases I read a book without giving up my place in the centre of my world: I am merely filling the gaps in this world of mine. When I close the book, there I am in possession of certain pieces of knowledge. Contrasted with this informative reading there is the reading by which one enters into a communication. Here the writer does not claim to provide me with knowledge but rather to convey the meaning, the sense, of his being in the world, and to do so by means of a single, unique world, his book. His existential experience cannot be reduced to concepts or notions: it does not instruct me. But while I am reading I live in another man's skin; and this may deeply alter my vision of the human state, of the world, and of the place I occupy in it. There is one fairly clear-cut criterion by which these two classes of books may be distinguished. I can summarize the informative work in my own words, thus providing a third person with a piece of universal knowledge; in a work of literature, on the other hand, language itself comes into play, for it is through the writer's language that his experience is conveyed in its unique quality – it cannot be communicated in any other words. That is why the blurb on the jacket of a good novel that claims to summarize it is always a betrayal; and that is why a writer is so worried and perplexed when he is asked about his work in progress – he cannot convey a knowledge of what is by definition un-knowledge.

Then again I often read neither to inform myself nor to enter into communication with the writer, but merely to pass the time – detective stories, science-fiction or novels about spies: books written solely for amusement.

I read a great deal to acquire information: I have always wanted to learn, and I am widely curious. I should like to keep abreast of everything that interests my contemporaries. Unfortunately my curiosity is limited by my own blanks – it is dependent on my earlier studies, on my investment in learning. The field of science is closed to me; and there are some forms of study, such as linguistics and political economy, that I have always disliked. I resign myself to being ignorant of many, many things. And even in the areas that are open to me I do not read everything that is published. Chance has something to do with my choice; people send me quite a lot of books, and I look into them: but generally speaking my choice is directed. What lies behind this direction?

A book attracts me straight away if it answers questions that I am asking myself. When I am getting ready for some particular journey, I wonder about the country I am going to see and I try to gather information about it. When I was working on the subject of old age I eagerly ran through gerontological studies that would have bored me a year earlier. But then again, just as the sight of an object often begets the desire for it, so hearing about some unforeseen event often makes me want to know more and to understand it better. Or else fresh discoveries about facts that I either did not know or did not care about will arouse my interest.

Above all I try to understand my own period. During these last ten years I have read a great many works on the USSR, the USA, Latin America, Cuba, the French working-class and the Italian proletariat. When important events such as the Six Days' War, May 1968, the invasion of Czechoslovakia and the Chinese cultural revolution take place I read almost everything I can find on the question. I am just as interested in books that help me to understand periods I lived through earlier. This decade has seen the publication of important revelations on Franco's Spain, the Greek resistance and the tragic failure of the partisans' war,[1] the Third Reich, the French Milice and Gestapo, the extermination of the Jews, and the wars in Indochina and Algeria. When I read books of this kind, I have the feeling of recovering my own history. They revive my knowledge of the subject and make it fuller; in doing so

[1] I am thinking of Eudes' fine book *The Kapetanios*.

141

they bring my pain and anger back to life, and with them my past, thus momentarily preserving me from time's erosion.

I also attribute great value to explanations of events that happened at a much greater distance from me. Later I shall describe the circumstances in which I read London's *On Trial,* a book in which I found the answers to so many questions I had asked myself. I already knew a good deal about the Soviet camps;[2] but Evgenia Ginzburg's *Into the Whirlwind* showed me certain aspects of them in greater depth; these memoirs of hers had been secretly handed about in the USSR long before they appeared in France, and Ehrenburg had told us of them with great respect. Evgenia Ginzburg – the mother of Axionov, the young anticonformist writer, very well known in the USSR – was arrested in 1937, a time when interrogation did not yet include torture. She signed no confession and she was not publicly tried. Nevertheless she underwent two years of imprisonment and seventeen in the camps. To pin her down, they made use of the tricks that were later described by London: 'You knew So-and-So, the Trotskyist, and you did not denounce his activities.' 'I did know Professor So-and-So, but I did not know he was a Trotskyist.' 'He was one. So you must sign "I knew So-and-So, the Trotskyist".' Evgenia Ginzburg was an unwavering Communist; she had lost all faith in Stalin, but she had never for a moment had any doubts about Communism itself. In the harshest, most rigorous surroundings, she fought strongly to survive and to help her companions; her tenacity and their gratitude enabled her to emerge from these shattering trials unharmed.

I knew that during the war the Soviet spy-network had done valuable service, but I had never really thought about the details of its work. Gilles Perrault's *The Red Orchestra* is one of those books that stimulate curiosity at the same time that they satisfy it. Although he irritates me at times, the author gives a vivid account of the fascinating adventures of Trepper and his colleagues – adventures that were sometimes ludicrous but more often tragic. As I read about these adventures, so I had a distinct realization of what I as a reader was doing: it was I who made all these characters scattered over Europe exist – the ill-fated Berlin network (all its members were tortured and put to death), the orchestra[3] in Paris,

---

[2] Among other books, I had read Solzhenitsyn's *One Day in the Life of Ivan Denisovich.*
[3] The spies who used clandestine transmitters to send out their information were called pianists: hence the name.

and the 'pianists' in Brussels. I went with the author as he made his inquiries; and I too synthesized the results he gathered.

There is one question I have asked myself about these books: how is it possible to experience the joy of reading when they are concerned with hideous or revolting events? The first condition is that they should be neutralized by their fall into the well of the past. When the papers tell me about the death-agonies of Biafran children or about the massacres perpetrated by the Americans in Vietnam, there is no question of feeling any kind of intellectual pleasure: the reaction is one of fury at one's impotence. And there are some revelations that can excite revulsion and dismay even in retrospect; I have known people who avoid them because they are afraid of being disturbed – among others an Italian Communist who refused even to look at *On Trial*. I myself have jibbed at descriptions of physical torture. But in tragic, heart-wringing accounts – *The Kapetianos, Into the Whirlwind, The Red Orchestra* for example – heroic or lovable characters often stand out; my longing for knowledge is so deep-rooted that the laying bare of some piece of reality, even of a hideous reality, almost always brings me a kind of exaltation.

The recent past refers me back to an earlier past, and I take an interest in those historical works that help me to a better understanding of France, of Europe, and of the present world. But during these recent years I have read almost nothing about very remote periods. On the other hand, I eagerly read ethnological reports and books: many have recently been published in France. I have a particular liking for monographs. Just as when one is on the Aventine in Rome and looking through the keyhole one discovers a garden and the whole city, so by fixing my attention upon a small corner of the earth, beyond it I see an entire country, together with its relationship with the world. Morin's *Plodémet*, Wylie's *Village in the Vaucluse*, Duvignaud's *Change at Shebika*, Mouloud Makal's *Un Village en Anatolie*, and above all Oscar Lewis's enthralling inquiries *The Children of Sanchez, Pedro Martinez* and *La Vida* interested me very much indeed.

The ethnological books I prefer are those which take one particular case to show a 'primitive man's' inward experience of his situation. There are few studies of this kind. Earlier we were given the astonishing *Soleil Hopi*; and in recent years I was enchanted by *Ishi*, the story of the last survivor of an exterminated Indian tribe, and by *Yonoama*, the dictated narrative of a white Brazilian woman who was kidnapped by Indians at the age of ten and who spent a great deal of her life among them.

Broadly speaking, I value all those works that throw new light upon the human state. I have been intensely interested in psychiatry ever since I was a girl. At present I eagerly follow the attempts of the 'anti-psychiatrists' at breaking the 'great closed ring'. I have read the works of Szasz, Cooper and Laing, and Basaglia's *L'Institution en négation*, in which he describes the experiment tried out at Gorizia. I liked the extreme vehemence of Gentis' pamphlet *Les Murs de l'asile*. I am now much more concerned than I was with the problems of childhood, for the longer I live the more I see the importance of the very first years in a human being's development. I found Bettelheim's *The Empty Fortress* particularly striking. Freud lays the primary stress upon the period of a child's life between the ages of three and four. Bettelheim shows[4] that a great deal has already been either won or lost by the age of two: it is in the first twenty-four months that what are called the gifts or the failings of the individual assume their definite shape. Normally it is at this period that the child must acquire that sense of reciprocity which is essential for his integration into society: if the attitude of those around him does not allow this to take place then he is condemned to schizophrenia or autistic behaviour, or else he becomes what is called a 'wolf' or a 'wild' child. The cases the writer brings forward are deeply interesting in themselves; they give rise to much reflection and they help one to understand a great deal.

The most astonishing of all the books on psychiatry I have read is L. Wolfson's *The Schizo Student of Language*, in which a young American schizophrenic describes the strange linguistic processes he used to defend himself against his mother-tongue, English, particularly when it is spoken by his mother, and against the food, which he looks upon as poisonous and dirty, that his mother wants him to eat. This obsessional theme is at the centre of the whole story of his life – his relationships with his mother, his father, and his stepfather. He handles his story both with an insane solemnity and with an ironic detachment that gives a curious charm to this account of a 'schizophrenic student of languages' as he describes

---

[4] Recently confirmed by a series of observations and experiments carried out in Israel in 1970/71. See p. 386.

144

himself. The outstanding preface by Gilles Deleuze sheds a great
deal of light upon this.

Then there is biography, a kind of writing that charms me
because it lies upon the frontier between history and psychology.
Here, as it happens with all monographs, a unique case refers me to
the world as a whole. I am particularly interested in knowing how
writers, men who followed the same calling as myself, saw their
position in that world. Painter's life of Proust did not help me to
know him better – his work brings one far closer. But by pointing
out the landscapes, faces and events that inspired him, the book did
tell me about his creative processes. That is what interests and
puzzles me most – the link between the daily life of a writer (a link
so different for each) and the books in which he expresses himself.
That is what I sought, with more or less success, in Lanoux's book
on Maupassant, Troyat's on Gogol, Julian's on D'Annunzio, and
Baxter's on Hemingway.

Another question that concerns me deeply is this: how does a
woman adjust herself to her womanly state, her female condition? I
took great pleasure in following Isabelle Eberhard's adventures in
Françoise d'Eaubonne's biography; and those of Madame Hanau,
recounted by Dominique Desanti. And I felt the warmest sympathy
for that astonishing woman Lou Andréas-Salomé when I read
H. F. Peter's rather clumsy *Ma soeur, mon épouse*.

But I can also feel interested in the fate of a character that is
utterly remote from me, and in the winter of 1970 I was delighted
with Orieux' *Talleyrand*. The history of his period conditioned
Talleyrand; and at the same time he was an expression of it.
Following him step by step gives one a distinct idea of a great
noble's position in society at the end of the eighteenth century – a
clearer impression than any generalities could give; and one sees
how his period's changes of regime were experienced from one day
to the next. Yet he was not only an incarnation of his century; he
was also a unique individual. He provides a striking example of the
part played in a man's life by his early childhood; and Talleyrand's
excuses a great many faults. There are some sides of his character,
such as his venality, that I find disagreeable. Others charm me – his
cynical intelligence, the acid humour of his 'cracks', his impassive-
ness, and his loyalty to his friends and to the mistresses he once
loved. His long and tolerant liaison with a niece forty years younger

145

than himself seems to me romantic; and I followed the curious story of his relations with Napoleon with intense interest.

There are some autobiographies that scarcely differ from lives written by a third person: they provide information rather than establish communication. In the successive volumes of her memoirs, Han Suyin gives a detailed account of the historical events that have formed part of her life; to be sure she also tells the specific and personal adventure of a Eurasian woman born in the time of Chiang Kai-shek – it is a very likeable narrative, but it is not one that admits the reader to intimate acquaintance. A book like *Papillon* does not make us take part in a piece of living experience: it shows us certain aspects of the penal settlement, and above all it amuses us with its more or less true, more or less fictitious, but in any case very well told, sequence of events.

In fact so marked a distinction between these three kinds of reading is somewhat arbitrary. All three are 'diverting', since they all engross my attention. When I read *The Red Orchestra* or the life of Lou Andréas-Salomé there are times when I get right inside the characters and see the world through their eyes. On the other hand, a literary work rarely provides me with no information at all. Yet what I have sought and found in the books I have mentioned so far, was essentially increase of knowledge.

My attitude is quite different if I am looking for a 'communication': when this is the case, I efface myself entirely, giving place to another. I try to realize Fantasio's dream – 'If only I could be that man passing by!' Here reading does not mean conversing, as Montaigne puts it, but rather making one's way deep into another person's monologue. Autobiographies, private diaries and collections of letters all make this intrusion easier. So do some novels. Narratives based on reality and those that are set in an imaginary world face the writer with problems of different kinds; but the part the reader has to play remains the same. The world the reader enters must possess sufficient coherence and interest for him to be concerned with its various phases and elements: it is of little importance whether this world belongs to past time, whether it exists at all, or whether it is entirely made up. In any event the reader makes contact with it by means of what Sartre calls an 'image-forming knowledge': words are as valid an *analogon* to the relevant object whether it still exists, no longer exists, or never has existed. Julien Sorel's prison is neither closer to me nor farther than

146

Oscar Wilde's. The cleavage lies elsewhere – between those books which do not affect my subjective position and those which take me out of myself. I very much dislike those that try to make me adopt both attitudes at the same time: the 'documentary' novel tells me little and communicates nothing at all; and the same applies to fictionalized biography.

What are the circumstances in which a writer can succeed in changing me into another person, and to what extent can he do it? First I shall look at those cases in which the writer yields himself most directly – memoirs, letters and private diaries. And afterwards those in which he recreates his world in the form of a novel.

I have already spoken of my particular relationship with the books of Sartre and Violette Leduc: I shall not return to the subject here, although in recent years few have enchanted me as much as *Words* and *La Bâtarde*. I was very, very pleased with *Fibrils*, too. It was easy for me to slip into the book because Leiris' world and mine intersect at many points. We live in the same city; I know many of his friends and I appreciate the books and the music he likes best. I too went to the China he speaks of, and at the same time. I know him personally and through his books; and these books charm me because of Leiris' meticulous observation of life, of the world and of himself, and because of the way he stands back from them all. There is humour in his scrupulous precision, and a close attention to exactness in his humour. He neither attempts to draw a pretty picture of himself nor to turn into an insect under the dispassionate gaze of an entomologist. He is both intimately concerned and an objective reporter, and what he shows us is a man – a unique person who happens to be himself. In *Fibrils* the flashing play of mirrors no longer carries on to infinity as it did in *Gear* and *Erasures*; his style is less complex, less dazzling; but it conveys his meaning more clearly; and the experience with which it deals is more harrowing than it was in his other books. I was deeply moved by those passages in which he describes the conflict between two sorts of love, *l'amour-fidélité* – love in faithfulness – on the one hand, and on the other *l'amour-vertige* – the immediate violent passion – a conflict that brought him to the brink of death. And I was even more touched by those in which he tells how he overcame the tragedy of growing old: going beyond the discouragement that the cruel shrinking of the future brings about at our age, he has succeeded in recovering his love for life and for writing.

I am happy too when my sympathy carries me into a world very unlike my own. This happened to me when I read Freud's letters. Although I challenge some of his theories, particularly those concerned with women, Freud is one of the men of this century for whom I have the greatest admiration. I knew him through Jones's biography, but his letters brought him closer. They took me into his family life, his friendships and his travels; I shared in the adventures of his mind, and I watched him struggle with fearless, indomitable courage against every obstacle that rose in his path. In spite of the quiet moderation of his tone, I could feel that there were times when illness, pain, bereavement and betrayals brought him to the edge of despair; yet out of love for his family he came to terms with suffering and with old age: there is something heroic in his resignation.

I am very imperfectly acquainted with Gramsci's work, but I do know its worth. I grew fond of him when I read a recently-translated biography, and the trials he underwent made me very sad. His letters from prison moved me even more. His wife forsook him; his children were taken away; he was misunderstood by his own people, and his body was a torment to him: in bitter loneliness he suffered an imprisonment that was in fact a slow murder.

I knew nothing whatsoever about Jackson until the day I had his letters in my hands. Genet praised them highly in his admirable preface, and they deserve all he says about them. When he was eighteen, Jackson was arrested for delinquency; at that time this young Black was only vaguely aware of political and racial problems, but gradually he came to understand them and then overcame them by his intellectual power. During these ten years one sees the formation of his character and the birth and the ripening of his ideas. He makes common cause with his brothers, the Black Panthers, and he gives a powerful explanation of his reasons for doing so. He rises up against the arbitrariness of racial discrimination within the prison. He is accused of killing a warder and he gets ready to stand his trial, together with two fellow-prisoners; but he knows that his life is in danger. By the end of his letters he has acquired a leader's education, experience and character. I followed his development with joy but also with extreme anxiety. I felt a particular bond with him, because both Sartre and I were to go and give evidence at his trial. And, like Jackson himself, I had a fore-boding of the end that was waiting for him: they killed him.

How deep must our understanding be before a writer can carry me along with him page after page? Although as far as he is con-cerned I may not have that total esteem which I feel for Freud, Gramsci and Jackson, I may yet sympathize enough to be able, on the basis of his past and his situation, to understand his aims and intentions, to rejoice at his good fortune and to feel for him in his sadness.

This is what happened when I read Oscar Wilde's letters. I liked his plays and his books, and I began these letters with a feeling of friendship. His frivolity, his aestheticism, his snobbery and his narcissism irritated me, particularly in the first volume. Yet I do feel intellectual affinities with him: he speaks of Art and the Artist with a vexing pomposity, but the fact is that art and writing were what he lived for. I often share his taste for certain books and pictures, and for Italy; I also share his refusal of conventions and of puritanism. He knew how to look at things and to see them; and I love his intense awareness of the happinesses in life, even though he may include pleasures arising from vanity, luxury and money that do not affect me at all. As a writer he knew how to stand up for himself and to attack – he had sharp claws; in his private life, I am touched by his generosity, his kindness, his want of bitterness and resentment. There is some masochism in this inability to hate, but it is chiefly goodness and an imagination that allowed him to enter into living contact with men as unlike himself as the Californian miners. His qualities as a writer are also to be seen in his letters; he is a charming correspondent. And often there is truth beneath his apparent paradoxes. 'Life is not a romance; one has romantic memories and romantic hopes – that's all. Our most burning ecstasies are merely the shadows of what we have felt elsewhere or of what we hope to feel some day.' These words truly express the existentialist idea of the impossible overtaking of being.

I find it difficult to understand Wilde when he is about to sue Lord Queensberry; but once he is in court, I admire both his audacious defiance of society and the dangerous elegance of his answers to the charges made against him. I re-read his *De Pro-fundis*, and it touched me deeply. His way of demolishing Douglas is somewhat unpleasant; but his situation was one that stimulated bitter reasoning of this kind. He cries out very powerfully against the poisonous sterility of hatred, contrasting it with the abundant wealth of love. When he blames Bosie for being 'superficial' one feels the depth of his own feelings, under their mask of frivolity. In extreme misfortune he discovers the truth of the human state and he takes a pride in assuming it; and he gains from his defeat. Yet he does not conceal those aspects of it that are ridiculous and even grotesque. He sinks to the very lowest pitch of abasement and in doing so he reaches a true greatness. He emerges from his sufferings not embittered but more human than he was before. Instead of saying nothing whatsoever about his stay in prison, he takes advantage of it to express his indignation at the administrative cruelty exercised upon the prisoners, particularly the children and adolescents. He writes to the editor of the *Daily Chronicle* to protest against the dismissal of a young warder guilty of having given biscuits to some children who were 'sick with hunger'. This wicked unkindness, he says, is not the result of devilish malignance; it is mere stupidity, a 'total lack of imagination'. For his own part, instead of sinking down into his own unhappiness, Wilde was capable of feeling the boundless horror that comes upon a child in the loneliness of its cell and of pitying it; and in his own flesh he experienced the bullying and knocking about that brought a youth to the edge of insanity. As he speaks of them, his voice takes on a tone of such true, poignant emotion that it forces us to make the same effort of understanding with regard to Wilde himself: he compels both our esteem and our friendship.

After this is there anything surprising about the fact that having suffered imprisonment for love of Bosie he falls in love with him again as soon as he is let out? In spite of his wife and his friends and against all his own interests, he starts living with Bosie once more; and in his letters we see his pitiful decline and fall. He is no longer able to write. He makes use of shabby little tricks to wring money from his friends – lies that he does not even trouble to make believable. He sheds not only the reputation and the outward appearances of the man he once was, but all notion of morality and even the most elementary decency. He reminds one of Lear tearing off his unmeaning ornaments and stripping bare the forked animal that is man.

Since I liked Wilde's books, it was natural that I should be fascinated by his history, as it could be made out through his letters. But there are also more surprising instances. Politically I very much dislike Clemenceau, that lackey of the bourgeoisie who was not ashamed to call himself 'France's chief cop'; and the philosophy that emerges from his books is nebulous, vague and insipid. Why then should I have taken so much interest in his 'letters to a woman-friend'?

At the age of eighty-two, he was politically neutralized. He no longer had any influence, but only opinions; though indeed these opinions gave him clear-sighted views upon the future. He hardly ever speaks of them in these letters. What this correspondence does show is the daily private life of a man who has known dazzling glory, who has been harshly 'retired', and who is now doing his best to fill the last years of his life as well as he can. He writes mostly about Bélébat, his house in the Vendée; I have seen it, standing alone by the sea, on a sandy coast. He grew roses there, and all kinds of flowers. What makes me like him in these accounts of his daily occupations is the freshness and sincerity with which he looks at things. He retains the same awareness of the world and the same eagerness for life that he had in his years of furious activity. He knew nothing about the good writers of his time, but he did understand the work of Rodin and Monet, and he defended them – he knew how to see. In these letters he is keenly alive to the sun and the wind; every day he looks at the sky and the clouds and the waves on the sea, seeing them with fresh and happy eyes; and using very simple words, he succeeds in showing them to us. Unlike so many old people, he does not withdraw himself and harden; he is warmly attached to his friends, to his sisters, and to Clotilde, his housekeeper; and he is interested in the people of his village.

But above all, what lights up these pages and what gives them their value is his liaison – platonic, no doubt, but passionate – with a forty-year-old woman. 'I shall help you to live; you will help me to die,' he says to her at the beginning of their love-affair. I know myself how much happiness a youthful friendship can bring into the life of an ageing person; and I can imagine the feelings of the eighty-year-old Clemenceau when he was with Madame B again – with her affectionate looks and her happy laughter. They wrote to one another every day, and he shared the smallest details of his life with her. Later she disappointed him a little; he thought her frivolous, vague and too apt to be sorry for herself. She 'scolded' him too often: though no doubt she did so because she worried about him – she knew very well that his death was close at hand. But at all events she never failed him, and he cherished her until his last moments. Although the two chief characters in this story are far removed from me, I am aware of the outstanding quality of their relationship. It would have left me unmoved, I believe, if I had not had a minimum of liking and respect for them. The feelings that exist between two utterly base creatures cannot be anything but depraved. Margarete's frantic love for Kent in *The Red Orchestra* merely fills me with repulsion.

If I am not in sympathy with a writer, my reading is not whole-hearted and what I read does not bite. I was enchanted with the eight volumes of George Sand's correspondence that Lubin brought out recently with a great wealth of notes and references: they bring a whole period back to life. Not long before I had seen Nohant and the Vallée noire, so my reading was more visually distinct than usual. But she irritates me. I like the young George Sand's determination to be independent, her eagerness in reading, educating herself, and travelling about the countryside; and I like the clarity of her decisions. When she was caught in the snare of a foolish marriage, she had the courage to leave for Paris to make a new life for herself and earn her own living.

Then later, I still respect her energy and her capacity for work. But she claps a virtuous mask over her face, and that sickens me. One may certainly have lovers, betray them and lie to them: why not? But if one does, then it is not right to proclaim one's love for the truth, utter shrill protests against evil tongues and give oneself saintly airs. She parades 'motherly' feelings for all her lovers: she goes to bed with Pagello, and at the same time she says they will both of them love Musset as 'their child'. Yet motherhood is not her strong point: she earns her daughter's hearty dislike, having humiliated her throughout the whole of her childhood, calling her 'my big fat girl', and telling her she is a fool, damping all her ardours with pedantic sermons, and granting her no more than a 'conditional' love – a terrifying thing for children, for whom emotional security is so necessary. Already at the age of thirty she poses as a woman broken by life and as one who devotes herself to others without reckoning the cost; in fact she is compelling everybody to wait on her hand and foot. What I forgive her least is the way she systematically falsifies her own inward language so that in every instance it transforms her behaviour into an edifying example. The lie is so

152

fundamental that I suspect even the attitude she displayed in 1848.[5]

It was also with an ambivalent mind that I read the three volumes of Anaïs Nin's *Journal*. There are some parts where I go along with her: when she speaks of Miller and his wife June, for example; when she remembers Artaud; when she gives a fairly penetrating description of people I have met; and when she honestly tries to recognize herself in her own past. But then all at once there she is under the domination of a wretched charlatan I once knew well, and I stop believing in her. I am embarrassed by her aestheticism, her narcissism, the narrowness of the world she artificially creates for herself, her immoderate indulgence in myth, and her silly passion for astrology. Her notion of femininity makes my hackles rise. All the time I was reading her, I wavered between candid acceptance and mistrust.

Reading the works of a writer whose values seem fundamentally erroneous sets a problem: for a text to have a meaning the reader must commit his freedom to it, silence his inner voice and instal another's within his own mind. This I cannot do if the falsity of the values accepted by the author is too staringly obvious and if his view of the world seems to me either childish or odious. Yet when I began Malraux's *Antimemoirs* I did hope that I should manage it. Given what he had been before the war, I was curious to know how he would justify the man he has become since then. What did he now think of the prophecies he uttered during the war in Algeria: 'We shall turn Algeria into a Tennessee Valley ... Fraternization has worked'? How would he explain the fact that it was possible for him to feel flattered at de Gaulle's tossing him 'a portfolio to gnaw', as Mauriac put it?

Did he really think he had done culture a great service by making people whiten the fronts of their houses, by having a ceiling painted, and by forcing *Son et Lumière* upon the dismayed Greeks, in the interests of Philips and Co.? I did not expect expressions of repentance, but I did hope that his book would provide me with answers to my questions.

How wrong I was! I was forgetting that the reason why Malraux's attitude since 1945 had seemed to me either grotesque or scandalous was that his entire conception of man, life, thought and literature was radically opposed to mine. At the very beginning of the book he warns the public that he is going to set himself on the

5 This edition stops at 1848.

highest plane – at the level not of individuals but of Civilizations, not of men but of their statues and their gods, not of everyday life and death but of Fate; in other words, that this world of ours, this earthly world, is to be spirited away in favour of humbug, of mystifying notions and concepts. Malraux spirits himself away, too. Apart from two or three episodes – the only parts of the book where I managed to follow him: passages that he must look upon as anecdotal and of minor importance – he is never there at all. 'What does that matter which only matters to me?' says he. When in spite of everything he does choose to define his position, this arrogance leads him to state that he is devoted to 'social justice', an expression dear to popes and dictators.

At the end of *Fibrils*, Leiris lays down the principles that he has tried to respect in his work as a writer – though without always succeeding, he says. Not to lie nor to indulge in fine words; to refuse all verbal inflation; to banish all purple patches; not to talk without rhyme or reason and turn writing into a meddlesome, busybody art; to write like a man who understands and appreciates the language, and to make use of that language only with the utmost rigour and fidelity. Malraux has taken the exactly opposite line. To claim that fraternization was anything but a mockery – to make that claim today would be a bare-faced lie, if the terms truth and falsehood had any meaning for him; but he does not distinguish the one from the other. For him words are merely *flatus vocis* – not that that prevents him from mistaking them for thoughts and supposing he has discovered an idea when he has merely chanced upon a formula. Looking at an object and telling honestly what he has seen is too modest an occupation for him: instead of facing up to it, he runs away. This is an exceedingly obvious tic or mannerism and it soon becomes unbearable: he always has to *think*[6] of something else. What does he think of this *other thing*? He never says: this something else makes him think of still another something; and he has no thoughts about that either. It is a continual series of hollow, meaningless intentions – nothing is made clear; everything is perpetually evaded. When he is in Cairo he *thinks* about Mexico or Guatemala or Antigua, where he *thought* about the beautiful baroque town of Noto. When he is with Mao, he *thinks* of Trotsky, of the Chinese emperors, of the 'deeply rusted carapaces of the army chiefs'. Confronted with the Great Wall, he *thinks* of Vézelay. In Delhi, he

[6] It is Malraux who uses the word 'think'.

thinks of the gardens of Babylon, of Cortez' soldiers, and the lotuses at Hangchow. He attends Jean Moulin's burial, and writes, 'I think of Michelet's account of the duel between Jarnac and La Châtaigneraie.' I could go on with this list for pages and pages. Paulhan advised writers not to enter the garden of literature carrying flowers. Malraux walks in loaded with wreaths, and he hides what he claims to display under heaps of rhetoric. Nor does he show us any one at all when he tells us about his meetings with Nehru or Mao. Everyone knows the value of meetings as official as these, even when they are well organized. But on top of that, Malraux is incapable of listening – he just talks: if he does ask any questions, he does so with such insistence that the other person is compelled to fit into a prefabricated frame – we never hear his real voice, but only that which Malraux forces upon him. In any case, Malraux is not concerned with informing his readers but rather with astonishing them, making them realize the breadth of his culture, the great extent of his travels and the quantities of well-known people he has met. The only function of his elaborate and often high-falutin' style is to mask the emptiness of what he has to say. It may be that in conversation these tricks give an impression of 'sparkle'; but when they are read the hollowness of these elegant flights is all too evident; and very often they conceal mere hackneyed truisms. Malraux has already made all he can out of themes such as realism in art, and all through the *Antimemoirs* he dishes them up again, together with commonplaces of right-wing thought – a thought that supports exploitation and that passes off the myths and values of the privileged classes as the truth about the human state. We hear emotional words about France, but none about the French people.

The most insidious form of lying is omission. Malraux says nothing about those periods of his life, those acts and words that he might find embarrassing to explain. It is impossible that he should not know that de Gaulle's government systematically covered torture and put men to death in the concentration camps by the thousand. I remember my interview with Michelet[7] and, when torture was mentioned, his embarrassed way of saying, 'I know, I know . . . It's a gangrene.' Malraux was equally well informed: from 1959 onwards there had been ever-increasing numbers of reports

[7] With reference to the Djamila Boupacha affair.

155

about the camps.[8] By giving the regime his unconditional support, Malraux set himself squarely on the side of the torturers. He is therefore flagrantly dishonest when, at the end of his book, he meditates at length upon torture, the camps and the techniques for bringing men down to the lowest pitch of abjection, as though he were placing himself on the side of the victims. Between 1940 and 1945 he, like many other Frenchmen, had friends who were among the victims; and when he was taken by the Germans in 1945 he may, for a while, have feared torture himself. But that does not authorize him to forget his complicity with those who tortured the Algerians. So this book, which is phoney from beginning to end, finishes with a huge imposture.

It is said that history never confesses. But for all that it has admitted certain facts since 1962. Never for a moment does Malraux take this into consideration. His mythomania exempts him from all need for justification.

As I have said, it is not only memoirs, letters and diaries that can communicate another person's experience to me, but also novels. Here I shall not speak of all that interested me during these last ten years; I shall only make use of a few examples to try to find out what it is that I look for and what it is that I can find in a novel.

A book that was a revelation to me was *Wolf Solent*, by John Cowper Powys, a writer of whom I knew nothing whatsoever until recently. The novel is both the description of a particular world and the adventure of a man; and this man, with whom the author wholly identifies himself, has many aspects, such as his fetishism and his animism, that remove him to a great distance from me. Yet for all that I moved into his world, and there I followed him step by step.

The action takes place in surroundings that are quite foreign to me, although at the same time they awaken memories in my mind. I can see those English villages with their embowered cottages where people drink tea and eat bread and honey, those green meadows, running streams and still, silent ponds: and there once again are the beloved country bedrooms, the candlesticks, the jugs and basins of my childhood. The characters upon this stage are shown to the

---

[8] In April 1959, Mgr Rodhain estimated the number of 're-located persons' at a million and a half; he gave an appalling description of their condition, and his words were confirmed by right-wing journalists and even by generals.

reader from so many aspects that at first he is taken aback; he wonders about them as though they were people he had actually met in the flesh. Their failures, their happinesses, their hopes and their disappointments really matter to him. Each of them has some painful secret deep within, usually of a sexual nature; each is haunted by memories and obsessions and each is inhabited by tormenting, shameful devils. (Their inner secrets are symbolized by the never-solved tragedy of the young secretary who throws herself into a pond.) Although Wolf Solent finds many of their aspects repulsive, he has an immense indulgence for all these people; for in them his anguished mind sees its own private torments.

Solent is at the centre of the action in all its phases, and all the objects and the people are seen through his eyes. He is a deeply selfish man, but he is capable of being haunted by an unhappy face seen for a passing moment, and he has that gift of fellow-feeling and sympathy which makes Powys a great writer. There is something of Rousseau about him, and the first link that joined us was his love for the countryside – a love like that which I felt in my childhood and adolescence, when it was the smell of the earth and the colours of the sky that showed me what my life was to be. I went with him on his lonely walks, and I too was fascinated by a pebble or caught up by the promise of far horizons. He has Rousseau's love for the immediate; and like Rousseau he will have nothing to do with technically practical, utilitarian, organized existence. He loathes the adults' ready-made words, order and systematic activity. Solent was dismissed from his post as a schoolmaster because, in a sudden outburst of verbal sincerity, he attacked the conventional values. He dreams of a life in which there are no orders or watchwords, a life in which routine would act as a background to freedom and leisure and in which he could give himself to his sexual fantasies and idiosyncrasies without restraint – sexuality pervades his entire world. He escapes from the shackles of daily existence through those illuminations granted him by nature; and these moments of perfect presence and perfect absence which for him are the absolute of happiness he calls his 'mythologies'.

From one end of the book to the other his essential concern is the search for his own truth; and by means of the unbroken continuity of his inner monologue he makes us take part in it. There are moments of sincerity in this search, but there are also points where he comes to a halt, where he runs away, and where he lies to

157

himself. One of Powys' particularly successful strokes is the way he manages to let us know the far side, the unlit side of his character, while at the same time that side remains unseen.

The adventure results in the destruction of his mythologies; and here, on the basis of a most extraordinary experience, he asks himself a question that concerns us all: 'How do men manage to go on living once their life-giving illusion is destroyed? What is it they patch together inside themselves so as to be able to drag on when this unique, incomparable resource dries up?' This is a question that confronts the ageing writer who has lost the illusion that writing will enable him to attain that fullness of being which all life reaches out for: when this happens he has to find sufficient reasons for living and even perhaps for writing again, and to find them in existence itself – in coexistence with the rest of mankind. Wolf Solent, at the age of thirty-six, saves himself from despair by basing himself upon the value of life itself, life taken at its most animal level. In fact the author must certainly have recovered other 'illusions', and among them, when he was about fifty-three, the joy of writing – it was at that age he began his first book. When he wrote *Wolf Solent* he was fifty-seven. One of the charms of this novel is its rich and glowing style, which comes through in the translation undimmed, and an immense narrative skill. Every other moment one stops, as one might in an enchanting walk, to admire the view called up by some passing phrase; and then the flow of the story carries one on.

This is an instance in which the novel is indeed a means of privileged communication. I found Powys' art, his personality and most of his themes once more in the autobiography he wrote some years after *Wolf Solent*. But here he dwells upon his peculiarities with greater insistence; and I was repelled by his self-centredness, his voluntary fixation upon his 'vices', the obstinate cultivation of his idiosyncrasies, and an indefinable complacency in the very style itself. The accounts of his travels are stubbornly confined within his self-chosen limits: they are depressingly meagre and inadequate. And the narrative is obscured by some odd prejudices: among others is his determination never to mention any of the women belonging to his family or his immediate circle – neither his mother nor his wife nor his women friends.

It was for completely different reasons that I liked Albert Cohen's

Belle du Seigneur. For him, nature scarcely exists; what interests him is the society that hems us in on every side. He describes a great love, the embodiment of one of this society's myths, and in doing so he throws a harsh light upon it.

1936. The sound of Nazi boots in the streets of Berlin. In the League of Nations plump officials yawn over their files, indifferent to what is happening in the world. The hero, Solal, is very like the author; he works in the League of Nations, and he looks at his colleagues with a dismayed irony. He makes us want to laugh and weep when he describes a cocktail-party at which superiors, inferiors and equals confront one another with a vivid sense of hierarchy – never a moment's respite from circumspection and devious, wary prudence. Decorations, promotion, social success: is it not ludicrous to attach so much importance to these baubles when one is a future corpse? Cohen is obsessed by the idea that every man is a corpse under suspended sentence. And to be sure no man escapes the grave. But if only one knows how to seize the fullness of the immediate instant, either in joy, action or revolt, then death draws back, and the corpse-to-be asserts itself as a living being in the present. There are few of those chosen souls. As the chief symbol of these silly, hollow ambitions, Cohen uses Adrien Deume, a League official; with merciless precision he tracks down his third-rate concerns and worries, his shoddy pleasures and his pointless, foolish panics. The system has dehumanized Deume; yet he might have been a man. He has a great fund of kindness. When misfortune strikes him (his beloved wife leaves him), Cohen, with a brotherly sympathy, gives him his own pitiful and touching reactions when he lost his mother.[9]

I have rarely read more amusing, nor more revengeful, passages than those in which Cohen brings Deume's parents on to the scene. He is sorry for little father Deume, who drags out his useless old man's existence under the harsh rule of his wife. But he hates mother Deume: he hates her false spirituality, her stupid vanity, her hardness, her pretentious vulgarity and her avarice. She is a perfect specimen of that grasping, selfish, hypocritical, racist bourgeoisie – the bourgeoisie that the Jew Solal feels is hunting him down.

Cohen contrasts this stuffy, futile society with the noisy, animal, carefree life of the Cephalonian Jews. I find the picturesque aspect of his 'Valeureux' irritating, yet they have to be there in order to

[9] He speaks of them in *Le Livre de ma mère*.

explain Solal. He and they have the same roots, but Solal has allowed himself to be contaminated by the western world; he condemns it bitterly, but he is unable to tear himself away.

This is the background to the development of the love-story, about which the novel hinges. Solal loves Ariane, Adrien Deume's wife; she is beautiful, noble by her birth and manner, and she finds the commonplace society around her very hard to bear. He seduces her and she leaves everything to go with him. Cohen manages to convey both the splendour of love and its wretchedness – the two sides of a single medal, as it were. He is wonderfully successful in making one feel the almost unbearable impatience of their waiting, the dazzling happiness when they do meet, the intoxication of seeing one's face reflected in loving eyes; and yet although for every single person these rapturous ecstasies are unique, they are also shown as wholly predictable and trite. Ariane clings to the myth of passion with a simple-mindedness that amuses Solal, touches his heart and exasperates him. For his own part, he launches into this affair with real fervour, but also with a grating scepticism. It does not save him from his isolation. He is alone when at the League he calls upon all countries to commit themselves to receiving the German Jews; he is alone when, sickened at their refusal, he anonymously denounces his fraudulent naturalization and is expelled from Geneva – he becomes a voluntary outcast, pursued by undefined but disgraceful suspicions. He is tragically alone when he walks through a Paris seething with anti-semitism and there puts on a grotesque false nose.

Ariane does not understand why they are wandering about France and Italy, living like gilded outlaws – for they are wealthy. They are cut off from the social dimension of life, and their passion has to supply all that is lacking. Ariane surrounds it with so many rites and ceremonies that she leaves no room for real affection. Each feels called upon to offer the other an idealized self-image, and this image strikes Solal as comic at first: these false refinements bore him and then they provoke an irritation that makes him very unkind. He contrasts them with love as it is experienced in Jewish marriages, love based on the giving and forgetting of self, on a common realization of human wretchedness, and on a common effort to take it upon oneself; a love that is frightened neither by ugliness nor disease. This too was the love that Mariette had known: she is their servant, and Ariane's artifices seem to her grotesque; she remembers her completely natural relationship with her husband, neither of them concealing the animality of their ordinary, everyday life. Why does Solal fall in with Ariane's game instead of trying to live with her in truthfulness? No doubt he feels that her background and upbringing make her incapable of doing so. His enmity for this impure society spills over on to her and also on to him; so he goes on cultivating the ethereal passion in which Ariane imprisons them both. But feelings as barren as these soon fade; to survive they have to turn to perversion, and if they want to be true to themselves they must end in death. Here again Cohen brings off a master-stroke. He shows us a cruel caricature of passionate love and yet at the same time he succeeds in giving it a pathetic dimension. Solal has a deep affection for Ariane. Although at times he treats her very harshly, torturing himself as he does so, he gladly looks after her when she falls ill, feeling not the least disgust for the physical squalor of her disease. And it is with an infinite tenderness that he nurses her dead body before he too kills himself.

It is easy for me to be pleased with a novel whose heroines are close to my heart: this was the case with Vitia Hessel's *Le Temps des parents*. Doris might have been one of my own friends; she is a left-wing intellectual, and she tries to maintain a balanced relationship with her husband, her children, her work and with politics, while at the same time remaining herself in the midst of all this piecemeal existence. She is very closely united with her husband and together they move through periods that mattered a great deal to me – the early days of the peace, and the war in Algeria.

Sometimes as I was reading, it seemed that I was with people I had known a very long while, and that we were exchanging memories. I am intimately acquainted with the physical background of the novel – the Latin quarter, the Luxembourg, the shops in the boulevard Saint-Michel, the quays along the Seine. I like being with the author as she walks about this city, describing it as though it were a landscape – the sky, the trees in leaf, the patch of white that is a wall, the colour of a house. The family that she speaks of is nothing like mine at all, yet it reminds me of my own childhood: this too is a home, a tightly-closed circle in which the grown-ups and the children live in a kind of symbiosis.

I have already said how concerned I am at present with the problems of very early childhood. Vitia Hessel treats the subject admirably. She shows how the adults were conditioned by their childhood and how they are conditioning their children's; the reader sympathizes with the parents, who devote themselves to the children but who at the same time try to preserve their own personal lives – sometimes, against their will, to the children's detriment; and he sympathizes with the children as they serve their difficult apprenticeship, sometimes with and sometimes against their parents. Vitia Hessel succeeds in a most unusual feat – that of letting us hear their inner monologue: she even carries us into one little boy's neurosis, using words to suggest that which lies beyond them – the void, the Unutterable, the Thing. We go through this child's horrible anxieties with him, and then through the slow crumbling of his resistance that leads to his healing. The author is also very good at describing the confusion and dismay of adolescence; she knows the great importance of friendship at this age, and the heart-rending sadness of a break; she brings back the restless unhappiness of a young heart that does not know how to express itself in words, and its horror of finding its secret detected, even if the detecting eye is intelligent and kind. Her characters' inner life is reflected and expressed by the outer world – she often shows a state of mind by speaking of the colour of the sky.

All the people in the novel are sharply distinguished, particularly Doris. Her husband looks upon her as a wholly unique being; yet she is also one of those countless mothers who hurry about the shops at the end of the holidays, buying shoes for their children. The book has a sociological dimension: it could be taken as an essay upon a twentieth-century French middle-class family. But that would be putting too low a value on it, for it also has a metaphysical dimension. It is not, as too many critics supposed, merely concerned with knowing *how* to bring up children but also with *why*. Most parents long to have outstanding offspring, but in the end they settle for less – the task of shaping a normal person, no more, is already hard enough. Is it worth all one's trouble and care? What is it that gives life its value, and what does the idea of normality really mean? Here it is the human state as a whole that is called into question.

But this novel does not yield up its wealth unless it is read carefully – between the lines. The explicit statement does not cover the reality of the actual experience, the feelings, the drives and the reticences. The subtlety of the relationship between the characters

162

lies in the fact that through a more or less deceitful and deceiving language they hear words that are true but that they interpret in their own fashion, more or less candidly. Some say that there is no communication between people – that they are opaque to one another; others say that there can be understanding: Vitia Hessel does not take sides. She rather points out that communication is never established once and for all, but is always yet to be achieved: and this achievement requires a great deal of love and candour.

I am also very fond of Claire Etcherelli's heroines, although I am less familiar with her world. I have already said what I like in her novels.

When I read Ehni's *La Gloire du vaurien* I found that my liking went to the writer rather than to his central character. I have nothing in common with the more or less homosexual young snob who travels all over Europe buying absurd quantities of clothes, luggage and knicknacks. I like seeing places I know – Heligoland, Munich and its monstrosities – in his company, but that is not enough to explain my pleasure in the book. The explanation lies in the skilful irony of Ehni's description of the wretchedness of a life entirely given over to being a consumer. Mani is a consumer who is most uncommonly good at consuming. He is wealthy, eclectic and sophisticated; he consumes whisky, silk scarves and pullovers; he also consumes landscapes, anecdotes, very good food, literature, music and pretty youths. He is aware of all the delicate shades that separate a tobacco-coloured from a cognac jersey. A young body can revive his memories of a masterpiece, and he can use his memories of a body to decipher a painting; and at the right moment he can recite to himself the appropriate poem. He meditates upon statues and Knoll furniture. He is likeable because of his sincere horror for everything that is ugly, that is to say vulgar and stupid. And also because he has an off-hand, insolent understanding of the paltry emptiness of all these amusements he deadens himself with: this gross excess of material and spiritual nourishment leaves a taste of ashes behind. Finally, amidst his pointless, silly activities, he asks the crucial question: what can one do here on earth? Why live? 'Here is my life: what am I to do with it? Help me: I am not competent.' Ehni chooses the easiest answer for his hero: one day his hand reaches out for a revolver.

I very much liked Solzhenitsyn's earlier books, *One Day in the*

Life of Ivan Denisovich and *Matriona's House*. Although I found *The First Circle* interesting, I did not recognize his voice in it; and there were many passages that did not ring true. But *Cancer Ward*[10] gripped me right away. It did not teach me a great deal, because I was already well informed about life in the Soviet Union; but mine was an abstract knowledge, whereas Solzhenitsyn's was immediate and concrete; and he made me share his experience. I made his disgusts and revolts my own; with him I felt pity, tenderness and hope; and I took part in his search for a truth that death cannot shake.

The ward is a microcosm, epitomizing the whole of the social, economic and political reality of the USSR. The time is 1955, the beginning of the 'thaw'. Manual workers, students, peasants, former deportees and one high official occupy the beds; and doctors, nurses and ward-maids revolve about them. They make up a world which is socialist in nothing but name – there is a glaring inequality in their earnings and their standards of living. The women have not shaken off the yoke of masculine oppression. Dontsova is a highly-qualified surgeon and physician, the equivalent of a consultant with us; nevertheless, when she goes home she has to do all her own housework, which is particularly arduous in the USSR. The individual reactions to this society vary widely: some of the characters are obstinately Stalinist, others do not care one way or another, and some are opportunists; Kostoglotov, an ex-deportee in whom the writer puts a great deal of himself, rejects it and even goes so far as to have doubts about socialism.

The one thing that is common to them all is their disease, cancer: at first they all react to it with an optimism that each derives from the feeling of his own uniqueness. 'It can't happen to me,' says Podduyev, the manual worker; and the high official Rusanov says just the same. Even the clear-sighted and courageous Dr Dontsova hesitates to believe it when she finds that she herself is affected. Rusanov's optimism is particularly stubborn: it is implicit in his view of the world, and this view is governed by his ideological interests. He is a totally-committed Stalinist, a profiteer and an informer – he has caused the deportation of a great many innocent people either because it was convenient to himself, or out of revenge, or out of mere wickedness. He is crammed with arrogance, and he has so thoroughly absorbed the privileges of his position that

10 Written between 1963 and 1967 and unpublished in the USSR.

even his body seems to him immune – it would be sacrilege if cancer presumed to touch it. He is one of the central figures in the book; and although Solzhenitsyn is sorry for him as suffering flesh gnawed by death, he uses Rusanov to attack everything he hates in Stalinism. Rusanov boasts of his working-class origins and parades his great love for the people; but he cannot bear being brought into contact with ordinary men and women, and by making use of his privileges he cuts himself off from them entirely. He thinks that there is a set reply to any question whatsoever, and he considers all free thought subversive. For him the golden age was 1937–8, when the public atmosphere was purified by means of the 'questionnaires' he was entrusted with drawing up. He trembles when History begins moving and when the rehabilitated deportees come home – he is afraid that one of his victims may find him and take his own revenge. His wife, covered with silver-fox furs, comes to see him in hospital; and both she and their daughter Aviette share his indignation. In spite of her youth, Aviette is as dehumanized as her father, wholly taken over by her family's ideological interests. She is scandalized by the 'dreadful' revision of the trials, and although she is delighted by the material progress that has been achieved in housing, equipment and clothing, she is censorious about moral decadence and Yevtushenko's poetry. She wants to be a writer, and through her Solzhenitsyn indirectly satirizes official Soviet literature. It is a subject he feels strongly about, and he touches upon it at the very beginning of the book, showing us Dyoma avidly reading the Stalin prize-winners and all the accepted 'masterpieces' yet at the same time being much upset by the contradictions he finds in them. Aviette is wonderstruck by the splendid position enjoyed by the members of the writers' union: they are wealthy, they are admired, and they hardly work at all – in three months they give birth to a novel. All that is needed for a thoroughly successful career in writing is a little skill – a little knowledge of how to take one's corners and to accommodate oneself to the times. When Dyoma asks her about sincerity in writing, she loftily explains that there is a danger that *subjective sincerity* may run counter to the truth – truth is that which *must be*, that which *will be tomorrow*.

Solzhenitsyn obviously enjoys lashing Rusanov's baseness, selfishness and wickedness; and he does so because Rusanov has been actively harmful. On the other hand he has an indulgence that goes as far as comparison for those opportunists who have merely gone along with the situation. Shulubin, for example, who confesses, 'I've spent my life being afraid.' Kostoglotov wonders whether enduring the rigours of the camps might not be better than living in dread and self-disgust.

The camps: once again Solzhenitsyn speaks of them. He shows the chasm that separates the detainees from the free members of the community – the night when the free men mourned Stalin's death was for the deportees a great outburst of joy that the guards could not suppress. Even now that he is free himself, Kostoglotov is isolated by what he has been through. He is not surprised when Aviette says that everyone who was sentenced must certainly have done something wrong; but even thoroughly good-natured women such as the intelligent Dontsova and the kind-hearted Zoya do not understand him when he talks about his past. On the other hand, there is an instant understanding between him and a ward-maid who was deported with her whole family in 1935, when a quarter of Leningrad's population was expelled. They *recognize* one another straight away.

It is against this historical and social background that we see the daily life of the hospital. Most of the doctors are women, and the author speaks of them with the greatest liking and sympathy: the staff is inadequate, and they are obliged to undertake an over-whelming amount of work, doing so with a high degree of profes-sional conscience and a great deal of human compassion. Yet many of the patients, including Kostoglotov, come into conflict with them. He feels that not telling the patients the truth means not treating them as free men – it is a kind of oppression; but when it comes to the point he cannot bring himself to reduce a fellow-patient to despair, although he knows there is no hope for him; and the patient leaves the hospital, believing himself to be cured. Kostoglo-tov also blames the doctors for not knowing what they are doing: the doctors are aware of their ignorance and of the problems that arise from this ignorance – the rays heal the tumours but later on they also damage and atrophy the tissues. Should treatment be withheld just because its consequences cannot all be foreseen? Then there is another source of disagreement. The doctors want to cure their patients at all costs. But is life worth living in no matter what conditions? That is what Kostoglotov wants to know. Should one agree 'to have one's life preserved at the price of everything that gives it its value, savour and feeling'? At first, when he learns that although certain injections improve his physical condition they also make him impotent, he refuses them: in the end he resigns himself to the treatment. Thus when the author is confronted with the question, he does not take sides. He understands both the doctors' point of view and the patients'. What he does show us is that they are on opposite sides of the barricade. This separation becomes strikingly obvious when Dontsova finds that she herself has cancer. At this point 'everything turns completely upside-down'. Her relationship with her body, with life, with death – everything is thrown into total disarray.

Most of the patients lull themselves with hope – a word or a smile from the doctor reassures them. They dream of miraculous cures. But there are times when they feel their death staring straight at them. Rusanov is the only one who will not look it in the face, so incapable is he of any attempt at sincerity. As his nightmares show, he is in fact eaten up with fear; but he clings to the idea that he will get better. He thinks his companions' discussions morbid and he tries to stop them. 'Why prevent a man from thinking?' replies Kostoglotov. 'Whether he belongs to a group or not, his death is his own business.' All of them feel that what is challenged is the very meaning of their life itself. Many of them, like Podduyev, thought that they knew what they were living for – for work and making money. Brought face to face with cancer, these reasons no longer make sense. Podduyev looks for a better solution in Tolstoy's *What Makes Men Live?*, and the answer 'it is love' satisfies him. Solzhenitsyn adopts it for himself: the worst plague on earth is wickedness; and this evil is symbolized by the person at the zoo who blinds a rhesus monkey by throwing tobacco in its eyes. A happy world would be one based on man's good-will towards man. Then everyone could enjoy all that makes life beautiful – work that you like doing, friends, domestic animals, an apricot-tree in bloom. 'It is not their standard of living that makes men happy, but rather the linking of hearts and our outlook on the world.' The author is of the opinion that asceticism suits men better than seeking after abundance.

There is a religiosity in the moral he points out that annoys me. And I do not accept the formula 'man is always happy if he wants to be' – a formula in which he obviously does not wholly believe himself. But I am entirely with him when he advises people 'to make do with what they have' and when he rejects the alienations, the tricks and lies that take man's humanity away from him. According to Solzhenitsyn, the more intensely aware one is of the world and the more one is concerned with helping others, the better one lives. I fully agree with these conclusions.

In his *The German Lesson*, Lenz[11] shows us a certain aspect of Nazism – that which millions of Germans lived through, in half-ignorance and total agreement, in the common round of daily life. The story begins in 1943 and it ends after the victory of the Allies. It is set in a remote corner of northern Germany – a vast windswept plain, dunes, a dyke, seagulls, the sea in the distance. The war is ever-present – air-raids, the radio pouring out false news, the un-savoury henchmen of the regime, its victims. Lenz shows it to us through the eyes of a child, perhaps because it was as a child, a little older than his hero Siggi, that he experienced the war and the years that came after it. In his reformatory-school, Siggi, now aged twenty, is told to write an essay on the 'joys of duty'. He moves back ten years to recapture his past, because the word duty instantly conjures up his father's face.

This father, Jepsen, is a policeman, and he is stationed at the last police post before the frontier. Not far off there lives a painter; his name is Nansen, and the authorities look upon him as a 'degenerate' artist. At first the regime made advances but he rejected them: his pictures were confiscated and the galleries where he exhibited were closed. He goes on painting.

In the first place Jepsen is told to confiscate Nansen's latest pictures and then to prevent him from carrying on with his painting. In their childhood they had been friends, and Nansen had even saved Jepsen's life: but orders are orders. 'It's nothing to do with me and I can't do anything about it,' he says to the painter. Another time he says, 'I have my orders: I'm only carrying them out.' Orders: when none have been given him from outside, he works them out for himself – he feels obliged to flog Siggi for trifling faults; and when his elder son (who has mutilated himself so as not to go to the front and who has run away from the hospital) takes refuge in his house, it is Jepsen who decides 'to do what must be done' – that is to say, to hand him over to the police. He is not exactly evil – his face turns grey as he picks up the telephone to call the station. But he knows

[11] A German novelist belonging to the same generation as Gunther Grass, with whom he is often compared.

168

no reason for living, other than a blind obedience to what he looks upon as the law. He is lifeless and empty: he is capable of spending days on end doing nothing and thinking of nothing, staring vaguely at a blank wall. He is happy only when he is given a clearly-defined task to carry out: then he feels useful and important; he assumes a martial air and his life takes on a meaning. He catches Nansen in the act of painting and denounces him: 'I am only doing my duty,' says he. 'When you talk about duty you make me feel sick,' says the painter; who also observes, 'Duty – I look upon it as so much blind assumption. People inevitably do more than it requires.' Just so: nobody requires Jepsen to be perpetually spying on Nansen nor to persecute him for the smallest details. The neighbourhood feels that he goes too far and that he is turning it all into a personal matter. In one sense this is not so: he does not care a damn about Nansen and his pictures; but it is true that the carrying out of a 'duty' removes him from his dim twilight and deceives him into feeling that he is a man of real importance in the world.

This illusion is so necessary to him that the idea of duty becomes an obsession. Once the war is over Nansen is loaded with honours. Jepsen spends three months in prison, but then he is given back his job; he doggedly persists in wanting to destroy Nansen's pictures; he searches his hut and burns his sketch-books outside it. Siggi, filled with disgust at his father's 'unshakeable good conscience', rises up for the first time crying, 'You've no right to do that.' His father hits him. 'A man must do his duty even when times change,' he replies. But there is a wild look in his eyes and a panic-stricken despair beneath his defiant attitude. He was dehumanized with his own consent, and this dehumanization is an irreversible process; the collapse of the values by which he lived does not show him the truth but urges him on to a wild flight forwards. He is overcome with blind rage; he sets fire to a mill in which Siggi has hidden some of Nansen's pictures.

Siggi speaks out only when his father's behaviour pushes him beyond all bearing. He is himself used to obeying, and he quietly submits to the beatings that are inflicted upon him. When his brother asks Siggi to hide him, he says, 'Father has the right to know.' He does keep the secret, but only because he has always obeyed the elder brother. He is perpetually on the watch, yet he never allows himself to form any judgment – he describes things just as he sees them; and his way of seeing them has nothing of the simplicity that is conventionally attributed to children. Siggi is very gifted, and so precocious that the painter is on terms of real friendship with him; he is the somewhat neurotic product of a sick society, and in his descriptions we note numerical exaggerations similar to those seen in schizophrenia – the painter's house has four hundred windows, his drawing-room can hold nine hundred people, and the sofa is a hundred feet long: there is something insane about the meticulous precision of his accounts. He almost never expresses what he feels. Yet in spite of the words' apparent lack of emotion one can make out the unspoken feelings that stirred within him, the unformulated experience that caused him to behave in unexpected ways, such as gathering the pieces of a painting torn up by his father, getting hold of some confiscated sketches, and hiding his collection in a mill. After the old building is destroyed by fire, he is afraid that other paintings of Nansen's may be burnt; he steals canvases from Nansen's studio and from galleries and hides them. No doubt this action, an expression of anxiety, is also a protest against the legality that he has come to hate because of his father. And this is the reason why, in spite of the painter's good-will, he is in his reformatory.

As well as the barren hell in which Jepsen has his being, the author also shows us glimpses of the joys that could light up the world if only hateful fanaticism did not stifle them – friendship, love, affection. Siggi and Nansen are often overwhelmed by the world's beauty, and at the painter's house the delight of seeing is combined with the noble pride of creating. The crime of Jepsen and of those like him is that of destroying the riches that can give human life a meaning.

The story is told with a simplicity that is in fact a very great art. Siggi's past and present, cleverly interwoven, throw a light upon each other. Our concern for the child carries on to the twenty-year-old prisoner, and it is reflected back again.

Lenz brings off the most difficult of feats: he shows us a painter in the act of creation. Generally speaking those novelists who attempt to bring an artist or a writer on to the stage fail dismally. In *The German Lesson*, when Lenz shows us Nansen in the act of painting, we actually see him, and we believe in his inspiration and his doubts. For us his work really exists.

The sober, almost neutral style is remarkably effective and alive. Throughout the book the writer lets the facts speak for themselves, never stepping in himself. Apart from two or three remarks by the painter, and Siggi's cry, there is no commentary to emphasize Jepsen's baseness: his behaviour seems ordinary and in a way normal. It does not unleash any disaster; but it does explain how disasters are unleashed. Preventing a painter from painting – what strikes one most about such an act is its meanness; but when the policeman says 'I have my orders; I am only carrying them out,' one sees that he would have used the same words if he had been given the task of exterminating hundreds of thousands of men. Hitlerism was possible because millions of Germans, either out loud or under their breath, uttered the same alibi as Jepsen: 'It's nothing to do with me, and I can't do anything about it.' Lenz denounces the falsehood of this alleged passive submission; carrying out an order necessarily means going beyond it; and neutrality always means complicity. Confronted with Nazism, Stalinism and the American massacres in Vietnam, I, like everyone else, have often wondered how a whole nation, a whole army, can possibly consent to such atrocities. Lenz's novel brings no new answer; but it does pinpoint what Hannah Arendt called the 'ordinariness of evil' when she was speaking of the Eichmann trial; and it conveys a fuller understanding of this evil than any merely factual knowledge.

I hardly read poetry at all: yet it is a very special means of communication. It was a great help to me when I was young: I loved repeating poems to myself. There are some that still haunt my memory; and I will quite often look into Baudelaire, Rimbaud or Mallarmé. I turn back with delight to the poets I loved when I was twenty – to Laforgue or Saint-Léger. Yet I cannot tell how – perhaps because I have not made the necessary effort to penetrate it – but the poetry of today awakens no echo in me. There may be a vicious circle here: since I doubt whether I shall enjoy modern verse, I do not try to get to know it. I think I am at fault. But there are so many other works that call for my attention that I have little hope of amendment.

Often enough, and particularly when I am on holiday, I will open a book without expecting to derive anything but amusement from it. At one time I liked science-fiction. It is fun, wondering about the possible variations of our world and state and travelling a great way off in time and space. But in recent years no book of this kind has satisfied me. It may be that the range of imaginable situations was

171

limited and that it has now been exhausted. The writers I have read lately lack fantasy; they deal arbitarily with worlds that are either too like ours or too vague, and with creatures whose peculiarities are modelled on worn-out patterns. I have never been able to take off for another universe.

On the other hand, I am easily involved in a detective, spy or adventure story. Just why is this, and what conditions have to be fulfilled?

In the first place the fictitious world I move into must be sufficiently coherent for me to take a firm footing there: sometimes this is achieved by a faithful imitation of our present world, as in the case of Japrisot's enchanting novel *The Lady in the Car with Glasses and a Gun*. Here the action of the book takes place along the Paris-Marseilles road, and I liked remembering it as I read about the adventures, which took on something of the road's reality. In the same way Patricia Highsmith's novels begin by creating surroundings, an atmosphere and a set of characters that are sufficiently probable for me to be able to belive in their existence; and the rest of the story profits from this belief. Yet I have noticed that among her novels I am really interested only in those where a murder has been committed: when there is no murder, her heroes' psychology seems to me conventional and I lose interest in them. For me to put up with their deficiencies there has to be suspense – I have to want to solve a mystery or to know the outcome of some terribly threatening event. It is only then that I will go along with the story, behaving as though I believed in the world it offers me. If a detective story grips me from the start – by vivid dialogue or a really cunning riddle or a challenge or a wager – then it does not matter if the plot is rather wild: so long as it is well constructed I will pretend to believe in it. Painting to know who did it, or whether the hold-up will succeed, or how the secret agent will manage to carry out his mission, I will consent to look upon a CIA man as a hero and to regard the Chinese, the Soviets or the Koreans as so many fiends. Yet to be really involved I must be able to identify myself with the hero and to want the story to end well for him. I found this easy with Japrisot's '*Lady*' and with Patricia Highsmith's likeable criminals. I readily join in the plans of the brave or sharp-witted private detective who is carrying out an inquiry. It is harder when the character the author wants me to follow is a policeman; in that case I am often unable to get inside him.

172

People will say I am wasting my time: but that is not a commodity I hoard. I will happily play draughts; I do crosswords; I try to work out puzzles. Why should I not read a detective story – a *Série noire* or the Italian equivalent, a *giallo*? Generally speaking I prefer books that give me something in addition to amusement. But not always. There are times when weariness makes me choose something easy to read. And then a book that I take seriously absorbs my whole attention and I lose myself in it; my pretence of going along with a detective story leaves me aware of my identity and of my physical situation – there are moments I value so very highly that I still want to remain fully conscious of them although I am doing something else at the same time. When I read books of this kind my mind has to be very free, because of the gratuitous nature of the diversion they offer: if I am taken up with other things they fail to hold my attention. They need reading straight off: apart from a very few exceptions, if I once close them there is no going back – my interest has weakened and I cannot bring it to life again.

I rarely turn to old books that I have never read. The very fact of my having neglected them so far diminishes my opinion of them – why should I find them interesting all at once? I know nothing about Paul-Louis Courier's works: they are within hand's reach, but I feel no urge to tackle them. In any case when I am in Paris I have no time to step into a world that for years I have never cared about and that is in no way connected with me. Sometimes when I am on holiday I do make up my mind to take the plunge. The stimulus is particularly strong if I am getting myself ready to see a foreign country that I want to know well. When I went to Japan I delighted in the admirable English translation of the *Tale of Genji* and I went through Tanizaki's books. But when I am on holiday I may also read French authors I either do not know well or have forgotten.

One year I was enthralled by Michelet's *History of the French Revolution*; when it is reprinted I shall gladly take his *History of France* to Rome with me. Although at one time I had studied Madame de Sévigné, my knowledge of her was very poor indeed: I took the utmost pleasure in discovering her as I read the three Pléiade volumes of her letters. On the enthusiastic advice of a friend, I read Barbey d'Aurevilly not long ago: until then he had scarcely existed as far as I was concerned.

Here I come back to a problem that I mentioned before: how can

I participate in the writing of a man whose opinions I reject? As I have said, most of the time I cannot do so at all. But I was charmed by Barbey d'Aurevilly's style, his fire, his verbal daring and his invention. I am not haunted by ghosts of the past as he is; but sometimes they do hover about me and I find it understandable that he should be obsessed by them. I can still feel the anxiety of twilight and the desolation of a naked moor; and when he speaks of the loneliness and the mists of the Cotentin I too am moved. He takes the side of the Chouans and the priests with so passionate a conviction that he arouses my curiosity, and while I am actually reading him he persuades me to see things in the same light as he does. Some of his pieces seem to me dull and tired. But when his imagination fires up and he takes off at a gallop, it is a delight to let him carry one along. There is a young noble who is in love with the daughter of the *married priest*; she will not have him, so to overcome her resistance the young man decides to bring about a spectacular accident in her presence. He harnesses two unbroken horses to a cart and makes them drunk: they knock down everything that stands in the way until they reach the steps outside the girl's house and there the whole thing is smashed to pieces. I shall never forget that furious headlong rush, wilder and more astonishing than the bravest car-driver's feats on the screen.

Often I do not feel inclined to re-read old books I already know. My eyes run along the Pléiade volumes in Sartre's library, and I turn away. To be sure, I am very far from knowing all Balzac, Zola, Dickens and Dostoevsky by heart, but I do know that they will take me into a world whose taste has gone stale. Even in the case of writers who are particularly dear to me, such as Stendhal or Kafka, I hesitate to open their books again. I know just how poor and thin my recollection is; but the idea of going to explore a country that I can no longer call to mind fills me with lassitude: as one re-reads one remembers what one should be discovering, or at least one has the illusion of doing so; and one is deprived of what constitutes the 'joy of reading' – that free collaboration with the author which is something very like creation. Yet I did take a great deal of pleasure in re-reading Diderot's letters to Sophie Volland. And there are two writers I love returning to almost indefinitely – the Rousseau of the *Confessions*, and Proust. I wait for some of their turns of speech just as Swann waited for Vinteuil's '*petite phrase*', and when they appear they give me an exquisite feeling both of miracle and inevitability. Some poets give me the same pleasure; as I have said, my relationship with poetry is almost solely that of re-reading.

Sometimes I find that I have entirely forgotten books that I read long ago; I discover them all over again, without their wakening any recollection in me at all. During these last years this has been the case with Lermontov, Goncharov and Shchedrin. At one time I was enthralled by Saint-Simon's *Memoirs*; I have just taken them up again and I find that apart from a few often-quoted lines I remember nothing. The first three volumes contain more tedious passages than I should have supposed – too many battles and family-trees. I was charmed, though not astonished, by the style, the rhythm, the racy descriptions of manners and morals and by the pungency of the anecdotes; but I was surprised by the complexity of Saint-Simon's portraits. They often begin with praise that is presently counterbalanced by criticism, and the criticism in its turn is qualified by more flattering views – one has to go right back over the whole picture from the beginning to find the true balance between these different strokes; and in doing so one sees that far from cancelling each other out they are in fact complementary, making up an extraordinarily living character.

My opinion of a re-read book often coincides with my earlier view. Sometimes I understand it better because good critical articles have provided me with useful keys. The recent French translation of Ellmann's biography of Joyce showed me the relationships between his writing and his past and certain places in Dublin and its neighbourhood; and this gives some passages a far greater wealth of meaning. It may also happen that what I had thought of as a faded, colourless book takes on an unexpected freshness, quite astonishing me. Thus not long ago I rediscovered the Bible. It was astounding to find that no more than three lines would contain episodes that I had thought of as very, very much longer, they being the source of so many pictures, plays and poems: I was astonished that accounts as short as these should so have bred and multiplied in the imagination of mankind. And characters my memory had rendered commonplace staggered me by their extraordinary behaviour – Abraham shamelessly pimping for his wife, for example. I knew that Jehovah was harsh and wrathful, but I had not thought him so mean and paltry. I remembered the Hebrews as a bellicose, chauvinistic people; but I was astonished at the extent of the massacres they perpetrated. In short, although the book was so

175

familiar to me from my earliest days, I found that I did not know it at all.

Re-reading may be a disappointment. Sometimes my memory has preserved confused, disconnected, dubious notions in the shape of some striking formula. Or, on the other hand, the few words I remembered had provided me with the basis for extensions and developments that never existed in the book. At a first reading, instead of going along with the author and his plan, one may listen to the reverberation of words that are in harmony with one's own fantasies and obsessions. That is what I used to do when I was twenty. Nowadays I try to be more objective. But sometimes a cross-check shows me that I have not been altogether successful. My memories of books, like my memories of reality, are incomplete and distorted.

My activity as a reader does not consist solely of gathering together the specific instants of one particular book, but also of relating various works that correct, complement or resemble one another. *The German Lesson* helped me to understand the high official in *Cancer Ward*; and as their epigraph both novels might carry Wilde's remark about wickedness being only a 'lack of imagination'. In this way I bring into being a bookish world that overlies and overflows the real world, lighting it up and enriching it; and in some cases this superimposed universe has greater depth and brilliance – Emma Bovary or Monsieur de Charlus exist more sharply for me than many people I have actually met. They also exist for other people, who see them from different angles but who communicate with me by means of them. It has been said, and very truly, that literature is the field of intersubjectivity. Alone in my room with a book, I feel in contact not only with the writer of it, but also, through time and space, with its readers.

Reading evokes no more than vague, uncertain images in my mind; those of dreaming may enchant me, but they are contradictory and evanescent. But those offered by the cinema have all the fullness of perception – they *are* perceptions, and perceptions grasped as the analogon of an absent reality. Apart from documentary films, they are usually so constructed that they make up a fictitious world; the director tells a story that takes place in time, as irreversible as a piece of music. As in reading, it is my presence that gives the story its unity and its meaning. But here mine is a less active role; I am not required to interpret symbols but to receive the impact of immediately-presented pictures. That is why seeing a film generally calls for less effort than reading a book. I only have to attend, and cheerfulness, anxiety, sympathy or disgust are imposed upon me. The feelings that affect me may reach such a pitch as to be physically overwhelming: spectators sometimes pass out at a particularly gruesome scene, which is something that does not happen during the reading of a book. (At the age of fourteen Colette did faint away when she was reading Zola's account of a childbirth, but this was an exceptional case.) And people cry more easily in a cinema than when they are reading a novel. Yet a director who wishes to set up a real communication with the audience will take the greatest care not to arouse a mental disturbance that might cloud their vision: like a good writer, he will make his appeal to their freedom.

The potency of images comes from the fact that they provide the illusion of reality, an illusion that I accept in a state of near-passivity. Even at those moments of my life when I am freest, most disengaged, there are plans and memories deep in my mind, and actions are taking shape. When I go into a cinema, I leave my actual self at the door; and although my past is certainly there behind me as I react to the film, it is not there as a conscious entity and my only project is to watch the scenes that go by before my eyes. I accept them as true, and I am not allowed to intervene in any way; my praxis is paralysed, and in some cases this paralysis emphasizes the unbearable nature of the pictures, while in others it makes them enchanting. Sitting there in front of the screen I surrender myself entirely, as I do in dreams; and in this case too, it is visual images that hold me captive – that is why the cinema awakens dream-like echoes in each beholder. If a film affects me deeply, it does so either because it stirs unformulated memories or because it brings unspoken hopes back to life. Sometimes, when I discuss a film with friends – friends whose tastes are the same as mine in other fields – I find that my opinion is quite unlike theirs: the film has certainly touched them or me or all of us in some intimate, entirely personal area.

The faces of the actors are of great importance to me. Faces elude analysis, conceptualization, words: almost no writer succeeds in making us see his heroes' features. Proust manages to suggest them, but the outline remains vague and indistinct. On the screen they are as sharply there as though they were present in the flesh before my

177

eyes. It is an ambiguous presence – that both of the actor and of the character he is playing. The relationship between the two varies. If the actor is really inside the character's skin, then the character alone exists, and I am ready to believe in his story. On the other hand, I find it hard to go along with him if I see the actor showing through the hero as he walks and talks upon the screen. This happens when I know the actor too well or when there is a disparity between his physical appearance and the part he has to play. Bad casting has spoilt some films for me; others, in spite of certain shortcomings, have delighted me because a man's or a woman's face has gone right to my heart. A special case is that in which the actor turns himself once and for all into the analogon of one particular character: on the screen, the distance between Mr Chaplin and Charlie is entirely done away with.

The cinema often shows me stretches of the countryside or urban landscapes that I did not know: it adds a great deal to my knowledge of the world. And it often carries me into surroundings that are familiar to me: I love seeing places that I have liked in their contingent aspect, made an essential part of a work of art which gives them a necessity – the streets of London, for example, or a square in Rome. Sometimes the cinema allows me to satisfy the childish desire to be in a place and yet at the same time not to destroy its solitude by my presence – the desire of seeing my absence with my own eyes. I seem almost to succeed in doing so when I am in a plane flying over a rocky island lying there in the blue sea. A film may give me the same kind of illusion. I do not belong in this moor that spreads out over the screen; although my eyes explore it, it still remains totally uninhabited.

It is not only landscapes that I catch unawares in this way. I slip silently into houses; I am present at events that cannot be seen. I sit by the bed upon which lovers make their love; I walk into a room where a man has taken refuge to hide his grief-stricken face. Then I have another privilege, that of gathering separate elements into one single spectacle. Here is a crowd, a crowd in which each individual is lost in the mass; yet my eyes embrace the whole. I pass through walls, I hover in the sky; I am endowed with supernatural powers.

As it is with books, the profit I derive from films varies greatly. They are an amusement in any event, and often I ask nothing more of them. Laughter is enough for me. The funniest book never produces more than a smile, because laughter is a collective form of behaviour. The conditions for laughter are fulfilled in a cinema, where the audience is made up of people who do not know one another – strangers sitting side by side. But for me to share in the general mirth, the film must not make me react in a way that is hostile to laughter – because of their vulgarity I carefully avoid French films that claim to be funny.

These last years I have had great fun watching old Buster Keaton films, *The Cameraman, Steamboat Bill Junior, Seven Chances, Spite Marriage,* and the one I like best of all, *The Navigator.* As Sartre has shown,[12] a comic situation is often the result of the contrast between the subject's inner experience and his state as a material object. Buster Keaton's face expresses the tension in a serious-minded, self-controlled man who asserts that he is competent: his dream is perpetually contradicted by the malevolence of inanimate objects and even of the very instruments he believes he has mastered; machines unexpectedly lash back, depriving him of that human dignity which his face nevertheless continues to express with a steady obstinacy. Keaton has spoken of 'the mathematical calculations required to work out a gag', and indeed his films give the same aesthetic pleasure as the elegant solution of a mathematical problem. They are wonderfull little mechanisms with perfectly adjusted gears. The Harry Langdon films such as *Tramp, Tramp, Tramp* and *The Strong Man,* that have recently been shown again, have less rigorous exactitude, but there are amusing things to be found in them, and I particularly like his character's ingenous charm – the baby face and the childishly affected gestures.

I took great pleasure in seeing Charlie Chaplin once more in *The Circus* and *Modern Times* – neither has lost anything of its freshness. In the second even more than in the first I rediscovered everything that I had liked so much before, and I was delighted to see that the audience, almost all young people, appreciated the film as much as I did.

Some adventure-films have kept me in suspense: there was *L'Homme de Rio,* with the cheerful Belmondo; some of Walsh's old pictures like *Murder Inc.* and *White Heart* in which James Cagney surpassed himself; some westerns, including films made by Italians, such as *The Good, the Bad and the Ugly;* and James Bond's adventures in *From Russia with Love* and *Goldfinger.* Stories that I should think ludicrous if they were written down can enchant me on

12 See Sartre, *L'Idiot de la famille,* pp. 816–17.

the screen – I could not be bothered with Bond in print. A film moves much faster than a book: my eyes grasp a situation that would take a long time to explain in words; yet if a writer hurries events beyond a certain limit he fails to make them convincing. Pictures on a screen are far more persuasive. There is an odd shift, a difference of phase, between the immediate evidence of one's eyes (the indestructible illusion of reality) and the unlikelihood of the facts. If a director uses this shift intelligently, he can make it produce the most delightful effects. That is the basis both of the humour of the Italian westerns and of the charm of Sean Connery's outrageous feats. But it has to be used intelligently. If the plot does not hold together, if the rhythm is too slow and if the actors do not fill their roles properly, then I will not go along with what I am shown. And if there is not fantasy and dash in the invention, then as far as I am concerned the flatness is too wearisome.

The Italian directors often come up with an ingenious combination of improbability and realism. *The Priest's Wife*, in which Sophia Loren and Mastroianni acted with mischievous subtlety, had some very amusing gags; but the film was also a serious attack upon the sanctimoniousness of priests and the hyprocrisy of the Church. *Jealousy Italian Style* makes one laugh heartily; yet here too the chief characters are drawn with great accuracy – a woman and two men who are insufficiently armed against the complications of their love and insufficiently helped by society to overcome the resulting disasters. At first glance the scenes in which Monica Vitti is taken to hospital after each of her suicides are very funny; but in fact they are both savage and heart-breaking. It is the ordinary people of Rome who move across the screen: one sees the setting in which they live, work and have fun. Theirs is a city very unlike the tourists' Rome: and we see Ostia not as a wilderness of ruins but as a general meeting-place for whores.

There are some ambitious directors who try to communicate their vision of the world to me; and mine is enriched if they succeed in doing so. This was the case with Pasolini's *Medea*. He answered a question that had worried me – how was it that some civilizations were able to reconcile a high degree of culture with the barbarous rites of human sacrifice? In *Medea* Pasolini brings forward no new evidence. But by means of a great deal of work and by the choice of astonishing landscapes and of Callas – an extraordinary actress in this film – he succeeds in re-creating the world of the Sacred. A superb young man is put to death, cut to pieces and devoured before our eyes: the sight is so gravely beautiful that we are not in the least horrified. As she hurries away towards the sea, Medea cuts off her brother's head and throws his quivering flesh behind her chariot; yet the act does not take away from the nobility of her face. Later, when she is set down in rationalistic Greece, Medea loses her magic powers: this second part seemed to me much less successful.

I was also struck by Arrabal's *Viva la muerte*, in which he speaks of Franco's Spain. I am very fond of his plays – I have not seen any, but I have read them – so I was eager to see his first film. In spite of some remarkably successful strokes, in the dream-like scenes he tends to give way to facility. But those which aim at displaying reality possess the dark and bitter poetry of a controlled nightmare: astonishing scenery, actors who entirely fit into their parts, and shots that are on the contrary strangely remote – all these lead the viewers into a squalid, ferocious world – a world seen through the naive, frightened eyes of a child. This child gradually finds out that his mother, so lovely in her black clothes, betrayed his father to the fascists: and he slowly dies of revolt and hatred.

In *Hara-Kiri* Masaki Kobayashi's intention is to destroy a certain mythical idea of the feudal era in Japan. The nobles do not form a heroic caste: they are profiteers, caring nothing for the wretchedness of the people or the poverty of the samurai. The great noble we are shown is odiously cruel: a samurai, reduced to the last extremity, comes to ask him for help, according to the usual custom, and swears that if his request is not granted then he will cut open his belly there in the very house. The noble condemns the samurai to an exceptionally horrible hara-kiri, since in his extreme poverty the man has sold his sword – the weapon in his sheath is made of wood. The dead samurai is revenged; and his avenger inflicts an atrocious humiliation upon those who caused his death before killing several of them during a battle in which he takes on the whole household single-handed. In this picture the simple, realistic description of poverty stands out against epic scenes of a fiery, passionate beauty.

Some admirable Hungarian films have been shown in Paris these last few years. Jancso's *The Round Up* showed me the nature of the nineteenth-century risings in Hungary better than any book could have done. I was not so pleased with his *The Red and the White*, a film in which he leaned more towards aestheticism. As I watched Kosa's *Ten Thousand Suns* I lived through the agrarian reform in

181

the Hungarian countryside: and here too the sight of the land, the farms and the faces gave me a better understanding of history than any printed text.

Visconti too tried to illustrate a page of history with his *The Dammed*: but in spite of its magnificence, his film left me unmoved. When it is well handled, improbability can make one laugh or smile: but it wrecks dramatic effects. Although the actor had great talent I did not believe in the character of Martin: he embodied altogether too many vices. The orgy before the Night of the Long Knives and the arrival of the boat loaded with black men at dawn were magnificent spectacles; but they were spectacles that did not correspond with historical truth. The baroque, ice-cold funeral ceremony that ended the film was a perfect example of plastic beauty. But I was too clearly aware of the presence of the director, and I watched the scene from a distance, not believing in it.

On the other hand *Z*, the film that Costa-Gavras based on Vassilikos' novel, is impregnated through and through with truth. I know Yves Montand's face too well, and for a moment this prevented me from seeing him as Lambrakis; but soon the actor and the character merged into one. I knew that the events that I was watching were authentic: it was a new experience to see an imaginative copy of reality on the screen, re-created so exactly that it preserved all the tragic weight of the original.

Films that bring historical events back to life interest me: so do those which show me certain new aspects of the society I belong to. Using a fictional plot in his *Les Coeurs Verts*, Luntz made me acquainted with a gang of youths who acted themselves – who were their own characters; they enabled me to share in their long boredom, their dismay and their bitterness. Beneath their affectation of cynicism one could sense feelings that they were unable either to put into words or to take upon themselves; and I suffered with them.

It is unusual to see the proletariat on the screen. Some Italian films have described their struggles or denounced the crimes of capitalism; but as it happens I have not seen them. Yet in 1965 I did see two excellent English films, both of which were about the revolt of a young man of the exploited class. The author of the scripts was Allan Sillitoe, a tanner's son who became a writer and who has kept closely in touch with the people among whom he was born and bred. I knew nothing about the actors who played the chief parts, which meant that I could identify them entirely with the characters. In *Saturday Night and Sunday Morning* a young working-man rises up in revolt against his state, his whole condition of life: he makes use of his week-ends in an attempt at escaping from it, but in vain. He goes out with friends, he loiters about, he drinks and gets into fights: but when work is an alienation, so too is leisure. It is no good his kicking over the traces – he cannot get free. In the end he falls into the snare of love and there is little doubt that soon he will be married, the father of a family, and that he will stop struggling. In *The Loneliness of the Long-Distance Runner* the hero has refused to work in a factory, looking upon it as unfair exploitation and a degrading oppression. He has robbed a bakery and now he is in a reformatory school. He is very good at running, and the headmaster encourages him to train – the reformatory and a private school are soon to compete for a cup, and it is hoped that the hero will win. In the race he does in fact outrun the whole field and he is on the point of winning when all at once he becomes aware that he is being exploited again: it is a hated institution that will profit by his victory. He stops and lets his astonished rival go by.

The class-struggle is shown more directly in Bo Widerberg's *Adalen 31*, a very beautiful Swedish film. Sweden, the summer of 1931: one of those moving northern summers when innumerable leaves and flowers burst out like a miracle and the sun sets only for a few hours in the very short night. 'If this were a Sunday, what a lovely day it would be!' says Thomas. He is a working-man, and the camera brings us into touch with him at the beginning of the film. But it is an ordinary day: a strike is in progress and it has been going on for weeks, with the workers asking for increased pay. They work in factories which are closed at present, but at the same time they are rural people, living in houses scattered about the countryside. Thomas lives in one, together with his wife (her blue eyes and her smile are very beautiful, but her skin is rather rough, and her hands are chapped) and their two good-looking sons of about fourteen and seventeen. Thomas himself gives the impression of strength and cheerfulness. The boys are on holiday and the men seem to be on holiday too: they go fishing in the nearby lake, they walk about, they talk together and they play cards; but at home there is almost nothing to eat. Maybe their claim will be granted: after all, as one paternalist boss points out, the raise they are asking for is not very great, and perhaps the employers might yield. Nothing of the sort. The bosses decide to take on Asians.

183

At this point the whole position changes: the tragedy begins: it moves faster and faster. The workers set about the Asians, harassing them, but without going so far as a lynching: there is no hatred in the workers and they do not suspect the existence of the hatred that their exploiters feel for them. The workers march in procession headed by red flags along a splendid high-perched road above the lake to argue their case with their employer. But there are soldiers hidden in the fields around his house – he has called in the military. Cavalrymen try to stop the procession; the workers break through; they march on, singing. Shots are heard: the officer has given orders to fire. 'They are blank cartridges,' says the leading worker confidently. He falls. Others fall too, weltering in their blood. Many wounded. Three dead. Thomas is killed. That evening the paternalist boss reproaches the officer for having opened fire. 'The soldiers fired, but it was you who bought the bullets,' says the officer. Thomas' son sees that calling in the troops meant accepting the risk that they might fire; indeed it was encouraging them to do so. Neither he nor his friends will ever be deceived again. The hatred increases. Next day there is a general strike all over Sweden. The government falls.

The film, never slipping into aestheticism, has great beauty. It is deeply touching and, without a hint of didacticism, it is convincing. Bo Widerberg's great success lies in his brilliant demonstration of the link between public and private life. We are affected by the love of Thomas and his wife – a love shot through with the fear of having another child they could not afford to bring up. We are touched by the budding idyll between Thomas' son and the boss's daughter: the scene in which they discover their bodies for the first time has a fresh tenderness that no film has ever equalled. The strike makes part of the workers' daily existence: all they want to do is raise their standard of living a little. But straight away it takes on a political dimension; it opens on to violence and death. Class-enmity can be covered over for a while, as it was during that particular summer in that particular part of Sweden; but it is there, it exists, and at the least opportunity it shows itself. The middle-class people the film shows us – and it does so without turning them into overloaded caricatures – are good fathers, good husbands, culti-vated men: but confronted with the class they exploit, they are potential killers and sometimes killers in fact.

I also very much enjoyed *The Ballad of Joe Hill*, by the same director, partly because of the excellent actor who played the part of

184

the hero. The film is about the workers' risings in the USA at the beginning of the century, outbreaks in which Joe Hill was the leading figure. Here you feel the crushing weight of the exploitation and the ferocity of the repression. But there is also a great deal of cheerfulness and humour in the way Joe Hill carries on the struggle; we see it in the forms of action he thinks up and in his songs and speeches. The scene of his execution – cynically contrived on the pretext of a crime he never committed – has a sinister, melancholy beauty. Yet because the story extends over years, this film does not possess the unity and the restrained density of *Adalen 31*. It is more anecdotal and it tends more towards aestheticism.

Among the many American films distributed in France, those that describe the America of today interest me most. I like travelling over those enormous landscapes with the two young motorcyclists in *Easy Rider*: the countryside, friendship, a few delightful meetings, a little grass in the evening – a fine life, happy and free. Their long hair and their cheerful clothes arouse hatred in the robotized, alienated Americans who are eaten up with rancour and who are ready to kill all who are not like them – the Viets, the blacks, the hippies. The two travellers are savagely beaten up and their friend is stabbed; and at the end of the film they are murdered.

Hatred and violence: that is the theme of *Joe*, too. Although they seem to be thoroughly settled in life, both the bourgeois and the working-man are filled with a neurotic fury against all those who challenge their values – the Asians, the blacks, the young. At the beginning of the story the bourgeois is guilty of the unpremeditated murder of a hippy; the proletarian Joe urges him to acknowledge his true feelings – they are both of them racists, both of them lynchers. The bourgeois allows himself to be drawn into the deliberate slaughter of a group of hippies, a slaughter in which he kills his own daughter.

The gulf between the generations: Forman, the Czech director, treats this theme much more lightly in *Taking Off*, which he shot in America. It is a cruel film, because all the characters are hopelessly doomed, both the grown-ups, hard-set in the parental roles, and the children, who try to escape from their parents but who can find no place for themselves anywhere in the world. With unloving hearts and empty minds, they are all consumed by boredom. Yet the film makes one laugh from the beginning to the end. Here again the comic arises from the contrast between the inward nature of the

185

characters and their external reality. They talk pompously, gravely, about themselves and their lives; and the truth the camera shows us is in ludicrous contradiction with what they say. The film throws subtle ridicule upon the habits, mannerisms, clichés and pretensions of a whole range of Americans. Even when some true feeling rises in them, it is instantly stifled by automatic reactions. The high spot of the film is the ceremony at which the parents set about smoking marijuana on the pretext of understanding their children's mental processes. Puffed up with self-importance, they proclaim their deep sense of their responsibilities; in fact they are doing nothing more than join in a parlour-game that amuses them for the moment.

Five Easy Pieces also has a picture of American life as its background. We see the hero as a man who is condemned to loneliness. In the oil-company where he is employed he knows nothing whatsoever about his fellow-workers and they know nothing whatsoever about him. He is scarcely interested in the pretty little waitress he lives with, and she does not understand him. He goes home to see his father, once a well-known musician and now half-paralysed, and there he has no real contact with anybody: he is drawn to his brother's wife, but he does not succeed in making her love him because she doubts whether he is capable of love. Empty-handed and desperately alone, he sets off for the icy forests of the north, where no doubt he will die. His solitude is partly accounted for by his character and his childhood. But it is also explained by the American way of life. It is the fate not only of the hero but of the other characters too, particularly the psychotic hitch-hiking girl who is obsessed by the problems of pollution and who is escaping to the Alaskan snows. And whatever the voluble blue-stocking in the film may say, turning to the mechanics of psychoanalysis is no adequate way of dealing with loneliness of this kind. It is the bitter fruit of a certain civilization.

What gives this film its value is the picture of the relationships between the various characters. It used to be thought that the cinema could not render fine psychological shades and subtleties; but that is not true – it shows them very well indeed. I was deeply struck by the relationship between the valet and his young master in Losey's *The Servant*; by that between the two brothers and between them and the caretaker in the film of the same name; by *Petulia*'s with the man who is hopelessly in love with her; by Mia Farrow's and Elizabeth Taylor's in *Secret Ceremony*; by that between the young Englishman and the Jamaican in *Two Gentlemen*; by those between the characters in *My Night at Maud's* and between the heroes of *Sunday, Bloody Sunday*. If a book were to deal with these stories, it would have first to make us acquainted with the chief characters and their surroundings; and then perhaps the over-expanded tale might seem a thin, light-weight affair. On the screen we see everything, the faces, the various settings, right away, and we can feel interested in the people immediately. A gesture, an expression, a particular tone of voice can tell more than whole pages of print, and do it faster.

Many films play on all these registers that I have just somewhat arbitrarily defined. They bring a period or a society back to life; they tell of adventures; they show us the feelings that bind people together.

Bonnie and Clyde displayed an era – 1929, the time of the great depression. It was a suspense-story; and it was also an astonishingly fresh account of the difficult love between an impotent young man and a young woman. *More*, a film that had excellent music, used a splendid landscape as the background for a picture of the strange creatures who inhabit Ibiza – former Nazis, hashish-smoking hippies, drug-addicts. It told the story of a young man who craved for all the delights of life, and who longed for them so furiously and so wildly that from the very beginning one felt he was doomed. He fell in love with a charming drug-addict; she persuaded him to take heroin; he became a slave to the drug and died of it. The tension, rising from the beginning to the end, created a terrible feeling of suspense.

Honeymoon Killers shows crime in all its extreme physical ugliness: the victims' death-agonies are revolting, and the killers have to batter them again and again to finish them off. They make up a monstrous pair, and the interest of the film lies in its persuading us that a monster is anything but a monster – he is 'my fellow-man, my brother'. The heroine is physically repulsive – a huge mass of flesh, although there is a pretty face in the midst of it all. She is sensual, morbidly greedy, pitilessly hard, and anti-semitic into the bargain; yet she touches us because of her exclusive passion for Ray and by her simple trust in him. She kills, twice out of insane jealousy and once in cold blood, but she does not value her own life much more than the lives of others and she is ready to lose it if she cannot have Ray entirely to herself, shared by no one, and in total harmony: she prefers having herself condemned to death with him rather than accept any compromise. This absolute quality sets her far above the drearily normal women whom Ray ensnares; we agree with her in despising them for their ludicrous coquetry, their squalid avarice or their inner falsehood. Ray is more commonplace and trifling, but even so he is capable of a tender love for this unlovely woman. I do not know whether the criminals who died in the electric chair at Sing Sing in 1951 resembled this pair: but these two succeed in making us feel for them, although the film hides nothing of the brutal horror of their crimes.

There are few directors who possess both a private world and the ability to charm me. In this last decade only two have produced works that I found moving – Bergman and Buñuel. Bergman's interest in women delights me: for him they are not objects but sensitive, intelligent subjects, and he is very good at drawing the relationships between them: friendship, complicity, hatred. As he sees it, their only weakness is that propensity which urges them towards those pitiful creatures, men. I rediscovered this feminine world, with its outbreaks of violence, its storms and furies in *The Silence*; and the film impressed me deeply. On the other hand, Bergman's mystic side, his obsession with Evil, seems to me boring. *A Passion* had some beautiful landscapes and some very likeable characters, wretchedly shut up in their inner loneliness; but the author's set purpose was too obvious. He symbolized the presence of evil in the world – men's wickedness – by the killing of sheep and the lynching of an innocent man. The story did not carry me along.

I really love Buñuel's films, but he bores me when he hypnotizes himself with religious themes. Although it had some very fine photography and a few enchanting scenes, I did not find *The Milky Way* interesting. But I did like *Tristana*: only the cinema could show this strange relationship between a beautiful and crippled young woman and an elderly charmer. Buñuel excels at uncovering what respectable people hide under the name of righteousness – bigotry and hypocrisy. He has only to show smooth-faced priests drinking their chocolate with a little too much smacking of their lips to make us hate them. There is more truth and humanity in the 'vices' of the old man, Tristana and the young deaf-mute.

A film I look upon as a masterpiece – and I said so when it came out – is *Les Abysses*, made by Nicos Papadakis in about 1953, with the dialogue written by Vauthier. Papadakis based himself upon the story of the Papin sisters, and although he always refrains from playing on the nerves of his audience, he carries the tale to the utmost pitch of violence. The tragedy takes place in the lonely country house where Monsieur, Madame and Mademoiselle lead their squalid lives: they are petits bourgeois, miserly, grasping and in any case half-ruined. We see them through the inimical eyes of these two sisters, their servants – parts admirably played by the Bergé sisters. Going into the kitchen with the maids is like going into a torture-chamber: Papadakis plays no tricks; he merely shows us the knives, the forks, the choppers, and the gas stove, and these familiar objects seem terrifying. The hatred increases, while the sisters' love for one another gives the feeling that a different life might be possible, a life in which there would be happiness, poetry and freedom. For a while the two servants persecute the family cruelly; for years they have had no wages, so they have them under their thumb. But in the end the middle-class coalition defeats them, and dressed up like stage maid-servants they obediently serve tea in the drawing-room. At this point they learn that they are to be dismissed and separated from one another: they turn back into furies and batter Madame and Mademoiselle to death with a flat-iron.

It is said that Papadakis had the Algerian war in mind when he told the story of this savage uprising. And indeed, he still had an intensely painful memory of that war in 1963, and a certain outline of the fight against colonialism can be seen in this private tragedy, which deals with one of those extreme situations described by Fanon,[13] a situation from which the oppressed can break free only by the slaughtering of the oppressor – by terrorism. Monsieur and Madame have the easy conscience – that is to say the unawareness and the ignorance – of the colonists who supposed that the Arabs tolerated and even liked them, and who were amazed by the discovery of their hatred. Mademoiselle is the personification of that paternalism that we used then to call the *gauche respectueuse* and that claimed it was granting the colonized people all that they were fighting for. And it is Mademoiselle, hurt at having her advances repelled and noble feelings scorned, who sets off the tragedy. (The film is so rich that at the present day Mademoiselle reminds one of the head of a certain university who was as understanding and well-meaning as she, even to the point of tolerating any insult or affront,

[13] *Les Damnés de la terre.*

and who ended up by calling in the police and having the students clubbed.) We saw this film at a private showing, and many of us who were writers recommended it to the public.[14]

I rarely take any pleasure in watching documentaries. They batter me with pieces of knowledge, quite divorced from any context, at times when I have no wish to absorb them. In these last years, only one has really enchanted me, and that was a piece on Benares, in colour. For years I had dreamt about the word Benares, and the pictures satisfied a long-lasting curiosity.

On the other hand, I am interested in films that try to bring an epoch back to life by selections from news-reels and so on. Straight away I went to see *36, le grand tournant*, which was about the adventure of the Popular Front. The commentary was often irritating, but I had never had a stronger feeling of recovering my own existence. I was present at some of the events of 1936, but generally speaking I knew about them from the papers or by conversation. The film provided me with a sum of the whole. Thanks to the impact of the pictures, I felt that I was carried back into my own past and that I could gather its various aspects into one single view.

The Sorrow and the Pity did not give me the same impression at all. It did not seem to me to reproduce the atmosphere of the occupation as I had known it: there was much more extreme anxiety in the air in those days. Besides, very few of the shots were directly connected with the past – there were survivors talking about a time already far away, and distance neutralized the intensity of their emotions. It seemed as though being a resistant or a collaborator was a matter of opinion; whereas in fact during the occupation the two sides were separated by heaps of dead bodies. Yet there were good sequences, such as the evidence of Mendès-France; the Comte de Chambrun's absurd, odious remarks, and the account given by the peasant member of the Resistance. What the German had to say corresponded so closely with what might have been foretold that hearing it actually spoken gave a somewhat grating intellectual pleasure.

Since 1962 I have seen other films, apart from those I have mentioned; and I often liked them. Yet I know I missed a great many

[14] Since then Papadakis has made another film, called *Les Pâtres du Soleil*: I have been told that it is very good, but circumstances have not allowed me to see it.

that were interesting. Nowadays I do not often go to the cinema. I am unwilling to take the trouble, to stand in a queue, and to undergo the news and the advertisements. And then, it is easy to break off when one is reading a book or listening to a record: but once I am settled into my seat in a cinema, particularly if I am with a friend, I feel compelled to stay there even if the film is boring.

These drawbacks would scarcely matter at all if the cinema brought me more than any other medium of expression: but it does not. It is the evident presence of the image that gives films their power or their charm: but then again the unescapable fullness of the picture cuts my dreaming short. As it has often been said, this is one of the reasons why adapting a novel for the screen is almost always a pity. Emma Bovary's face is undefined and multiple; her unhappiness goes beyond her particular case: yet on the screen I see one specific face, and that lessens the story's range. I do not feel the same kind of disappointment when the piece has been written directly for the cinema, and I like seeing that Tristana has the features of Catherine Deneuve: the reason is that I was resigned beforehand to this story's having no more than the dimension of an anecdote. And then the importance assumed by the visual image often impoverishes the places it shows me: on paper, the 'flower no longer to be seen in any posy' is absent in its scent and in the texture of its petals just as much as in its form and colour; it is the entirety of the flower that words endeavour to encompass. On the screen I see a landscape, I hear its sounds; but I do not catch the salt smell of the sea, nor does the spray splash on my skin. The centring of the pictures often cuts them off from the rest of the world. When I read the word Toledo, the whole of Spain is there before me: for the very reason that they were photographed so perfectly, the streets of Toledo in *Tristana* gave me nothing but themselves. Sometimes a director's art allows him to go beyond these limitations – I may see a countryside so much alive that I feel its coolness on my face: I may be walking, not in a street but in London with all England around me. But even at the best, there is a certain degree of complexity that no film can attain. The written word is less expressive than the image and therefore, when it confines itself to making the reader see, it is slower; but when it is concerned with conveying knowledge, then it has very great advantages indeed. If a work is rich, it communicates a piece of actual experience that rises upon a basis of abstract knowledge: without this context, the experience is

191

mutilated or even incomprehensible. But visual images are not enough to provide it: if they try to suggest it, then they do so clumsily and they almost always blunder. This was evident when Costa-Gavras made *The Confession*. He had succeeded with Z, because in that case the plot was very simple and the context was known – just one more piece of unscrupulous plotting by the police. But *The Confession* has a meaning only if it is placed in a situation that harks back to the whole of post-war history in the USSR and the eastern countries. The characters do not exist only at the time of the trial: each has a whole political life behind him. In the book one knew exactly who one was dealing with and one understood the reasons behind each move. Reduced to something that was merely to be seen, London's tragedy lost its weight and its meaning.

I believe that the main reason why I prefer books is the fact that ever since childhood my investment has been in literature. I feel words more than I feel pictures. I am more sensitive to words than to images.

One of the commonplace remarks that is repeated over and over again in some circles is that from now onwards literature will have only a secondary part to play; the future belongs to the cinema, to the television – to the image. I do not believe it for a moment. For my part I have no television and I never shall have one. For a moment the image is enchanting; but then it fades and loses strength. Words have this immense privilege: you can take them with you. When I say '*Nos jours meurent avant nous*' I am precisely re-creating Chateaubriand's line within myself.

It is language that makes the presence of other men within each man a fact; and that is one of the reasons why I believe that literature cannot be replaced.

I go to the theatre much less often than to the cinema. The cinema's raw material is perfectly homogeneous – visual images perceived as an analogon of reality and as immediate as that reality. I can settle down into the imagery and follow the film without ever being jerked into the real world for a moment. In the theatre, the relationship between the imagery and the real seems to me lame and halting – incomplete. It never happens that the whole cast performs perfectly: I catch sight of the actor beneath the character he impersonates. The settings, the costumes and the stage-properties are all there in their materially contingent aspect, and they bring me back to that everyday life from which the text, in one way or another, is trying to withdraw me. For a while it does succeed in carrying me into a fictitious world, but presently there I am back again with my feet on the ground, watching a show. Even if I find the play fully satisfying and even if the staging is unusually successful, I never feel entirely at ease.[15].

In spite of these reservations, there were some plays I did enjoy. Gatti's *La Vie de A. Geai*, which was produced at the Odéon in 1964, had a good theatrical idea – that of showing us the same character at four different ages. This has sometimes been attempted in books, but the effect of simultaneity is much more striking when there on the stage before me I see the adolescent, the young man, the man in his prime, and the ancient-to-be, and all of them the one individual. When the curtain rises, a forty-year-old dustman, recently wounded in a demonstration, is struggling for life in a hospital bed. He sees his past over again; and at the same time the pensioner he dreams of becoming sits in the doorway of a pretty little cottage and begs him, in vain, to stay alive. If we were not moved by his fate, then all this would be a mere stage trick with no significance. But Gatti succeeds in making us feel for the dustman Auguste Geai, a character largely based upon his father, whose grossly underprivileged life he sums up with tenderness and indignation.

Georges Michel's *Les Jouets* is a cruel, amusing satire on our consumer society, on the environment we are forced to live in, and on the slogans the radio infects us with. The piece was successful because the dialogue, built up of clichés, was in perfect harmony with the form of acting, for the actors' mimes and voices rendered them quite inhuman. The setting and the production also helped in carrying out this shift, this removal to a distance, by which the only too commonplace reality could be recognized so clearly.

This shift: as we know, it is the mainspring of Brecht's art; he is the only writer whose plays I should rather see than read: the written text usually seems dull, and it only really comes to life on the stage. I realized this once again when I went to the TNP to see *Maître Puntila et son valet Matti*, which I had read with no particular enthusiasm. The play was cleverly staged and it was very well

15 Here I am speaking of the Western theatre. There are forms which elude this criticism. I shall speak of them later on.

acted by Wilson, Denner, and Judith Magre; it made me laugh a great deal, and it left a bitter taste behind.

At the little TNP I also saw Walser's[16] *Chêne et lapins angora*, and I liked its restrained pathos. The poetic, heart-rending character played by Dufilho, deported for anti-Nazism, has been so thoroughly transformed by a brain-operation followed by re-education that he goes on shouting 'Long live Hitler' when all his fellow-countrymen are bawling 'Long live America' at the tops of their voices. In the grip of a helpless despair he sees himself gradually stripped of everything that made life pleasant; while at the same time the former Nazi, played by Wilson, grows steadily more and more prosperous. The play is close-knit and tense; and without ever falling into symbolism or allegory it throws a dark light upon the whole of that post-war Germany in which the good were punished and the wicked rewarded.

Mnouchkine put on Wesker's *The Kitchen* in a circus that had been turned into a theatre. The setting was scrupulously exact: you really believed you were in a kitchen and you felt you could make out the restaurant the other side of the door. Yet the food and most of the kitchen implements were just not there – the actors supplied them by their gestures. Cooks roasted invisible joints, stirred ghostly dough and gutted absent fishes. The play's strength and originality came from this combination of mime and of realism in expression, intonation and movement. One felt entirely with these harassed men and women as they worked at this appalling rhythm, and one saw the breadth of the gulf between them and the boss, who was incapable of understanding their furious discontent. The only thing I regretted was that the plot turned to melodrama. Here again, the acted play was far better than the written text.

Somewhat later Mnouchkine produced *A Midsummer Night's Dream* in the same theatre. It is not my favourite Shakespearean comedy, and most of the actors had been chosen for their plastic qualities: the dances and mimes were done with the utmost grace, but the text was not well handled. The most successful thing was the setting: the whole stage was covered with fur as thick as moss in a pictured forest, and it seemed to be lit by the glow of a night-sky, filtering through the branches.

Two of Sartre's plays were produced at the TNP. In 1965 Cacoyanis put on *The Trojan Women* which Sartre had adapted

[16] A German novelist and playwright.

194

from Euripides, carefully respecting the text though at the same time giving it a very modern accent. Podromides had written music for the play in New York, and he blamed the words for not fitting in with his rhythms. Sartre had influenza, and he could not go to the rehearsals. The first time we went to the theatre, a few days before the first night, we were horror-struck – shattering music completely drowned the actors' voices. They acted well; Judith Magre was an outstanding Cassandre. But the choruses were very badly trained. When Hécube said 'Strike thy head!' all the supernumeraries beat their bosoms with movements reminiscent of a class doing rhythmic gymnastics. 'Anatomical error,' murmured the scene-painter, a very amusing elderly Greek who had painted beautiful settings. Sartre persuaded them to cut certain disastrous theatrical effects. At the first night the audience clapped, but we and our friends were far from enthusiastic.

On the other hand, Wilson's production of *Le Diable et le bon Dieu* in the autumn of 1968 was excellent. Instead of built-up scenery he had an ingenious arrangement that allowed the actors to come in, go out, and move about with the greatest freedom. The choice of the actors was fortunate. In the first act, Périer, playing the part of Goetz, was as good as Brasseur, though no better; and in the second act he had much more sincerity. The play as a whole was far superior to Jouvet's production. The circumstances of the time gave it a very modern note – the lessons droned out by the inhabitants of the Cité du Soleil reminded one of the collective recitations from Mao's little red book. The young people who filled the theatre every night discovered quantities of allusions to current events in the text, and they applauded madly.

In spite of some innovations, all these plays were still fairly traditional. Later on I saw others whose break with the past was far more sharp and distinct.

In October 1968 I saw a performance of *Akropolis* at the little Epée-de-bois theatre. In the nineteenth century a Polish dramatist who meant to glorify our humanistic culture had the idea of making the heroes of the Homeric or Biblical scenes in the tapestries of a castle step down from the walls and act them out before us. The Polish producer Grotowski based himself on this play, but with the intention of holding humanism and traditional culture up to ridicule. In his version the play is put on in a concentration camp by deportees in striped clothes. They are busy with arduous and meaningless tasks, carrying heavy pipes and putting up scaffolding. Then all at once their gestures and their words evoke the great figures that stand there far back in our past: and there is a grotesque contrast between the prisoners' abasement and the legendary nobility of the heroes whose parts they play. In fact they are scoffing at all this nobility. The idyll between Helen and Paris becomes strangely sodomitic, both the actors being men. The most striking episode is Rachel's marriage: it does not correspond with the Biblical account at all – instead of submitting to Laban, Jacob kicks him to death and runs off with Rachel. Her part is taken by a tube covered in a plastic material as white as a bride's veil. Jacob goes right round the theatre with this on his arm, followed by a wedding-party chanting songs. The audience sat on benches round the stage, and the actors often mingled with them. What grieved me was that I could not understand the words. Our Czech friend Liéhm, who knows Polish, gave us a short version, and he said the original was very fine. The double transposition – false prisoners playing the parts of heroes of antiquity – utterly removed the play from all reality, thus doing away with the awkward difference of phase between the imaginary world and this.

In 1970, in the cathedral square at Milan, Ronconi produced a free, popular show adapted from *Orlando Furioso*. In May he brought it to Paris, to one of the unused halls in the central market: one had to pay to go in, and the audience was smaller. The evening I went, the setting delighted me at once – an iron architecture, harmonious and open to the sky on every side. The standing spectators took part in the action; they represented the crowd through which charged the fighting men and women on their iron horses – they raced after one another, defied one another and fought over our heads, for their chargers were perched on wooden cages: the cages had little wheels, and a man squatting inside pushed them along at a run. All the machinery had this same ingenious simplicity – one might have been back in the sixteenth century, when marvels were conjured up by the most rudimentary means. There were stages at each end of the hall and trestles along the walls. At times one's whole attention was taken up by one single action; at others two, three or four scenes were going on at the same time. You could choose one, or move from that to the next, or relax and smoke a cigarette. In many old novels this profusion of incongruous adventure stuns and bores me, but here I was delighted: the real temporal relationship between adventures of this kind is simultaneity, whereas reading compels a wearisome sequence, one necessarily coming after another. My Italian is poor and I could not catch the words, but the stories were easy to understand and they could do without any text. Everything – the fire and dash of the actors, both men and women, the brilliant costumes, the gaiety, the speed of the movements—everything contributed to my happiness. It was a happiness which resembled that which I experienced in my childhood, not so much at the theatre as when I was reading wild, extravagant stories whose illustrations enchanted me.

I was happier still in February 1971, when I went to see *1789*, produced by Mnouchkine and acted by the forty-odd members of the Théâtre du Soleil. Here again the setting was wonderfully well chosen – the old cartridge-factory deep in the Bois de Vincennes, where once they made a poison-gas called vincennite. Five connecting platforms had been erected in the enormous building, and the audience could either sit on rising rows of benches against one of the walls, or stand in the middle of the hall, or find places on the gangways or the trestles when they happened to be unoccupied. The play was written collectively by the whole company after a long and serious study of the Revolution, and its argument is this: the day after the firing on the crowd at the Champs-de-Mars in 1791, the mountebanks act the history of the last two years: they show it as the people might imagine it themselves, and this allows every kind of exaggeration and burlesque and the freest interpretation of events. Sometimes different scenes were going on on each of the five platforms at once; sometimes a single action occupied the entire theatre, the gangways allowing the actors to run from one point to another and the audience representing the crowd.

After a rather slow beginning that described the wretched state of the country, the show took on a furious rhythm that never slackened as the evening went on. A great variety of techniques were used: the mountebanks represented the summoning of the States General by puppets, manipulating them openly; then immediately the puppets came to life, acting away in a world of their own; and at the same time the wild caricatures of Marie-Antoinette, and Polignac and Lamballe danced round Cagliostro. All at once there was a great silence. From one end of the theatre to the other, actors scattered among the audience began to whisper the story of the taking of the Bastille in their ears. This was accompanied by very beautiful

197

music, and at first the tale was no more than a murmur, not wholly synchronized so that the same word *Necker* was heard at different moments and in different places – it seemed to flit about the theatre. The voices rose; they mingled, though still remaining separate – it was the voice of the triumphant people, atomized through space and time. It was a brilliantly orchestrated uproar, as necessary and as overwhelming as a Bach cantata: all these voices, confident and enthusiastic, all together and each in turn, cried 'And that was how we took the Bastille!' This was one of the greatest moments of theatre I have ever been privileged to experience. It awoke deep echoes in me, because in this story I recognized the one we and our friends had often told the evening after some demonstration that we thought successful and full of promise. And now, after these voices, an immense fair and merry-making broke out: the trestles turned into fair-ground booths with wrestling, games, dancing and dumb-shows, accompanied by the pom-pom-pom of a rowdy band.

It might have been feared that after this paroxysm the show would decline. Not at all. One astonishing invention came after another, and then that would be followed by something equally unexpected. There was the strip-tease of the night of 4 August, when in a frenzy of generosity the nobles tore off their plumed hats and splendid coats, stripping themselves almost bare; then filled with horror at the extent of their sacrifice, they hurriedly gathered up their things and rushed off with them. The women of Paris, wearing white dresses and waving green branches, pushed through the crowd to bring back the king and queen, who were represented by bladders floating over their heads. Then to the sound of a wedding-march, the rich quarrelled over the possessions of the clergy in a ludicrous dumb-show. One of the last scenes took its pattern from Punch and Judy. There were bourgeois sitting on a platform to watch a farce; and opposite them, on another stage, there was a chest, standing between a great noble and a cardinal, both absurdly got up. A mountebank opened the chest and let out the People, who instantly knocked down Privilege and Superstition. The bourgeois clapped, and they clapped even more when the mountebank shut the People in the chest once more: when they saw the lid beginning to lift again they were terrified and shouted 'Look out! Look out!' just as children do to Punch. But the People shot up behind the showman and strangled him. A success with no future to it. When the People called for the deposition of the king after his flight (shown by one of the most brilliant sequences of the evening) the National Guard fired upon the crowd, and the Order of the wealthy triumphed.

Here too there was double transposition, since the actors were meant to be mountebanks who themselves were playing parts. Because of this expedient, no caricature nor parody seemed outrageous. And in fact both caricature and parody were at the service of the only valid truth – the People's truth. It was no calumny to show the king and queen stuffing themselves like gluttons, getting drunk and staggering about while the people were starving; for even if you behave well at table, eating as much as you want at a time of famine is gormandizing. What Mnouchkine and her company were really showing us by means of their astonishingly funny gags and burlesque was in fact a tragic tale – the strangling of the Revolution by the rising class, which destroyed the nobility only in order to take over its prerogatives, the aristocracy of wealth replacing that of birth. This class fooled the People and made use of them; and in the end the People gained nothing from it at all. The demonstration was carried out with remarkable exactness in its details, and the process was hardly noticeable. There were those who denied that the play had any revolutionary value because one had to pay to go in; yet it certainly did have one, because of the emotion and the indignation that it aroused.

In June 1971 a most unusual performance was to be seen in Paris; this was Robert Wilson's *Le Regard du sourd*, a series of tableaux in which motionless or moving images followed one another in silence. They were the slow, dream-like evocations of a deaf and dumb black child's fantasies; and into it the author had also projected his own world. In spite of the tedious passages and the repetitions, I, like almost all the people who saw it, was enthralled by this phantasmagoria. But presently I found that I had retained nothing of it. The pictures faded, yielding no meaning that I might at least have remembered in part. As far as I was concerned, this 'river of silence', as Renée Saurel called it, had flowed in vain.

Music still has great importance in my life. I never go to concerts: I loathe their pompous solemnity. I prefer waiting until the work that interests me is recorded. Still, I did go twice to the Opera. I had liked Berg's *Wozzeck* for a great many years, and I did not want to

199

miss the performance with Boulez conducting; I thought it magnificent, and what is more I was delighted with Masson's beautiful scenery and Barrault's excellent staging – he had most successfully patterned himself on Brecht. It is rare for an opera to achieve this artistic synthesis; although indeed the form requires it. In 1969 I also saw the Moscow Opera's *Boris Godunov*. It is a work I know well. The choruses were admirable and the actors not only sang but also acted with consummate art. The splendour of the costumes made one forget the conventional aspect of the scenery.

But these were exceptions. My true relationship with music is a much more everyday matter. During the evenings I spend with Sartre, we listen to records. Nowadays they rarely bring me any exciting revelations, because I am well acquainted with the great composers of former times. But it is a delight to hear works that I love over again, and to discover those that had not yet been recorded – works that enlarge my knowledge of a composer or a period. Thus in 1970 I heard Gesualdo's lovely madrigals: before that I did not even know his name. I revive my earlier knowledge and I acquire new; I see some pieces in a new light; my opinions and my tastes change, sometimes more, sometimes less. At present, as I have already said, one of my preoccupations is to sum up my past and to find just where I stand.

Another, as I have also said, is to keep myself up to date. I keep a close watch on my contemporaries' creative work. Stockhausen, Xenakis, Penderecki and Ligety have given me new emotions of great value; I also like Boulez, Berio, Nono, Henze and some others. It is an odd experience, listening to composers who are still young, when one knows that it is in their later middle years or even in their old age that musicians usually write their masterpieces. Which of these young men will go farthest? Which will be considered the greatest at the end of this century? I am intensely interested in their future, whether it is to be in their life-time or after their death. Other productions that neither they nor I can foresee will retrospectively change the meaning of their works, just as these composers now help me to understand the research of those who went before them. Xenakis enables me to make a fresh interpretation of some of Beethoven, Ravel and Bartok.

Sometimes I try my luck – I turn the knob of my transistor to listen to France-Musique. I may chance on a piece that I really like: but it does not happen often and that is not what I am looking for. A friend once said to me that the pleasure of fashionable cocktail-parties lay in meeting people you did not want to meet; in the same way I amuse myself with the radio by listening to music I do not want to hear. But it is a pleasure that does not hold me for long. I prefer to go back to my records.

I dread the swarming crowds at big exhibitions. And then the objects that are exhibited are cut off from their roots, and they therefore lose much of their value. The exhibition of Negro art at the Grand Palais in 1966 was very rich and there were magnificent things to admire; but they were arranged in a somewhat arbitrary order that did not clarify their meaning. That too was the fault of the Gothic Europe exhibition[17]: the rooms were well lit, there were not too many people, and I could stroll about as I liked. Yet the works brought from every part of Europe and standing there side by side gave something of the impression of a curiosity shop, of bric-à-brac. The recumbent figures lying in these impersonal halls were much less touching than they are at Saint-Denis or Bourges or Dijon, sleeping in the darkness of the church where they prayed when they were alive. Most of the sculptures were too much like those I already knew and they were too much like one another. There were some strange wooden figures, daubed with many colours, that astonished me: but almost all of them were very ugly. The most striking thing I saw was a huge Christ, entirely black, and crucified upon a gibbet. It came from Westphalia. He had a brigand's face and an immensely elongated body. It made me think of all those unhappy people in Germany who were hideously tortured, nailed to the trunks of trees or hanging from their branches at the time of the peasants' risings. Upon the whole I prefer provincial museums to these great displays – modest provincial museums such as those at Provins, Autun, Dijon and so many other places, that offer the visitor a homogeneous collection.

Still, I was glad to renew my memories of Yugoslavia at the Grand Palais[18] in 1971. There were coloured photographs projected on to a screen, and they reminded me of the monuments I had seen. I saw the lovely frescoes of the Byzantine churches once again, this

[17] At the Louvre, in 1967.
[18] I did not have to go to the immensely popular Tutankhamun exhibition in Paris; I was in Cairo at the time, and the museum there had sent Paris only a very small part of the objects found in the tomb.

time in reproduction; and I discovered many works that I did not know at all – stone statues found on the banks of the Danube, rough representations of fish-men that no doubt went back to prehistoric times; a charming little bronze-age terracotta votive chariot drawn by ducks; the marble head of a girl with a pure face and carefully plaited hair, carved in the second century AD. And I was enchanted by the gallery of painted Slovene wood-carvings – female saints with naive faces, set in unexpected attitudes.

Since I love painting, I shun *vernissages*; but every year I spend a fair amount of time in galleries or museums. In 1964 I saw an exhibition of Nicolas de Staël, that great painter who opened so many new directions for his art and who could not be satisfied with any of them: it was not as rich as that which I had seen some few years earlier and which had revealed him to me, but I saw some very fine pictures there.

I already knew Dubuffet quite well. I had very much liked his *Matériologies* of 1950–60, studies of raw material on canvas: stones, pebbles, earth, grass, sand. Later, with *Paris Circus*, he returned to earlier themes. I went to see *L'Hourloupe*: in this series he meant to 'humbug' the public, to bewilder them in a 'comedy of errors'. All the pictures were based on flat cells, strongly contrasting in colour, with red and blue dominating; the outlines of the cells were as exact as the leads in a stained-glass window, and in many cases they were filled with black hatching. Their juxtaposition gave the space an abstract character. The swirling whole was ambiguous; according to the way one looked at it, it might be figurative or it might not. This world was removed from reality by a deliberate artifice; yet gesticulating silhouettes could be seen through the blue and red cut-outs, dances, farandoles whose gaiety contrasted with the pitiful absurdity of the bodies and faces. Beyond our world there was another, mocking yet joyful.

Somewhat later, in 1966, I saw and liked Bissière's subtle, meticulous canvases, Pignon's powerful compositions, and Singier's, which were not figurative, although their splendid colours, their transparencies and opacities called blue seas, coral and watery depths to mind.

In 1967 the greater part of Bonnard's works were shown at the Orangerie. I was quite well acquainted with Bonnard, and this time too it was his latest pictures that pleased me most – those which are, in his own words, 'a series of interconnecting patches of colour'.

Some, reduced to their bare essentials, are an almost abstract play of luminous yellows and delicate whites; the outlines are hardly to be seen, yet nature is suggested here, nature in its mute solitude or its overflowing wealth.

My taste for summing up was satisfied by the exhibition that gave me back the broad outlines of Picasso's whole work, from the beginning up until today. It merely strengthened both my admiration and my reserves. His virtuosity is staggering – he does whatever he wants to do: but I do not always like what he wants. In my opinion he reached his highest point in the period that goes roughly from 1930 to 1950. At this time he found himself entirely, and he kept continuously rediscovering himself. Later there was more self-repetition. He still often succeeds brilliantly; but these successes grow more mechanical.

I was also very pleased to see the body of Chagall's work at the Grand Palais. It is somewhat monotonous and it can be rather affected; but it grows deeper with time. 'I had to wait until I was an old man . . . before I understood the importance of texture,' he has said. This is very evident when one compares his recent and his earlier pictures. They have the same poetry, but their matter is richer, the colours are more carefully worked out – they have a more precious 'texture'. The great originality of Chagall's work lies in its autobiographical aspect. He paints Vitebsk, his native town, with its houses and its snow and the creatures he was familiar with from his childhood – fishes, cocks, cows, horses. He lovingly paints Paris as he discovered it – the quays, the roofs, the Eiffel Tower. Deeply imbued with his own culture, he illustrates Hebrew proverbs and he sets folklore down on canvas. His landscapes, flowers, fabulous animals, mountebanks and lovers are seen as in a dream; often there is an open window with the sleeper flying, taking to the air; although he does not show himself, the painter nevertheless invites us to step into his dreams, where the fishes are blue and the horses green, where fiddlers are perched upon the roof and where bridegrooms lie stretched out in the sky. There is a sensual tenderness in this world of naive forms and shimmering colours.

Another great pleasure was seeing a retrospective exhibition of the painting of 1918–20 at Strasbourg. It was by showing me pictures of this period that my cousin Jacques first gave me some notion of painting; though indeed my initiation did not occur until the late 1920s. I remember the reservations and the enthusiasms of myself at twenty, as I first looked at the painters who are now so familiar to me. I was happy to see them again, but they did not surprise me. What did surprise me was to find that at that time I hardly knew anything about a painter whom I now place among the greatest – Robert Delaunay. He had a considerable influence on his period: and upon Klee, among others. The colour in his rigorously-composed pictures is so generous, so candid and so brilliant that it is a physical delight to behold.

I am very fond of Vieira de Silva's painting; and in the autumn of 1969 the Musée d'art moderne had a great retrospective of her work. I am particularly moved by her second period – very white or very grey pictures whose straight, hard lines evoke the extreme anxiety of our modern urban landscapes.

I had often heard of Delvaux, but he is little known in France and I had only seen a few reproductions of his pictures. The retrospective at the Musée des Arts Décoratifs in June 1969 was a revelation to me. Straight away I was at home in that oneiric world, so remote from my own dreams and yet all at once mysteriously close – a disturbingly serene universe in which the strange seems familiar and where our everyday world makes one uneasy. It is filled with delicious female bodies: beneath their severe black dresses or their high-necked white tuckers, some of these young women are as naked as their chastely unclothed sisters, who wear nothing but a big hat, a necklace, a vast bow of ribbons or just their hair. They make one think of pictures – often of Cranach's Lucretia – or of marble busts, yet at the same time they are made of tender, succulent flesh. They dwell in suburbs, whose roads, paved with little dark square stones, have rails running along them, and ancient trams rumble by: they sit there, naked, in little stations, and watch the trains go past. One of them is sitting naked in the middle of a path, at a table covered with a green cloth and lit by an oil lamp like those of my childhood. Bowler-hatted gentlemen with spectacles pass close by without seeing them in streets where candles flicker, or among ruins. For in Delvaux' world, the little smoke-blackened towns of the Nord are next door to marble landscapes, where dark cypresses grow beneath deep blue skies. There too, women made of flesh and marble dream gravely under their high-plumed hats while short-sighted scholars and men blinded by their own importance pass by uncaring. Like many other painters, Delvaux has not ceased making progress as he grows older. The pictures he painted between 1960 and 1969 are among those I like best: his colour has never been so profound, nor the reality he shows us so immediate and yet so remote. Above all I like *Les Extravagantes d'Athènes*, which he painted when he was seventy-two: naked or half naked women are standing or lying in an antique landscape with a little tram passing through it. Many of these images still haunt my memory: time may have taken away their richness, but it has not robbed them of their charm.

In the winter of 1969–70 I made several long visits to the Klee exhibition. I had already seen shows of his work in Paris – the exhibition in February 1948, among others. And at Basle and in other galleries I had stopped dead in front of his pictures. Already I thought him the greatest of all modern painters. But nevertheless I was still dazzled. For Klee, painting means colour above all. 'Colour and I are one. I am a painter!' he said one day in a burst of enthusiasm. His pictures are a feast of colours and subtle shades. Towns, houses, gardens, fauna and flora are all a pretext for him to shatter the rainbow and put its pieces together as he thinks fit: what he gives us in his paintings is happiness itself, laid open to the view. He patterns himself on reality, but he discovers it afresh. He liked children's drawings: 'At the origin of their gifts there is a wisdom,' he said. He retained that wisdom. His vision was never distorted by the adults' practical hide-bound way of seeing. His is above all the vision of a world in gestation, begotten by vectors, arrows and vortices. 'Adventures of the line,' as Michaux rightly puts it. To bring the wonderful *Vieillard calculant* into being before our eyes, no more than a single skilfully modelled stroke was required; and it is the wild saraband of lines and colours that makes the charm of the *Saltimbanque*, the *Fou dansant*, the *Créateur* and so many other pictures. Even the one called *Intériorité* is no more than a play of lines. What is more, man has no privileged place in this world. Animals, plants and all living forms have the same value, and there is a continual interchange between them. A face may be built up from shells, insects and flowers, like that of the *Cantatrice dans le rôle de Fiordiligi*. The human being, stripped of pretensions and reduced to its simple truth, has something comic, ludicrous and touching about it, and at times something mysterious, as we see in *Senecio*: the name calls to mind both old age and the flower of the coltsfoot (senecio) and the picture shows us a lunar, childish face.

This title makes one think: for although there is nothing literary about Klee's painting, words have great importance in it – he brings printed and written letters into his pictures and he chooses his titles with great care, so that they form part of the painting and modify its meaning. It is these interchanges between the written language and that of painting, between the various earthly creatures, and between nature and architecture that give Klee's world its poetry. His process is the opposite of Picasso's, for Picasso's painting breaks reality down and analyses it. Klee sees it as a universal presence that goes beyond its apparent limits: everything is bound to the cosmos as a whole, and it is the painter's task to make this connection visible by isolating the analogies that exist between all things.

His last pictures no longer have the gaiety and humour of his earlier work; they do not tell us about happiness any more. I like them none the less for that. In 1939–40 he was very ill; he knew it, and those were dark days for him. The presence of death can be felt in his *Germination pathétique*, in the restrained, disturbing *Signes sur fond blanc*, and in *Labyrinthe détruit*: far down in all these pictures, death is there, lying in wait. Yet, by the beauty that it inspires, death is overcome and sublimated.

Giacometti once told me that whenever he came out of an exhibition of paintings he was delighted at being immersed in the contingent variety of the real once more: coming as a contrast to the circumscribed necessity of works of art, this profusion dazzled him. On me, Klee has the opposite effect. He is neither a pure painter nor uniquely a poet, but he is both at once, and he gives me a world beyond the reach of my eyes, beyond what they are capable of seeing. He gives me everything that I do know in the world and everything that I do not know; everything that has a name and everything that has none.

At about the same period, a hundred or so of Goya's pictures were shown at the Orangerie: they were not in the Prado, and it was the first time I had ever seen them. Since Goya is one of the painters I admire most, I was delighted to increase my knowledge of him. At that time I was working on my book on old age; I had read several works about him and I had looked at reproductions of his last pictures – I was very fortunate to be able to gaze at the originals of those terrible portraits of old women. But many of his pictures gave me a more direct pleasure – their beauty enchanted me.

It was also at the Orangerie that I discovered Max Ernst: this was rather later. I had seen some of his pictures in 1947, mostly in

New York. The impression I had retained was that of an inspired surrealist who happened to paint. Now I found myself in the presence of a great painter, influenced by surrealism.

Unhappily I had missed Rebeyrolle's exhibition, *Les Guérilleros*, in 1969. Sartre had praised it warmly and I did see some very fine pictures in reproduction. Then some friends who knew us both put him in touch with Sartre and me and we went to see him in his studio, which was then in Montrouge. He showed us his earlier pictures, and at last I saw *Les Guérilleros*. Recent canvases were leaning against the walls: I saw them again at the Galerie Maeght, where Rebeyrolle showed a fresh series called *Coexistences*, for which Sartre wrote a preface. In 1969 Rebeyrolle had denounced the evils of imperialism: this time he attacked socialism, guilty not only of the crimes perpetrated in Prague and Moscow, but also responsible for those which are now being committed in Brazil, Greece and Vietnam, since in the name of coexistence it does not attempt to prevent them. In his pictures the red of the flag, once the sign of such great hopes, mingles with the colour of spilt blood and of gaping wounds. Rebeyrolle does not treat these shattered bodies in abstract terms: it is in their immediately material aspect that he compels us to see them with his own profound fury and horror. The reason why these feelings, although they move us deeply, still remain bearable, is what Sartre calls the pictures' 'alacrity': Rebeyrolle makes us share in the joy he felt in painting – a joy he felt through his rage.

Francis Bacon is almost unknown in France; I was not acquainted with him at all. In November 1971 I went to see the exhibition of his works at the Grand Palais, and I was taken aback. 'We are all potential carcasses,' he said in an interview. 'Every time I go into a butcher's shop it seems to me astonishing that I am not hanging there instead of the animal.' There in the Grand Palais I was surrounded by bleeding sides of beef and tortured carcasses. In the pictures called 'crucifixions' the bodies had undergone almost unbearable mutilations and distortions. There were others that seemed less violent – a man or a woman lying or sitting on a sofa: but their limbs were convulsed, their flesh quivered, the sofa was a rack and the walls were those of a prison-cell. Many of his pictures were portraits: the faces seemed to have burst apart, and the mouths were open in a shriek. A few were calmer – two very fine bull-fights and some landscapes with grey grass. But the exhibition

207

as a whole offered a tragic and sometimes even a horrible image of man's estate – man as a tortured body, as a prisoner stifling in his cage, as one who lives in terror and who feels like screaming. This terribly distressing impression is strengthened by the choice of colours – muddy purples, greys and dingy yellows. 'I have never tried to be horrible,' says Bacon. 'I believe you only have to look at things and think about life as a whole to see that what I have done does not really exaggerate that side of life.' Merely leafing through a newspaper is enough to be convinced that he is right. At this very moment thousands of mouths are shrieking, thousands of bleeding bodies are in the throes of death. The astonishing thing is that Bacon's pictures, pitilessly showing us these appalling truths, nevertheless give us real joy by what must in spite of everything be called their beauty.

I rarely miss a great exhibition of paintings or an important retrospective. But I know less about contemporary painters than I do about composers and writers. I cannot spare the time to go to galleries. And often I am bored when I do go to them. I appreciate Vasarely's 'optical sadism', but not the hundreds of pictures that are based upon it. It is now a very long time since Duchamp invented 'ready-mades', and I can detect no originality in the innumerable versions that are to be seen today. Apart from a few exceptions, I find little to interest me in anti-art. But at present it spreads and multiplies, whereas painting properly so called grows rarer and rarer.

So I still go on cultivating my mind. Am I more informed than I used to be or less? I never stop learning, but knowledge grows so fast that at the same time my ignorance increases. And my memory lets a great deal of the learning I have stored up leak away. It was above all between the ages of twenty-five and fifty that I lost so much – almost everything I knew of mathematics, Latin and Greek. I remember only the broad outlines of the systems of philosophy that I studied in former days and I have not read the books devoted to them these last twenty years. In literature I still feel very close to the writers I like. In painting and music, I have continually enriched and strengthened my knowledge: even during these last ten years I have acquired a great deal. On the whole I see where I stand in the world more clearly than when I was forty. I understand the structure of society and the course of history better than I did before;

and I am better at making out people's intentions and their reactions.

But at present what value do I place upon the culture I possess? I must confess that I am not one of those intellectuals who were deeply shaken by May 1968. In 1962, when I was finishing *Force of Circumstance*, I was already aware of the contradiction between the intellectual's universal aims and the particularism in which he is imprisoned – a contradiction exposed by Sartre.[19] It worried me once again when I began this book. I make use of language, a universal instrument; I am therefore addressing myself to all men. But I reach only a limited audience. At the present time many of the young, whom I should particularly like to reach, look upon reading as pointless. So I no longer see writing as a privileged means of communication. And yet I have carried this book on to the end and no doubt I shall write others: I may indeed challenge the worth of the writer that I am, but I cannot tear myself from that writer's personality. I cannot toss my past overboard and deny everything I have loved. During the war in Algeria I learnt to distrust music, painting and all the arts which sublimate men's pain and thereby conceal it; but nevertheless they are still very important in my life. I do not believe in the universal and everlasting value of Western culture, but it has been my food and I love it still. I should like it not to vanish entirely but to be handed on to the rising generation – most of it, at any rate. I quite see that most young people will have nothing to do with some aspects of it and I understand their having rebelled against the way it was taught them. But is there not some way of communicating that which remains valid and which might help them to live?

It is hard, I know. Several of my friends – Bianca, Sylvie, Courchay and many more – are teachers, and we have often talked over their difficulties together. Their position is wholly unlike mine in the thirties. In a few respects it is better: a teacher is allowed to deal much more freely with the subjects that interest him – he can attack what is real and immediate. There are no longer sexual taboos that he must respect. My fourteen-year-old pupils used to titter when they read the word *femur* in a Latin text, and I remember how awkward I felt when I had to explain Valéry's line 'the piercing shrieks of tickled girls' to an older class. When I talked about psychoanalysis I was compelled to approach it indirectly and

19 In an interview in *L'Idiot international* reprinted in *Situations VIII*.

209

make it insipid. Nowadays these questions are treated with a much greater openness and simplicity. But my friends tell me that the advantage does not amount to very much, because of the lycée pupils' resistance to the transmission of knowledge and particularly of philosophy.

Classes are bigger than they used to be, which makes it harder to know each pupil personally and harder to initiate discussions that do not degenerate into a general uproar. When I had twenty or thirty girls in my class I could let them express themselves as they chose: they would all want to talk at once and they would contradict one another vehemently, but I never had any difficulty in bringing them under control: keeping forty children in order is quite another matter. But this is not solely a question of numbers; far from it. I sometimes had unusually big classes, yet they were both disciplined and quick to react. It is the attitude of the pupils that has changed radically, and it is this present attitude that prevents all dialogue.

What I liked when I taught philosophy was being in the presence of minds that were completely virgin as far as this field was concerned; I saw them gradually come to life, open and grow richer; and if a pupil happened to contradict me then she did so on the basis of what I myself had taught her. Nowadays things are not the same at all. The pupils in the terminal classes of the lycées are more mature than they were in my time; they have watched the television and read the papers for years and they think they know everything – or, which gives the same result, they think there is nothing to be known about anything at all. However you look at it, man is conditioned, say some of them: and that being so, what is the point of study or thought? They distrust adults and anything a teacher may say is already discredited beforehand. They do not realize that it is the adults themselves who, by means of the mass media, have taught them the facts that they bring up against the teacher. What interests them most, no doubt in reaction to this technocratic society, is the occult sciences and 'science-fiction' worlds. But on the whole they are wanting in curiosity. The picture my friends give me is more or less gloomy according to the lycée; but they all deplore their classes' inertia and their total lack of participation. Those who teach the children of twelve and thirteen are more in contact with their pupils; they succeed in holding their attention and making them react, but they can only do so by freeing themselves from programmes that do not suit the children and by working out new relationships with them, taking no account either of discipline or the rules. This results in conflict with the authorities and with the parents. In short, teaching, which I found a pleasure, has become a thankless task at the best and often an exhausting one. The reason for this is that the nourishment provided for the young is fundamentally inadequate for their needs: the lycée has become a place of constraint, both for those who are compelled to swallow this pabulum and for those who have to serve it out. The position is so rotten that no mere reform can make it better; it would need a positive revolution to give the young the wish and the means to integrate themselves in society – either the society would have to be different or the moulding of the younger generation by the older would have to be conceived in a totally different fashion.

In the present state of affairs, I find it perfectly comprehensible that most young people no longer value knowledge at all: yet I am sorry for it. For my own part, as I have said, my curiosity is still wide open. I have already spoken of most of the fields in which it operates: now I shall turn to another – travel.

4

I love travelling as much as ever I did. In 1962 I had lost my appetite for it, but the taste has come back to me. During these last ten years I have visited and revisited a great many places. What have these explorations brought me?

In the first place they form an integral part of a much wider project that still means a great deal to me – the project of knowing. To be sure, seeing is not enough: one can pass through towns and countryside without understanding anything about either. I need conversation and reading to give me a clear notion of a country, but they alone cannot provide me with the equivalent of the flesh-and-blood presence of things. When I walk about the streets, mingling with the crowd, a town and its inhabitants begin to exist for me with a fullness that words cannot possibly convey. And then I am far more interested in places that have a connection with my actual life than in those that I have called to mind only by means of words.

Generally speaking, the journeys that I undertake for the purpose of information follow programmes that have been worked out for me by those who have invited me or who offer themselves as guides: when this is the case, it may sometimes happen that I find the things I am required to do wearisome. But more often I have the agreeable feeling of being given presents without having to make any effort beyond that of receiving them. With journeys of another kind, when it is more a question of travelling for pleasure than of gathering information, I plot the route myself; and when I do so I feel the same pleasure that filled me in former times, when I used to go for very long walks – the joy of creation. And I am always enchanted, astonished, when I actually come to places and monuments that were until that time merely abstract signs upon the map.

A journey is also a personal adventure, a change in my relationship with the world, with space and time. It often begins in bewilderment: the novelty of the place and the people make me lose my head and I am filled with a desire to do a very great many things and to do them all at once. Some of my friends are thrown into a state of anxiety when first they see an unknown city: for my part it fills me with rapture. Thanks to my sanguine habit of mind, I am persuaded that I shall soon manage to conquer this reality that is overwhelming me for the moment. Its immense abundance takes me out of myself and gives me an illusion of infinity – for a while my consciousness of my own limits and of the limits of things is done away with. That is why I treasure these moments so.

The hours I spend driving or – far less often – sitting in a train are rare and precious. A book or a film shows me the world without my seeming to have to make any personal effort – I forget my own existence. In a car, I am present and I have the feeling that it is I myself who, by my bodily movement, give rise to the visions that are presented to me – there is something intoxicating about motion when it makes the flow of time coincide with the unfolding of a space rich in meaning. It is the memory of the past and the promise of the future that most surely give the living person the illusion of catching up with his being. As I drive smoothly along a road I am perpetually at the meeting-point between memory and fresh dis- coveries; I am both memory and expectation, intensely aware of what is leaving me and of what is just about to come.

In time this perpetual flight forwards grows wearisome: sorrow at forgetting things almost as soon as they are seen outweighs the pleasure of remembering. I long for a pause and for that other great delight of travelling – contemplation. This too gives me the illusion of overtaking my being: I melt into the object I am looking at; I take over its permanence and the depth of its reality. I live in a moment that embraces eternity.

When I stop in front of a picture, a statue, the apse of a church – in front of what is called a work of art – I try to grasp its creator's intention and to understand the means he used to carry it out. I am therefore obliged to place the object in its historical and social context and to be aware of the techniques that were employed: I turn to my culture – a culture that is enriched by this new aesthetic experience. Contingent scenes – landscapes, streets, crowds, and even works of art themselves when I see them as elements in a setting in the same way as the trees and the sky – are given to me in a more surreptitious manner, and one that is harder to define. Here the spectacle that delights me has been assembled by no single intention whatsoever: it is I who endow it with a meaning by seeing it as the analogon of something other than itself. To look at this world of ours with the deliberate intention of finding aesthetic pleasure and no more surely argues an indifference to one's fellowmen or even a loathing for them. Yet the world would be a very dreary place if we were not to work out the allusions, symbols, and likenesses that refer us back to its history, to ours, to art and to literature; if it did not awake memories in us; if it did not offer us ways of escape; and if it did not suggest forms of creation to us. There are times when, in the contingence of that which is given, I catch a glimpse of the necessity of a work of art. In those lovely winter days when dawn lingers until the evening, it seems that a Breughel has assumed material form. Or the reverse may happen – in this bunch of flowers I discover a picture that has never been painted. Take these two men, walking along the saltings down by the estuary of the Seine: leaning out of my hotel window I watch them; and there I am at the beginning of a very good film. At night the curtains are drawn; the windows glow yellow, red or orange; and in hidden privacy behind those curtains the characters of a novel end their day. The whistle of a train racing through the darkening countryside comes to me from the farthest limits of an imaginary world. That is why, from a distance, I can be enchanted by places I do not want to live in and by things I do not want to possess. A provincial square: for a while I like strolling under its plane-trees and going to its cafés; I should be horrified if I were to be banished there. When I am travelling and I pass by very pretty houses – French manors, Provençal farms, chalets in the Tyrol – I feel a kind of longing: I should like to sit in that garden, to lean on that balcony and to be at home there; I should like to, but I do not want to at all. I do not really desire these imaginary delights.

That is what charms me about travelling – dream life prevails over life as it is actually lived: I tell myself stories and I play at being a different person. Yet for a long time now these shimmering mirages have no longer satisfied me. I indulge in them only at long intervals. What I want above all is to know the truth about the places I travel through.

Here there is a great deal of difference between the two kinds of journey I spoke of earlier on. In both cases I enjoy the pleasures I have just mentioned: but when I am gathering information about a country I explore it methodically, I meet a great many people, and I make inquiries about its political, economic and social problems. When I am travelling for fun I generally do so in parts of the world that I know fairly well on the theoretical plane. It is interesting to grasp certain aspects of that reality as it is actually lived. But what I am mainly concerned with is discovering sites and famous buildings. And it is these more or less haphazard explorations that I shall talk about first.

When I was younger I was greedy for a continual stream of fresh sights, of new things to be seen. For a long time now I have found a happiness in seeing what I have seen before. For me, seeing a place again means mingling the faded sweetness of memory with the smile of what is new – inserting the brilliance of fresh discovery into a resuscitated past. Things are almost never quite the same as my recollection of them; or if they are, then they show me a different aspect of themselves. Sometimes the encounter makes me sad: I miss the peace of the old Provençal villages, the solitude of places now invaded by hideous great buildings, the tranquillity of those little Roman squares that have been turned into car-parks, and the rasping sweetness of a countryside that is now ringed by concrete.

But time is not always a destroyer; in France, Italy and Yugoslavia I have seen frescoes and buildings brought to life after long neglect or natural disasters had hidden or ruined them.

In former days I liked travelling alone; I enjoyed the pleasure of organizing my own solitude. At present I far prefer sharing my experiences with someone who matters a great deal to me – usually with Sartre, sometimes with Sylvie. In the following pages I do not differentiate between *I* and *we*; but in fact, apart from a few short periods, I always had someone with me.

Sartre and I have continued to spend the greater part of our summers in Rome. L'Albergo Nazionale, at the far end of the Piazza Montecitorio, by the parliament building, has installed air-conditioning; and that is where we stay now. I used to like living at the edge of the city, but I like being in the very middle even more. There we were once again, breakfasting and reading the papers every morning by the Pantheon. That was the square from which we first set out to discover Rome, almost forty years ago. We had stayed in several of the hotels either in this square or very close to it. The scene had not changed and it was still the same waiter who brought us our coffee: his fair hair was now white. Yet every year some details slightly change the city's face. In 1964 the obelisk in the Piazza Montecitorio was railed off and hidden by scaffolding: it was in danger of collapsing, and they were strengthening it. A new bar called the Navona had opened in the square of the same name, and in the evening we saw its little lamps glowing red under their silk shades.

In the afternoons we went for a stroll. We revisited our favourite places and we rediscovered some that we had rather forgotten – the inside of the Castel S. Angelo; the Golden House, whose stuccoes and decorations inspired the artists of the Renaissance when they painted their 'grotesques'; S. Agnes and S. Costanza, where the naive mosaics enchanted us long ago. Once again we saw the Caravaggios in their various churches and we liked them more than ever. Sometimes we drove about the suburbs that have invaded the Roman Campagna with astonishing speed, now reaching the foot of the Alban hills. 'A ring of concrete: even the climate in Rome is changed,' said Pajetta. Or we would go farther, out to Ostia, Tarquinia, Cerveteri or the Castelli Romani. In 1964 we took the brand-new autostrada that runs across the Sabine hills beneath high-perched villages, sometimes almost touching their low-roofed houses. We had lunch at Orvieto and saw the Signorellis once more. How memory fails one! All I remembered of those frescoes, which I had seen several times, was the resurrection of the dead: certainly, it is a most striking picture, but that of hell, with its blue-bottomed fiends cheerfully torturing the damned and its armoured archangels looking like the Teutonic Knights in *Alexander Nevsky*, is no less impressive. The angels with aerodynamic wings diving towards the earth at the speed of a jet might have come out of science-fiction. And how could I have forgotten the Anti-Christ with his face looking false and evil as he harangues a gullible crowd? Another surprise: since I was a methodical traveller, I must in former times have been to see that well, where two spiral flights of steps plunge more than two hundred feet for asses to go and fetch the water. Seen from above, it is an astonishing spectacle; and I had no recollection of it whatsoever.

Yet we also spent many hours in our rooms. Generally speaking I did not work. As others abandon themselves to the warmth of the sun and the sound of the sea, so I bathed myself in Rome. From my

216

window I could see tiled roofs, green bowers, and terraces covered with pots of flowers, watered every morning by a nun. Sometimes I gazed at this charming urban landscape: more often I lay on my bed, soothed by the hum of the air-conditioner; and as I turned the pages of my book I would see the blue of the sky on the other side of the panes. I read a great deal in Rome. I brought all the interesting books that had come out during the year and that I had not had time to look at: or older books that I had either neglected or forgotten. And I also devoured detective stories, in French, English, or above all Italian. It was a way of keeping myself occupied without leaving the spot. I did not believe in them enough to fly away far from Rome, yet the progress of the adventures filled the time.

The most precious hours for me were the evenings, which we carried on far into the night. We would dine and then we would have a few drinks in the places we liked. We left the Piazza S. Eustaccio because there was too much laughter and noise round the sellers of pissing dolls, preferring the Piazza Navona and the Piazza Santa Maria in Trastevere. Unfortunately, until 1967, they were invaded by cars, tourists' coaches, men who sold red balloons, and caricaturists. The square by the Pantheon was much quieter, and as a new bar had been opened there, that was where we often spent our time. Although my feelings have grown less easily moved with age, the beauty of the Roman nights can still strike right to my heart. There on the Piazza Navona, between the stone fountains and the red-brown houses, stood two horse-drawn cabs, close against the pavement; their coachwork was a gleaming black, and against it the red of the wheels made a violent splash of colour; I felt a joy as inexplicable and as piercing as anguish. 'It is anguish in reverse,' I said to Sartre. The presence of the world dazzled me; and in doing so it showed my future absence in counter-relief.

Sometimes when we were sitting on the terrace of a café, people would greet us or ask for autographs. This they did very gracefully. Once, in a little street near the hotel, where you can eat the best ices in Rome, but a street so narrow that the cars almost brush the tables, a red car suddenly stopped. An elegant young woman, dressed entirely in red, darted towards me. '*C'é lei o non c'é?*' I smiled, without answering. Then in French she said, 'Are you Simone de Beauvoir?' 'Yes.' She seized my hand and she shook it for quite a while, laughing; then she ran back to the car. Sometimes

217

young men asked Sartre for an appointment, particularly revolutionaries from Latin America.

When French friends passed through Rome we spent some time with them. And we saw some Italians, too. Carlo Levi had moved. Now he lived in a huge studio full of books and pictures in the middle of a semi-public park: he often used to ask us to lunch. We also saw the Communist leaders – Pajetta, Alicata up until the year he died, and Rosana Rossanda, who was in charge of cultural policy in Togliatti's days and with whom we got on very well. It would have delighted us if culture had been in such good hands in the French Communist Party.

The summer of 1964 was marked by Togliatti's death. At the interval of a few days the papers gave the news that both the president of the republic, Segni, and Togliatti had had a stroke. People did not say much about Segni, who gradually recovered; but every day there were huge headlines and long articles on the state of Togliatti's health. He had collapsed when he was travelling in the USSR and he was in a coma. One morning the walls of Rome were covered with posters: *E morto Togliatti. Togliatti é morto.* Sartre had met him several times: he thought it remarkable that Togliatti, though he was entirely a man of action, should also have remained an intellectual; and that he had managed to ensure the Italian Communist Party a fair degree of independence with regard to Moscow. The people worshipped him. The attempt on his life a few years after the war had very nearly set off bloody reprisals. It was he who whispered the words of appeasement from his sick-bed 'No adventures, comrades, no adventures.' The Italian workers were overwhelmed by his death. His body was brought back to Rome: it lay in state and it was watched over by comrades at the party's headquarters in the via delle Botteghe Oscure. The street was closed and all day long an immense crowd of people filed past the coffin: many men were in tears. On the morning of the funeral, coaches poured armies of peasants into the Pantheon square: most of them had bottles of red wine in their hands, and every now and then they would take a long pull. Claude Roy and Loleh Bellon came from San Gimignano; in their coach there were perhaps a hundred peasants, singing the *Bandiera Rossa*. One of them had come to Rome for only the second time in his life: the first had been to join in a demonstration against the attempted assassination of Togliatti. Presently in all the streets we saw groups marching by, carrying red

218

flags still furled about their poles. They leant them up against the wall while they had a drink on a café terrace or picnicked sitting on the kerb. Many of them settled down in the Piazza di Venezia, under the balcony where once Mussolini used to hold forth. An immense sun blazed down on this funeral feast. We stood on the top of a little flight of steps at the foot of Trajan's Column, waiting to see the coffin pass by. An immense procession stretched as far as the Coliseum and beyond, their red flags floating in the breeze. All along the route groups came from side streets to take their appointed places. Behind the hearse walked the woman who had shared Togliatti's life, with his adopted daughter, then the important members of the party, followed by a huge crowd. The procession lasted until nightfall, but we left before the end. All the streets and squares of Rome were filled with excitement and restlessness, and men in black clothes invaded all the café terraces.

During our stay, the year after that, Italy was devastated by terrible floods. Torrential rivers tore over the autostrada between Orvieto and Florence, carrying cars away – eight tourists were drowned. Walking about the middle of Rome, one saw no sign of the disaster at all. But the island in the Tiber was half under water and the Milvio bridge was closed – it was a furious, threatening river that tore beneath it. The Porta Prima district was almost entirely destroyed; the people had lost everything they possessed and they had no roof over their heads.

It was that summer I first went to Bomarzo. In the eighteenth century a sadistic sculptor carved baroque monsters there, and they amazed the people who came unexpectedly upon them in that wild landscape. I thought them curious; but now the park in which they stand has been done up for tourists; there were quantities of Romans eating their picnics there and the monsters astonished me less than people had foretold.

Before going back to Paris, we set off on a little tour to see some of the Italian towns again. This was both a recapitulation and a rediscovery: the reality coincided with some of my memories, but it always brought me something new. At Perugia we sat at the same café where thirty years before I had delighted in an apricot sorbet, and the same landscape stretched out at our feet; but I had forgotten the singular aqueduct that runs across the lower town, and I did not know the underground street, lined with sixteenth-century houses, that runs right through the Rocca Paolina. I had often been to

Bolgona, and there it was again; but I had known nothing of one of its greatest beauties, and I discovered it only then – the Piazza S. Stefano, surrounded by palaces and churches, two of which go back to the eleventh century. The circular church of the Calvary belongs to the twelfth, and its architecture is of the most touching purity. I knew the Giottos in Padua well, but I had not remembered the very fine Mantegnas. Mantua, Verona and Cremona were their old selves; but the wealth and the freshness of their immediate presence quite wiped out the old images that I had retained.

In 1966 we did not stay in Rome as long as usual because we were to go to Japan; my thoughts were already there; I read books about the country from morning till night and Rome was less with me than it had been in other years.

The year after that we came into Italy by way of Venice. I always love the moment when the gondola first turns into a small canal: the entire city opens itself to you, with its faded pinks, its pinkish greys, its scaling brick and stone. I spent some particularly happy hours at the exhibition of the Vedutisti: as I was there, walking about in this painted Venice, I could sense the real Venice stretching all around me. I liked the Canalettos very much indeed and the Guardis even more, as I always do. The young Canaletto, the Canaletto whose pictures helped in the rebuilding of Warsaw, carried me away to Germany and to Austria. And I was delighted with those paintings called *Fantasia* or *Capriccio* in which the artist arbitrarily brought various ruins together, and even some that did not exist at all: a column stands next to a triumphal arch and a half-fallen wall, the whole in a great wealth of foliage – a scene created by the artist's fantasy, for he had never set eyes upon it anywhere at all.

I remember Rome of that year above all for its violent storms. One burst on a September night when I was in the Piazza Navona. From the first floor I beheld the deserted square in all its baroque purity – never a soul in sight and the asphalt gleaming in the rain.

We went back to Venice for the festival: Sartre wanted to be present at the showing of *Le Mur* because he liked the film that Serge Roulet had made from his story.[1] For the first time I flew over the city: we came down through the clouds just as the plane was directly above it. The dyke, the lagoon and the islands could be seen perfectly, and then, as the plane lost height and turned, I made out the Grand Canal, the Campanile, the little canals and the streets

[1] *Intimacy* in the English edition.—Tr.

as clearly as on a model – one glance gave you Venice whole. Roulet was waiting for us at the airport, and we skimmed across the lagoon in an outboard. Fishermen, up to their knees in the water, stood in a half circle stretching a great net fixed to boats over against them: their movements harmonized so well with the water and the sky that the whole might have been a show put on by some inspired producer.

We had lunch at the Fenice with the Roulets and Goytisolo; he had been at the festival for several days and he was infuriated by the quantities of children in the films as well as by all the promiscuous fornication, each example just as conventional as the rest in its carefully-dosed audacity. When Godard's *La Chinoise* was shown, Goytisolo happened to be sitting next to the Soviet critic. 'When the little Vietnamese girl began calling out "Help, help, Mr Kosygin!" I was so embarrassed for him that I dared not look,' he told us. But the Soviet had remained totally unmoved.

Chiarini directed the festival, and he was much criticized for his severity; he had based his selection on the intellectual qualities of the films rather than upon the starlets' charms. He took us to the Lido in a launch. At the landing-stage we took a horse-drawn cab to go to see Maheu, the director of UNESCO. He was an old friend of Sartre's, but they had lost touch for a while; however, now they saw one another quite often. He was staying at the Hôtel des Bains, where Mann situated *Death in Venice*, and we were delighted with its old-fashioned charm. We had a drink on a terrace looking out over a big garden. We were deeply interested in his account of the reasons why Venice was threatened with very serious damage. The protecting dykes were destroyed in the eighteenth century, and when there is a wind the sea flows into the lagoon. The town is built on piles, and it stands on a spongy subsoil; when the water presses upon the foundations, this subsoil swells and the ground cracks, which is the explanation of those geysers that burst out between the paving-stones in St Mark's Square in times of heavy rain. Then again the dust and waste from the factories have accumulated, and the land has eaten into the lagoon. What is more, so much refuse goes into the canals that their beds are rising year by year: at the least flood, water flows into the cellars and even the ground floors. Measures could be taken to lessen all these dangers – among other things, dykes might be rebuilt. But there is another peril for which no remedy is known: gases from the factories attack not the brick but the stone; and the better the quality of the stone the worse the attack – it is above all marble that crumbles away. And so long as it is not known why this happens, nothing can be done to avert the danger.

Late that afternoon we saw *Le Mur*. The cast acted very well, particularly Castillo, who had spent his childhood in a camp for deportees and who slipped into the role of a prisoner without any difficulty. The part of the Belgian doctor was taken by a commercial traveller; he gave a perfectly natural performance of the character, whose odious nature he had never grasped. The setting was restrained and effective. Only the end of the film worried me: in the story it amounts to no more than ten lines and it is taken as a literary artifice of no consequence; on the screen it lasts longer, and the images have too much importance.

The lounge of the Excelsior at eight o'clock in the evening – what a circus! Rubbing elbows in the crowd there were ancients, young men, women in ordinary town clothes, and others who seemed to be in fancy-dress, with long, long gowns, either exceedingly severe or exceedingly low-necked. I saw Christiane Rochefort, gay and friendly; Moravia, whose hair had grown much whiter; Odette Joyeux, who was still wonderfully fresh and elegant. We had dinner on the terrace with Basso and his wife – they go to the festival every year. Our table was against the parapet, and without stirring I could gaze at the vast expanse of smooth water, gentle in the falling dusk.

A few days later we were sitting in the Piazza Navona after dinner when a young man came up to us. 'I'm Michel del Castillo.' He was slim, young and smiling – very unlike the Pablo whose part he had played so well. 'It was easy for me to take that role,' he said. 'I only had to remember.' He told us briefly about his childhood – a childhood described in his first book, *Tanguy*: a Spanish Communist mother, denounced by his father, a French bourgeois; the years spent in camps in France and in Germany; then in a Spanish reformatory from which he escaped when he was sixteen. He was writing a book about Spain: later we published part of it in *Les Temps modernes*, an interesting chapter in which he shows how in Spain the notion of honour is linked with that of the Old Christian, the *viejo cristiano*, as opposed to the converted Moor or Jew.[2]

[2] He later wrote a fine book on Gabrielle Russier: the family of the young man had it confiscated.

The two following summers we did not leave Rome at all, and it had never seemed to us more delightful. We were on the top floor of the hotel, in rooms that gave on to a terrace; from there we had an immense view over the roofs of Rome and its hills, and the noises of the town scarcely reached us. In the morning we had our breakfast up there: scattered round us, five or six teams of masons and tilers were repairing chimneys, building pent-houses, mending roofs; they seemed to be merely twiddling their thumbs, yet gradually the work went forward. In the day-time it was too hot to be outside. But almost every evening I went to watch the sun setting behind St Peter's in a blaze of fire. After dinner, we often came back to the hotel. We had a refrigerator that we filled with ice and drinks, and we sat late on our flat roof, drinking and talking. In the silent night the illuminated monuments shone out – Victor-Emmanuel's, alas, but also the Capitol, the Quirinal, the Castel San Angelo and St Peter's.

We walked about less than we had in other years because we had the feeling of being in all the streets and all the squares of Rome at one and the same time. Yet in the evenings we also liked lingering in the Piazza Navona. A new regulation fortunately meant that it was forbidden to cars. The very evening we arrived, the owner of the Navona Bar – a handsome dark young man with emerald-green corduroy trousers, a violet shirt and a broad studded leather belt – got us to sign a petition asking for the measure not to be revoked; some shopkeepers were against it and the police would have liked to oppose it too – in that summer of 1968 they were afraid that subversive young people might take possession of the square, and indeed a few days before they had provoked some fighting. For our part we were enchanted – no more noise, no more reek of petrol, no more cars blocking the road along the pavements. There were many young people in the big space in the middle: left-wingers who met at the Navona Bar; hippies, pouffes, homosexuals and guitar-players by the central fountain; and by another fountain painters who spread their horrible, very academic daubs on the ground. There were a few pretty girls in miniskirts, but it was chiefly men who paraded about, tightly clothed in silk, satin and brilliantly coloured lamé: we might have been back in the days of Pinturicchio. Drugs were sold, but no doubt little more than around the Trevi fountain or on the Spanish Steps. One night it rained. From our sheltered café terrace we saw the boys and girls run off barefoot, dragging

223

their guitars, rucksacks and bed-rolls. (Where, in fact, did they sleep?) Others flattened themselves against a wall or huddled under balconies: through the curtain of rain their red, pink, orange, violet clothes gleamed against the ochre of the stone.

That summer we had many conversations with our Italian friends. Rosana Rossanda was no longer in charge of culture for the Italian Communist party; now she had time to devote to her theoretical work. We talked about the *mouvement de Mai* in France and the student movements in Italy and the rest of the world; she had a deep understanding of the question. Basso, one of the leaders of the PSIUP, discussed the policy of the PCI with us. He told us about an affair that was making a great deal of noise just then: a homosexual had been convicted of committing the crime of *plagia* against two boys and he had been sent to prison for nine years. In Italy, *plagia* – that is to say bewitchment – takes place when a person induces another to do what he wishes by means of captivating his will. If a girl (even though she may be of age) or a married woman leaves home to go with a lover, the family can accuse the seducer of *plagia*. Basso would have liked to have this mediaeval law done away with, but the official men of law would not agree. After 21 August we were all wholly taken up with the fate of Czechoslovakia.

The summer of 1969 was so very like that of 1968 that there were times when I wondered whether the year that lay between had ever really been. Yet a few changes had come about. The police had carried out great sweeps among the drug-traffickers in the Piazza Navona; there were fewer young and they were not so dashing. In the evening the whole of one side in the middle was invaded by painters who tried to sell their pictures, and by men selling red balloons: there was even one fire-eater. Fortunately the other half of the square was given over to solitude and quietness. The Piazza Santa Maria in Trastevere had also become an *isola pedonale*, and it was possible to gaze at the lovely baroque fountain and the gold of the mosaics on the front of the church in peace. That year the Romans hardly left their city, in spite of the *afa;* on 12 August, under the glaring sky and in a humid heat, the streets were still packed. We saw a great deal of Rosana Rossanda, who had just started a magazine called *Il Manifesto* with some of her friends. She was very much concerned with the problem of the relationship between the masses and the organization of the party, and the PCI did not think her views orthodox. She was afraid of being excluded from the party and in fact this happened a little later.

1970 was like the earlier years. In its turn the Piazza Farnese had been decreed an *isola pedonale*, and one could enjoy the beauty of the fountains and the palace at one's leisure. But the Piazza Navona was invaded by painters and tourists; it was much the same mob that one sees in the place du Tertre. The great attraction that year was the campaign in favour of divorce. A lorry stood at one of the entrances to the Piazza Navona, covered with posters, caricatures and slogans exhorting the senators to vote for the divorce-bill. Men and women paraded up and down in front of the Senate carrying placards that said 'Courage, senators. Do not let yourselves be frightened by the priests. Vote for the divorce-bill.' Some militants went on hunger-strike. Others held meetings or collected signatures. Basso and Levi thought that the bill would be passed in October but that in fact a divorce would be very hard to get; whereas for a modest sum the Church quite freely annulled religious marriages. So if one chose to keep a way out, a religious marriage was better than a civil one.

We made a splendid trip to Fara in Sabina, a very old village perched on a hill in the middle of the Sabine range that has a view over a vast rolling landscape. I visited Rieti, which I did not know, and I revisited Aquila. I had meant to come back by the autostrada which was indicated by green notices on the way out of Rome. But apart from a short stretch it did not yet exist. We saw workmen and bulldozers busy high above us as we went along the bottom of a valley, keeping to a little crowded road.

In 1971 part of our terrace had been transformed into a room separated from the open roof by a glassed partition; it was even more agreeable than it had been in the earlier years, because now it was possible to stay out even in the heat of the day. We spent most of our time there, either in the shelter or in the open air. I know nothing more beautiful than this city when the dusk falls and the stars prick out above the dark roofs and the outlines of St Peter's, swimming in fiery mists, seem to enclose its immaterial spirit.

During the war in Algeria, it became impossible for me to travel about France for pleasure. Now, although I have not recovered much liking for my fellow-countrymen, I no longer find their presence oppressive.

225

So having acknowledged this country where I have my roots as my own again, I wanted to possess it once more. I had explored the outskirts of Paris on a bicycle during the war and by car once I had learnt to drive. But now, thanks to the motorways, these outskirts stretch out much farther than they did in former times. Making little trips of a day or so, I rediscovered the Ile-de-France and the surrounding provinces. These regions have so often been devastated by war that there are not many old villages left, nor many old quarters in the towns. Here and there one may catch sight of half-timbered houses with oriel windows, their woodwork decorated with carving: at Troyes there are some mediaeval streets with tall, narrow houses topped with gables that almost meet across the lane. In a few squares covered markets are to be seen, built of wood and roofed with tiles. The bigger private houses, being built of brick or stone, have resisted time better than the rest. At Sens and Chartres and Meaux there are streets in which I have strolled with the greatest pleasure. But, in under two hours from Paris, the only urban landscape that has really impressed me very deeply is at Arras – the whole formed by the Grande and the Petite Place, which have both been excellently restored. This is one of those cases where time renews instead of destroying. When I was a child and I went to Arras, where my father had relations, I was shown photographs of the town as it had been before 1914: all that then remained of the centre was a few blackened stones. I went back not long ago. I saw the belfry and the arcaded squares designed by Flemish architects influenced by Spain, a union that produced a masterpiece.

Yet the greater part of the buildings that have survived the disasters of war in the Ile-de-France and the surrounding country are châteaux and churches. The interior decoration of the châteaux leaves me unmoved; what I am interested in is the building and its surroundings. Even at this modest pitch, my curiosity is not always easy to satisfy. Often entry to the park is forbidden. When this is so, I sometimes tiptoe into the forbidden ground, either hiding or mingling with a group of authorized tourists. Once, at the lovely château of La Grange Bléneau, where La Fayette lived, an enraged caretaker set a tiny dog on me, fortunately far too late. In other cases, caretakers have asked nothing better than to be bribed. And then seeing the place is often officially allowed or at least tolerated. In one way or another I have managed to visit many very fine châteaux that I knew nothing about – the eighteenth-century Le

Marais, whose elegant façade rises at the far end of an immense rectangular sheet of water – Boni de Castellane gave famous parties there. Vaux, on which Fouquet spent eighteen millions and where Le Nôtre designed the magnificent park. The keep and the towers of Septmonts, abandoned in a garden full of weeds and nettles. Vivier en Brie, where Charles VI was shut up; its ruined walls are covered with ivy, and it stands there mirrored in a lake. La Grange-le-Roi, built of brick and stone at the end of the sixteenth century and still intact; it is surrounded by moats, immense lawns and leafy trees. But to all those I have mentioned and to many more I have passed over in silence I prefer Champ-de-Bataille, another sixteenth-century brick and stone château. Two main buildings face one another in the middle of a grassy plain; they form the sides of a great courtyard which is closed at one end by an immense wall with a magnificent gateway in it, and at the other by a kind of triumphal arch. I saw it in the setting sun, and the long low lines of the pink façades and the vastness of the court, edged with wrought-iron railings and with porticoes, made a scene of deeply stirring grandeur.

There is less hazard in going to see churches: there is always a little door that opens in the end. One plunges into the cold, the smell of candles and incense: the nave is decorated with faded lilies and dusty artificial flowers. Often the architecture is plain and beautiful. Among others I liked the little fortified churches that dot the countryside to the south of Laon; they are all alike, but each has some detail that sets it off from the rest. Always, even in the humblest of them, there is something to attract my attention – stalls, misericords, an altar-piece, a rood-screen, statues carved in wood or stone, tombs. At Houdan a charmingly naive fresco shows pilgrims on their way to the distant monastery of Montserrat. At Villemaur the steeple is covered with oak shingles from top to bottom; it looks like a prehistoric animal with scaly armour. On the floor of the beautiful collegiate church of Ecouis I found this inscription 'Here lies the child, here lies the father, here lies the mother, here lies the brother, here lies the wife and the husband; there are only two bodies here. 1502.' I wonder who invented the incredible story to which these words allude: Berthe, the daughter of the Comte de Chatillon, married the lord of Ecouis. By him she had a son who went to Italy with Charles VII. At Bourges he met his mother, did not recognize her, and got her with child – a girl. As fate would have it, eighteen years later he married this girl who was also his sister. They discovered the truth and died of anguish!

One of the most curious sanctuaries I know is the crypt of Jouarre, which dates from the seventh century. It has two funerary chapels, the one dedicated to Saint Thelchilde, the other to Saint Ebrégisile. The first is the finest Merovingian monument that we possess. The vaults rest on six antique columns, made of coloured marble and ornamented with splendid capitals that follow the Byzantine tradition. The remains of Saint Thelchilde lie in a sarcophagus decorated with water-lily leaves. Others hold Saint Agilbert, Saint Ozane and other small saints with strange names, such as the Venerable Mode, and Saint Balde.

Valéry was right when he compared architecture with music. When I walked into the cathedral of Soissons – rebuilt after the 1914–18 war exactly as it had been – I felt a joy very like that which music sometimes gives me. How harmonious it is, that hemicycle rising in one of the cross-braces! I knew Rheims cathedral from photographs: I thought the building itself cumbersome. But I was wonderstruck when I discovered Saint-Rémi. I admired the inside of the famous cathedral at Laon – the pattern for so many others – but the façade seemed to me flimsy. (I had seen it in the days when Sartre was teaching at Laon: I remembered absolutely nothing of it whatsoever.) I also went to see some of those abbeys which are scattered about the countryside – Bec Hellouin, which was the intellectual centre of the West from the eleventh to the thirteenth centuries. Royaumont, of which I had heard so much. I love the way their towers, their cloisters, their ancient stones mingle with the grass and the trees and the running water of a brook.

I knew the broad outlines of the forests, valleys, hills and plateaux that I travelled through in these journeys. But one day, driving along deep lanes through the lovely forest of Saint-Gobain, I was astonished by the sudden appearance of a melancholy pool, surrounded by trees, with a deserted monastery on its bank – Le Tortoir. It was a vision that seemed to lie outside this world: no road could ever take me back to it. The old caretaker who lived there quite alone showed me what were once the monks' quarters, a chapel, and a ruined hospice. It was once a place of pilgrimage, and it received a great many visitors. There is talk of restoring it. But Le Tortoir will never be so touching as it is in this state of abandonment.

228

I made a rather long tour in the Ardennes. The forest of Arden: because of Shakespeare, I dreamt of an enchanted place. And it was an enchanted place. A very blue and very gay young morning: snow carpeting the ground, clothing the branches of trees, the bushes and the undergrowth with its glittering crystals. The car glided along through the solitude and the silence. I got out, and my feet crunched as I walked along a path to a viewpoint that showed me an infinity of whiteness. When I left this magic spot I travelled up the valley of the Meuse; I saw its dark waters and its slate-quarries, Givet, its roofs covered with slates of a violet-pink, and Charleville, whose ducal square is almost as beautiful as the Place des Vosges.

I wanted to know Champagne. Verdun, where my mother lived all through her girlhood, is rather sad, but for me it was peopled by the memories she had so often talked about. I went to see the nearby places whose names had caused my childish heart so much pain – Apremont, Le Mort-Homme, the Eparges ridge, and the Argonne. Now the trees were all in leaf and the bushes were green; but everywhere there were old photographs for sale, showing burnt, blackened landscapes, shattered trees, woods torn apart – images familiar to me from films about the war. Notices showed where there had once been villages and where not a trace remained. I saw *buttes* and *côtes* whose names reminded me of the old communiqués: how many men had died to take or to defend those scraps of earth! The forest of Vaux, the fort of Douaumont, its graveyard, its huge ossuary, the Trench of the Bayonets, where a whole platoon of Bretons were buried alive – all that is to be seen is the rusting points sticking out of the ground. The heroic places of my childhood. Rosalie;[3] our gallant *poilus*; dead men, on your feet! Places whose horror overwhelmed me in my adolescence, when I sobbed over the films and the books that told of this enormous slaughter. And still, when I think of the five hundred thousand dead at Verdun, I am filled with nausea and my heart rebels.

The days that followed were quieter. I saw Domrémy in the sun, Vaucouleurs, little forest tracks, churches with pure lines, almost all of them containing fine statues of Our Lady or various saints. At Avioth, whose style lies between fourteenth-century Gothic and flamboyant, there is a curious little monument called the Receveresse, where the pilgrims' offerings were received. I wandered about the upper town of Bar-le-Duc, where almost all the

[3] Pet name for bayonet.—Tr.

229

houses are old and well preserved; and in the church of Saint-Etienne I looked long at a masterpiece that to my shame I did not know at all – Ligier Richier's *Le Décharné*. It is a dead body, half flayed and half skeleton, in which the soul still dwells – a man living yet already mummified. He stands upright, holding his heart towards heaven.[4] I saw more of Ligier Richier's sculpture in those parts. He was born at Saint-Mihiel, and in a church there thirteen statues, more than life-size, stand round the Holy Sepulchre. He combined the influences of Champagne with those of Italy, uniting the macabre taste of the fifteenth century most successfully with the realism of the Renaissance.

I stopped at Langres, and from its ramparts I had an immense view out over the valley of the Meuse : I loved the massive towers of Langres, its fine town houses, and Saint-Mammès, the cathedral : here Burgundian Romanesque mingles with the new-born Gothic, and the whole is curiously influenced by the many Gallo-Roman ruins that are to be seen in the neighbourhood. I passed through Châteauvillain. It was exactly like the picture I had retained, with its neat little houses and their brightly-coloured shutters held back against the wall by clasps in the shape of little people. I found Jacques' house again, and the tree-lined avenue and the gateway of the park where we had seen the deer. But not the tower covered with wild roses.

The pleasure I took in these trips induced me to make quite a long journey in France during the summer of 1969. There was one region that I hardly knew at all – the west of the country, between the Loire and the Pyrenees. That was the part I chose. I had always left the plains to one side, but now the peaceful landscapes south of the Loire delighted me : the shadows of the clouds quarrelled with the sun for possession of the greens and golds of the meadows, and above my head the huge torn sky was a sight as continually varying as the sea – clouds drove across, joined company, drew out in wisps; now the light came filtering through and now it shone down with all its force. I never grew tired of watching those lofty evolutions. Farther on I liked the up-and-down of the Bocage Vendéen and its deep, hedge-lined lanes that suddenly open out at the top of a hill and offer you an immense view in every direction. The wind-

---

[4] On a tomb in the little Romanesque chapel of the Templars at Laon I saw a recumbent figure, and this body too is just about to turn into a skeleton. It was striking, but less so than the upright corpse of Bar-le-Duc.

mills the Vendéens used for signalling the movements of the republican troops are still to be seen on the top of the Monts des Alouettes. I glided, charmed, over the still waters of the Poitevin marsh; it was hard to believe that on Sundays it becomes a confused, noisy mass of boats that block the canals. That morning I was alone with the boatman as he rowed miles along watery lanes lined with poplars and peopled with crowds of blue dragonflies. A few cows (they are moved by boat, trembling with fear) browsed in meadows surrounded by water on every side. At long intervals the canals intersect, making vast liquid crossroads. What a silence! A silence broken only by the plash of the water on the oars. The solid earth seemed a great way off.

I went to see Nohant. It so happened that I was reading the letters of George Sand at the time, and they bring not only her but the whole period back to life. The little square is charming, particularly the minute church that looks like a toy, with its hooded porch. What interested me most in the house was the two theatres, above all the marionette theatre and the collection of puppets made by Maurice and dressed by George Sand. I also saw some of the places she loved – those great grey rocks that are called 'les pierres jaunâtres'; Gargilesse, where she had a house; the château of Crozant; and the whole valley of the Creuse. Twenty years before I had ridden along this valley on a bicycle; yet it did not bring me the slightest echo of my past. Still farther south, I came to a sudden halt: there was the Gironde before me, and from the height of the citadel of Blaye I could see the lead-coloured river flowing away as far as eye could reach.

But even more than the rivers and the meadows, even more than the forests and their secret pools, it was the frescoes in the Romanesque churches that enchanted me. I had not known of their existence. I discovered those of Montoire, Vic, Lavardin and Gargilesse: the brightly-clothed figures in the crypt of Tavant seem to be dancing above the columns. The loveliest paintings are those that decorate the wonderful barrel-vaulted roof of Saint-Savin; they date from the beginning of the twelfth century, and in a naive, poetic epitome they tell the stories of the Creation, of Abraham and of Moses.

All through Poitou, Saintonge and the Angoumois I found treasures of an architecture that I hardly knew at all. In order to assert its own personality against the north, where Gothic was coming into flower, the country south of the Loire remained faithful

231

to Romanesque until the end of the thirteenth century. But the builders wanted their churches to be able to compete with the huge Gothic cathedrals, and they were obliged to invent new techniques that would allow Romanesque to attain equally vast proportions, as it does at Saint-Savin, Poitiers, Angoulême and Aulnay. And there are also swarms of very little churches – six hundred in Saintonge alone – which in many cases astonish one with their delicate grace, the harmonious wealth of sculpture surrounding their main doorways, the tracery of their apses and the originality of their capitals. When I came to compare them with one another, I was deeply impressed by the fact that, on the basis of a few plain, rigorous principles, it had been possible to work out so many subtle variations : and once I had understood the difference between the barrel-vault and the line of cupolas, both in the part each plays and the consequences that follow, then the connection between the functional and the aesthetic became obvious. As my comparisons and my experience grew, so my interest increased. I learnt to distinguish the Romanesque of Poitou from that of the Périgord, and to recognize the variants to be found in Saintonge and the Angoumois; I marked the difference between cupolas with pendentives and those with squinches, between pine-cone and classical bell-towers, and between porches in the form of a triumphal arch and those which have a tympanum. I identified the various arches – the semicircular, segmental, high-pitched, dropped, horseshoe and cusped; and once I could name them I saw them far better.

I found these churches in towns, large and small, in sleepy villages, and sometimes even in total solitude, at the end of a path, surrounded by woods, fields and silence. One that I liked best was the round church of Neuvy-Saint-Sépulcre, which contains a complete circus, that is to say a series of columns forming a perfect circle : many others have these circuses open in front. One of the strongest emotions I ever had came to me at Salignac. Employing the system of a line of cupolas, the Romanesque architects succeeded in building churches with a single very broad and very high nave. When I walked into that of Salignac I found myself at the top of a flight of twelve steps, dominating a long and most impressively majestic nave. At the far end of this vast space sat twelve black-robed monks, facing the door : standing opposite them there was a priest, and he was chanting. It was as though I had been projected far back through the centuries – it was exactly like a session of the Inquisition.

Once again I saw the wonderful statues in the doorways of Beaulieu and Moissac, elongated like so many El Grecos. In many of the churches there were small, homely, familiar figures made of painted wood; among others the little coloured saints of Saint-Junien delighted me, particularly the enchanting Saint Barbara. When a sculptor works on a capital, the lack of space obliges him to adopt an ingenious compression: sometimes the carving is patterned on Eastern monsters or on symbols, but one often sees realistic scenes too – Delilah cutting off Samson's hair, for example. Often the artist has fun, and his work touches upon the ludicrous; among some rather astonishing bas-reliefs in the cloister at Cadouin, there is one corbel that shows Aristotle mounted by a courtesan.

Next to the church in some villages I saw an object that I had never come across before – a lantern of the dead. It is a tall, tapering, hollow tower ending in a stone lantern in which a light was placed every evening. At Fernioux, a very small hamlet lost in the green countryside, it looked like a delicate reflection of the church's bell-tower.

Nor had I ever heard of monolithic churches, cut into the living rock of a cliff. There is one hollowed out in a precipice above the Charente: at one time the river washed the rock, but now it has receded, and meadows stand between the two. The monks who lived in this troglodytic hermitage ferried pilgrims across the river, on their way to Saint James of Compostella – many of the churches and monasteries in this region stand along the road to Compostella, and carved on their porches one sees the scallop-shell. Saint-Emilion has another, a very large one: it harboured the stained glass from Chartres during the last war. The rock-church at Aubeterre was excavated in the twelfth century and it remained in use until the eighteenth. They are strange constructions: they look like immense natural caves; yet the columns, the vaulting and the altars were all cut in the rock by the hands of men.

It was a moving day when I crossed into the Limousin. I did not know the Blond or the Ambazac hills, but there I once more found the bracken, the chestnut-trees, the grey rocks and the blue distances of my childhood. In those days La Souterraine, Salignac, Le Vigan and Saint-Sulpice-Laurière were merely names of railway-stations; I was quite taken aback to find that they also belonged to little towns as real as Uzerche or Saint-Germain-les-Belles. They often had fine, severe churches, built of a dark stone. Once again I saw Beaulieu; Collonges the red with its beauty still untouched; Uzerche, whose centre is the same, but whose suburbs have grown so that the notice showing the name of the town now stands at the beginning of the Meyrignac avenue.

I visited Oradour. It had been left as it was after the massacre: the little station is still there, and the rails; in the courtyards lie old bicycles and wrecked cars; you see the familiar tools, burnt and rusting, in the baker's, the butcher's or the ironmonger's shop, and pothooks and saucepans in the hearths. Everyday life is there, as it is in certain parts of Pompeii, suddenly turned to stone by death.

Driving south, I saw the first *cornières*, those tiled galleries with wooden pillars that run round squares; and sometimes these squares have old covered markets in them, also built of wood and tile. Perhaps the finest is at Monpazier, but I am also fond of the more countrified example at Auvillar, with its round markets, and of the magnificently red great square of Montauban.

This region was poorer in churches, but what quantities of splendid châteaux! We had already come across some magnificent specimens – Rochechouart in the Limousin, for instance, where one great hall is decorated with charming sixteenth-century frescoes of hunting scenes. At the Château of Labrède, completely surrounded by moats with running water in them, we went to see Montesquieu's room. But none was as striking as the feudal castle of Bonaguil: with its slender keep and its thirteen towers it looked like the castles in the illuminations in the *Très Riches Heures du Duc de Berry*. In the Gers, many of the villages have resisted the attacks of time; they have kept their fortifications, their markets and their old houses. At Castres too an entire old quarter is untouched: on either side of the Tarn rows of ancient houses gaze at themselves in the water.

Again I saw that marvel, the great cathedral of Albi; and then Toulouse, Mont-Louis and many other places that I had seen before. But I had never climbed up to the entrancing church of Serrabone. To get there, one has to take the most terrifying road I have ever driven on – steep, bristling with stones and hairpin bends, and so narrow that there is no passing except in a few places, and even then only with great difficulty: nearly five miles, and once you are on it there is no possibility of turning. On the top stands the priory of Serrabone, built in the eleventh century and deserted in the

234

fourteenth. It is a severe church – the material is schist – but inside it has an extraordinary graceful tribune, raised on little pink marble columns whose capitals are decorated with flowers, animals and human heads.

The hills of Lacaune, the road to L'Espinouse – there are few landscapes in France as beautiful as these. The Minervois: I had stayed overnight at Minerve forty years before, during my first walking-tour. This astonishing little town is built on a platform at the junction of two torrents, and only a narrow strip of land links it with the plateau: it has remained exactly as it was. I also recognized the little roads of the Minervois and the scent of the bare, stony, sun-drenched hills. I wandered for a while among the harsh land-scapes of the Corbières and then went on to Perpignan, where I was able to see the palace of the kings of Majorca – when I was young the public were not allowed in. Then I hurried away towards Italy.

La Rochelle, Poitiers, Saintes, Périgueux, Angoulême, the Limousin, Bordeaux, Albi, Toulouse: I had revisited many places that I already knew. Sometimes I remembered almost everything, sometimes nothing at all. Generally recollection and new impres-sions mingled, and I liked that interchange of the past and present. I also discovered many places and buildings that I had only heard of or whose existence I did not even suspect. I have spoken of only a very, very few. I have left unmentioned countless lakes, pools, ponds, marshes, canals, streams, rivers and brooks: none was like the others, but words would betray their variety. I saw forests, valleys and mountains each of which had its particular physiognomy. No town had the same colour as another. The red of Montauban is not the red of Albi. For me everything was a surprise.

Once again I experienced the pleasure of remembering and of learn-ing when I took Sylvie to Burgundy at the end of the winter of 1970: now that the autoroute du Sud has been finished, the country is almost at the gates of Paris. Dijon: it was long since I had stopped there. It is a secular town, a layman's town: the religious architec-ture is interesting, but it is far less important than the fine town houses built between the thirteenth and the eighteenth centuries or the old half-timbered and often gabled dwellings of a humbler kind. The town's heart is a secular building, the ducal palace, whose courtyard gives on to a beautiful semicircular *place* dating from the seventeenth century. In the palace I went to see the former kitchens, which date from the fifteenth century, and the huge guard-room, with the tombs of Philippe le Hardi, Jean sans Peur and Marguerite of Bavaria. Once again I saw Claude Sluter's statues, splendid carvings grouped together under the name of Moses' Well. But what I liked most was wandering about the archaeological museum, which I had never visited before. In a basement smelling like an old cellar there is the 'treasure' found in the source of the Seine between 1933 and 1963. Some of the beautiful roughly-made little figures are bronze, and they remind one of those which are to be seen in Sardinia; others are stone or wood. They represent pilgrims, human heads or animals. The most curious are the ex-votos that sick people whom she had restored to health laid up in the goddess Sequana's sanctuary – a bust of the patient, or the organ she had healed – liver, heart, lungs. There was also a fine model galley as an offering.

Autun once more, and its magnificent tympanum with the Christ in majesty. In the chapter-house the capitals from the cathedral can be seen close to, which is a rare piece of good fortune; in churches you have to crane your neck cruelly for an imperfect and distant view of the detail. Here they are at eye-level. I particularly liked the three kings being woken by an angel as they sleep under neatly-folded cloaks, wearing their crowns.

I did remember the Hôtel-Dieu at Beaune with its famous roofs of glazed tiles with green and red patterns on a golden background, and the kitchens and the old dispensary. But I doubted my memory when I went into the great hall and looked at its polychrome ceiling in the form of a reversed hull: on either side there were rows of four-poster beds whose red curtains contrasted strongly with the pure white sheets. How had I contrived to forget this striking scene? In fact I had never set eyes on it: before the war the room was not open to the public.

We went to see the Romanesque church of Paray-le-Monial, beautiful and golden, with its high barrel-vaulted nave and the elegant ambulatory they call the angels' walk. And then we saw a whole string of little Romanesque churches: a notice on a very small one announced proudly 'Here all the figures in the tympanum have preserved their heads.' Indeed, the statues in all the other porches were decapitated during the Revolution; and under Napoleon, Cluny, whose monks had been hated for their exploitation of the local people, was entirely wrecked. The abbey must have been extraordinarily beautiful; even its vestiges are still magnificent.

I was touched by the Burgundian landscapes, now rugged, now peaceful; now boundless, now domestic. We climbed the still icy Mont Beuvray: and looking from the top of Mont Dun we could see a vast plain with blue horizons on the one hand, and on the other the hills of the Lyonnais; they were still covered with snow, which gave them the air of high mountains.

What pleased me most was two small fortified towns that have remained almost unaltered through the centuries. Brancion, high on a wind-swept promontory, has an undamaged castle and a Romanesque church; and it looks out on to a vast expanse of forests that still seem completely wild. Châteauneuf has not only retained its nobly-towered castle, but also a great many pretty old houses; meadows stretch below, and through them creeps the Burgundy canal, lined by a double row of trees.

A year later we rounded out this journey by a short stay in Lyons. Forty years had gone by since my Sirmione cousins showed me the town, and thirty since I stopped there with Sartre during a bicycle tour. Later I had often driven through on my way to the south, but now I wanted to walk about the city at my leisure. I went along the quays, wandered about the shopping streets, lingered in the fine place Bellecour, and on the place des Terraux I admired the splendid hôtel de ville. I took great pleasure in the Romanesque church of Saint-Martin d'Ainay and its carved capitals. From the top of the hill upon which there stands the hideous basilica of Fourvière, I gazed out over the dark roofs and the two grey rivers. I went carefully through the old part of Lyons, where once the richest families lived. The façades have been restored: the old stones, with their bas-reliefs, carvings and modillions can now be seen. I was all the more surprised when, allured by a notice that said 'courtyard, tower, *traboule*',[5] I walked through an outer door. A dark, low-roofed passage led me to a courtyard; there stood a tower, and inside the tower a spiral staircase: the architecture was elegantly simple, but a layer of filth blackened the high yellow walls; and the windows in those walls were very dirty: behind them one could sense damp and lightless rooms.

Yet in spite of their decline, these ancient dwellings are palaces in comparison with the houses of the Croix-Rousse. I went right down the hill from top to bottom, taking the *traboules*. In other parts of

5 A kind of alley peculiar to Lyons.—Tr.

the town these passages that link one street with another, passing through the blocks of houses, are merely corridors; but here, because of the slope, they form a complex system of alleys and open stairways surrounded by galleries with rooms opening on to them. In one of these, the height of the house walls and the number of galleries rising one above the other, made me think of Piranesi's prisons; but the overriding impression was one of a filth and a dilapidation that I had never met with before on such a scale in any French town. In courtyards strewn with rubbish I passed men on their way to empty slop-pails in the privies – there were no lavatories in the flats, nor even on the landings. The walls were even dirtier than they had been in the old quarter. The clothes drying in the windows were protected by a piece of plastic stretched above them, and upon this covering there was heaped soot, dust and every kind of falling dirt. Formerly these slums were inhabited by the *canuts*, the poor silk-weavers; now North Africans are crowded into them.

I walked round the Musée des Beaux-Arts, once an abbey: it has a few striking and a great many tedious pictures. The Musée des Hospices was much more interesting: it gives one an idea of what a hospital must have been like between the sixteenth and nineteenth centuries, and it is enough to make one shudder. I saw one of those beds for four in which patients and corpses lay packed together side by side. I saw instruments used by surgeons and physicians that look as though they were meant for the torture-chamber – clysters, specula, forceps, trepans, monstrous great pincers. The operating-tables and delivery-chairs made one think of hideous torments. I came to a halt in front of an astonishing figure in a show-case: it was a life-sized dummy dressed in the clothes worn by doctors when they went to see those suffering from the plague – a long black robe, a broad-brimmed black hat and a mask with two glass disks for the eyes and a long hooked beak to contain aromatics that were supposed to protect him from contagion.

Lyons is exceptionally favoured in its situation: it is bounded by two hills and it is traversed by two great rivers. And the buildings and the quays along the Saône form a whole of great architectural beauty. Yet in spite of a very blue sky, the city left me with a feeling of sadness: it is so decayed and so little cared for that it seems unwholesome.

These last three years we have reverted to an old tradition of ours – that of spending a fortnight in Provence every spring. The first time, we went to Antibes and the next two to Saint-Paul-de-Vence. From Saint-Tropez to San Remo and from the snowy slopes of Valberg to the Turini pass I revisited this country, where so many of my memories lie packed on top of one another. Some no longer correspond with reality: Madame Lemaire's villa at Juan-les-Pins has been turned into a nursing-home and it is shut in by a mass of new and ugly buildings. The Baie des Anges is disfigured by an enormous construction that can be seen from every angle as it sits there like a great wart on the edge of the sea. But once again from the ramparts of Antibes and from the top of the hills I saw the lovely mountain landscapes running gently down to the blue of the sea just as they always did; and at that time of the year they gleamed white with their covering of snow. The ridge-path from Gassin to Ramatuelle, which I had walked so often, is now fit for cars; but it is still silent and lonely, and the outline of the peninsula has not changed. Unchanged too the gorges of the Cians and the Daluis, with those lovely reds, and that 'aerial road' as the Guide Bleu calls it, which I had walked along with Olga – it is an extension of the Var corniche and it runs at a height of three thousand feet, looking down on magnificent panoramas on either hand. Gourdon, standing on a little peak above the gorges of the Loup, has made concessions to the tourists: all along the streets there are shops that sell rubbish. Visitors swarm over the café terraces at Cagnes and Cabris; but the heart of these little towns remains intact. I recovered my past at Broc, on the Var corniche; at Saint-Agnès, from where the orange-groves can be seen, running down towards Menton; and even Saint-Paul-de-Vence looks like its former self at nightfall, when the tourists have left it – it is dark and quiet; the shops are shut and all you hear is the sound of your own footsteps and the murmur of a fountain. Over on the far side, a hill lit up: the first evening I was puzzled by this festive brilliance – they were hot-houses, violently illuminated by electricity.

While I was bringing my more or less distant past back to life, I also made some fresh discoveries – a hillside road in the Maures that wound through the pinetrees, and others in the mountains between San Remo and Ventimiglia, studded with wonderful villages. In a remote spot near Tende, an astonishing chapel, its interior entirely covered with naive frescoes by an Italian painter:

the guide speaks of them as 'realistic', but they are in fact a weird evocation of hell and its torments.

I also went to the Galerie Maeght, which I did not know. There, better than anywhere else, I could really see and gaze at Giacometti's walking men. And a great many very fine paintings.

But often I did nothing but sit on my balcony, reading under the blue sky and absorbing that familiar landscape.

One of the amusements and sometimes one of the vexations of travelling is the guides who show the sights. In churches, one can walk about freely; but generally speaking not in abbeys or châteaux. There are some pleasant guides: the country-girl in a remote hamlet who showed me the fine abbey of Villesalem, for example; she was angry about the damage done, not by the Revolution, but by the nuns who set up their quarters there at a later date. The one in the château de Rochechouart gave interesting explanations, always punctuating them with the same little phrase – 'at least, according to what the authorities say'. The woman who looked after La Grange-aux-Dîmes, the Provins museum, uttered one remark that would have enchanted Proust. When I said what a pity it was that the beautiful Romanesque church should have had a hideous eighteenth-century bell-tower clapped on to it, she replied with great conviction, 'True enough, it's not pretty. But from the top you have an absolutely *hor*-rifying view.'

Quite often it was senile old women who explained things for me: the one in charge of the troglodytic hermitage at Mortagne was a gentle dodderer, carefully dressed and with beautiful white hair, and in a mechanical voice she uttered the little speech she had learnt by heart: as soon as she had finished she began again in precisely the same words; and she went on repeating it as long as the visit lasted.

The owner of the abbey of Flaran,[6] a crazy, ill-tempered woman, attended to the tourists herself: she was lame, and she thumped the ground furiously with her stick. She spoke angrily, and when she pointed out a black place on the ground where, according to her, monks had been burnt during the Revolution, she almost had a fit.

At Charroux the work that was going on in the shattered abbey made it impossible to reach the remains: a guide, standing in front

6 In January 1972 five persons were found guilty of setting fire to this abbey, one of them being the owner's grandson—he wanted the insurance.

of a plan in a corridor, was giving a hypnotized young couple a detailed description of what he ought to have been able to show them and could not. I escaped. But where I was really vexed was at Bonaguil: we had to wait half an hour for a guide dressed up as a Montmartre artist – long white hair, floppy bow-tie, corduroy trousers. He said the guided tour would last two hours: I followed him through the door to get a view of the castle as a whole from the inside, and then after ten minutes I turned round and walked off, to the great scandal of his audience.

There is another pleasure in which I indulge when I am travelling in France, and that is eating. In their fashion the cooking and often the wine are an expression of the province that produces them: they are better in their own country than the imitation produced in Paris – I had no idea of what a *quiche* really was before I ate one at Verdun, a *quiche* as firm as a tart and as light as a soufflé; nor had I the least notion of a *quenelle* before I had lunched at Dijon. It is only in country inns that trout from mountain streams are still to be found, and crayfish in abundance, My heart rejoices when I sit down to table at the end of the morning or the afternoon, satiated with monuments and sights and hungry for earthly nourishment; and it is a delight to run through the bill of fare in search of un-known or at least typical dishes.

I like the moment of reaching the hotel at the end of those days that go by so quickly but whose fullness makes them seem so long when one looks back. Often it is a pleasant old house in a courtyard or a garden or on a quiet street; or sometimes it is a mill by the waterside. I walk along the warm silence of passages lined with doors that enclose lives I know nothing about and I am eager to open mine. The unexpected and often charming room in which I settle down forms a kind of parenthesis in my life: I am at home in the quietness and the solitude of a space enclosed by walls, with a few of my own belongings; and yet my real home is far away – I am elsewhere. From my window I look out at a provincial square, at ivy-covered walls, at flowerbeds or at a stream, none of which belongs to my life. I wake up in a place that has already grown familiar but that I leave at once; and this leaving starts a day that will end in another arrival – I feel that it is I myself who set the hours in motion rather than I who am subjected to their course.

It is not only France that I have revisited during these last years; I have also gone back to other countries that I knew. One of these had undergone a total transformation between my first visit in 1953 and my second – this was Yugoslavia. What is more, this time I saw it from a very different angle.

In 1953 I did not go to Dubrovnik: in March 1963 I landed there with Sartre, and our friend Dedijer was waiting for us. He had booked us rooms in an hotel on the coast, quite near the town: every morning we made the enchanting discovery of tall towers, gleaming white on a rocky headland washed by blue water. Dubrovnik is completely surrounded by its walls, and we took the rampart-walk high above the golden roofs, looking down into the streets, squares, courtyards and gardens. Cars are forbidden inside the walled town, and one can walk about there as peacefully as in Venice. There are some interesting buildings, but the city's greatest beauty is its streets. There is no street in the world to rival the Placa, which runs right through the old town. This part of Dubrovnik was destroyed by an earthquake in 1667, and in their rebuilding the inspired architects imposed a rigorous unity upon it. The Placa is paved with time-polished slabs of the same mellow stone that is to be seen on the fronts of the houses; they are all built in the same style, but the difference in their carved decoration gives them individuality. On one side of the town the streets climb the hill in steps. They end in a thoroughfare that runs parallel to the Placa; this street is narrower than the Placa, but it too is paved with cut stone and lined with old houses of the same material, with highly ornamental balconies. At night, when these parts were silent and deserted, we seemed to be in a city belonging to another age, yet miraculously lit by street-lamps. We liked sitting on the quay of the old port, which runs right in among the walls – the fishing-boats are moored there. We had our meals either in the little restaurants of the town or on the terrace of our hotel, looking out at the nearby islet of Lokrum.

We hired a car, and either alone or with Sartre and Dedijer I went for long drives. We all three went to the mouth of Kotor, a kind of deep fjord surrounded by naked cliffs. The car climbed up to the top, and from there, at a height of four thousand five hundred feet above the sea, we looked over a desert of tormented stone with a snowy range of high mountains rising behind it. We came down to Cetinje, a shabby little town of two thousand inhabitants: it was hard to believe that it had once been a capital. On the way back we saw Kotor and Budva: they are neither so big nor so well laid out as

Dubrovnik; but they too are surrounded with walls, and cars are not allowed; their flagged, level streets are lined with stone-fronted houses. We followed the coast both coming and going, and it was planted with cypresses and olives all the way.

I went back to Sarajevo: this time I went into the town by the Turkish side, and I did not feel that I was in central Europe at all. I saw the mosque again, the caravanserai, the swarming bazaar and the little stalls, one specializing in kebabs, another in feathery little pastries filled with meat, while its neighbour filled them with cheese; and I drank Turkish coffee in a little coffee-shop. The hotel was quite transformed – its heavy furnishings had disappeared, giving way to an Italian style of interior decoration. Mostar was much as I had remembered, with its cupolas, minarets, hump-backed bridges, the whiteness of its Turkish houses and the brass trays in the cafés. I ate roast mutton by the side of the road in the open air: an ingenious device caused a little waterfall to turn the spits.

Dedijer had often told us about the Bogomil cemetery at Radimlje, and we went to see it with him. The Bogomils or Patarins were Manichees, and in the twelfth century their heresy reached the south of France. This cemetery we visited was the largest they had: from the fifteenth century onwards they decorated their tombs with rather coarse but singular carvings – weapons, tournaments, dances, invocations to the sun.

The Dalmatian coast is one of the most beautiful in the world, with its string of golden islands sparkling against a background of the purest blue. I had only seen part of it in 1953, because then great stretches of the road were unusable. Now it is a splendid corniche, and now there is heavy traffic where once no mortal stirred. The day of the 'door-men' who had the keys of both the petrol-pumps and the over-night rooms is over: service-stations and hotels are to be found everywhere. Opatija was my greatest surprise. In 1953 the tourists had nothing but one solitary and very modest restaurant in the little port. Now all the old hotels have been opened again and a great many new ones have been built; it is a spreading, luxurious watering-place, and since it has a great many late nineteenth-century villas and gardens it reminds one somewhat of Menton.

One of the main reasons for Dalmatia's look of prosperity is the considerable effort that the country has made to encourage tourism. But I also noticed that the peasants in the Yugoslav villages and hamlets were much better dressed than they had been in 1956, when

243

their poverty shocked us as we passed through the country on our way to Greece. Now the children were dressed in comfortable, brightly-coloured woollens. In most restaurants the food was still frugal; and there was not much to be seen in the shops – the clothes, the material and the shoes were monotonous and far from attractive. Yugoslavia is far from the overflowing abundance of Italy. Nevertheless, a very great advance has been achieved.

In one of my books I said that as people grow older they do not notice the changes in the world around them; its new appearance tends to be taken for granted right away. That is true for the places or things one sees frequently. But sometimes, when several years have elapsed between two journeys abroad, the contrast between the past and the present is strikingly apparent. In such cases the passage of time becomes a reality as tangible as that of distance when you are driving and the road fleets away behind you. From that point of view, our March in Yugoslavia was a remarkable experience.

For me, one of the pleasures of these journeys is the driving. I like short runs and on occasion I also like really long ones. I have often driven down from Paris to Rome by myself: it bores Sartre, and he joins me by plane. One evening, in the days when cars were still allowed in the Piazza Navona, I saw a big Citroën drive up; it had a Paris number-plate and it was covered with mud. An exhausted-looking woman got out. She sat down on a café terrace and opened a book about Michel Leiris. It seemed to me that I was seeing my own somewhat blurred reflection in a glass. I have often arrived in Rome just like that, alone and worn out after having driven all day long: I would go and sit in the Piazza Navona and I too would read.

During these journeys I liked the sensation of being both so governed by my time-table and so free: my time was limited and yet I could spend it as I pleased. On each trip I took slightly different routes that nevertheless coincided at long intervals; in this way I enjoyed both the pleasures of repetition and those of new discovery. Even on the roads I knew, there was room for the unforeseen; for although I was following a routine, I was at the same time in the midst of adventure. There were times when driving was an exacting task and one that called for my whole attention; and when this was the case my pleasure in the landscape was all the sharper for being given me over and above the bargain, as it were – almost surreptitiously.

I remember one of those journeys in particular delight. My sister expected me that Friday evening at Trebiano, a little village near La Spezia I had never seen, where she has a house. I left Paris at two o'clock in the afternoon on Thursday by the autoroute; in those days it was interrupted before Fontainebleau. It was black with traffic: overtake, fall back into line, overtake again – I had to keep a continual watch behind me in the driving-mirror. The ordinary road was just as crowded. Fortunately a new stretch of motorway had recently been opened between Auxerre and Avallon and most of the drivers disliked the idea of paying the two-franc toll. I drove along an empty road, enjoying completely unknown and splendid views of the rolling Morvan, dry and golden at the end of July. Another novelty: an artificial lake just outside Dijon, its shores crowded with people bathing. I stopped at a café in the town, then drove on until I reached Pontarlier, fresh and pleased with myself: and there I stayed the night.

As usual, I started off early in the morning. I love that time when the villages are still asleep and when the sun is just beginning to draw the dew off the fields. In Switzerland, at Lausanne and all along the lake, the traffic grew very thick. Friends had advised me to take the newly-opened tunnel under the Great St Bernard: this was a mistake. A solid line of cars crept up the steep road to the pass, and I crept after them. Now the sun was blazing down: the sky and the countryside were veiled with the heat haze. On the other side of the tunnel, caravans, cars and lorries cluttered the Val d'Aosta road. I wanted to reach my sister before nightfall so that she should not be worried and I should not have to drive with headlights on unknown mountain roads: so I had to get along at all costs – overtake, fall back, overtake again, always without taking any risks or losing any chances. The tension was all the more dangerous because I felt myself growing tireder and tireder and because my fatigue meant I could not take a rest – it would have needed more energy to make up my mind to stop than to continue. I drove on and on. As I was passing Ivrea about one in the afternoon I did make an effort and force myself to go into the town. For some minutes I drove along the baking streets with my mind a total blank. The moment I saw a café I pulled up. And sitting there in a little square with a sandwich and a cup of coffee in front of me I

245

enjoyed the full savour of my halt: the motionless buildings and the quietly-moving passers-by were quite enough to fill me with pleasure. I still felt rested as I drove along the deserted autostrada. But then I had to take the difficult Milan bypass to reach the southern autostrada. I left that to take the road that winds up to the Cisa pass and then plunges abruptly down again – a road used by a great many lorry-drivers. I was tired, but now I was sure of getting there before night and I stopped again in a village, sitting there with a glass of beer. Then I drove on. At Pontremoli a funeral halted all traffic for ten minutes: men in black carrying torches that flamed dismally in the falling dusk. At last I reached the little town from which a road led up to Trebiano: from below the village looked magnificent with its castle, its majestic baroque church and its great walls dropping sheer. But I lost my way for a while, until someone showed me the beginning of the lane that wound up into it. At the entrance to the village there were a few cars parked in a grassy square; I left mine with them and walked in through the arched gateway. What a reward to be there at last, with my sister, sitting on a terrace and looking out over the countryside and the sea! I should never have enjoyed the immobility, the silence and the tinkle of ice in my glass so much if I had not had that long day of urgent striving behind me. I had dinner, and went to sleep with the pleasant feeling of a task well done.

All next morning I wandered about the steep streets with my sister, between white walls: the village is still unknown to tourists, and only peasants live there. In the old days Eze and Saint-Paul-de-Vence must have been like that. I left for Rome after luncheon, and I went along the coast. There were swarms of half-naked bodies on the sandy beaches, swarms of cars on the road. The driving absorbed me entirely. But now and again a fleeting pleasure took me by surprise. Once a waft of damp, salty air blew in, laden with imprecise memories. (The morning air at Copacobana had just that smell.) Farther on, dark pine-trees stood out along the blue ridge of a headland that jutted out into the sea. In the midst of heavy traffic I caught a sudden glimpse of Tarquinia's walls and towers, very high above me and white against the whiteness of the sky. I had just seen two wrecked cars by the side of the road when all at once there was the dome of St Peter's; and St Peter's too was white against a white sky. Never had I been so deeply touched by its beauty. I drove through Rome, reached my hotel and collapsed in the Piazza

Navona, more or less destroyed but with my heart bubbling over with joy.

I remember another drive down to Rome with violent winds and blinding rain almost all day long. In the evening, a little before Annecy, I was going along a mountain road in the middle of a line of cars: the wind was blowing in furious gusts. Suddenly the car in front of me stopped: a huge branch had fallen immediately in front of it. Everybody got out of their cars; lorry-drivers set about the branch with an axe and in two minutes the road was clear.

Twice disagreeable things happened to me as I was coming back from Rome. One rainy Sunday I was on the Colmar road, on my way to see my sister in Alsace. Behind me I heard the wailing of a siren, but I paid no attention; then a little while later I stopped at a halt sign and a police-car drew up beside me. It had been following me for the last five miles, and I was accused of three serious offences. The first I had not committed at all: I *had* waited for the yellow line to end before overtaking. No doubt I was guilty of the others – of having exceeded the twenty-five miles an hour speed limit as I went through two villages – but it would never have been noticed if I had not had the police-car just behind me. (The police followed one seventy-year-old driver who had never had a conviction in his life, and he was found guilty of having committed ten offences in half an hour.) I tried arguing about the first charge but then for the sake of peace I gave in and signed the report. As I was passing through a village three miles farther on at the legal speed, a gendarme asked me for my papers. I then found out why the police had been following me: my car was a blue Simca, and they were looking for a blue Simca with just one person in it – a woman who had kidnapped a child.

The second incident was more serious – an accident. This was in 1965. I had gone for a tour in northern Italy with Sartre and then I had left him in Milan one morning: we were to meet in Paris the next day at about seven in the evening. The weather was splendid. I crossed the Mont Cénis pass, drove through Chambéry, and had lunch on a terrace overlooking lake Le Bourget. I dined and spent the night at Chalon-sur-Saône, in one of those pleasant, welcoming hotels that are part of the charm of the province.

The next morning there was so thick a fog that I wondered whether I should leave or not – I had plenty of time to spare. But the town was remarkably disagreeable and I thought the fog would thin out farther from the river. In fact I had to keep my headlights on for two hours as I crept along the edge of the road through the blinding mists. From time to time a sunlit patch of countryside would appear, and I thought it beautiful, merely because it was visible. Then everything grew light. I took the Avallon to Auxerre motorway, passed Auxerre and drove on, following the ordinary road. It was early and I did not drive fast; I was happy to be going home and I began to work out how I should spend the afternoon. Then, just as I had turned a corner and I was beginning to climb a hill, all at once I saw an aggressively red tanker coming down towards me. I was on the wrong side of the road. I scarcely had time to think 'Something's going to happen' before the crash came, and there I was, unhurt. The driver got out and blamed me vehemently – I had taken the curve too fast: fortunately he was going slowly and he had managed to swerve to the left, otherwise he would have squashed me flat. A whole crowd of people had already gathered round me. There was only one thought in my head: 'I'll no doubt catch a train to get me back to Paris before seven.' Ambulance-men appeared with a stretcher. I refused to lie down on it: they insisted and as my back hurt a little I thought it would be sensible to have myself examined – it would certainly not take long. They carried me away. I noticed that there was blood on my arms and legs. As soon as I lay down on a bed, I began to feel dizzy. They X-rayed me: four ribs were broken behind. A doctor put a stitch in my eyelid, and several in my knee, having anaesthetized it. I felt really ill and I was slightly sick. I no longer thought of going straight back to Paris, but I did want to tell Sartre myself, so that he should not worry. A nurse came and said that Lanzmann and Sartre had just telephoned: they had learnt about my accident from the television and they were on their way. A little later they walked into my room: I realized that my face had swollen. One of my eyes was completely shut. I told them about my accident in an excited, garrulous way that proved I had had a shock. The announcer had said I was only slightly bruised, but even so Lanzmann had raced down the motorway at a hundred miles an hour. While we were talking a policeman came in with my baggage; and he gave me back the papers they had taken away. Almost every day, he said, the hospital received drivers who had had an accident in the same place as mine: some had been killed. It was a dangerous curve because it was sharper than it seemed and because there was a long stretch of straight before it. In my opinion, the reason why I took it carelessly was that I was not driving fast: if I had been, I should have been more tense and watchful.

A little later I heard that my sister and some of my friends had been shocked at hearing the news of my accident on the radio: they ought to begin by saying that the victim has only been slightly hurt before they go on to give the name and the facts.

Sartre took me back to Paris the next day in an ambulance that drove at ninety miles an hour. I did not suffer, either lying down or sitting up. I needed help only when I had to change from one position to another. I stayed in bed for about three weeks. I read; people came to see me; I was not bored at all. It seems that an accident is a social event – never have I had so many letters, tele-grams, telephone-calls or bunches of flowers, often sent by people I knew only by hearsay.

On thinking it over, I saw that the driver of the tanker had saved my life and I wrote to thank him. He had taken a serious risk in swerving over to the left, because if another car had struck him at the moment he would have been in the wrong. In spite of his swerve, the whole front of my car, a sturdy Peugeot 404, was smashed: when I saw the photographs I was astonished that I had got off so lightly.

At present my journeys between Paris and Rome are devoid of incident. The autoroute du Sud is much longer now. The Mont Blanc tunnel has been finished and a very short distance on the other side there is the Val d'Aosta autostrada, which joins the autostrada from Turin to Milan; and there it is easy to get on to the southern autostrada. I am not one of those people who find motor-ways boring. I do like wandering along little roads in particular regions, but when it is a question of moving myself from one place to another, I like getting there fast. I was enchanted the first time I did the Milan-Bologna run in two and a half hours. Then the stretch linking Bologna with Florence over the Apennines was opened. I waited impatiently for the motorway from Florence to Rome to be finished and then for the opening of the Val d'Aosta autostrada. As I come from France, it is one of my great pleasures to stop at about two o'clock at one of those 'Pavesi' that straddle the road and to renew my acquaintance with Italian ham, wine and pasta.

I rarely go anywhere by train; and because it has grown unusual, this way of travelling enchants me – the smells, the rhythm of the wheels and the noise of the stations as one runs through them at night send me back to my childhood.

But when I go abroad I generally travel by plane. It is a long time now since I first flew – that was in 1945 – but I never tire of gazing at the earth from the sky. I love seeing its mountains, lakes and rivers, all geographically exact. But above all it is the cloud-scapes beneath my feet that fascinate me. Vast polar plains, rent by dark chasms; or maybe ice-banks covered with rolling snowdrifts and multitudes of budding white bushes. Gossamer floats between their jutting rocks – crests and peaks so solid that it seems the plane must be shattered against them. When the machine flies low above the snowy carpet it seems to me very slow, very heavy and just about to crash upon it. The plane dives towards this carpet and pierces through, the strong sunlight flickers on the wings. Through a gap in the clouds I catch glimpses of a golden plain – I discover a château hidden deep in a wood on the edge of a lake. In earlier times I should have been incapable of even imagining these visions or so many others. Exploring this planet I live upon still gives me as much pleasure as ever it did; and in this respect time has given me as much as it has taken away – perhaps more indeed.

5

Some of my journeys with Sartre have had a political significance; for some of our political activities required us to travel. Later on I shall speak of these complex undertakings, our journeys to the USSR, Czechoslovakia, Egypt and Israel, and our stays in Stockholm and Copenhagen at the time of the Russell Tribunal. But first I will talk about our voyage to Japan. We gathered a great deal of information on every aspect of the country; we met left-wing intellectuals and we had very interesting exchanges of views with them. But the country's problems concerned us only very indirectly, and our main reason for going there was to increase our knowledge of the world – our visit did not cause us to adopt any political attitude. That is why I am putting it immediately after those trips that I took just for my own pleasure.

Our Japanese publisher, Mr Watanabe, and the university of Kyoto invited Sartre and me to visit Japan during the autumn of 1966 to see the country and to give a few lectures. I prepared the journey carefully. That spring Mr Watanabe had brought me a huge pile of magazines and books in English dealing with the history of Japan and above all with the country's post-war economic, social and political problems. I obtained all the ancient and modern literature that had been translated into French or English – among others, the admirable *Tale of Genji* in the English version. And it was then that I discovered the great Japanese writer Tanizaki, who had just died. My initiation into the Japanese way of life came largely from his novel *The Makioka Sisters*. I also learnt a great deal from Tomiko Asabuki, who translated my books into Japanese: she was my sister's friend and she became mine too. She was born and brought up in a wealthy aristocratic family that had a beautiful house surrounded by a park right in the middle of Tokyo.

Before her marriage she had pursued her studies very far, particularly in French. Most of the war she spent in Tokyo, while the city was being devastated by air-raids and enormous fires. In 1945 she was pregnant, and, like all the rest of her family, penniless. She sold her kimonos to buy a little food on the black market. After the birth of her daughter she ran a tea-room. She was so very clever with her needle that she could make her own clothes, so she thought of setting up a dress-shop; and after the dissolution of her marriage she came to France with the idea of learning about the great Paris fashion-houses. Her journey through more or less war-shattered countries was long and interesting, and she wrote a series of articles about it that had a great deal of success. She abandoned dress-making for journalism and then for translation. She stayed in France for fifteen years, marrying a Frenchman but retaining her maiden name. She was then about forty-five and she spoke French perfectly. It was she who was to act as our guide and interpreter during our voyage; she knew her country well and she had many friends there. She went off to Japan at the beginning of the summer.

We set out, one hour late, at three in the afternoon of 17 September in a plane belonging to the Japanese airline. Two enchanting hostesses dressed in magnificent kimonos helped us to settle in. The seats were covered with a very pretty brocade matching the folders that contained our tickets. Eight UDR senators occupied seats nearby. After a late but excellent luncheon we came down at Hamburg: the town had been entirely rebuilt, but under the grey sky it looked very dreary. Then we took off again in the direction of Alaska. The hostesses handed round cotton robes: the senators put theirs on with noisy laughter and facetiousness. They tried their French charm on the hostesses, who very gracefully kept them at arm's length. I am not yet blasée and I thought flying over the north pole something perfectly extraordinary: for hours on end I saw nothing beneath me but a white immensity, striated with black crevasses. After a sumptuous dinner, we came down at Anchorage: tall snowy mountains overlooked a plain dotted with dark pools and covered with a thin gold-coloured scrub. It gave the feeling of being at the aftermost end of the earth, far from all civilization. (Later I was told that almost all the people who live there have a little private plane to link them with the rest of the world.) The huge circular airport building was scarcely a welcoming place, but it had windows all round and they gave a fine view of this strange, beautiful landscape. By way of souvenirs, there were objects made of ivory and seal-skin for sale. As soon as we set off again, which by French time was at five o'clock in the morning, a huge meal appeared, based on fillet steak: the senators devoured it. We just had whisky. It is shattering, the way these hours run into one another, whirl about and overlap. Since we left there had been no night at all, only a long twilight followed by a brief sunrise. And then all at once, when it was eleven in the morning in Paris, night came down. We landed in total darkness.

The Japanese read prodigiously. Compulsory education was introduced in 1871, and by 1910 ninety-eight per cent of the population attended school. In 1966 ninety-nine per cent of the children were studying for at least nine years; there were virtually no illiterates, and the working classes were intensely eager for culture. The Japanese devour newspapers and magazines, and they take third place in the world for the production of books, coming immediately after the USA and the USSR. In 1965 the number of works published reached the figure of twenty-five thousand and the number of copies printed about two hundred and eighty million. The paperback series have increased and multiplied. They produce a very great many translations from foreign languages. And to protect themselves from American influence – the government follows US policy, but America is deeply unpopular, especially among the intellectuals – they pay particular attention to French culture. All Sartre's books and all mine have been translated. In 1965 *The Second Sex* came out as a paperback, and it was a best-seller. We knew all this; yet I had never imagined anything like the welcome we received. At the foot of the gangway more than a hundred photographers lay in wait. the senators were led out first, then Sartre and me. 'Nothing for us, but they machine-gun Simone de Beauvoir and Sartre,' said one of them furiously, to the great amusement of Madame Asabuki. She sheltered me under her umbrella, for the rain was coming down in torrents. The photographers walked backwards in front of us, blinding us with their flashes so that we blundered into puddles. The other side of the customs, hundreds of young people lined the passage. At first they only smiled in silence; then they began to call out our names and to catch hold of our hands and our arms, pulling, pushing and smothering us. We were taken into a tiny room, where a hundred sweating journalists bombarded us with questions while press and film photographers directed powerful lights at us.

We took the motorway that runs through Tokyo above the level of the streets. There are now many of these express throughways, but they only date from 1962. They were begun to ease the traffic problems for the Olympic Games which took place in 1964; and since then the building has continued. Sometimes one drives along higher than the roofs, sometimes in tunnels that have replaced former canals. Then our car turned off into densely crowded avenues and streets and we reached a charming hotel: it was in the Western style, but the decoration followed Japanese patterns – in the lounge and the corridors I noticed those wonderful bouquets whose arrangement is a highly formalized art. We had a quiet dinner with Tomiko Asabuki and her brother; he had worked at UNESCO in Paris for a long while, he had translated several of our books and he speaks French as well as his sister. We had Western food, but I drank saké, a very weak drink that is prepared from rice and served warm in little bowls – it is like the Chinese rice wine. At midnight we went to bed, and although it was only four in the afternoon in Paris, I had no difficulty in going to sleep.

The next day Tomiko and her brother showed us Tokyo, on foot and by car. The city has eleven million people in it. The very modern central districts remind one of the USA – skyscrapers, enormous blocks, streets swarming with people dressed in Western clothes, very heavy traffic. We went round the outer walls of the imperial palace; it is being rebuilt and the public are not allowed in. Deep in an immense park smelling of autumn we saw an imposing Shinto building, the temple of the Emperor Meiji. We walked along the cheerful, highly-coloured streets of the Ginza, the fashionable shopping district. There were big stores, the equivalent of the Louvre or the Printemps in Paris but far more welcoming, for in addition to the attentive shop-girls there were smiling hostesses, who came forward to give information or to show you the way: these stores sold both the latest kind of modern goods and the traditional wares – splendid kimonos, among other things. But the streets were also lined with astonishing numbers of very small boutiques rather like those in the Faubourg Saint-Honoré. In many of the restaurant windows I gazed curiously at strange, brilliantly-coloured dishes. We had our own lunch in a very small place with no more than three or four scrupulously clean wooden tables: and there we ate excellent chicken brochettes.

As early as six o'clock we went to the dinner-party that the rector of the university had arranged for us in the city's best-known restaurant. We were received by the woman who owned it and the waitresses, who knelt to each guest, touching the ground with their foreheads. We took our shoes off before treading on the wheat-coloured tatamis – rectangular mats lying either parallel or at right angles to one another, so that the uniformly coloured ground looked like an abstract picture – the room seemed to bathe in the light of a summer sun.

The rector had invited professors, writers and producers, and he had sent for geishas. We all sat on the ground at a long low table. The women who wore kimonos – the rector's wife and the geisahs – sat on their heels in the Japanese way: Tomiko told me that this was very tiring. She and I were dressed in Western clothes, and they covered our knees with a cloth. Each guest had two geishas, one on either side; they were neither young nor beautiful, but they have been chosen from among the most cultivated. A few of them played music and sang, but their main function was to fill their neighbour's glass with saké and to talk, which made any more general conversation almost impossible. One next to me asked in careful French whether I preferred ancient or modern art. Another asked Sartre to autograph a heap of books belonging to her husband. Meanwhile a succession of dishes appeared on the table, none readily identifiable. The fried fishes were pleasant; but I suffered when I was compelled to swallow blood-red raw tunny; and I suffered even more when I felt the pale, slimy flakes of what I believe was raw sea-bream gliding down my throat. Although Sartre has the same aversion to all raw shellfish as I, he seemed to be getting along very well with all these dishes; he was smiling and laughing, and looked quite relaxed.

The meal lasted three hours. Then we were back at the hotel, exhausted at having eaten so many strange things while listening to foolish prattle and uttering it. We sent for a bottle of Japanese whisky, which is very good. Sartre did not touch his glass: all at once he turned pale. He felt his pulse and found that it was beating at a hundred and twenty to the minute – twice the normal rate. What was the matter with him? He had never felt so ill. This was a disaster, because he had to give a lecture the next day. Suddenly he darted into the bathroom: absurdly enough, he had never felt sick before in his life, and he had not recognized the symptoms. Out of politeness he had managed to overcome his repulsion, but now thinking about it had brought it back and he threw up his entire

255

dinner. For two days he was incapable of swallowing anything whatsoever.

This did not prevent him from feeling quite well, and the next afternoon we went to the university together. Did they do it to make sure that we should both have exactly the same number of hearers? My lectures always took place either immediately before or immediately after Sartre's. In the university courtyard the students received us as warmly as they had at the airport: they waved welcoming placards and surrounded us, calling out our names and seizing our hands. Yet when Sartre had finished speaking, and when my lecture was done, their applause was only very moderate: we were told that the rules of good manners required this restraint. And indeed we were often struck by the contrast between the spontaneous violence of the Japanese and their somewhat formal reserve in the more deliberate, codified forms of behaviour.

The days we spent in Tokyo were well filled. We questioned politicians and intellectuals on the situation in Japan, and we talked with writers and teachers, thus increasing the knowledge we had derived from reading. We had studied the Meiji revolution and we were aware of the circumstances that had allowed Japan to escape from the domination of the West. But what we were primarily interested in was the Japan of today, the country, tragically devastated in 1945, that had become the world's third great economic power.

This story had a paradoxical beginning. The Americans were eager to democratize Japan, so they released the imprisoned communists and socialists, the opponents of the militaristic regime, and relied on them for support. They also enforced agrarian reform, broke up the trusts and encouraged the creation of trade unions: but very soon they reversed their policies – the general strike desired by the workers in 1947 was forbidden. Political power fell into the hands of the conservative party, which retained it from that time on. The trusts have been built up again. The unions do have a fairly large number of members – the Sohyo, which is vaguely based on Marxism but which rejects communism, has four million – yet they have hardly any influence upon the country's economic life.

In view of their limited space, the main preoccupations of the Japanese was to halt their galloping birth-rate. They launched great campaigns in favour of contraception and they made abortion almost universally available. But for all that the increase in the population has been close on a million a year. According to the 1956 census, Japan had 98,211,935 inhabitants.

How did this country, whose gross national income was ten thousand million dollars in 1953, manage to reach the figure of a hundred thousand million in 1966? The 'miracle' is explained largely by the boldness and the imagination of the new managers who replaced the trusts dissolved by the Americans in 1945. They did not hesitate to plunge deeply into debt: and in spite of the risk the banks did not hesitate to finance them. They immediately re-invested their profits, thus creating what the Japanese economists term a 'virtuous circle' – in no country in the world has investment reached such proportions. The reason why the banks can lend large sums of money is that the rate of saving in the population as a whole is very high, perhaps because Japan is a young country – only 8.5 per cent of the people are over sixty. No foreign investment was allowed. To a large extent the boom was also due to the quantity and the quality of the workers' production and to their low wages.

Here we have the most characteristic feature of the Japanese economy. The country's industrialization was not preceded by the total destruction of the feudal structures. It was the samurai themselves who carried out the Meiji revolution; transformed into bureaucrats, they retained feudal values, patterns of behaviour and social relationships, and they obliged the workers to adopt their ethic of self-denial – the worker owes the same absolute loyalty to the firm that the vassal owed to his lord.

In fact the worker has no way of escaping from this position: he belongs to the firm body and soul. Permanent tenure of a job is the universal rule in Japan, and when a clerk or a worker enters a firm he does so for life, climbing from rank to rank until he retires. If an employee were dismissed he would not be able to find another position – the labour-market is practically nonexistent. This almost never happens in fact; but the threat is there, and it results in an enforced and total submissiveness on the part of the worker. He is required to do overtime; he does not claim the holidays to which he is entitled – if he were to do so there would be a black mark against him and he might lose his situation. At the most he may take two or three days now and then. Even the Zengakuren,[1] who are such ferocious revolutionaries in their youth, conform to this way of life as soon as they have a job.

[1] Members of the students' association.

The job itself is very badly paid, especially in the small and medium-sized firms: for another characteristic feature of the Japanese economy is the 'double structure'. In the industrial sector only thirty per cent of the labour-force is employed by factories having more than three hundred workers: thirty-three per cent work in factories with less than thirty. If trade and business are also taken into account, then ninety per cent of the firms fall into the category of those with less than thirty, counting office staff and workers; 6.4 per cent into that of from thirty to a hundred; and 2.9 per cent into that of from one hundred to a thousand. Only five hundred and fifty firms, or 0.1 per cent of the total, employ more than a thousand.

The small and medium firms belong to two classes. There are those that produce traditional consumer-goods such as tatamis, white socks, kimonos, clogs, soya sauce, lanterns and sunshades. They are usually family enterprises in which the working day begins early and ends late – towards half past ten or eleven – and the profits are very small. Others are sub-contractors working for the big concerns; there are a very great many of these sub-contractors, because they mean the possibility of diminishing production-costs. Their workers do not enjoy such facilities as canteens, company housing, bonuses, etc, by which the big firms do a little to compensate for the low level of the wages. Often they do not have even one free day in the week; health measures are inadequate; the workers are underpaid and for them there is no social security whatsoever. Even in the big firms wages are low; and there are some grossly under-privileged categories – the women and the 'temporaries' who are taken on for short periods.

The people of Japan, taken as a whole, have a very low standard of living; they eat very sparingly and they are badly housed, the building-programmes being totally inadequate. Although the country's national income places it among the world's first three, the income per head of population classes it twenty-first, at about the same level as Venezuela. And it should be added that the infrastructure has been neglected: there are not enough roads, there is an insufficiency of transport and there are too few trains – to cram the travellers into the carriages every morning and evening, karate experts are employed as 'shovers'. There is therefore a great deal of discontent among the mass of the Japanese; and this discontent is crystallized and made evident in the students' revolts.

It was with this basic information that we set out to discover

Japan. And to begin with we spent a great deal of time walking about Tokyo. It is not a beautiful city. Innumerable cars hurtle along its noisy avenues and there are perpetual traffic-jams. The flow is controlled by lights and policemen, of course; but in some places there are also little yellow flags placed in baskets on the edge of the pavement. If you wish to cross, you take one and wave it at the traffic, which is then supposed to stop. Having crossed you leave it in a corresponding basket on the other side. The reek of petrol pervades the air, which is also polluted by fall-out of every kind. The drainage-system and the street-cleaning arrangements are so defective that every day the river Sumida, which runs through the town, carries one million three hundred thousand tons of refuse and filth.

We avoided the main thoroughfares as much as we could. We liked the quieter districts where the traditional wooden houses are still to be seen: some of their streets were full of teeming life, with stalls and booths on either side, each having a paper lantern or a banner covered with elegant Japanese characters by way of a sign. And if any had just been opened there would be immense wreaths of gaily coloured artificial flowers in front of it. Tokyo has innumerable little shops, for although Japan has become a great industrial power in the forefront of progress it nevertheless retains certain archaic aspects, and craftsmanship still flourishes. This coexistence of the traditional past with modern life was strikingly evident in the huge covered market that Tomiko took us to see. Over the entry there hung an enormous lantern made of red paper; and on the stalls either side of the passage there was a mixture of hand-made and of mass-produced goods – fans, belts, kimonos, cotton materials and baskets, but also factory-made hardware, utensils and clothes. When we left the market we came out into a sports-ground with a Buddhist temple in the middle of it. On the following days we went to see the port, the central markets, the university quarter, and a very fine ultra-modern church with metals walls and roof: it was the work of Kanso Tange, a young architect who has also built a remarkably elegant covered swimming-pool. We strolled along the pleasant, quiet streets of the old residential district, where there is an interesting folk-lore museum. And we spent several hours in the fine arts museum.

In the evening Tokyo lights up with splendid fire. Neon signs blaze on all the roofs and walls: they have colours I have never seen

259

anywhere else – deep violet, orange, a golden yellow and a night-dark blue. They are as carefully composed as pictures, and indeed they are often framed in a rectangular outline. They do not blaze as they do in New York: they burst out and then fade away, or else they slowly spread and then retract. In the shopping streets there are countless paper lanterns in the form of globes or fishes; they are either white or red and they often have inscriptions. (There were some Americans who came to learn about Zen; they bought lanterns that they thought the perfect expression of the Japanese soul, and the writing upon them in fact said *Noodles*.)

The most agreeable time is eleven o'clock in the evening, when life comes to a stop; for the Japanese are early risers. At half past six in the morning eighty per cent of the inhabitants of Tokyo are out of bed. At eleven, the last stalls close; the customers all leave the bars, restaurants and cabarets in the Ginza and the street fills with young women, many of them ravishing, dressed in Western clothes or kimonos. These are the hostesses from the bars and the dance-halls, far prettier than the geishas. You hear laughter and fluting voices. After this rapid, charming flight, silence falls upon the town.

Yet in Shinjuku, which is reminiscent both of Saint-Germain-des-Prés and the Latin quarter, some places stay open much later. The centre of the district is an enormous station that serves several different railway and underground networks. The building contains a big store, offices, restaurants, cinemas and many boutiques; and in the streets and alleys all round there are countless bars, night-clubs, strip-tease joints and music-halls. Some are enormous, others minute. I was struck by the number of places for playing pachinko: this is a kind of pin-table, but it is set upright and not flat, like ours. In some of these halls there are hundreds side by side with a narrow passage between the ranks; not one of them is free, and the players work the knobs with a contained, silent frenzy. These streets also have numbers of restaurants, most of them highly specialized – one will be for fish, another for chicken brochettes and another for fried prawns. We dined at a place that served nothing but pork. As the papers, the television and the news-reels had made our photographs quite widely known, some people recognized us. One girl kissed Sartre's hand and offered him a packet of biscuits – a traditional gift, said Tomiko: she also told us that in Japan people are perpetually exchanging presents, and these generally take the shape of food. A friend or a neighbour would send her a dish of spaghetti, and the next day Tomiko would have her taken some fruit or a cake. In the street a young man silently proffered me a flower. And we were pursued by a cloud of students asking us for autographs. Every cultivated Japanese possesses an arsenal of large square pieces of cardboard, white one side and grey the other, upon which they practise calligraphy or write their own poems. They also use them for collecting autographs.

We went into a thoroughly working-class tavern where a man was singing traditional songs. We drank beer. The waitresses wore cotton kimonos with the sleeves rolled up: they were fine stout wenches. When a customer had had too much to drink and grew noisy they seized him, laughing heartily, and chucked him out. After that we went to a cellar that reminded me rather of the old Tabou – very young men were listening to jazz and dancing in a smoke-laden atmosphere. They recognized us, but at a word from Mr Asabuki they discreetly looked away. We finished the evening in a very prettily decorated homosexuals' place. There was a big photograph of a naked man behind the bar and an advertisement for one of Genet's plays: the barman asked Sartre to sign it.

We went back to Shinjuku one Sunday afternoon: Tomiko took us to a kind of working-class cabaret. It was a bare room with a platform in it; the audience sat on the floor; some were asleep, some dozed and others drank tea, listening to a man telling stories – very licentious stories, said Tomiko.

One evening we went to a big music-hall in the Ginza. The programme included dances, strip-tease numbers and comic sketches. One of these held the bonzes up to ridicule with what seemed to me a surprising lack of respect. The stage bonze, a lecherous-looking character, was drawing obscene pictures on a wall; when a passer-by came near the bonze made them innocuous with one clever stroke; and as soon as he was alone again another stroke transformed them into still more obscenities.

We wanted to learn something about the traditional Japanese theatre. This was by no means easy, because it no longer attracts any considerable audience – the theatre-going public prefers plays in the Western style, written either by Japanese authors or by foreigners. But Mr Watanabe arranged a private *no* performance for us at a little theatre, and he invited about a hundred guests. The stage was covered by a roof supported on four pillars: on the back

261

wall was painted an ancient pine-tree – an image that has become the symbol of *no* and that is inseparable from it. The stage was prolonged by a kind of very long roofed bridge running along the wall as far as the curtain that separated it from the wings. It was by this bridge that the actors made their entrance.

The show began with a short comic piece, a *kyogen*, the traditional accompaniment of the *no*: I thought it insipid. The *no* proper is a kind of funeral oratorio that attained its most perfect form in the fourteenth century; it was a court spectacle, reserved for the aristocracy and influenced by Zen Buddhism.

First the orchestra took their places on the stage – a flute and two drums. The musicians wore the town clothes of the Tokugawa period (seventeenth to nineteenth centuries), a dark silk robe with a very wide divided skirt over it, and a sleeveless outer garment with wide upward-curving shoulders. A chorus, dressed in modern clothes, sat on the right of the stage.

The play, *Aoinoue*, was taken from an episode in the *Tale of Genji*. Aoinoue, Prince Genji's wife, is very ill. She was represented by a kimono lying on the ground at the front of the stage. Rokujo, the prince's former mistress, has cast a spell on her. The orchestra created a tragic atmosphere, the musicians accompanying the drums with piercing cries. At this point Rokujo's evil spirit appears – the *shite*, the chief character in the play. The *shite* is often a spirit that comes back from the other world, but it may also be the incarnation of a passion, such as remorse or anger or, as in this case, jealousy. It was magnificently dressed in a richly embroidered silk tunic and widely-flared trousers. It wore a wooden mask, tied behind the head by two black strings and somewhat narrower than the face, which gave the actor an elongated appearance; and the openings for the eyes were so small that he could not move without taking his bearings from the pillars that support the roof. The *shite*, its words emphasized by the music and the shrill cries that accompany the drums, complains of having been abandoned by Genji. Its jealousy grows even more frantic. It bends over the sick woman and strikes her furiously with its fan. (We had been told that the mask's expression varied according to its angle and the lighting, and to our astonishment we found this to be true.) The chorus proclaims its indignation and sends a messenger for a highly respected priest who will exorcise the evil spirit. The priest appears: this is the *waki*, the traditional opponent of the *shite*; he wears no mask and he is

262

dressed in a plain black robe. (The *waki* usually comes on to the stage first, and it is he who provokes the appearance of the *shite*.) The priest starts praying. The *shite* makes off and then comes back in its real form, wearing a demon's mask. It confronts the priest and challenges him to a duel – a verbal duel in which the demon shouts and roars while the priest prays. Finally it runs away, defeated. The passionate voices of the chorus, contrasting with the hieratic gestures, the obsessive rhythm of the orchestra and the piercing cries of the musicians, built up a lasting tension that kept us in suspense from the beginning of the play to the end. *No* is said to be difficult for Westerners to understand: it seemed to us that one had but to let oneself go to be enthralled.

It was not easy to see the puppet-show called *bunraku* either. The company was on tour and we had to content ourselves with two short single-character pieces put on before an almost entirely Western audience in one of the drawing-rooms at the Imperial Hotel. Yet the performance impressed us deeply, and two years later, when the *bunraku* came to the Odéon in Paris, we hurried to see it, taking Tomiko, who was then in France. It is an art of such a particular beauty that I should like to speak of it here.

Bunraku evolved chiefly in the eighteenth century, among the rising middle class of Osaka. It is the only puppet-theatre for which literary masterpieces have been written. The plays usually date from the eighteenth century: they sometimes deal with feudal legends and sometimes with middle-class tragedies – but tragedies in which noble feelings are carried to their highest conceivable pitch: a servant kills his own son in order to save his master's; two lovers who are forbidden to marry commit suicide together. The puppets move about on a narrow stage. Behind it there is a pit in which the men who manipulate them are partly hidden. The painted backcloth suggests a landscape or the inside of a house. The first people to appear and to take their places, sitting beside the stage, are a samisen-player and a singer: the singer has a very important part to play; he situates the action and he speaks for the characters. Then come the manipulators, carrying the puppets, which are understood to be walking on the stage. They are two-thirds the size of life, but their heads are not in proportion, being relatively smaller. Each puppet has three manipulators: the first has both his hands inside the body and he moves the head, the body and the right arm; his face is unhidden but it remains strictly expressionless. The second

263

moves the left arm and the third the legs: these two wear hoods. All three are dressed in long black robes. I had always loved puppets, but hitherto they had never entirely satisfied me; either they were so stylized that I could not wholly believe in them or they were prodigies of virtuosity in which there was no longer any room for art. The Japanese had succeeded in finding a perfect balance between realism and otherness. In the eighteenth century, when the rough old puppets of earlier times had become entirely alive, when even their faces were animated and the plays were based on everyday life, then the once-hidden manipulators, the samisen-player and the singer started to perform in full view of the audience. One very soon moves into the puppets' world: at first they look rather like invalids in constant need of attention, but in a few moments the men who handle them no longer count. These belong to another world: they are unseen gods, the forces of destiny, the reverse or negative aspect of the adventure passionately and freely lived out by those other beings, the only ones who exist for the audience – beings who do not know they are being manipulated. The feelings of the characters are expressed with extreme violence: when one of them is deeply grieved, the singer utters shrieks that have nothing human about them. He emphasizes the meaning of the words and the tone with mime and facial expression of great intensity; one has the feeling that the emotions he expresses come from the puppets themselves and that it is they who are in control of their movements. One of the pieces they played in Paris was an episode from the well-known story of the forty-seven ronin (the full version lasts twelve hours). At the end, one of the ronin commits harakiri. He slowly takes off his many tunics, one after another, until only his white robe is left. When he grasped his sword and cut open his belly, it was more moving than if there had been a flesh and blood actor on the stage, because in that world to which we were removed death was as believable as life. For the first time in the theatre I saw a corpse that really was a corpse. It lay there, abandoned on the front of the stage, utterly dead.

Why am I so fond of *no* and *bunraku*? I have already given the reason – in the Western theatre the relationship between the real and the imaginary seems to me lame and halting, inadequate.[2] In both *no* and *bunraku* one straight away enters a world that is *other* and all of a piece throughout. The chanting, the songs and the cries

2 See p. 192.

in no way resemble ordinary means of verbal communication. The faces, masked or carved in wood, are inhuman. Emotions are expressed not by the usual mimes and gestures but by conventional signs. In *no* these are very restrained: when the hero is in the grip of the most appalling unhappiness he merely gives his forehead a quick touch with a fold of his long sleeve. In *bunraku* they are exceedingly violent: the singer rolls his eyes like a maniac. In both cases there is a refusal to imitate reality. It is through a total shattering of this reality that the meaning of the drama is isolated in a brilliant purity.

The *kabuki* theatre is the offspring of the *bunraku*: in the eighteenth century plays written for puppets were performed by flesh and blood actors. In 1955 a Japanese company was passing through Pekin, and we saw an example of *kabuki* that charmed us. In Tokyo we devoted a whole evening to it. The chief actor, elderly, fat and very well-known, invited us to his dressing-room while he was putting on his make-up. We took off our shoes in the doorway (we soon got used to living without them half the day), walked in and sat on the floor. We watched him smear ceruse on his face, cover his head with a wig, and put on his kimono – a long, complex operation that needed the help of several dressers. Once the transformations was complete, there before us, instead of an old and ugly man we had an old and hideous woman. The play was a tasteless mixture of coarse farce, laborious realism and earthbound fantasy. I was deeply bored.

I have no liking for the rather vulgar Japanese prints that were all the rage in France at the end of the last century. But in the Tokyo museum there are works of an entirely different quality; here again there is that balance between stylization and realism that is so characteristic of *bunraku*. A few strokes evoke a landscape of mountains and clouds; and against this background people painted with the most scrupulous precision live their everyday life. This is so in the beautiful eleventh-century silk-paintings that show the Buddha's disciples, and in the twelfth-century rolls that recount a legend based on the burning of the imperial palace – two hundred and twenty-seven figures drawn in Indian ink, all in panic-stricken flight. A lovely seventeenth-century paper screen has scenes from the *Tale of Genji*, painted on a background of gold: a two-wheeled carriage drawn by a cow moves towards a tower. And there are some very careful portraits of ministers: they too stand out against a golden background, and they too have this otherness.

The evening we watched the *no* performance, the supper after the show was cut short – a typhoon had been announced and everybody was in a hurry to get home. We were already in bed when, at about one in the morning, the wind began to howl. When we woke up, our rooms were full of dust – the hurricane had forced it in through the window frames. Outside, trees were lying uprooted on the pavement. Tomiko's mother, and those of her friends who lived in low, Japanese-style houses in Tokyo, had spent a very anxious night, with the walls and the window-panes trembling around them. The typhoon had caused deaths in the surrounding country, and a village at the foot of Fujiyama had been engulfed by a torrent of mud. Disasters of this kind are scarcely looked upon as exceptional – they are a normal part of Japanese life. During the occupation, typhoons were given American women's names: now they have numbers. They usually come from the south and travel northwards. Tomiko remembered one several years before; she was in the country when it struck and she had been terrified. It was like the Flood all over again – water came into the house and her mattress was soaked: huge trees were uprooted.

We came to know Tomiko's sister-in-law, Yoshiko. She is the daughter of the minister of justice, and she is one of the best-known singers in Japan – every time she appears on television it is an event. She had lived for a long while in Paris, where she sang – 'I *sang* and that was all,' she stated firmly – at the Cabaret des Nudistes. She had been a close friend of Giacometti. She is now an impresario as well, and the evening we met her she was in a state of some alarm because she was expecting seventy Red Army singers the following week. She asked us to lunch at a luxurious restaurant that had nothing but private rooms: we sat on the ground at a low table and then we discovered that there was a place for our feet – a kind of trench in the floor – so that although we looked as though we were sitting in the Japanese manner, we were spared the discomfort. This was a piece of camouflage that we thoroughly appreciated. We were given a delicious steak: beef is rarely served in Japan, because it is exceedingly expensive. By this time our raw fish was no more than a distant memory. In the Tokyo hotels we found excellent French cooking. The city also had some German eating-places – in one of them the blond waitresses were dressed in Tyrolean costume.

Our friends wanted to show us the surrounding countryside. By train and then by car we reached the little town of Hakone, and from there we went to a hotel that stood above a lake surrounded by hills. The vegetation was both luxuriant and carefully tended. In the villages I was struck by the cleanliness of the houses and the roads, and by the elegance of the flowers that the peasants grew round their neat vegetable-gardens. We went to Tomiko's country house, and we dined at another belonging to a friend of hers: I love those bare sparsely-furnished interiors with their gently glowing wheat-coloured tatamis and the country flooding into the room on all sides. Yoshiko cooked the dinner herself; it was Chinese food, and it was delicious.

The next day we drove along a splendid hillside road above the lake, the same road that the merchants used to take in former times when they travelled from Tokyo to Kyoto. On the border between the districts belonging to these two towns there stood a customs-post. It has been turned into a museum, and there we saw life-sized figures of samurai in the clothes they wore in the eighteenth century, standing as they would have stood when they were on duty.

One of the greatest pleasures of the Japanese is going to watering-places. We stopped at Atami: there the people do not bathe in the sea but in the many public baths, which have swimming-pools, hot baths and rooms for massage. Sometimes men and women bathe separately, sometimes together: for although in most respects they are very reserved about anything to do with sex, the Japanese see no harm in displaying their nakedness bathing at home or in public. I had a look at one bath reserved for women, and Sartre at another reserved for men. After that we went down to see the fortress that commands the town, dominating a long stretch of the coast. We lunched at a hotel whose lawn, sloping gently down towards the sea, was studded with rhododendrons, pines and strangely-shaped dwarf palm-trees. In the lounge I saw a *sumo* match on the television: the Japanese are very fond of this sport. The opponents are huge, hideous masses of flesh; bare to the waist, they confront one another in pairs; and the winner is the one who flings his adversary out of the ring in which they grapple. I personally found the show exceedingly dull; there was a long ceremony before each bout, and the wrestling itself usually lasted no more than a minute.

We went back to Tokyo and then left almost at once for Kyoto, taking the fastest train in the world, the 'flashing express' that eats up the three hundred and thirty miles in three hours, sometimes reaching a speed of more than a hundred and fifty miles per hour. The raised, electrified track has no level crossings or points and it carries no goods-trains, being reserved for passengers. The traffic is controlled electronically. We very nearly missed our train, because we were held up by traffic-jams and Tomiko rather lost her way in the enormous station. We could easily have taken another – about fifty-five leave Tokyo every day. But we had appointments with friends; we ran like hares to catch it, while as a great favour they kept it waiting for three minutes. We saw green rice-paddies and villages charmingly poised at the foot of the hills; but Fujiyama was shrouded in mist. Our friends pointed out that neither in this train nor in the one we had taken earlier did the passengers carry suit-cases: a bundle was all they needed, since they never left their work for more than two or three days.

Kyoto is so famous for its beauty that the Americans did not bomb it. It has preserved its old quarters and one thousand seven hundred temples. From our hotel window we looked out over low, ancient, dark-roofed houses, the little river that runs through the town, and streets lined with covered stalls. We loved Kyoto from the moment we set eyes on it.

We gave a lecture in a big hall. The Japanese have such delicacy, such artistic feeling, that even a lecturer's platform is a delight to the eye. On either side of the reading-desk there was one of those wonderful bouquets that only the Japanese can arrange, and behind us a gilded screen with our names in elegant black characters above it.

We met a great many people – writers, art-historians, philo-sophers, students and teachers – and our conversations often took place while we were eating together. There were many charming garden-restaurants in Kyoto: a few trees and bamboos are so arranged on the far side of a glass screen that they give the illusion of a spreading landscape. There, sitting at little tables, we ate national dishes whose names I forget – beef you cooked yourself on little stoves or by plunging it into a boiling liquid on the end of a fork.

On our arrival in Japan we had given a press-conference; Sartre told the reporters of his high opinion of the works of Tanizaki, and his widow asked us to go and see her. Before she married Tanizaki, who had already written erotic novels in his youth, she had been the wife of one of his friends: for a while, with her husband's consent, she was Tanizaki's mistress. Tanizaki himself was married at that time: he sent his wife to live with still another friend and then he married the present Mrs Tanizaki. This had caused a certain amount of scandal in literary circles. In his *La Confession impudique* and *Diary of a Mad Old Man* he speaks of his erotic experiences in old age; in the first novel his partner is his wife; in the second his daughter-in-law. We were curious to meet them.

Mrs Tanizaki lived in the neighbourhood of Kyoto: wearing a kimono, she welcomed us in the doorway of her house, exchanging deep and prolonged bows with Tomiko. She took us to the cemetery that contains the writer's tomb and then she invited us to have tea in a temple. Like some of our monasteries in earlier times, temples are often 'hostelries' where one can eat and drink – there are those that do not even possess a sanctuary. A bonze received us in a kind of drawing-room; he sent for large bowls of a horribly bitter green soup, quite thick; and we were told that this was Japanese tea. He played with a rosary while Sartre discreetly questioned the widow about her late husband's sexual life – was it anything like that which he had described? The fact of the matter was that Tanizaki had wanted them both to try out some of the practices described in his account of the blind female musician; at first she had refused, but then, because she admired him so, she agreed. But he was an artist; he experienced things primarily in his imagination; his morals were very pure. From time to time, as she spoke, she wiped away imaginary tears with the corner of her handkerchief – exactly the same gesture as that of the old actor whom we had seen playing the part of a tearful heroine. A few days later Mrs Tanizaki asked us to a geisha-house: there were dances and songs, none of them particularly interesting. Her daughter-in-law came, but we did not talk to her.

Every evening we strolled about the huge covered market – souks lit by neon – where all manner of things were sold: local craftsmen's wares, manufactured goods, clothes, food of every kind. We also wandered along the streets where the geishas live; there are a great many in Kyoto and their houses are in a charming old part of the town. In this same quarter there were many restaurants and many pleasant-looking bars. Tomiko, Sartre and I went into one: immediately two 'hostesses' came and sat at our feet. They said nothing, but their presence was so inhibiting that we left almost at once.

Tomiko told us that even if women went out together without men, these hostesses still made a nuisance of themselves. Our only refuge was the tea-rooms, where fortunately whisky is served as well as other things.

The imperial villa is very fine – single-storeyed buildings roofed with green tiles and stretching away and away. The park in which it stands is even finer. Everywhere the gardens and the architecture form a whole. The landscape has been as it were carefully worked upon: skilful pruning has dictated the size and shape of each tree; the form and placing of every rock, bridge, flowerbed and stone lantern has been studied with the utmost care. These are so many microcosms in which each element has a symbolic meaning; yet there is nothing pretty-pretty or finicking about them and they charm the beholder at once. They usually rise against a background of 'borrowed landscape' – that is to say, the distant mountains and forests seem to belong to them.

There are also 'stone-gardens', where strangely-shaped rocks are gathered together in a limited space. The most striking was a Zen garden I saw in a temple. Zen is a severe, highly-refined form of Buddhism that aims at giving a man complete control over his mind and body by means of a quietistic detachment. All the arts have felt its influence – archery, the theatre, painting. And there is a style of garden-planning that derives from Zen. The famous stone-garden near Kyoto is a rectangular court paved with white sand; lines, ridges and circles are drawn in this sand with a rake; and in the court stand fifteen black rocks of different sizes. They are so placed that it is never possible to see more than fourteen at a time. We were enchanted by this austere spectacle, and we gazed at it for a long while. You can see it as so many small islands rising from the sea or sinking into it; or as mountain-peaks viewed from a plane, stabbing through the clouds; or as the abandonment of being in the heart of the void; or just as black rocks on a background of white sand.

We went to see a great many temples in Kyoto, in the surrounding country, and at Nara, the former capital, some twenty-five miles away. These are of two kinds, Shinto and Buddhist. Shinto believes that gods, men and everything else in nature all descend from common ancestors; and it used to hold that the emperor was the reincarnation of the Supreme Being. There was therefore a very powerful link between this religion and the state – a link that the

Americans broke after the war. They were of the opinion that Shinto was responsible for Japanese nationalism and warmongering, and a 'directive' enforced total separation between Shinto and the state. The result was that the priests, deprived of the government's financial support, turned to the people, and there was a sudden wave of popular enthusiasm for the religion. Shinto is therefore thriving. It honours the divine as it is made manifest through natural forces. Buddhism worships the Saviour who removed men from the infernal cycle of successive reincarnations so that one day they might enjoy the peace of Nirvana or the delights of Paradise. The Japanese practise both religions. The Buddhist priests are concerned primarily with theology, while the Shintoists perform the ceremonies, particular those of marriage: though funeral rites are carried out by Buddhists. The priests of each religion take part in the worship of the other.

The Shinto temples are of a democratic nature. They are wide open to the people. They may be as small as a beehive but usually they are as big as a village. On going in, one passes beneath a *torii*, a gateless gateway made of two upright wooden pillars that sustain two horizontal beams. Inside the temple walls, other torii or streams or fences mark off the various zones. The buildings and the torii are made of wood, often painted in brilliant colours – red or vivid orange. They are almost always surrounded by a garden with a lake and tall stone lanterns in it. Often there are goldfish in the pool and animals in the park: one that we saw had fallow-deer that came and took food from the visitors' hands. A temple usually has many buildings – the monks' quarters, the pavilions where they house guests, and the sanctuaries, which are closed to laymen. The doors of these *horden* are guarded by fantastic beasts. On the open ground in front of the sanctuaries, peddlars sell amulets – sheets of paper, small bells, little animals. The worshippers offer up twigs with pieces of white paper attached to them: these are placed outside the shrine. The Shinto priests often have great celebrations with music and sacred dances, either in the courtyards or in certain buildings.

The Buddhist temples are more restrained in both form and colour. The area they cover is usually less, and their gardens are more austere. But they often possess beautiful frescoes and above all admirable sculpture – bronze or wooden statues of Buddha, Kannon, warriors or musicians. At Nara I saw some ancient statues of Buddha that were as beautiful as Greek korai.

271

One glorious piece of architecture at Kyoto is the Golden Pavilion. It is a Zen temple that was once a palace, and the upper two of its three storeys are covered with gold. It stands reflected in a little lake dotted with minute islands, like all Japanese pools. For reasons known only to himself, the young priest in charge set fire to the temple; it was rebuilt in 1955. The writer Mishima based a novel upon the incident – a novel that is very well-known in Japan.

In all these temples there were swarms of schoolboys and school-girls, laughing and chattering: all of them, even the very youngest, had cameras, and they never stoppped taking photographs.

We left Kyoto, and drove through magnificent country up the Koya mountain. It is covered with pine forests, and among the trees a very ancient cemetery stretches mile after mile; it is wrapped in silence and in deep shadow, pierced here and there by a ray of sun. The funeral monuments are very simple – steles or columns. They often represent the five elements, spheres standing one upon another to symbolize water, earth, fire, air and sky. Sometimes they stand alone, sometimes in groups. Occasionally the little laughing god that watches over children is to be seen: he wears a white or a red bib and he carries red flowers; this is the only touch of colour among the dark tree-trunks and the grey rocks. (This little god is often found at temple gates: he is not allowed inside the sanctuary.) A black-robed lama with a shaved head showed us the tombs. All the lamas we met took an interest in Sartre's work, and the nature of their interest surprised me: this one had tears of emotion in his eyes as he shook Sartre's hand. Another, and in another place, spoke to me warmly about *The Second Sex*. He ended by saying, 'But you know, according to our religion a woman cannot go to paradise; first she has to be reincarnated as a man.' He said it with a laugh and obviously he did not believe a word of it.

Our guide led us to one of the temple halls; it was sheltered but it stood open to a garden, and there we ate the picnic we had brought. Then we took a newly-opened mountain-road that runs from a point high above the sea and down to Shima, on the Pacific coast. We reached the town in the darkness, so discovering the landscape next morning was a surprise. We were at the bottom of a long bay whose deeply-indented sides were covered with dry, proliferating vegetation. On the narrow tongues of water that ran into the wooded shores there floated hurdles or rafts that were in fact oyster-parks – an immense and perfectly flat armada of them. Beyond this kind of fjord, we could sense the distant ocean. We took a boat in spite of the rain, and it rowed us about the bay. In floating huts women were making cultured pearls: they opened the living oyster a little way, slipped a morsel of mother-of-pearl under its flesh and closed it again. The oysters are then put into baskets; the baskets are tied to the bottom of the rafts and the creatures therefore bathe in sea-water. The longer they are left the bigger the pearls become; but at the same time there is a greater risk of the parks being destroyed by a storm: the culture usually lasts five years. At Shima no one dives for pearl-oysters on the sea-bed, but we did see one woman going down for those big molluscs the English call abalones – they have excellent flesh and beautiful nacreous shells.

I lunched at the hotel off a crayfish taken in the bay, and then we went to the temple of Ise, the most ancient and revered shrine in Japan. It is a Shinto temple, austere in its architecture of unpainted wood. Here, and by the medium of this holy place, the union of mankind with the forces of nature is brought about; but in order that these forces should remain perpetually vigorous, the temple must be always young, and it is rebuilt every twenty years. Beside the present building lay a stretch of land upon which the outlines of the future temple were taking shape. The temple stands amidst those tall, massive pine-trees that are one of the natural beauties of Japan. It is a place of pilgrimage and there were a great many visitors. The sanctuary is not open to the public; but in a nearby building a bonze arranged sacred dances for us.

When we were back in Kyoto, Tomiko was very anxious for us to stay in a Japanese inn. She chose the best in the town for us, but we were not happy there. The bedroom was pleasant: it was entirely empty, yet it ran on into a verandah, and there, at a lower level, we had a table and two armchairs; through the glass wall, we could see a dense thicket of bamboo. But we had to take off our shoes to go into the hotel, and every time we came or went the staff knelt and bowed to the ground; our door had no lock and the manageress would walk in without the least warning – the first day she was very insistent that we should have a bath at five o'clock in the afternoon. We preferred the impersonality of 'Western' hotels. But in any case we only stayed two days, during which we revisited those parts of Kyoto we liked best.

We spent one afternoon in Oṣaka. There we saw a densely-populated quarter where many of the faces seemed to us gloomy and withdrawn. After dinner we set off in a taxi for Kobe, where we were to take ship on the Inland Sea. For twenty-five miles the road ran through a landscape of factories. Tomiko asked the driver to go slowly. It was not that he was driving too fast, but rather with an unskilful jerkiness that we found alarming. Japanese taxi-drivers are dangerous. They are overworked, starting their day at eight one morning and finishing it at two o'clock the next. Then they rest for more than twenty-four hours. But as they earn very little, they do extra (and illegal) work on their day off. They often have accidents. The accident-rate for cars as a whole is exceedingly high in Japan – the country holds the world record, with 3.3 deaths for every thousand cars on the road. One cause is the inadequacy of the road-network; another is the way the Japanese drive – they have been called the kamikaze of the road. They are rash, they are violent, and they deliberately disobey traffic regulations. So I was deeply relieved when we reached Kobe and I saw our hotel in the distance. The taxi was nearly there when on the right I saw a car racing towards us. Our man drove on without giving a damn. I cried 'The idiot! This was bound to happen!' and then bang: the two cars collided. The taxi had jumped a red light. Tomiko, Sartre and I were in the back, and we were not much hurt. But in the front a young colleague of Mr Watanabe's was bleeding profusely, and he looked stunned. A passer-by called a police-car, and it took him to hospital. He was not seriously injured and he was able to leave for Kyoto the next day. But the two cars were shattered. The news spread quickly: journalists watched for us all night and Tomiko had a great many telephone-calls.

The next day we went aboard a large, comfortable ship and glided over the Inland Sea – a calm sea, with deeply-indented shores and a scattering of rocky islets. We stopped several times in little ports. For the first time in his life Sartre was travelling with a camera, and he plied it with the ardour of a Japanese.

We stayed the night at Beppu, a spa. The hotel was on the top of a hill, and below us we could see the town and the steam rising from the various hot springs. The next morning we went to see them. There was one whose water was red; another in which a boiling geyser shot up at regular intervals; another was covered with water-lillies whose leaves were so big that one might have sat upon them. From Beppu we travelled to Mount Asu in a car lent and driven – carefully and skilfully – by a friend of Tomiko's: in order not to thrust himself upon us, at the beginning of the journey he carried delicacy so far as to pretend to be a hired chauffeur. Eventually Tomiko told us the true state of affairs.

Mount Aso is a volcano with an up-heaved, swollen crust; its immense crater belches thick smoke and fumaroles; and its folded, twisted, fissured sides have the colours of the pit – whitish-grey, poisonous green, and greyish black. It often shoots out lava and stones; and all around it stretches a desert of ashes. Gradually, as one goes down, one sees the beginning of a stunted vegetation, then comes grass and handsome pink thistles.

We slept at the little town of Komamuto. From my bedroom window I could see little tables on the hotel lawn, and at these tables sat men accompanied by geishas. Wives are not usually invited to banquets and geishas look after the womanly side of the entertainment. These were less stiff than any we had seen. They sang cheerful songs, laughed a great deal, and put up with having their bottoms slapped.

The next day we went for a wonderful drive in a most unusual countryside – an archipelago whose islands were linked by five enormous bridges. The road had just been opened. Our friends were glad to be able to show it off to us: for until very recently the Japanese roads were among the worst in the world. As I have already said, this expanding society has neglected the needs of the community as a whole. But the state is now seeing to the construction of important lines of communication, and toll-paying motor-ways are increasing fast. This one was quite astonishing. Sometimes you seemed to be on lakes surrounded by land and sometimes on islands surrounded by water.

That evening we reached Nagasaki. This was the town by which the West first made its way into Japan, and the preaching of the missionaries left a lasting mark upon it; it still has a great many Catholics and the shops sell dolls dressed as nuns. We went to see 'Madame Butterfly's house': it is a villa deep in a garden with a fine view over the harbour; and for many years an Englishman lived there with a Japanese woman. We walked about the port and the quarters where the European merchants lived in the nineteenth century. In the middle of the town there is an immense covered market, a maze of shop-lined alleys where things of every kind are to be had – goldfish, balloons, masks, birds, artificial flowers, lanterns, and every imaginable type of utensil, garment and food.

275

We climbed up to the temples that stand in their beautiful gardens on the top of the hill. And we went to see the 'Park of Remembrance' in a suburb, just where the atomic bomb fell. A gigantic, hideous statue has been erected.

At the end of the day we took a light plane and for twenty-five minutes we flew over a striking panorama of mountains, rice-fields and villages: the green crops covered the plain and ran right up the valleys, dying away at the far end, where they met the barren scree. We landed at Fluoka, a very ugly industrial town that is nevertheless transfigured at night, when the neon blazes out. We had dinner with a woman writer who, with her husband, has elected to live in a neighbouring village near to a mine, in order to help the workers in their struggle. And in fact their condition is deplorable. Those who work directly for the mine are protected by a union. But most are *kumifu*, provided by the *kumi*, the labour-contractors. The union does not concern itself with them. They earn scarcely half the normal pay and they are not entitled to social benefits. They are given the most dangerous work – many are killed or wounded by falls of stone. They are housed in camps patrolled by armed guards, who are usually recruited from common-law criminals in the prisons. It is impossible for these outcastes to run away. When a labour-inspector is due, they are hidden in a gallery so that they shall not be able to make contact with him. The young woman who was talking to us and her husband live among them and encourage them to unite in order to be able to resist. To begin with the miners distrusted them, but gradually they took to asking for their advice. Together they built a 'house of solidarity' with the aid of money provided by left-wing intellectuals; and this institution helped out-of-work miners to qualify themselves for new jobs when the management closed down a certain number of pits.

This system of forced labour is widespread in Japan: the dockers, the day-labourers and the building-workers form a sub-proletariat controlled by a middleman who provides firms with labour. They usually come from the country, mechanization having thrown them out of work. They live herded into what amounts to ghettoes near the place where they work, and the boss employs strong-arm men who prevent them from leaving.

The next day we travelled by train – an hour's journey through an industrial region – to a port where women did the work of unloading cargoes: I was to interview some of them for the television. A launch took us alongside a large ship and we climbed aboard by a ladder. At the very bottom of the hold, in a cloud of acrid dust, ants were to be seen – women shovelling chemical fertilizer into sacks that were carried off by a crane. They came up on to the deck: they were sweating heavily, and one of the women was over sixty. I questioned them. In a rancourous tone one said she could say a great deal if she chose to speak out; but in fact their answers were invariably timid and unassertive. Yet for all that the harshness and injustice of their state were none the less flagrant: they worked eight hours a day in exhausting conditions – eight hours every day, including Sundays. (Indeed, that day happened to be a Sunday.) In spite of the official regulations they were paid less than men. And on top of that, it was they who did all the household work – as women do in all countries. They complained both of that and of the unequal pay. This inequality is a widespread phenomenon in Japan: official statistics show that in 1962 the average pay for women was sixteen thousand yen a month as opposed to thirty-five thousand for men. Thirty-five per cent of the Japanese labour-force consists of women.

That evening we landed at Hiroshima. A tourist folder that I read in the plane began with these words: 'Hiroshima is above all famous for the five rivers that run through it.' The fact that the town had been destroyed was mentioned in passing. Hiroshima has been entirely rebuilt; its broad avenues intersect at right-angles; in the evening it blazes with light and of all Japanese towns has the greatest number of restaurants, bars and night-clubs. That evening we were invited to a luxurious Western-style restaurant: a band was playing jazz and I found it hard to persuade myself that I was actually in Hiroshima.

In spite of the tourist folder, Japan in fact retains a horrified memory of the atomic bombs, and at present it is a deeply pacifist country. Towards 1951 the Americans authorized and even urged rearmament: Japan refused. All the government agreed to do – and the population as a whole blamed them vehemently for it – was to set up a reserve police force; it has since become the Self-Defence Force, but in 1966 it amounted to no more than two hundred and fifty thousand men divided between the army, the navy and the air force.

No one in Japan would so much as contemplate the making of an atomic bomb. A very important section of public opinion, including the biggest trade-union, the *Sohyo*, advocates neutrality. To be sure, it was thanks to Japanese bases and Japanese economic aid that the Americans were able to carry on the war in Korea and in Vietnam: but the government's pro-American policy has aroused violent opposition.

There are two peace-movements in Japan: one condemns all atomic weapons, the other only those owned by America. They are both very active, particularly in Hiroshima, which has been baptized 'the city of peace'. The next morning our hotel lounge was full of representatives from both organizations: as Sartre did not wish to hurt anyone's feelings, he refused all their invitations. We set out to tour the town, guided by Mr Tanabe, the head of the 'Foundation to help the victims of the bomb' that was set up by an American named Morris. First he showed us the ruin that commemorates the disaster: it is the shell of a large building in the Austrian style, a bank or a store – I forget which – of such solid construction that it alone escaped destruction. There was nothing very striking about this relic, except on reflection – it was in fact the only *ruin* that we ever saw in Japan. When the old wooden buildings collapse they are rebuilt, thus remaining perpetually young. By this ruin there was the Memorial, where fresh victims are still buried every year: they usually die of leukaemia. Then we visited the museum. In the show-cases we saw views of the devastated Hiroshima – vast charred expanses. Other photographs showed mutilated people, with their backs burnt, their bodies covered with those horrible skin-tumours called cheloids. I was afraid that our next visit was going to be even more painful: a taxi took us to the hospital. In the way someone stopped the cab to buy a bunch of flowers: and they were put into my hands. The director received us in his office; it was filled with journalists and photographers. He told us that in case of illness the hospital provided free treatment for the people who were within a certain radius the day the bomb was dropped. At present there were two hundred and fifty of them, the majority suffering from leukaemia. 'Should you like to go and see the patient, or should you prefer her to come down?' he asked. We went up, followed by the troop of journalists, and we went into a room with two beds in it. In the first, lying on her back, there was an old woman; her hand was on the sheet, and it trembled without a pause. A sad-faced woman of about forty was sitting up in the other bed. They thrust me towards her and I gave her the flowers, machine-gunned by the photographers. This absurd ceremony verged upon gross indecency. We agreed to visit other patients on condition that we should see them without an escort. And we cut this unpleasant expedition as short as possible.

In the afternoon we went to the Foundation. It is a modest little building in which the victims of the bomb can meet together or apply for assistance. We were to see some of them. We had supposed that the encounter would be private and we were disagreeably surprised to find that we were expected to sit on a dais with microphones in front of us, while the people we were to talk to sat on the ground at our feet. At the back of the room there were journalists, photographers and a television-team. Holding anything like a conversation was not easy. Yet we did so. And here again we were astonished. We had expected these survivors to be bitter and resentful: they were humble and resigned. Indeed, they were even ashamed – ashamed of their infirmities, their scars, their inability to work. Some leave for other towns, where they conceal their misfortune as though it were a shameful blemish – if they told the truth they would not be employed. The government gives them no pension unless they were civil servants; none of the civilian victims of the war receives any compensation – and there were as many of them in Tokyo as at Hiroshima. In Hiroshima itself, many of the survivors live in a wretchedly poor district that we were not shown.

It was with a deep feeling of relief that we took the train that evening for Kurashiki, one of the very few towns in Japan to have been spared by wars and earthquakes. All the next day we walked about it: a narrow willow-lined stream crossed by little bridges runs through the middle of the town; on either side of the old streets stand low houses with green-tiled roofs; beautiful signs with black characters adorn the larger shops; and in open stalls craftsmen make sunshades, lanterns and fans. A cloth-merchant showed us his house: it had several inner courtyards and gardens with wooden pavilions in them. We also went to see the village some miles away: the farm we visited was remarkably clean and comfortable.

In some parts of the country the peasants are still very poor; but on the whole their condition is much improved. Since the agrarian reform ninety per cent possess their own land. Thanks to irrigation, to the quantities of fertilizer they use, and to the mechanization of agriculture, their harvest from the same piece of land is two or three times greater than it was at the beginning of the century – that is to say, it is now five times the French yield from an equal area. Furthermore, the members of a peasant family usually have a subsidiary job in the nearest town – manual or clerical work. Their living standard is therefore higher than it used to be: they have enough to eat; they take a pride in their homes, their gardens and their clothes; and they read.

Back in Tokyo we attended a great meeting in protest against American intervention in Vietnam. The Japanese have an ambivalent attitude towards America. Economically, they accept an alliance that they find profitable; but on the political and military plane they think it dangerous. In the event of a conflict it exposes them to the treatment not of a neutral but of a hostile nation. They protest against the occupation of Okinawa and against the presence of air bases. The left wing is determinedly anti-American – it was in the anti-American demonstrations of 1960 that the Zengakuren first made themselves known. Most Japanese students and intellectuals feel that the war in Vietnam concerns them very deeply indeed: they have a strong fellow-feeling for that little scrap of Asia. The Americans' criminal interference not only offends their pacifism and their sense of justice; they also know that the imperialism of the United States is a direct threat to them. There are frequent demonstrations against the Vietnamese war. In 1965 twenty-eight intellectuals founded a movement for peace in Vietnam; its leader was Oda, a writer we had often met. The meeting to which he invited us took place in an ampitheatre, strangely situated on the top floor of a big department-store. Sartre and I each said a few words. The main speakers were teachers and writers. The numerous audience listened most attentively, but, according to Japanese custom, their applause was very discreet and subdued.

I was told that several of those labour-camps in which the subproletariat live their wretched lives were to be found in Tokyo itself: obviously there was no question of going to see them. There are also exceedingly poor districts where people are crowded three and four to a room in wooden shacks without water, heating or light: we were told about them, but nobody suggested taking us there. Generally speaking the Japanese are very poorly housed. In the neighbourhood of Osaka I visited a teacher's flat in the equivalent of a council block, and was struck by its lack of space and its ugliness. The pretty houses that delighted me at the beginning of my journey

280

belonged to privileged people; but even so they are very uncomfortable in winter, being impossible to heat.

Although Japan is rich, the Japanese are poor: all our meetings confirmed this fact. The teachers, even those in the universities, are very badly paid. There are a great many university-students and almost all of them manage to take a degree: but these degrees are of no use to them – they become minor clerks, and their living-standard is very low. The twenty million craftsmen who carry on their calling in their own family workshop scarcely make a living. In the big companies the workers are decently paid; but we have seen what a small percentage of Japanese industry these large firms represent.

A very considerable proportion of the population is not only poor, but wretchedly poor: twenty per cent of the homes – that is to say, about twenty million persons – live at 'subsistence-level', or in other words they are under-nourished.

We were also told about the strange condition of those outcasts of society called Etas. There are three million of them, and although they belong to the same race as the other Japanese they form a despised and separate body. The origins of this discrimination are little known; but it is rigorously carried out. Some few Etas are wealthy – I was told of one who owned important shops – yet no Japanese would ever grant one his daughter's hand: marriages between Japanese and Etas are strictly forbidden. Almost all are exceedingly poor, because the Japanese refuse to employ them. They live in ghettoes, without water or sanitation.

Our return journey confused me entirely: it was eleven o'clock in Tokyo when we took off, and it was dark; then when we landed at Anchorage the clock said eleven and it was broad daylight – the landscape was snowier and more desolate than it had been a month earlier. Then it was night again as we flew over the Pole and day when we landed at Paris.

6

During our journey to the USSR in 1962 it had seemed to us that we were seeing an even more definitive 'thaw' than that of 1954. Sartre had gone back to Moscow at the beginning of July 1962 to take part in a Movement for Peace congress. There he had broached the question of culture. Taking Kafka as his example he showed how culture had been made use of for partisan ends in the Eastern countries: but culture was not a weapon, he said. Instead of rejecting Western culture outright, it would be to the Soviets' advantage to make it an integral part of their own. On the political plane, Khrushchev asserted the necessity of a coexistence based upon peaceful competition. Thus the two cultures, though still in opposition, were to live side by side, not attempting to destroy one another. This idea of a unity in the struggle charmed those intellectuals who were called liberals or progressives and who were opposed to conformism. They wanted to carry on a dialogue with Sartre. And that was one of the reasons that decided us to make frequent returns to the USSR. Until 1966 we spent several weeks there every summer. We were interested in following the country's evolution; and we were attracted both by the variety of its landscapes and the beauty of its former cultural wealth. And above all we had made many friends: we were all the more anxious to maintain links with them since year by year they were losing ground in their struggle with the conformists. Sartre had considerable sums in royalties in Moscow and he paid all our expenses. Thanks to invitations from the Writers' Union we obtained our visas; and the Union placed an interpreter at our disposal – it was always Lena Zonina – who saw to all the material arrangements, working through Intourist.

We were on terms of the warmest friendship with Ehrenburg. It was he who told us all about Russian cultural life and its hidden sides. He often came to Paris. When we were in Moscow we went to see him at his dacha, a pretty, very simple house surrounded by a garden – he loved growing flowers and vegetables himself and he was very proud of having introduced a plant unknown in Russia: the artichoke. We also visited his flat in Moscow, near Gorki Street. It was a positive museum. Before the war he had been *Izvestia*'s correspondent in Paris for years, and he had known all the painters in Montparnasse: he had an immense collection of pictures they had given him, including many paintings, drawings and lithographs by Picasso. There were also Chagalls, Légers, Matisses and pictures by Russian painters such as Falk and Tishler. He knew a great deal about painting and in Moscow he supported the avant-garde artists. As far as writing was concerned, he was less receptive. He saw no merit in Kafka, Proust or Joyce and he had no more than a partial appreciation of Sartre's work. Yet as he grew older he became more and more tolerant and there was never any subject that we could not discuss. In the USSR he protected young writers who were looked upon as anti-conformist. He was popular with the rising generation. He was less elegant than he had been in Helsinki and he had aged physically – only one tooth left. His lack of a false set was no doubt due to the Russians' dread of their dentists: either from want of skill or because they do not care, they make their patients suffer cruelly. Intellectually he had retained all his charm; he chose his anecdotes well and he told them admirably.

On every visit to Russia we dined two or three times with the Cathalas. He had been at the Ecole normale with Sartre: during the war he supported de Gaulle, and in 1945 he became a Communist. He was now supervising the publication of Russian works in French; and he was an excellent translator. His Russian wife was a very dark-haired woman, lively and agreeable: she worked on a magazine. They lived in a delightful flat – a great many books and prints and a remarkable collection of pipes. Both of them were open-minded, clear-thinking people with a well-developed critical faculty. They knew a great deal about what was happening in the country: they also had a great many contacts and they passed the benefit of their wide acquaintance on to us.

We were also much attached to Doroch, of whom I have spoken in *Force of Circumstance*: he was an art-historian and he was also interested in agriculture – he wrote articles on the subject for *Novy Mir*. Intellectually he was more open than Ehrenburg: he liked

Brecht and Kafka as soon as he read them. Unhappily he spoke no French, and our conversation was rather slow.

We knew other writers too, and translators, interpreters and people who worked for the Writers' Union. Our closest friend was Lena, a handsome dark woman of about forty, exceptionally cultivated and intelligent. She told us a great deal about her life. Her father, mother and uncles had been ardent Bolsheviks – there was a photograph of them all with Lenin. At the time it was taken Lena's mother was twenty: Lena was the living image of her, with twenty years added. Shortly after Lena's birth her parents separated; she saw her father often but she actually lived with her mother. She was educated in Moscow, going to the university, where she specialized in French language and literature. Her teacher foretold a brilliant future for her, and she hoped to teach and write herself. When the war broke out she joined up; and she was sent to a place north of Leningrad, where she worked in an office. She showed us a snapshot of herself in uniform, wearing a forage-cap and a martial air. As we were sitting on a bench in the Champ de Mars in Leningrad, she told us how she had once crossed it when she was on leave, meaning to go and have her hair waved: suddenly the shelling began and she tried to retain an upright, soldierly bearing while at the same time striding out to reach the hairdresser's as quickly as possible. She wanted to be nearer the front, and she had herself transferred to Pskov. After the victory she returned to her studies at the university.

At that time she was an out-and-out Stalinist: in her eyes he was the incarnation of the revolution and of the fatherland, and he had saved the country. Her best friend criticized him, and Lena threatened to kill her with her own hands if ever she became a counter-revolutionary – she never saw this friend again. A few months later she happened to run into a man who knew her father; he told her that her father had been sent to a camp. She was so utterly taken aback that for three days she lost the power of speech. A little later she was told that her father's deportation meant she could no longer attend the university. Her mother was excluded from the Communist party for another reason: a friend of hers had a post abroad, and according to the logic of the period that was enough for him to be considered as an enemy of the regime and one fine day to be arrested. She herself fell under the same suspicion. Lena was completely overwhelmed at having to give up her studies and even more so at being the victim of such injustice. She never entirely recovered from the blow. Her faith in Stalin was dead.

She heard that Ehrenburg was looking for a secretary and she applied, warning him that her father was in a camp: he took her on. It was an act of courage for which she was deeply grateful: she was very fond of the 'old man', as she called him. She worked with him for several years, and then he found her a job with the Writers' Union.

After Stalin's death the camps were opened, and Lena's father came home: he died soon after. Her mother rejoined the party.

Lena had married an architect, but they did not get along together intellectually. She divorced, and married a critic for whom she had a great respect. But he could not give her a child, and after some years she wanted one. She had an affair with another writer. When her daughter was born she divorced again, but she declared the baby under her own name alone – a common practice in the USSR – and did not go to live with its father. She wanted her independence, and like many other Soviet women she had a lively feeling of superiority to men. She settled down with the baby and her mother in a little flat near the Writers' Union. Her mother did not work, being ill, and she helped to bring up Masha, Lena's child. Lena herself was very busy; she worked long hours at her office; she did some translations and she wrote highly praised critical articles for the reviews.

In about 1960 her daughter fell so ill that Lena was afraid she might die. The child recovered, and when she was well Lena travelled to France. She was deeply moved at seeing a country that meant so much to her, but she felt uneasy all the time she was there: she loathed the capitalist system, but although the richness of the West sickened her she also found it fascinating – the contrast between this opulence and the austerity to which her own people were condemned wounded and oppressed her. When she was back in the USSR she had an attack of diabetes; it was no doubt due to her fear of losing Masha and to the emotion of seeing Paris. She took to her bed, and the disease grew worse – the doctors had not made the correct diagnosis at first. They just managed to save her. From then on she had to give herself an injection of insulin every morning, and she was obliged to take many precautions.

We liked one another as soon as we met, and I valued her the more the longer I knew her. I admired her strength of character.

Her career had been wrecked and the life she led was not the life she had wanted: yet she was never sorry for herself. She shirked no responsibility and she refused all compromise. When she took French writers to the mausoleum where Stalin lay until 1962, she would never go in. There was nothing lukewarm about Lena. She had a passionate feeling for truth and justice. But she never indulged in dogmatism or priggishness; she was gay, ironical, and sometimes very funny. Above all there was a bond between us that is hard to define – an understanding, an instant communication, a way of having the same opinions about things and people, and of laughing or smiling at the same moment. It was a great pleasure, walking about with her or sitting in her flat, talking and drinking vodka.

The liberalization of culture went on during the autumn of 1962. In October, with Khrushchev's consent, *Pravda* published Yevtushenko's poem *Stalin's Heirs*, which denounced the continuing existence of Stalinism – the poet called for the tripling of the guard over Stalin's tomb to prevent him from coming to life again. Khrushchev also allowed *Novy Mir* to publish Solzhenitsyn's book *One Day in the Life of Ivan Denisovich*, which described his experiences in the Stalinist camps. In his *Memoirs*, which were coming out in the same magazine, Ehrenburg spoke very freely about Western art. Nekrassov wrote an article about his journeys to the United States and Italy – an impartial account, in which he mixed a great deal of praise with his criticism. Voznesensky published a collection of poems called *The Triangular Pear* with nothing conformist about it whatsoever. We had seen him in Paris,[1] together with Nekrassov and Paustovsky, and all three were delighted with the new climate in Moscow. This finally decided us to return for the Christmas holidays. Yet by December things were already turning a little sour. There was a great exhibition of modern painting and sculpture in the Manège, and when Khrushchev went to see it he violently condemned formalism and abstraction in art. The propaganda chief, Ilyichev, made a speech against 'ideological coexistence' – a speech in which he attacked Ehrenburg in particular and uttered a number of anti-semitic remarks.

However, by the time we reached Moscow the exhibition had not yet closed, and we were able to see it. There were many academic

[1] We had first made his acquaintance in Moscow in 1962.

works, but there were also some pictures by Falk and Tishler, those painters of the nineteen-twenties whom Ehrenburg liked so much. And works by contemporary artists who were seeking new paths – among others Weisberg, the painter, and the sculptor Neizvestny. A little later these works were withdrawn. Ehrenburg wondered whether the conformist painters had not been thoroughly Machiavellian when they invited the avant-garde artists to exhibit, hoping that the decadent nature of their art would thus become evident and that it would be proscribed more severely than ever.

How gay Moscow was, under the snow and the blue sky! The branches of the trees and their delicate twigs were powdered with a sparkling whiteness. Many people went about on skis, and where the streets sloped down they glided happily along. The passers-by, carefully wrapped up, were all loaded with parcels; and in their brilliantly-coloured quilted coats the children looked as though they were going to a fancy-dress party. In the squares stood tall snowy Christmas-trees. All the streets had a holiday look – an air of festivity. Simonov and his wife invited us to a Christmas Eve party in the foyer of a theatre near Mayakovsky Square. It was minus twenty degrees centigrade. When we got there, fat young women were arriving; they hurried to the cloak-room, shed their fur coats, boots and thick wool skirts, and reappeared, slim and elegant in light evening dresses and slippers. Almost all the people there were young; and there were many very pretty girls – actresses and models. As we had our supper at a little table we watched the couples dancing; they danced modern dances, and danced them very well, to the sound of excellent recorded jazz. It was only a privileged few who were concerned: but we thought it a good sign that they were allowed to wear these elegant clothes and to listen to this Western music.

In comparison with Moscow, Leningrad seemed dreary: the sun did not rise until ten, and it shed but a faint light on the greyish streets. It described a short curve in the sky and then at about three o'clock it vanished. But the frozen Neva was very beautiful – Italianate palaces on both sides of a polar icefield with a timid trickle of water shimmering here and there.

In 1968 an organization called COMES[2] was set up in Italy: its aim was to encourage exchanges between European writers from the

[2] Community of European writers.

East and the West. The undertaking was in complete agreement with the cultural programme put forward by Sartre in Moscow in July 1962, so a little while ago we agreed to join it. Its president was the Italian poet Ungaretti and its secretary-general the Italian writer Vigorelli, whom we had known since 1946: the organization decided to hold a congress in Leningrad in July 1963. Ever since his initiative of July 1962, Sartre had been looked upon by the Writers' Union as a person with whom a worthwhile dialogue could be established, and the Union sent us an invitation. (It also invited André Stil, but for other reasons.) The French delegation, led by Frénaud, was made up of Robbe-Grillet, Nathalie Sarraute and Pingaud; Caillois represented UNESCO. Among the English were Angus Wilson, John Lehmann and Goyen; among the Italians Piovene and Vigorelli. Enzensberger, a charming young German and a member of Group 47 was also there, and Tibor Dery, the aged Hungarian writer, some Poles and Romanians and a great many Soviets, including Simonov, Fedin, Sholokov, Ehrenburg, Surkov, Axionov, Granin and Tvardovsky.

The cultural situation had deteriorated since the winter. On 8 March 1963 Khrushchev had addressed an audience that included party and government leaders, writers and artists; it was a speech twenty thousand words long in which he defended Stalin and made a vehement attack on formalism and abstraction in writing and the fine arts, firing several broadsides at Ehrenburg, Nekrassov, Yevtushenko and even Paustovsky. Friends had told us of a film about the conflict between the generations called *The Lenin Barrier* that they had seen at a private showing; and they praised it very highly. Khrushchev tore it to pieces. Of all the writers, Ehrenburg was picked out for the severest criticism. When they were talking privately together, Khrushchev blamed him for having had a bad influence on Sartre – for having incited him to leave the Communist Party. Ehrenburg observed that Sartre had never belonged to it; but it was no use: Khrushchev remained unconvinced. Ehrenburg's position was very worrying. The authorities would not let the rest of his memoirs be published and the printing of the complete edition of his works was suspended. There were consolations – whenever he addressed an audience of students they gave him an ovation. But it was a hard blow from the material point of view. He had nothing but his royalties to live on and to maintain his wife and two old sisters – they lived in his dacha. If he were not published, it would mean extreme poverty. He told us that he spent a great deal of time working in his garden to calm his mind, but that nevertheless he was still very uneasy.

No doubt it was because of Khrushchev's speech in March that the opening session of the congress was so very strange and disconcerting. The Soviet writers began by expressing their bitter contempt for Western literature and particularly for Proust, Joyce and Kafka, and they upheld the excellence of socialist realism as compared with the work of these 'decadents'. There was little hope that this fanaticism would subsequently allow any worthwhile 'interchange'.

The tone of the other sessions was in fact more moderate; but there was no dialogue whatsoever between the East and the West – it was as though neither listened to what the other was saying. On the Western side the French had a good deal to say, and they defended the *nouveau roman*; on the Eastern side all the speakers with the exception of Tvardovsky, Ehrenburg and two or three others proclaimed their faith in a literature that should help 'to beautify men's lives'. Fedin compared the writer to a pilot whose duty it is to fly his passengers to their right destination. Robbe-Grillet replied that 'the novel was not a means of transport . . . that by definition a writer did not know where he was going'. But the Soviets went on and on with their comparison of author and pilot. Leonov was the most vehement: he denounced not capitalism but the rotten, corrupted West. 'The West has reached the point at which Dostoevsky's thesis is realized to the full – anything and everything is allowed,' he said; and he went on to expose and deplore the degeneration of the literary character among the Westerners, the increase in crime, the decline of social principles, the decay of ancient taboos and the open, corrupt cynicism. He castigated all our vices, especially our passion for strip-tease.

To prevent the congress from fizzling out altogether, during the last session Surkov suddenly asked Sartre to make a coherent summing up of the proceedings. Sartre took off his earphones, and without leaving his place he quickly drafted a general statement. He brought it off very well and he was loudly applauded. But this hasty reconciliation in no way altered the facts – the attitude of the Soviet writers was far more closed than we had imagined. The watchword had probably come from above.

Nevertheless Surkov persuaded Khrushchev to receive a COMES delegation at his country place in Georgia. We spent two days in

Moscow and then we went aboard a special plane. There was Sartre and myself, Ungaretti, Vigorelli, Angus Wilson, Lehmann, Enzensberger, Putrament the Pole, a Romanian, and a great many Soviets, including Surkov and Tvardovsky. Sholokhov was already with Khrushchev. We left with empty stomachs at seven o'clock in the morning and we were not even given a cup of coffee on the plane: nothing at the airport either. We were bundled into a coach that lurched dangerously along a high coast-road with sudden, perilous corners. I was astonished by the southern warmth and by the luxuriant vegetation that flowed down the hillside to the very blue sea. And I was faint with hunger. At about eleven the coach came to a stop: there in the dining-room of a big hotel stood a table covered with smoked fish, cold meat and blinis. We were almost there and we were soon to have luncheon; so I limited myself to a few cups of coffee. An hour later we climbed out of the coach at Khrushchev's place – a vast wood, planted with the rarest and most beautiful trees in the whole Union. Khrushchev greeted us pleasantly. He was wearing a light-coloured suit and a Ukrainian shirt with a high-buttoned collar. He took us to see the swimming-pool he had had made by the shore; it was immense, and all round it had a glass wall that could be made to disappear by pressing a button – he did so several times, with great satisfaction.

Then we sat at little tables in the conference-hall and with growing surprise we listened to Khrushchev's address. Since he had asked us there, we had supposed he was going to be friendly. Not at all. He abused us as though we were so many henchmen of capitalism. He extolled the beauties of socialism; he claimed responsibility for the Soviet intervention in Budapest. After this outburst he did manage to bring out a few civil words: 'Still, you are against war too. So at least we can eat and drink together.' A little later Surkov said to him privately, 'You were very rough on them.' 'They must understand,' he replied sharply.

We went to the house, following a lovely flower-lined drive that ran along the sea. Bathing-costumes had been laid out for us: Vigorelli and Surkov had a short swim while the others talked. Then we went into the fine old Georgian house, walked upstairs to the first floor, and there we had a splendid meal. Khrushchev remained very sullen: he scarcely uttered a word.

When dessert appeared, Tvardovsky, at Khrushchev's request, brought a poem out of his pocket and began to read it aloud. Now

Khrushchev began to laugh – a deep, full-throated laugh – and all the Soviets followed suit. All our friends had invariably spoken of Tvardovsky with great esteem. He had a rather babyish face, with a pink complexion and very light blue eyes. He was fifty-three. He had written long humorous and lyrical poems and they had won him the Stalin prize: he owed most of his reputation to a poem he had written in 1942 on the good soldier Tiorkin, the Russian equivalent of the Good Soldier Schweik. When Stalin died Tvardovsky wrote a sequel called *Tiorkin in the Other World*, which was thought to be unpublishable. Some of his friends considered this the right moment for it to be read to Khrushchev, and I imagine Khrushchev knew what it was about when he agreed to hear it. An interpreter whispered that it was a satire on socialism; and we thought it rather amusing that Khrushchev should be so heartily amused by the poem immediately after he had treated us to such an extravagant eulogy of the regime. Later I found that much of the poem made fun of the administration's slowness and the delay; but that it also contained biting parodies of the clichés of Soviet propaganda.[3] The 'liberal' camp was delighted with the friendship between Khrushchev and Tvardovsky, for Tvardovsky had considerable influence in the literary world. He was the editor of *Novy Mir*, the most interesting and open-minded of the literary reviews; and with great courage he supported the writers he liked, including Doroch. And like Doroch he was particularly interested in the problems of the peasants. But any really worthwhile piece of writing would always find a defender in him.

Nevertheless we were profoundly bored during the reading of his poem; it lasted three quarters of an hour and we did not understand a single word. Immediately after the meal we took our leave of Khrushchev: he embraced the Soviets and vouchsafed the others a smile. Just as Sartre was getting into the coach Sholokhov, who was not going with us, flung his arms about him. No one was more zealous in denouncing 'subversive' literature than Sholokhov, and his great talent of earlier days was no more than a memory. We did not like him at all.

In Moscow a friend told us why Khrushchev had received us so very coldly. Thorez was spending his holidays a few miles away; he had come to see Khrushchev that morning and he had put him on

---

[3] The poem came out in *Novy Mir* the following October. *Les Temps modernes* published a translation.

291

his guard against these dangerous anti-Communists he was about to meet: he should be all the more wary of them because they pretended to belong to the left. Khrushchev had taken notice of this warning. Another surprise: the papers carried enthusiastic reports of our meeting. Had other influences come to bear overnight? We never did make out the reasons for this change of face.

Moscow smelt of summer. People stood in queues by tankers that sold beer or kvass, and they crowded round those brightly-coloured machines that gush fizzy drinks or plain cold water in return for a coin. There were some new cafés: most were low, roughly-furnished, glassed-in buildings. They served no vodka: some had brandy, others no spirits at all. The restaurants were more cheerful and there were many we liked; unfortunately they had dancing in the evenings and the bands were so loud we could scarcely hear ourselves speak. We hardly knew what to do with ourselves after dinner, except when we went to see friends, which was often the case. We renewed our contacts with almost all of them; they were exceedingly eager to know what was going on in the West, and they told us all about the changes that had occurred in the USSR.

We knew that a certain number of studies were forbidden because of their Western origins. Scientists could make only a surreptitious use of cybernetics, a discipline essential for their research. But the psychiatrists would have nothing to do with psychoanalysis. What were their methods? What results did they obtain? We asked if we might visit the Psychiatric Institute.

A team of doctors received us and they began the interview by warmly praising Kraeppelin, Clérambault and French psychiatry. Then they took us to their laboratories, all of which were engaged in the study of schizophrenia. They showed us encephalograms and the machines that took them; we saw cats with electrodes implanted in their heads and research-workers handling test-tubes and carrying out analyses. The doctors told us how they regretted their inability to isolate the chemical factor common to all these cases: they had no sort of doubt that one existed. Since they classed all mental illness under one single heading their failure seemed the less surprising.

Then we visited the hospital. I believe that in all countries the patients are now treated with tranquilizing drugs, some very powerful: these patients, sitting on benches or wandering about the wards and corridors, looked like so many zombies. But there was one woman sobbing and calling out; she was a new arrival and there had not yet been time to dose her.

In our presence the doctors spoke to a patient whom they looked upon as cured and who was about to leave. She was a former schoolmistress of about forty, married and the mother of a family: severely dressed; hair scraped back; pale, cold eyes. In a lifeless voice she thanked the doctors for having looked after her so well: she now understood the errors she had made in the past. She spoke without the least conviction – it might have been a prisoner reciting a pre-arranged confession before his judges. The psychiatrists asked her a few questions and she obediently produced answers that she seemed to have learnt by heart. After an illness and a period of overwork she had begun to suspect her husband of hating her and of trying to do her harm. She was suspicious of everyone around her. When she was in the bathroom, she thought her father was watching her through the keyhole. She gave up all activity, doing nothing at all; she wept; she wasted away. Her husband brought her to the hospital; she had been treated for a nervous breakdown consequent upon overwork, and now she no longer thought herself persecuted: at least that was what she said and the doctors believed her; for my part I was by no means so sure of it. It seemed to me that having learnt what she had to say to be let out she was saying it.

As the psychiatrists walked with us to the door, Lena whispered 'Ask them whether there is not a sexual factor in her illness.' 'Not me. I don't want to be taken for a corrupt Westerner. You ask.' Later she did so and she told us about their conversation. Her question made the doctor start. 'A sexual factor? What an idea! This woman is married, she has two children – her life is completely normal.' 'Married women are not always satisfied.' 'She gets along very well with her husband.' 'Still, the father watching her through the keyhole . . .' 'What of it? She was persecuted and she thought people were spying on everything she did. As she said, she suspected everybody. What are you trying to get at?' Lena did not press the matter.

We left Moscow for the Crimea. At Simferopol an Intourist car was waiting for us, but there was no driver in it. 'He's shaving,' we were told. 'This is the South all right,' said Lena with a laugh. The South, the Taurida: I found it hard to link this name with the USSR. It was hot. We drove along between low flat-roofed houses, sparsely shaded by false acacias and eucalyptus-trees; we passed an artificial lake, hard blue in its ring of red stone, and then there was the coast—a fine corniche road cut into white rock; blue sea; tall black cypresses. It was the South; but it was not the Mediterranean – there were no olive-trees. Yalta: another of those names too closely bound up with history for me to imagine them as geographical realities. Yet there I was, seeing Yalta with my own eyes – walking about it, indeed. It was a garden rather than a town, with flower-beds, and walks winding in and out of little groves. From the very first evening I was delighted with it. Some people were walking slowly along the sea-front; others sat on benches, talking or meditating. They were nothing like the holiday-makers on the Côte d'Azur: for me their unaffected faces and unpretentious clothes made a startling contrast with the luxury of the silken sea and the gorgeous many-coloured flowers.

The next day we went to look at the town. It stands in terraces upon a hill. From a distance the higher parts seem entirely wooded, but when one gets there houses appear among the trees. They are old wooden houses and their fronts are often extravagantly carved; many of them have balconies and verandahs decorated with stained glass. In former times they belonged to wealthy people. Now several families share them, but they have retained all their charm. Each is hidden from the rest; and each seems lost in its own jungle. We went into one that had belonged to Chekov: his presence was still very much to be felt.

At Yalta itself there was a public beach so thickly strewn with naked bodies that not a free inch was to be seen. The women's forms were quite distressingly ample; only the very young took care of their figures. We went to the almost deserted Intourist beach. The car that took us followed a fine lofty coast-road (dotted now and then with bravely-smiling kolkhoz girls, made of stone) and then dropped down through the vineyards. The Tartars of former days understood their cultivation and they produced a delicious wine: Stalin had all the Tartars deported to Central Asia for collaborating with the Germans, and a great many of them died there. The Crimea is now inhabited by Ukrainians, and they are but indifferent vine-growers.

Going by way of Simferopol – for the direct road was forbidden to foreigners – we visited the former capital of the Tartars: at present it is a small town with low houses and narrow cobbled streets. The palace is countrified and charming: it is built of wood and stucco with Moorish decorations; it has barred windows, a fountain that inspired Pushkin, and sparsely-planted gardens – an Alhambra for a penniless prince. On the walls we saw huge pictures of battles between Cossacks and Tartars: in the end it was the Tartars who were beaten.

We went for many other excursions, driving along all the corniche roads and visiting all the little ports. I loved those bare white mountains sloping steeply to the sea. Along the shores, surrounded by immense gardens, stood palaces and villas that had once belonged to nobles or wealthy merchants: now workers of all kinds come there to recuperate. Each house had its own beach, and upon many of them there were lines of beds: during these warm months – they are called the 'velvet season' – the people who stay there often sleep in the open air. We went to see the palace where the pact was signed, and this too is a rest-home. The magnificent park, with its flowerbeds, rare plants, fountains, paths and flights of steps, falls in terrace after terrace to the shore; and everyone can walk about it freely.

We stayed a week. We had breakfast in the open air at a self-service café next to the hotel. People competed for the tables and one had to stand in a queue for twenty minutes to fill one's tray. Every meal raised its own problems. The food was very bad that year; even the caviare tasted muddy. At Yalta it was impossible to get a table unless one booked. There were two restaurants we liked: one was in the town itself and it formed part of the Hotel Taurida. Chekov often used to dine there, having driven through Yalta in a carriage; and the place can hardly have changed since his time. There was a vast over-decorated lounge, then a covered patio full of green plants, which was used as a dining-room; and as the hotel was built into the side of a hill terraces rose one above another, with interior staircases linking them. The topmost had a bar, and there we drank very strange cocktails in the evening, watching the flickering lights in the harbour. But even more than that we liked taking a taxi to a height crowned by an imitation Greek temple; there we would have dinner on a terrace that looked out over the whole town, with its lights and the neon signs and the dark water. Sometimes a sweeping beam would pick out a boat or a ship, and for a moment it would gleam there before it melted back into the darkness. We used to walk down by a steep little path.

Every evening at dusk a large white ship with its portholes lit up came into the harbour: it had different names, but it always seemed to be the same vessel. One evening we went aboard: we were leaving Yalta for Sochi.

Sochi was a modern town, devoid of interest and with over-crowded beaches. What struck me most was the sight of a man in bathing-trunks walking along the jetty and puffing out his broad chest: Lenin's portrait was tatooed on the one side and Stalin's on the other.

A train took us through splendid mountain scenery to Tbilisi, the capital of Georgia. Nizan had given us an enthusiastic description of this half-oriental town; he had been there before the war, in the days when it was called Tiflis. It lies on both banks of the Kura, and mountains surround it on three sides; it still has some fine monu-ments and a very agreeable old quarter – steep narrow streets lined by wooden houses with decorated balconies. But it has lost its exotic character: the streets where the Muslims live are winding and filthy, and their houses are wretched. At the gates of Tbilisi we caught sight of a kind of shanty-town. We did not take many walks in the city; the president of the Writers' Union had taken us in charge and he kept us away from it as much as possible, there being a great shortage of food in Georgia that year: long queues stretched out in front of the bakers' shops; the housewives grumbled; and for two or three days there was no bread. One evening the writers asked us to dinner in a restaurant on Mount Mtatsminda, high above the town: we admired the view – the lit-up streets, the churches, the river. And we waited two hours before sitting down to a pitiful meal: in spite of great exertions the chef had only managed to get hold of a very little food. It sometimes happened that at our hotel we were only given one meagre portion of fish.

Although we did not see much of the capital, we did make some interesting excursions to other places. The first was to Mtskheta, the former capital, a dozen miles from Tbilisi. It lies at the junction of two rivers and it is surrounded by late mediaeval walls. It has some beautiful churches: the finest is Djivari (the Cross), a very well preserved sixth-century building; it is decorated with bas-reliefs showing its founders, various other characters, and religious symbols. Another time we went to see a wine-making centre, driving along a pretty road that wound along at the foot of vine-covered hills – it reminded me of the one in Alsace they call the *route des vins*. As I walked into the building I had a shock: there were heads rising from the ground, as though men had been buried alive. In fact they were only cleaning out some of the vats in which the wine was fermented. Other vats were full, and their appearance was far from attractive – a greasy, muddy layer covered the whole surface. One of our hosts plunged a tube through this murk and brought it up filled with a pleasant-looking amber-coloured wine. The evening before we left, the president of the Writers' Union – he was called the Prince, because he was descended from a princely family – gave a big dinner-party for us. We went with Alexia, the Georgian girl I had known in Paris and who was writing a thesis on Sartre – we liked her very much. I do not know how the Prince managed it, but the meal was sumptuous. He had promised that there would be musicians (there are wonderful choirs in Georgia – six unaccompanied men's voices, as harsh as flamenco, against a background of plain-chant: I had heard them on records). But he had not been able to assemble one of these groups, and all we had was two young women who sang national songs and an old actress who declaimed pieces from her repertoire, provoking ill-concealed giggles. The evening was not unpleasant; but generally speaking banquets of this kind wear me out. The Georgians have the custom of appointing a 'tamada', who presides at the feast, proposes the toasts, makes jokes and tells funny stories. The appointment is much sought after, and it almost always fell to the Prince. The tamada's fine flow of sayings and anecdotes was all the more boring as far as we were concerned in that they needed a double translation, since many Georgians do not speak Russian and Lena knew no Georgian. No doubt this custom has peasant origins: people unused to talking invented it as a way of enlivening their feasts. It must have been very useful in those times when any conversation was dangerous – before the war Stalin had had almost all the Georgian writers and intellectuals deported and shot.

We drove on, taking the very beautiful road from Tbilisi to Erivan, the capital of Armenia. It ran through fields of cotton and then through green pastures fringed with dark pines. We reached a pass, and all at once the landscape changed entirely: before us stretched a pinkish, chaotic desert with a bright blue lake in the middle of it. While we were gazing at it in admiration we saw a

297

black car coming towards us: it was the Armenian writers who were to welcome us. We got into their car and they took us to a hotel on the shores of Lake Sevan. It was a very fine day, and really hot although we were at over six thousand feet. They had ordered trout; fish as long as one's arm, pink as salmon and so delicious that I could hardly manage to eat any of the dishes that followed. The Armenians told us about the archeological discoveries that have been made on the shores of the lake – many remains going back to a very ancient civilization. And about the birth of the Armenian alphabet: until the fifth century it did not exist, and they used Greek and Persian characters. Then, in order to encourage the spread of Christianity, Saint Mesrop invented an alphabet that made it possible to transcribe the Bible. Many works appeared in the course of that century. Our Armenians said that the following year would see the publication of a French version of *David of Sassoun*, the great epic poem about their legendary hero: it had been handed down by word of mouth since ancient times, growing richer in the course of ages, and it had been committed to writing in the nineteenth century. And indeed a year later I was able to see that the Armenians were right in being so proud of it: the poem holds its own in comparison with the very greatest works.

It was an interesting lunch, and after it we should have liked to go straight on down to Erivan but our hosts were eager to take us to see a friend of theirs who was giving a house-warming party. We drove through a dusty village, apparently quite deserted, apart from one anxious-looking woman sitting on a flight of steps with some emaciated children round her. Then we reached a garden with a large, new-built house at the far end. About fifty guests were at a horseshoe table loaded with dishes: it was five o'clock in the afternoon and they were still eating. The guests included ministers, a man representing the president of the Armenian republic, and some important civil servants: I sat next to a minister, bewildered by the deafening noise of shouting, laughter and clattering of dishes. It seemed to me astonishing that private property should be celebrated in such a thorough-going and official way in a socialist country: but even more, this ostentatious display of food at a time when the whole country was suffering from hunger was indecent. I had already eaten to satiety and I impatiently refused to touch the food with which my neighbour forcibly filled my plate. What on earth were we doing there? One of the writers who were looking after us advised Sartre to propose a toast. Sartre spoke of the friendship between France and Armenia, and his remarks dropped into an icy silence. If one of the people present uttered two or three words, that was the full extent of their efforts. They did not like us: no doubt they had not followed the development of Russian opinion as far as Sartre was concerned.

Erivan is built in the form of an amphitheatre upon a plateau facing Mount Ararat: the upper town lies a thousand feet above the lower. The houses are made of the local stone whose colours range from salmon-pink to copper, rust and bull's blood: the façades look like slices of gelatine, and the effect is more remarkable than charming. The town dates from 1924 and its plan was progressively modified as the number of inhabitants increased; it is a modern, widespreading place. We did see some remaining shacks and hovels, built into the side of the hill; but only a very few. The people seemed full of life – black-mustachioed men with velvety eyes; dark-haired, olive-skinned and often beautiful women. There was little for sale in the markets, but they were crowded with people. Our hotel stood on the big Lenin Square, and in the evenings couples or groups of friends strolled about, talking and laughing. It was a comfortable, modern hotel, but the orchestra made such a din that we asked to have dinner in one of our rooms; it was pleasant sitting there talking and watching the people go to and fro outside.

One morning we were taken to Echmiadzin, the Vatican of Armenia, the residence of the Catholicos. The road runs along the frontier with Turkey for miles and miles and for a long while it gave us a view of the majestic Ararat, upon which Noah's ark was stranded: its snowy peak stood out brilliantly against the blue of the sky. We went to see two churches, as red as the town: one dated from the fifth century and the other from the seventh. They were both more compact and more complex than those of Georgia, yet they were quite as beautiful. We also saw the ruins of Zwartnotz, a Christian sanctuary that was destroyed by an earthquake: broken columns still remain, and some enormous capitals.

The monastery of Echmiadzin contains the oldest church in the world, built in the fourth century: it was being restored, and it was surrounded with scaffolding; but even so we could see its beautiful, faceted cupolas, so often imitated. Behind the church lies the great building which houses the head of the Armenian church. We passed through halls and galleries filled with green plants and crystal chandeliers and we climbed marble staircases. 'This is too luxurious for a priest,' said Lena disapprovingly. The Catholicos was a man of about fifty, bearded, and very carefully dressed in robes like those of an Orthodox priest. On his table there was a telephone and a dish full of translucent amber-coloured grapes: he gave us each a bunch. The Catholicos told us about Gregorian Christianity. The Armenians were converted in 302, and in 374 they broke with Rome, thus bringing about the first schism in history. They refused to adopt the Athanasian creed laid down by the Council of Nicaea: they had a different concept of the relationship between the human and the divine natures of Christ. As in the Russian Orthodox Church, the priests marry. After this the Catholicos spoke about the very friendly relations between the USSR Armenians and those who live elsewhere – great numbers of them fled from the Turkish persecutions. We were told that politically he was the most influential man in the republic; and of course he is an unconditional supporter of the regime, otherwise he would not hold his present position.

The Armenian radio is said to utter a great many cracks against socialism. Yet as we travelled about the country we saw that it had benefited much from its union with the USSR: huge irrigation schemes have transformed what was formerly barren ground into a fertile countryside. The mountains are still very wild, however. A road carried us through vast bare landscapes to a monastery that used to be the Christians' place of refuge from the Turks. A half-Christian, half-pagan celebration was in progress. Outside the church stood white, curly-coated lambs with red ribbons round their necks: presently they would have their throats cut and they would be offered to God in sacrifice; then the congregation would eat their flesh. From the top of the hill to the bottom there were fires burning under enormous pots; and gathered round a great bowl, families were devouring stew.

Two days later we flew high above a sea of clouds with chaotic, snowy peaks thrusting up through them: the highest was Mount Kazbek. Then came Moscow, and then Paris.

In May 1964 we were invited to the celebrations that were to take place in Kiev to honour the hundred and fiftieth anniversary of the birth of Shevchenko, the great Ukrainian poet. We hesitated. A professor at the university of Kiev by the name of Kichko had just published a virulently anti-semitic pamphlet, *Judaism Undisguised*, illustrated with caricatures that would have delighted the Nazis. We were tempted to refuse and to say why.

Lena was Jewish. She would not have it that this fact had ever been to her disadvantage. Yet perhaps it was not entirely by chance that her father had been deported for no reason after the war. A little incident that happened during one of the stays I am talking about showed us that in Moscow itself anti-semitism is not unknown. We were having dinner at the Sovietskaya, a big hotel that we rarely went to because it is some way from the centre. The people at a nearby table listened to our conversation. One of them spoke to Lena, 'Your friends are talking Jewish, aren't they?' 'Not at all,' said Lena, surprised. 'They are talking French.' 'But they are talking French with a Jewish accent.' She shrugged and said, 'Do you speak French?' 'No.' 'Then how can you tell whether they have an accent?' The man made no reply. They probably had the impression that Lena, with her black hair and huge dark eyes, was Jewish. At all events there was something very disagreeable about these stupid remarks and she was quite overcome.

So we procrastinated. Then we heard that the USSR had officially disavowed Kichko;[4] our Russian friends wrote, urging us to come, and so did Bajan, the Ukrainian poet, whom we liked. We accepted.

We flew to Moscow and then took one of those Soviet trains that shake you about so horribly, reaching Kiev after a night's journey. It was 1 June. Among the writers who welcomed us was a man who had written a fictionalized account of Balzac's relationship with Madame Hanska called *Balzac's Marriage*: he had managed to make his anti-semitism evident in the very first pages. Bajan deplored the Ukrainians' racism. 'It is sad to feel at odds with one's country and be unable to love it,' he said to us. Yet during the celebrations that were now coming to an end he had felt a good will and a generosity in the Ukrainian people that had comforted him.

Once again we saw Kiev, with its old streets and low houses in the deep shade of chestnut trees; it was spring, and the gardens were full of the scent of lilac in full flower. That evening there was a monstrous great banquet, attended by something like a thousand people: parallel rows of tables filled the whole length of the hall and another ran across the top for the praesidium. Deeply-rooted self-satisfaction could be read on every face.

Charming young women in national costume waited on us. There

4 His pamphlet was republished in 1969.

were songs, very badly sung. Guillevic, a somewhat surprising figure with his little fringe of beard and his bow tie, read his translation of Shevchenko's *Testament*. A large number of toasts were drunk. The Ukrainians kept harping on their country's wealth and how useful it was to the Soviet Union: their hostility to the Russians was staringly obvious. Sartre was in a bad temper: his neighbour, Korneichuk, had just told him the name of one of the writers with whom he had shaken hands before dinner – it was a certain Tikhonov, who had written a venomous article about him in 1962, after his speech at the Movement for Peace congress. The article accused Sartre of wanting to set himself at the head of a gathering of intellectuals who were to rule the world. Sartre worked his anger off on Korneichuk: he complained that the attitude of the USSR towards him was ambiguous – did the Soviet intellectuals accept the idea of cultural coexistence or did they not? If not, why did they invite him, and what was he doing here? Korneichuk protested – friendship between the USSR and the Western intellectuals was now more necessary than ever, because of the danger of China.

The next day we glided along the broad and peaceful Dneiper, its melancholy banks dotted with sandy beaches where cows were drinking. We disembarked and went to see the Shevchenko museum in the village where he was born. His life was told by a series of objects and by pictures that he had painted himself – some of them really quite inspired. He was born a serf, and some Russian writers who admired his poetry bought his freedom. When we reached the picture that showed his liberation, the curator observed in a resentful tone, 'Nowadays in our country a poet of such merit would need no aid.' It was obvious that he was thinking 'No foreign aid'. Later the poet struggled against the regime; he went to prison and he was banished. When he died the people raised what must, from the photographs we saw, have been a very moving monument to him by piling up great stones. It has been replaced by a totally uninteresting official memorial.

We were happy to be back in Moscow, free from all constraint at last. Never had the characteristic smell of petrol been so strong: this was no doubt because there was more traffic – not only more lorries and trucks but also more taxis, whose numbers had doubled since 1963, and by night their little green eyes were often to be seen twinkling in the streets. In theory, they were not allowed to pull up along the pavement and they often had to be fetched from a rank. Most were driven by beginners who had little notion of the town. The system of one-way streets was so complicated that once, when we were on the other side of the street from our hotel, the Pekin, we had to go half a mile round to reach its door.

Moscow was changing as one looked at it. Quite near the hotel a broad avenue had been driven through, and in the middle of the town a great many old houses were being pulled down to make room for modern blocks. In the part of Moscow where Dostoevsky's house is to be seen there were still quiet streets lined with old isbas, but they were soon to disappear. What pleased us very much was finding that Red Square was now forbidden to cars. It is quite lovely, that vast bare expanse with the store called GUM on one side and a great red wall on the other, while the brilliant colours of Saint Basil's glow down at the farther end. One night we found bands of boys and girls, all of them about fifteen, dancing and singing there in the middle of the square: they had passed their examinations and they were celebrating the event.

Moscow has many squares. They have fine trees in them, particularly poplars, of a kind rather different from ours. There was one moment during our stay when they all came into season. Downy catkins hung in clusters from the branches; the breeze scattered them and a kind of cotton-wool came snowing down, filling our ears, eyes, mouths and noses – it was as though the sky was an immense eiderdown that someone had ripped open. There were streams of fluff along the pavements, and in the gardens we walked upon a carpet of white. And I remember another day when we were stitting in a park near the Moskova and we watched children and grown-up people picking dandelions; they made wreaths and put them upon their heads.

Food-supplies had improved. Shoppers could no longer buy flour or kasha; but there were street-sellers by the dozen offering cabbages, cucumbers, strawberries, tomatoes and oranges. Fruit was very dear, however: in a restaurant an orange cost as much as a large helping of caviare. In all the restaurants we went to the food was very good, and the caviare had gone back to being delicious once again.

The cultural situation was far from encouraging. *The Lenin Barrier* was still under the censors' ban: the film only came out much later, and then in a deformed and mutilated version.

303

Tarkovsky was making a film about Rublov: they compelled him to rewrite his scenario, and he foresaw that there were going to be great difficulties. The 'accursed' painters no longer exhibited. Some few of them made a meagre living by selling their pictures to foreigners, who were allowed to take pictures, ancient or modern, out of the country so long as the Tretyakov gallery certified that they had no commercial value.

One of Kafka's stories, *A Report for an Academy*, had been translated, and there was talk of publishing *The Trial* – talk that came to nothing, however. In 1962 Brecht had been suspect: he strayed too far from socialist realism. In 1964 the theatres were opening to him: in Leningrad there was an excellent production of *Arturo Ui*. Lena had translated Sartre's *Words* and there was a suggestion that the book should be published first in *Novy Mir* and then in volume form. The people who worked on the review and even Tvardovsky himself were hesitant. They thought the book 'indiscreet' and 'exhibitionist'. Speaking of oneself so harshly was tantamount to disobeying the watchword of optimism; it was speaking evil of mankind. Doroch liked *Words* and it was no doubt he who swayed Tvardovsky: in the end the book was printed.

Ehrenburg's situation had righted itself. His books were being published once more. He gave us the inside story of the Brodsky affair: it was one that all our friends found very painful indeed – some went so far as to speak of a 'return of Stalinism' – but they did not know the details. Brodsky was a young red-haired Jew who lived in Leningrad and who wrote poems; he earned his living as a translator, but he was not part of any state organization and he did not belong to the Writers' Union. Ehrenburg liked him and thought he had talent. Brodsky was accused of 'parasitism', a charge that is brought against almost nobody but whores and their protectors. The trial took place in Leningrad. A woman journalist who attended managed to take notes, and the detailed account she drew up was handed about privately. Ehrenburg translated it for us. The judge was a woman. When Brodsky stated that he was a translator and a poet she asked, 'Who has established the fact that you are a poet?' 'No one. And just who has established the fact that I am a human being?' At a later stage she very strangely reproached him with not making enough money. 'Can anyone possibly live on what you earn?' 'Yes. Every morning since I have been in prison I have signed a certificate that the state is spending forty kopecks a day on me. But I can make more than forty kopecks.' 'There are people who work in factories and who also write. Why don't you?' 'Not all people are the same: some have red hair, some are blond and some are dark.' 'We know all about that.' There were comparatively few witnesses for the defence and several of them were Jews: the judge pretended not to be able to read their names and ostentatiously spelled them out. Three members of the Writers' Union defended Brodsky: they stated that he was a highly talented poet and an excellent translator. But then appeared an overwhelming number of witnesses for the prosecution: they said that Brodsky's supporters were all idle, cunning rogues. Brodsky did not love his country: he had spoken of the 'grey crowd' that flows along the streets. He was a counter-revolutionary: he had called Marx 'an old glutton crowned with fir-cones'. He corrupted the young by his example and by his poems: one father complained that his son had read Brodsky's verse and now refused to work. Brodsky was savagely attacked both as an intellectual and as a Jew. He was sentenced to five years of forced labour and sent to a state farm near Archangel.

This account shocked us deeply. What is more, Sartre had the impression that ideologically the young were losing their grip. There were students and young teachers who questioned him about Berdyaev and Shestov: for many of them, in a more or less disguised fashion, the idea of God seemed to be coming back to life. We talked this over with a group of intellectuals – our friend Alicata, the editor of *L'Unità*, was there. What he regretted, as did Sartre, was that this search for a freer expression was accompanied not by an attitude more revolutionary than that of the establishment but by one that was on the contrary more retrograde. They should have transcended the 'scientific' dogmatism imposed by Stalin and his heirs and have gone back to the true Marx: instead of that they were turning their backs on him. 'Marxism?' said a forty-year-old teacher. 'We have been utterly disgusted by all we have been made to swallow under that name!' 'Find someone who knows Marx through and through and organize a training-centre.' They burst out laughing: 'There's not one single person in the whole of the Soviet Union who knows Marx through and through. Not a single one we'd really trust.'

A question that we often discussed was that of the black students. There were serious conflicts between them and the Russian students. Fighting often broke out, and during the winter some young blacks had been mortally wounded. We talked about the subject with Ben Yaya, the Algerian ambassador, when we were having dinner with him. Their governments give the black students considerable grants, and that makes the young Soviets look upon them as exceptionally privileged; yet since the Africans were promised the moon when they were sent to Moscow, they find their status as students all the harder to bear. All the students are very badly housed; they sleep in hostels whose supervisors are mostly former warders from the camps; the Africans are not used to the food and they think it uneatable. They find the climate very harsh, and since their grants do not allow them to dress warmly they suffer from the cold. They protest angrily at this state of affairs – a state of affairs that their Russian companions bear more easily because they are more used to it. The Russians think the Africans' grievances exaggerated. On top of all this come difficulties over girls. The blacks cry racism if a white girl will not dance with them: the Soviets are indignant if an African goes out with a Russian woman. Have the Soviets a racist attitude or not? Given their distrust for all foreigners, to a greater or a less extent, they have. The white foreigner feels himself suspect merely because he is a foreigner: the black thinks that the colour of his skin is involved and often he reacts violently.

As far as consumer-goods and services are concerned, the public meets with little tenderness in the USSR: I had already noticed this, but I regretted it more than usual as we left for Vladimir. The train comes in in one direction and leaves in the other without bothering to turn the carriages round: so the seats either side of the central corridor have their backs to the engine. I cannot bear travelling backwards, so for three hours I knelt there on my seat. But I did like the monotonous landscape of grassland and little woods. As we went along the sky began to redden; the interminable sunset went on and on, and when we arrived at ten in the evening there were still wafts of pink on the horizon.

Vladimir is one of the oldest towns in Russia, founded by Grand Prince Vladimir in 1108. His grandson made it the capital of the country and so it remained for a hundred and seventy years: after that it became the centre of an extensive province. In the nineteenth century many revolutionaries were banished there. At present it is a large town, important both from the industrial and the cultural points of view. The very first evening we were there we walked about the upper town. We took the rampart-walk that runs along the kremlin walls: far below us lay the river and the brilliantly-lit lower town; we walked through leafy gardens with beautiful white churches standing in them; and on the benches sat loving couples, lost to the world.

The next day we revisited the churches: the Dmitrievsky cathedral dates from the twelfth century; its white exterior, topped by a single gilded dome, is wonderfully decorated; and the beautiful five-domed cathedral of the Assumption has frescoes by Rublov. We also saw the fortified Golden Gate, as white as the cathedrals and crowned by a gilded dome; and ancient streets, lined with noble trees and wooden houses, each with a little garden in front of it. A car took us out of the town for a view of the very simple and lovely church of the Intercession mirrored in the waters of the Nerl. Then we went on to Suzdal, a town even older than Vladimir; its walls enclose a very great many churches, and there was one, a tall building of considerable size, that was made entirely of wood, with a shingled dome. One morning as we woke up, beneath our windows we saw lorries going by: they were filled with girls in white dresses and boys with red ties, all holding branches of birch. In the USSR many Christian feasts have been replaced by secular holidays: this was the day of Corpus Christi, and they were celebrating the Feast of the Birch-Trees. A considerable part of the upper town is occupied by a park, and in this park there were processions of people singing; others were amusing themselves with various games, still others strummed their balalaikas; and all this gaiety seemed both spontaneous and yet at the same time carried out to order. A summer-house had been turned into a café; there were tables around it, and inside one could buy cakes in abundance and rolls filled with hard-boiled egg or onion. There were some women who carried off bags stuffed with food, and wreaths of pretzels. We sat at a table and ate steadily, on and on. It was a godsend, for at the hotel there was nothing. The bread was neither white nor black and the mineral water was as salt as the sea. (Nowhere in the USSR can one drink the ordinary water except in Moscow, where it has a strong not unpleasant taste of mint.) The dishes were inedible, apart from the eggs; but eggs very rarely appeared. In front of the hotel a crowd pressed eagerly around a hawker who sold dusty biscuits. The cheerful, lively market had almost nothing in it whatsoever. So where did this sudden plenty come from? And if it was possible here, what was the reason for the extreme shortage in the rest of the town? In Moscow, which was quite near at hand, it was possible to eat decently; which made the whole thing even less comprehensible.

For our return we should have liked to take one of those collective taxis that are called 'road-walkers'; but for some mysterious reason they were forbidden to foreigners. So we took the train: this time the seats were the right way round.

Friends worked out a splendid journey for us: we were to go to Tallinn, the capital of Estonia, by way of the ancient Russian city of Pskov and the Estonian university-town of Tartu; then we should take ship back to Leningrad and so go on to Novgorod. Intourist told us that the idea was not feasible, because we were foreigners. Foreigners might go to the capitals of the Baltic states, but to the capitals only: it was impossible to travel to Tallinn by way of Tartu. The only permissible way of reaching Tallinn was by taking the train from Leningrad: and the return journey had also to be made by way of Leningrad and again by train. Why? We did not even ask. We took the plane for Leningrad.

Leningrad is a city I love, above all when the evening light grows soft and its beautiful Italian colours take on a northern coldness. The 'white nights' were as moving as ever. In Kiev the lilac must surely have been over, but here spring was just coming in and the bushes were in full flower: the Champ de Mars was covered with a Japanese variety with a discreet peppery smell and with others much the same as our own fresh, heady-scented kind – such a wealth of leaves and flowers under the clear midnight sky! Few things on earth have ever touched me as much as these midnight wonders.

Then came Tallinn, and it seemed to us that we had moved into a different world. Estonia only had about twenty years of independence, and that was between 1921 and 1940. For five centuries the country was under foreign rule, first that of the Germans, then of the Danes, the Poles and the Swedes, each change accompanied by bloody war. From 1721 it was controlled politically by Russia and economically by German feudal overlords who Westernized it. After the war the country was annexed to the Soviet Union. But it has retained the bourgeois traditions of the 1921–40 republic. Our very elegant hotel was in the European style, and its cooking was excellent; we liked sitting there in the dining-room, looking out at the luxurious foliage of the park; and the evening orchestra played

308

quietly. We were welcomed by a charming couple – Monsieur Semper, a very brisk old gentleman who had translated *Intimacy* into Estonian before the war, and his wife: at sixty-two she was as pleasant to look at as she was to listen to. She was a music expert and she thoroughly appreciated the avant-garde composers. They had lived in France a long while and they had a perfect knowledge of the language and the literature. They were always at hand when we needed their help and they left us alone whenever they felt that we should like to be by ourselves – we could stroll about Tallinn in complete freedom.

The upper town was built by the Danes at the beginning of the thirteenth century; and with its towers, battlements and turrets it has remained much as it always was: from a distance it looks like a Victor Hugo drawing. Its ramparts enclose narrow cobbled streets lined with ancient houses, and little squares that are silent by day and deserted by night. At Tallinn too the white nights touched me to the heart: far away under the pale sky one could see the pale sea and its ghostly shipping. A garden with a winding stream ran down from the walls to the road, and this garden was filled with the scent of lime-trees and of the lilac, which had travelled northwards with us.

Below lay the merchants' town. Once its narrow streets were crowded with shops and stalls, and they led to immense squares where the great markets were held. Now the shops are few (though they are comparatively well-supplied) and the squares are empty. Tallinn gives the impression of a town whose true function has been taken away – an occupied town. The inhabitants live better than their Russian counterparts, but not so well as they did before the war. A particular feature is the great number of cake-shops filled with appetizing pastries, and the existence of cafés in the Western style. The biggest, the Café Tallinn, is on the first floor of a building, and it is reminiscent of those at Innsbruck and Vienna: it is spacious, dimly-lit and quiet, and it is divided into boxes, each with a large round table. These cafés close at eleven in the evening; and they provide cakes, tea and coffee – no vodka.

In several shop windows we were astonished to see posters showing views of Australia. The reason is that after the war many Estonians emigrated to that country, and to Canada. People spoke of these emigrants with a kindness and a liking that at first we found surprising. A journalist who asked Sartre for an interview

said, 'Our paper is chiefly intended for our countrymen abroad.'
The 'home' Estonians have a feeling of inferiority with regard to the
emigrants: they look upon them not as having refused socialism but
as having displayed their patriotism – what they had fled was the
yoke of Russia, the age-old tyrant; and although no one said it in so
many words, we could sense that those who had stayed approved of
their action. The Russians deported many Estonians immediately
after the war merely because they were Estonians and therefore
suspected of enmity to Russia. Thus we met a writer who for no
other reason had spent several years in a camp. A huge and very
ugly nineteenth-century church, visible from all around, stands
there as a massive symbol of the earlier Russian presence. It was to
protest against that presence – and against the German barons –
that the peasant choral societies were formed, societies that sang
national songs. We were shown the huge auditorium in which they
still meet every three or four years, all their members wearing the
traditional Estonian dress.

The Sempers introduced us to editors and publishers. They
enjoyed a certain degree of independence from Moscow, and were
more liberal than the Russians – they had published Camus' *The
Plague*. Yet one of the writers we spoke to was faithful to the
Zhdanovite optimism. He was a Lenin prizewinner and a great
talker, and he told amusing stories about his speciality, the Ant-
arctic; but his literary tastes were unlike ours. Speaking of *Intimacy*
he criticized Sartre for its pessimism: and he disliked *One Day in
the Life of Ivan Denisovich* – 'It is written in too gloomy a tone,' he
said. 'And just how would you have written it?' asked Sartre. He
paused. 'I don't know,' he admitted. Obviously he thought it should
not have been written at all.

We had no right to enter Estonia by way of Tartu, but there was
nothing illegal in being taken there from Tallinn by the Estonian
writers. It was a fine drive, about a hundred and twenty miles
through flat but agreeable countryside – meadows, woods, long low
farm-houses.

Our rooms at the Hôtel du Parc were modern and cheerful and
there were no supervisors in the corridors, something I had never
seen in the USSR. We had luncheon with Professor B in a café, and
he told us that between 1945 and our arrival only one solitary
Frenchman had been to Tartu. In the lower town he showed us
some pretty wooden houses: he regretted that the municipality had

not blown them up; but fortunately most had been destroyed in the war. Clearly he was no great lover of the past. Tartu had first been built on a hill, like Tallinn; but the wars that ravaged Estonia, ruining so many of its fine buildings, had almost entirely wiped out the upper town. All that was left was the beautiful shell of the red brick cathedral. We went up to see it with Professor B, who uttered a few superior disdainful remarks. Part of the church had been done up to house the university library, and this we visited; then our guide took us to see a sculptor, whose house and garden were filled with hideous statues. Twenty years ago he was almost an 'accursed' artist, an outcast: some of his groups were criticized for their eroticism. Now he was mainly occupied with turning out funeral monuments; he was loaded with honours, and all the travellers who passed through Tallinn were expected to call upon him and to record their impressions in his visitor's book.

On the whole we found little to interest us in Tartu; but we did enjoy our midsummer's eve in the nearby country. Professor B, still just as superior and just as glum, took us to a big lake surrounded by wooded hills and dotted with little islands. There a forestry official received us: he was entrusted with 'showing' us the lake; in the USSR everything has to be 'explained' by a specialist and this has often vexed me extremely. In fact, although he was a little too talkative, this new guide was less dreary than the other. He suggested taking a boat, and we rowed among secret little islands over water so smooth that the reeds stood in their own reflections. High overhead, jet-planes left vapour-trails that the setting sun touched with pink.

Then the car took us up a steep hill overlooking the lake. Some young men had erected a tent on the top and they had lit a huge fire: they were playing accordions. Our driver gathered armfuls of dead wood and threw them on the flames. A young Estonian who had come with us from Tallinn produced a bottle of vodka; it passed from hand to hand, and he danced with Lena to the sound of the accordion. On other hills there were other fires; and below us the silent lake floated in the milky light.

We returned to Tallinn and then to Leningrad, where an Intourist car took us to Novgorod, a city that was once a great centre of trade. The Kremlin, with its lofty red walls, overlooks a broad, sluggish river that winds away out of sight across an endless plain. Inside the walls stands a very beautiful cathedral. On the far bank there is to be seen a series of arcades, the remains of an eighteenth-

century market, and a multitude of entrancing little churches –
every wealthy merchant had one built. In one morning's walk we
counted twenty-five. They were covered over with a white rough-
cast; but one has been restored to its original state, with its red and
pink brick showing. A great many more are to be seen in the surrounding countryside. We went to see a monastery that stands all by
itself on the bank of the Volkhov, as broad as a lake at that point.
In Russia many fine buildings are half-abandoned: we wandered
round a great church with wonderfully pure lines, stumbling
through weeds and rubble.

For two days we strolled about Novgorod without seeing a single
official. On the morning of the third day an indignant journalist
telephoned Lena – we ought to have made our presence known so
that we could be 'shown' the town. 'But I have a book that explains
everything,' said Lena. 'A book! That's nothing like as good as the
living word.' We made an appointment with a woman from the
museum and in lifeless words she told us about the cathedral. Still,
it was thanks to her that we were able to see the beautiful bronze
doors of German origin and the mysterious little scenes that are
carved all over them. The museum itself has a fairly rich collection
of icons.

We went back to Moscow, stayed there a few days, and then took
the plane for Paris.

From 1963 onwards China and the USSR were in open conflict.
Pekin denounced the policy of peaceful coexistence as collusion
with capitalism: Moscow accused the Chinese of wanting a war.
This mutual hostility increased when the Americans started bombing North Vietnam in February 1965. Khrushchev was no longer in
power, but his successors carried on with his foreign policy and
instead of sending Hanoi massive consignments of arms they left
America a free hand. The Chinese Communist Party denounced the
Russians' neutrality, calling them collaborators and revisionists.
The Russians became more and more convinced that the Chinese
wanted to set off a world war and that they were preparing to
invade the Soviet Union. All our Russian friends shared this
opinion: they attributed no rational, tactical or strategical motive to
the Chinese but only a diabolical urge to do harm; they saw the
Chinese as the incarnation of pure evil, and they were terrified. No
argument on this point was of the least avail.

Both the Soviets and the Chinese were to attend the Peace Congress at Helsinki in July 1965. When he was passing through Paris, Ehrenburg asked Sartre to take part in it too: he might be helpful to the Soviet cause. We decided to go to the USSR in July; and from there Sartre would go to Finland for two or three days.

On our arrival in Moscow it seemed to us that Khrushchev's fall had had fortunate consequences as far as culture was concerned. *Novy Mir* was publishing Solzhenitsyn's stories, Akhmatova's poems, and that part of Ehrenburg's memoirs in which he spoke of the days of Zhadanovism. Tvardovsky had produced a kind of manifesto in which he called upon writers to renounce faking and disguise, to speak out against error and to tell the truth without concealment. Pasternak's work was appearing again. It was not total victory nor anything like it. Kafka was still not translated, although indeed he was now presented as a victim of capitalism and not as a decadent pessimist. And Tarkovsky still could not get permission to make his film of Rublov. But it did seem that hope was allowable.

Mikhalkov, who had worked with Tarkovsky in the production of *The Childhood of Ivan*, had just made a film called *The First Teacher*. Would it be authorized for distribution or would it not? The censors were hesitant. We saw it at a private showing and we were enthralled. The film was adapted from a book by a Kirghiz novelist called Aitmatov, whom we met a little later when he was stopping in Paris. The book begins in the present day, and the scene is a prosperous kolkhoz in Kirghizstan, where they are celebrating the anniversary of the foundation of their school. In the midst of the festivities a man observes, 'There's someone missing here today – the first schoolmaster.' And then his story is told: it is a dramatic tale, but one knows that it ended well since now the village is happily integrated with the USSR. The film was altogether tougher: here the action takes place immediately after the first world war, when Kirghizstan was inhabited by wretched peasants oppressed by brutal and ignorant overlords. This first teacher, an ex-soldier of the Red Army and a fanatical Leninist, is sent among them to set up a school. The lords, mounted on horseback, greet his arrival with ill-natured laughter; the peasants view him with distrust. He turns an old barn into a classroom, and with dogged courage he succeeds in gathering some pupils together. But since he is blinded by his passion for Lenin, and his head is filled with ill-digested reading, and since he is oppressed by the magnitude of his responsibilities, he does not adjust himself to the present state of affairs. He cries out against the conflict between the proletariat and the bourgeoisie although at this period Kirghiz society is still feudal. One day when he is speaking to his class about death, a pupil asks whether Lenin too will die eventually: he loses control of himself, seizes the boy and knocks him about, shouting and bawling as he does so. These neurotic outbursts set the schoolchildren and all the people against him. Yet one pupil, a very beautiful girl of about fifteen, shows a great deal of affection for him. The all-powerful Bey sends men to carry her off to his tent, where he rapes her. The schoolmaster is profoundly moved; he has her rescued by Red Army soldiers and sends her for protection to the nearby town. The enraged Bey revenges himself upon the peasants; they then burn the school, blaming the master for having spurned all their traditions and for bringing misfortune upon them. The master feels that he has lost the battle and he decides to go away. But as he is leaving his spirit suddenly revives and he turns back: he will stay, struggling against himself and the rest of the world. Grasping an axe, he starts cutting down the only poplar in the region to rebuild his burnt-down school. The peasants watch him dubiously, and then some of them start helping, thereby showing that he has won at last.

The author describes the hidebound, high-principled militant with as much sympathy as he does the peasants, obstinately wrapped up in their immediate interests, the slaves of ancient, set forms of behaviour: this drama was seen often enough when official organizers tried to plant socialism in the countryside. It was said that the authorities were doubtful about letting the film be distributed because they were afraid of wounding the feelings of the Kirghiz. It was also thought that the censors might have been shocked by the scene of the heroine bathing naked in a stream. I think that more than anything else it was Mikhalkov's frankness that irked them: perhaps too clearly for their liking, his touching and intensely disagreeable hero exemplified the complex nature of revolution, the complexity of the revolutionary act.[5]

We heard news of Brodsky. He was getting along well with the peasants, and his work was chiefly to do with horses, which he did not dislike at all. At Ehrenburg's suggestion Sartre sent Mikoyan a letter through the Writers' Union, asking for Brodsky to be

5 In the end the film did come out. Later it was shown in Paris.

pardoned. Did this help to influence the government? Shortly after, Brodsky was allowed to return to a normal life in Leningrad.

That year we visited Lithuania. In many respects its fate has been much the same as Estonia's. First it was annexed by Poland, then by Russia; and its only period of independence was between the two wars. The Germans occupied the country from 1940 to 1945, and it was not incorporated in the USSR without difficulty, for bands of peasants, supported by broken remnants of the German army, violently opposed the union. They took to the woods, living as brigands and terrorizing the countryside.[6] The situation remained confused for a long while. At present it does not appear that the Russians are much loved in Lithuania: the country has just cele-brated the twentieth anniversary of its union with the USSR, but with so little enthusiasm that Intourist hesitated before allowing us to go there.

In Moscow and Leningrad we lived just as we chose; but as soon as we arrived in any of the republics there was always a delegation of writers who took us in charge. There was no one waiting at the Vilno airport, however, and we were delighted to be spared this attention. We were just about to have a quiet dinner when a head-waiter came up: 'Monsieur Sartre? There is a table ready for you.' He opened the door of a private room and there was a table laid for more than twenty: our hosts had made a mistake about our landing-time, and a little later they appeared. From the next morning onwards they never left us alone for a minute: once we timidly suggested that we should be allowed to stroll about the city by ourselves. That evening, in a somewhat offended tone, they asked 'Was it better without us?' We liked them; but we took no pleasure in walking about accompanied by an escort five or six strong.

Vilno was of but moderate interest – a few pretty streets and picturesque courtyards; an old brick-built church of complicated but harmonious design; a baroque church far from the centre, the whole of its interior carved with plants, animals and human figures in which one could make out the typical features of the Lithuanian peasant.

One morning when we came down into the lounge of our com-

---

[6] There was a rather curious Lithuanian film about these guerillas. We saw it at a private showing in Moscow.

paratively stylish hotel we were astonished to see that it was full of peasant women with kerchiefs tied under their chins. As in Estonia, and for similar reasons, the 'overseas Lithuanians' are highly esteemed at home; and they can come and go quite easily. A boat-train had just reached Vilno and the emigrants' families had hurried to the hotel to welcome them. There was an odd contrast between the 'home Lithuanians', most of whom belonged to kolkhozes, and the exiles in their middle-class clothes. We talked to some of them: the majority belonged to the lowest, most underprivileged strata of American society, and they loathed it.

We made one or two excursions: I remember an elegant brick château standing on an island in the middle of a lake, with a string of other vast melancholy sheets of water carrying the landscape on to the horizon.

Our drive from Vilno to Palanka, on the shores of the Baltic, was tolerably wearing. At Kaunas, the second most important town in Lithuania, we had to see an exhibition of very ugly modern stained glass, a textile-mill, and an interesting museum of antiquities. In this museum I saw a fine wooden figure of Christ; very ugly reproductions are to be seen all over the country, but the original is very beautiful. It is a sitting figure, crowned with thorns, and it leans its cheek upon its hand: it is the very picture of desolation. We had lunch at a charming café in the Viennese style and then we went to see a fortress in which members of the resistance had been imprisoned by the Germans. On the walls of some of the cells Frenchmen had written their names. Many of the prisoners were shot, and their bones were buried in the fields for miles around. Sartre was obliged to lay a wreath at the war-memorial. Then we passed through Klaypeda, the former Memel, a town of ponderous German architecture. Memel: another of those names that astonish me by possessing an actual, physical being. Throughout the journey we and our escort discussed French writing and Italian films. When we reached Palanka, very late, we were utterly exhausted. Lena was the first to go into the hotel: she came out again, appalled – the mayor wanted to invite us to dinner. However, we managed to excuse ourselves.

Palanka was of no interest, but the sea was lovely – huge coffee-coloured or dark grey waves thundered on an endless beach – sand as far as eye could see. In spite of the temperature – it was about 55°F – people were bathing. There were even some nudists. Once

316

when we were walking along the shore, some fat, voluble women flung themselves upon Sartre – we were approaching the beach reserved for women. In the USSR men and women often practise nudism on separate beaches. On mixed beaches, of course, bathing costumes are insisted upon.

One morning we saw a strange sight: a man in yellow oilskins wading up to his middle in the sea, pushing something before him with a pole. It was a net, and when he emptied it on the sand, delighted children squabbled for what he had brought up. It was amber that he was looking for. Most of the transparent or opaque amber that is made into such beautiful necklaces in the USSR comes from this coast.

Some way from Palanka we saw a house where Thomas Mann had stayed. It stands high above the sea on a cliff, entirely by itself at the edge of a wood: at present writers use it. The position is very beautiful; but even more beautiful are the tall white dunes a few miles away. A strong wind was blowing and it made us stumble as we climbed them: we sat down on the top and gazed at the vividly blue sea lapping against the feet of steep hills of a sand as brilliant and sparkling as snow.

We flew back to Leningrad: we wanted to visit Pskov – we had missed it the year before. It was arranged that an Intourist car should come for us on Saturday morning. At ten o'clock on Friday evening, Lena was summoned to the hotel office: the Pskov road was closed. Impossible to get the Writers' Union to intervene: everyone was away for the week-end. What was the reason for this prohibition? Were there troop-movements or army manoeuvres? The next day Lena, who was determined to take us to Pskov, played her trump card. She told the hotel manager that Sartre was going to Helsinki: if the Soviets wanted him to support them against China, then petty annoyances must not endanger his friendship for the USSR. An hour later we were authorized to leave for Pskov, and after luncheon that was what we did.

We drove along an entirely empty road. At Pskov the cultural delegate welcomed us in the friendliest way. She apologized for having no flowers for us – a little while before the British ambassador and his wife had arrived and she had given them her bouquet, mistaking them for us. She proposed showing us Pushkin's house the next day, some thirty miles from Pskov. Lena had had orders that no foreigners were to be taken there. 'I'll assume entire responsibility,' said the delegate. Lena had been in Pskov during the war, but she could not find the parts she had liked – most of the old houses and fine buildings had been destroyed.

Pushkin's estate did not affect me much – he is so little known in France. But I did like the sunlit countryside and the vast horizon beyond the spring-smelling woods and meadows. On the way there we did not meet a living soul; nor did we do so on the road back to Leningrad.

Sartre spent two days in Helsinki. When Lena and I went to meet him at the station we found it full of people carrying bunches of flowers. They formed little groups. When the train came in they darted towards the carriages, and at the same time a band began to play patriotic airs. Some of the delegates were mobbed by journalists and photographers. The Japanese had more round him than anyone else. People began to make speeches. Sartre managed to escape. At the hotel he told us about the congress. The Chinese had been exceedingly hostile: during the sessions they never applauded any speakers at all other than the Vietnamese. On the night of 14 July the French delegates had a little private celebration, and one of them scored a hit by singing '*Nuit de Chine, nuit câline, nuit d'amour.*' Relations between the Chinese and the Russians were particularly strained: the Soviets remained on the defensive, but the Chinese kept attacking them again and again. These attacks were so violent that on one occasion, when Ehrenburg was arguing with them, the effort he had to make to control himself very nearly gave him a stroke: he left the room, and in the corridor he fell down, damaging his face quite badly. The next day, during another debate in which the Chinese accused the USSR of deviationism, revisionism and a return to capitalism, Ehrenburg completely lost his temper. The Chinese called upon the Soviet delegation to apologize; they refused – Ehrenburg's words and his anger were entirely his own responsibility. 'That is unacceptable,' said the Chinese. 'We know how things happen. Individual reactions are forbidden: everything is settled beforehand. If a delegate loses his temper that is because it was decided that he should lose his temper.' And indeed their behaviour showed that they themselves observed this rule.

Sartre also told us about his speech to the congress. He had said that there should be no yielding to American blackmail but that there should be whole-hearted support for Vietnam: that was the only way of preventing escalation. The Vietnamese applauded heartily. Ehrenburg reproached Sartre with having taken sides with the Chinese. The fact of the matter was that Sartre regretted that Russian aid to Vietnam should be so lukewarm. In his opinion Russia could have counter-attacked the USA vigorously without starting a world war – the Americans had no more desire for that than the Russians.

On his way back Sartre was in the same carriage as a young woman who spoke French and a general who was nicknamed 'the peace-general'. 'When I was young,' said the general, 'I was taught how to surround and wipe out ten thousand men. Then how to wipe out a hundred thousand. But now it is a matter of wiping out millions: I prefer fighting for peace.' The idea that the Chinese possessed the atomic bomb terrified him: one fine day they were going to drop it just anywhere at all, so as to start a world war. 'For my own part I don't give a damn. I live in the middle of Moscow and I shall be killed right away. But I am thinking about the people in the suburbs!' The young woman too was horrified – there were such a very great many Chinese! Diffidently, she asked, 'Couldn't the Americans be persuaded to bomb – oh, not the Chinese towns but the factories, before it's too late?' 'No,' said the general firmly. 'In the first place that would be criminal. And then we and the Chinese are allies – if they were attacked, we should have to help them.' Sartre had great fun with his old general.

At a COMES meeting in Rome in October 1965 we met Simonov, Surkov, Tvardovsky and other less well-known Russian friends. They told us that an affair far more serious than that of Brodsky was about to come to light in Moscow: two writers, Sinyavsky and Daniel, were accused of having published anti-Soviet works abroad, using the pen-names of Abraham Tertz and Arjak.

Ehrenburg explained that the most important form of publishing in the USSR at present was *samizdat* – self-publishing. Those writers whom the censors condemned to silence would not submit; helped by their friends they had their manuscripts typed and handed about. A full-blown and exceedingly interesting clandestine literature, said Ehrenburg, was developing side by side with official writing. Some of Daniel's stories had been passed through the iron curtain and they were published in France under the title of *Ici Moscou*: the same had happened to stories and a study written by Sinyavsky, which appeared under the title of *The Icicle*. I had read *The Icicle*: I had not felt particularly enthusiastic about it, but I had detected no attacks against the USSR. They were ironical, critical tales; but they were not anti-Soviet. For his part Daniel denounced the terrorism of the Stalin regime, but he did not attack socialism as such. Yet those in authority were of the opinion that Daniel and Sinyavsky had slandered their country.

In October they were arrested. *Izvestia* and the *Literaturnaya Gazeta* attacked them violently. On 13 December some students attempted to demonstrate in Moscow, shouting 'a public trial for Sinyavsky', but the police dispersed them. The trial took place in February 1966 before a carefully-chosen public composed solely of party-members. The defendants were allowed to speak, and they pleaded not guilty; but the papers did not publish their defence. The court considered their case jointly with that of Tarsis, who had in fact written very violent works against the regime and who had been allowed to leave the country three days before the trial, labelled as a paranoiac. The court declared that Sinyavsky and Daniel were guilty of having damaged the social and political regime of the USSR – the subversive perversity of their actions was proved by the manner in which the bourgeois press had exploited their propaganda. They were sentenced to re-education in a tough labour-camp, Sinyavsky for seven years and Daniel for five. On Ehrenburg's initiative sixty-two writers signed a petition calling for the release of the condemned and offering to be responsible for them. Seeing that the Writers' Union had six thousand members, the figure of sixty-two was derisory. It called for a great deal of courage to sign: putting one's name to this petition meant taking the risk of never being sent abroad again, of losing one's job and of remaining unpublished for ever. Our friends Doroch and Lena accepted these risks. At the Twenty-Third Congress of the Party, which was held immediately after the trial, Sholokov expressed his extreme regret that the guilty men had not been punished more severely: in Lenin's time, said he, they would have been shot. He also criticized the intellectuals who had stood surety for them. 'I feel doubly ashamed for those who offered their services and who asked for these renegades to be released under supervision.' He asserted that the only people to protest against the trial were the 'bourgeois defenders' of Daniel and Sinyavsky. Yet on 16 April *L'Humanité* published a declaration in which Aragon, speaking for himself and for the French Communist party, condemned the trial. The Italian party adopted the same attitude. *L'Humanité* was banned in Moscow for a week. We arrived on 2 May. 'What are you doing here in the midst of all this?' asked Ehrenburg. According to him, the present position of the intellectuals was disastrous. All we met expressed their indignation at the trial, even those who had not signed the petition. They told us that Sinyavsky was being very harshly treated in the labour-camp, and Daniel even worse. Throughout our stay in Moscow almost every conversation revolved about this subject. Our friends were exceedingly upset, worried and anxious. Those who used the *samizdat* only did so with extreme caution: no interesting work was appearing. Tarkovsky had at last finished a scenario for Rublov that was acceptable to the authorities: but Doroch told us that he had been obliged to make so many concessions that the result was not at all satisfactory.[7]

In 1963 we had published Solzhenitsyn's admirable *Matriona's House* in *Les Temps modernes*, translated by Cathala; before that the tale had appeared in *Novy Mir*, but it had been severely criticized. We had also brought out two of his other stories, and we should have liked to know him. A common friend suggested that he should arrange a meeting. Then one day Lena told us that Solzhenitsyn had telephoned: he wanted to see her. We thought it was to fix an appointment with us. But when she came back having talked to him for an hour she was quite out of countenance. 'He does not want to see you,' she said to Sartre.

Why not? Solzhenitsyn had not explained himself very clearly. In effect what he had said was this: 'Sartre, do you see, is a writer whose work has all been published. Every time he writes a book he knows it will be read. So I really do not feel that I can talk to him: I should suffer too much.' His reaction surprised us. There was no doubt that Sartre knew him better than he knew Sartre, few of whose books had been translated into Russian – only some plays and *Words*. From that point of view they would meet on an equal footing. Perhaps Solzhenitsyn wanted neither to look as though he were making the best of his lot nor to tell a stranger of the ideas that he expressed a year later in his letter to the Writers' Congress. What we did see quite clearly was the fact that for a writer the greatest curse of all was being condemned to silence, to darkness.

---

[7] I was of the same opinion when I saw the film in Paris during the winter of 1969. The critics praised it extravagantly: but was not this because it was forbidden in the USSR?

We had never been to Central Asia, the summers being too hot. But in May the temperature is still quite mild, and I delighted in the thought of seeing Samarkand. Just as we reached the USSR an earthquake ravaged Uzbekistan – there was no question of travelling about those parts as tourists. So we changed our plans.

We went back to Yalta. It was less crowded than in 1963, and cooler. In the parks and gardens spring was bursting out in an explosion of countless violet flowers – great swathes of wistaria and lilac, Judas trees and Japanese cherries. Roses and petunias everywhere, filling the air with their scent, sometimes obvious, sometimes subtle. We went for our old walks and we skimmed over the sea in a hydrofoil. And once again we went aboard a white ship one evening and watched the coast glide by in the sunset. The captain asked us to an exceedingly poor dinner in his cabin. (The same cabin in which Maurice Thorez had his fatal stroke.) Half in earnest he asked Sartre whether he had come to the USSR because of the Sinyavsky-Daniel affair.

Odessa. For me it meant above all the famous flight of steps of *Battleship Potemkin*. From above they are not very striking: from below, although a few have been taken away to leave room for the road running along the quays and although it no longer plunges straight into the sea, it is as impressive as it was in the film. I had just read that volume of Paustovsky's memoirs in which he describes the days immediately before the Red Army entered the town – the dark, empty streets where one had to creep cautiously along if one did not wish to be robbed of one's coat or shot by the Cossacks; the people's rush to the harbour – bundles and wicker trunks being slid down the sloping streets, crammed suitcases spilling lace and ribbons; the murderous crush and trampling on the gangways of the ships escaping to Constantinople – ships that steamed away without even pulling up these gangways, so that the masses of people clinging to them were thrown into the sea. Then the great silence of the abandoned city, and the Soviet cavalry advancing through streets littered with dead bodies. Huge rats swarming in the deserted shops. These pictures all came to my mind as we explored Odessa, either on foot or by taxi. The crowded business centre was alive with people: there were also quiet residential districts, where innumerable acacias in bloom filled the air with their scent and covered the ground with their petals. On either side of the unpaved streets stood elegant houses with uniform façades,

322

unaltered since the beginning of the nineteenth century. The past seemed to have perpetuated itself without the slightest change. Yet the people were not the same. Formerly a great many of the inhabitants of Odessa were Jews or Levantines: now most are Ukrainians. Yet in a part of the town where the pavements had yawning gaps in them and where the acacias rose from deep mud, we did hear Yiddish spoken. Swarms of little jet-eyed Kafkas played along the side-walk.

The train carried us through an agreeable countryside to Kishinev – meadows, little thatched houses with blue-washed walls, carefully-cultivated kitchen-gardens, an air of happy abundance. The town had been almost entirely razed to the ground during the war: judging by the few painted wooden houses that had survived, it must have been charming. The writers who welcomed us asked why we had come; they sounded a little surprised. Sartre, caught off his guard, replied that the earthquake had made it impossible for us to go to Uzbekistan; the explanation did not seem altogether to their taste. Yet we all remained on very friendly terms for the two days we spent there: they showed us the surrounding country – immense black-earth fields alternating with pasture; villages like those we had seen from the train, carefully tended and prosperous. Before the war this region belonged to Romania; many of the people spoke Romanian and most of the intellectuals knew French.

We drove along the Prut, the present frontier, following a road lined with sweet-scented white acacias. At the entrance to each village the car stopped; we got out and wiped our feet on a kind of mat soaked with disinfectant – foot-and-mouth disease was raging, and there was a danger we might carry it from one part of the country to the next. The romantically-named Carpathians were clearly in sight.

When I was young Stépha had often told me about Lvov, the town where she was born and which then belonged to Poland. How remote it seemed to me in those days! And how the world has shrunk since then, seeing that I found it so natural to be there! The town is more akin to central Europe than to Russia. Its finest buildings were in the Austrian baroque manner, and they had lovely double-hipped green roofs. We went into a Catholic church; it was full of people all singing beautiful hymns, many of them young.

The students at the university of Lvov asked Sartre the same questions as the writers of Vilno the year before and of Kishinev this year: they were interested in Italian films, above all Antonioni's, and in French writing, particularly Sagan and the *nouveau roman.*

During this short journey we had still another experience of the suspicious attitude towards foreigners. Before reaching Lvov we stopped in a town at the foot of the Carpathians; we wanted to take a trip into the mountains. Intourist told us that an excursion had been laid on: four hours' drive up to a certain pass, where we should lunch at a hotel, and then four hours down. But Lena cannot stand winding roads for long, so I suggested that the trip should be curtailed – we should have a picnic half way up to the pass. Impossible: foreigners were not allowed to get out of the car before reaching the pass. We had to content ourselves with spending two hours in the forest, never leaving our seats. The Carpathians are like the Vosges—pines, fresh green grass, high blue ridges. I should have liked to breathe their scented air.

When we totted up all the prohibitions we had come up against, we were staggered at their absurdity. At Yalta the eastern coast was forbidden to foreigners, and so was the direct road to the Tartar capital; they were not allowed into Sevastopol; they were not permitted to take taxis from Vladimir to Moscow. The Baltic states might not be entered except by way of their capitals. It was forbidden to go from Leningrad to Tallinn and back again except by train. Our journey to Pskov had shown the utterly witless nature of these regulations. 'It's like that bench in Madrid,' said Goytisolo, whom we met in Moscow. 'There was a notice saying "It is forbidden to sit here". Someone was sufficiently curious to make inquiries: five years before, the bench had been repainted; the notice had been put up and no one had had the sense to take it away again.'

No doubt some of these regulations are mere relics of former times. But the Russians' mistrust of foreigners goes back a long way, and the Soviets are only returning to a very old tradition. In one of the churches at Vladimir there was a fresco by an unknown hand that seemed to us particularly significant. It was a picture of the Last Judgement: on the right of the Lord stood a troop of angels and of the blessed, wearing long robes of no particular period; and on His left, doomed to perdition, were seen to be gentlemen with pointed beards, dressed in black jerkins, breeches and lace collars – Catholics; behind them were men in turbans – Muslims. Here the discrimination was based upon religion: but difference of religion blends with difference of nationality. All foreigners dwell in error; and all foreigners are damned.

In 1967 we refused to attend the congress of the Soviet Writers' Union: if we had gone it would have looked as though we approved of the condemnation of Sinyavsky and Daniel and of the way in which Solzhenitsyn had been reduced to silence. The proceedings of the congress and the repression exercised against a great many liberal intellectuals during the following year did not encourage us to return to the USSR in 1968. But it was the events in Czechoslovakia that determined us to break with the Soviet Union for good and all.

Czechoslovakia. We had caught no more than a fleeting glimpse of the country in 1954, when a little secretly-whispered phrase, 'Terrible things are happening here,' had filled our minds with apprehension. But in 1963 we felt the wind of freedom blowing through Prague. The gigantic, hideous statue of Stalin had been thrown down long since. Kafka was read and loved. A great many foreign books had been translated, including some of Sartre's and mine. In a densely crowded tavern we heard young men playing jazz and reading poems by American beatniks. At the university, Sartre could speak to the students with complete openness and freedom. Many intellectuals had that immediate, living knowledge of Marxism that was so regrettably wanting in the Soviets. They remained faithful to socialism, but their minds, their way of thought, had grown critical and demanding. They were not afraid of looking the past in the face and denouncing its errors. A commission was set up in 1962, and in April of the following year it came to the conclusion that the Prague trials had been based upon completely fraudulent evidence: it demanded that the sentences should be quashed and the defendants rehabilitated. Some rehabilitations were refused, but the process was under way and it seemed that nothing could reverse it.

Our two most usual contacts were Hoffmeister, who welcomed us at the airport, and Liehm, who acted as our guide and interpreter. Hoffmeister was a man of about sixty and one of the best-known figures in Prague. In his youth he had written poems, plays and essays, and exhibitions of his caricatures had been very successful in Paris and Prague in 1927 and 1928. In 1939 he left Prague for Paris: he was interned in the Santé prison and then deported to

Germany; there he escaped and made his way to the United States. After the war he was put in charge of cultural relations and then from 1948 to 1951 he was ambassador to Paris. During the period of the trials he had remained aloof from public life. Now he was a professor at the school of decorative arts, and at the same time he carried on with his writing and drawing.

Liehm was younger: he was a highly talented essayist and journalist, and he had translated a great many books from French. They were both very well-informed, open-minded, keen-witted men; they both spoke perfect French; and in their company we could discuss no matter what subject without the least reserve.

In the beautiful château near Prague belonging to the Writers' Union we met the Slovak author Mnacko: his book *The Delayed Report*, in which he describes the abuses of the Stalin era, was held in great esteem. He was passionately alive, he felt things very strongly, and he had a remarkably independent mind. We were glad to meet him again in Bratislava.

This was a town I did not know. We were shown it by a very likeable couple, Monsieur Ballo and his wife. He had been an attaché at the Paris embassy and it was he who had provided us with the official information on Slansky's trial. Now he was the editor of a literary review.

Bratislava gave the impression of being poor. At the foot of the castle there was a wretched district inhabited by gypsies. In order to bring in foreign currency, the nearby frontier had recently been opened on Saturdays and Sundays, and there were floods of Austrian tourists in the streets. The manager of our hotel told us that he knew some of them very well indeed by sight – twenty years earlier they had been wearing German uniforms. Slovak resistance had been heroic and the repression bloody: neither Germans nor Austrians were looked upon with any liking. One evening Mnacko and his friends took us to a restaurant called 'the thieves' cave' in the heart of a forest; it was a huge log-cabin with dark wooden furniture, and spitted joints turning in front of a fire in the middle of the room filled it with an appetizing smell. While we were eating our dinner and drinking white wine a party of tourists came and sat nearby, and they began to sing in German. Our table retorted with the song of the partisans. There was tension in the air, but after a while Mnacko went over and spoke to the Austrians and in the end they shook hands.

326

On our way from Bratislava to Prague we passed through immense, spreading landscapes – green hills and dark forests, where wealthy foreigners come to shoot big game in the autumn. Most of the villages have beautiful baroque columns erected by survivors of the plague to thank God for having spared them.

We only stayed a short while, but afterwards we kept in touch with our Czech friends. In 1964 we published Kundera's cruel, ironic story *Personne ne va rire* in *Les Temps modernes*. We saw Hoffmeister in Paris. In 1967 Liehm brought out an account of the Russell Tribunal's proceedings in *Literarni Noviny*, the magazine he edited. We saw him again in Paris on this occasion, and he told us that painting, music and writing were then reasonably free.in Czechoslovakia: indeed, some excellent books on the Stalin period had been published. The cinema was not so well placed: films were not censored, but subversive producers were encouraged to leave for Hollywood. Liehm told us that the explanation for this state of affairs was that the leaders never read books and knew nothing whatsoever about music or painting, but from time to time they did see a film in their projection-rooms.

A political crisis was brewing. The country was in a bad economic situation, and to rectify this, Ota Sik had worked out a new system: he wanted to adapt production to the country's needs and its resources. But these reforms were incompatible with the extreme centralization of power and they called for a certain liberalization of the system: the result was conflict between the new and the old bureaucrats. The working class, which had lost all political awareness, seemed to side with the latter, although the reformists intended to provide the workers with a certain control over production. The intellectuals, seeing that authority was paralyzed by internal dissension, urged the workers to insist upon a socialist democratization. *Literarni Noviny* openly criticized the system. Before the Fourth Congress of the Writers' Union, which opened in June, the Stalinists launched a campaign against Liehm and his review; but their attack came to nothing. The congress was stormy: the writer Vaculik denounced the ruling circle's hidebound incompetence; others supported him; Hendrych, the former secretary of the central committee and an out-and-out Stalinist, walked out. The leadership of the Communist Party refused to recognize the governing body of the union, although it had been elected by an overwhelming majority. Between the party and the intellectuals there was therefore a total break. The intellectuals distributed great quantities of pamphlets attacking the regime.

After the Six Days' War Prague adopted a violently hostile attitude towards Israel. It was forbidden to express any opinion that differed from the official line. The anti-semitism that had served as the background to the Slansky trial came to life again, now calling itself anti-Zionism. In September 1967 Mnacko left Bratislava for Israel amidst a great deal of publicity: he was not a Jew, but he would not tolerate being prevented from writing what he thought. A great number of Czech writers signed a manifesto in which they demanded freedom of expression, both upon Israel and upon all other questions.

During its plenary session at the end of September, the central committee barred three writers from the party, including Liehm. At the end of October there was another session, and it happened to coincide with a student demonstration. This was alleged to have a political character, although in fact it was concerned with questions of heating and lighting. Then again, Slovakia was a centre of unrest, the Slovaks rightly considering themselves to be oppressed by the Czechs. Novotny and Dubcek clashed over the Slovak problem and Novotny's blundering conduct drove several members of the central committee into opposition. Dubcek and Cernik informed Brezhnev how things stood in December: he did not promise Novotny his support.

During the December session the central committee brought pressure to bear on Novotny to resign. On the night of 4 January he gave up his post as head of the party, retaining only that of president of the republic. Dubcek was the new secretary. This change had been carried out on the initiative of the central committee in a perfectly democratic manner.

This was the beginning of the 'Prague spring', and then came its full flowering. The chief voice heard between January and March was that of the intelligentsia. The intellectuals were trying to swing the masses over to the side of the reformers, but their writings in fact went much further – they showed that it was impossible to put an end to the 'abuses' of the regime without doing away with the entire system. Now that the working-class were informed about the true situation of the country and about the errors that had been committed, they gradually became politically conscious once more, and returned to the old maximalist demand of all power to the soviets. Censorship was abolished; the press and radio enjoyed total freedom; and the intellectuals redoubled their attacks upon the system. In March Novotny resigned: the leaders decided to summon the party congress and to hold parliamentary elections. In June Vaculik brought out the 'Two Thousand Words Manifesto', proclaiming that democratization must be carried out by the workers themselves. In their dialogue with the new regime the workers secured the right of management; it was clear to them that this victory was the result of the discussions that had been going on since January, and therefore the right to total information as well became one of their basic, essential claims – the factories set up 'workers' committees for the freedom of expression'. And thus the difficult alliance between the intellectuals and the working class became an accomplished fact.

But the Soviet Communist Party had taken fright. On 1 June the Czech Communist Party's central committee unanimously decided to summon the Fourteenth Congress in September, whereupon the Soviet and Polish armies began to patrol the Czechoslovak frontiers. On 1 July the USSR, Poland, Hungary, Bulgaria and East Germany signed the 'Letter of the Five Powers' in Warsaw, calling on the Czechoslovak Stalinists to oppose Dubcek's policies. This was an entirely fruitless gesture: it did nothing but strengthen the unity of the party and of the people.

We followed these events with passionate interest. I had read *The Joke*, in which Kundera described the general atmosphere in Czechoslovakia during the fifties with grim humour. He based his novel on an incident that had really occurred in 1949: Nezval, whom the young Czechs admired as a poet but much less as a man, published a work in which he extolled both sensual pleasures and Stalin; and some young men wrote a parody of it for fun. The 'joke' cost them dear. Their pamphlet was described as a tract directed against the state; the reviews that had distributed it were attacked; its authors and their accomplices were accused of being Trotskyists and agents of imperialism. They performed their public self-criticism; and often they did so sincerely, for the mere fact of being intellectuals made them feel guilty. In his book Kundera transposed this story, describing the years of forced labour to which the joker has been condemned. In April *Les Temps modernes* published several articles by Czech progressives. And Sartre gave long talks on the Czech television.

329

On 21 August, when we heard that the Soviet tanks had entered Czechoslovakia, we were in Rome. Sartre at once gave the Communist paper *Paese Sera* an interview in which he called the Soviets 'war criminals': our relationship with the USSR was broken off for ever. All our Italian friends were overwhelmed and horror-struck. The Italian Communist Party dissociated itself very strongly from the Soviet aggression: the French party did the same, but with less conviction. In both countries the rank and file, accustomed to admiring the USSR without the least reservation, were deeply shocked by the central committee's attitude. For our part, we were exceedingly distressed by the position adopted by Castro. Rosana Rossanda had just received the original text of his speech and she showed it to us: she was as amazed and as grieved as we were at the spectacle of Castro enthusiastically approving of the invasion of a small country by a great power.

The Soviet writers sent the Czechoslovak intellectuals a letter in which they entirely supported the Soviet government. Among the big men only Simonov, Tvardovsky and Leonov refused to sign. (Ehrenburg was dead.) We thought of our Russian friends with pain and grief. When we were back in Paris we met Svetlana, a young Russian communist whom we knew slightly. She had been on holiday with her sister in a Black Sea resort when she turned on her transistor to listen to the news and heard of the aggression. 'I never cry,' she said, 'but when I heard I burst into tears. So did my sister.' At their hotel they lunched with a young officer. 'Don't look so sad,' he said to them, 'the Germans shan't enter the Soviet Union. We'll chase them back into their own country.' Like so many others he thought it was a question of fighting the Germans. 'The masses blindly support the government,' said Svetlana. 'We intellectuals are completely isolated now.'

At about the same time I met a Romanian friend who had just come back from Bucharest. On 22 August she was at her chiropodist's: the woman switched on the radio and then she too burst into tears. 'We're done for!' she cried. Ceausescu announced that he was going to speak and the whole city gathered to listen to him: he protested against the aggression with extreme violence. Sartre's declaration to *Paese Sera* appeared on the front page in all the papers. Then, after secret bargaining with the USSR, silence gradually came down. The Romanians who happened to be in Czechoslovakia returned home with their cars battered and dented – the

Hungarians had stoned them as they passed through the country. Enlightened opinion in Hungary had condemned the intervention; but there had always been a deep enmity between Hungary and Romania, and as pro-Soviet propaganda had inflamed their minds, the peasants thought it permissible to express their hatred.

In October we saw Liehm again and we had long conversations with him. He told Sartre that the Prague producers invited him to come to see *The Flies* and *Crime Passionel* performed. Sartre accepted, but we were doubtful – would not the plays be banned? Should we be granted visas?

In fact we landed at Prague at eleven on the morning of 28 November. It was a cold, wet, clouded day. The director of the theatre, his colleagues and a party of writers took us to the charming old-fashioned Hotel Alkron, once a centre for international spying. Then we went straight to the theatre, where the dress rehearsal of *The Flies* was just coming to an end. As we entered the foyer we heard the crackle of applause. We went on to the stage, and some of the many students in the audience asked Sartre questions. Liehm had told him he might speak openly, without the least precaution; but even so I was surprised by the freedom of the interchanges. As the audience urged him to give his views, Sartre stated that he looked upon the Soviet aggression as a war-crime; that he had written *The Flies* to encourage the French to resist; and that he was glad that his play was now being performed in occupied Czechoslovakia. A few days earlier the students had gone on strike, and he asked them why they had done so. 'Monsieur Sartre, you have only just arrived; you don't understand the conditions we live in. We could tell you about the strike in private, but not in public – there is auto-censorship here you know,' said one young man. Another, red-haired and bearded, a mathematician, stood up: 'Auto-censorship or not, I'm going to answer.' He came on to the stage. He spoke in Czech, and our interpreter, a charming, sad young woman with bright blue eyes, translated what he said. The students were not against the government, but they did want to prove their political importance and prevent the leaders from starting along the road of concessions. The workers had struck for an hour to show their solidarity with the students. The discussion, moving from subject to subject, went on for two hours.

We had a very late luncheon with the director of the theatre and his colleagues, and then we rested at the hotel. At about seven o'clock we went out. It was very cold; there was a fog; and in spite of the cheerful colours of the neon signs the streets were tolerably grim. At the foot of the statue which stands at the upper end of Wenceslas Square wreaths were piled high, bunches of flowers lay on the ground, and round them glowed a little field of candles. People stood there in silent reverence, or murmured prayers in memory of the victims of the aggression.

The next morning our interpreter drove us about the city. The streets were packed with cars, most of them small. Once again I saw the castle, the old parts of Prague with their delightful baroque houses, many charming squares, and far off the bridge with the magical statues – we could not cross it because it was being repaired. I went over the fine Hus chapel; and we paused for a long while in the great square where he was burnt: I had retained a clear picture of the clock, the beautiful old houses, and, a little farther back, the two bell-towers of the church.

We lunched with a group of writers in a pretty restaurant decorated with imitation trees – that is the fashion in Prague, just as old beams are with us, by way of reaction against plastic. We saw Hoffmeister again, and I met the young philosopher Kosik: Sartre had spoken highly of him. Here again the conversation was perfectly free. No one mistrusted anyone else and the atmosphere was one of total unity. Later there was a meeting at the Writers' Union attended by about a hundred people: this was far less interesting – those we should have liked to meet, including Kundera, were away from Prague.

Then in the evening we went to the first night of *The Flies*. The theatre was packed. Both the production and the actors seemed to us excellent. Some of the lines were received with wild applause. When Jupiter says to Orestes and Electra 'I have come to help you,' laughter broke out all over the house. And when Electra, having heard Jupiter's alluring promises, asks, 'What will you require of me in return?' there was more laughter at his reply, 'I shall ask you nothing . . . or almost nothing.' An enthusiastic reaction too, when Jupiter says, 'Once freedom has exploded in a mortal heart the gods can no longer do anything against that man.' In many other places the audience saw allusions to the situation in Czechoslovakia and they applauded vigorously. At the end of the play they gave Sartre an ovation.

After that we had a supper of cold meat washed down with

vodka, white wine and beer. We sat opposite Cisak and Hadjek (who had been vilely slandered).[8] Cisak was a broad-faced, thickset man with a crew cut. Hadjek looked like a moulting bird. He called the Russians 'our allies', and he counselled prudence – 'We must not alarm our allies.' In his opinion there had been too much talk: intellectuals loved talking too much. From now on it would be wiser to act in silence.

The next evening the audience also gave *Crime Passionel* a most enthusiastic reception. They found many allusions to the recent happenings in the play. When Hoederer says that an army of occupation is never loved, no, not even if it happens to be the Red Army, there was frantic applause. Someone told me that in a comedy an actress had set off a storm of laughter by saying to a friend on the telephone, 'Call me back later, I'm busy.'[9]

Our day had been well filled, and so was the next. We were shown the news-reels taken by the Czechs during that tragic night and the following day: I had read a great many special articles, but seeing things with one's own eyes is altogether different. They also showed us news-reels shot by the Russians: they had been distributed in the USSR with commentaries that completely falsified their significance – weapons found in cellars of a ministry were alleged to be a counter-revolutionary arsenal, for example. This Soviet version had been shown in Prague with the trickery and falsification exposed.

When Bartosek interviewed us on the television we avoided expressions that might be too compromising, but we did speak in veiled but perfectly obvious terms of the 'misfortune' that had descended upon the Czechoslovak nation, and of the nation's 'justifiable bitterness'. Bartosek wanted us to meet some workers. He thought that the spring of 1968 had prepared the way for a radical change in their way of life and that at least to some extent they were going to wrest power from the bureaucrats and participate in the management of the factories. That was why they were supporting the new government against the Russians. Unfortunately we could not stay in Prague long enough to visit any factories.

We had lunch in a restaurant called the Moscow of all things,

---

[8] He was accused of being an old social-democrat, a Gestapo agent, and a Zionist although he was not even a Jew.

[9] There is a play upon words here, the French being *occupée*, which can mean either busy or occupied.—Trs.

with some theatrical people. And we spent an agreeable time with the Hoffmeisters in their big flat filled with splendid objects from every corner of the earth. He showed us some of his recent drawings and amusing caricatures of present-day progressive intellectuals and politicians, and he told us anecdotes about the occupation. At Bratislava, on the morning of 21 August, a Russian officer said to the head of the television, 'I am posting men on your staircase. They will defend you against the counter-revolutionaries.' Coming back that evening he cried out in astonishment, 'What? Not a single counter-revolutionary has appeared?' Then all at once he saw the light. 'Why then, it's *you* who are the counter-revolutionary!' But in the course of that day the television team had had time to remove all the equipment to a place of safety. He also told us of a news-paper the Russians had banned. They put sentries at the door of the building and occupied the entrance-hall. They did not know of the existence of a door at the back. Even the police refused to collabor-ate with the Russians, which was why they found it so very difficult to be harshly effective.

All the people we spoke to told us a great deal about the Four-teenth Congress which the Czechoslovak Communist Party had held secretly, in open defiance of the occupying Russians, the very purpose of whose intervention was to prevent this meeting. Its intention was to legalize the renovation of socialism and to strengthen the guiding role of the Communist Party; and this made it dangerous in the eyes of the Soviet bureaucrats. Nevertheless the congress was held, in the most surprising circumstances, and with more than two thirds of the delegates attending. The call was sent out on the radio, and on 22 August they gathered at a great factory in Prague; from there the workers took them to Vysocany, a suburb secretly chosen as the meeting-place. Their proceedings lasted for several days, and the congress established a protocol.

All our conversations confirmed what we already knew – the Czech spring had not been directed against socialism. What the new regime had wanted to do was to abolish the Stalinists' bureaucratic rule and their police-methods; to substitute persuasion for coercion; to have the central committee elected by the secret vote of the people instead of being appointed from above; and to give the workers political power and economic responsibility – they had wanted to bring an authentic socialism into existence. In any case it was only after the event that the Soviets thought up their theory of 'counter-revolutionary threat'. The reason for the existence of anti-socialist forces in Czechoslovakia over the years was in fact Novotny's dogmatic and inefficient policy: these forces collapsed entirely when the Communist Party brought forward its new political programme. The Party was doing its utmost to win the whole country over to socialism; and from May onwards, when it decided to hold the Fourteenth Congress, its authority steadily increased. The entire working class were behind Dubcek, and they expressed their support and agreement in thousands of resolutions. Now to the last man they were solidly opposed to the occupation.

So what was the true reason for the Russian intervention? Our friend Svetlana thought the Soviet bureaucrats had been thrown into a panic by the idea that Prague intended to bring the trials fully to light; the masses upheld the government as a whole but no single one of its members in particular; and those responsible for the trials were in danger of being ousted by competitors less compromised than themselves. Then again, Moscow could not tolerate the abolition of censorship – 'More especially as the Ukrainians understand Czech,' said a Hungarian opponent of the intervention. The Czech example would have encouraged Ukrainian nationalism. The leading groups in the USSR Communist Party dearly loved their supremacy, and that alone would be enough to explain the aggression: they had to keep all the socialist countries in subjection and they could not accept Czechoslovakia's claims to some degree of independence.

We left Prague more hopeful than when we arrived: how could the Russians break so unanimous a resistance?

It was on my return to Paris that I read London's *On Trial*, whose dedication included 'all those who carry on the struggle to give socialism back its human face'. We had never been deceived by the Rajk and Slansky trials; we had never believed in the 'confessions': but in no book had I ever found a satisfactory answer to the question 'How do they bring themselves to confess?' Some spoke of torture, others of blind devotion to the party, and still others of the hope of making a public defence. Only London showed the whole process in a completely convincing way: the reader shared his feeling of being caught in a machine from which there was no escaping. His fast-moving, restrained and affecting account was the work of a true writer. He completely clarified a problem that had puzzled me when I heard of him many years before: how could he bear to go on living with a woman who had dissociated herself from him during the trial? The fact of the matter was that she had believed him right up until the moment she actually heard him confess his crimes. He had not talked when the Gestapo tortured him: how could she possibly have imagined the methods the Czech police used to extract confessions from all the defendants? Overcome with pain and bitterness, she disowned him. But as soon as he managed to tell her very briefly of his innocence during a visit, she was convinced and she set everything in motion to have him rehabilitated. In the streets of occupied Paris, she openly launched an appeal to the women against the Germans: she escaped death only because she was pregnant – she had her baby in a German prison. In other words she belonged to her party heart and soul; she believed in it as the believer believes in God. It seemed to me unfair that she should be blamed for not looking at it with a critical eye, and I said so when I spoke of this moving story on Radio-Luxembourg.

Lanzmann arranged for London and me to meet at luncheon, and I liked him very much. Lanzmann asked, 'Would you still be politically active now?' 'On condition of never lying,' replied London, and he laughed. He hoped his book would be translated into Czech and filmed by a Czech producer. No, alas: by 1969 the springtime of Prague was no more than a memory. Costa-Gavras did make a film in France; it had merit, but it failed to convey the full complexity of the drama. In my opinion one of the great qualities of London's book is that for the future it deprives any extorted confession of all credibility: but still that hardly worries the authoritarian regimes – they simply condemn without a confession.[10]

I am writing these lines in May 1971. All the Czech and Slovak intellectuals we knew have been expelled from the Communist Party. They have lost their jobs and they find it extremely difficult to live. Or else they are in exile. And the Czech leaders are once more completely under the thumb of the Soviets.

The Russians have finally disappointed all our hopes. Never has the situation of the intellectuals been so critical. None of our friends can obtain permission to come and see us any more, and we know that they all feel completely powerless. Amalric, for having told the

[10] Some have even returned to the system of confessions.

336

truth about his country, has once again been sent to Siberia, and there he is dying.[11] The Leningrad trial has clearly shown the anti-semitism that is so rife at government level in the USSR. Not without regret, I believe I shall never see Moscow again.

[11] Since I wrote this, many other intellectuals have been deported or shut up in asylums.

7

The Franco-Vietnamese war had mattered a very great deal to me;
I was deeply involved and I rejoiced at the victory of Hanoi. After
June 1962, when I was no longer haunted by the war in Algeria, the
fate of Vietnam once again occupied the forefront of my mind – I
was utterly disgusted by the Americans' interference and their contempt for the Vietnamese people's right to self-determination.

It will be remembered that at the signing of the Geneva agreements in 1954, a provisional demarcation-line was drawn to allow
the forces to regroup, the Vietminh to the north, the French to the
south. There was absolutely no question of a frontier dividing two
separate states. The agreements provided for the reunification of the
country, which was to elect a president in July 1956. It was obvious
– and Eisenhower admitted it in his memoirs – that at least eighty
per cent of the population would vote for Ho Chi Minh. The Americans cynically decided to prevent these elections. In opposition to
Ho Chi Minh, the French set up a 'state of Vietnam', with Bao Dai
as president. The Geneva agreements, which the Americans had
undertaken to honour, did not admit the existence of this state:
nevertheless the Americans affected to look upon it as a nation, and
at its head they placed Diem, a creature of their own. To oppose
Diem the people formed a National Liberation Front. The Pentagon
sent in ever-increasing numbers of troops to crush the guerillas.

The American left wing cried out against this interference, with
the university of Cornell spearheading the movement. The professors sent Johnson a letter of protest and they organized a pacifist
demonstration. At the beginning of 1965 they invited Sartre to give
lectures at Cornell. The entire left wing wanted him to come – his
presence and support at their meetings would be of the utmost
value. He accepted.

On 7 February 1965 the Americans bombed the Democratic Republic of Vietnam on the pretext that the North was taking part in the war, which in fact affected the entire country, the division between North and South being nothing but a piece of American humbug. They did so again on 2 March and after that they continued without a pause.

Sartre felt that in these circumstances he should not go to the USA; the attacks on the North amounted to a violent escalation of the war, an irreversible qualitative change. He wrote to Cornell explaining his reasons. He also gave *L'Observateur* an interview on the subject, and the interview was reproduced in America by *The Nation*. He was especially glad that he had come to this decision because shortly after there occurred the American intervention in Santo Domingo. At first the American left wing criticized Sartre for his attitude: people wrote saying 'This is desertion! You are letting us down!' How hard it is for Americans, even Americans of good will, not to consider themselves the centre of the universe! They felt that Sartre was answerable to them alone, whereas he was thinking of the scandal it would cause in the underdeveloped countries, in Cuba and Vietnam itself, if he accepted Cornell's invitation at this juncture. Gradually the American left saw things more clearly. In letters and articles they admitted that Sartre's refusal had made more impact than any amount of speeches. Militants said, 'He has been immensely useful to us; it has served as an example.'

There were now massive demonstrations in the USA, and a great many debates in the universities. Twenty writers refused an invitation to the White House. Meetings and processions against the war increased and multiplied.

In July 1966 I was called upon by a young American who lived in England and who was one of the chief secretaries of the Russell Foundation: his name was Schoenman. He told me about a plan of Lord Russell's – the setting up of a tribunal, based on that of Nuremberg, to bring American action in Vietnam to trial. The Foundation would send commissions of inquiry to Vietnam; it would ask the American left wing to supply documents; and it would organize a trial at which a number of 'judges' would weigh the facts and pronounce a verdict. The aim was to arouse public opinion all over the world and particularly in America. Would Sartre and I agree to be members of the tribunal? Schoenman specifically stated that the hearings would be held in Paris; that we should not have to attend all of them; that we should be provided with accounts of the proceedings; and that we should only be asked to be present for two or three days, when the final decisions were taken.

Tito Gerassi urged us to accept. As I have said, he was actively campaigning against the war in Vietnam. We had confidence in him, and his advice decided us.

In November 1966 a meeting against the war was held at the Mutualité. An enormous crowd packed the entrances and the hall was filled with a younger and more enthusiastic audience than usual. They frantically applauded the speakers as they came on to the platform, especially Max Ernst, who had designed the poster that decorated the auditorium. Sartre aroused a storm of applause when he said that we should support Vietnam not from moral considerations but because the Vietnamese were fighting for us. After the speeches there were films with a commentary by Gatti, ballet by Nono, and some music.

Meanwhile the plan for the tribunal was being implemented. On 1 December Sartre wrote an article announcing its existence and denying the claim that a trial of this kind would have no significance because its outcome was known in advance: our methods would be those of all other courts – on the basis of a strong a priori case we should establish whether the USA had committed war-crimes or not. Our decision would be founded on the laws applied at Nuremberg and also on the Briand-Kellogg pact and the Geneva convention. Cuba sent Alejo Carpentier to North Vietnam to carry out an investigation for the Russell Tribunal. We lunched with him on his return. He told us that most of the small towns had been wiped out: the planes selected the schools, hospitals, leper-colonies and churches for attack because they were solidly built and were therefore better targets than straw huts. Hanoi expected to be bombed from one day to the next, and the children had been evacuated. People did their shopping between three and five in the morning, supposing that to be the least favourable time for a raid. He described the individual shelters dug alongside the pavements, the fragility of that city built of bamboo, and the courage of its people. He also showed us photographs of civilians burnt by napalm.

In January 1967 Sartre went to London to meet Schoenman and a certain number of the judges, and they laid down the tribunal's statutes and defined the questions we should be called upon to answer. Other meetings were held in Paris, and at these Lanzmann, whom Sartre had named as his deputy, sometimes took his place.

A delegation that included Tito Gerassi and the lawyer Matarasso came back from Vietnam bringing with them a quantity of most impressive evidence; others followed.

We had expected the tribunal to hold its sittings in Paris. But when Dedijer wanted to come to France in February he was refused a visa, although it had always been granted before. Sartre wrote to General de Gaulle asking whether this refusal was based upon a desire to prevent the tribunal from sitting in Paris. De Gaulle replied with a letter composed of two antithetical sections, like his speeches. The first said 'Yes, of course': the second said 'certainly not'. In spite of his apparently anti-American policy de Gaulle did not choose to antagonize the government of the United States. The refusal was confirmed by a letter from the prefect of police.

The tribunal then got into touch with Stockholm. The Swedish government's answer was no. But the next day it stated that a refusal to allow us to meet there would be unconstitutional: Sweden would receive us unwillingly, but the country's democratic principles obliged it to do so. So there was no longer any question of carrying on with our ordinary lives in Paris while at the same time following the sessions more or less closely. But ever since the undertaking had taken on a real existence we had become deeply involved and we were ready to devote ourselves to it unreservedly.

During the days just before we left for Sweden in May 1967 we were somewhat disturbed by telephone-messages from Stockholm telling us that Schoenman was holding three press-conferences a day and that he was talking very wildly. Together with a great many other delegates, we landed one Saturday afternoon. A reception-committee was waiting for us, standing by a large poster that said *Tribunal*. At a meeting held in the drawing-room of a big hotel I first learnt the exact composition of the tribunal. The honorary chairman was Bertrand Russell, whose great age obliged him to stay in England. Sartre was executive president. Dedijer, assisted by Schwartz, was to preside over the sittings. I had known Schwartz during the Algerian war: Dedijer I had recently met in Paris for the first time. Before our meeting I had read his book *Tito Speaks* with the greatest interest. He and Tito had fought in the resistance together – the day Tito was wounded Dedijer's wife was killed.

Later a shell-splinter struck Dedijer in the head, and the surgeons have never been able to remove the whole of it.

He was a historian and a doctor of laws; he represented Yugoslavia at the United Nations in 1945, and subsequently he held other important posts. In 1955, when Tito banned Djilas' writings and threw him into prison, Dedijer protested vigorously: it was not that he shared all Djilas' ideas, but he felt he should be allowed to express them. This brought about Dedijer's disgrace; he was given a suspended sentence 'for having spread information harmful to his country in the American press'. A year later he was given permission to leave Yugoslavia; he went to the United States, where he taught first at the university of Manchester and then at Harvard and Cornell. For the last year he had been living at Ljubljana once more, and he had returned to his work as a historian. Dedijer was the only member of the tribunal who belonged to a socialist country: he was a very tall, broad-shouldered man, and he gave an impression of strength and solidity. In fact he was neither as robust nor well-balanced as he seemed: from time to time his old wound gave him violent headaches and every year he was obliged to make a long stay in hospital. Sometimes he would fly into rages that he could scarcely control. His intransigent character, his life and warmth quite won us over. He became a friend of ours.

The other judges were Gunther Anders, a German philosopher and writer; Aybard, a Turkish professor of international law and a member of parliament; Basso, an Italian jurist, a member of parliament and a specialist in international law; Cardenas, the former president of Mexico, who did not come to Stockholm; Carmichael, the Afro-American who launched the slogan 'Black Power' and who was represented by another Afro-American named Cox; Dellinger, an American pacifist and editor of *Liberation*, the protesting, anti-conformist paper, whose political struggle had led him to prison; Hernandez, a Philippino poet, who had spent six years in gaol on political charges; Kasuri, a barrister at the Pakistan supreme court; Morihawa, a Japanese legal expert; Sakata, a Japanese physicist; Abendrath, a German university teacher and a doctor of laws, for whom a Swedish novelist, Madame Lidmann, deputized; Baldwin, the Afro-American novelist – he neither came to Sweden nor was he represented; Deutscher, the well-known Trotskyist historian; and Daly, the secretary-general of the Scottish miners' union, who did not come until the end of the sittings. New judges were coopted:

Ogleby, a young American pacifist; Melba Hernandez, who had taken part in the attack on the Moncada barracks at Castro's side; and Peter Weiss, who to begin with was only the secretary-general of the Swedish committee. The judges were assisted by a legal committee that included Gisèle Halimi, Jouffa, Matarasso and Suzanne Bouvier. Schoenman and Statler represented the Foundation. Amazingly competent voluntary translators enabled us to understand one another; and the languages used were English, French and Spanish.

On Sunday morning I was woken by a strange device fixed to the wall: you set it at night and at the stated time next day, it uttered a harsh yapping until its hand was put back to zero. Looking out of the window I saw a broad avenue and a café with people sitting on its terrace; the idea of spending ten days here, far from my own life, made me very pensive. But as the taxi took me through the city, I was immediately captivated by its charm – the arms of the sea reaching into the town, the docks with their water shining in the sun, the green roofs of the churches and the palaces, the modern but very beautiful red-brick town hall.

The tribunal had hired the fourth floor of the House of the People – a large amphitheatre and a great many offices. The corridors were filled with girls in miniskirts and long-haired young men; they were voluntarily carrying out the thankless jobs of translating, typing and roneoing documents. Melba Hernandez, the Cuban delegate, was much struck by these young people: she was going to tell Castro about them, for they proved that the Carnaby Street style – strictly forbidden in Cuba – was not incompatible with revolutionary commitment. We particularly noticed one charming person who attended all the sessions, sitting in the front row of the public seats. We could not determine his sex until one day we met him at Peter Weiss's – it was his son-in-law, and Alejo Carpentier was sadly confused at having greeted him with a '*Bonjour, mademoiselle*'. There was also a young couple who always carried a kind of portable cot with a baby in it: this was Statler and his wife. At the hotel one evening the baby was perfectly seriously refused entry to the bar: 'Minors are not allowed in.'

The first day we had a private meeting. To begin with we had to repair a tactless blunder committed by Schoenman during a press-conference: on their front pages all the Swedish papers accused the tribunal of having insulted the prime minister, Erlander. Schoen-

343

man had denied that Erlander had sent Russell a welcoming message, whereas in fact he had done so – he had sent a .polite cable. Schoenman wrote a note of apology for the press and it was decided that four spokesmen, chosen from among the judges, should be the only people authorized to communicate with the papers.

During these ten days we had a great many private meetings: they took place after the public sessions and they often carried on late into the night. And indeed we had a great many things to discuss – the exact programme for the following days; the precise wording of the questions we were to answer; the position to be given to the minority in the event of our decisions not being unanimous; and other points of less importance.

Our meetings provided me with an interesting experience in group-psychology. These people, coming from every corner of the earth, were all opposed to American imperialism; but their standpoints varied very widely indeed. Kasuri and Hernandez represented the left wing of under-developed countries whose governments were on terms with the USA. The anti-Americanism of the Japanese had its origin in the memory of Nagasaki and Hiroshima and in the current occupation of Okinawa; they were particularly affected by an aggression carried out against an Asian country. Melba Hernandez stood for Cuba, whose triumphant revolution was being threatened by the USA; she was emotionally stirred by the struggle of a small country against the enormous strength of the United States. The Americans spoke in the name of the opposition within their own country. Aybard and Basso reacted as jurists; Deutscher as a Trotskyist. Sartre, Schwartz and I belonged to the French non-Communist left wing. Dedijer's position was very close to ours and also to Peter Weiss's. To begin with there was a certain amount of mutual distrust. Kasuri and Hernandez, especially, showed some degree of hostility towards the Westerners. And then again each member had his particular idiosyncrasies and his own likes and dislikes. There were combinations and changes of alliance, hidden conflicts and violent outbursts. Sometimes I had to hold myself in, but generally speaking our disagreements interested and even amused me.

Their violence was largely due to the curious personality of Schoenman. Without him, I believe the Tribunal would never have existed: with astonishing tenacity he had travelled all round the world explaining his plan, recruiting the judges and setting up an organization. He could work for days on end without rest and if necessary he would sleep on the floor. But he had the defects of his qualities, with some more added. He was energetic and efficient; and he was the only man I have ever met who hid his chin under a beard not to mask the weakness of his features but on the contrary to hide their stubborn arrogance. He wanted to exercise a positive dictatorship over the tribunal: he was its secretary-general and he also claimed to sit as Russell's representative. Everybody opposed this plurality of offices. He was furious, and at the first session he sat among the judges: the next day he was compelled to take another place. But in private he still tried to boss everything, sheltering behind Russell's authority – 'Lord Russell would not allow ... Lord Russell insists that ...' One day Sartre lost his patience and said, 'Don't carry on like de Gaulle, who says *France* when he means *I*.' Although he was capable of leading an ascetic life, Schoenman's vainglory led him to display an outrageous extravagance. For instance he continually made long, useless telephone-calls from Stockholm to London or Paris. And in spite of our decision he went on talking to the journalists. His overbearing manner and vehemence often angered Schwartz, Dedijer and Sartre. But even so we liked him for the strength of his convictions and his desperate eagerness to get results.

On Monday the journalists were invited to the amphitheatre and we told them about a certain number of practical decisions. It was on Tuesday that the sitting of the court really began. We sat in alphabetical order at a horseshoe table with the three presidents in the middle. Every morning we were given a summary of the newspaper reports and of the previous day's proceedings. There were some two hundred people in the hall – all the secretaries and technicians, the journalists and two television teams, one Swedish and the other American. We were unpleasantly dazzled by their powerful lights. Each of us was provided with a microphone. The translators could be seen in a kind of glass cage which hung from the roof; whenever a speaker grew over-enthusiastic a powerful voice from on high adjured him to slow down, and Dedijer beat on the table with a mallet. Ha Van Lau, representing the National Liberation Front, and Pham Van Bac, representing the Democratic Republic of Vietnam, attended the sessions as guests.

In August 1965 Russell had asked the USA to send lawyers to plead their cause before the tribunal. He received no answer. Sartre wrote to Dean Rusk, making the same request. Rusk made no direct reply, but he told journalists that he would not 'play childish games with an old Englishman of ninety-four'. Sartre publicly read his response to this observation, a response in which he made a comparison between Russell and Dean Rusk, 'that commonplace State Department official'. He added that we should object to any semi-official American counsel for the defence – it would be only too easy for the American government to disavow him and even to accuse us of having engineered the whole thing.

However, we had begun our work. At this first session – which was to be followed by another in some months' time – we were primarily concerned with North Vietnam. We replied to two questions:

1 Had the United States committed an act of aggression as defined by international law?
2 Had there been bombing of purely civilian targets and if so to what extent?

Two American specialists in international law produced reports, at times long-winded but exceedingly interesting as a whole, that condemned the manner in which the United States had disregarded the Geneva agreements and had artificially set up a state of South Vietnam; they dissected this piece of humbug, which had deceived so many people, and they came to the conclusion that aggression had in fact taken place. The French historians Chesneaux and Fourmain and a Japanese legal expert delivered interesting accounts of the progress of this war; and they reached the same verdict.

Many of the reports dealt with attacks on the civilian population. Vigier, the French physicist, exhibited specimens of anti-personnel bombs and showed how they worked; and he conclusively proved that they could not be used against military targets – one sandbag gave adequate protection. These were weapons of a new kind: a mother-bomb contained some six hundred and forty smaller ones shaped rather like a guava or a pineapple; they were made up of a hollow metal shell with little spheres or needles inside. They exploded on hitting the ground, scattering these projectiles with great force; they could do no significant material damage, but they could kill or wound great numbers of people when they went off in all directions in the middle of a market or a village square. These anti-personnel weapons were specially designed for the massacre of under-developed communities: neither the roofs nor the walls of straw huts offered any resistance. The Pentagon denied these statements, and Vigier repeated his rigorous proof with an even greater wealth of detail.

Doctors and journalists who had carried out inquiries in Vietnam confirmed Alejo Carpentier's evidence, producing figures and names: leper-colonies, hospitals and schools had been deliberately chosen for attack. And churches too: no doubt the Americans hoped to rouse the Catholics against Hanoi – the manoeuvre had completely failed. Dr Behar and two Japanese, Totushimo and Kugai, particularly emphasized the systematic destruction of the dykes. Gisèle Halimi produced an excellent report on the two provinces she had visited: everything, place-names, figures, opinion-polls and statistics, was remarkably precise. So were her replies to the tribunal's questions: for the court interrogated all these witnesses at length. Their evidence was carefully sifted both to emphasize the important points that arose from it and to avoid any ambiguities that might be exploited by our opponents.

Other testimonies followed: we were told of many villages and cooperatives, far from any military objective, whose inhabitants had been killed in hundreds by fragmentation bombs, napalm or phosphorus; and doctors described the hideous wounds caused by these weapons. The evidence of Madeleine Riffault, a journalist who had lived in Vietnam for many years, was particularly interesting.

These reports were confirmed by diapositives and films, several of them made by Pic. They showed the burnt and mutilated corpses of civilians, and living, but horribly wounded, men and women. The most unbearable part of this was the children – children with their arms torn off, their faces a shapeless wound, their bodies eaten by napalm; children gazing out with bewildered eyes. The bodies burnt by napalm or phosphorous were like those we had seen in the photographs at the Hiroshima museum.

Two civilians who had come from North Vietnam to give their evidence appeared before us. The first was a young schoolmistress: she had been sleeping in the school at Quang Linh, a small, densely-populated agricultural town, when an explosion woke her. She hurried her pupils to the shelters. All at once something hit her on the back of the neck and made her shiver. Shortly after, she lost consciousness – a little ball had pierced her brain. It could not be extracted: she suffered from violent headaches and she was half blind. Her evidence was restrained and she spoke only of what she had experienced personally. Then a twelve-year-old boy took off his clothes to show us his horribly burnt body.

Van Dong, one of the leaders of the Front, brought forward two terribly wounded civilians from South Vietnam. One was so exhausted that he hardly spoke at all. His legs were covered with cheloids – they looked like still-raw wounds. The other replied to the tribunal's questions. He had a family to support, so he was not a combatant; but from time to time he helped repair the damaged dykes and bridges. He was burnt with napalm as he was going from one village to another in a coach that contained civilians only. One of his ears was seared away, his left arm adhered to his body, and his back was covered with cheloids – the whole surface was one huge purplish swelling. The doctors told us that there was a grave danger of these cheloids becoming cancerous.

As well as interesting or terribly moving moments such as these there were also some of deep boredom – evidence badly delivered or providing no new information. Since I got up earlier than usual in the mornings, there were days when I found it hard to keep awake: I drank mineral-water, I smoked, and I stared at the people who had come to watch. I noticed that some of the others made efforts of the same kind, not always successfully.

Some of the inhabitants of Stockholm were in favour of us; some were not. One day when we were having lunch at a little café near the tribunal with Alejo Carpentier, a man came up and handed me a flower. Another at a nearby table congratulated us warmly. Yet one morning a man appeared high up in the amphitheatre, shouting in Swedish, 'Get out! Clear off! Get out of here!' Then he ran away. At six o'clock every day, whether it was fine or snowy or wet, a few young men marched up and down in front of the House of the People carrying placards that read, 'The president of the tribunal to the gallows!' 'Long live the USA!' 'What about Budapest?' They too had long hair, and they seemed very peaceable. One day they organized a demonstration against the tribunal. We met them in the streets, carrying streamers and flags. Our supporters replied with a counter-demonstration. Both passed off without incident.

When the previous afternoon had been particularly wearisome, I began my exactly programmed day with some apprehension – a day in which there would be no chance of reading anything interesting nor of talking privately with Sartre. But there were many restoring

348

moments. Our breakfast, to begin with, which we had in the hotel restaurant: boiling coffee, carafes of fruit-juice, food and crockery were laid out on a big table; people helped themselves and took their things to a table. We usually sat with Dedijer, and the conversation went on afterwards as we travelled through Stockholm, touchingly beautiful in the morning mist.

And then after all I did manage to take a few walks with Sartre and then with Lanzmann, who had come to replace him for a few hours. In the very middle of Stockholm there is now a big ultra-modern shopping district with splendid glass buildings; but most of the time I strolled along the little streets in the old town. They were quiet and narrow and they called to mind the strictness of provincial ways; yet quantities of strip-tease joints were to be found there as well as cinemas that, to judge by the photographs outside, showed films for which daring is far too mild a word. Once I stopped in front of a bookshop: one of the windows was full of books about plants or animals; the display in the other was the most obscene I have ever seen in my life. Either directly or through keyholes were to be seen couples (all heterosexual: that was the sole restriction) engaged in every imaginable kind of amorous exercise. The photographs were in colour, and they were staggeringly specific.

I loved the nights at Stockholm. Sometimes they were icy cold; indeed, it sometimes snowed. Many of the buildings, particularly the restaurants, were lit by the flickering blaze of great torches; a row flamed all along the façade of the enormous opera-house. Next door there was a dance-hall with crystal chandeliers and a pompous restaurant adorned with green plants; it had an *art nouveau* bar on the first floor, with mosaics and plaster-work – festoons and astragals – that would have delighted Giacometti. Most of the customers were young – miniskirted girls and long-haired youths. We often dined there off smoked salmon and akvavit. Peter Weiss and his wife had taken us the evening we arrived. I had very much liked his play *Marat-Sade*, and it gave me great pleasure to meet him. He looked younger than his fifty years; he was very dark, he wore horn-rimmed spectacles, and his subtle, reserved features came to life when he talked. When we were with him we spoke not only about the tribunal but also about plays and Sade and all kinds of things. His very pretty, fair-haired, sharp-faced wife seemed very young, although she had a seventeen-year-old son by her first marriage; she was a sculptor and she also designed sets, particularly for

349

her husband's plays. She had a great deal of talent, as I saw when we went to lunch with them. The little flat was decorated with fine ceramics and ingenious model stage-sets. They had also invited Gisèle Halimi, Schwartz, Dedijer and Alejo Carpentier. The table was laid in the big kitchen; and as we talked we ate salad, cold meat and smoked fish.

One of the pleasant sides of our stay was being once more with people we knew and liked – with Alejo Carpentier and the Slovak writer Mnacko—and meeting others whom we also liked – Dedijer, Peter Weiss and his wife, and Basso, whom we often saw later in Rome.

And then again, in spite of some tedious moments, our work was utterly absorbing. Every day we made progress. Our presumptions became certainties; and our certainties were frequently and tragically confirmed. Even those of us who understood the question best, including Dedijer, said they had learnt a great deal. And what had been known beforehand took on a fresh value by forming part of the picture as a whole.

The local papers were ill-disposed: they spread the rumour that the tribunal was ruining itself by paying its interpreters whereas in fact the interpreters did not receive a penny; and instead of publishing photographs of the child whose body was one vast scar, they wrote that he was 'slightly burnt'. The French papers only gave rapid summaries of our sessions. But the *New York Times* provided long accounts of several. Trombadori gave very full reports day after day in *L'Unità*; and Radio-Luxembourg and the French radio spoke about the tribunal fairly regularly.

Our deliberations lasted a long while. The first evening we met in the amphitheatre at nine o'clock: and we stayed there until half past one the next morning. It was strange, sitting there in one's usual seat facing nothing but empty galleries. We set up committees to draft various reports that would give the grounds for our replies. I did not eat any of the indigestible sandwiches nor did I drink any coffee, for fear of not sleeping; and perhaps that was why I did not stand the strain as well as the others – by the end of the meeting my head was spinning and I was no longer sure of where I was or what I was doing there. At eleven the next morning we met again to discuss the exact wording of the questions. We took a vote and unanimously accused the USA of aggression and of attacking the civilian population. We did not reach agreement as to the responsibility of their allies. In the afternoon there was a public session at which Basso read out an excellent general synthesis. At half past nine that evening we continued our discussion in one of the offices: and this time I had crammed myself with coffee and corydrane. We unanimously condemned the complicity of Australia, New Zealand and South Korea; and all votes except for Kasuri's found the United States guilty not of aggression against Cambodia but of carrying out attacks upon that country. Yet when we came to deal with the documents prepared by the committees we could not reach agreement. Outside, day was beginning to dawn: above the empty town the sky changed from a dark to a vivid blue. 'It is growing light,' observed Kasuri, 'but in here the confusion is increasing.' At four o'clock we reached the end at last, and then we travelled through Stockholm in the coolness of the dawn. I slept like one of the dead for four hours. Many of the secretaries had worked all night. The interpreters were exhausted: they found these discussions where everybody talked at once far more trying than the regular meetings: one of them had to spend two hours in hospital having his throat treated.

At half past eleven we met again in the amphitheatre: Sartre read out a paper giving the grounds for our decision and then the questions and answers. The hall broke into applause. Everybody embraced everybody else. The Cubans wept openly; the Vietnamese had tears in their eyes.

I went to the Swedish television with Sartre, Dedijer and Dellinger. They refused to allow themselves to be made up. The Swedes asked us ill-natured, stupid questions which in any case had been answered at length during the sessions of the tribunal. 'Have you not attended a single sitting then?' asked Sartre. Never a one, they admitted. Dellinger spoke particularly well: he had gone to prison for pacifism and he had organized several non-violent demonstrations; so his statement that it was necessary to oppose violence with counter-violence had all the more weight.

For a while, when I was back in Paris, I had quite a nostalgia for this period that had just come to a close. The daily, conscientious work as a team – a work far removed from my own life – had given me the impression of a religious retreat: furthermore, I had felt totally committed – not the least vagueness, never a moment of lost time. Now it seemed strange to be able to arrange my days just as I chose.

351

It had been agreed that our last session should take place that autumn. In September 1967 Sartre and I went to Brussels for a preparatory meeting. We had all appointed to meet at the Auberge de la Paix; but some Maoists, feeling that their premises were more suitable than this Christian establishment, carried off the first to appear. There was a longish pause while a secretary recovered them. Ours was a surprising meeting-place – a dilapidated room with a big table in the middle of it, and upon the table glasses and bottles of water; a crucifix on the wall, the doors strangely painted and framed in silver-paper – one, which could not be induced to remain shut, opened on to a courtyard, and the place was terribly cold. After some time Gunther Anders, Statler and another Englishman appeared, then Halimi, Jouffa and the members of the secretariat. It had been suggested that we should hold our sessions in Copenhagen, and a couple of Danes were present. We discussed the recent meeting in Tokyo, the results obtained by the latest commissions sent to Vietnam, and the work of the committees. Dr Behar and Dr Dellinger arrived in the afternoon: Dellinger asked that the session should not begin before 21 November, because from 21 October onwards there were to be great demonstrations against the war in the USA, and it was hoped that would persuade some American servicemen to come and give evidence before the tribunal.

The demonstrations of which he spoke did in fact take place. On 21 October Dellinger led the great pacifist march that culminated in the siege of the Pentagon.

On 19 November 1967 we took the plane for Copenhagen. We did not wish to abuse the hospitality of the Swedes, and Denmark had agreed to receive us. There was no suitable hall to be found in Copenhagen, and the tribunal took up its quarters in a trade union building at Roskilde, some twenty miles from the capital. But as no hotel in that little town would house us, we put up in Copenhagen. I preferred this solution: the idea of being shut up day and night in a place the size of Roskilde had very little charm for me.

Dedijer was waiting for us at the airport. He told us that Schoenman was in the United States and that he would no doubt have difficulty in entering Denmark; so much the better—our discussions would be much less stormy without him. The tribunal was made up of roughly the same members as before. But Deutscher had died of a heart-attack in Rome; Hernandez had not come; and Fukishima deputized for Shorchi Sakata. That same day Sartre and Schwartz gave a press-conference.

The sittings began on the twentieth. Every morning a kind Danish woman, Madame Nielsen, brought her car to fetch us from our hotel. We drove along a motorway that ran through uninteresting suburbs and then a somewhat dreary countryside. On a bank at the side of the road stood an imitation windmill: a little farther on there came an immense lake, covered with white birds. Soon after this we reached Roskilde, whose streets were decorated with festoons and coloured lights, for they were already looking forward to Christmas.

The kings used to be crowned and buried at Roskilde, and in the middle of the town there is a fine fourteenth-century red-brick cathedral, the oldest in Denmark; it has green roofs and two very tall bell-towers. The interior is enormous and icy-cold; it contains some particularly ugly tombs and very beautiful wrought-iron screens. The restrained and majestic royal palace is just at hand, built of an elegant yellow stone. From the cathedral square one has a distant view of the fjord, its water lead-coloured or blue, according to the play of the light. Whether the sun shone or the snow was falling in heavy flakes, I always loved our arrival in this little town, with its two bell-towers reaching up towards the sky.

The trade union house, Fjord-Villa, was only a few yards away. At the door fair-haired bearded Danish youths with red arm-bands checked the people as they went in. We went upstairs, passed through an immense dining-room, followed a corridor that also acted as a restaurant, and reached the ceremonial hall, which was a ballroom on Saturday evenings: this was where the tribunal sat. The secretariat was installed on the floor above. The restaurant was very cheerful, with its great windowed bays opening on to the sky, the trees and the distant promise of the sea. Our court-room was rather curious: we sat on the stage, behind a long straight table; railings shut off the dance-floor, and raised galleries ran along three sides of the room. Three prodigious clusters of candelabra hung from the ceiling, and two red lamps were fixed to the balcony opposite us. As at Stockholm, we were arranged by alphabetical order, with the three presidents in the middle.

The first day the head of the trade union house made a short speech of very moderate welcome in Danish. Sartre repeated the

M*

tribunal's invitation to the American government. Neither the morning's nor the evening's session was particularly interesting. Nor were those on the two following days. Subjects that had already been dealt with in May were brought up again and we had the unpleasant feeling that we were going to bog down. Then again several of us, including Sartre and myself, were uneasy: three questions were on the agenda this session:

Had the American forces used or tried out new weapons forbidden by the laws of war?
Were the Vietnamese prisoners subjected to inhuman treatment forbidden by the laws of war?
Had there been acts tending towards the extermination of the population and coming within the legal definition of acts of genocide?

We were much concerned by this third question. If our answer was to be *no*, then it would be better not to put the question. And when we considered Hitler's extermination of the Jews we hesitated to liken the war in Vietnam to genocide. At the beginning of the session we had many private conversations on this problem; but we did not reach a decision. The first days the press said we were marking time. But in fact we were not. On Thursday a Japanese delegate brought forward a fresh subject, and he handled it in a most striking manner: this was the subject of defoliation. On the pretext of ensuring the army's safety along the roads and depriving the guerillas of shelter and of food, the Americans were spraying poisonous substances not only on the forests but also on the fields of rice, sugar-cane and vegetables. The operation in fact consisted in destroying the vegetation and of poisoning the population. It was a direct and an efficacious form of genocide.[1]

From that moment on our interest never slackened. Gisèle Halimi had been to America; the left wing provided her with important documents – newspapers, magazines, and a book on the village of

[1] On 1 January 1970 *Le Monde* reported: 'American scientists have recently called upon the Pentagon to stop the use of certain defoliants that cause malformations in the foetus. According to a Saigon journalist quoted by the *New Haven Register* of 1 November 1969 the South Vietnamese government is trying to keep public opinion in ignorance of the increasing number of babies who are born deformed. The American administration has just banned certain potentially dangerous defoliants in the USA, but they continue to be used in Vietnam. So although it has all the scientific information the White House accepts the risk of employing defoliants that may cause malformations in Vietnamese babies.'

Ben-Suc, which the Americans razed to the ground after having killed some of the men and deported all the inhabitants – and she passed on their contents to us. She had also recorded the evidence of American ex-servicemen. Taken as a whole, her material formed a crushing indictment. What is more, she brought three witnesses, and in the course of the following days they gave their evidence before the court.

The first, Martinsen, was studying psychology at Berkeley University; he had belonged to the 'special services' – that is to say he had taught Vietnamese government troops the art of torturing, and he himself had tortured prisoners. He was twenty-three and he was quite good-looking. At first he was very tense and even inhibited. Gradually he relaxed. He seemed to be in the throes of a very serious psychological conflict and to be easing his conscience by speaking out. 'I am an average American student and I am a war-criminal,' he said in an anguished tone. His evidence lasted an entire afternoon. The Americans claimed that only the government soldiers tortured and that all this was a matter between 'yellow men'; but this was 'just lies – pure falsehood'; he had beaten up prisoners himself; and he had seen American officers torture them by thrusting pieces of bamboo under their nails. It was usually enlisted men who actually did it, but always in the presence of a lieutenant or a captain, and the senior officers knew all about it. The victims often died. Martinsen gave a list of the methods used in interrogation. Everyone in the hall listened in tense, horrified silence.

The second witness was a young black named Tuck. He had not himself inflicted torture but he had been present both at torture sessions and at massacres. On the orders of an officer he had killed a woman who had not joined the group gathered on the village square quickly enough: if he had disobeyed he would have been shot at once. He described the 'interrogations'. He had seen one prisoner thrown from a helicopter and he told us how the wounded were finished off. 'Our officers think the only good Vietnamese is a dead Vietnamese.' He also said, 'Another very common thing was that if we were fired on from a village we had our "crazy moment" – the tanks and machine-guns blazed away for quite a while, firing at everything in the village, living or not.' He was asked how many of these 'crazy moments' he had witnessed, and he replied, 'I've seen them so often! A great many times – it was what you might call

355

quite usual.' He also spoke of those camps of deportees the Americans call 'strategic villages'. 'All the people I saw looked as though they were starving, and they were all in rags.'

After that we heard the evidence of Duncan, a 'green beret' and the author of *New Legions*, a book in which he exposed a great many American war-crimes. He was working for *Ramparts*, a magazine based on Christian principles and actively opposed to the war. First he described the training of the young recruits: on the pretext of teaching them to hold out against torture, they are shown all the different ways of inflicting it. He asserted that the Americans massacred all prisoners in Vietnam except for the officers, who were 'questioned'. They were then handed over to the government forces, who sent them to death camps. After this he gave us a long account of the 'strategic hamlets': he called them 'garbage dumps'. There are no beds or bedding, no water, no latrines. The stench is abominable. One third of the population in the south has been taken to them. The people have nothing to do. The women and old men just lie on the ground all day; the children beg and filch what they can from the American soldiers; the young women and even the little girls prostitute themselves for food.

All this evidence was exceedingly painful to hear: these men had actually seen the horrors they described, and this brought them tragically close to us. Their different accounts repeated one another in many points, and there was something both wearing and at the same time cruelly convincing about this reiteration. Even the journalists were impressed, and they gave full reports of these sessions. Martinsen in particular became very popular. At a press-conference he most ably explained the reasons for his presence at Roskilde. Pictures of him were to be seen everywhere.

Bardolini, a French journalist, also spoke of the hell of these 'strategic hamlets', and he showed us a film in colour – huge red tents with old men, women and children crowded into them. They were to be seen there in the doorway, sitting listless, quite despairing and bewildered. Theft and prostitution: this entire peasant population, accustomed to a strict code, had been torn away from all that had made up their lives, and they were losing not only their culture but also their code of ethics. It was a positive moral murder.

We also listened to the evidence of two Vietnamese women who had been tortured. One was an 'intellectual'; she was a pharmacist very well known in Saigon, and this had meant that she was tried

356

before being condemned to life-imprisonment, whereas so many others were executed without any process of law; it was also thanks to her wide-spread reputation that she was released after seven years. In her dark blue velvet national dress she was very beautiful and she spoke with great dignity and restraint. She had been appallingly flogged; her chest and belly had been trampled upon; the soles of her feet had been beaten; she had been subjected to the 'trip in a submarine', a variation of the mediaeval torture of the funnel; she had been hung up by her wrists; and one day they had tied her half-naked to a tree swarming with ants whose slightest bite causes intolerable burning pain and swellings. She also described the treatment inflicted upon other victims: when she spoke of the sufferings of one of her uncles her eyes filled with tears. She was sent to the notorious death-camp of Pulo-Condor. Among other forms of mal-treatment, one day she had a bowl emptied over her head – a bowl full of pus, the expectoration of consumptives, vomit, and water in which lepers had washed: I found this episode even more revolting than all the torture: one's imagination fails to encompass physical pain, whereas disgust can be relayed. The judges asked a great many questions and we admired the way in which she weighed her replies and declined to assert anything that she had not observed herself. The second witness was a Communist who had been burnt with red-hot irons and tortured to the point of becoming an epilep-tic. But she was less interesting than the other, because she read from a report that she had obviously not written herself.

Of all the evidence we heard, the fullest and most satisfactory was that of Dr Wolff: he had come straight from Hué, where he had been working as a surgeon in a hospital for the last two years. He was a West German: triangular face, fair hair, broad forehead, blue eyes, a cool, unemotional air. In January 1966 he had sent *Les Temps modernes* a remarkable unsigned article on the Americans in Vietnam. He spoke for an hour and he answered all our questions with striking precision and wealth of detail. He began by describing the appearance of the country seen from a plane – it was like the skin of a smallpox patient: eruptions everywhere, vast areas devastated by chemicals, a landscape of dust and ashes. He told us about the military sweeps and searches – the young men taken off by helicopter to interrogation centres, tortured and flung into prison, where they died. Whole territories were completely emptied of their inhabitants: there were four million 're-located' Vietnamese

357

in the South. Then he spoke of the wounds, the burns and the mutilations inflicted on civilian populations by the various anti-personnel weapons such as fragmentation bombs, napalm and phosphorus. He told us how, to amuse the nurses they were pursuing, American officers would take them 'hunting Viets' in a plane or a helicopter: all they did in fact was to machine-gun peasants.

This testimony was confirmed by an appalling film that Pic showed us: most of it had been shot by American soldiers themselves.[2] He used two screens, the one to show the moving pictures and the other to show the stills. Both were almost unbearable. In a hospital we saw the faces of adults and children literally melted, seared away, by napalm – faces in which the eyes, staring with horror, were the only remaining human features. Charnel-houses. Bulldozers destroying whole forests. Big leering Americans killing the little Liberation Front soldiers by kicking them in the genitals, shooting them in the back of the neck or, just for laughs, in the anus. And others cheerfully setting fire to straw huts.

Our public sessions alternated with private meetings, as they had done at Stockholm; and seeing that Schoenman had not managed to enter Denmark the private discussions went along quite calmly. He had landed one night at Copenhagen, but having no passport he had not been admitted. He went to Amsterdam and from there to Finland, where he spent a night in prison; and then to Stockholm, where he was arrested. Every day the papers gave news of his tribulations – they called him the Flying Dutchman.

Our deliberations on the subject of genocide continued. During one meeting in the villa of one of the tribunal's Danish supporters, Gunther Anders, Dedijer and Sartre produced interesting analyses of the whole idea; but still we remained divided. Sartre, myself and some others were persuaded that the Americans were war-criminals; but we nevertheless doubted whether they could be accused of genocide. The Cuban and Japanese delegates were indignant at our hanging-back: for them it was a political matter and our intellectual scruples seemed to them out of place and unnecessary. The meeting broke up without our having reached any decision.

But then gradually we became more and more convinced, above all after the reports on the 'strategic villages'. The Convention of 1948 defines genocide as a 'serious attack upon the physical and

[2] Pic had obtained photographs and films when he was in the USA.

mental integrity of the group – Deliberate subjection of the group to living-conditions that must bring about its partial or total physical destruction – Measures necessarily tending to hinder births within the group – The forcible removal of children.' Now the breaking-up of the families in these 'villages', their reduction to a totally aimless life, and the appalling sanitary conditions to which they were condemned had exactly these effects. And then again, the massive, lethal bombing and the spraying of poisonous substances amounted to extermination. As for the North, the bombing of the densely-inhabited districts of Haiphong and Hanoi no less clearly proved the intent to exterminate. Bost came to report the trial for *Le Nouvel Observateur*, and when he arrived he said, 'Above all, don't talk about genocide.' After three days he was convinced that we were obliged to talk about it. At the beginning of our deliberations Sartre read a paper he had written on this subject, and we all thought it absolutely conclusive. He established that this genocide was intentional and premeditated, for it represented the only possible reply to the rising-up of a whole nation against its oppressors. By its choice of this war, this total war, carried out *by one side alone without the slightest reciprocal action,* the American government had decided upon genocide. Up until this point, Gisèle Halimi and Matarasso had had reservations, but now, in a burst of enthusiasm, they cried, 'You have convinced us.'

I found the day's routine easier to cope with than I had in Stockholm. My room, like all the others in the hotel, had a table, a desk, and a bed that vanished behind a wooden screen during the day – a bed in the German manner, with an immense quilt instead of sheets and blankets. It was not yet light when I got up at seven in the morning, still heavy with sleep – we never went to bed before one o'clock. I loved watching the dawn break and the monotonous road slide past. Sometimes I had to struggle against drowsiness during the sittings: there were times when people were openly sleeping in the hall. But then all at once some piece of evidence or a film would revive my attention. During the early days we lunched at the Villa-Fjord; but the meals there were very bad and it was very noisy. We took to going to a quiet, old-fashioned hotel nearby – one of those that had refused to take us in, though nevertheless the manager had asked Dedijer to sign his visitor's book. Sometimes we would take a short walk, going down to the fjord: then back to our seats. When we left we walked out into the night, though we had never seen it fall. Madame Nielsen or her son drove us back to Copenhagen. She told us of some agreeable restaurants and we dined in them with Lanzmann, who had come to take Sartre's place for a few days, with Bost, sometimes with Schwartz and Dedijer, and sometimes just by ourselves. There were some charming places, including one called the Seven Nations, which had seven rooms, each decorated in the style of a different country: one was an igloo. But all the food was Danish. The cost of living astonished us: the cheapest bottle of wine was thirty francs and a bottle of whisky a hundred; the coffee was horribly expensive in spite of being very bad; even beer and akvavit cost a great deal, and the price of the meals was exorbitant. The reason for this was that all luxury articles are heavily taxed – the taxes go to fill the coffers of the social security and to maintain hospitals and old people's homes.

One aspect of the Danish way of life took us very much aback, for at that time the famous Copenhagen fair had not yet taken place. I went to buy papers at a little bookshop and stationer's in Roskilde, and there I saw a display of infinitely more remarkable books than those which had astonished me in Stockholm. In the window and inside the shop the jackets showed coloured photographs of people exhibiting themselves in every imaginable position – heterosexual and homosexual couples of both sexes, and little orgies of three or four partners. There were magazines and advertisements all beginning with Porno – *Porno-Magazine, Porno-Week-End* and so on. The children who went by paid not the least attention to this literature; they were far more interested in the toys and children's comics in another window. Bost was sufficiently curious to buy a porno weekly; he asked for it at a kiosk. The respectable old lady of the booth looked through her wares to find the most lurid and she asked the advice of her grand-daughter, a charming eighteen-year-old, who made her choice with the same unconcern as her grandmother. Yet by the time Bost had leafed through the magazine his eyes were as round as saucers. It seems that in *Porno-Week-End* and publications of that kind, individuals and couples offer their services and advertise for partners. I asked Madame Nielsen whether sexuality were particularly highly-developed in Denmark. No, said she, but the Danes will have nothing to do with secrecy, and everything happens openly: the explanation did not entirely satisfy me.

As in Stockholm, public opinion was divided as far as we were concerned. In a restaurant one evening some miniskirted young giantesses very gracefully offered us a bottle of champagne. Yet one afternoon I heard two reports, one after the other, and through the open door into the passage I saw two red flashes behind the glass – two charges of explosive. And on the evening of that same day a stone was thrown at the windows of a Danish friend who had entertained us.

We saw nothing of Copenhagen, because we were staying at the far end of the town and every morning we hurried straight off to Roskilde. But when Sylvie came to spend a weekend with me I took a short holiday. We hired a car, bought a guide to Copenhagen, and on the Saturday morning – a lovely blue day – we set off for the heart of the city. We walked along little streets, many of them forbidden to cars: some, bordered with old houses, were very pretty and the Christmas-trees, coloured lights and tinsel gave them a festive air. In the street with the bookshops, Sylvie fairly gaped with astonishment. We saw palaces, churches, monuments: the finest was the Exchange. It is an eighteenth-century building at the side of a canal; it has a long flat façade, green roofs, and a steeple made of three serpents' tails entwined. I found the Hôtel d'Angleterre, where I had stayed with Sartre in 1947, and the canal lined with old houses of every colour, and the sailors' bars where we had gone for a drink in the evenings. There were still plenty of bars along the quay but there were also boutiques that sold brilliantly-coloured men's shirts in shiny satin, obviously intended for Danish pouffes. I was told that by night the district reminds one of Saint-Germain-des-Prés: the sailors' bars had all disappeared. We also found a beautiful, solemn square, completely round and ringed with palaces. And the citadel – bright red eighteenth-century barracks with immense roofs and countless windows; they were lonely and silent, surrounded by earthworks now covered with grass and trees.

After that we drove out for a quarter of an hour to see a charming little port with narrow cobbled streets and colour-washed cottages – we might have been in one of Disney's prettiest cartoons. We lunched off salmon and akvavit on the verandah of a hotel looking out over the sea: at a nearby table two people were talking about the 'Flying Dutchman' in English. Then we went on to Elsinore. I had retained a fairly clear image of the elegant eighteenth-century castle; it was admirably placed right over the sea, but it did not call Hamlet to mind in the very least. We looked at the port and its great ships, and we saw the distant Swedish coast: it seems that the Swedes and Danes spend a great deal of their spare time going from one country to the other, the Danes buying their neighbours' coffee and the Swedes buying Danish butter. We came back by the beautiful road that runs along the coast. Night had fallen. A long street took us back to the hotel, and from one end to the other we passed under a series of arches of coloured lights – we might have been in a palace.

The next morning we went down to the sea, going right along that promenade where Sartre and I had wandered dismally in the midst of a Sunday crowd sweltering in the heat; now it was cold and there was no one about apart from a few anglers; the little mermaid seemed frozen stiff. We took refuge in the Glyptothek, which has many French Impressionists, some fine Rembrandts and Frans Hals, including the little portrait of Descartes that everyone knows from the reproductions.

Towards the end of the session Dedijer, Weiss, Sartre and I had luncheon at the Hotel Prinser with the affable, easy-going, friendly Stokely Carmichael. He had just finished a lecture-tour in Scandinavia, speaking against the war in Vietnam. It was too late for him to vote with the tribunal as a whole, and we agreed that he should make a separate statement: later, at a private meeting, we discussed its terms. 'I shan't look at it from a legal expert's point of view, because I don't believe in legality,' he said, smiling. Aybard gave a start: 'If you are a member of a tribunal you must not say that legality is nonsense,' he observed. This was the last of our meetings. It was decided that the tribunal should continue to exist but only in the restricted form of a centre for documentation and liaison, dealing solely with Vietnam.

This time too our deliberations took a great while. They were held in a Roskilde hotel, where a large room had been reserved for us. Halimi and Matarasso had prepared questions concerning the guilt of Japan, Thailand and the Phillipines, the aggression against Laos, the treatment of prisoners and civilians, forbidden weapons, and genocide. It took us the whole afternoon merely working out their definite phrasing, and after a hurried dinner in the hotel dining-room, the arguments went on. Some of the points in Sartre's paper on genocide aroused passionate reactions: were we to allude to other genocides, and if so to which? Some insisted upon addi-

362

tions or changes while others were bitterly opposed to them. It was five in the morning before we reached a compromise.

The last public session took place that afternoon, and the hall was crowded. Proceedings began with the projection of Pic's horrifying film, which was shown in deathly silence. Then Sartre read his report and Schwartz the court's verdict and its motivations, which had been drawn up by Halimi and Matarasso. Our unanimous decision was that the Americans did make use of forbidden weapons, that they did treat prisoners and civilians in an inhuman manner contrary to the laws of war, and that they were committing the crime of genocide. We also unanimously condemned their aggression against Laos and the complicity of Thailand and the Philippines. Three members of the tribunal considered that Japan helped the USA but that it was not an accomplice in the aggression against Vietnam. When the replies to all the questions had been delivered there was applause in the hall and on the platform, and people embraced one another.

I retain a lively recollection of this session. As at Stockholm, there was the pleasure of working as a team and that of keeping our friendships up to date; and we learnt even more than we had at the earlier meeting. The distressing side of it all was that because of the negligence of the press there were so few of us to profit from this impressive collection of documents, evidence and explanations. The essence was summed up in two paperbacks published by Gallimard: but too few people read them. American public opinion was overwhelmed by the revelation of the My Lai massacre in March 1968. But Tuck had already spoken of the 'crazy moments' that were 'ordinarily' allowed the soldiers. The number of victims at My Lai – 567, including 170 children – was certainly very much higher than the average; but these murders still formed part and parcel of a routine system: GI's had been fired on from the village; one had been killed; thereupon they had charged and wiped out the population. It was no doubt because these methods were so wide-spread that Nixon had the man responsible for the massacre of My Lai released – among so many war-criminals why choose him as a scapegoat rather than another?

Opposition to the war increased. With the presidential elections coming closer, many politicians declared themselves in favour of peace. It was heartening to see that a little country could victoriously resist the most powerful state in the world, and prove by its heroism that money, bombs and brute force could not accomplish everything. But in spite of its victory Vietnam must remain a devastated country for a great while. Its people have paid too high a price: my memory is too full of appalling images for me to be able to think of them without a stab at my heart.

During these last years the political event that affected me most, after Vietnam, was the Six Days' War. It interested me all the more because *Les Temps modernes* had just prepared a collection of documents on the conflict between Israel and the Arabs, and in this connection I had travelled to Egypt and to Israel with Sartre. Before describing my personal reaction to the Six Days, I shall first speak of these two visits.

We had never been to Egypt nor to Israel. After the war I followed the struggle of the Jews against the English with passionate attention: the tragedy of the *Exodus* moved me deeply. It was a great relief to me when the survivors of the death-camps found what I believed to be a safe refuge in a state that the United Nations had recognized, largely because of pressure from the USSR. But after that I had no particular desire to go to Israel. Egypt on the contrary, was a country I had longed to know ever since my childhood – the Nile, the Pyramids, the colossal statues of Memnon had enchanted me from afar at an age when impressions sink in so deeply that they can never be erased. The persecution of the Communists under Nasser's regime prevented us from going there. By 1967 he had become reconciled with his left wing and even those who had formerly opposed him urged us to visit Cairo. We had often met Lufti el-Kholi, a man of about forty who had spent long periods in prison under Nasser, but who now, without giving up his Marxist convictions, supported the regime. He was the editor of a left-wing review, *Al Talia*. He pressed us to come and see his country. Then again, the articles collected by Claude Lanzmann for our file had reawoken our interest in Israel. We decided to visit both Egypt and Israel, each country accepting the idea that we should also go to the other. Immediately before leaving for Cairo we learnt that eighteen young men accused of trying to reconstitute a Communist Party were still in prison: their families asked us not to give up our plan but to see whether we could induce Nasser to intervene.

We had been invited to go to Egypt by Heykal, Nasser's friend and spokesman and the editor of *Al Ahram*. He also asked Lanzmann. Ali el-Saman, an Egyptian journalist who was working on a thesis in Paris, had actively collaborated on the Arab part of the *Temps modernes* documentation – indeed, it was thanks to him that it had been brought into being. He went with us. On 25 February we all four took the plane.

Dusk was falling as we landed. We were welcomed by Heykal, a short, broad-shouldered, jolly man, very brown and energetic, and by the elderly Tawfik al-Hakim (his name means the philosopher's success), whose amusing *Journal d'un substitut* had been published in *Les Temps modernes* fifteen years before: he was primarily a playwright, and he was very well-known in Egypt. On his white head he wore a beret. He was said to be a misanthrope, but he cheerfully went about with us whenever it was not too tiring. Lufti el-Kholi was also at the airport, together with his young and agreeable wife Liliane, who belonged to the state tourist organization – she was to be our guide and interpreter. We were also introduced to Dr Awad and his wife. After a short press-conference we got into Heykal's car and he took us to Shepherd's Hotel, with the Nile only a few steps away. The river looked much the same as any other, but this was the true Nile, and it seemed fabulous that I was actually seeing it with my own eyes.

The next morning I hurried to my window. There it was, flowing along and looking green – but not eau-de-nil, however. On the other side of the water I saw some rather ugly houses, palm-trees, and on a bridge flags streaming in the violent wind. Followed by a positive escort – Ali, the el-Kholis and some journalists – we went to the Cairo museum. Afterwards we went back again and again, but even so we were far from having seen everything. It is much too small for the wealth of objects that it contains; it is badly lit, badly arranged, and the piled-up treasures are not shown to anything like their full advantage: yet none of this prevented us from being more and more amazed as we moved on. We were struck above all by the beauty of the ancient Egyptian sculptures, from 2778 to 2423 BC. They were carved in schist, diorite, limestone, pink, grey and black granite, or wood; and they were both realistic and magical. They represented kings, queens, priests, scribes, couples and families; all these people seemed to have been taken from the life and yet at the same time they were endowed with something of a sacred nature. One group, made of copper, showed a father and his son; another, the strangest of them all, a dwarf with his wife and children. There were also animals, genii, gods. In the later periods the statues became more conventional. The pharaohs all had to look like the god Ammon and all the other subjects were treated academically. The statues of Akhenaton – a whole room is devoted to them – are an exception to the rule. This revolutionary pharaoh, who reigned from 1370 to 1352, abandoned the name of Amenophis IV, renounced his ancestors, left Thebes, and turned government and religion upside down: he insisted that the sculptor should depart from the royal formula and show him as he really was: his statues, far larger than life-size, represent him as a man with a fat belly and a long, enigmatic, degenerate face. His court and family followed his example, and these works made a striking contrast with those of the preceding centuries.

We could only take a hurried glance at the bas-reliefs, usually found in tombs, that commemorate warlike expeditions or religious ceremonies, or that give a detailed picture of everyday life in ancient Egypt. We were shown the treasure of Tutankhamun.[3] We saw the wonderfully wrought gold mummy-cases that fitted over one another in the tomb; golden beds, chariots and sarcophagi: and alabaster canopic jars, unbroken throughout the centuries – it was one of the only burials that was never looted. It contained thousands of little figures, ornaments and objects; they are now to be seen in the show-cases and they give an extraordinarily living idea of the Egyptian civilization. Farther on there was a little room where the mummies of pharaohs and high officials sleep in their bandages. We lingered in front of cases filled with masked mummies and coffins belonging to the Graeco-Roman period. They came from the oasis of Fayum, Antinoë or Alexandria. There were also portraits, painted in wax on wood or canvas, that decorated the sarcophagi; they were mass-produced pieces of work, but they were striking in their modernity.

I had so often gazed at photographs of the Sphinx and the Pyramids that my first sight of them caused me no surprise. I had known that they stood in the outskirts of Cairo, but even so I was upset by the proximity of the dusty suburbs and by the number and the commotion of the tourists – Americans, dressed up as Palestinians, rode about on camels. Lacking perspective, I saw little more in that harsh light than so many stones piled on top of one another.

We went into the largest of the tombs. To reach it we had to creep

[3] As I have said, only a very small selection was sent to Paris.

on all fours up a steep corridor; the hot, vitiated air was stifling, and we came out again very quickly indeed. But I did admire the Pyramids when I plunged into the desert and saw them from a distance. There was one particular day when I was coming back from Alexandria and they loomed up in the most astonishing way. The setting sun lit up their sides and they looked quite small and transparent – wonderful abstract sculptures. Then they grew larger: their cold severity gave them the air of pure geometrical entities; and their rigid presence in the middle of a flat, bare landscape made me think of certain surrealist paintings.

The pyramid of Sakkara stands a little farther from the city, in the midst of the majestic ruins of a temple. Inhotep, the architect who built it, was deified after his death. Like most other tombs, it was broken into and robbed. The builders and the priests were in league with the thieves – it was one way of recuperating the wealth of the pharaohs.

As early as our first day, and often after that, we wandered about the streets of Cairo. In the modern town there are handsome avenues and luxurious shops; but it lacks charm. The old town swarms with life. In the crowded Sharia Mehemet Ali, lined with stalls and little restaurants, I noticed large tents made of richly-embroidered red cloth: they were something after the nature of funeral parlours, being set up to receive the dead man's friends and relations as they gather round his coffin. All the streets in this district have a mediaeval look: one seems to be in a big village rather than in a capital city – children play among the geese and chickens, and as Easter was approaching sheep stood tethered in the doorways of the little shops, waiting for the time of sacrifice. They all belonged to one particular breed, and the huge tail that hung between their legs seemed to be afflicted with elephantiasis. Now and then we would meet with a flock of ducks, or a cow. The streets were narrow, and sometimes the overhanging gables on either side reached out so far that they almost formed a roof. In the souks they sold jewellery imitated from Queen Nefertiti's ancient splendours – necklaces, earrings, brooches and bracelets made of gold and silver, sometimes set off with coloured beads. And amusing linen squares embroidered with pyramids, camels, asses and palm-trees. We had a drink at the Café des Miroirs, a famous place in Cairo that has inspired many writers. It stands in a lane that has now been roofed over, closed off with two doors, and provided with chairs and little

367

tables. It is crowded with knick-knacks and tinselly little objects of every kind, but above all with mirrors, all more or less cracked and tarnished. The owner sleeps on an old sofa from dawn till dusk, so well hidden under his blankets that Liliane told us she had once sat down on him. We went up to the citadel, which gives a very fine view over the town and its countless minarets.

There are a few splendid fortified gates remaining from the ancient city walls; but it is the mosques that are the most remarkable buildings in Cairo. Most of all I liked that of the Sultan Hassan, with its triple-galleried minaret, its majestic flight of steps rising to a monumental doorway, and its beautifully-proportioned interior. Seventy chains for great lamps hung from the ceiling – the lamps themselves have been taken to the Arab museum. In the Al-Hazar mosque, students were sitting in a ring round their teachers of theology: they stood up to shake Sartre by the hand.

Although Dr Awad had told us that the Egyptians were not Arabs, since intermarriage with the Arabs had scarcely influenced the indigenous race at all, Arabic civilization has left many traces in Cairo, quite apart from the mosques. One of the museums has collections of carved and inlaid wooden objects, copper, ceramics, terra-cotta, faience, carpets, lamps and miniatures. There is also a very beautiful house filled with Arab furniture and ornaments, silk, glass, and rock-crystal; the architecture is typically Arabic, and the first floor contains the harem, where the women could look through the mushrebiya and watch the festivities going on in the immense rooms below.

Kasr-esh-Shama, 'the castle of the candle', which is also called 'the Christian monastery', is the oldest part of the city, and it is entirely surrounded by walls – one goes in through a gateway between two towers. Here there is the Coptic museum, with beautiful examples of primitive Christian art, including pictures and masks from the Fayum. Nearly all the Coptic churches of the town are gathered within these walls. In the crypt of Saint Sergius we were shown the place where the Holy Family is said to have taken shelter during the Flight into Egypt. We also went to see the Ben Ezra synagogue, which is just at hand: it is built on the spot where, by tradition, Moses saw the Burning Bush.

Nothing in Cairo impressed me as much as the City of the Dead. It is a positive town, with buses running through it; but the houses have only one room, where the friends and relations of the dead man gather, and a courtyard, in which he is buried. As housing is scarce and expensive, families – caretakers or relatives – settle in; and at long intervals in the silent, deserted lines of tombs one sees washing hung out to dry, a child, a dog, or a hen. It seems that there are nights when this simulacrum of a town is strangely disturbing. Groups of people come to watch over their dead; they eat and they pray, and in the darkness one hears low murmurs and whispering.

The government put a light plane at our disposal, and we set off for Luxor and the ruins of ancient Thebes. A swarm of journalists and photographers went with us. When our flying drawing-room took off, at last with my own eyes I saw that landscape I had so often tried to imagine when I was a child – a vast desert, and in the middle of it a thin winding green oasis, the valley made fruitful by the waters of the Nile.

We stayed in a modern hotel next to the Winter Palace with its old-fashioned charm, where once the English used to come to warm their bones. Between us and the Nile lay a broad, palm-lined avenue; horse-drawn cabs stood along the side, and on the grass under the trees sat students, reading in their books or writing. The river was calm and wide, and sails passed up and down. On the far side a dry, broken landscape stretched far away into the distance. I found the peace wonderfully restful after the noise and bustle of Cairo. The sun shone down, but it was not too hot.

First we went to see the very beautiful temple of Amenophis II, just by the hotel. Then at sunset we took a boat and glided along the Nile, gazing at the lights on its banks. After dinner – immensely copious, as usual – as a special favour an archaeologist took us in a cab to see the temple of Karnak by moonlight. The first thing that struck me was its prodigious size: for more than two thousand years the architects never stopped making it still more complex and enormous. It is the biggest columned building in the world. You lose your way in a forest of pillars, and then all at once you are brought up in front of a pink granite obelisk or a colossal statue. I was astonished by the beauty of the papyrus-capitals. We walked through great courts and halls in a darkness pierced here and there by rays of moonlight. Then we went back to the cab, and as we drove through the soft night I listened with keen pleasure to the clip-clop of the horse's hoofs.

The next evening we returned to Karnak, and this time we walked along the avenue of great stone rams in front of the temple – it was

369

once a part of the long road stretching as far as Luxor. But when the god Ammon moved from the temple at Luxor to Karnak at the new year, he did so by boat, and with splendid ceremonies: deep in the Karnak temple there is a granite sanctuary where the sacred vessels lay – they are shown on some of the bas-reliefs that decorate the walls. We had not seen them the day before, and now we inspected them thoroughly. They give detailed accounts of the battles and victories of Seti I) and of his son Rameses II. The delicacy of these carvings contrasts admirably with the massive, somewhat overwhelming nature of the character of the architecture. The cylindrical columns and squared pillars are covered from top to bottom with figures of gods or symbolic patterns. Within the temple walls there is a sacred lake, and a little café has been built on its bank: we went there for a drink.

In the morning we crossed the Nile in a boat whose seats were covered with cloth printed with 'pharaonic' patterns. It was hot, and Sartre, Lanzmann, Ali and Lufti put on canvas hats that made them look like imitation cowboys. An archaeologist in a white cap and sun-glasses came with us. We drove to the Deir el-Bahari temple, founded by the powerful Queen Hatshepsut and dedicated both to her *ka* – her double – and to her father's. The sadly ruined building, rising in terraces, has been over-restored, but its decoration is exceedingly interesting. The queen often appears on the walls, and she is always represented as a man. She had a particular cult for Hathor, the cow, who has a shrine inside the temple: a bas-relief shows her suckling the queen. Another relief, a coloured one, describes Hatshepsut's no doubt peaceful expedition to the Land of Punt, that is to say Somalia. Others tell of her youth and of the festivities at her ascension. One perfectly preserved shrine, with a blue ceiling studded with stars, is dedicated to Anubis. And I remember carvings of Horus in the form of a bird that may be fairly compared to some of Brancusi's work. Hatshepsut was Thutmose II's wife and sister; she was regent in the time of her stepson and nephew Thutmose III, and when he succeeded he had her name erased from all the cartouches in the temple.

Then we went to see the necropolis of Sheikh Abd el-Gurnah, which stands upon a hill: from a great way off the mouths of the rock-tombs can be seen standing out black against its side. This was the burial-place of high Theban officials of the eighteenth dynasty. I had not expected the wealth of frescoes and bas-reliefs illustrating

370

their functions. We walked into the tomb of Khaembat, a scribe in charge of the granaries of Amenophis III: it contains six statues of the dead man, his wife and other relatives. On one wall he is to be seen presenting his accounts to the king. Another depicts scenes of country life. Menna was also an important scribe of this period: brightly-coloured frescoes show him carrying offerings to Osiris. Others again represent rural labours and the inspection of the harvest. In the tomb of Bekhmara, the governor of Thebes, remote tribes and nations wearing strange clothes and head-dresses bring him tribute. There were also various scenes from his life and a representation of his funeral feast, attended by his mummy. The most interesting tomb in the Valley of the Kings was that of Seti I. Several flights of steps lead down to it; then comes a corridor, ending in a little tomb with a shaft. In most burial-chambers the access is by a shaft, and this was sunk to mislead thieves; for in fact there is a carefully-hidden opening that leads to another room. From this second room a maze of passages and stairs runs off to other chambers: all their ceilings are painted and the walls are covered with bas-reliefs, paintings and drawings. These include seventy-five different representations of the sun; the king, Osiris and various other gods; the nations of the world, and some solar boats. This tomb is a museum in itself. Tutankhamun's astonished me by its smallness: when it was discovered, the treasures now shown in the Cairo museum were heaped up on top of one another. They had remained intact because one attempt at theft had been firmly dealt with and because rubble from a neighbouring tomb had subsequently blocked the entrance.

I was quite stunned by having seen an entire civilization pass by in front of my eyes in the space of a single morning – an entire civilization, with its wars, its ceremonies, sacred and profane, its occupations and its ordinary round of daily life. I can still see the faces of those women following the funeral procession and weeping passionately, and those dancing-girls and musicians with a scented cone on their lovely black hair. There were some periods when the figures were treated academically, but they are usually both hieratic and yet living, painted in clean, vivid, delicate colours. We should have liked to have had time to see them again and again; they were masterpieces, and for us their aesthetic value outweighed even their interest as documentary evidence.

On our way back, in the middle of a plain where herds were

grazing, we saw the colossi of Memnon; they represent Amenophis III, and with their plinths they rise to the height of a six-storey house. One, which was split to the waist by an earthquake, used to sing at the breaking of the day. But Septimius Severus had it repaired, and it has been silent ever since. These gigantic figures stood at the entrance of a temple that has now disappeared.

The next day our plane flew over the Nile and the old Aswan dam; the pilot brought us into his cabin so that we should have a comprehensive view of the new barrage before we landed there. At the airfield women in black veils and black clothes covered with shining embroidery offered us baskets filled with dates and hazelnuts. Then straight away a public-relations officer took us to the site: there, on foot and by car, he showed us the whole project, explaining it as he went. The dam was not yet entirely finished, but already it provided irrigation for a great area of desert. In the midst of the din we watched the prodigious activity of bulldozers, cranes and labourers. That evening a short film in colour showed us the inauguration of this enormous undertaking. It will be remembered that the USA refused to finance it – a refusal that led to the nationalization of the Suez canal in 1956 – and that the USSR gave the necessary assistance: and there at the opening ceremony was Khrushchev, standing next to Nasser. The main body of the dam was built by two separate teams of workmen, the one starting from the left bank and the other from the right; we saw them meeting in the middle and shaking hands – it was a time of immense, triumphant rejoicing both for them and the public. The workers we spoke to the next day still had this feeling; they were happy and proud at having carried out a labour that would mean a hitherto unknown prosperity for their country. For they knew very well that the huge reservoir called Lake Nasser would allow barren land to be brought under cultivation and that it would provide the electricity needed for industry.

As at Luxor, our hotel was modern; it had been built next to the old Cataract Hotel on a headland some way from the town, overlooking the Nile. There was a great stretch of rushing broken water – the cataract – with rocks sticking out of it: upstream the river was calm, and upon the smooth water boats moved gently along, their white sails rounding in the wind. The sun blazed down. A boat took us along by Elephantine Island to the little Kichenev Island, which is covered with an enchanting tropical garden. We saw the upper part of the temple of Philae: the island upon which it stands was submerged when the first dam was built.

Now the whole upper Nubian valley is under water. A coloured film showed us pretty white villages with brightly-decorated houses whose inhabitants have been taken elsewhere – the villages are now beneath the surface. I knew that UNESCO had launched a plan by which engineers from different countries should preserve the temples of Abu Simbel, and I very much wanted to see them. In the hydrofoil usually taken by tourists the journey is long and wearing; but the Ministry of Culture had arranged for the engineers' light plane to come and fetch us. There was just room for the pilot and three passengers – Sartre, Lanzmann and myself. We took off in the morning. For an hour we flew over a desert of white or pale yellow sand dotted with black rocks; it reminded me of parts of the Hoggar. Then we followed the Nile, which is now a vast, pure blue lake, and we flew just over the water. Here and there we could make out the top of a drowned palm-tree and abandoned houses on the water's edge – they would soon be engulfed, because the level was still rising.

An archaeologist was waiting for us at the airfield, together with Hochtief, the German engineer in charge of the work. Of the various plans put forward since 1959 it was the Swedes' that was chosen, and it was being carried out with the help of an international group. It consists of cutting out the temples and rebuilding them at the top of the cliff. First they showed us the original site and the steep path rising some hundred and fifty feet, up which the separate elements had been hauled. Huge, carefully-numbered blocks of stone lay about on the plateau in a vast roofless depot. Hochtief told us that in two years the temples would be entirely rebuilt, and the largest would stand at the water's edge, just as it had stood in ancient times, for the river would reach the top of the cliff. It looked very nearly complete already. At the entrance stood four colossal statues of Rameses II accompanied by very much smaller figures representing the Pharaoh's mother, wife and daughters. Above the façade sat twenty-two dog-faced baboons; and above the great gate stood another colossus, the hawk-headed god Re. The whole formed a most impressive and yet perfectly proportioned mass. In spite of the scaffolding that cluttered the inner halls, we were able to see the frescoes and bas-reliefs: they recount the wars of Rameses II, and one scene shows the great battle in which he overcame the Hittites. The temple will be set against an artificial cliff, and the site will therefore look exactly as it did in former times.

In front of the temple dedicated to Hathor rose six more colossi, representing Rameses II and his wife Nefertari, with smaller statues for their children. The interior of this temple too was decorated with bas-reliefs.

We had a quick look at the little town where the workmen lived and then Hochtief asked us to his house for a drink. We sat on the verandah while he told us more about the work in progress. We watched the Nile flowing gently below us between the sheer cliffs: I could have stayed there for hours, gazing at it. But we had to go back to the plane. The return flight was even more wonderful than the outward journey, because this time we followed the river all the way.

That was our last important visit to ancient Egypt. Not far from Aswan we were shown a chemical factory; and from Cairo we were taken to Helwan, where a great iron and steel complex has been set up. There we watched the pouring of the molten metal, forging-presses at work, machines that grasp the red-hot metal and shape it, and others that finish the object, delicately removing any roughness. New buildings were being erected, larger than the old. These are Egypt's first full-scale industrial achievements. They are not yet commercially profitable, the cost-price of the goods being too high.

Our friends wanted to show us the results produced by the irrigation of the desert in the Delta. They took us to Alexandria by car, and there we had luncheon in a dreary great hotel on the shores of a bay. All around us stretched the park of Montarah, which contains the former palace of King Farouk; it is a huge three-storeyed villa, as ugly as it is pretentious, and now it has been turned into a museum. Then we took the coast road. Most of the houses were shut up, because the people rarely come except in the summer. In the city we walked about busy, crowded streets, all rather wanting in character. Round a mosque a somewhat dismal local fair was going on. After dinner we went to watch belly-dancing at a cabaret. At the next table tall, fair-haired, blue-eyed young men gazed about them in bewilderment: they were United Nations soldiers. Two women danced, and they danced very well. Nowadays the law insists that the belly should not be naked, and they had veiled theirs with transparent muslin. The show was nothing like the debased imitations I had seen before; it was as abstract as a true flamenco and its interest was on the technical plane – the dancer must be in such perfect control of every muscle that her body remains motionless while her shoulders tremble and her belly quivers. It is a very tiring performance: when they stopped the two women were sweating heavily and they seemed exhausted.

The next day we left Alexandria by the desert road. We passed through the marshes that Durrell describes at the beginning of *Justine*. (That is the only part of the book I like.) Here there was once a lake, mentioned by Strabo, Virgil and Horace; and it still existed at the beginning of the nineteenth century, although by then it was partly dry. For strategic reasons, the English destroyed the dam that held back its waters, and they flowed out over a vast area. These last few years the government has been reclaiming the land. An agronomist explained the techniques employed. They have succeeded in bringing part of the arid country beyond the marshes back into cultivation; but it is in the part called the province of the Liberation that the most remarkable results have been achieved. Thanks to the Aswan dam the flow of the Nile has been regulated, and now a network of canals draws off a great volume of its waters. At the headquarters of the undertaking we were shown models of the new system of irrigation; we also saw one of the main canals. Then we were taken in charge by a general. In a private car we travelled over miles and miles of straight roads that intersect at right angles. On either side vast fields of wheat and barley showed green: the coming summer would see the first harvests. We were also taken to admire splendid newly-planted orchards. It is the army that cultivates this land, because the peasants are unwilling to leave their villages; but it is thought that they will come in great numbers once the houses have been built. The idea is to set up vast cooperatives, or preferably state farms. Soldiers had been lined up on both sides of the road and they waved little French and Egyptian flags. This tour of inspection was exceedingly interesting at first, but in time its monotony grew wearisome; our agronomist realized this, and he told the chauffeur to turn back. The general flew into a rage; he threatened to leap out of the car – men were waiting for us, flag in hand, some miles farther on; we could not leave them in the lurch. After a great deal of talking he agreed to shorten the trip. We were then taken on to an agricultural workers' centre: they too had been lined up, and as we passed through the ranks they waved flags and cried in unison, 'Long live Sartre! Long live Simone!' After a luncheon attended by forty guests, an official presented us with medals. 'Tell the world about the work we are carrying out,' he said to Sartre and me. And to Lanzmann he said, 'Tell our enemies and our friends the work we are carrying out.' This was the first and last time in our journey that anyone alluded to his being a Jew. He was always treated with the same courtesy that we met with ourselves.

We were the objects of a highly-organized – though more spontaneous – acclamation again some days later, when we visited the village of Kamshish, which had become famous because of its struggle against the feudal landowners. Nasser's attempted agrarian reform forbade them to hold more than about a hundred acres. But they easily got round the law by transferring part of their estates to the nominal ownership of members of their family, their dependents or their employees: it was difficult to foil their manoeuvres. A Kamshish schoolmaster, a local leader of the Socialist Union, set about the Fikki family and denounced their fraudulent activities. He wanted to have their houses requisitioned for the social services of the village. One night he was shot down in the street. His wife called for justice and she carried on with the struggle led by her husband. The government arrested the whole Fikki family, and it set up a commission for the liquidation of feudalism, which discovered many cases where landowners had murdered peasants. The commission launched an anti-feudal campaign in the villages, holding Kamshish up as an example. We went there, accompanied by our usual escort and by the prefect of the region. An immense crowd came out to meet us. They unfolded banners that said 'Long live Nasser! Nasser is the peasants' friend!' And as loud as ever they could they shouted 'Long live Sartre! Long live Simone!' A hysterical schoolmistress made a placid group of black-clothed peasant-women cry 'Long live Simone! Long live Simone!' Yet the villagers did feel a genuine interest in us. Our bodyguards found it hard to clear the way. We were shown several houses made of unbaked brick that the peasants had just built themselves. Then we went into a large farm building that could only hold a small part of the crowd: those who were left outside tried to burst open the door that had been closed in their faces, not without difficulty. The schoolmaster's widow, a very dark young woman with a gentle yet energetic face, sat beside us on a dais together with the prefect and some other officials. She made Sartre the present of a djellaba and she gave me a necklace. We had an uninteresting conversation with the audience. The prefect and his wife took us off to lunch.

The visit did not tell us anything about the condition of the fellahin. The fact is that throughout our stay we never came near them. We only observed that the villages we passed through on our way to the pyramids were exceedingly poor. The houses were built of mud; the camels and oxen were very thin; and under the black veil that framed their faces the women, though often beautiful, were emaciated. The great problem that Egypt has to deal with, if the rural standard of living is to be raised, is that of over-population. Nasser had launched a campaign in favour of birth-control. I saw the centres for advice and consultation. There were many of them. But a young peasant woman could never consent to use contraception until she had at least five or six children. The fellah looks upon his sons as his greatest wealth; when he grows old – and he ages quickly – he needs them to work the land. In spite of the achievements in the desert areas the perpetual increase in the number of mouths to feed allows no improvement in the peasants' way of life.

On a different plane, there is another problem by no means properly solved – the status of women. The charter upon which Nasser based the regime in 1962 calls for equality between the sexes. But the tradition of Islam is opposed to this equality, and for the moment it is tradition that prevails. At the beginning of my stay I met a few Egyptian feminists – doctors, lawyers, journalists. Among them was a woman who had been the first to declare war on the veil,[4] before 1914; she was a very old lady, but she was still fighting. They gave me a great deal of exact information. Women's social, civic and economic rights are by no means the same as men's. When a father dies his daughter receives a much smaller share of the inheritance than his sons. It is very hard for a woman to get a divorce, whereas her husband can repudiate her almost without formality. In ordinary life the gulf is still wider. There are very few women who work away from home, and when they do they earn less than men. They rarely go out. I never saw any women on the terraces of the Cairo cafés. My informants were disgusted by this discrimination. I attacked the question when I spoke to the students at the university in Alexandria. According to the Charter, I said, socialism could not exist so long as women were not equal to men.

[4] As it is generally known, this war was won.

'Within the limits of religion,' cried some male voices. I returned to the subject at length in a lecture I gave in Cairo. I accused the Egyptian men of behaving like feudalists, colonialists and racists towards women. I showed that the arguments they advanced to justify their conduct were exactly the same as those used by the former colonists against the people they colonized; and I condemned their attitude in the name of the battle that they themselves had fought for their own independence. The very large number of women in the audience applauded frantically. Several of the men were displeased. When I left an old gentleman accosted me; he was carrying a paper he had written on the Koran. 'As for women's inequality, madame, it forms part of religion – it is written in the Koran.' I left him arguing with the old journalist who had been one of the pioneers of feminism. Other women came up to thank me, sometimes behind their husbands' backs.

Yet we did know one pair, Lufti and Liliane el-Kholi, who seemed to be on a footing of perfect equality and who were entirely in favour of it. She was thoroughly typical of the still far from numerous class of truly liberated women. She was pretty, stylish, very 'feminine', and she looked after her child and her home; but she also had a job. She was a Copt, that is to say a Christian. She lost her faith when she was fourteen, during a pilgrimage to the Holy Sepulchre. A nun showed her a hole where the Cross had been set up; just as Liliane was about to put her pious hand into it, the nun thought again: 'But now I come to think about it, are you Roman Catholic or Orthodox?' 'Orthodox.' 'Then for you, it's the hole over there.' And she pointed out another. For Liliane everything wavered, and afterwards she stopped believing. She had carried her studies to a very high level and she wanted to go to Paris to work for the *agrégation* in philosophy: her father forbade it, because Paris was a place where people kissed one another in the streets. But in spite of that she had a profound knowledge of French language and literature.

We took part in the many discussions on Egypt's current problems. We met the editorial staff of *Al Talia*; the minister of culture; Ali Sabry, the head of the Socialist Union, the single party to which all Egyptians automatically belong; some Marxists and a variety of public figures. When we were present, no one questioned the existence of a single party, the absence of trade union activity, or the policy of state-direction. They were essentially concerned with the difficult struggle against the feudal landowners, with over-population, and above all with the existence of a 'new class' which has taken the place of the former bourgeoisie but which is also composed of privileged people. The greater part of industry has been nationalized, but the state needs large numbers of executives and technicians, and to obtain their services it is forced to pay them highly. The more the country develops the larger becomes this category of profiteers; and they have to be tolerated because they are necessary. The members of this 'new class' are individualists and reactionaries who formerly belonged to the petite bourgeoisie.

Towards the end of our stay Nasser received us at his residence in Heliopolis. Lanzmann, Ali and Heykal came too. We talked for three hours, sitting in a large drawing-room and drinking fruit-juice. Nasser had nothing of the 'white-toothed grin' that some ill-natured photographs gave him: his voice and his expression had a quiet, somewhat melancholy charm. It was said that his friend-ship for Heykal was explained by the contrast between their natures, the one overflowing with jovial vitality, the other uneasy, worried and turned in upon himself. Nasser listened attentively; and he answered without haste, weighing his words. I asked him about the status of Egyptian women. He was a feminist, and he had encouraged one of his daughters to carry on with her studies to an advanced level. When the section of the Charter that called for equality between the sexes was being discussed, someone raised the objection, 'So every woman will have a right to four husbands, then?' Nasser replied that Islam first appeared in what was a widely polygamous society and that in fact the Koran, far from encouraging polygamy, tried to make it impossible by laying down a great number of restrictions. For his part, he would like to see it disappear. He believed in God, he added; but as far as religion was concerned it had thwarted him at every step. Sartre mentioned the eighteen young men who were then in prison: he asked whether it would not be possible to hasten their trial. Nasser had obviously been told of this approach by Heykal; he smiled and said, 'A trial? By all means. But they run the risk of a ten-year sentence. Our idea was that it would be better to keep them in a little longer and then let them go quietly.' 'That would be the best solution, of course,' said Sartre. At the end of our conversation Sartre broached the Palestinian problem. 'There is no question of the Arab states taking charge of the refugees,' said Nasser. 'But if Israel took them in, would you recognize Israel?' 'With one million two hundred thousand Palestinians, Israel would no longer be Israel: it would burst apart. It is impossible for them to agree.' 'What then?' 'What then?' repeated Nasser in a puzzled tone. 'War? But it's all very difficult.' He did not seem in the least inclined to run the risk of an adventure of that sort.

From the beginning of our voyage it had been agreed that we should go to see the refugee camps in Gaza. Once more we and all our troop climbed into a plane and flew over the desert: beneath us stretched the only road across it, perfectly straight, its macadam shining in the sun. We passed low over Ismailia, the Suez canal with its embankments and its ships, and the Bitter Lakes. Unfortunately a violent wind buffeted the plane: Lufti was green and I was horribly queasy by the time we landed at el'Arish. A Palestinian couple who had lived for many years in Lebanon took us in their car and we drove across a beautiful desert landscape. At long intervals we saw tents among the tumbled rocks – Bedouin and their black-clothed, heavily jewelled women. At the frontier of the Gaza strip the car stopped. Before we set off again we were given flags of the 'Palestinian liberation forces'.

The camp that we visited in Gaza was in fact a village, and a very wretched one. It was most disagreeable walking about its streets with a whole band at our heels – our Egyptian escort and the Palestinian leaders. They took us into disused barracks crowded with families of refugees, and into other equally bare, cramped dwellings. Men and women told us how they longed to see their own land and houses in occupied Palestine once more. In the street we spoke to some children: one wanted to be a doctor, another a soldier. Our guides noisily lamented these people's appalling situation; but were they not to some degree responsible for it themselves? Were they making the most efficient use of the considerable relief distributed by UNWRA?[5] There was no lack of space. Why had not the refugees been encouraged to build houses like those put up by the peasants of Kamshish, for example? These questions occurred to me at the banquet given by General Hoshi, the Egyptian governor of the Gaza zone, for a hundred guests: I also wondered why there was this great spread of food. It took away my appetite.

We were taken to the frontier. Far off we could see the Israeli flag,

[5] United Nations Work and Relief Administration for the refugees in the Near East; it was set up by the United Nations in 1949, and most of its money comes from America.

and in the no-man's-land between the two countries, blue-helmeted UN soldiers. We visited a school, an embroidery workshop, and an institution where the sons of Palestinians killed fighting the Israelis are brought up. The children wore their national costume, and to the sound of a trumpet they sang a warlike song about returning to their own country. Many cafés in Gaza are called 'the café of the return'.

At dinner there were even more guests than there had been at lunch, and the meal was still vaster and more lavish. With a disgusted air, Liliane whispered, 'And all this while the people outside are starving!' Afterwards everybody gathered in a large room and there was a discussion between Sartre and the Palestinian leaders. He asked them what would happen if the Arabs won a war against Israel. Why, in that case all the Jews would be sent back to 'their own' countries, except those from the Arab states – they would have the right to stay. The Nazis' extermination of the Jews had been a crime; but, said one of Shukairy's lieutenants, a crime was not put right by committing a 'greater crime'. So, he added, without realizing his own inconsistency, we should not hesitate to bring about a world war in order to obtain justice. The conversation was tense, because Sartre hoped that a means might be found of reconciling the right of the Palestinians to go back to their country and Israel's right to existence: the return of the refugees might be spread out over several years, for example. But the Palestinians insisted that the Jews should be expelled from occupied Palestine. Their indignation and their hatred were no doubt sincere, but they were expressed in a high-flown bombast that rang false. Sartre ended by saying, 'In Paris I shall give a faithful account of the opinions I have heard here.' 'That's not enough,' said one of the Palestinians angrily. 'We should have liked you to share them.'

Liliane and Lufti had felt most uneasy at the Palestinians leaders' violence and want of logic. They too found the atmosphere of Gaza stifling. We were wholly persuaded of the reality and the gravity of the problem; but the incessant propaganda to which we had been subjected all day long wore us out. And the leaders who had entertained us so much too lavishly appeared to be living in an unreal world of words, totally remote from the destitution of the masses.[6]

[6] After the Six Days' War these leaders, together with Shukairy, lost all influence. The new men are of quite a different kind.

The next morning we went for a drive in Gaza: the shopping street and the market gave an impression of poverty. When we had driven along by the sea, the chauffeur suggested taking us to a densely-populated part of the town. It was in fact another refugee-camp, but it seemed distinctly less wretched than the first. There were piles of oranges at the edge of the pavement. We got out of the car. Liliane stopped a woman and began talking to her; Liliane was as eager as we were to have a free, open conversation with someone who seemed free from pressure. Of course the refugees hated Israel. But what did they think of their leaders? What assistance did their leaders obtain for them? How did they live from day to day? They had barely exchanged more than a few words before we saw two local bigwigs hurrying towards us. This woman was incapable of answering us, they said: what she had said did not count. We did not press the point, but our uneasiness increased. We had the feeling that the day before the refugees' misery had been displayed with altogether too much zeal and satisfaction; that their groans and complaints had been firmly put on to order. It was pointless, because the problem was quite unchanged even if they did eat oranges occasionally and if some of them were not too discontented with their lot. On the return flight we talked it over with Liliane: this visit had depressed her, too. As she rightly said, Egypt was too poor to take care of all these people: but she also said that the Jews should have stayed in 'their own countries' after the war, thus showing that she knew nothing whatsoever about the Jewish question as it existed in the West.

In Cairo Heykal told us that Nasser had freed the eighteen prisoners of whom Sartre had spoken. No doubt he had intended to do so long before: but nevertheless it was very handsome conduct.

The journey was coming to an end. It had been as pleasant as it was interesting. The only drawback was the swarm of journalists who followed us everywhere. But we got along very well with our usual companions, the keenly intelligent and cheerful Ali; Lufti, entirely devoted to his ideas; and Liliane, as kind and as attractive as she was highly cultured. Heykal, who enchanted us with his gay vitality, was with us less often. Almost all the Egyptians we met spoke French. French-speakers had been chosen to accompany us; but quite apart from that many Egyptians have their children taught the language out of reaction against English domination.

We had been splendidly entertained by the Heykals, the el-Kholis and the minister of culture. At these parties we dined at small tables, which meant that one could change places and partners during the meal. The buffet of hot and cold dishes was always magnificent – among other marvels I remember a huge turkey and a whole sheep, cut up in the kitchen and then put together again. One evening Heykal asked us to a restaurant-ship moored in the Nile. As we ate we heard the lapping of the water, and through the portholes we could see the lights of Cairo : he had sent for an excellent dancer, and once again I admired the genuine belly-dance. One evening the aged Tawfik al-Hakim invited us all to a restaurant near the pyramids; it was run by former landowners who were friends of his, and he wanted to see how they were fitting into their new way of life. They were away, which was a disappointment for him; but we had great fun. The pleasant dining-room was all upholstered in red, lit by lamps with pleated shades and filled with soft music. Tawfik was the object of a great deal of teasing : he had been married these last twenty years and yet no one had ever seen his wife. He explained that as his plays were so misogynistic he was afraid the papers would make game of his marriage. He had made his wife promise never to go out with him anywhere at all. One of the guests terrified him by threatening to make a surprise visit to see his wife at last and to find out what was at the bottom of it all. We also ate chick-pea rissoles and skewers of meat in popular restaurants; and in one café in the middle of the town Sartre and Lanzmann puffed at a hookah without much result – Lufti and Ali smoked theirs very skilfully indeed.

The last evening we were asked to a farewell dinner in the House of the Arts – a sixteenth-century Arabic building with beautiful Arabic furniture and painted ceilings. Almost all the people we had met were there, gathered about big low round tables covered with brass trays. During the meal there was a wonderful show – belly-dancing, a conjuror, a whirling dervish and above all a marvellous male dancer. We were given two funerary masks from the Fayum.

No airlines operated between Egypt and Israel, so the next day we took a plane for Athens. Nobody was waiting for us at the airport. This was both unusual and restful. We spent the morning on the Lycabettus and the Acropolis, and then we boarded another plane for Tel-Aviv. Lanzmann went with us, but only for three days.

We were somewhat alarmed at the idea of having to face still more welcoming-ceremonies, of having to get used to new faces and going back to life in public. But we very, very much wanted to see Israel. We had been invited by a reception-committee that included figures from the political, university and literary worlds. Flapan, a member of Mapam whom we had met in Paris, had organized our journey; and he was one of the group waiting for us at the airport. Lanzmann introduced Monique Howard, an agreeable dark young woman who was to be our interpreter. A young man with reddish hair spoke to me and suggested that he should act as our guide and protector from pests; I thought he might be one himself, but in fact Ely Ben-Gal soon became one of our friends. Sartre had a brief talk with the journalists in all the noise and heat. Then Schlonsky, an elderly writer born in Russia, took us to the Dan, a hotel on the sea-front.

When I opened my window in the morning, there was the sea, and it was beautiful. It is Tel-Aviv's only charm. The town is full of life, but its straight streets are quite devoid of character. The richest, Dizengoff Street, is far less luxurious than the great avenues of Cairo. There are many shops, but the clothes and the other goods displayed in their windows are not of high quality. The cafés and restaurants are reminiscent of those the students go to in the Latin Quarter.

We visited Jaffa, just outside Tel-Aviv; we liked its fortifications, its ruined castle, old houses and broad flights of steps; and it was fun to wander about the flea-market.

Then we travelled about all over the country. Flapan preceded us to the places on our itinerary and arranged each visit. As he did not speak French well, he was afraid he might be in our way, and he seldom made an appearance. It would be impossible to imagine a more discreet way of looking after us.

I knew that the inhabitants of the kibbutzim amounted to no more than 4% of the population of Israel, that most of the settlements were no longer made up of pioneers, and that they were kept artificially alive in a capitalist economy. But they had stood for such a stirring adventure at the beginning that I was exceedingly eager to see them; and we did in fact spend quite a long time in these communities. At the Merharia kibbutz we were welcomed by the Mapam leader Meir Yaari, who had a long conversation with Sartre while I was talking to a group of women. At Degania B, the 'mother kibbutz', the oldest of them all, our host was Kaddish Louz, the president of the Knesset; we lunched with him in the communal dining-room and then had coffee at his house. His wife spoke most feelingly of the first days of the little community, long ago, before any of the trees had been planted or the houses built and when there was no road; and she told us how they had built it all up from nothing by the sweat of their brow, the women working as hard as the men. The frontier kibbutz of Laavat Habashan lies at the foot of a hill, on whose top the lights of the Syrian forward posts can be seen shining in the darkness. Once, Syrian shell-fire had destroyed the dining-room: fortunately it was empty at the time. After the meal we gathered in the basement, which serves as a club and a shelter; they also showed us deep, well-equipped trenches where they took refuge in times of danger.

The two questions that interested me most were the status of the women and the attitude of the young. I had already discussed the first with a group of professional women in Tel-Aviv: one was a former pioneer, now aged sixty. In the early days, she told me, their motto was 'never mind' – they ignored all differences and behaved as though they were men. This is not the case at present; some younger women – an actress and an architect – told me that they accepted the division of tasks. They felt that they served Israel just as well by carrying out their 'women's work' as by competing with the men; and that was what really counted in the end. In their opinion, the question of feminism did not therefore arise in Israel.

In the kibbutzim my informants confirmed the fact that heavy labour did wear women out. There were exceptions – Ely Ben-Gal's wife insisted upon driving a tractor, like a man. After two failures she was accepted as a tractor-driver; but her stubbornness aroused little praise. At Degania B the women complained that theirs was not a very interesting life. They might be teachers, or they might look after crèches or infant-schools or the chicken run, or they might do the cooking; but they did not play a direct part in production. They also admitted that politically they were more timid and less active than the men. Yet nevertheless they felt that it was they who had the greatest social responsibility: the men look after the land, they told me, but we look after the community. According to them, the women of the earlier generation had made a mistake in giving up too much of their womanliness: in this generation they were calling for free time to take care of themselves. At Merharia the opinions I heard were rather different. The part they played within the community did not satisfy the young women I met there, and they wanted to fulfil themselves, to express their personalities in a home of their own. They disapproved of the communal way of bringing up children with the parents only seeing them for a few hours a day. One little dark-complexioned woman wanted to look after her children herself; she felt frustrated, not having complete charge of them. A beautiful blonde girl told me that she was full of complexes because she had not lived with her parents; she was now a children's nurse, and she thought it was not very good for the very small ones to sleep away from their mothers, with an attendant who changed every week.

This view is contradicted by Bettelheim in *The Children of the Dream*, which is devoted to the upbringing of children in the kibbutzim; according to him the absence of the mother is amply counterbalanced by the constant presence of the other children.[7] Yet on the other hand his inquiry does support the conclusions that I regretfully drew myself: it seemed to me that the women of the kibbutzim accepted the traditional division of tasks and that household work was despised, being unproductive – men were never to be seen in the laundries. Even though a man may serve in the canteen from time to time or do the cooking, he looks upon these jobs as of secondary importance – his real life is elsewhere. Whereas the women have no prospect apart from keeping the daily routine in motion.

The real feelings of the young are hard to discover. For them the kibbutz is no longer an adventure. 'We feel too sheltered,' said some of them. At Laavat Habashan they also told us that many would leave if they dared; but they feel the eyes of the community upon them, and they dread its disapproval. Even so, a fair number do go away, either to form new kibbutzim in the Negev desert or to settle in Tel-Aviv. At Degania B only one of the Kaddish Louz's three children has stayed – he is a teacher: another is in the USA, while his daughter, a well-dressed young woman with lacquered nails, far more elegant than the others in the kibbutz, is studying philosophy at Tel-Aviv. She was asked why she had made up her mind to leave,

---

[7] Bettelheim shows that this 'peer-companionship' amounts to a bringing-up unlike that within the family and that it produces different results. But there is no room here to give a full account of his book: those that are interested in the problem should read it.

386

but she did not like to answer with her parents there; her father said with a laugh, 'She's working at philosophy so as to discover her reasons.'

Ely told us that there were great differences between the kibbutzim. There were the 'good ones', where the people got along well together and which throve; and there were the 'bad ones', where the production was inadequate and the morale low. The system might be either more communal or less: the possibility of travelling, of having use of a car, and freedom of consumption are not the same in all. In Ely's kibbutz, near the Lebanese frontier, all the members were young and progressive, and they practised the strictest equality; it was, said he, an excellent kibbutz.

Besides kibbutzim there are the moshavim, villages where the life is not communal. The two can be told apart from a distance, because a kibbutz has large buildings where this life goes on, whereas the moshavim have none. We went out to see one; it was inhabited by English-speaking Indians and by immigrants from North Africa, with whom we conversed. They had been employees or small shopkeepers, and at first they had found it hard to adapt themselves to their new occupation of growing flowers. But they soon learnt how to speak Hebrew and cultivate the land, and now they are satisfied with their life. They lived in comfortable little houses, furnished in a petit-bourgeois style. The women looked after their homes and children.

Patish, a member of Mapam, took us to a factory that made metal pipes; there too most of the workers came from North Africa, though some were from the Yemen: of all the Eastern Jews it is the Yemenis who adapt themselves best. We watched them at work and afterwards we talked and drank coffee with them. They spoke angrily of the Arabs, who prevented them from corresponding with those members of their families who had remained in Tunisia or Algeria. If there were a war, they would be ready to fight. (That was the only bellicose remark that I heard in the entire journey.[8]) They all said they were satisfied with their pay and their work. This was no doubt true, because the factory belonged to the Histadrut, which treats its employees unusually well.

The Histadrut is the great labour organization and its primary

[8] Writing in *Le Nouvel Observateur* at the end of April 1970, Vidal-Naquet states that the only Israelis he heard express a decided hostility for the Arabs were those from Arab countries.

function is to defend the interests of the wage-earners. The social
security administration is under its control: if the worker is not a
member of the Histadrut he does not receive social insurance benefits, so the great majority belong. It cannot be looked upon as a
trade union, however. It was set up some fifty years ago, on a
national, not a class basis. Its aim was to create an economic infrastructure that would allow the creation of an Israeli capitalism. It
became the country's largest employer, controlling a quarter of the
national production. It is the only 'trade union' in the world whose
statutes include a political programme; and its elections are carried
out upon the basis of political parties, not of trade organizations. It
is neither revolutionary nor even reformist; on the contrary, it
represents the surest guarantee of the established order. Politically,
economically and socially, the Histadrut plays a very important
part; and it supports the government's programme. It brings pressure to bear on the workers to prevent strikes. If ever a class-war
were to develop in Israel, it would be in spite of the Histadrut and
in opposition to it.

We had a conversation with the Histadrut leaders on the top floor
of a tall building in Tel-Aviv. Several heads of department were
present, but they scarcely uttered a word because the general secretary talked all the time. He was a member of the Mapai, and he
gave us propaganda instead of information. By dint of hard questioning I did make an official – she too was a member of the Mapai
– admit that in the labour-market there was a great difference
between men and women. Far fewer women are employed; they are
given the least interesting work; and the principle of equal pay is
evaded.

We got on very badly with the members of Mapai and generally
speaking with all the right-wing Israelis. The situation was by no
means the same as it was in Egypt, where only one party existed
and where no one argued about the government's policy. As Sartre
had been invited by Nasser's spokesman everyone, apart from the
Gaza Palestinians, was friendly. Israel is a democracy: it has many
political parties and within each party there are different tendencies.
Obviously the right wing was hostile to Sartre. The right wing with
one exception – Yigal Allon, then the minister of labour and a
member of the Ahdut Avodah. His feats of arms are legendary and
he is the idol of the right and of many of the young; we did not
share his ideas in the very least, but the conversation was so lively

and so cheerful throughout the dinner and the evening we spent with him, and he spoke to us so openly and frankly, that we liked him very much indeed. In fact during our journey we met scarcely anybody who did not belong to the left – members of the two Communist parties and of the left wing of Mapam: Amos Kennan; Bloch, the historian, and a bearded young man called Levi. The last two belonged to the committee against the war in Vietnam and they organized a meeting on the subject; Sartre addressed the audience, and General Dayan was present.

We took a great liking to Monique Howard. She had come from France some years before and she had become an interpreter: she was married to a musician, with whom she led an uneventful life in Tel-Aviv. Ely Ben-Gal's case was more unusual. He was the son of a Lyons manufacturer, and he and his parents had spent the war in hiding at Chambon-sur-Lignon. His grandparents were deported and they died in a camp; but he was too young for it to affect him much. The whole village was kind to his family. The baker's wife let them have bread without ration-cards: when the war was over they went to thank her. 'Oh, it was natural enough,' she said. 'You are Jews, but even so ...' He was nine at the time, and it left a deep, lasting impression. In the years that followed he realized that the French did not look upon him as one of themselves, and he decided to emigrate. First he went to Brazil, where he married; then he came to Israel. His wife was Jewish too, and they settled in a Galilean kibbutz; when we met him he was looking after the sheep. He used to take them to graze on the Lebanese frontier. He knew a little Arabic and he talked to the Lebanese shepherds – they would exchange bread and cheese. Yet even so, one of them cried eagerly, 'The day will come when all the Jews will be flung into the sea.' 'Me too?' asked Ely. The other hesitated for a moment, and then said, 'You too.' Ely carried a rifle when he went out with his sheep: an attack was always possible. He also took a book. Not a novel: there was a danger of his forgetting his flock – they had to be kept on the move all the time and never allowed to go to sleep. But a philosophic work suited very well: he would break off after two or three pages and think about what he had read while he looked after the sheep. In this way he worked through Plato and the *Critique of Dialectical Reason*. Politically he was to the left of the Mapam. He hoped that Israel would find a way of absorbing the refugees, and in home politics he defended the interests of the Arab minority. One of our chief concerns was the Arab question, and we were given every facility for gathering information. At Guivaret-Haviva, a centre for advanced studies that works for better relations between Jews and Arabs, we met Mohamed Wattad, the editor of *Al Misrad*, Mapam's Arabic publication. After the day's proceedings at the seminar he took us home for coffee. He was still very young, and he had a son whom he had named Castro. It was then that for the first time I saw an Arab village in Israel. How very unlike the moshavim! The Jewish villages, aseptic and built according to the rules of logic, look like housing-estates. This one was rooted in the earth – it looked as though it had grown naturally from it; and its steep narrow streets wound their way among houses that seemed to have a history. Women passed up and down, dressed in their vividly-coloured national costume. As we drank our coffee, Wattad told us about the very difficult situation of the three hundred thousand Arabs in Israel. They were looked upon with distrust, being considered more or less as a fifth column. The Arab countries regard them as traitors who collaborate with the enemy. He had two brothers the other side of the frontier, and the family gatherings which are so important for Muslims were therefore impossible. 'It is very sad for my mother,' he said. The government makes scarcely any effort to improve the minority's lot. There is discrimination that cannot be avoided: the Jews have no wish to arm the Arabs, and the Arabs will not fight against their own brothers – they therefore do no military service. But there are many deplorable injustices. All Israelis have the same political rights, but the Arabs are too few in number to use these as a weapon. Some Arabs do sit in parliament, but they amount to only a very small proportion of the assembly as a whole. The Arabs have virtually no means of accomplishing anything. There is no attempt at providing them with any technical qualifications; they work at the roughest and hardest jobs and they are the first victims of unemployment. The day we arrived in Tel-Aviv there was a noisy demonstration because eighty thousand building-workers were out of work: they were almost all Arabs.

A few days later we heard Arabs express their bitterness with far more violence than Wattad. The Mapai municipality of Kfar-Rama received us officially in the village school; then the municipality of Kfar-Yassin, which was partly Mapam and partly Communist, did the same, also in a classroom. Some of the Arabs in the audience angrily spoke out against the ill-treatment they suffered. Land belonging to Arabs was confiscated by the state on the pretext of public interest and the peasants were forced to leave their houses. They were given derisory compensation and they were rehoused in the wretched shacks we had seen on the outskirts of the village – it was one of the men who had been 'regrouped' who told us of these facts with such furious resentment. Others complained that they were condemned to the most unpleasant kinds of work and that they were the first victims of the recession. Still others cried out that they had been put on the black list for no reason at all so that now they had to get special permission to move about. Formerly they were under the supervision of the army: this has been replaced by a no less strict supervision by the police. The next day some of the Tel-Aviv papers carried denials of these statements; but all our friends told us that they were perfectly true, and this was confirmed by the day we spent in Nazareth.

The town is almost entirely inhabited by Arabs. In a hotel at the gates of Nazareth we met one of the mayor's deputies, Abdul-Aziz-Zuabi, and other Arab public figures. They drove us to the middle of the town and there we got out: a great 'spontaneous demonstration' had been organized, I do not know by whom, and the crowd of men – there were no women at all – shouted and cheered, waving placards with various claims and grievances written on them. We were surrounded on all sides and so hemmed in that we gave up our idea of walking about the old streets. We returned to the car: when it turned round there was more shouting, accompanied by hoots, because the demonstrators wanted us to be shown some outstandingly wretched district: Zuabi promised to take us there later. And indeed, at the end of the day, after a short walk in the old part of Nazareth, we did visit a kind of vacant lot with shacks made of wood or corrugated iron. There were not a great many of them. But the whole town seemed very poor from one end to the other.

We spent the afternoon at the hotel, and in one of the rooms Sartre received Arab delegations representing a variety of different tendencies. The Gaza Palestinians had foretold that we should not be allowed to meet several figures, whom they named: they were allowed to come, however, and we did have talks with them.

Summing up his impressions a little later in an interview with the *New Outlook*[9] team, Sartre said, 'I never met a single Arab who felt

9 Review edited by Flapan.

satisfied with his life in Israel. I never met a single Arab who said that at the present moment he had the same rights as an Israeli citizen.' The confiscation of land had been stopped a year before, thanks in part to the action of Mapam; but those who had been evicted had not been compensated, nor had they been properly rehoused. All the grievances that we had already heard we now heard again, and with fresh evidence to substantiate them.

In Jerusalem we had one last contact with the Arabs. Amos Kennan, a Jew who had defended the rights of the Arabs for years and whose militant activities had cost him a stay in prison, came to see us at our hotel, together with his brother and two Arab students. Both these students came from very poor villages. They were disgusted because they were refused the right to set up an Arab students' union – the authorities were afraid that it might be a centre for subversion. They could of course join the Students' Union; but they were too few to have the least influence in that body. We met many Israeli Jews who were extremely worried by this problem and who were trying to break the barriers that kept the minority apart and isolated. But the situation could never be changed by private initiative alone: the government itself would have to refrain from any form of discrimination.

As we talked and argued and gathered information, so we explored the countryside and the towns of Israel. Galilee, Mount Tabor, the Jordan, the Mount of the Beatitudes, Lake Tiberias: these holy places that I had dreamt of with such fervour when I was a child were now no more than secular localities; and they were very unlike what I had imagined them to be. In these green landscapes I could not recognize the arid hills where the feet of Jesus had trodden in the dust. The Jordan seemed to me pitifully narrow. Only Lake Tiberias was like its legend. From the balcony of our hotel we could see it as a whole; and over against us rose the Syrian hills. We went to the far end of the lake to visit the well-preserved ruins of the temple of Capernaum and the Byzantine mosaics in the little church of Topha: the prettiest were those of ducks drinking out of flowers.

We wandered about Safed, an ancient city that saw the birth of the Cabala. The Jews took refuge there in the sixteenth century, when the Turks seized Palestine, and they settled in different quarters, according to their places of origin. Safed was not only a weaving and cloth-dying town and an important entrepot for trade but also a centre for theological studies that drew hundreds of learned men and rabbis with a leaning towards mysticism from Spain and Portugal and Sicily. It stands high on a hill, and it has a very beautiful view of the mountains of Canaan and Galilee. Sartre and Ely had to put on paper skull-caps to go into the synagogue – they were to be borrowed at the door. As we went down the little streets and climbed flights of steps, so we talked: Ely told us the tale of the four rabbis of Safed who had seen truth face to face. The first became impious: he rode his horse on the Sabbath. The second, his disciple, followed him at a run; he was a good man and compassionate, and when truth revealed itself to him he went mad. Two centuries later another rabbi had the same revelation: it killed him. The fourth alone became a wise man, a great sage who is still revered to this day.

From Safed we drove down a delightful road through olive-groves to Acre: this is where the greatest number of Jews congregated during the two centuries when the Crusaders barred them from Jerusalem. It was the Crusaders who built the walls and towers whose ruins still stand, and when we had looked at them we went down to the sea to have lunch in the sun. Most of the people who live in Acre are Arabs. We visited the mosque and wandered about the rather squalid but very busy souks. We passed the night at Haifa, on the top of Mount Carmel; and there we dined with two members of the 'new Communist party', the Rakah, which is largely made up of Arabs. Then Professor Heinman and his wife took us for a drive in their car. The town seemed dead. But the next morning the harbour and the streets around it were swarming with life. It was there that both Monique and Ely had first landed, with some years between them; and both of them, with an intensity of feeling that other Jews have told me about, had thought, 'This is perfectly extraordinary! Everybody here is Jewish!' They were astonished that the people they saw walking did not seem to be amazed too: how could they possibly refrain from falling into one another's arms?

A few hours later we were in Caesarea. The port was founded by the Phoenicians and enlarged by Herod the Great, who gave it the name of Caesarea in honour of Augustus Caesar. He built a palace, and from that time on the Roman procurators resided there. The town's gate and its walls date from the middle ages. The ancient ruins stretch down as far as the sea; and at the edge of the bright blue water the brick glowed in the blazing sun.

At Jerusalem we stayed at the well-known King David Hotel: in the days of the mandate this was the headquarters of the civil and military administration. In 1946 a Jewish terrorist organization blew up one wing, an outrage that caused a great deal of noise in the world. First we went to see the Knesset, a large new building in a new quarter. A somewhat uninteresting discussion was going on in the assembly and the audience was sparse. A Palestinian had told us that there was a map of 'Greater Israel' on the walls; we observed that this was not so. Barzilai, the minister of health, received us in his office; he was a member of the Mapam, and he was friendly and very open and frank. He thoroughly understood the gravity of the refugee problem and he thought a solution had to be found. He was against the 1956 expedition; but at the same time he did point out the obviously biased way in which the USSR recalled the Soviet ambassador from Israel but not from Paris or London.

From a hill near the hotel we looked out over Arab Jerusalem: its old walls and fine buildings could be seen very clearly. A few yards from us, on the other side of the barbed wire, Jordanian soldiers kept guard; some were on the roofs, others crouched behind walls or heaps of sand.

We lunched at the university with some of the professors and then we were taken to see the Meah Shearim district, a kind of ghetto where the orthodox Jews live. I had often been told about it, but even so I was astonished at the sight of the men's long black coats, side-locks and round hats: all the women were dressed in black, with a scarf tied over their wigs: the children, with their side-locks and black skull-caps seemed to me unnatural: and the spectacle of an adolescent boy with a girlish complexion who was already forced to wear men's clothes, struck me as dismal in the extreme as he walked along, looking crushed, beside his mother, a ponderous woman with a majestic pace. The Meah Shearim Jews are hostile to the state of Israel: in their opinion the rebirth of Zion cannot take place before the coming of the Messiah. They think it sacrilege to use Hebrew for secular purposes, and they speak Yiddish. The day before we reached Tel-Aviv they had held a violent demonstration against the dissection of human bodies. All the walls of the religious quarter had placards and inscriptions saying that dissection was an offence against the dead, and through them an insult to God. The women look after their homes and children: the men spend their days in prayer and religious discussion – they live on money sent from America. They are fanatical respecters of the Sabbath. On Saturdays they prevent cars from moving about – a motorcyclist had been killed by a chain stretched across the road. On that day some of them go so far as to pin their handkerchief to their sleeve, for taking it out of their pocket would be work. Monique had seen some going to the synagogue wearing their prayer-shawls, because carrying them in their hands would also amount to breaking the Law.

We strolled about the shopping districts and the markets. We spent an interesting evening with Professor Shalem, who has an immense library entirely devoted to the Cabala: some professors from the university were also there, and the writer Claude Vigée: we talked about Jewish traditions and mysticism. During the following days we each of us gave a lecture. And we spent an afternoon in the place where the memory of the 'final solution' is perpetuated. We went down into the crypt where blood-stained clothes are laid out. On the floor one sees the names of some of the victims. Then we went to the 'mountain of memory', walking along a drive lined with trees, each of which was planted by a 'saver of Jews', that is to say someone who had helped Jews to cross the frontier or to hide. And it so happened that just then a Swiss was being received in the impressive great Memorial Hall. He was standing by the flame of remembrance; behind him were grouped a large number of Jews who owed their lives to him; and all the people present chanted religious songs. Carved in huge letters on the flagstones there were the terrible names: Treblinka, Dachau, and so many others. A series of smaller rooms contained photographs: here again I saw one of those that had touched me most – children with shaved heads standing round a little violin-teacher with a heart-broken look on his face – and then another photograph showing a cart loaded with their bodies. Statistics gave the number of victims country by country. Six million.

Another place that affected me deeply was the kibbutz of Lohame Hagetact,[10] where the survivors of the Warsaw ghetto had been assembled. We were received at the club, and first a woman gave us a brief account of the community: she told us how difficult it was

10 The Ghetto Risings.

for the members to readjust themselves to ordinary life. She had been a commanding officer during the rising. On her arrival here, more than twenty years before, she had spoken of the history of the ghetto and its revolt for twelve hours on end. Since then she had never alluded to it. She talked in a monotonous voice, with her eyes half-closed. Some of the women wept. Another member of the kibbutz showed us a model of the ghetto and gave us a quick history of the rising, pointing out the places where the chief events had occurred. Then we went into a museum with a large collection of photographs – Jews electrocuted on the barbed wire; others lying on the ground, as thin as skeletons, with huge mad eyes in their emaciated faces; German soldiers, laughing as they beat old men; others watching the 'last Jew' die.

To round off our journey, Monique and Ely had organized a trip to the south for us. We were to take a helicopter and fly over the fortress of Masada, but wind and rain prevented this and we set off by car. Presently the sun came out. We stopped for lunch at a lonely little hotel from which we had a view of the Dead Sea far below us. After our meal we went down to it. We passed the notice that shows sea-level and still we went on, down and down to the shimmering water, blue or green according to the play of the light, at the foot of the bare Jordanian mountains.

First we went along the shore; then we branched off and drove inland to the foot of the 'fortress', a huge natural cliff upon whose top Herod built an enormous palace. During the rebellion against Rome that ended in the destruction of the temple of Jerusalem the Jews seized this fortress, and in spite of the small number of fighting men they held out for two years. When they saw that they were about to fall into the hands of the Romans, the nine hundred and sixty members of the garrison killed themselves. Only five women and three children remained alive. From the bottom of the cliff it is impossible to reach the top, where the ruins of the palace are still to be seen; but the landscape in which we stood was so extraordinary that I did not regret the helicopter: all around us were pedestals and columns of glowing stone whose form and brilliance reminded me somewhat of the Painted Desert of Colorado. We went back to the coast road, meaning to look at the springs of En-Geadi – an angel made them burst forth in order to save Ishmael – but the violent rains had turned the narrow brook into an impossible torrent of mud: its coffee-coloured stream could be seen flowing out into the blue of the sea. Cars stood motionless on either side. We turned back. A gale was blowing, and it raised waves of a strange, unnatural hue; a square tin drove before the wind, and it bounced along as though the surface were made of asphalt. We dipped our hands into the water, and when we took them out they were sticky. The car drove on along the coast. Where Sodom had been there is now a factory. Many of the rocks there are supposed to represent Lot's wife turned into a pillar of salt. A winding road brought us to Beersheba.

We passed the night there, in an icy-cold hotel. Beersheba is a very ugly town. Each district has been built in a different style, and one has the feeling that the architects tried to find themselves and never managed it. Some of the streets are very poor. After a quick visit we set off in the morning to cross the Negev. When we had driven over an enormous basin – the Great Mortar – we walked a little way to look down at the springs of Ain-Avdat far below, at the bottom of a vertiginous ravine. The desert grew wilder and even more tormented: great hollows alternated with plateaux studded with sharp bare peaks and ragged crests. The shifting light – clouds and sun – brought out all their strong and lovely colours. At long intervals we caught sight of new kibbutzim, set up by young people. A little road took us to King Solomon's mines – columns and pillars of naked rock, cliffs like fortresses: they look as though some barbaric, slightly demented giant had painted them red, pink, ochre and golden yellow.

At Eilat the Queen of Sheba Hotel was cut off from the sea by a building-site cluttered with cranes and bulldozers: it is an uncomely little town, wedged between Egypt, Saudi Arabia and Jordan – the mountains surrounding the bay belong to those countries. Looking westwards we could clearly see the little neighbouring Jordanian port. Out at sea two ships lay at anchor, one Israeli and the other Jordanian. We were shown an aquarium near the water's edge, full of weirdly-shaped and extraordinarily-coloured fish: the strangest of them all were tight black balls covered with prickles: two points gleamed on the surface – their eyes. We had dinner by the harbour in an agreeable restaurant decorated with nets and large stuffed fish.

Although we had refused to visit the Israeli army, a small military plane was put at our disposal for our return to Tel-Aviv; we therefore let our chauffeur drive off without us. He was a Sabra, about thirty years old, reactionary and chauvinist. He often refused to follow Monique's directions; more than once she had to employ guile to attain her ends. He protested when she asked him to take a road that ran along the frontier. He was angry if we were shown the poor parts of a town, and he became even more furious when we talked to Arabs in the villages – when we left a meeting he would call them all liars.

So we took the plane. Ely sat next to the pilot and Monique, Sartre and myself behind. We were inside a glass bubble and we had a limitless view in all directions. The horizon was blackish, and for a while I gazed at the shattered, tormented desert with some apprehension. But in fact we glided through the air without so much as a bump. We did not fly high, and we could recognize the details of the landscape we had driven across the day before. The pilot made a turn over the ancient city of Avdat and we clearly made out the colonnades and the ruined houses. The desert ended. Gaza came into sight. We flew over cultivated ground. Our view embraced immense orange-groves, and we could even distinguish the freshly-gathered heaps of fruit.

From this height we could see the lay-out of the fields, the kibbutzim and the villages. We flew over the port of Ashdod, which has recently been constructed to the south of Tel-Aviv: many parts of it looked very strange – on the bare earth stood out the tracing of roads and traffic circuses, a wilderness of lines that appeared to have no justification. The reason for this was that the town was not yet finished: the main roads had been worked out before the houses were built. Then there was Jaffa; and we landed at a little military airfield on the edge of the town.

On our last day we were received by Eshkol. Sartre gave a press-conference, and at a party organized by *New Outlook* we met almost all the people who had been kind to us during our journey. Throughout our stay Sartre had spoken to everyone we met about the Palestinian question and the condition of the Arabs in Israel. He pursued the subject during these last encounters.

Our journeys in Israel and in Egypt were made in very different conditions. In Israel the governing class lived far less luxuriously and in any case they were not the people who entertained us. Although it had been arranged that we should stay at the best hotels, we lived more simply altogether; which was something that we by no means regretted. No private plane, no magnificent banquets. Only Monique and Ely travelled with us; not a single journalist followed behind. Apart from the grapefruit and the avocado pears, in which I delighted, the cooking at the Tel-Aviv hotel was indifferent. (And since it obeyed the religious laws in order to satisfy the American Jewish tourists, meat and cheese could not be served at the same meal.) We usually ate at pleasant little restaurants in the Yemeni quarter or in the Arab part of Jaffa: the bill of fare was never particularly varied nor abundant.

As we flew towards Athens, we felt more sanguine than otherwise. The demands of each country were unacceptable to the other. Egypt would not recognize Israel: Israel would not take in a million Palestinians. Yet to us war seemed no more than a distant threat. 'War? But it's all very difficult,' Nasser had said. And all the Iraelis told us again and again, 'All we want is peace.' Egypt needed a long peaceful spell to carry out the great undertakings it had begun – industrialization and the irrigation of the desert. Israel had nothing to gain from a war.

So we spent two happy days at Athens. We sat there on the Pnyx or the Acropolis, saying nothing, bathing in the pleasure of silence recovered. For a month we had seen nothing that we were not shown and told about. Everything had taken the form of words. And this was necessary, just as it was necessary for us to conform to exactly-detailed programmes. But now we found it delightful to let time just flow by unchecked.

The frontier between Israel and Syria was often the scene of more or less serious incidents: a few days after our return to Paris there was a very grave outbreak of violence. From our hotel on Lake Tiberias, Ely Ben-Gal had shown us the narrow stretch of Israeli territory on the far bank, a strip running along the foot of the Syrian mountains that is called de Gaulle's nose, because of its shape. The Syrians often attacked this region. On 7 April the members of a kibbutz set about cultivating it. The Syrian forts fired upon the tractors. Seventy Israeli planes instantly pounded the enemy positions. Syrian Migs attacked: the Israelis shot down three and they plunged flaming into the lake. Four hours later the Syrians opened fire on a frontier kibbutz. The Israeli air force destroyed their forts and brought down three more Migs, one of them over Damascus. Nasser did not react, and this confirmed us in the idea that he was primarily concerned with improving his people's lot and that he wanted to preserve the peace.

But a month later his attitude changed. He was convinced, after the Greek coup d'état on the night of 21 April, instigated by the CIA, that the United States were going to make use of Israel to bring down first the Syrian government and then his own. Then again his role as leader of the Arab world compelled him to prefer force to conciliation. And no doubt he was also prompted by still other motives. The fact is that he massed his troops in Sinai. Jerusalem's traditional military parade on 15 May was very discreet that year, for Israel wanted to avoid making it look like a provocation. Nevertheless, Nasser felt that it confirmed his suspicions. He asked the United Nations to withdraw their troops from the frontier between Egypt and Israel. To the general surprise, U Thant not only agreed to do so, but he also evacuated Sharm el-Sheikh: it was at once occupied by Egyptian troops. Eshkol did not react vigorously, and his moderation encouraged Nasser to close the Gulf of Akaba. From that day on – 23 May – war seemed unavoidable. The Egyptians accepted responsibility for it. On 26 May Heykal, Nasser's spokesman, wrote, 'It is no longer a question of the Gulf of Akaba but of something more important – the Israeli concept of security. That is why I say Israel must attack.' In a speech on the same day Nasser declared, 'The taking of Sharm el-Sheikh meant a clash with Israel. It also meant that we were ready to launch into a full-scale war with Israel.'

A few days' respite followed. Abba Eban was touring the European capitals: perhaps some way of settling the conflict peaceably would be found. But when on 30 May Hussein arrived in Cairo to assure Nasser of his support all hope of peace was lost. A few of us, including Laurent Schwarz, Lanzmann, Sartre and myself, signed an appeal calling upon both Israel and the Arabs not to engage in hostilities; but we had no illusions about the effect of our action.

I lived through those days in a state of extreme anxiety. I had just been to Israel and Egypt: for different reasons I felt a friendship for both countries, and the idea that their armies were about to start killing one another and that their towns were going to be bombed was hateful to me. Above all I was afraid for Israel. For there was no equivalence between the two possible issues of the conflict. If Egypt were beaten, she would survive. A defeated Israel, even if her citizens were not flung into the sea, would cease to exist as a state.

Many people told me that Israel must necessarily win; but none of them said this before the fighting began – only after the cease-fire.

One would have had to be remarkably clearsighted to have picked Israel as the winner at the beginning. All the Arabs were certain of her defeat, and apart from a few generals, almost all the Israelis feared it. Afterwards we learnt that the government had had thousands of graves dug in the suburbs of Tel-Aviv. The country was completely surrounded: the Jordanian frontier stretched for nearly four hundred miles and Hussein's Legion was the most formidable armed force in the Arab world. Every day Soviet ships unloaded cargoes of arms in the Egyptian ports. The Egyptian generals preached a holy war to the cheering people. The Arab radio howled for blood. Shukairy spoke of the total extermination of all Israelis, both Jew and Arab. What shall we do with the Zionists when the time comes? asked the Jordanian radio. Then, after a silence, a burst of machine-gun fire and the sound of laughter. (Subsequently the Arabs and their friends tried to minimize the importance of these statements. But on 1 July Heykal admitted, 'We always make a great many mistakes. Our words, for example, often say more than we mean and more than we intend to do. That was how our radio behaved when it called for blood and for the crushing of Israel.') All my Jewish friends were overwhelmed.

It appeared that salvation could come only from intervention by the great powers. It was with this in mind that Lanzmann uttered the words for which he was so strongly criticized – 'Are we going to be forced to shout "Long live Johnson"?' The form of the question itself and its context show that he thought the notion scandalous; but in his opinion it was also a scandal that Israel should be condemned to annihilation without anyone raising a finger to help.

Every morning for some days I opened the paper with the utmost anxiety. On Monday, 5 June, in the taxi that was taking me to the Bibliothèque nationale, I was amazed to hear the radio giving the news that Israel had bombed Cairo. I imagined shattered houses, fires, bodies lying in the streets. What sudden madness had urged the Israelis to commit such a crime? And what price were they going to pay for having done so? I found it hard to concentrate upon what I was reading. At midday the news was different. The *France-Soir* headlines read 'Egypt attacks Israel'. All the next edition had to say was 'It is war. Cairo does not appear to have been bombed.'

In the evening we learnt that Israel had wiped out the entire Egyptian airforce without a fight. The Jordanians were shelling Jerusalem: in Tunis synagogues were in flames. The next day Israeli armies surrounded Gaza; the Egyptian general who had entertained us surrendered. The Israeli advance continued: victory was already theirs. To my extreme distress, in certain districts of Paris this was the pretext for an outburst of anti-Arab racism: once again we heard the cars hooting and the slogans that had been the rallying-cry of the supporters of a French Algeria. The noise jarred upon me inexpressibly. The tragic flight of the Egyptian soldiers across the desert grieved my heart. But when the moment of the cease-fire came I rejoiced that Israel had been spared the fire and the sword.

On the afternoon of Friday, Nasser resigned. Like all my friends, I was dismayed. He had been induced to start this war by an unfortunate series of events: he had surely never expected U Thant to react as he did, and this reaction left him with no other way out. But quite certainly he was no warmonger. What he was trying to do was to raise his country's standard of living and to destroy feudalism in Egypt. Once he was gone his place would no doubt be taken by soldiers, by men belonging to the right wing. Happily the overwhelming pressure of public opinion obliged him to change his mind.

Some days later we had luncheon with Liliane and Lufti el-Kholi. They had just spent a hideous fortnight in Paris. They had no news of their family or their friends and they were consumed with anxiety. They had seen anti-Arab demonstrations and they had been the object of hostile remarks themselves. 'If Egypt had won, we should have been torn to pieces,' said Liliane. Their reaction took the form of a feverish exasperation. They were convinced there had been an Anglo-American plot to overthrow the governments in Damascus and Cairo. They assured us that the Israeli planes had been heavily reinforced by the American airforce: this was the version that Nasser would have liked to propagate, but the USSR would not endorse it and everyone knew that the tale had no basis whatsoever. The el-Kholis found our scepticism intolerable. They blamed us angrily for not having loudly and publicly taken Egypt's side against Israel. It was a painful interview. At our second meeting they had a more level-headed Egyptian friend with them, a former Communist whom we had liked very much in Cairo; and this time the conversation was more relaxed. They acknowledged that the Arab countries had made a grave diplomatic error in clamouring for the destruction of Israel. Later we heard that on returning to Egypt Lufti was arrested and imprisoned, charged with belonging to the

402

opposition: the police had recorded a telephone-conversation in which he criticized Nasser.[11]

In August of that same year we met Monique Howard in Rome. She was thin and she looked worn: she had only just come out of hospital. The war had so deeply worried and disturbed her that it had affected her heart; she had also had a serious lung infection. She had been working on a telegraphic instrument that allowed simultaneous transmission in both directions, and from dawn till dusk she listened to the murderous threats the Arab radio poured out against Israel. At a distance and after the event it was easy to say that these were no more than verbal excesses arising from the fiery Arab temperament: but at that time and in that context, she told us, the hatred behind them froze everyone's heart. There had been no panic in Israel on the eve of the war, but everyone was profoundly anxious. At the first signs of hoarding the government threw open all the stores of flour, oil and sugar, which reassured the housewives at once. All the women took first-aid courses to be able to look after the wounded. The cemetery had been enlarged, making room for sixty thousand dead. It was feared that Egypt might use secret weapons, either rockets or the paralysing gas that had been found stored in Sinai. Monique also told us that the victory had not been received with any exuberant demonstration. Not many people had been killed; but in a small country everyone knows everyone else and nearly every family lost a relative or friend. Monique had had her share of losses, too. Another thing that wounded her was the attitude of the European left, which spoke of Israel as imperialist and of the Arab world as socialist. She wondered how such wild ideas were possible.

The USSR had supplied arms to Egypt and supported her in the United Nations. When Kosygin spoke against Israel in the United Nations, the Soviet television cut the Israeli delegate's reply. The Eastern countries could not but follow Moscow's lead. When some Polish Jews rejoiced in Israel's victory, all the thirty thousand Jews of the country were denounced as Zionists. Prague insisted upon anti-Israel declarations from the intellectuals. The only exception was Romania, which stood aside more out of animosity for the USSR than sympathy for Israel.

Opinion in France was so divided and so passionate that some

[11] After Nasser's death he was released and he is now carrying on with his political struggle.

people said it might have been the Dreyfus affair all over again. Families quarrelled most bitterly: friendships were broken. On the right wing, the Gaullists fell into step behind the Leader and declared against Israel. But there were also many belonging to the right whose anti-Arab racism outweighed their anti-semitism. The Communists took the same side as the USSR, of course. On the non-Communist left wing there was a great variety of attitudes. Again and again one saw a brisk volte-face: many left-wingers would have been very sorry for Israel if she had been destroyed or if she had had to pay an exceedingly high price for survival; but the Israeli victory suddenly and disconcertingly did away with the traditional image of the Jew as victim, and their sympathies shifted to the Arabs. All the extreme left, from the Trotskyists to the Marxists, supported the cause of the Arabs and more specifically of the Palestinians.

Among the Jews there was often a conflict between the generations, with the parents, whether they belonged to the right or the left, being entirely for Israel, and the children coming out against Zionism.

I was not in complete agreement with any single one of my friends, and with some of them I was in total conflict. I did not consider Israel as the aggressor, since by international law the closing of the Gulf of Akaba constituted a casus belli, as Nasser himself had acknowledged. I also denied that Israel was colonialist; the country did not exploit a native labour-force and it did not carry off raw materials and send them back to a mother-country that would sell the manufactured products to the colonies at a high price – there was no mother-country. I did not look upon Israel as a bridgehead for imperialism: the USA certainly helped the country to live, but the Americans had no base there, nor did they draw any wealth from the country; whereas they did have military bases in the Arab states, they did exploit Arab oil, and they did provide the Arabs with important economic aid. It is not true that Israel's existence hindered the development of the Arab countries – it neither prevented Algeria from winning its independence, nor Nasser from building the Aswan dam, nor Libya from successfully carrying out its revolution. As to its being an impediment to the unity of the Arab world, why, the existence of Israel is the very reason why that unity is at least to some degree achieved; the only factor that these states, strangers to one another or even enemies, have in common is their hatred for Israel. It is a capitalist country and it has committed grave mistakes; but it is not the only one, and the others do not see their existence called into question. For my part, I find the idea that Israel might vanish from the map of the world perfectly hateful. Men and women, confident in the assurances of the United Nations – particularly those of the USSR and the Eastern countries – have built up this country with their own hands; they have founded families there and sent down their roots: tearing them from it would be iniquitous. It would be even more iniquitous since anti-semitism is still widespread and virulent throughout Europe and for the Jews Israel is the only safe refuge against the threats that that implies.

My journey to the Near East showed me the full importance of the Palestinian question. I understand the claims of Arafat's nationalists; but unlike many of the left wing I refuse to see Al Fatah as a movement that embodies the hopes of socialism. I am sorry that only a small fraction of the Israeli left attempts to negotiate with the Palestinians. And the fact that the Arab leaders, having urged the Palestinians on, now display mere indifference or hostility or even have them massacred must necessarily arouse one's indignation. The Palestinians must be offered solutions that they themselves consider valid. But I cannot support the answer which their leaders have chosen and which is in fact the destruction of Israel.[12]

This does not mean that I approve of Israel's policy. I could wish that Israel would not stubbornly insist upon direct negotiations; that it would immediately undertake to give back the occupied territories; and that it would show itself as determined to make peace as it was to win the war.

The positions I have taken up on the problems of the Near East almost always make my relationships with left-wing militants uneasy. I am entirely for the Black Panthers and I admire Cleaver's *Soul on Ice*; but I was deeply depressed when he attacked the Jews in his *Les Temps modernes* interview. I regret that the non-Communist left should have grown as monolithic as the Party itself. A left-winger must necessarily admire China without the least reservation, take Nigeria's side against Biafra and the Palestinians' against Israel. I will not bow to these conditions. Yet this does not

---

[12] I say *in fact* because the Palestinian propaganda directed at the French left wing uses circumlocution to disguise this aim.

prevent me from being very close to the gauchistes in the area in which they are most directly concerned – in the action they carry out in France.

Before dealing with my relations with my own country, I should like to define my attitudes towards the rest of the world as they have been these last ten years and as they are today. But first I must say this: not all foreign countries matter to me equally. There is one which I have not the least desire to visit and see with my own eyes, although it is among the most important: and that is India. It seems to me, from the studies and articles I have read, that the extreme and general poverty there must be unbearable. I am discouraged by the complexity of the country's economic and political problems. I was not, of course, unmoved by the tragedy of Bengal, and I was pleased by the defeat of the Pakistani oppressors. Yet these struggles have but a faint echo in France; and I have no direct relationship with the countries involved. I am no more than remotely affected by what happens there. Here I shall speak only of those countries with which, for one reason or another, I am personally concerned.

I have already said how far I have moved from the USSR and how very much I felt the tragedy of Prague. I draw no comfort from anything that is happening in the European socialist countries: I have never had any link with Romania or Bulgaria, where the regime is still dictatorial and the standard of living very low; in Hungary the atmosphere is less oppressive and the standard of living higher, but apart from some very fine films that were shown in France, I know almost nothing about that country – a country where literature is still strictly censored. But on the other hand I do have Polish friends, I was there in 1962, and I have enjoyed many books written by Poles: I was very deeply grieved to see the hopes of 1956 all brought to nothing. In every field Gomulka behaved as a dictator, particularly with regard to the intellectuals. They sent him a letter asking for some measure of freedom; by way of a reply he launched a campaign against them and banned a great many publications. A little later two young Communist intellectuals were thrown into prison for having written an open letter criticizing bureaucratic socialism. In October 1966 the philosopher Kolakowski[13] denounced the retrogression he had observed during

[13] His works include the remarkable *Chrétiens sans Eglise*.

the previous ten years – the slowing-down of economic expansion, the decrease in social mobility, the growth of inequalities and the consequent feeling of insecurity and frustration throughout the entire nation. He was dismissed from the university and expelled from the party, a procedure that provoked many reactions in his favour among the intellectuals.

Gomulka's government was anti-intellectual: from 1967 onwards it also proved itself to be violently anti-semitic into the bargain. By the end of the war only three hundred and fifty thousand Polish Jews had survived out of the three million: most of them emigrated, either out of their horror of the past or from fear, for the Polish fascists had perpetrated a bloody pogrom at Kielce in 1946. By 1967 no more than thirty thousand were left. Yet this did not prevent Moczar, the minister of the interior, from preparing an anti-Jewish campaign: it was launched in 1967, with the government seeking to deprive the Jews of their posts, thus striking at the intelligentsia through them. On 19 June 1967, immediately after the Six Days' War, Gomulka made a speech at the union congress in which he accused the Jews of forming a fifth column. In the following months the papers, the radio, television and speakers at public meetings all denounced the Zionists as Poland's worst enemies – and every Jew was suspected of being a Zionist. The press and the army were 'purged of Jews'. In addition to all this furious abuse of Israel, the Jews were also declared to be responsible for the extermination of their people by Hitler.

On 30 January 1968 the performance of Mickiewicz's play *The Ancestors* was banned; students demonstrated in front of the theatre, and a great many of them were arrested. To protest against this they held another demonstration at the university of Warsaw on 8 March: the police reacted with brutal force and once more many students were arrested – the Aryans were released and the Jews imprisoned. Moczar sorted the Jews into three categories, a classification that left the way open for every kind of arbitrary act: first, the Zionists, who were to leave Poland; second, those Jews who felt as much Jewish as Polish; and third, those who felt more Polish than Jewish.

Twenty thousand Jews left Poland between the summer of 1968 and the summer of 1971. The rest are trying to follow their example. But although they are being forced out, the continual persecution to which they are submitted makes it very hard for them actually to leave. Israel is the only country they are allowed to go to: as soon as they have handed in their request for an exit-permit they lose their citizenship and all prospect of work; they have to pay five thousand zlotys, which is about two months' good pay; they have to hand over their dwelling 'in perfect condition', which means a considerable outlay; and they have to refund the cost of their children's education. They are forbidden to take even the smallest sum of money with them. They are required to draw up a highly-detailed list of their luggage and the customs officials submit them to long and humiliating searches. All the Polish friends, Jewish or not, we have met in Paris were utterly sickened by the treatment of the Jews.[14]

Meanwhile there is no improvement in the position of the country as a whole. In December 1970, after the bloody repression of the Silesian workers' rising, Gierek took Gomulka's place. It seems that the USSR had long desired this change and that the riots had been artificially provoked; although indeed the rise in the cost of living provided a valid reason for them. Gierek has nothing of the democrat about him: there is little hope that things will change for the better.

Up until this year of 1972 Yugoslavia was the most liberal of the socialist countries. Papers expressing different shades of opinion appeared side by side, and some even published severe criticism of the regime. The intellectuals argued freely and openly. Since the events in Croatia everything has changed. Croatia is the most industrialized region of the country; it exports more than the other republics and brings in the greatest amount of foreign currency. A law, which was supported by Tito himself, requires that each republic should have the disposal of the currency it receives: but in fact the government centralizes all the incoming money and wastes a great deal in spectacular undertakings whose value is open to doubt – the huge Danube dam, for example. In spite of its industrialization, Croatia is not rich. Seven hundred thousand Croats work in West Germany, unable to find jobs at home. The students live in

[14] In 1970 *Les Temps modernes* published *Western*, an excellent story by a non-Jewish writer about a Jewish family leaving Poland. The review also carried a long article, *Le Pogrome à sec*, by an exiled Polish Jewess, dealing with the question as a whole. Trepper, the head of the intelligence organization the Red Orchestra, has been denied a permit to emigrate to Israel. He was expelled from the Polish Communist Party for having asked to leave and he lives under continual police supervision.

deplorable conditions: they sleep on the ground, crammed together in miserable little rooms. In November they organized a demonstration: they claimed that the law should be obeyed and that Croatia should use its foreign currency for its own purposes. There does exist a chauvinistic and reactionary Croatian nationalism, backed by a clandestine, terrorist organization of Ustachis; but the students had the support of the progressive socialists, and they were not asking for Croatia to be detached from Yugoslavia but merely to be given some degree of autonomy. Tito sent in squads of Serbian police and they beat up the students savagely. Tanks surrounded Zagreb. All the Croat intellectuals were seized and other arrests were carried out in Belgrade itself. The press was gagged; the central authority strengthened. I have met Croats who had belonged to the Communist party for more than twenty years and who were nevertheless forced into exile. They say that the situation can only grow worse in the years to come.

There is one country that we looked upon, for a while, as the very embodiment of socialist hopes – Cuba. It very soon stopped being a land of freedom – homosexuals were persecuted and the least trace of nonconformity in dress made the wearer a suspect. And yet on the whole the air was easier to breathe in Cuba than in the USSR. The cultural congress held at Havana in January 1968 was directed against the 'hide-bound, pseudo-Marxist church' as Castro put it when he launched an appeal to the 'new pioneers'. The discussion at the congress was perfectly free and open; and some of the painters showed abstract pictures. All our friends who had attended the congress spoke of it with enthusiastic approval on their return.

Very soon they were obliged to eat their words. In that same year Castro adopted a more cautious attitude. He stopped supporting Castroism in Latin America. In May, in order not to vex Moscow nor to encourage challenge or contestation in his own country, he refused to send the French students the least message of sympathy. In July he uttered no word of favour of the Mexican students murdered by the police, and Cuba took part in the Mexican Olympic Games. His speech after the entry of the Soviet troops into Czechoslovakia showed that he was now unreservedly following the policy of the USSR. He has never diverged from this attitude since then. It was no doubt inevitable: Cuba depends upon Moscow, particularly for its supplies of oil. But it is sad, because the Cuban economy has steadily declined. Moscow condemns the island's agriculture to the production of one single crop, whereas diversification – a change of various food-crops – would give its people a plentiful living. Since they are condemned to near-famine, the people are unsatisfied, and their discontent leads to repressive measures.

In an atmosphere of this kind, intellectuals are allowed no freedom of any sort. As early as 1969 the museum of modern art was closed and the cultural budget cut to a minimum. Five hundred youths were arrested for having long hair. In January 1971 Castro promulgated his own version of the Soviet law against the 'idle' which led to the arrest of Brodsky and Amalrik, among others. The charge of 'parasitism' allows the most arbitrary forms of persecution and imprisonment. In April the poet Padilla was denounced as a counter-revolutionary and gaoled; he was released after having signed a 'self-criticism', a document filled with utter nonsense from beginning to end – it accuses René Dumont and Karol of being agents of the CIA! If that was so then Castro should clap himself in prison too, because he gave them a warm welcome and talked with them for a great while. Castro has also threatened other counter-revolutionary intellectuals. The 'honeymoon of the revolution' that had so enchanted us is over and done with.

A disappointment of another kind was the evolution of Algeria. Of course no one could look for a miracle that would suddenly bring about the reign of socialism and prosperity: the war had killed more than a million people; the finest leaders had been killed in the guerrilla fighting; and the departure of a million Europeans who ran the country left it in economic confusion. At the time when the Algerians won their independence, eighty-five per cent of the adults were illiterate. The reorganization of the economy could not fail to be a difficult task. The disasters foretold by the colonists did not occur; but a third of the male working population is underemployed, another third unemployed altogether, and five hundred thousand have emigrated. The circumstances were unfavourable for the setting-up of socialism, but the leaders have made no serious effort in that direction whatsoever. What they have done is to instal a state capitalism that has nothing socialist about it apart from the name. In agriculture they have not encouraged the collectivization of the land; in industry they have not encouraged management by the workers. Instead of attempting to make the masses politically conscious they have urged them to return to the values of the Arab, Islamic world. Unlike Tunisia and Egypt, Algeria has made no attempt at checking the birthrate – a birthrate so high that the population is increasing far more rapidly than its resources. The condition of women is deplorable, and one of them has spoken out against it in a courageous book. They are given no more than a minimum of education, and this is justified by Muslim tradition; they still wear veils; and they are confined either to their father's home or to that of the husband they are obliged to marry. Fanon was profoundly mistaken when he foretold that the Algerian women would escape from male oppression because of the part they had played in the war. Algeria's foreign policy is held out as 'progressive' and it is indeed anti-colonialist and anti-imperialist. But the country's home policy is both nationalist and reactionary. There is nothing to show that it is likely to change its nature for a very long while.

And what is happening in China? That is a question I really should like to be able to answer. I went there in 1955 and when I came back I wrote a book about it. Since then I have learnt all I could about the period of 'the hundred flowers', the great leap forward, and the experiment of the communes. Whereas the USSR advanced a model of a wealthy socialism and preached patience to the under-developed countries, China put forward a model of a poor socialism and encouraged the oppressed nations to violent action: and our sympathies went to China. As I have said, Sartre supported the Chinese view at Helsinki. But when the cultural revolution broke out, no one could give us a convincing explanation of the reality that underlay the words. The Russian and the French papers gave disconnected, contradictory scraps of news – Mao had gone for a swim in the Yangtze; young Red Guards were cutting off girls' plaits; they switched the red and yellow of the traffic-lights; they were defying the army; it was civil war – no, it was only small-scale rioting. In a facetious tone they related anecdotes which were quite droll in fact, when they were completely divorced from any context. We did not trust the ill-disposed and spiteful press but we were equally sceptical about the propaganda-articles published in English or French by the Pekin reviews.

Those with a special knowledge of China offered interesting interpretations; but they were all guesswork. According to one, it was all

411

a matter of economic conflict; according to another everything was to be explained by political rivalries; while a third said it was a struggle against the bureaucracy. No doubt all these explanations were partially correct: but none was certain, and none gave us the key to what was happening – to these events which reached us as vague echoes.

The people we knew who went to China came back in a state of utter confusion: all they had seen was the outermost aspect of the cultural revolution, and they could make nothing of it whatsoever. In December 1966 Alejo Carpentier[15] returned from Hanoi by way of Pekin. He had been there the same year as ourselves, and he had liked everything he had seen. Now it was another city, he told us, another world, and one that he found quite frightening. In the plane the hostesses waved the book that was only just beginning to be known in France under the name of 'the little red book', and every half hour they said, 'I am going to read you one of Chairman Mao's thoughts.' As they drove, the Pekin taxi-men recited Mao's thoughts, and Carpentier's interpreter translated them to him. He was kept waiting at the airport for four hours, and all the time he heard instructors reading Mao's thoughts to the passengers: they lined them up in two columns and made them say the thoughts over again. Thirty-five million pictures of Mao had just been printed; each household was to put one up and a leaflet explained how and where the picture was to be placed. Carpentier asked a publisher what books were to be published that year; the man replied, 'Thirty-five million copies of the works of Chairman Mao; nothing else.' 'But still, you will bring out some technical books and manuals too?' 'I said nothing else.' During his brief stay there was a campaign in favour of dung-gatherers, who were looked upon as the most typically proletarian workers. The one who was thought to be the most exemplary gatherer of them all was chosen, and he was brought to the university to give a lecture in the presence of all the professors.[16] The cinemas and theatres were shut, and in spite of the young people who filled the streets, Carpentier found the city gloomy and ominous.

About a year later we saw Kateb Yacine, who had spent a month

---

[15] The great Cuban writer.
[16] Now we understand: this episode was part of a great campaign to re-establish manual labour in the public esteem and to do away with the excessive prestige of intellectual work.

in Pekin during the autumn of 1967, staying in the Algerian embassy. Neither he nor the diplomats he met understood anything about what was happening either. Like Carpentier he had heard the loudspeakers roaring out slogans and he too had seen the air-hostesses and the taxi-drivers waving the little red book. Yet the streets had been full of life all day and late into the night, and they had given him the impression of cheerfulness. No doubt they were cheerful for the Chinese, he added, speaking more exactly. But the foreigners lived in fear: for the merest trifle they would be ill-treated (except, of course, for government guests, who walked about surrounded by Chinese). The Algerian ambassador, who had red hair, no longer dared go out. The Bulgarian ambassador went shopping in a big store with his chauffeur; an assistant wanted to sell the chauffeur a picture of Mao; the man refused – a mistake – and to make things even more disastrous the picture fell to the ground. They were very nearly lynched. The police did protect them, but that evening the embassy went up in flames – the fire lasted three days.

I had read some of Mao's works with great interest; but the 'little red book' sent me to sleep. No doubt the quotations with which it is filled were the beginning of a fuller treatment that was later suppressed: what remains is a quantity of depressingly platitudinous elementary truths. I am told that it is a question of teaching a population still infected with superstition to think rationally. Clearly the Chinese must have some reason for attaching such importance to this catechism. But even now, in May 1971, I can hardly understand what it can be.

We visited the Chinese embassy in 1967, but I came away none the wiser. We dined there with the Bourdets and the Vercors. Whisky was not served, as it had been before: some days earlier young Chinese had demonstrated in front of the embassy, accusing the ambassador of luxury and corruption. During the meal we drank wine and rice-spirit. I have often listened to those who practise the art of talking for hours and saying nothing: I had examples in China in 1955, and at official banquets in the USSR. But never have I heard it carried so far as it was that evening. Neither the cultural nor the press attaché opened his mouth. To try to thaw Huang Chen, the ambassador, Ida Bourdet talked to him in Russian; but he pretended not to understand. Through an interpreter he explained that they were not burning Shakespeare's works in Pekin, nor Beethoven's, but that they were trying to adapt this old culture to the present times. In spite of the fact that all the theatres were closed in Pekin, the ambassador's wife told me about the beauty of the new operas that were being performed there now. We drank green tea after dinner, and to avoid any conversation the ambassador showed us an album of drawings that he had made many years ago, during the Long March. It was obvious that he had not dared to cancel an invitation issued some weeks earlier; but he entertained us most unwillingly. He was worried: so were the other Chinese. The next day we learnt that the chief of the Pekin press-agency had been dismissed. Shortly after, the ambassador was recalled.[17]

It was only after 1970 that books and articles gave me a satis-factory explanation of the cultural revolution, and then I found it a fascinating story. Unlike the Soviets, Mao rightly thought that socialism produced its own contradictions and that nationalizing the means of production was not enough to ensure that power was really in the hands of the workers and the peasants. Whereas Liu had a Stalinist view of the party, looking upon it as the monolithic expression of the masses, Mao wanted to reveal the conflicts that existed both within the party and between the party and the masses. He encouraged the *dazibaos*[18] and thereby gave the people the right to speak. He mobilized the Red Guards against an inner circle of bureaucrats, economic experts and gradualists. He used the support of the army, not as an instrument for violent coercion but because under Lin Piao's leadership it had become a first-rate revolutionary propaganda machine. The struggle brought with it a great deal of disturbance; but these upheavals in no way showed the weakness of the regime – indeed, they were almost welcomed and their develop-ment was tolerated. Yet in these conflicts between the party, the revolutionary committees and the Red Guards, a final arbiter was required; and that was the function and the meaning of the 'person-ality cult' which grew so strongly at this period. Only Mao could decide which of those who 'waved the red flag against the red flag' was authentically Maoist.

The cultural revolution came to an end in April 1969, when the

---

[17] Subsequently he returned. He was one of the few diplomats to be reappointed to an earlier post after the cultural revolution.
[18] Posters on which anyone could express his opinions in large letters and denounce the enemies of the people.

Ninth Congress of the Chinese Communist Party met in Pekin and drew up the balance-sheet. But Mao holds that the struggle between the masses and the bureaucracy will last for decades: he launched the notion of 'the continuous revolution', that is to say of an ever-lasting revolution within the revolution, with contradictions perpetually coming into being. However, it does seem that a great many of the desired ends have already been attained. The Chinese are doing their utmost to transfer the basic responsibilities to the masses in many fields, such as medicine, teaching and the management of commercial enterprises. They are also trying to do something towards abolishing the distance between the manual workers and the intellectuals: theoretical teaching must always be linked to actual practice, which takes precedence over mere book-learning. In this way they hope to create a 'new man', not unlike the being Marx wished to see.

Preventing a new privileged class from coming into existence; giving genuine power to the masses; turning each individual into a complete being: such a programme must necessarily win my support. Yet I cannot grant China that blind confidence that once the USSR aroused in so many hearts. The publications China directs at the West dismay me by their dogmatic naivety. When I am told that the workers have a right to three weeks of holiday but that they give them up because of their socialist enthusiasm, what stays in my mind is the fact that they do not take holidays: enthusiasm cannot be institutionalized. Saying that China is a paradise is all the more absurd since the revolution has not yet been carried through, as Mao himself admits. But there is no need to make a myth of China in order to feel great sympathy for the country.

For a short while it was possible to hope that the emancipation of the under-developed countries was about to open unexpected horizons for mankind. There was the promise that the Africans would bring fresh life to civilization, adding 'a new colour to the rainbow'. At present these hopes seem to have been illusory. It is now some years since Dumont said, 'Black Africa has made a bad start'; and events have confirmed his gloomy forecast. In the first place Africa has not really been emancipated at all. Apartheid lives on in South Africa – with the blessing of several African states. The authority of the Portuguese has been shaken in Guinea, Angola and Mozambique, but still it endures. In spite of their new political

415

status, the de-colonized nations are still exploited economically. When they won independence in about 1960, their rural population amounted to something like eighty or ninety per cent of the whole. During this last decade the population has grown far more rapidly than the economy, with the result that year by year the mass of the people have grown poorer and poorer. In their attempt at fighting exploitation and overcoming poverty, some African leaders tried to change the institutions bequeathed to them by the colonists: they were attacked and isolated, and now almost all the truly progressive regimes have been overthrown. The black continent remains tragically under-developed, and it is torn by internal dissensions, often fomented by the capitalist powers which stand to gain by these divisions.

This was the case during the thirty-month war that Biafra waged against Nigeria in an attempt at winning independence – an independence that the Ibos had been claiming since 1945. The Ibos had the richest, most highly-developed culture of any African nation, and they found it hard to bear the domination of the northern feudalists, who were supported by the English. They committed a serious political error in 1960, just after independence, when power was seized by the Hausas, the feudal party that governed the northern Nigerians; instead of forming an alliance with the Yorubas, the second most important southern race, the Ibos let the authorities dismantle the party grouped about Awolowo, the Yoruba chief. The mistake cost them dear. In 1966, after a coup d'état, young Ibo officers made General Ironsi head of the state, and upon this the Yoruba combined with the Hausas. Ironsi, all the Ibo leaders, two hundred officers and thirty thousand civilians, men, women and children, were massacred, while hundreds of thousands more were cruelly maltreated. Two million fled to the east of the country, which was under the authority of Ojukwu, an Ibo. The pressure of public opinion led Ojukwu to declare a state of secession; and in May 1967 he proclaimed the independence of Biafra, a country of fourteen million inhabitants. Biafra was recognized by the most truly revolutionary Africans – Julius Nyerere of Tanzania and Kenneth Kaunda, the president of Zambia. China's recognition came half-way through 1968. But since there were rich oil-deposits in Biafra, the capitalist powers interfered. England wanted to retain Nigeria as a neo-colony and therefore supported the Lagos government, providing it with bombs and planes. For reasons of prestige

416

the USSR and Egypt did the same. The Federals invaded Biafra: eight million people were surrounded in a confined area cut off from the rest of the world. Lagos would not allow the Red Cross to take them medicine and food. Starvation and air-raids killed two million. Even after Biafra surrendered in January 1970, the Nigerian government, alleging that it would offend the nation's pride, refused the help of foreign Red Cross organizations, thus condemning tens of thousands of children to death. Before and after the defeat of Biafra I met a great many returning doctors and journalists: they were utterly sickened with the horror of it. Sartre and I joined several left-wing figures in signing a document that said 'now that the hopes of Biafra have been murdered, the reign of political gangsterism has indeed taken on global dimensions ... Let the murderers and the hired ideologists rejoice: their rule stretches right round the world.'

Lagos propagandists tried to persuade me that to bring about socialism it was necessary to maintain the frontiers that the English had laid down in the interests of colonialism. A large proportion of the French left fell into step behind the USSR and approved of what Marienstrass, writing in *Les Temps modernes*, called 'genocide in the historical meaning of the word'. Yet the Ibos were a nation, and the left wing, which now looks upon the nationalist claims of the oppressed as the surest path to internationalism, should have recognized their right to self-determination. And even if they had thought that politically Lagos had the sounder argument, still they should never cheerfully have accepted the wiping out of an entire culture and the extermination of two million people, including a whole generation of children. This indifference makes one suspect the indignation they display when the child-victims of the Vietnamese war are concerned. Scarcely ever, during these last years, have I been so sickened as I was at the magnitude and the appalling nature of these massacres – killings encouraged, condoned, or placidly accepted by almost all the 'progressives' in France and the rest of the world.

For years too, and in an equally placid silence, they have passed over the genocide of the Nilotic peoples of the south by the Sudanese government. They were stirred only when Nemery launched his savage repression against the officers and unionists who had tried to overthrow him in July 1971 – torture; massive, bestial executions; the hunting down of Communists.

When I turn to Latin America, I find no great comfort there, either. Nobody could have hoped for the miracle of the Cuban revolution to repeat itself. I had contacts with revolutionary circles in Venezuela, Bolivia and Colombia; in each of these countries the left wing was divided, guerrilla warfare was difficult to wage, the repression savage and the chances of success almost nonexistent. Even so it was a comfort to know that there was a very widespread opposition to the governments supported by the USA. Many a time have I been delighted by the feats of the Tupamaros in particular. Then again Allende's election in Chile was a victory for the left; though in all likelihood there is no future in it, alas.

When Sartre and I came back from Brazil in 1960 we were both convinced that there was no possibility of a socialist revolution in that country for a long time. Prestes, the well-known Brazilian Communist, had asserted that this was not the case, and a Trotskyist economist told me how he had come to the same conclusion: both based themselves upon an abstract Marxist appreciation of the state of affairs, coming out with the answer that socialism must inevitably conquer. We had in fact observed that the Brazilian proletariat, highly favoured in comparison with the peasants, had no sort of wish for a revolution; the peasants of the Nordeste were indeed in a revolutionary condition, but they were wholly powerless. The violent measures of 1964 took us completely by surprise, however: our Brazilian friends had assured us that for a great many reasons the army was entirely harmless and that it was incapable of seizing power. As it happened the soldiers overthrew Goulart and put Castelo Branco at the head of the state. The Americans encouraged this coup d'état, and it brought the country's entire economy under their control: the battle against socialism led to the suppression of all freedom – terror reigned in the trade unions and among the peasants; there was a general lowering of wages; and habeas corpus was suspended. A great many democrats and intellectuals left the country. A resistance did take shape; but everyone knows how hideous the repression was and how hideous it actually is today – imprisonment, torture, murders carried out by the 'death squad'. In Paris I have met a certain number of Brazilians, members of the opposition who were themselves tortured, and others whose relatives suffered horribly in prison or disappeared

418

altogether. They have told me of the general atmosphere of suspicion throughout the country; of people coming to visit relatives in prison and pretending not to know one another, each fearing that his neighbour might compromise him; and of students not daring to tell their companions of their ideas if there were the slightest hint of subversion about them.

Some of my Brazilian friends have also given me highly-detailed accounts of the methods that have been used for years to exterminate the Indians. They can do nothing whatsoever against these organized massacres, and they feel utterly desperate. Nowadays the subject is so well-known and all protests are so useless that I believe there is no point in speaking of it again here.

Quite recently – in January 1972 – I learnt that there had been a wave of arrests in the Argentine; those who were against the regime and those who were suspected of being against it were imprisoned and shockingly tortured. I had a letter from a friend whose son had been subjected to long sessions with a magneto. In reply to protests the government said that it was the prisoners who wounded themselves by beating their heads against the walls: 'We cannot pad the cells, after all,' they said.

The United States was responsible for the Brazilian coup d'état; and in Spain it supports Franco's regime, which is still founded upon the arbitrary power of the police, as the Burgos trial has proved in so ugly a fashion. What the us has set up in Greece is still another hideous police dictatorship. At American instigation the soldiers seized power in Athens on 21 April 1967. Because of the general discontent throughout the country, parliamentary democracy had become dangerous for the oligarchy. The economy was at the service of the great controlling monopolies, not of the people: the workers, the peasants, the lower-middle and part of the middle class were beginning to form an alliance, and at the elections the democratic forces would have won an overwhelming victory. To deal with them, the army set in motion the 'plan against subversion from within' that all NATO countries are to apply. Once again the economic oligarchy has crushed the masses, who can no longer even express themselves politically, since there are no longer either parties or parliament. The regime deliberately plunges them into obscurantism. For utilitarian ends it does educate managers and executives; but thought and creativity are stifled. The cult of traditional ways and mediaeval religious dogmas has been revived. To escape the extreme poverty of the countryside, the peasants flock to the towns, where they are reduced to unemployment. And in the meantime all opposition is brutally put down. The police oppression that has always existed in Greece has been made even harsher. All those citizens who are suspected of sympathy not only for Communism but for democracy have been imprisoned, appallingly tortured, deported. Some of those who have fled from Greece live the unhappy lives of exiles in Paris.

The moment a nationalist or a popular movement seems to threaten its interests, the United States crushes it. Millions upon millions of men are kept in a subhuman condition so that the United States may plunder the wealth of the under-developed countries at its ease. What is so scandalously absurd about it all is that as economists have proved the billions of dollars thus extorted by America do nothing to help the well-being of the American people as a whole. A large proportion of them, particularly the blacks, live in poverty and even in extreme poverty. The huge profits are invested in war-industries and the main result of its frenzied exploitation of the planet is that the US government is capable of destroying it.

As for life within the States, the situation of the blacks, which disgusted me the very first time I was ever there, has merely grown more and more unbearable; this has caused an escalation of violence in the Afro-American communities and consequently an escalation in repression, with the Black Panthers being hunted down, imprisoned, murdered. It seems that the police have succeeded in dismantling a great many organizations or in rendering them powerless, among others those white revolutionaries called the Weathermen, who favoured terrorism. Yet most of the Americans I have spoken to feel that the regime is no longer viable: such a climate of violence reigns in the US, unemployment has reached such proportions, and the number of people maintained by the social security organizations is so great, that the economy is about to collapse: insoluble conflicts arise even at the technical level. 'It must necessarily break down because it can't go on,' friends have told me. Perhaps this collapse may set off a revolution on a worldwide scale? I do not know whether I shall live long enough to see it, but it is a comforting outlook.

8

I paid little attention to what was happening in France between 1962 and 1968. The right wing, united and happy to be in power, had no thoughts beyond retaining it; the divided left was making fruitless attempts at coming together round a coherent programme. Their confrontation was not calculated to arouse enthusiasm. I did feel a certain pleasure when de Gaulle was made to run a second time in the presidential elections of 1965; but I had little sympathy for his most serious rival, Mitterand, whose ideas were completely opposed to mine and who represented groups that were equally remote. I no longer lived in a state of intense distress, as I had during the war in Algeria; but I was not proud of my country. France had renewed its relations with Franco's Spain at a time when that country was murdering Grimau. It imprisoned thirteen Martiniquans who were of the opinion that Martinique was not a French *département*. The country was dishonoured by the Ben Barka affair: none of the scandals that had sullied the Third and Fourth Republics were as squalid as that police-conspiracy, so eagerly and willingly covered by the government. I was interested in the struggles within the Communist Party and in the great mass movements, such as the unrest among the peasants and the miners' strike in protest against the closing of the pits. But none of these things affected me directly.

Because I had been a teacher and because I am fond of the young I did keep a close watch on the problems that were coming to the fore in the student world. In February 1964, Kravetz, the president of UNEF, the students' union, wrote an article for *Les Temps modernes* in which he attacked the system of lectures; he called for a different conception of culture and of freedom, one that should involve a complete transformation of the relationship between

421

teachers and students. The UNEF rejected all subordination of rank, and it launched the slogan 'The Sorbonne for the students'. In 1965 *Les Temps modernes* published a debate on the question. Kravetz and some of his friends denounced the way in which the students were made subservient to the technocracy. Not all the members of our editorial team were in agreement with these views, but Sartre and I approved of them – new means would have to be used for the handing-on of knowledge, and there would have to be an attempt at defining these means.

Tendencies of a similar nature appeared in other countries, and they too were linked to political commitment. In the United States a student revolt over civil rights broke out at Berkeley in December 1964. In Germany, egg-throwing students gathered outside the American embassy to protest against the war in Vietnam. A little later they invaded the university buildings, to mark their rejection of the reforms based on selection. Gradually they reached the point of challenging, 'contesting', capitalist society, root and branch. The SDS, the Social-Democrat students' organization, distributed revolutionary tracts. In April 1967 it organized a demonstration against Humphrey, and another in January against the Shah of Persia. A policeman shot and killed a demonstrator, and this led to an immense student uprising. In spite of the rapidly-increasing repression they set up action-committees and a 'university of criticism', and their movement spread throughout Germany. They were furiously opposed to the war in Vietnam, and at home to the Springer newspaper trust. Violent disturbances broke out in the English, Dutch, Scandinavian, Italian and even Spanish student worlds.

In France the incidents reported in the press were far less spectacular. In 1967, when Misoffe went to the university of Nanterre to open the swimming-pool, he was tackled by an unknown young man called Cohn-Bendit. It was also at Nanterre that the men students, who were forbidden to go into the buildings reserved for the women (the reverse was allowed), burst out, roaring 'Down with sexual ghettoes.' In February 1968 they invaded the women's quarters. They denounced the miserable conditions in which they had to work. The papers devoted little space to their claims and for my part I did not appreciate their real importance.

Like everybody else, I only began to suspect it in March. After charges of explosive had been set off on the night of 17 March, four lycée boys were arrested: they all belonged to committees against the war in Vietnam. On 22 March, the Nanterre students, led by Cohn-Bendit, occupied the administrative buildings: they worked out a plan of action against the war in Vietnam and against the oppression to which they felt they were being subjected. During the following days they distributed tracts and disturbed lectures and examinations. When Grappin, the rector of the university, closed Nanterre for the week-end, they held a meeting in the Descartes amphitheatre at the Sorbonne. On 12 April they demonstrated in the Latin Quarter to show their solidarity with Rudi Dutschke, the leader of the SDS, who had been seriously wounded by a German fascist the day before.

Everyone knows what happened then, with Grappin closing Nanterre to bring the 'hot-heads' to heel, the hot-heads invading the Sorbonne, and the rector, Roche, calling in the police. The students evacuated the Sorbonne, and a great many of them were arrested as they left, The SNESUP, the union of teachers in secondary and higher education, called all its members out on strike. The UNEF organized a demonstration for 6 May, the day when Cohn-Bendit and several other ringleaders were to appear before the disciplinary council at the Sorbonne.

Throughout the morning and afternoon of 6 May there were clashes between the students and the police in the Latin Quarter, and the smell of tear-gas – soon to become so familiar – drifted along the boulevard Saint-Michel. In the evening I turned on the radio, a thing I rarely do, and for four hours on end I never stopped listening. Europe No 1 and Radio-Luxembourg were giving a minute by minute account of the battle in the boulevard Saint-Germain: behind the somewhat breathless voice of the reporters could be heard the roar of the crowd and the crash of explosions. Extraordinary things were happening: the demonstrators had thrown up barricades and with paving-stones as ammunition they were forcing back the riot police and even the fire-hoses that had been sent against them. The next day we learnt how brutally the police had clubbed them, chasing them even into the houses where they took shelter: they were savagely beaten up in the police-stations and at the Beaujon centre, where they were taken in police-vans. But could repression deal with these new forces that had just been unleashed? My friends and I hoped that they were going to shake the regime and perhaps even bring it down: the riot had turned into an insurrection.

The next day between twenty and fifty thousand demonstrators marched from Denfert-Rochereau to the Etoile, singing the Internationale, some waving red flags, others black. The Sorbonne was surrounded by the police and there was no reaching it; but Cohn-Bendit and his friends did not appear before the disciplinary council.

The story of the epic night of 10 May has been told again and again, with the barricades in the rue Gay-Lussac, the cars burning and the police behaving like hounds at the kill. The local bourgeois were horrified by this orgy of violence – they were the victims of it themselves, for many peaceable passers-by were knocked about – and they tried to help the students. Public opinion as a whole was outraged.

During the first days the Communists had attacked the students: *L'Humanité* condemned many of them, including 'the German anarchist Cohn-Bendit'. On 8 May talks began between the great labour unions, the CGT and the CFDT on the one hand, and the teachers' and students' unions on the other. On the tenth, a little before the barricades went up, the two workers' unions, the FEN (a teachers' union) and the UNEF issued orders for an unlimited strike and demonstration against the repression. Although Pompidou, back from Afghanistan, had the Sorbonne opened on the morning of the thirteenth, on the afternoon of that same day an enormous procession marched from the République to the place Denfert-Rochereau: it was composed of a host of students, numerous workers' delegations and the leaders of the left-wing parties. Sauvageot, Geismar and Cohn-Bendit (whom the CGT had vainly tried to exclude) marched at the head of a parade that numbered between five and six hundred thousand demonstrators. They chanted slogans written up on banners: 'Students, teachers, workers, all united', 'Ten years is enough', 'Popular government'. But the workers were carefully shepherded by the CGT, which did its best to limit their contacts with the students. In the place Denfert-Rochereau the CGT, using megaphones and loudspeaker vans, gave the workers the order to disperse. About ten thousand students, together with a certain number of workers, went to the Champ-de-Mars and held a meeting there: the students and the workers did not speak the same language, and the dialogue between them failed. But their success in mobilizing the unions in ten days was a great victory for the hot-heads of Nanterre. Their movement had become very popular.

The students had the support of many of the teachers; Laurent Schwartz was one of them, although a little while before he had been booed at Nanterre because he favoured selection. Professors Kastler, Jacob and Monod took the students' part and stood by them during the night of the barricades. We were not teachers, but we felt deeply involved. In a manifesto published on 9 May we expressed our solidarity with those who were challenging the established order, the *contestataires*, congratulating them for wishing 'to escape from an alienated establishment by every possible means'. We added that we hoped they would be able to maintain 'a power of rejection' that might open a new future. On 12 May, Sartre spoke on Radio-Luxembourg and said that the students' only valid relationship with the university system was to smash it and that in order to do so they had to come out into the streets. His statement was reproduced in tracts distributed in the Latin Quarter.

As soon as the Sorbonne was reopened, the students occupied it. Neither in my studious youth nor even at the beginning of this year of 1968 could I ever possibly have imagined such a party. The red flag flew over the chapel and the statues of the great men, and the walls blossomed with the wonderful slogans invented some weeks earlier at Nanterre. Every day new inscriptions appeared in the corridors, new tracts, posters, drawings. Clusters of people argued passionately on the stairs or standing in the courtyard. Each political formation had its own stand for the distribution of tracts and papers. The Palestinians' stood next to that of the 'left-wing Zionists'. The young and the less young crowded the benches of the amphitheatres; and anyone who chose to speak could state his case, explain his ideas or suggest tasks or watchwords, while the audience replied, approved or criticized. Press offices were set up in lecture-rooms, and in the attics a crèche. Many of the students spent the night there in their sleeping-bags. Sympathizers brought fruit-juice, sandwiches and hot meals.

I often went there with friends, and we wandered about the corridors and the courtyard. I always met people I knew. We strolled about and talked and listened to the discussions: many of them centred about the conflict between Israel and the Arabs, about the Palestinian question. From 15 May onwards the party spread to the place de l'Odéon; the students occupied the theatre, and the black flag flew from the roof. Here too there were passionate discussions, and here too people came forward to speak. Orchestras played jazz and dance-music. Young or old, everybody fraternized.

Yet the students saw that in order to defeat the regime they needed the working class. They had acted as a detonator, but they could not accomplish the revolution all by themselves. On 17 May they carried the Sorbonne red flag to Billancourt: on a streamer they had written 'The working class takes the flag of battle from the frail hands of the students.' And indeed, strikes broke out at Nantes and all over France. For some days Paris presented a very strange appearance. On 18 May the métro and the buses stopped running. Cigarettes grew scarce. The banks closed and people had no ready cash. There was a shortage of petrol: long lines of cars stretched out in front of the few filling-stations that were still working. The dustmen came out on strike: the streets and pavements were covered with rubbish from the overflowing bins. By 24 May the number of strikers reached nine to ten million. Their claims went far beyond demands for higher pay: they hoisted the red flag over their factories and occupied them. They shouted slogans: 'Ten years is enough', 'The factories for the workers', 'Power to the working class'. The students tried to get into contact with them. Groups of young people from the universities went to the factory gates: the unions would not let them in. The FEN strike went on: it was an unlimited strike and the teachers, against all tradition, stayed out for a month.

On the evening of the twentieth several writers were invited to come to the Sorbonne for discussions with the students. Sartre and I, together with a group of friends, met a young student leader in front of the Balzar at ten o'clock. He seemed very anxious. 'It won't be at all conformist,' he told us. 'Indeed, it will be very hectic.' The speakers would have to sit in the hall, in the midst of the audience; and since there was no microphone they would find it very hard to make themselves heard. No doubt Sartre would be booed to a certain extent – some of the students did not like him and as the hall was crammed with people eager to make trouble there might even be serious fighting. I was a little apprehensive as I went up to the first floor, to the 'cultural agitation centre'; Marguerite Duras, Duvignaud, Claude Roy and some other writers were there before us, together with several organizers and the head of the centre, the

426

sociologist Lapassade. He too told us that the session would be noisy; indeed, it was possible that we should not be able to get into the amphitheatre at all – it was made for four thousand, and that evening it held seven. Someone suggested that we should all go into the courtyard and speak there: it was crammed with people and we refused. Besides, how could we even manage to get out of this room? The corridors were impossibly crowded. We stayed there, marking time for a while; and then all at once Sartre had vanished – they had taken him to the sound room, we were told. So they had: and there at a window, with a microphone, he spoke to the students massed in the courtyard. Then there was a rumour that he had disappeared; I was beginning to worry when I heard that they had managed to get him into the amphitheatre. Would he ever be able to get out again? Might not things take an ugly turn? A few minutes later a student came to tell us that the discussion had begun and that everything was going very well. Some of the writers grumbled, vexed at having come for nothing. 'I'm fed up with the star-system,' said Marguerite Duras.

My friends and I waited for Sartre at the Balzar. An hour later he appeared, followed by a horde of students, journalists and photographers. He told us that when he first went into the amphitheatre the audience was rather rowdy, but after he had said a few words they quietened down. He told them of his hopes in 'this wild democracy that you have created and that upsets all established institutions'. And for an hour he answered questions. At the end they applauded him heartily. Other friends joined us: they had gone to the amphitheatre as early as eight o'clock and had watched it gradually fill. By nine a mouse could not have got in: there were students sitting in the arms of Descartes and others on Richelieu's shoulders. The curious thing was, they told us, that although these people had all obviously come to hear Sartre, not one, out of horror of the 'star-system', had uttered his name.

After this we kept in contact with the movement. We met Geismar more than once, and Sartre interviewed Cohn-Bendit for *Le Nouvel Observateur*. Our young friends and colleagues all belonged to action committees. They sold the paper *Action*, distributed tracts and took part in all the demonstrations.

To protest against the expulsion of Cohn-Bendit, the students built barricades on the night of 23 May, and there were violent clashes. On the twenty-fourth the CGT organized two demonstrations in support of the strikers; they passed off in perfect order and the demonstrators dispersed without incident. That evening the students gathered in great numbers outside the Gare de Lyon. On their transistors they listened to de Gaulle's speech announcing a referendum on participation, and they booed him. Thousands of them, led by Geismar, went to the stock exchange and set fire to it: the 'forces of order' burst out with extreme fury – clubbing, rapes and no doubt murders that were subsequently disguised as car-accidents. On 27 May there was a huge meeting at the Stade Charléty, in the course of which Mendès-France and Mitterand were reconciled: in spite of the absence of the CGT, the event seemed full of promise. Two days later the CGT held a demonstration. It seemed likely that the union of the left wing might be accomplished, and that this united left might confront the bourgeoisie with an anti-capitalist programme and a transitional government.

In fact from that day on the tide began to ebb. De Gaulle, back from his secret consultation with the army at Baden-Baden, dissolved the Assembly. On 30 May a Gaullist procession marched down the Champs-Elysées. Now that petrol was available again, countless people left Paris for the week-end. For his part Séguy, boasting of having won 'remarkable gains', decided to end the strikes; and he called the students who supported the strikers *provocateurs*. Nevertheless a great many students went out to Flins to protest against the occupation of the Renault works by the police: one of them, Gilles Tautin, was drowned escaping from the 'forces of order'. At Sochaux the next day the police killed two workers. That evening the UNEF called the students to the Gare de l'Est to protest against the repression. The police sealed off the whole district. Very violent fighting broke out in the Latin Quarter: the demonstrators attacked the police vans and stations, cut down trees, burnt cars and smashed shop-windows; more than four hundred of them were wounded. Their violence frightened the ordinary people, who now stopped sympathizing with them. The police had perfected techniques that made large gatherings impossible. Demonstrations were forbidden; gatherings were broken up. As Citroën remained on strike, nine hundred monthly-paid workers were dismissed. A strike broke out in the ORTF, the French radio: all the members of the staff who had taken part in it lost their jobs.

I paid my last visit to the Sorbonne about 10 June. There I met Lapassade, who was in a great state of excitement. 'Terrible things are happening here,' he said. 'I'll show you.' The cellars were full of rats, and he told me that they might cause a serious epidemic. 'As for epidemics,' said a young doctor, 'there's only one here, and that's lice.' They both complained that the whole situation was going sour: at night the Sorbonne was filled with beatniks, whores and tramps. At all hours drug-traffickers came to peddle their wares in the corridors – the amphitheatres stank of hashish and marijuana. We climbed to the upper floors where the students had set up a 'parallel' infirmary, which the doctor accused of having stolen ampoules of morphia from the regular establishment; Lapassade said that drug-trafficking and even abortion went on up here. He stopped in front of a door locked from the inside; he got them to open it, and there we were in a little room furnished with a chest of drawers and a bed. He introduced me pompously and asked what went on here. 'This is where we look after weary writers,' said a girl, insolently looking me up and down: to tell the truth I really did look as though I were trying to interfere in things that had nothing to do with me. As we went down the stairs the doctor said that he was leaving to stir things up at Rennes and that he would bring back potatoes for the strikers – he was sick of the Sorbonne. Then Lapassade showed me some of the 'Katangans', helmeted and armed with iron bars: they were defending the Sorbonne against possible attack by the right-wing Occident movement, and they proved very tough in clashes with the police. But Lapassade thought it was dangerous for the students to be more or less in the hands of these mercenaries, wholly devoid of political convictions – many of them were really former *affreux*, hired thugs with a terrible reputation. Lapassade urged me very strongly to come down into the cellars to see the rats, but I refused: I also refused to write the article he wanted on 'the decay of the Sorbonne'. I did not share his indignation; and in any case it was not for me to denounce the students. The article in question appeared in Le Monde on 12 June over the signature of Girod de l'Ain.

Shortly afterwards, the Sorbonne and the Odéon were evacuated. Once again the Latin Quarter swarmed with cops. A few students still threw Molotov cocktails from the roofs. Then calm came back again – a deathly calm. Paving-stones in the streets were covered over with tar. Workmen on ladders systematically scraped off the inscriptions and the beautiful posters. At first the country had sympathized with the students or had at least felt kindly towards them; then it had taken fright, and it longed for order. The elections were a brilliant success for the Gaullists. The revolution was still-born.

The most enlightened among the students had never thought it could succeed. They almost all belonged to pro-Vietnamese committees and they had been influenced by the resistance of Vietnam – it proved that a determined minority could hold superior forces in check. That was what had led them to play the part of the detonators. But they knew that the great movement they had initiated would not go so far as to overthrow the regime straight away. Cohn-Bendit had said, 'The revolution will not be achieved in a single day, and it is not tomorrow that the students and the workers will unite.' But although they acknowledged their failure they were still hopeful: 'this is only a beginning: let's carry on with the fight.'

In several interviews Sartre spoke of what had seemed to him to have constituted the original aspects of the May explosion. The prime mover in revolutions had always been poverty: the students had replaced this by a fresh requirement – that of sovereignty. In our technocratic society the notion of power had become more important than that of ownership, and it was power that they were claiming – the power of being masters of their own fate. They saw that in our dehumanized world the individual is defined by the object he produces or the function he fulfils: they rebelled against this state of affairs and they claimed the right to decide for themselves what part they should play. The young workers had followed their example: they had rebelled against the proletarian condition, and this was a new and very important fact.

All that the lovers of order had chosen to see in the events of May was a youthful and romantic outburst: the truth of the matter is that these events expressed not the crisis of one generation but of society as a whole. The students, grown more and more numerous and seeing no future ahead of them, formed the focus at which the contradictions of neo-capitalism exploded: this explosion meant that the entire system was at stake and this directly involved the proletariat. And of course that was why between nine and ten million workers came out on strike. For the first time in thirty-five years the question of a revolution and of a transition to socialism had been raised in an advanced capitalist country. May had proved that the struggle for control by the workers was possible and that the creative initiative of the masses was a necessity. It had also shown the conditions in which a battle for socialism might be effective – it had shown the indispensible necessity for creating a vanguard capable of carrying a revolution in the developed capitalist countries through to a successful conclusion.

Indirectly it was the movement of May that brought about de Gaulle's defeat on 27 April 1960. We welcomed it heartily. And the dismay of the team in power amused us very much indeed. La Malène was so upset that when he spoke on the radio that he called Waldeck-Rochet Baldeck-Wochet. These gentlemen told us that 'disturbances' were about to take place. Nothing of the kind happened. But we were not interested in choosing between Poher and Pompidou. We attached no importance to a change of men that would in no way alter the working of the system. Like many other people in France, we abstained from voting.

We wanted to keep in touch with the gauchistes. In *Les Temps modernes* might they not find a forum where they could express their various points of view? During the summer of 1969 we met the two Cohn-Bendit brothers, Kravetz, François George and several of their companions in Rome. They had spent their holidays by the Italian sea. They seemed all on edge and more or less hostile to one another. They spoke nostalgically of the events of May, each dwelling on the part he had played, and each accusing the others of having an ex-serviceman's state of mind. What struck us most of all was that they did in fact have the state of mind of defeated men. There they were, after the great days of May, empty-handed. They harshly criticized *Les Temps modernes*, accusing it of having become an institution. So the plan of bringing the micro-groups together came to nothing.

Yet from time to time Sartre still saw the gauchistes. In April 1970 the *Gauche prolétarienne*, feeling isolated and threatened with disappearance, got in touch with him. Its paper, *La Cause du Peuple*, was being systematically confiscated and its two editors, Le Dantec and Le Bris, had just been arrested, one after the other: apart from the days of the occupation, no editor had been arrested in France since 1881. What could be done against a repression as shameless as this? Having considered various solutions, Sartre suggested that he should take over the editorship of *La Cause du Peuple*. He let it be known that he did not agree with all its views: in particular he regretted that the *GP* likened its activities to those of

the Resistance and the Communist Party's to those of the collaborators, and that it spoke of the 'occupation' of France by the
bourgeoisie and of the 'liberation of the country'. It appeared to him
that these analogies were as unsound as they were clumsy. But
basically he sympathized with the Maoists. He approved of their
desire to bring revolutionary violence back to life instead of putting
it to sleep after the manner of the left-wing parties and the unions.
Legitimate activities – petitions and meetings – had no effect: what
had to be done was to move on to illegal action. So he decided to be
the official editor of *La Cause du Peuple*, that is to say to assume
responsibility for all the articles appearing in it. He should therefore
have been arrested at once: he was not. When an issue was confiscated the authorities contented themselves with making a charge
against X – some unknown person.

At the end of May I went with him to the trial of Le Dantec and
Le Bris. The Palais de Justice was ringed with police-vans and the
court was packed; behind me sat two rows of police in civilian
clothes, and their uniformed colleagues stood all round the room. I
recognized many faces I knew, including Gisèle Halimi's. Sartre
was not called upon to give evidence until the end of the afternoon,
and we had lunch in a nearby restaurant. Some journalists came
and asked him for a statement on the banning of the *Gauche
prolétarienne* – the decree had been issued that very morning. We
knew nothing about it. A little later Gisèle Halimi joined us. She
told us that while the incriminated articles from *La Cause du
Peuple* were being read out, the many lawyers and apprentice-
lawyers in court shuddered with horror. 'How can such things be
allowed to be printed!'

When we went back to our seats a former miner was giving
evidence: his father had died of silicosis; he described the miners'
way of life and accused society of reducing them to despair; he
congratulated *La Cause du Peuple* for giving the workers the right
to speak whereas the bourgeois press stifled them. He was
succeeded by a long-haired os[1] who defended the *Gauche
prolétarienne's* action in getting hold of a large number of métro
tickets, which it distributed to working men. Another spoke of the
brutalities committed by the police at Flins. A Franciscan
demanded that he too should be charged, since he edited a paper in
which he maintained the same arguments as *La Cause du Peuple*. A
well-known Dominican, Father Carbonnel, basing himself upon

[1] *Ouvrier spécialisé*: one of the lowest-paid classes of worker. Tr.

papal encyclicals, accused the rich of being thieves. All the witnesses were eager and convincing, but they might have been speaking to the empty air. The presiding judge had taken his decision beforehand.

Sartre emphasized the scandal of his being in the witness-box while the two other editors were in the dock. He did not ask that he should be arrested, but that Le Dantec and Le Bris should be released. The lawyers asked him how he explained that the *GP* should have been banned on the very day of the trial; but the judge forbade him to reply.

Prosecuting counsel asked the court to suspend *La Cause du Peuple* definitively: this was refused, and the paper retained its legal existence.

The students held meetings: they clashed with the police at Censier, at the Faculté des Sciences, and in the Latin Quarter and the boulevard Saint-Germain until three in the morning. The next day, after the verdict that sent Le Dantec to prison for a year and Le Bris for eight months, there were outbreaks of violence, carried out by small commandos – the police chased them on motor-cycles. Geismar was accused of having encouraged the 'smashers' by words uttered at a meeting, and a warrant was issued for his arrest. The police began looking for him.

A few days later they surrounded Simon Blumenthal's works, where *La Cause du Peuple* was printed – seventy-five thousand copies of the paper had already been taken to a place of safety. They wanted to take Blumenthal away for 'supervisory detention', but his workers would not allow it. The next day we held a press-conference in my flat to protest against these arbitrary actions: Blumenthal was within his rights when he printed a paper that had a legal existence; the illegality lay in coming to harass him in the exercise of his calling. Radio-Luxembourg and several newspapers – including *Le Monde*, at length – gave accounts of this meeting.

The friends of *La Cause du Peuple* formed an association, presided over by Michel Leiris and myself. The Prefecture of Police refused to give us an official acknowledgement. We took them to court. At first we were nonsuited, but in the end we won the case. Together with Davezies, Tillon, Halbwachs and many others, Sartre joined the *Secours rouge*, whose function was to help the victims of this repression. By doing so they hoped to bring about a union of the various non-Communist left-wing groups.

Thirty sellers of *La Cause du Peuple* were in prison on the charge of trying to reconstitute the *Gauche prolétarienne*. Some of the friends of *La Cause du Peuple* decided to go out and distribute the paper in the streets. What we wanted was not, as Monsieur Dutourd and *Minute* alleged, to get ourselves arrested but to put the government in a state of self-contradiction by reason of its failure to arrest us. There were only about ten of us, but a great many journalists and photographers came too: so we occupied a good deal of space. In the familiar background of the rue Daguerre, and outside one of the shops where I ordinarily buy my food, we unloaded sacks of papers and tracts from a car and shared them out. It was half past five and many people were doing their shopping. We pushed through the crowd, crying, 'Read *La Cause du Peuple*. Support the freedom of the press!' and handing out copies: then we went along the avenue du Général-Leclerc, which was even more crowded. Some people refused the paper with a disapproving look: 'It's banned,' said one man. Others took it without caring one way or another: still others called out for a copy. A fishwife, sitting in front of her stall, said, 'They sell medicines that poison us: does your paper talk about that?' 'It talks about all the wrongs they do to you.' 'Then give me one.' A crowd began to gather: a young cop came up to Sartre, took a packet of papers from him and grasped his arm. Instantly the photographers took a great number of shots, as we set off towards the police-station someone in the street called out, 'You're arresting a Nobel prize-winner!' The cop let go; Sartre followed him while our friends shouted 'Stop thief!' But the cop walked faster and faster, almost running. So we went back and carried on with our distribution. The people were amused and interested; they almost fought for the papers. By the time we reached Alésia we had none left. We gathered in a quiet spot to draw up a communiqué for the press. Radio-Luxembourg was already reporting the operation: our voices could be heard calling 'Read *La Cause du Peuple*', and Sartre's explanations as he walked along – *La Cause du Peuple* was not banned; it was illegal to arrest those who sold it. We had managed to hold out for thirty-five minutes. On 22 June *Le Monde* gave an excellent account of this little demonstration.

We did it again on Friday, the twenty-sixth. This time there were many more of us. We gathered on the boulevards, by the Rex – just opposite *L'Humanité* – and we walked towards Strasbourg-Saint-

Denis, accompanied by journalists and photographers. We handed out our copies to the passers-by and to the people sitting on the café terraces. They looked at us with indifference, hostility or sympathy: many of them smiled. After a quarter of an hour we crossed the road and worked back again along the other pavement. Four or five policemen came up and then went away. They returned with a police-van. 'You are not being arrested. You are being taken to have your identity checked,' they told us. When our van stopped in front of the police-station we were all made to go in – all of us except Sartre: to him they said, 'You are free, Monsieur Sartre.' About a dozen of our companions were already there, inside; we numbered perhaps twenty altogether. While they were looking at our papers. Sartre appeared. Having been left all by himself on the pavement with a packet of papers under his arm, he started distributing them. So they brought him in.

They began filling out our dockets. 'Apart from Monsieur Sartre, you're none of you public figures? Bertrand de Beauvoir – that's not the writer . . .' In a chorus we replied, 'We are all public figures.' 'I don't know a single one of you.' 'It's not our fault if you are ill-informed: we are all public figures.' 'Well then, so am I,' said the exasperated cop. He asked Sartre and me to go into an office with him: he meant to release us and keep the others. We refused. At this the cops grew upset: they telephoned in all directions and one said very loud, 'It's a crazy, crazy business!' 'You are the one who says so,' said one of us. We were having great fun. They were obviously given orders to release Sartre at any price and to keep the others, and our attitude made this impossible. An hour later some plain-clothes men appeared, together with an officer in a silver-braided uniform. Speaking aside to Sartre he told him that we should all be released within half an hour. Very well: but we made it clear that Sartre and I would be the last to leave. We were let out in little groups. I left two minutes after Sartre, and I found him at the corner of the street, surrounded by journalists and speaking into microphones. I spoke too. Again Sartre said that his wish was by no means to get himself arrested but to place the government in a state of self-contradiction: he had succeeded perfectly, as could be seen from the total confusion of the police. These statements and an account of the incident were passed on to Truffaut, who was speaking on Radio-Luxembourg that day, and he passed them right on to his audience. So the operation was quite widely publicized. That evening the French television showed some shots and gave an impartial report. The Swiss, German, Italian and English television also reported the affair; and no doubt that was why the French papers produced long articles – a whole page in *Combat*, and long pieces in both *Le Monde* and *Le Figaro*. The front page of *France-Soir* showed Sartre and me behind the bars of the police-van. *Paris-Presse* was the only one to make poisonous remarks, saying that Sartre was furious because he had been left at large.

In Paris and in Rome that summer, Sartre remained in close touch with the gauchistes. He gave an interview to *Idiot International*, a publication of which I had agreed to be the official editor, making the same reservations as Sartre in the case of *La Cause du Peuple*. Back in Paris, Sartre assumed responsibility for two more gauchiste papers, *Tout* and *La Parole au Peuple*. He also did a great deal for the *Secours rouge*, which had been established in several towns in France.

Since the government went on obstinately confiscating *La Cause du Peuple* – which was nevertheless widely distributed – we had another demonstration in the autumn of 1970. The day number 37 came out, the friends of *La Cause du Peuple* gathered at the printing-works. One of them came to fetch me: 'There is a police-car at the corner of your street,' he said. Although I knew they were keeping a watch on Sartre, I could not believe it. But the moment we drove off, the other car followed us; and when we stopped outside Sartre's block it stopped too. By a cunning manoeuvre our driver shook it off. The weather was quite beautiful, blue and gold, and it was a pleasure to drive through Paris. In the workshop a noisy machine, threshing away at a great pace, folded and printed sheets of *La Cause du Peuple*. By about noon a great many people had gathered, including quantities of journalists and reporters from the various television networks. Maspero, Blumenthal and Sartre spoke to the press and made recorded statements. We carried three thousand copies of the paper to Maspero's shop: the plain-clothes police we had shaken off found us again, and they followed us, but without interfering. We stacked the papers in *La Joie de lire* and then we distributed them in the street. A police-van drew up a few yards away, but it left us alone. Yet three young men who had ventured as far as the boulevard Saint-Michel were picked up. Godard, Delphine Seyrig and Marie-France Pisier voluntarily went with them. We all hurried to the police station in the place du

Panthéon and stood there outside the door, talking to the journalists and being filmed by the foreign television networks until our six friends came out again. The police-car that had been given the job of following us was there, and one of the cops posted at a first floor window took several photographs of each one of us. Their car followed us to the restaurant where we had lunch. This was such an absurd waste of the tax-payer's money that I could scarcely believe my eyes.

A much more important action was that which the *Secours rouge* organized at Lens in December. In February 1970 sixteen miners had been killed and several others injured by an explosion of fire-damp at Hénin-Liétard. The employers were obviously responsible for the accident and by way of reprisal some unidentified young men tossed Molotov cocktails into their offices, starting a fire. Without the slightest shadow of proof the police arrested four Maoists and two habitual criminals. The criminals admitted having thrown the explosives and accused the four Maoists of being their accomplices. The trial of the 'incendiaries' was to take place on Monday, 14 December, so the *Secours rouge* summoned a people's court in the biggest room in the town hall on Saturday the twelfth. Sartre went to Hénin-Liétard to make enquiries on the spot in preparation for this investigation, and he stayed in a mining village.

Lens is a mining town, black and ugly. Christmas was coming, and the streets were decorated with tinsel, festoons and coloured lights. At four o'clock in the afternoon the great hall of the Hôtel de Ville, a huge modern building in the main square, was full of people, between seven and eight hundred of them. Huge photographs of the miners killed in the accident were posted up on the walls. Above the stage, which acted as a platform, stretched a banner reading 'Pit-managers murderers'. Sartre sat on the platform at a little table next to a bearded schoolmaster with a great deal of reddish hair, the *Secours rouge* chief for the northern region. He limped and his face was scarred, because a couple of days earlier two unknown men had tried to run him down with his own car.

At a large table sat a kind of jury: Madame Camphin, terribly thin-faced, old and half blind, the mother and widow of miners who had belonged to the Resistance and who were shot by the Germans during the war; an engineer; a doctor; and an ex-miner. The engineer read out a printed paper that gave the employers' point of view. Another engineer took the microphone and tore this statement

437

to pieces; other witnesses supported his accusations. The responsibility of the Coal Authority was glaringly obvious. On the day of
the accident a fan had been removed; it was to be replaced by a
more powerful model. In the meantime the fire-damp accumulated
in the shaft. But in spite of this the miners were sent down the pit.
The operation should either have been carried out on a holiday or
work should have been stopped until the second machine was working. But as usual profit took precedence over safety. No more than a
single spark was needed to set off the fatal explosion. Other witnesses proved that accidents at work were not due to that 'inevitability' behind which the management tried to shelter, but to the
employers' indifference to the miners' danger – there were never any
accidents when bigwigs went down a mine, because in that case all
precautions were taken.

Then some doctors gave a striking account of silicosis. It kills
nine hundred miners a year and turns others into semi-invalids or
very sick men before the age of forty. They exposed the self-seeking
complicity of the majority of their colleagues: so that the employers
shall not have to pay a pension, these men refuse to diagnose silicosis even when the patient is already severely affected, and they send
him back to the pit. If he dies, the widow receives a pension only if
her husband had an affection of more than fifty per cent; and this
has to be shown by an autopsy at which she must be present – the
hope is that she would rather give up her pension. Former miners
spoke of their own cases and angrily denounced the dangers to
which they were exposed, the mutilating results, and the bad faith of
the doctors upon whose decision their pensions depend. Sartre
summed up all these accusations in an indictment of the state as employer. He demolished the management's argument – 'It is the
workers themselves who neglect the necessary precautions.' For if
the miner ensures his safety, he reduces his output and he is paid
less. It is the state as employer that is responsible for industrial
accidents and diseases: and it makes the worker himself pay for his
own defence against these evils. At the top level security-regulations
are issued; but it is known that the miner will not carry them out
thoroughly – if he did his pay would dwindle catastrophically. 'If
you keep to the safety-regulations,' said one to his companion, 'your
children will never eat meat.'

Sartre was criticized for having 'set himself up as a judge'. In fact
he produced the indictment: he did not judge. It was the audience as

438

a whole that pronounced the verdict. Others have said, 'What's the point, seeing there can be no sanction?' Yet a condemnation of this kind has its effect: it is an urgent warning to the employers and it is a way of arousing public opinion. People are killed in the name of profit: the more this is publicized the less easy these killings become.

On the following Monday the six alleged 'incendiaries' were acquitted, including those who had confessed and falsely accused the Maoists. There was obviously so much shady police intrigue in this whole affair that it was thought better to cover it all up by letting everybody go free.[2]

At the end of January I took part in a meeting organized at the Mutualité by the friends of *La Cause du Peuple*. Our association had just been officially recognized and the government had grown tired of confiscating the paper: we wanted to tell the public about these victories. Michel Leiris presided; Sartre was not present. I spoke on the subject of governmental illegality within the framework of pseudo-legality, and the audience laughed very heartily when I told them about our dealings with the police when we were distributing the paper.

The other speakers were chiefly concerned with the political detainees' hunger-strike, which was directed at obtaining better conditions. Although Geismar – the police had managed to arrest him – enjoyed a comparatively privileged status, he joined in. They were claiming, both for the common-law prisoners and themselves, a more bearable regime, including the right to have books and to receive visits.

A certain number of gauchistes decided to go on a hunger-strike to support these demands. The priest of St Bernard's chapel under the Gare Montparnasse agreed to shelter them. Michèle Vian was among the fasters, and I often went to see them; they were camping in a roomy reception-centre, next to the priest's office. They had covered the walls with posters, drawings, slogans and manifestos; they had also put up placards in the corridor and on the station wall to explain what they were doing. Their daily diet was no more than two and a half pints of mineral-water and five lumps of sugar. Yet unlike most hunger-strikers they did not stay in bed. They talked

---

[2] It is usual to release informers when those they have denounced are in fact guilty. But hitherto the denunciation of innocent men has never led to the release of persons who have confessed to a crime.

among themselves and received journalists as well as visitors, to whom they sold left-wing papers from a heap on the table; they renewed their posters, drew up documents and invented new slogans. Every afternoon they went out to take the air for a while.

One night at about twelve someone rang my bell: it was Michèle and another woman, also a hunger-striker; they were pale and distraught. A fascist commando had broken in; the women had been flung out and they did not know what was happening to their companions. They telephoned the priest, who came to fetch them. Fortunately the strikers had managed to barricade themselves in his office and from there they had given the alarm by telephone. The commando had gone away, having smashed the bottles and pots and torn down all the posters. They came back some nights later, but this time the left-wingers had guards and they could not get in. It was never known whether they were members of Occident or – which was more likely – agents provocateurs sent by the police to start trouble. Soon even the bourgeois papers took the strikers' side and Pleven gave in. He granted the detainees their special status and appointed a commission to define the circumstances in which an offence was to be considered political and to improve the condition of the common-law criminals.[3] The strikers in St Bernard's chapel had held out for twenty-one days. They had grown thinner, but they were quite well.

It was during this period – on 6 February, to be exact – that the paper *J'Accuse* asked me to go to Méru to write a special article. It was about an exceptionally horrible 'industrial accident'. On 11 May 1967 the Rochel works blew up: it was a factory that packed gaseous substances for the manufacture of insecticides and beauty products. Horrified witnesses saw girls rushing out, in flames from head to foot, half-naked, screaming as they rolled on the ground. Out of the eighty-seven workers present that day – most of them very young girls – fifty-seven were taken to hospital as urgent cases. Three died. The others had to be given horribly painful courses of treatment for months – some for no less than a year and a half. All of them remained more or less handicapped.

When the papers with a large circulation reported the disaster they spoke of a tragedy due to misadventure. Yet the responsibility of Monsieur Bérion, the director of the works, was so obvious that the court found him guilty of an 'unpardonable error' and sentenced

[3] By 1 May 1971 six weeks had gone by and nothing had yet been done.

him for manslaughter by negligence: yet it limited the penalty to a year's imprisonment with suspended sentence and a fine of twenty thousand francs. (Monsieur Bérion has in any case benefited from an amnesty and he is now running a new and prosperous concern.) It was evident to me, from my conversations with the workers and with Monsieur P, the manager who had thrown up his job in disgust in February 1967, that Monsieur Bérion deserved to be called a murderer.

Since it made use of inflammable gases, the Rochel works belonged to the category of especially dangerous establishments: it had twenty-seven tons of these gases in stock instead of the authorized fifteen. Because of faulty equipment and the inadequacy of the checks there were often leaks; and this escaping gas spread on the ground because the pipes ran through unventilated channels. What is more, it often happened that the taps of the propane and butane containers were not turned off properly. Several fires had broken out. The person entrusted with opening the factory at seven in the morning and checking the installations was a boy of fifteen (!) named Marc Vinet. When he arrived on the morning of 11 May 1967 everything seemed to him normal. But at about a quarter past eight he noticed that a deep layer of gas had leaked from the main machine. ('You could see the gas escaping,' a work-girl told me. 'As it reached the air it made little white crystals. A friend said "It's freezing my back".' Another girl told me, 'There was a layer of gas; you could see it. It was a white – no, sort of grey, like a mist.') The boy warned a foreman: the foreman turned off the tap and told him to get the labeller going. Marc refused, saying, 'It'll blow up.' 'No it won't. You do as you're told,' said the foreman, and he added, 'That's an order.' Marc Vinet obeyed. There was a spark. The gas caught fire. Everybody fled. But the passages were not clear and several of the doors were wedged with cardboard; according to the regulations they should have opened outwards, but these were sliding doors. The double ceiling was made of nylon: it caught fire and collapsed. The management made the girls wear polythene overalls and these caught fire too. The whole workshop went up in flames.

What was the reason for the spark? The answer puts an overwhelming load of guilt on Bérion. The regulations required that the electrical equipment should be sealed and that the electric motors should be provided with anti-sparking devices. But to save two thousand five hundred francs Bérion deliberately ordered a labeller

441

(the machine that caused the explosion) of the ordinary kind. The electrical equipment was so faulty that no local firm would carry out the hasty repairs that Bérion wanted done: the works ought to have been closed for several days and the entire system replaced. Bérion knew that several short-circuits had already occurred that year. In May 1966 the Association of Owners of Steam and Electrical Machines examined the equipment and called for a large number of alterations, for the machines did not possess the required safety devices. The relevant services of the Social Security had also remonstrated with Bérion on the subject. He took no notice of any of these warnings. Monsieur P told me that when he reminded Bérion of the safety-measures, he replied, 'Don't be a fool. Just keep them at it, that's all I ask of you.'

And what about the labour-inspectors? 'We never saw any.' 'At any rate they never came in,' the work-girls told me. The Amiens court itself denounced the 'failure' of the inspection-service. The fact of the matter is that throughout France the inspectors, who should in theory ensure the workers' safety, are in league with the employers. Eighty per cent of French factories do not observe the security-measures required by the labour legislation: if the inspectors exposed these abuses, productivity and profit would fall.

There was another scandalous side to this affair – the attitude of the law. The trial did not come on until two years after the disaster. Bérion got off very lightly. The foreman who gave the order to start the machine was not charged at all.

A third scandal is the behaviour of the Social Security. When the rate of incapacity is less than fifty per cent the sufferer receives only half the pension that this rate would entitle him to: for an incapacity of fourteen per cent he receives seven per cent of his salary. The Social Security's medical consultants support the interest not of the victims but of the organization. The majority of the victims injured at Méru were stated to have an incapacity ranging from fourteen to twenty per cent and they receive something in the nature of four hundred francs a quarter. And they are not granted even this unless they go back to work; if they do not they are accused of trying to sponge on the state.

Why did they not sue the Social Security to get their pensions increased? Because if they lost they would have to pay all the costs!

Another monstrous aspect, as a local doctor told me, is that the only thing the Social Security sees fit to take into account (and even then most inadequately) is actual incapacity for work. But other factors come into play. Many of the girls are psychologically marked by the appalling sufferings they had to endure for months on end. They have nervous breakdowns. They live in dread. The aesthetic damage matters a great deal where young women are concerned: they are ashamed of their bodies and their faces. And lastly for many of them the future is most disturbing. There is the danger of circulatory disorders and, for some, of cancer.

The likeness between this case and that of the Lens coal-mine is evident. In both the employers have been able to get away with murder. The labour-inspectors, the doctors and the courts are in league with them. And these two cases are not exceptions; they are tragically typical. In eighty per cent of factories in France, safety is sacrificed to profit and the workers risk their lives every day.

The reason why I was asked to go to Méru four years after the accident was that the victims were trying to combine so as to obtain an increase in their pensions. I am very glad I agreed, in the first place because I believe that scandals of this kind should be denounced and that public opinion should be informed, and secondly because this journey taught me a great deal. I met young working women, went into their homes, saw how they lived, listened to them and their families. It was only a very limited experience, because the Méru factories are small undertakings in a rural area and the girls are almost all peasants' daughters; but it gave me a more immediate, realistic view of their way of life than I could ever have obtained from books.

I also realized how necessary it was that the left-wing press, persecuted by those in power, should exist: no one else troubles to give a truthful, detailed account of the workers' state, their daily life and their struggles. The gauchiste papers do try to tell the workers about what is happening within their own class – a subject that the bourgeois press either ignores or misrepresents.

In spite of certain reservations (particularly my lack of blind faith in Mao's China) I do sympathize with the Maoists. They assert themselves as revolutionary socialists in contrast to the revisionism of the USSR and the new bureaucracy set up by the Trotskyists: I share their rejection of these things. I am not so naïve as to suppose that they will accomplish the revolution in the near future, and the 'triumphalism' of some Maoists seems to me childish.

But whereas the whole of the traditional left wing accepts the system, defining itself as an alternative team or as a respectful opposition, the Maoists stand for a root-and-branch denial of it. In a country whose arteries have hardened, that is resigned and half-asleep, they stir things up, they arouse public opinion. They try to focus 'fresh forces' in the proletariat – the young, the women, the foreigners, the workers in the small provincial factories, so much less under the influence and control of the unions than those in the great industrial complexes. They encourage action of a new kind – wild-cat strikes and sequestrations – and sometimes they foment it from within. They set the problem, the immediate and effectual problem, of the existence of a revolutionary vanguard. If the country continues on its downward path and if the contradictions within the system grow more and more obvious, then this vanguard will have a part to play. In any case, and whatever the future may bring, I shall never regret whatever I may have done to help them. I should rather try to help the young in their struggle than be the passive witness of a despair that has led some of them to the most hideous suicide.

At the end of 1970 some members of the *Mouvement de Libération des Femmes* got in touch with me; they wanted me to speak on the new abortion bill that was soon to come before parliament. They thought it far too half-hearted and they wanted to launch a campaign for free abortion. They suggested that to arouse public opinion, some women, well-known or obscure, should declare that they personally had had abortions. Twenty years earlier, in *The Second Sex*, I had protested against the repression of abortion and I had spoken of the tragic results of this repression; so it was natural that I should sign what was called the *Manifeste des 343*, which appeared in *Le Nouvel Observateur* in the spring of 1971. It was not, as some hostile critics pretended to believe, a question of introducing abortion into France, nor even of encouraging women to have abortions; but seeing that they did so on a very large scale – there are between eight hundred thousand and a million abortions every year – the intention was to allow them to undergo this operation in the best physical and psychological conditions – conditions that are at present the privilege of a certain class. Of course, contraception is preferable. But until contraceptive methods are widely known and practised – only seven per cent of Frenchwomen of childbearing age use them at present – abortion remains the only solution for those who do not want to have a child. The fact of the matter is that they do turn to abortion in spite of all the difficulties, humiliation and danger. This manifesto was criticized as having been signed only by well-known women: that was untrue – there was only a handful of them, the majority of the names being those of secretaries, office-workers and housewives.

To continue this campaign, the Movement organized a march through Paris on 20 November, a day when feminist demonstrations were to take place all over the world. Our march was in support of freedom of motherhood, birth-control and abortion. I took part. Our placard-carrying procession went from the République to the Nation, filling the whole roadway;[4] some of the militants waved floor-cloths, some lengths of wire with dirty washing hanging from them, paper dolls or balloons. One of them handed out parsley, the symbol of clandestine abortion, which others put in their hair. There were about four thousand of us, mostly women, though some men joined in, nearly all hairy and bearded. We released balloons, sang, and chanted watchwords: 'A wanted baby is a loved baby. Freedom of motherhood.' Some parents had brought their children and there were six-year-olds who piped with the adults 'We shall have the children we want to have.' Under the cold blue sky it was all very lively and gay – full of imagination. One interesting thing was that most of the women the demonstrators spoke to said they were entirely on our side, and they cheered and clapped. As we went by the church of Saint-Antoine a bride, dressed in white, was going up the steps. We shouted 'The bride's one of us! Set the bride free!' And the vanguard of the procession, leaving the street, darted into the church. The priest spoke to the militants for a while and then we went on towards the Nation.

A little before we reached it we met some conscientious objectors carrying anti-militarist placards. Their demonstration had been forbidden, and some of them had the idea of joining us. Upon this our procession began shouting 'No children for cannon-fodder! Debré, you swine, the women will get you!' And we all sang the Internationale. At the Nation some women climbed to the plinth of a statue and there they burnt floor-cloths, symbols of the feminine state. We danced in a round and there were more songs: it was a happy, companionable celebration.

4 The demonstration had been authorized.

445

Another action in which I had a share concerned the technical college, the CET, at Le Plessis-Robinson. I had been told about the place as early as the autumn of 1970. This college was opened in 1944, and it was for unmarried girls of between twelve and eighteen who were pregnant for the first time. When these girls are expelled or withdrawn from their state schools they are sent here on the advice of a social worker. It has room for thirty-five, and every year about two hundred future mothers succeed one another at Le Plessis: if the girl belongs to a poor family and has several brothers and sisters she is taken in for nothing. Three or four teachers prepare the boarders for the BEP[5] or for jobs as municipal or office workers; but they only deal with the first-year course, and the girls who are already in their second or third year waste their time. In any case, the working conditions are deplorable – no more than eight typewriters altogether and the mathematics class being held in the laundry. Some brilliant lycée pupils have their future completely wrecked. There is no library. As far as visits and going out are concerned, the girls are treated as though they were delinquents. The family-planning organization offered to give free lectures on birth-control: the headmistress refused. To protest against this state of affairs, the girls asked to be allowed to join a delegation of unmarried mothers who were to see the educational authorities: the headmistress forbade them to go. On Thursday, 16 December, they decided to boycott the lessons and the meals. The headmistress sent their parents a short, imperious telegram: 'Come and fetch your daughter at once,' and she announced that she was closing the school. Some of the parents came for their daughters: one father hit his, knocked her down and dragged her along by the hair without anyone's interfering. At this point one of the mistresses called in the MLF. I joined the group which occupied the school on Sunday morning: it was a hideous château, completely isolated in the middle of a park. A school inspector and a woman from the educational authorities were there, but in spite of them we talked to the girls. Some active members of the MLF stayed all day and even that night. Under pressure from them, the inspector telephoned the rector,[6] who fixed an appointment for the next day. I went with the mistress and some of the pupils; Halbwachs and Charles-André Julien of the

[5] An elementary examination usually taken at about fifteen.—Tr.
[6] From the educational point of view, France is divided into *académies*, and the head of each of those regions is the rector.—Tr.

Secours rouge came too. When she was asked to explain, Lucienne, one of the future mothers, said that what they were claiming was freedom from parental control and a grant that would allow them to bring up their baby. And indeed, whereas marriage automatically frees a girl of fifteen, the unmarried mother remains under her parents' authority even when she is over seventeen – it is they who decide whether she shall keep her baby or abandon it. They often prefer giving it up, and it is society that compels them to make this choice: it looks upon the baby as belonging to the mother of the girl who has borne it, yet instead of giving her extra help it withdraws that part of the family allowance which she had for her daughter, on the pretext that the girl is no longer attending school! It is so iniquitous a measure that it absolutely staggered both me and all the people I have told about it. Lucienne's demands were therefore totally justified: nevertheless the rector gave a start. 'You claim a privileged status on the pretext that you have committed – I will not say an offence, because that is a word I do not like, but a mistake.' I stopped him: 'According to what code do you decide that it is a mistake to have sexual relations at thirteen?' He did not know what to reply, but I could feel a scandalized shiver passing through his numerous staff. Our society does not accept juvenile sexuality. A priest had said to Lucienne, 'You assume that thirteen-year-olds have sexual instincts: I don't.' Lucienne and her friends also demanded that a pregnant girl at a lycée or a collège should not be automatically expelled by the headmaster or mistress. 'But what is done is for your own good,' said the rector. 'The other children's parents insist on your being sent away.' Certainly: so that the parents can deny that a girl of thirteen has sexual instincts, those who have yielded to them must be treated as scabbed sheep. The parents, who refuse to give their children, and especially their daughters, any sexual education whatsoever, are afraid that the experienced girl may do away with an ignorance the parents prefer to call innocence. But why does the university give way to them? That is what I asked the rector; and Charles-André Julien reminded him of the case of Senghor – some parents did not want their children to be taught by a black man, but for all that Senghor was kept at his post. The truth is that the university shares the anti-quated notions of the virtuous parents and looks upon pregnant girls as guilty. The guilty people in this matter are the parents and society as a whole. In France today there are more than four thous-

447

and minors between thirteen and eighteen who are pregnant: if they
had been given sexual education most of them would have been
more careful. Yet when one of the future mothers complained that
they were taught nothing about birth-control there was a kind of ill-
natured snigger among the authorities: 'It's rather late now!' They
seemed to think that if these girls returned to the same mistaken
ways then it would be right for them to be punished again. 'Family-
planning is not allowed, but the priest is,' observed the mistress.
'That is a juxtaposition as uncalled-for as it is revealing,' said the
inspector. And he explained at length that it was for the parents to
decide whether a school should or should not accept the family-
planning organization's lectures. 'Is there a parents' association at
the CET at Le Plessis-Robinson?' 'No.' 'Then it is the headmistress
who decides on her own authority.' The rector reproached the girls
of the CET for wanting to be treated as adults, free to dispose of their
children as they saw fit, yet at the same time to be kept and cared for
like minors. I pointed out that it was society that thrust this contradictory status upon them. If they were children then the law affecting adults should not be applied to them, but they should be allowed
to abort, their cases being regarded as exceptional; or if on the other
hand they were adults, then they should be freed from control and
helped. At last, to bring things to a close, the rector made some
vague promises about the improvement in the working-conditions,
visits and going out. He also promised to receive another delegation
at the end of January. Whatever happens, things will certainly go on
as they did in the past as far as the heart of the matter is concerned.
I wrote an article on this subject for *La Cause du Peuple,* and I did
my best to expose, among other things, the moral hypocrisy of the
righteous, the abuse of parental authority and the tragic situation
inflicted upon the young in our society.

The reason why I have taken part in demonstrations and committed
myself to specifically feminist activities is that my attitude with
regard to the state of women has evolved. As far as theory is concerned my opinions are still the same; but from the point of view of
practice and tactics my position has changed.

As I have already said,[7] if I were to write *The Second Sex* today I
should provide a materialistic, not an idealistic, theoretical foundation for the opposition between the Same and the Other. I should

[7] In *Force of Circumstance.*

base the rejection and oppression of the Other not on antagonistic awareness but upon the economic explanation of scarcity. As I have also said, this would not modify the argument of the book – that all male ideologies are directed at justifying the oppression of women, and that women are so conditioned by society that they consent to this oppression.

'You are not born a woman; you become one': I take this statement over – it expresses one of the leading ideas in *The Second Sex*. Of course there are genetic, glandular and anatomical differences between the human female and the male; but they are not an adequate definition of femininity, which is a cultural formation, not a natural datum. This conviction has not been shaken by Madame Lilar's cloudy scientism; on the contrary, it has been strengthened by the increasingly elaborate and far-reaching research on childhood carried out these last years. This work proves that my argument is correct and that it only requires completing with the statement 'You are not born a male; you become one.' For masculinity is not given at the beginning, either.

Freud is concerned with children only from the moment at which, according to him, the Oedipus complex appears – the age of three or four. But works such as Bruno Bettelheim's *The Empty Fortress* show that the individual's earliest months have a decisive influence upon his future. This has been confirmed by experiments carried out in Israel by the Hebrew University of Jerusalem. A psychologist and a physician studied groups of three-year-old children, some born in well-to-do, cultured Ashkenazi families, others to poor, badly-housed, over-worked Sephardi parents: the first were active, communicative and full of imagination, and they defended their territory and their toys; the second were apathetic and closed in upon themselves, they did not know how to play together and they had so little sense of their own existence that they pointed out their companions on photographs but not themselves. For two years both groups were submitted to intensive education: at the beginning the handicapped children blossomed out and made progress; but the privileged children profited even more from the teachers' efforts and at the end of the two years their advance was even more distinct than it had been at the start. The 'integration' failed: the backward children still played only with other backward children. At the age of three it is already too late to equalize opportunities. According to the work of Benjamin Bloom, an American neurologist, and of some European scientists, fifty per cent of the subject's potentiality for development and acquisition is fulfilled by the age of four: if the child has not been stimulated to develop his faculties during these years then their evolution and coordination will never be brought to the same degree of perfection. So all that is required for important differences between boys and girls to appear as early as three or four years of age is a failure on the part of the parents to 'stimulate' male and female babies in the same manner.

Rosenthal and his colleagues carried out another series of experiments which led to similar conclusions – those who bring children up play an important role. When he was directing work on white rats at Harvard Rosenthal made some curious observations;[8] it appeared to him that the results obtained depended upon the research-worker's initial bias – he found what he expected to find. To confirm this hypothesis he formed two random groups of rats: he told the workers that group A was composed of rats conspicuously successful in making their way through mazes, whereas the rats in group B were stupid. The workers obtained brilliant results with group A; very poor results with group B. Their optimism or defeatism had obviously influenced the way in which they performed their experiments. Rosenthal submitted some professors to a similar experiment.[9] He asked students to complete intelligence-tests and then drew up two lists, so arranged that the average IQ of the subjects was the same in each. He stated that the first list contained the most talented students, the second the average or mediocre. The professors put the students through fresh tests: those in the first category achieved a very high IQ, those in the second a most indifferent mark. All teachers know that one has to believe in a pupil if he is to succeed: if one has no confidence he loses heart and fails. Rosenthal's experiment – and he made many others, all coming to the same conclusion – makes it strikingly obvious that the master's attitude towards a learner in the course of his apprenticeship plays a decisive role: the master obtains what he expects to obtain. But in the cradle itself and even more afterwards, parents expect one thing from a girl and another from a boy.

Mothers 'handle, caress and carry boys differently from girls'

[8] Rosenthal, *Experimental Effects on Behavioral Research* (New York 1966) and Rosenthal and L. Jacobson, *Pygmalion in the Classroom* (New York 1966).
[9] Rosenthal and K. L. Fole, *The Effects of Experimental Bias on the Performance of Albino Rats* (1967); Rosenthal and R. Lawson, *A Longitudinal Study of Experimental Bias on the Operant Learning of Laboratory Rats.*

said the American psychoanalyst Robert J. Staller, who has made a particular study of male transexuality. He firmly dismisses[10] 'the discredited notion that masculinity and femininity are biologically produced in humans at the beginning'; and he recalls 'the many natural experiments which have shown that the effects of the apprenticeship that begins at birth determine the greater part of the identity of the sex.' He states 'It is not because of some inborn force that the baby knows that he belongs to the male sex and that he will become masculine. His parents teach him this, and they might just as easily teach him something else ... The choice of name, the colour and style of clothes, the way the child is carried, nearness and distance, kinds of games – all this and much else begins almost at birth.'

A particular point is that mothers do not treat the sexual organs of a boy baby in the same way as those of a girl. Not all play with their son's penis as freely as Gargantua's nurses or those of Louis XIII; but they are proud of it, they give it a pet name, and at times they stroke it. Nothing of the kind for the little girl, whose sex remains a hidden region. This, and not some mysterious instinct, is the explanation of the difference between the forms of behaviour in boys and girls as early as the age of two. A young woman who works in a crèche has told me how marked this difference is: when the boys go to the lavatory they freely display their sexual organs; the girls have already learnt to 'hide that' and they are awkward and ashamed; the boys peep at little girls when they wash or relieve themselves, but little girls do not watch the boys. I repeat that it is nonsense to suppose that their modesty can be produced by their hormones: it has been taught and learnt in just the same way as all those other qualities that are called specifically feminine will subsequently be taught and learnt. In *The Second Sex* I tried to show how this education is carried out in detail. The toys children are given dictate specific roles to them; the little girl accepts the mother's as her own, the boy the father's. In all these fields the parents encourage differentiation, because one of their greatest fears is to have a homosexual for a son and a tomboy for a daughter.

For Freud, of course, the difference between men and women is entirely explained by the difference between their anatomies, the little girl envying the boy's penis and attempting throughout her life

---

[10] In an article in *La Nouvelle Revue de psychanalyse*, no. 4, autumn 1971, in which he sums up the essence of his arguments.

451

to compensate for this inferiority. In *The Second Sex* I said that I rejected his interpretation: many little girls know nothing whatsoever about boys' anatomy; when they do discover the penis they often do so with indifference or even disgust. Kate Millett, dealing with this argument in her *Sexual Politics*, asks why the little girl should on the face of it consider one object superior to another merely because it is bigger. According to Freud she regards it as a better organ for masturbation: but the little girl has no notion of the penis's masturbatory function. And does she even know that she possesses a clitoris? Freud knew about women only through clinical cases; his female patients were suffering from sexual inhibitions and they were discontented with their lot. He tried to explain the second fact by the first. But the inferiority that society imposes upon a woman is revealed to her by society itself. In any case towards the end of his life Freud admitted that he had never understood anything about women at all. From his time and his surroundings he derived a 'machist' preconception that made him look upon women as incomplete men. This notion, which many modern psychologists reject, has been widely used by the post-Freudians: if a woman does not keep to her 'proper place', they instantly endow her with a 'masculine complex'.

For both in France and America, since the publication of *The Second Sex*, there has been a spate of books that endeavour to persuade women of their 'particular vocation'. They claim to 'demystify feminism' but in fact they succeed in mystifying their female readers. They say that feminism is old-fashioned, out-of-date – an overwhelming argument in an age terrorized by modernity. They say that women themselves deny its validity – those who work get nothing but disappointment from their jobs: they prefer staying at home. When two sets of people are in conflict there are always some members of the less favoured group who join the privileged side out of personal interest.[11] Then again one has to be wary of sociological inquiries, which are usually carried out in a conservative spirit[12]: the way the question is phrased very often dictates the answer. Furthermore, it is true that in present conditions a job, which she combines with household tasks, does not

---

11 'Women raise their value in their own eyes and in those of men by adopting the men's point of view.' G. Texcier in 'Les enquêtes sociologiques et les femmes', *Les Temps modernes*, 1 December 1965.
12 Idem.

bring a woman the rewards it brings a man: it is society that refuses her these rewards, and at the same time it does everything it can to give her an uneasy conscience. Lastly, the housewife, the woman who stays at home, is usually very far from really feeling the satisfaction that she displays: she is discontented with her lot and she does not want her daughter's to be any easier; the more she suffers from it, the louder she called for the preservation of her status. As for men, they stubbornly continue to assert their superiority. Machism is so firmly anchored in the hearts of French men that some of them do not hesitate to bring forward the fact that they piss standing as a sound basis for it – a statement that is not altogether kind to Muslims. Speaking with great enthusiasm of the 'new society', Monsieur Chaban-Delmas affirmed that here women would be equal to men; but, of course, in their equality their difference would still remain. It appears that this difference devotes women primarily to the act of wiping – of wiping babies, the sick, the old; that is the 'social service' offered them by Monsieur Debré. The fact is that the status of women has scarcely changed at all in France during the last ten years. They have been granted an easing of matrimonial legislation. Birth-control has been authorized: but as I have said, scarcely seven per cent of Frenchwomen of child-bearing age make use of it. Abortion is still strictly forbidden. Household tasks are still done exclusively by women. Their claims as workers are stifled.

In the USA some women have become aware of this oppression and have rebelled against it. In 1963 Betty Friedan brought out an excellent book, *The Feminine Mystique*, that created a great stir. She described a sickness that dares not tell its name – the sickness of the housewife. She showed the means by which capitalism manipulates women so as to confine them to the role of consumers – it is in the interests of both trade and industry to increase sales-figures. She denounced the way Freudian teachings and post-Freudian psychoanalysis are made use of to persuade women that in the nature of things they must fulfil one specific function, that of looking after the house and having babies. Three years later, in 1966, Betty Friedan founded NOW, a liberal, reforming feminist organization that was soon outstripped by more radical movements set up by younger women. In 1968 there appeared the Scum Manifesto, put out by the Society for Cutting Up Men: it is not to be regarded as a serious programme, but rather as a furiously indignant pamphlet such as Swift might have written, in which the revolt against men is carried to the point of absurdity. Much more important than this was the appearance of Women's Lib in the autumn of 1968 – the Women's Liberation Movement, which was joined by very large numbers of them. Other groups were formed too. This new feminism made itself known by means of demonstrations, some of them spectacular, others less so, and by a flood of literature – quantities of articles and books, including Kate Millett's *Sexual Politics*, Shulamith Firestone's *Dialectic of Sex*, Robin Morgan's collection of studies called *Sisterhood is Powerful*, and Germaine Greer's *The Female Eunuch*. What these women are demanding is not a superficial emancipation but the 'decolonization of women', for they look upon themselves as having been 'colonized from within' – the victims of colonization at home. They are exploited in their role as housewives, people from whom society extorts unpaid work; and in the labour-market they are the victims of discrimination – the pay and opportunities enjoyed by men are denied to women. The movement spread far and wide in the USA, and it has reached other countries, particularly Italy and France, where the MLF (Mouvement de Libération des Femmes) has been growing since 1970.

Why did this explosion occur? There are two main reasons. The first is that in an advanced capitalist society women see their status, which is economically very profitable from the men's viewpoint, as a contradiction. In a society based upon the production of saleable goods, household tasks are not looked upon as real work: to be so considered they would have to be transformed into production for public consumption. The survival of housework performed in each home (even though it may be done with the help of machines) clashes violently with the way of life of a technocratic society in which other forms of labour are increasingly rationalized. The second and more important reason is that women have seen that socialism and the left-wing movements have not solved their problems. Changing relationships in production is not enough to change the relationships between individuals; and more specifically women have not become the equals of men in any socialist country whatsoever. Many active members of Women's Lib and of the French MLF have first-hand knowledge of this: even in the most authentically revolutionary groups women are only given the most unpleasant tasks and all the leaders are men. When a handful of women raised the standard of revolt at Vincennes, left-wingers invaded the hall, shouting, 'Power is at the tip of the phallus.' American women have had similar experiences.

In their tactics and their forms of action the feminists of today have been influenced, in the USA, by the hippies, the yippies and above all by the Black Panthers, and in France by the events of May 1968: they aim at a kind of revolution other than that of the traditional left, and they are inventing new methods of bringing it about.

I have read the American feminist literature; I have corresponded with their militants; I have met some of them, and learnt with great pleasure that the new American feminism quotes *The Second Sex* as its authority: in 1969 the paperback edition sold seven hundred and fifty thousand copies. No feminist questions the statement that women are manufactured by civilization, not biologically determined. Where they do differ from my book is on the practical plane: they refuse to trust in the future; they want to tackle their problems, to take their fate in hand, here and now. This is the point upon which I have changed: I think they are right.

The Second Sex may be useful to some militants; but it is not a militant book. When I wrote it I thought the state of women and society would evolve together. I wrote, 'By and large, we have won the game. There are many problems that we look upon as more important than those which affect us specifically.' And speaking of women's condition in *Force of Circumstance* I said, 'It depends on the future of labour in the world; it will change only at the price of an upheaval in production. That is why I have avoided confining myself to feminism.' Somewhat later, in an interview with Jeanson,[13] I said that the most accurate way of interpreting my opinions would be to stress the feminist component. But I remained on a theoretical plane: I totally denied the existence of a feminine nature. Now when I speak of feminism I mean the fact of struggling for specifically feminine claims at the same time as carrying on the class-war; and I declare myself a feminist. No, we have not won the game: in fact we have won almost nothing since 1950. The social revolution will not suffice to solve our problems. These problems affect rather more than half mankind: at present I regard them as essential. And it astonishes me that the exploitation of women should be so readily accepted. When one thinks of the ancient

13 Francis Jeanson, *Simone de Beauvoir ou L'Entreprise de vivre.*

455

democracies, deeply attached to the ideal of equality, it is difficult to see how they can possibly have thought the status of the slaves natural: anyone would suppose that the contradiction must have been glaringly obvious to them. Perhaps one day posterity will wonder with the same astonishment how the bourgeois or popular democracies of our day can conceivably have maintained a basic inequality between the two sexes, and have maintained it without the least qualm of conscience. Although I see the reasons perfectly well, there are times when it amazes me myself. In short, I used to think that the class-war should take precedence over the struggle between the sexes. Now I think that they should both be carried on together.

In her excellent little book *Woman's Estate*,[14] Juliet Mitchell gives a very good description of the divergences between radical feminism and abstract socialism.

Radical Feminists	*Abstract Socialists*
Men are the oppressors.	Men are not the oppressors: it
All societies have been male	is the system.
supremacist.	Capitalism oppresses women.
It starts with a psychological	It starts with private property.
power struggle—which men win.	We've got to discover 'our rela-
Socialism has nothing to offer us.	tionship' to socialism.

etc.

Some years ago I should have upheld precisely these abstract socialist propositions; now, with Juliet Mitchell, I think neither of these two sets of statements adequate: the one has to be completed by the other. Certainly the system crushes both men and women, and it incites the first to oppress the second: but every man takes it over for himself and internalizes it; even if the system does change, he will still retain his antiquated notions and his claims. The rebellion of the young in 1968 could not, all by itself, lead on to revolution; nor can the women's revolt overthrow the regime of production. But then again it has been proved that socialism – as we see it today – has not emancipated women. Would a truly egalitarian socialism succeed in doing so? For the moment all that is Utopian, whereas the condition to which women are subjected is a present reality.

[14] Published in 1971: it resumes and completes an interesting article, 'The Longest Revolution' which appeared in the English *New Left Review* some years earlier.

The feminists differ on many points. They are undecided about the future of the family. Some, including Shulamith Firestone, think its destruction necessary for the liberation of women and also that of children and adolescents. The failure of those institutions that take the place of parents proves nothing – they are mere rubbish-dumps on the fringes of a society that must be radically reconstructed. This is true; and I find Firestone's criticism of the family equally sound. I deplore the slavery inflicted upon women through their children; I also deplore the abuse of authority to which the children are exposed. The parents bring their children into their sado-masochistic games, projecting their own fantasies on to them, their obsessions and neuroses. It is a profoundly unhealthy state of affairs. The parental tasks should be fairly shared between the father and mother. It would be better if the children were left to them as little as possible and if their authority were limited and strictly checked. Would the family, thus reorganized, retain a useful purpose? There are communities in which all the children are looked after by all the adults, with excellent results; but there are too few for one to be able to look upon them as a solution to the problem. Like many feminists, I wish for the abolition of the family, but without being quite sure what to replace it with.

There is another point at issue – the relationship between men and women. All feminists agree that love and sexuality must be redefined. But some of them deny that men have any part to play in a woman's life, particularly in her sexual life, whereas others wish to keep a place for them in their lives and in their beds. I side with them. I utterly revolt at the idea of shutting women up in a feminine ghetto.

Some feminists, basing themselves upon the laboratory experiments carried out by Masters and Johnson, claim that the vaginal orgasm is a myth and that the only true orgasm is that of the clitoris – a woman has no need of a man to experience sexual pleasure – Freud was wrong when he said that she did. There is not the least doubt that on this point Freud's attitude was prompted by his patriarchal notions of the relationship between the sexes – it was a question of refusing sexual autonomy to women and of placing them under the domination of men. He went so far as to write, 'Masturbation of the clitoris is a masculine activity and the elimination of clitoridian sexuality is a necessary condition for the development of femineity.' Seeing that the clitoris is an exclusively female

457

organ the absurdity of the first words is startlingly obvious. It is mere prejudice to imagine that a woman who prefers clitoridian pleasure, whether in homosexuality or in solitary enjoyment, is less well-balanced than others. Then again the notion of eliminating clitoridian sexuality is aberrant: the clitoris is intimately connected with the vagina, and it may be that it is this connection which makes the vaginal orgasm possible. However, coition with penetration of the vagina does provide pleasure of an undeniably specific kind, and this is the form that many women find the fullest and most satisfying. Laboratory experiments that isolate the internal sensitivity of the vagina from its reactions as a whole prove nothing. Copulation is not an intercourse between two sets of genital organs, nor yet between two bodies, but between two persons, and the orgasm is in the highest sense of the word a psychosomatic phenomenon.[15]

Nor do I accept the idea that every copulation is a rape. Indeed I even think I went too far in *The Second Sex* when I said, 'The first penetration is always a rape.' I was thinking primarily of those traditional wedding-nights when an ignorant virgin is more or less clumsily deflowered. It is true that quite often, and at all levels of society, a man 'takes' a woman without consulting her wishes, and he may even make use of his strength to do so: if he inflicts himself upon her without her wanting him, then the coition is a rape. But there may also be an exchange, freely agreed to by both sides; and in that case likening penetration to rape means relapsing into all the masculine myths according to which the membrum virile is a ploughshare, a sword, a dominating weapon.

Hatred for men incites some women to deny all the values men recognize and to reject everything that they call 'masculine patterns'. Here I do not agree, because I do not believe that there are specifically feminine qualities, values or ways of life: to believe this would mean acknowledging the existence of a specifically female nature – that is to say agreeing with a myth invented by men to confine women to their oppressed state. For women it is not a

---

[15] In *Le Sexe de la femme* Gérard Zwang gives a most exact description of the conditions in which the vaginal orgasm takes place and the manner in which it does so (pp. 125–9). He observes that there are a very great many cases of vaginal masturbation: the Andeans' use of the *guesquel* and the way in which the Polynesians and many other nations clothe the penis would have no meaning if the vagina were insensitive. Cf. also Mary Jane Sher Fey, M.D., *The Nature and Evolution of Female Sexuality*, Random House, New York 1972.

458

question of asserting themselves as women, but of becoming full-scale human beings. Refusing 'masculine patterns' is nonsense. The fact of the matter is that culture, science, the arts and techniques were created by men, since it was men who stood for universality. Just as the proletariat makes its own use of the heritage of the past, so women must take over the tools forged by men and use them for their own interests. What is true is that although civilization set up by men aims at universality it nevertheless reflects their machism – their very vocabulary bears its traces. In the wealth that we take over from them, we must very carefully distinguish between those things which have a universal nature and those which are marked by their masculinity. The words *black* and *white* are as fit for our use as for theirs: not the word *virility*. I think it is perfectly safe to study mathematics and chemistry; biology is suspect; psychology and psychoanalysis even more so. From our point of view it seems to me that what is called for is a revision, not a repudiation, of knowledge.

Personally or through their writings, I have met a great many feminists whose opinions are the same as mine, and that is why it has been possible for me to take part in their activities, as I have recounted, and to connect myself with their movement. And I have every intention of continuing to do so.

There is one point upon which my position has not changed, and here I wish to speak of it again – it is my atheism. Many worthy souls have deplored the unhappy chance that caused me to 'lose my faith'. In articles or in letters I often read, 'Oh, if only she had lived among real Christians!' 'If only you had read the Gospel rather than the *Imitation*!' 'If only she had met an intelligent priest!' What they really mean is, 'If only she had met *me*: she would have been edified by my example, convinced by my arguments.' My religious instruction was in fact very thorough: as for the Gospel, I knew long passages of it by heart. I have known intelligent Christians both in my childhood and in my later life; and for the very reason that they were intelligent they never supposed that their influence could save my soul. Faith, in their opinion, depended on God, on the divine intention and on the grace that He might grant. And indeed it is a theological error to explain His presence or His absence by contingent or merely natural causes.

Yet I who do not believe in the hereafter think myself authorized

459

to search for the social or psychological factors that underlie the attitude of practising Catholics. Most of the time they are merely reproducing a form of behaviour that was inculcated by their upbringing and that is observed in their circle. Like the character played by Trintignant in *My Night at Maud's* they might say, 'I was a Catholic, so I have remained one.' Faith is often an appurtenance that is given in childhood as part of the middle-class equipment, and that is unquestioningly retained together with the rest of it. If a doubt arises, it is often thrust aside for emotional reasons – a nostalgic loyalty to the past, affection for those around one, dread of the loneliness and banishment that threaten those who do not conform. Zaza had a critical mind and many aspects of her religion puzzled her; yet because of her painful, unconditional love for her mother she did not renounce it – she did not wish to move farther away from her in her own mind. She was tormented and unsure of herself; for her it was necessary to trust in a supreme being. Generally speaking, ideological interests come into play. Habits of mind, a system of reference and of values have been acquired, and one becomes their prisoner. Even if deep thought urged him to do so, a priest would revolt against breaking with his former life. Material interest may also step in: a Daniel-Rops or a Mauriac could not possibly question the firmness of his convictions – his entire career would be in danger.

I shall be told that in some cases it is unbelief that is given first: then one day the subject suddenly finds God – 'He came into my room. He spoke to me in a garden. He exists: I have seen Him.' Generally speaking – and Simone Weil is a striking example of this – the convert is going through a crisis at the time. His conception of the world is crumbling, his own idea of himself falling to pieces. Believing in God allows him to reshape the world and his own image. Catching a glimpse of a way out of the depths of his own confusion and unhappiness overwhelms him with joy and he takes his emotion for a revelation. Believers often dwell upon the difficulty of living in God's presence: I have observed that they find it very convenient. The miseries and injustices with which this world is overwheimed are all part of the divine scheme of things and they will be made up for in the next; believers do not have to worry about them. God forgives their faults, and He is very ready to say that they are in the right because it is they who make Him speak. There are exceptions: for Sister Renée, whom I met in a *favela* at

Rio, God was not an alibi but an imperative demand: He required her to struggle against poverty, against exploitation, against all the crimes that men commit against their fellow-men. Here and there priests and laymen fight the same kind of battle. But there are not very many of them.

I have often asked believers how they justify their faith. Some reply with outworn philosophical arguments – 'The world did not come out of nothing ... The world is not just a matter of chance.' Others with a pitiful 'There really must be something after life ... Without God there would be no point in living ... It would be too utterly hopeless ...' Still others speak of the kind of experience that I have already mentioned. A theologian told me, 'The day of my confirmation I felt the presence of God as distinctly as I feel yours now: the memory has never faded.' The question is, why, for the whole of the rest of his life, did he attach so much importance to a childish impression? Many simply observe, 'Faith? Why, there is no explaining faith.'

I know what a child's faith amounts to: for him, believing in God means believing in the adults who tell him about God. When he no longer trusts them his faith is no more than a dubious compromise that consists of believing that one believes. At fifteen I was too direct and plain-spoken to be satisfied with that. Later the study of philosophy showed me that a being existing both in the mode of the in-itself and in that of the for-itself was unthinkable. For me there was never any question, there never will be any question, of going back to the fables that enchanted my earliest years.

Many of the readers who chose to regard the epilogue of *Force of Circumstance* as a statement of failure eagerly put it down to my atheism. Seeing that I was deprived of that circumspect faith which allows sixty-year-olds to spend happy hours in the night-clubs of Paris, I must have felt all the horror of an existence that does not transcend itself in God. The arrogance of some Christians would close heaven to them if, to their misfortune, it existed. If the unbeliever is happy and well-adjusted, they accuse him of under-standing nothing whatsoever about the enigma and the tragedy of man's estate – he is a Monsieur Homais, and they despise his narrow-minded, commonplace conceptions. Yet if he does possess a sense of death, of mystery and of tragedy, then that is against him too. Either he is informed – and who has not had this experience? – that fundamentally he *does* believe in God; or else his rebellion, his

461

distress, are taken as a proof of his error. The void horrifies: so we are all immortal.

A curious reasoning that reveals the part played by religion in most cases – flight, desertion. Faith allows an evasion of those difficulties which the atheist confronts honestly. And to crown all, the believer derives a sense of great superiority from this very cowardice itself. From an immense height he stretches out a charitable hand to us: 'One day the voice of God will reach you: I am certain of it.' If one were to reply, 'I hope that one day you will stop talking humbug to yourself', he would be scandalized.

In what colours do I see this Godless world in which I live? Many readers tell me that what they like in my books is my delight in happiness, my love of life – my optimism. But others, particularly when they write to me about my last book, *Old Age*, deplore my pessimism. Both these labels are over-simplified. As I have already said, my childhood endowed me with a vital optimism. I have almost always felt happy and well-adjusted and I have trusted in my star. Indeed there have been times when I carried my confidence in the future to the point of foolishness – I did not believe in the war until it actually broke out. Since then I have grown more cautious. But even so I have often cherished hopes that have come to nothing: my high expectations of socialism – in the USSR, in Cuba and in Algeria – have not been fulfilled. When I wrote *The Second Sex* my belief in the coming victory of women was premature. And even though it is on its guard, my imagination is always outstripped by the horror of such tragedies as those of Biafra and Bengal – they take me by surprise. My natural bent certainly does not lead me to suppose that the worst is always inevitable. Yet I am committed to looking reality in the face and speaking about it without pretence: and who dares to say that it is a pleasant sight? The letters I received from old people after the publication of *Old Age* proved to me that their state was even darker and more wretched than my description. It is just because I loathe unhappiness and because I am not given to foreseeing it that when I do come up against it I am deeply shocked or furiously indignant – I have to communicate my feelings. To fight unhappiness one must first expose it, which means that one must dispel the mystifications behind which it is hidden so that people do not have to think about it. It is because I reject lies and running away that I am accused of pessimism; but this rejec-

462

tion implies hope – the hope that truth may be of use. And this is a more optimistic attitude than the choice of indifference, ignorance or sham.

Doing away with humbug and telling the truth: that is one of the aims I have pursued most stubbornly throughout all my books. This obstinacy has its roots in my childhood: I hated what my sister and I used to call 'silliness' – a way of smothering life and its joys under prejudice, set habits, pretence and empty phrases. I wanted to escape from that oppression, and I inwardly swore that I should expose it. Early in my defence I relied upon my own self-awareness: even when I was very small the mystery of its first appearance, its evident and yet disputed sovereignty, and the scandal of its future extinction haunted me, and they have an important place in my books. Somewhat later, when I was about fourteen, I identified myself with Louisa M. Alcott's Jo and with George Eliot's Maggie; I longed to assume that imaginary dimension which made these story-book heroines and the writer who projected herself into them so fascinating, and to assume it before an audience. I did not begin by writing a novel about an apprenticeship to life, because between the ages of twenty and thirty I was detached from my past. But later I did try to recount my life, endowing my experience with an artistic necessity.

Sartre once told me he did not feel he had written the books that, at the age of twelve, he hoped he would write. 'But after all,' he added, 'why should a child of twelve be privileged?' My case is different from his. It is of course very difficult to compare a vague and limitless plan with a realized, finite body of work. But I do not feel a gap between the intention that incited me to write books and the books that I have written. I have not brought the shimmer of feelings back to life nor caught the outer world in words. But that was not my aim. I wanted to make myself exist for others by conveying, as directly as I could, the taste of my own life: I have more or less succeeded. I have some thorough-going enemies, but I have also made many friends among my readers. I asked no more.

This time I shall not write a conclusion to my book. I leave the reader to draw any he may choose.